REEL PLEASURES

NEW AFRICAN HISTORIES

SERIES EDITORS: JEAN ALLMAN, ALLEN ISAACMAN,
AND DEREK R. PETERSON

LAURA FAIR

REEL PLEASURES

CINEMA AUDIENCES AND ENTREPRENEURS

IN TWENTIETH-CENTURY URBAN TANZANIA

OHIO UNIVERSITY PRESS   ATHENS

Ohio University Press, Athens, Ohio 45701
ohioswallow.com
© 2018 by Ohio University Press
All rights reserved

Printed in the United States of America
Ohio University Press books are printed on acid-free paper ⊗ ™

27 26 25 24 23 22 21 20 19 18   5 4 3 2 1

A version of chapter 3 appeared as "Making Love in the Indian Ocean: Hindi
Films, Zanzibari Audiences and the Construction of Romance in the 1950s," in
Cole and Thomas, eds., *Love in Africa* (University of Chicago Press, 2009), 58–82.

A version of chapter 6 was previously published as "Drive-In Socialism: Debating Modernities and Development in Dar es Salaam, Tanzania," *The American
Historical Review* 118, no. 4 (2013): 1077–104.

Library of Congress Cataloging-in-Publication Data
Names: Fair, Laura, author.
Title: Reel pleasures : cinema audiences and entrepreneurs in
  twentieth-century urban Tanzania / Laura Fair.
Other titles: New African histories series.
Description: Athens, Ohio : Ohio University Press, 2017. | Series: New
  African histories
Identifiers: LCCN 2017043710| ISBN 9780821422854 (hc : alk. paper) | ISBN
  9780821422861 (pb : alk. paper) | ISBN 9780821446119 (pdf)
Subjects: LCSH: Motion picture industry–Tanzania. | Motion picture
  audiences–Social aspects–Tanzania. | Motion picture theaters–Tanzania.
Classification: LCC PN1993.5.T34 F35 2017 | DDC 791.4309678–dc23
LC record available at https://lccn.loc.gov/2017043710

Dedicated to
Sabri and Nassir

for the joy they brought to the journey
and for teaching me about the important things in life

May 2005

CONTENTS

CONTENTS

ILLUSTRATIONS

MAPS

ACKNOWLEDGMENTS

Few authors work in isolation, and this book would certainly never have been completed without the support of individuals and institutions on numerous continents.

A year of intensive research was funded by a generous Fulbright faculty research award to Tanzania, during the academic year of 2004–5. A number of three-month preliminary and subsequent research trips were made possible by financial support from the departments of history at the University of Oregon and Michigan State University. The staff and collections at the National Archives of Zanzibar and the Tanzanian National Archives were invaluable. And without the residential fellowship and warm collegiality offered by the Netherlands Institute for Advanced Study, which provided the opportunity to spend nine full months focused solely on writing, it is doubtful that I would have ever managed to wrangle together a complete draft manuscript. I am also extremely grateful to those who wrote on my behalf for grants and fellowships over many years, as I struggled to transform a hunch into a book.

The critical comments offered by friends, colleagues, audience members at talks, and anonymous reviewers were instrumental in helping me refine (and often find) my arguments. The insights and encouragement provided by members of my writing groups strengthened not only the text but my resolve to keep on writing and rewriting and rewriting. Graduate students at Michigan State University were also key interlocutors, turning me on to new ways to think about my subject matter and innovative fields of historical enquiry. I am sure that all of them will see their fingerprints in the pages that follow.

The men and women who shared their experiences and understandings of the past also deserve a special note of thanks. While published and archived material were essential in allowing me to piece this picture together, without these personal stories the image I came to see would have remained utterly flat. It is their stories about what moviegoing meant to them that brought this history to life. Many generously shared not only their time and insights but also their private papers and photo collections, adding depth, richness, diversity, and personality to the view presented in official archives.

My deepest personal debt is to those who helped us survive Nassir's sudden death near the end of a glorious year doing research in Tanzania. From those who gently washed his body and helped lay his remains to peaceful rest at our home in Zanzibar, to those who comforted us and shared their memories of his joy-filled, goofy days on earth I am eternally grateful. The few who dared to mention Nassir's name after he passed also deserve special recognition, as do those who taught me to keep his soul alive by continuing to act on his best qualities, acknowledged my sorrow and sent good bourbon on his birthday, or encouraged me to keep putting one foot in front of the other and took me on high-altitude hikes on the anniversaries of his death. I am thankful to have had friends and colleagues who told me it was okay to stay away from writing when I could not bear to touch this research, as well as others who gently pushed and prodded me to get back to work.

I am truly blessed to have had Sabri's company on this journey. His exuberant embrace of beauty and wonder has been a daily reminder that life deserves nothing less than to be lived to its fullest. His generous willingness to give, accept, and adjust is something I both admire and aspire to someday emulate. Rare is the researcher lucky enough to have a child who appears to move effortlessly back and forth between continents or who is willing to spend his first year of high school in a new, foreign country without the slightest complaint. I have been truly blessed. Sabri was two years old when I began this project. His name is derived from the Arabic word for patience, and as he used to bounce around like a little kid, disrupting interviews, I teased him that he was a test of my patience. But sticking with me through the process of writing this book has certainly been a testament to his patience and fortitude. I just dropped him off at college. The refrain my grandfather used to sing from one of his favorite player-piano rolls keeps ringing in my head: "The years go by as quickly as a wink. So enjoy yourself! Enjoy yourself! It's later than you think!"

A NOTE ON USAGE

In 1964, President Julius Nyerere of Tanganyika and President Abeid Karume of Zanzibar joined their previously independent nations in a union known as the United Republic of Tanzania. Prior to 1964, individuals, families, and businesses frequently straddled and traversed the national boundaries, and cinematic entrepreneurs and their industry in both countries were joined long before the political union occurred. In using the term *Tanzania* throughout this volume, even when discussing events prior to 1964, I imply that the reference is to what was taking place both on the mainland of Tanganyika and in the isles of Zanzibar and Pemba. If speaking more narrowly, I use the name of the particular town being discussed or terms such as *the mainland*, *the isles*, or *Tanganyika* or *Zanzibar*. The word *Zanzibar* can also be confusing: it is the name of a town, an island, and an archipelago that includes several islands, most notably the two large ones of Zanzibar and Pemba. Context will illuminate the one to which I am referring.

INTRODUCTION

FOR GENERATIONS, going to the movies was the most popular form of leisure in cities across Tanzania. On Sundays in particular, thousands of people filled the streets from late afternoon until well past midnight, coming and going from seeing the week's hot new release. Films from every corner of the globe were shown during the week, but on Sundays, it was always Indian films that stole the show, serving as the focus of these large public gatherings in city centers across the land. In the final hours before a screening, the scene outside the ticket windows could became crazy, as crowds of patrons jostled in desperate attempts to secure the last remaining seats. The meek and gentle often hired agile youth to fight to the front of the line on their behalf, and many later reminisced about the strategies these young men employed to score tickets in the face of such crowds: slinking along walls, crawling between legs, or forming human pyramids capable of catapulting companions to the front. In Zanzibar and Dar es Salaam, two towns with particularly avid fans, demand was so intense that a vibrant black market in cinema tickets burgeoned. At its peak, Dar es Salaam's population sustained nine different cinemas with a Sunday capacity for nearly sixteen thousand fans, yet inevitably, some were turned away. From the early 1950s through the 1980s, black market tickets for films starring popular actors easily sold for two to three times the ticket window price in the final hours before the show. To avoid the unfortunate fates of those who waited until the last minute to secure a ticket, most people booked their seats well in advance. In towns across the country, many individuals and families even had reserved seats at a favorite theater, which they occupied each Sunday, week in and week out, for years on end. Going to the movies was a central preoccupation for millions and a significant way in which people enjoyed and gave meaning to their lives.

Films became the cornerstone of urban conversations as friends, neighbors, and complete strangers debated the meaning and artistic style of what they had seen on screen. On a continent where literacy was always the preserve of an elite few, films provided a narrative spark that lit debates that quickly engulfed a town. Audiences were never passive. Their active engagement with on-screen texts began inside the theater itself, where youth in the front rows frequently talked back to characters, sang and danced along with lovers in the film, and delivered punches and karate kicks to villains on the screen. Older members of the audience were typically far more reserved, saving their energy for the animated analysis that erupted during intermission and continued to escalate after the show let out. The skills of various actors and actresses were rated, the social worth and deeper meaning of their characters debated. For days, weeks, and sometimes months after a premier, people talked about the message of a film and its implications for their own lives. Generational tensions, the meanings of modernity, class exploitation, political corruption, dance and fashion styles, and the nature of romantic love were just a few of the topics films raised that people avidly analyzed and discussed. As Birgit Meyer has poignantly argued, films become hits because they give form to socially pervasive thoughts, dreams, and nightmares. Movies, she asserts, "make things public"—visible, visceral, material, and thus available for tangible public debate.[1] On street corners and shop stoops in Tanzania and in living rooms and workplaces, people engaged both global media and each other as they sifted and sorted, weighed and deciphered, and determined what they did and did not like about the places, the people, and the styles they encountered on the screen. Whether you went to the movies or not, said many, there was no escaping these discussions. For much of the twentieth century, films were the talk of the town in Tanzania.

From the early 1900s, when the display of moving pictures first became a regular feature of urban nightlife in Zanzibar, local businessmen struggled hard to meet audience demand. Not only were they often pressed to accommodate more fans than their venues could hold, they also had to work hard to build dynamic regional and transnational networks of film supply to secure and maintain the enthusiasm of local audiences. A steady crowd could never be taken for granted; it had to be consciously and continuously fashioned. The men who pioneered and built the cinema industry were typically avid film fans themselves as well as knowledgeable entrepreneurs. They kept abreast of the latest global developments in the art, craft, and industry of film and exhibition, and they committed themselves to providing products and services that resonated with local aesthetic demands. The East Africans who ran exhibition and distribution had to keep their fingers on both the local and the global cinematic pulses simultaneously. Building on precolonial trade links spanning the Indian and Atlantic worlds, Zanzibari entrepreneurs in the twentieth century developed networks of global film supply reaching to India, Egypt, Europe, Japan, Hong Kong, and the United States. As a result of their efforts, Tanzanians enjoyed access to a far more diverse range of global media products than most audiences anywhere else in the world.[2] Although Indian films were perennial favorites, each generation had different genres and national film styles that caught its fancy. During the colonial era—particularly along the coast—Egyptian musicals were nearly as popular as their Indian counterparts. Elvis, kung fu, and blaxploitation films were favorites of the young, postcolonial generation. Cowboys, from the American Alan Ladd in the 1940s and 1950s to the Italian Giuliano Gemma in the 1960s and 1970s, consistently drew a sizable young, male crowd. *Globilization* may have emerged in the late twentieth century as a new buzzword in academia, but the transnational movement of goods, ideas, and technologies has long been part of East Africans' mental and material worlds. And in the case of celluloid, it was Tanzanians who were driving and directing these flows.

This book interweaves the local, national, and transnational. Some chapters offer close-ups illustrating the richly textured experiences of specific audiences and how they reworked particular films to give them meaning in individual and communal lives. Other chapters take a broader view, exploring how audience experiences varied across sociological categories, space, and time. And then there are the panoramic views that situate Tanzania within the context of twentieth-century transnational media flows and global cosmopolitan connections. Often, these local, regional, and global entanglements are brought together in a single chapter to highlight their interconnections. In other instances, such relationships are best revealed through paired chapters, one of which is more ethnographic or temporally and spatially focused, whereas the other tracks change over time. Audiences and entrepreneurs are the central characters in the story. Throughout, cinematic leisure and the political economy are viewed as two sides of the same coin; business and pleasure are intertwined. The changing social, cultural, and political context of exhibition and moviegoing is examined from the early colonial period through the socialist and neoliberal eras, demonstrating the importance of historical and political-economic context for understanding cultural consumption, leisure practices, and the relationship between media and audiences.

Films and moviegoing are the central focus of this book, but the bigger picture reveals much about key issues that have long been at the core of Africanist historiography. Gender and generational tensions and transitions figure prominently, as do states and the politics of development. The social construction of masculinities and the values and characteristics of a "good man" are examined in various contexts and across time. Cities and citizenship are also central. One prominent argument is that cinemas were major nodes of urban social and cultural life, places where urban citizenship was physically and discursively grounded. Theaters brought together young and old; rich and poor; male and female; Muslim, Christian, Hindu, and Parsi; and African, Asian, Arab, and the occasional European. After the show, they took their interpretations of the film onto the streets, where they engaged others in animated debates about the movie and its relevance (or lack thereof) to local lives and society. The most popular films provided viewers with material they could blend, bend, and refashion to speak to their own dreams and desires. The cinema was a space of encounters—a borderland if you will—where Tanzanians engaged with media cultures from across the globe and a diverse range of people from their own towns.

CINEMA, CITIES, AND COLONIALISM

By the late 1950s, Tanzania had more cinemas than any country in eastern and southern Africa—with the notable exception of South Africa—and one of the richest African and Asian moviegoing cultures on the continent. At the end of the colonial era, Tanzania boasted nearly forty theaters, the rough equivalent of all the theaters in French West Africa combined.[3] Uganda had only twelve theaters, the Rhodesias (today's Zimbabwe and Zambia) eleven, and Malawi a mere four.[4] Every major Tanzanian town had at least one theater, and many towns had several. Kenya was a far richer colony, but it had only half as many theaters. What accounts for this disparity?

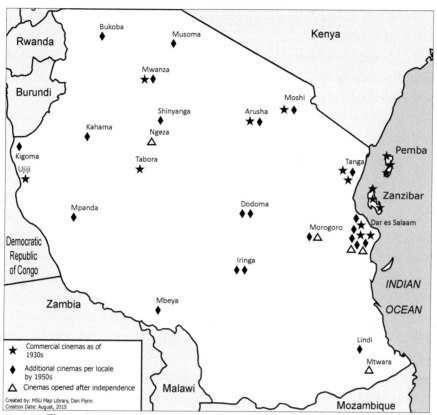

Map I.1 Tanzanian cinemas

The relative degree of urbanization is one important factor that helps explain such variations. Zanzibar—the epicenter from which cinema spread throughout the region at the turn of the twentieth century—had the most urbanized population in sub-Saharan Africa, with more than 50,000 people living permanently in town long before the British Empire claimed the isles.[5] The first records we have of cinema attendance indicate that by the mid-1920s, some 2,700 people were going to the cinema in Zanzibar each week, and in the neighboring isle of Pemba, a somewhat smaller but no less impressive 1,500 patrons took in a show weekly.[6] According to historian James Burns, in neighboring Kenya and nearby Zimbabwe going to urban cinemas was largely unheard of among Africans at the time.[7] In Kenya, less than 8 percent of the population was urban at independence, which partly explains why many Kenyans only began going to the cinema in the 1960s (and many actually never went at all). By the 1960s, one-third of Zanzibar's population was living in the capital city; by contrast, only

5

2 percent of all Ugandans were living in Kampala.[8] Moviegoing was an urban phenomenon.

Africans' historical relationship to the city was an equally important factor impacting who went to the show and how often. Tanzanian towns with permanent cinemas in the 1920s—including fairly small ones such as Chake-Chake, Tanga, and Ujiji—existed well before European arrival on the continent: they had permanent populations who considered the town home; many residents who earned their living independent of European employers; and long historical traditions of large-scale, urban, public entertainment at night. When entrepreneurs began offering itinerant shows featuring moving pictures in these towns, crowds welcomed the new arrivals with the enthusiasm they historically extended to dhows pulling into port or caravans marching into a market square.[9] Traders brought not only goods but also news, stories, music, dance, and other cultural styles from across the region and indeed the world. Urban residents of these trade-based towns had long been engaged connoisseurs of the cosmopolitan. Moving pictures were a novel form of cultural product in the first decades of the twentieth century, but urban residents appropriated them and made them their own just as earlier generations had done with Islam, the *kanga*, (cloth) or the *msondo* and *unyago* drums. After World War II, the number of cinemas in mainland Tanzania grew exponentially, as up-country entrepreneurs diversified their holdings and invested their capital assets to put their towns on the cinematic cultural map. The fact that cinemas sprang up all across the country illustrates the immense value Tanzanians placed on enjoyment of this cultural form. Local exhibitors delighted in their ability to bring global media products to local doorsteps and also in their capacity to bring their community together and their town to life at night.

All across the continent, people appreciated celluloid spectacle and drama, but the nature of colonialism, capitalism, and urban civic life was not always conducive to the growth of a vibrant moviegoing culture. The literature on screenings offered by colonial film units and mining compounds demonstrates that film and collective viewing were widely appreciated all across the continent.[10] But as Odile Goerg's 2015 book on commercial cinema in colonial French West Africa reveals, audience size varied greatly from town to town.[11] It was not that Africans in Dakar, Bamako, or Cape Town did not appreciate this form of leisure as much as their counterparts in Tanga or Ujiji; the issue was having the opportunity to take in a show.

Settler colonies had stringent policies restricting Africans' access to town. Urban housing was limited, and pass laws and police harassment constrained Africans' freedom of movement at night. Many towns were also largely colonial creations. The Kenyan towns of Nairobi and Kisumu, for instance, were established by Europeans and relied on a largely migrant labor force. Structurally and administratively, Africans were made to feel as though they did not belong. In Nairobi, they needed a special, government-issued permit before they could buy a ticket to a show. A patronizing list of rules and expectations—detailing a dress code and mode of comportment while in a theater—handed out with the special pass also hampered Africans' desire to go to a film.[12] In the 1950s, as moviegoing blossomed in Tanzania, Kenya was largely under lockdown due to Mau Mau. One can only imagine that in the tense political climate of the Emergency—with more than fifty thousand Kenyans arrested in a single week in Nairobi during Operation Anvil—few were venturing downtown to see what was playing at the cinema. In Zambia and the Belgian Congo too, Africans were prohibited from entering commercial, indoor theaters until just a few years before independence.[13] In many cities across the continent, mining compounds, colonial social centers, and church facilities served as the primary venues for Africans' engagements with film.

Tanganyika's status as a League of Nations Mandated Territory and Zanzibar's status as a Protectorate, rather than as formal colonies, gave Africans in these areas a few more protections than those living in Kenya, Zimbabwe, and the Congo, but colonialism was never benign. Across the continent, official colonial opinion was that unless they were required for menial labor Africans belonged in the countryside. Most authorities were convinced that urban Africans were idle or lazy or, worse still, criminally inclined.[14] Tanzanian officials were no exception. Efforts to "protect" the sanctity and security of the cities were constant. Africans had to struggle to make their housing legal, and common strategies for earning an independent living in town—such as selling food on the street, raising a few goats or chickens, hawking fish door to door, or selling beer and sex—were criminalized. Offenders were not only arrested or fined but also frequently returned to "where they belonged." According to Andrew Burton, the capital city of Dar es Salaam was regularly hit by allegedly curative purges to cleanse the city of so-called undesirables.[15] But despite official efforts, Dar es Salaam's population grew, from approximately twenty-five thousand

7

when the British took control from the Germans after World War I to nearly one hundred thirty thousand at the end of colonial rule.[16] Colonial authorities had the power to criminalize African urban lives and livelihoods, but clearly, they could not control them.

In Dar es Salaam, Tanzanians also fought for Africans' rights to go to the movies. James Brennan and Andrew Burton have written masterfully of Dar es Salaam as viewed and imagined by colonial officials and urban planners, where urban space was neatly divided into exclusive racial zones. The city center—where the cinemas were located—was officially outside the "'African zone," and any African found there by police after dark was subject to arrest.[17] But thousands of Africans went to the cinemas in Dar es Salaam nonetheless, pursuing their pleasures as they desired and giving little heed to administrative imaginary lines. Cinema patrons and owners protested against colonial efforts to keep Africans away from the show, and within a few years of the British takeover of the territory, they had won certain concessions pertaining to Africans' rights to the city (see chapters 1 and 5). By the 1930s, one of the few "legitimate" excuses Africans could offer to escape arrest when caught in the city center after dark was that they were coming from the cinema or escorting a friend home after a show.[18] In other towns, however, African attendance was more constrained. One of the key arguments developed in *Reel Pleasures* is that cities have their own histories and cultures. Examining regional variations in cinema attendance allows us to see how and why Tanzanians' experiences in cities differed, as well as how their relationships with urban space changed over time.

The nature of cinematic capitalism in Tanzania also enhanced Africans' access to the show. All the theaters in the nation were owned by local businessmen. These entrepreneurs invested substantial sums of money building and outfitting their theaters; to make the venture profitable, they needed to sell as many tickets as possible, and many patently rejected administrative calls to restrict African attendance. Equally important, exhibitors lived in the communities where their cinemas operated. They established theaters as a sign of their investment in building social community and bringing people together through a shared appreciation of the arts. Providing attractive and enjoyable entertainment for their communities was a source of great pride. Excluding people because of race or class would have undermined these principles, as well as their bottom lines. At theaters run by industry pioneers, Africans comprised the majority of the audiences from the earliest days.[19] In Tanzania, cinemas were independent enterprises, free of the constraints imposed by large exhibition and distribution chains. This too altered their relationship to people in the neighborhood. It was local customers, not distant corporate managers, who determined if a theater would succeed or fail.

Elsewhere, the industry differed. In Dakar and Accra, the first cinemas were owned by Europeans, and they used both exclusive pricing and location to deter all but the most "civilized" from taking in a film.[20] Only when ownership and location diversified did audiences diversify as well. In the settler colonies of South Africa, the Rhodesias, and Kenya, white capital dominated the industry, and segregation of facilities and audiences was the norm. By the 1920s, South Africa had more cinemas than the rest of the continent's countries combined, but it took another thirty years before people of color had regular access to theaters in many towns. The South African exhibition and distribution industries were dominated by a white-owned monopoly, and according to David Gainer and Vashna Jagarnath, even when independent theater owners wanted to offer screenings for mixed or nonwhite audiences they were hampered by the monopoly's control of films, not to mention the enforcement of apartheid.[21] Small-town theater owners had only limited control over the nature of their own shows.

Mobility was central to many Africans' conceptions of modernity and citizenship. With the end of colonial rule, traversing earlier social, physical, and economic boundaries became a source of newfound delight. Urbanites took great pleasure in walking through previously exclusive parts of town and spending late nights downtown. In Tanzania, urban populations also soared after independence, and going to the movies became one of the premier national pastimes (see chapters 4, 6, and 7).

FILM, SPACE, AND COLLECTIVE PUBLICS

This book builds on a long and rich tradition of African urban social, cultural, and leisure history that emphasizes the vitality and creativity of average men and women and their power to fashion their own lives. Generations of scholars have demonstrated how landless men, disgruntled wives, assertive teens, and even dutiful daughters traveled to towns across the continent in pursuit of particular goals and opportunities and how, despite the odds, they built not only personal homes and individual families but also communities and the social and economic institutions that sustained them. Today's scholars take as an unspoken premise the fact that Africans shaped the physical and social structures of the urban environment. State officials may have deemed African housing or leisure activities illegal, but rarely did they succeed in keeping people from building, drinking, dancing, selling, playing music, or raising their children in town. This study adds to this vibrant tradition of scholarship by examining how cinemas—as a particular form of urban space—figured in these negotiations between authorities, entrepreneurs, and urban residents over the shape that Tanzanian cities would take. It also demonstrates how individuals and groups utilized cinematic space to create social and intellectual communities and bring joy to their individual and collective days and nights.

Going to the movies provided people with far more than a legal pretext for walking the streets after dark; it gave them a reason to inhabit areas beyond their immediate neighborhoods and a means of establishing both a physical and an emotional bond with the city at large. Walking through the streets on their way to a show with friends, family, and lovers transformed their relationships with urban space, binding people and place together with affective ties. As they laughed with friends on the way to the movies, wiped tears from their eyes outside the theater after the show, or filled alleyways with the sounds of filmic love songs, moviegoers transformed abstract urban spaces into places imbued with sensual, aesthetic, and emotional attachments.[22] Theaters— and the urban streets in which they were enmeshed—became invested with tangible, deeply personal meaning. These residual affective bonds between people and place remained long after a fleeting show had passed. In the interviews I conducted for this book, recollections of nights at a favorite theater brought tears of joy and longing to many people's eyes. Others smiled deeply and said, "That's where I spent some of the happiest, most meaningful days of my life." Cinema halls were not lifeless chunks of brick and mortar; they resonated with soul and spirit. They were places that gave individual lives meaning, spaces that gave a town emotional life.

Cinemas were considered by many to be the anchor of the community, and in fact, entire neighborhoods were frequently known by the cinemas in their midst. Urban landmarks, rather than street names and addresses, served to orient one around town. North and south, east and west meant very little to most; far more meaningful directionals in the capital city of Dar es Salaam were the Avalon, the Empire, the Odeon, the Amana, and the New

Chox. These were points on urban mental maps that resonated; these were spots that everyone knew.[23] In Mwanza, Dodoma, and Mbeya too, a visitor could ask anyone he or she met and be pointed to a family member's house or a business in the vicinity of the Liberty, the Paradise, or the Enterprise. These were not banal, soulless spaces surrounded by acres of empty parking lots left lifeless after customers walked out the door. These were buildings in the heart of urban neighborhoods, deeply integrated with adjacent homes, schools, mosques, markets, and ports. Disparate urban spaces and people were linked together through the city's cinematic beating heart.

Across generations, cinemas were central to community formation. It was there, more than at any other place in the city, that a diverse array of a city's population came into contact. Going to the movies together in no way erased class, gender, race, or religious differences; indeed, at the movies many were forced to acknowledge the immense diversity among people in their town. But through the process of enjoying the same leisure activity and then talking about the same films at work, in the shops, and on the streets, urbanites created "in-commonness," doing something much bolder than ignoring or eliding difference, creating something shared despite it.[24] At the movies, older, established urban residents met on a weekly basis and many new urban immigrants were introduced to people who could help them find housing, work, and scarce materials of all sorts (see chapters 2, 5, and 7). These networks then extended into the larger physical and social landscape of the town, as those who gathered at the cinema returned to their respective neighborhoods and shared their new insights, friends, and connections with others who were sociologically more like themselves.

Boundaries of gender were also negotiated in the interest of attending the movies. In colonial urban Africa, public recreation was largely gendered male; cinemas were sometimes an exception to this general rule. Where cinemas were located, women's historical relationships with urban space, as well as local cultural and religious norms, were decisive factors affecting female attendance at shows—and not just in Africa but across the globe.[25] These issues are explored in detail in chapters 3, 5, and 7, with particular attention paid to how cinemas and cities were perceived across the country as well as how women's attendance changed over time and varied according to the types of films screened. Typically, however, Sunday shows were family affairs in Tanzania. Everyone, everywhere, regardless of gender or age, attended these shows. Sunday screenings often gave women

11

and children their sole opportunity to venture downtown. Along the coast, theater owners went a step further and responded to women's clamoring for additional public leisure opportunities by offering gender-segregated, ladies-only (*zanana*) shows. There was nothing inherently immoral about moviegoing or watching films; it was the possibility of encounters with random men that threatened a woman's respectability. The ladies-only shows provided women with the opportunity to enter the public realm without jeopardizing their reputations. These all-female matinees, attended by hundreds each week, were a blessing to women who otherwise found few patriarchally sanctioned opportunities to cavort downtown. In Zanzibar, women from the royal family joined with hundreds of less prominent citizens to watch Indian and Egyptian films. Such outings were the highlight of the week. Whether women lived in purdah or not, ladies' shows gave them a chance to dress up, stroll through town, and make public space their own (see chapters 3 and 5). Thus, even being in purdah did not prevent women and girls from participating in the film-inspired debates that engulfed households, kitchens, and shops.

Cinematic content came to life in the city, further enlarging the networks of people brought and bound together through their engagement with film. One could spot other fans of a favorite star at the market or on the street if they rolled up their pants just like Raj Kapoor did in *Awara* (Kapoor, 1951) and *Shree 420* (Kapoor, 1955); donned a hat like Dev Anand's in *Guide* (Anand, 1965); or coifed their hair like Elvis, Geeta Bali, or Pam Grier. In the 1960s, two men who were utter strangers might meet at a shop because they were both in hot pursuit of limited, underground supplies of James Bond underwear with "007" emblazoned on the elastic band. Later, when they met again at a football match or on the city bus, they might nod and acknowledge that they had more in common than the obvious. Men who dared to sport "Pecos pants" (wide bell-bottoms) when such transgressions often resulted in public assaults by members of the Youth League or Green Guards or even a stint in jail signaled, as they walked down the street, not only their love of Guliano Gemma and Italian westerns but also their membership in a larger group of youth at odds with the socialist state's efforts to control the most mundane aspects of life (see chapters 5 and 7).[26] Across generations, fans adopted looks, stances, and language from the movies, but as they did so, the audience they had in mind for their performative engagement was always local. Adopting the latest in cosmopolitan

Figure I.1 Jaws Corner. Photo by Sabri Fair, December 2014

fashion demonstrated their knowledge of global trends and at the same time conveyed their desire to set their own city's style.

Films were also physically inscribed on urban space. Jaws Corner is certainly one of the more enduring examples. Jaws Corner is a well-known *baraza*, or neighborhood spot where men meet, drink coffee, play board games, socialize, and debate local and world events. This corner, where six major streets intersect in the narrow, winding way of Zanzibar's famed old town, had long been a major meeting spot. In the 1970s, the area was renamed by a group of young men after they watched the blockbuster hit *Jaws* (Spielberg, 1975).[27] The following day, they painted the first shark on a wall and christened the area Jaws Corner. Forty-some years later, this area is still referred to by that name, and the symbol of Jaws is still regularly repainted on the walls of the buildings to mark the territory.

Jaws Corner powerfully illustrates the complex ways global film products are interpreted, inscribed, and given meaning at the local level. Like
audiences across the globe, these young men in Zanzibar were thrilled,
scared, and fascinated by *Jaws*, one of the first movies to successfully employ mechanical stunts. The film became a global cult classic, filling theaters on return runs not just in the United States but also in South Africa,
Australia, and Tanzania.[28] When *Jaws* made a two-day repeat run at the
Majestic in Zanzibar in 1978, it filled the theater with a midweek crowd of
more than twenty-five hundred fans, marking it as one of the most popular Hollywood films ever screened in the isles.[29] Some of the young men
who established Jaws Corner were fishermen; others swam regularly at the
nearby waterfront. They teased and terrified each other, screaming "JAWS!"
or humming the infamous tune that foreshadowed the shark's attack while
they worked and played in the water.[30] They engaged each other as well
as anyone who stopped for coffee or a board game at this busy corner in
debates inspired by the film. Was Jaws real or fake? Could a shark really
chomp a boat in half? How did those fishermen in the village of Nungwi,
known for catching the sharks regularly sold in the market, manage? What
mistakes did the old fisherman in the film make that resulted in his defeat?
Did Zanzibari fishermen have better strategies for outsmarting the fish?

But these young men who painted Jaws on the walls of their baraza
and pestered everyone with their incessant questions about how to defeat
a shark also had some big local fish in mind. According to people I interviewed, *Jaws* was a fitting metaphor for political life in the isles. Like many
in Zanzibar in the 1970s, the lead character in the film was a fisherman
who had to use his wits to stay alive and remain a step ahead of his ad-
versary. He had to be constantly prepared for an unexpected assault and
continually rethinking strategies and new ways to maneuver. Although this
character was killed in the end, he provided the knowledge and inspired
tenacity that allowed his younger compatriots to defeat the shark.

Many residents and shopkeepers in the neighborhood of Jaws Corner
were targeted in the pogroms that wracked the isles after the 1964 Zanzibar
Revolution, and relations between actors of the state and neighborhood
residents have been tense ever since. The trauma suffered by families,
friends, and neighbors in the 1960s was kept from healing by regular assaults, both petty and grand—a situation that has persisted to the present
day. The founding members of Jaws Corner were politicized by the initial

attacks on their community, and many have been harassed, arrested, and imprisoned over the years. Jaws Corner eventually became synonymous with vocal opposition to the ruling political party. In the topography of urban place-names, it became a landmark, an emblem of a collective resolve to kill the monster who attacked the defenseless. In the 1990s, during the early years of multiparty politics, Jaws Corner was one of the first public spaces associated with the opposition Civic United Front (CUF), and often, there were more posters for CUF in the vicinity of Jaws Corner than there were in the rest of the city combined. For decades, then, *Jaws* has served as a local metaphor for the relentless, bone-crushing power of the state. But like Quint, the rugged fisherman and less-than-noble hero of the film, those who inhabit Jaws Corner refuse to concede to naked, terrorizing power. They have resolved to defeat the beast or die trying.

CAPITALISM, SOCIALISM, AND RACISM

Examining the role of Tanzanian entrepreneurs in building, running, and sustaining the cinema industry provides a necessary counter to broad-based stereotypes of Africa as a continent in need of external aid to foster economic development. In this book, we see instead men who recognized an opportunity and ran with it. They provided a service their townspeople clamored for and earned a respectable living in the process. Like the wealth of literature on the African "informal economies" that burgeoned in the 1970s and 1980s, this study highlights how local businesspeople mobilized vast local, regional, and transnational networks to meet local demand. By illustrating how Africans have continued to provide for their own most important daily needs—from housing materials to food, clothing, transportation, and leisure—this literature recognizes and gives credit to the plethora of small-scale entrepreneurs who have built the continent.[31] Historians have given renewed attention to studies of business, and literatures on the "varieties of capitalism" have burgeoned, but to date, these varieties include few people of color and even fewer from the African continent. Historical studies of business and capital in Africa are necessary to illustrate how economic change has occurred over time, how cultural matrixes impacted business practices, and how individual and communal values structured the accumulation of profit. Neither capitalism nor socialism is a fixed system; both change over time and vary across cultures. And no economic system exists without the individuals who bring it to life. This examination of the cinema industry in Tanzania over the course of the twentieth century allows us to see the concrete ways individuals in specific places and times influenced the forms that capitalism and socialism took, illuminating variations, inconsistencies, and contradictions that force us to rethink the norms presumed by economic *isms*.

The men who built the exhibition and distribution industries in Tanzania during the first half of the twentieth century were businessmen, of course, but also showmen and civic boosters. Profit was important for them, but equally significant was the desire to enhance the splendors of urban life and show their friends and neighbors a good time. As chapters 1, 2, and 8 elaborate, returns on investment in a cinema were slow to materialize at best, but the personal satisfaction gained by sharing a passion for film and turning others into fans was immense. The admiration entrepreneurs earned by building beautiful, prized cultural institutions was also priceless. Colonial officials gave little attention to enhancing the aesthetic qualities of urban Africa, but the entrepreneurs who built theaters created architectural forms that were not just functional but also attractive, innovative, and inspiring. Cinematic capitalists wed their desire to earn money with an equally powerful desire to endow their community with an effervescent social, cultural, and built environment.

A related component of Tanzania's cinematic capitalism involved building social ties and feelings of reciprocity between entrepreneurs and people in the community at large. In many parts of Africa, there were generalized expectations that economic power came with communal obligations. Precolonial chiefs accumulated wealth through taxes and labor, but if they wanted to be seen as legitimate political officeholders, they needed to redistribute some of the wealth they amassed; this was often accomplished through periodic feasts or alms to the destitute. This ethos was carried into the twentieth century and applied to capitalists. A "good businessman"—and certainly not all were good—shared his wealth via ritual gifts or endowments to public institutions. In his pioneering work on East African philanthropy, Robert Gregory notes that many of the first libraries, gardens, hospitals, and sports grounds to welcome members of all races in colonial East Africa were financed by gifts from successful businessmen and their families.[32] Cinematic entrepreneurs gave to their communities by building places where people came together to find pleasure. They also

Figure I.2 Sultana Cinema in Zanzibar, c. 1953. Photo by Ranchhod T. Oza, courtesy of Capital Art Studio, Zanzibar

gave to individuals—and particularly children and youth—by letting them into the shows for free. Cinema seats were a commodity to be sold, but the passions and ethics that guided many entrepreneurs pushed them to share rather than to hoard. Selling a seat was certainly the most preferable option, but an exhibitor made no money by letting a seat go empty—yet he earned social capital as a good man if he gave it to someone with pleading eyes and empty pockets. In the words of Bill Nasson, who was well ahead of his time in writing about the significance of local theaters to community life in African towns, this was "penny capitalism with a chubby face," where cinema owners represented family-owned businesses deeply integrated into the social fabric of urban neighborhoods.[33]

Situating the business history of exhibition and distribution in Tanzania within a larger context highlights that there was nothing inherently generous about the cinema industry at large; the varieties of capitalism that permeated the business varied immensely across the globe, the continent, and even within Tanzania over time. In the United States, exhibition,

17

distribution, and production became a vertically integrated industry dominated by a small oligarchy of players in the 1910s and 1920s. Indeed, five large monopoly producer-distributor-exhibition chains controlled 75 percent of box office receipts in the nation by 1930.[34] In Britain, the industry was not quite so integrated, but three major exhibition circuits (Gaumont, ABC, and Odeon) controlled the rights for the first-run releases of all the major studios.[35] In Australia and South Africa, vertical integration of distribution and exhibition also held sway. In South Africa, the industry came under the monopoly control of Isador William Schlesinger, an American-born Jewish immigrant who relocated to Johannesburg in 1894. Schlesinger made a quick fortune in insurance, real estate, and citrus before turning his attention to building an entertainment empire that eventually included film production as well as print and broadcast journalism.[36] In 1913, Schlesinger began buying up South African theaters. He then moved to consolidate the seven independent suppliers of film in South Africa into one organization in which he was the dominant partner.[37] He continued the process of centralizing the industry through the 1940s. According to David Gainer, by the time of World War II Schlesinger controlled the first-run release of nearly all the major British and American studios in South Africa; in addition, he owned the vast majority of the most lucrative theaters in the country and had exclusive distribution contracts with all but twenty of the four hundred cinemas outside the major metropolises.[38] He also made valiant and repeated efforts to monopolize distribution across the entire African continent.

In South Africa, independent theaters and film importers had no chance against the economic and political power exercised by Schlesinger's monopoly. He made a sport of forcing men out of business if they dared challenge his power to determine what films they screened or the terms of their rent.[39] According to Gainer, if an exhibitor ever dared to show a film provided by an independent importer or did not follow the screening schedule set by Schlesinger, he would be "starved" of product until he left the business. Others were denied films because they dared to purchase new projectors from someone other than Schlesinger, who dominated equipment sales in South Africa as well.[40] Even two of the major powerhouses from Hollywood—Metro-Goldwyn-Mayer (MGM) and 20th Century Fox—fought lengthy, costly, and largely unsuccessful battles to break Schlesinger's monopoly. By the late 1930s, both studios capitulated to Schlesinger's terms, finding it more profitable and easier to work with him than against him. Together, "The Big Three" came to control 90 percent of the South African market, leaving little room for importers of films from India, continental Europe, or elsewhere.[41] The monopoly capitalism and vertical integration of the Gilded Age was on full display in the cinema industry in many corners of the globe.

But the monopoly model was not the only way to organize the industry. Denmark, for one, took an aggressive stance against vertical integration, legally banning related practices in 1933.[42] There, distributors were explicitly prohibited from owning cinemas. In India too, individual proprietorships held sway. In neither case did the lack of consolidation hinder the development of robust film production and exhibition industries. Actually, India has always rivaled, if not exceeded, Hollywood in terms of the number of films produced. By the mid-1920s, Indians were producing 100 films a year, a figure that grew to 300 per annum by the 1950s and peaked at more than 900 a year by 1985.[43] The number of exhibitors, distributors, and producers in India was similarly large. By the late 1940s, there were more than 600 producers actively making films. In the 1990s, the number of producers was beyond count. As film distribution consolidated in the United States, it democratized in India, growing from 11 distributors in the 1920s to more than 800 in the 1940s to over 1,000 by the late 1950s.[44] Exhibition has also been historically characterized by independently owned enterprises. In the 1950s, there was just a single vertically integrated production-distribution-exhibition company in India, but it controlled less than 1 percent of the nearly 4,300 permanent cinemas in the nation.[45]

Given the large number of distributors and independent exhibitors in India, the profits derived from ticket sales were much more widely shared there than in countries where the industry was monopolized by a few key players. The diversity of distributors in India also afforded greater power to exhibitors, giving them more room to negotiate for better films and film-rental terms.[46] In India, exhibitors have historically enjoyed the most stable and consistent profits in the industry, whereas in the United States and South Africa, distributors swallowed the lion's share of earnings. Block booking, a system whereby exhibitors were required to take a large number of low-quality films for the privilege of securing each hit they wanted, was a standard practice in the United States until outlawed in 1948, and it was a common element in Hollywood and South African international contracts for much longer than that.[47] Exhibitors worked essentially as the servants of big distributors rather than as autonomous entrepreneurs. Today in India, Denmark, the Netherlands, and a host of other countries, independent theaters screening films from a range of producers and various national cinemas remain an important part of local and national cultural economies. Clearly, political and economic policies shape not only industrial forms and the accumulation of capital but also leisure and cultural options.

The exhibition and distribution industries in Tanzania occupied an intermediary zone between the Indian and American models and changed somewhat dramatically over time as new political regimes, guided by different economic goals, rose to power. During the colonial era, both the exhibition and distribution industries were run by independent, local entrepreneurs. With but a few exceptions, all the theaters in the nation were individually owned and run by local men who lived in the towns where their businesses operated. As in India, the state paid little heed to the development of these small enterprises. So long as the theater owners abided by fire codes and adhered to censorship rules and regulations, the state did little to govern, direct, or restrict how the industry developed. The colonial state considered most small businesses in Tanzania too petty to bother with, and cinemas, shops, fishmongers, and carpenters operated largely beyond the official gaze. Although colonial officials surely noted the large numbers of people streaming in and out of the cinemas each day, they somehow could not even imagine that it might be worth their while to tax admissions or business profits. There was a duty imposed on films as they entered the country, but no official attention was ever paid to what these films earned once imported.

The situation changed radically with independence. Rather quickly, the cinema industry was brought under state control. Movie theaters continued to be individually operated, but the buildings themselves were nationalized, in 1964 in Zanzibar and 1971 on the mainland. In the 1960s, the socialist state became increasingly directive about all aspects of the national economy. The 1967 Arusha Declaration marked the official beginning of the nationalization of key industries, banking, and trade. The following year, film distribution was formally nationalized. The impact this had on film imports and what was seen by urban audiences was less significant than those familiar with socialist film policy in the Soviet Union or Cuba might imagine, but the profits gleaned by monopolizing distribution were enormous (see chapter 8). Net profits recorded by the Tanzania Film Company Ltd. (TFC) grew from just under 400,000 shillings (TSh) two years after incorporation to nearly 8 million in 1985, a twentyfold increase in a fifteen-year period after adjusting for currency devaluations.[48] Oddly, the nature of the industry came closest to the American and South African monopoly models of vertical integration under state socialism. Structural changes allowing for a concentration of capital were deemed good for socialism. Meanwhile, political rhetoric vilified cinematic entrepreneurs as bloodsucking, alien capitalists because nearly all the men in the business were of South Asian descent.

The racist rhetoric of the postcolonial era paid no heed to the facts that not all Asians were capitalists and that capitalists came in immense varieties. The South Asians who immigrated to East Africa were diverse in terms of religion, class, caste, and region of origin. There were also huge variations in the relative degrees of economic success they achieved in East Africa. Some rose to become the captains of industry, but others worked as *dhobis* (clothes washers) whose daily labor earned them little more than their daily bread. As Richa Nagar has pointedly argued, racial stereotypes often erase the class diversity found within the South Asian communities of East Africa.[49] Postcolonial racist rhetoric lumped all Asians into the category of *dukawalla* (petty, conniving shopkeepers) or economic saboteurs, completely ignoring the class and personal diversity within the Asian community: neither all Asians nor all shopkeepers were greedy racketeers.[50] The literature on minorities in East Africa tends to emphasize racial antagonisms between Africans, Asians, and Arabs. Fueled by the racism of the nationalist era, the historiography has sought to explain why East African minorities have been stigmatized as "blood enemies," to quote James Brennan, stereotyped in political discourse and journalistic accounts from the independence era as ruthless exploiters, slave traders, and foreigners who did not belong.[51]

There were certainly Asians and Arabs who exploited Africans economically or whose actions aided imperial or subimperial conquest. And extrapolating from these cases to entire populations served the political interests of many early African nationalists. Vilifying minorities, political leaders from Zanzibar, Tanganyika, Uganda, and to a lesser degree Kenya were able to craft a common enemy and distract attention from other concerns. This discourse fueled racial antagonisms, hatred, and assaults. In Zanzibar, in addition to the thousands of Arabs who were murdered, the Asian population of the isles dropped from 18,000 to 3,500 due to persistent assaults in the first decade after independence.[52] Many initially joined family and friends on the mainland, but after the Acquisition of Buildings Act of 1971 nationalized property, tens of thousands once again felt compelled to move on.

The personal and collective impact of racism directed at Tanzanian Asians was enormous, but it is also only part of the picture regarding Asian experiences in Tanzania. Equally important were the personal bonds and social networks that allowed immigrants to transform foreign soil into home. By and large, cinema owners were not, to use Gijsbert Oonk's term, *settled strangers*—people who lived within African communities but not among them and who remained, even after generations, somehow "other." Cinema owners and managers were individually named and personally known by nearly everyone in their communities. They were recognized for their individual foibles, quirks, passions, and acts of kindness. As critical members of their local social community, they were deeply integrated, not segregated, and perhaps this helps explain why the vast majority of cinema owners remained in Tanzania long after their buildings were nationalized and most of the Asian population had left the country. Like those who fled between the 1960s and the 1980s, these men endured immense personal and communal trauma. They watched as homes and businesses were seized, daughters and sisters were raped and forcibly married, fathers and sons were imprisoned, and most of their family and communal members went into exile. But for reasons that even they have difficulty explaining, they could not leave. This was home.

I refer to the men who built and ran the cinema industry as they considered themselves: Zanzibaris and Tanzanians. This is not to deny their status as minorities descended from immigrants but to emphasize how they worked to build institutions where anyone who wanted it had access to a seat and to foster communities where people mobilized not only around difference but also around what they had in common. The literature on Asian and Arab immigrants and minorities in East Africa is paltry, given the size of these communities and the fact that they have lived in the region for some two hundred years.[53] It is also surprising how dominated the literature is by images of othering minority populations. Our failure to fully examine the diversity of immigrant experiences in Africa, combined with the preponderance of studies emphasizing conflict, has granted normativity to the racism of nationalist rhetoric. *Reel Pleasures* elucidates how South Asian immigrants and their children developed not only businesses but also social and cultural institutions that built bridges rather than divides.

Socialism, like capitalism, is both an ideology and an economic system that exists only because human beings animate it and bring it to life. Socialists, like capitalists, also come in many different colors and stripes. The political economy of the cinema industry changed enormously after independence, but different actors within relevant state bureaucracies and ruling parties had varying interests that were often at odds. These complexities and contradictions are explored in chapter 6 in the context of the state-owned drive-in theater and in chapter 8 where struggles between industry bureaucrats and others are highlighted. The state was no monolith, nor was the party all-powerful. Socialism had different meanings and measures, and individuals invoked the term with particular outcomes in mind. Race also had little bearing on political predilections. There were Asians and Arabs who were staunch socialists and Marxists and many Africans in the postcolonial governments who were neither. Being a self-described Marxist also did not necessarily mean that one disavowed cinematic pleasure or even Hollywood: a leading comrade in the Tanzanian Defense Force was known by his self-chosen nickname, Tony Curtis, and Hafidh Suleiman, a hard-line member of the Revolutionary Council in Zanzibar, adopted the nom de guerre Sancho after a villain he idolized in Italian westerns.[54]

The study of moviegoing allows us to hear variety in the voices of postcolonial socialists and see the complicated and divergent ways in which rhetoric and reality intertwined. If some of the narratives presented here seem contradictory, that is because they were. The world is messy, and history no less so. You will not find the straight lines and neatly mapped socialist world depicted in James Scott's *Seeing Like a State* here.[55] Examining postcolonial cinema policy is more like looking through a kaleidoscope. Every time you turn the lens, you see a different image, distinct but entangled in some difficult-to-discern way with the images before and after. Socialists did not all agree.

CINEMATIC MODERNITY AND MOVIEGOING: GLOBAL TWENTIETH-CENTURY PHENOMENON

This book focuses on the issues and practices that made the business and pleasures of moviegoing in Tanzania distinctive, but it is vital to recognize that in many ways the Tanzanian experience was also part of a much larger global phenomenon. All too often, Africa is ignored or marginalized

23

in studies of worldwide developments. The continent is consigned to the "global shadows," as if Africa were tangential, rather than central, to the unfolding of truly global experiences.[56] This exploration of the cinema industry in Tanzania destabilizes historiographies of underdevelopment and depictions of Africa and Africans as always scrambling to catch up to the rest of the world. Instead, we see that Tanzanians' experiences were actually commensurate with global trends in technological appropriation, the rise of commercial public leisure, and engagement with transnational media flows. From enraptured nights enveloped in the cocoon of a picture palace in the early twentieth century to midcentury evenings in the family car at the drive-in to late-century retreats to the couch to watch a video or DVD on the family television, Tanzanians' film watching was in step with both the aesthetic and the technological standards of the time.

Films and stars that took other regions of the globe by storm were equally popular with Tanzanian crowds. Charlie Chaplin and Laurel and Hardy delighted silent-movie audiences everywhere. In the 1950s, the superb acting and impeccable production values of Raj Kapoor's films ensured sell-out crowds not just in India and Tanzania but also in Russia and Turkey.[57] By the 1960s, Elvis Presley was the hottest thing around, and youth from Mexico City to Melbourne, Memphis, and Moshi flocked to the theaters to see his latest moves on screen, which they then emulated on hometown dance floors.[58] A decade later, Bruce Lee was the world's leading screen icon among young moviegoers, including those in East Africa. In the 1980s, the disco craze took the world by storm. But from Tanzania to Dubai, Singapore, and Hong Kong, it was the dance moves of India's Mithun Chakraborty, who starred in *Disco Dancer* (Shubash, 1982)—not those of John Travolta or the Village People—that inspired. As Brian Larkin has persuasively argued, twentieth-century media cultures were transnational phenomena with multiple, shifting metropoles.[59] We can only understand transnational media by appreciating Africans' roles in making them truly global.

The mechanical technology of moving-picture display was nearly identical across the world, yet how this technology was negotiated as a social practice was incredibly diverse. Technology is always imbedded both in space and in society. To say that moviegoing was a global twentieth-century phenomenon is not to say that it was the same everywhere. James Burns's recent book on cinema across the British Empire brilliantly reveals some of

Figure I.3 Dar es Salaam Cinema ads. *Sunday News*, May 8, 1966

the key similarities and profound differences in the cinematic experience during the early twentieth century.[60] Likewise, Lakshmi Shrinivas's *House Full* and Sudha Rajagopalan's *Indian Films in Soviet Cinemas* profoundly destabilize Western moviegoing habits as the norm. A host of factors affected the social practices of exhibition and moviegoing. I situate the Tanzanian experience within this global context.

At the turn of the twentieth century, moving-picture technology was a revolutionary invention. It mesmerized audiences the world over. Inventors in the United States, Germany, and France were all experimenting with different ways of displaying moving pictures in the 1890s, but the Lumière brothers, Auguste and Louis, are generally credited as giving birth to "cinema" with their first public display of moving pictures on a screen in Paris, in 1895. Unencumbered by patents and pushed by demand, the new technology quickly enveloped the globe, as regional artisans and inventors built on and combined various initial designs.[61] Photography itself was fairly new, having been refined only in the late 1870s, and many who went to see moving pictures at the turn of the century had actually never even seen a still photograph. The ability to seemingly capture people on film was deemed magic; watching people and objects move on a screen was spellbinding. When editors of the *East African Standard* ran a two-part article explaining what a moving picture was and how it worked for their English-speaking, literate audience in 1911 and 1912, the obvious assumption was that few of their British readers had yet experienced this novelty themselves. Though itinerant shows were by then somewhat common in caravan towns and ports in Tanzania, isolated British settlers living on rural farms in Kenya could only imagine what such a spectacle was like. The technological mysteries of moving pictures remained unfathomable to many, even for those who had seen films. In 1917, the *swadeshi* "father of Indian cinema," Dhundiraj Govind Phalke, made a short documentary, entitled *How Films Are Prepared*, to educate the public. He included footage from some of his earlier features as well as shots illustrating the physical and technical processes involved in making these films. In the early decades of the twentieth century, Europeans, Africans, and Asians all marveled at this new technology with equal delight.[62]

Quickly, however, moviegoing grew from an utter novelty to a mass form of leisure and one of the most popular "cheap amusements" found in burgeoning cities across the world. During the first decades of the twentieth century, urban populations exploded, and mass entertainment was born. Initially, the *mass* in *mass media* did not refer to a message pegged to the lowest common denominator; it referred to the huge publics that gathered to see a show. Nickelodeons—so named in the United States because of the nominal fee required to go inside—spread like wildfire in American cities in the first decade of the 1900s as millions of new urban immigrants flocked to the show.[63] A similar phenomenon could be found in China, Japan, Thailand, Iran, Egypt, Turkey, Tunisia, Lebanon, Singapore, Jamaica, and India.[64] By the time of World War I, overflowing nightly shows were just as common in Zanzibar and Dar es Salaam. The fact that the first films were silent and thus intelligible no matter where they were shown aided the spread of moving pictures. The standardization of film technology and projection equipment furthered the ease with which films circulated: it made no difference, technically speaking, whether the films imported into Zanzibar were produced in India, France, Japan, or Britain. The cheap cost of entrance—typically just a few pennies—made it possible for the working poor in cities from Calcutta to Chake-Chake and Chicago to indulge in an evening's delights at the moving pictures.

The thrills and spectacles offered by this new visual medium were not its only draw; equally enticing was the ability to vicariously travel to exotic places and explore new surroundings, to access news and information, and to learn about people and customs different from one's own. Again, readers must appreciate the limited availability of other forms of mass media at that time. Prior to the 1920s, radio broadcasting was extremely limited even in Europe, and many people in the world did not gain access to wireless transmission or affordable receivers until well after World War II. Newspapers and magazines were relatively inexpensive sources of news and information, but most of the world's population was not literate, making access to print media irrelevant to most. American journalists frequently referred to movies as "the workingman's college" and lamented that more people got their knowledge of the world beyond their doorsteps from film rather than newspapers.[65] In Tanzania too, the desire to learn about new people and places and see how others lived was one of the common reasons respondents cited when asked why they went to the show. An old Swahili maxim said, "Travel to learn/open your mind." Film offered a slice of the traveler's vision to those who never left home.

Movie houses also offered patrons access to modern splendors and delights. Inaugurated in Europe in the 1910s, picture palaces swept the globe in the 1920s as the industry sought to cultivate a "higher-class" audience and distance itself from the urban working classes who comprised the majority of viewers during its first two decades.[66] Picture palaces evoked glamour and opulence, encouraging patrons to identify with the dream world on the screen.[67] I grew up hearing stories from my great-aunt and great-uncle about their adventures dressing in their finest clothes and taking the streetcar downtown to the Tivoli Theater or the Chicago, while courting in the 1930s. For them, these were rare adventures, and their reminiscences focused on the exotic: the opulent theaters with their gilded ornamentation and antique statuary, as well as the extravagant use of electrical lighting—three thousand bulbs in the marquee that spelled *Chicago* and the largest chandelier in the world in the theater lobby—all of which was a world away from their working-class tenement and single-bulb daily life. Going to the movies allowed them not only to see films but also to physically and emotionally experience a life of affluence and plush indulgence, if only for a short time.

East Africa's first picture palace, the Royal, opened in Zanzibar in 1921, the same year that the Tivoli and the Chicago debuted. (See fig. 1.2.) Following global aesthetic standards, Zanzibar's picture palace encouraged patrons of every class to enter a space where they too were royal. According to Mwalim Idd Farhan, a teacher and musician from Zanzibar who attended the theater in his youth, "The way you were treated at the cinema made you feel proud, like you were *someone*. Just being in the building made you feel like a Sultan.," He added, "At home we had no electricity, or even a chair. The cinema was lit up both inside and out, and the chairs were upholstered, something unknown to us Swahili back in those days."[68] The American movie moguls A. J. Balaban and Sam Katz, who operated the Tivoli, the Chicago, and one of the first national chains in the United States, would have been proud of the theatergoing experience in Zanzibar. In the 1920s, they were among the first in the United States to inaugurate an elaborate corporate policy of treating moviegoing patrons as kings and queens, which was part of their effort to attract wealthy and middle-class audiences to the picture show.[69] Mwalim Idd recalled that "at the cinema everyone was treated like royalty. You had an usher, like a servant, who politely guided you to your seat. He called you sir or madam, and made certain you were comfortable. Nowhere else were you treated so grand." The fact that the Royal also boasted box seats for the sultan of Zanzibar's large extended family and the British resident's entourage further enhanced the feeling of moviegoers like Mwalim Idd that there, if nowhere else, they were experiencing the same indulgence as the wealthy and powerful.

Prior to World War II, movie theaters were among the rare public venues where working-class and wealthy patrons encountered each other and enjoyed the same entertainments as relative equals. Few places in the world were as democratic in this regard as the United States, where patrons all paid the same price for a ticket and sat wherever they chose—so long as they were white.[70] In Britain, India, and Tanzania, theaters—like ships, trains, and other public amenities—were divided not by race but by class. The elite typically occupied the balcony, if there was one, and paid substantially more for a ticket. "Second-class" patrons occupied the rear of the main floor, and the poor sat closest to the screen. Such seating arrangements allowed middle-class and elite patrons to maintain their sense of propriety, while simultaneously giving the poor and working-class patrons the satisfaction of knowing that they were traveling the same journey and arriving at the same destination, for a fraction of the cost. Despite—or perhaps because of—divisions by class within the theaters, cinemas were one of the few public places that brought patrons from residentially restricted neighborhoods and clearly distinct class backgrounds into the same space. Whether the cinema was in Bombay, India, in Bukoba, Tanzania, or in Bristol, England, it was while waiting in the queue for a ticket, milling in the lobby, or buying concessions that many encountered the most diverse cross section of people from the town where they lived.[71] Exposure to the novel and foreign—on screen, in the city, and within the crowd—was part of the thrill of any adventure at the cinema during these early years of mass commercial leisure.

Film viewing was a collective form of entertainment, and the collective sense of engagement was enhanced by the fact that it seemed nearly everyone was watching—and then talking about—the same film. Opening day frenzies generate a lot of buzz the world over. But in this regard, the Tanzanian experience diverged from the global standard in several important ways. First, Tanzanian audiences took their obsession with being part of the opening day crowd to the extreme. No one with the means to attend would ever agree to be turned away on opening day. Long-standing coastal social conventions of wanting to claim attendance at the biggest and most elaborate public gatherings—be they weddings, dance competitions, or football contests—parlayed into public excitement for filmgoing. Moving-picture technology was incorporated into a long-established cultural milieu that placed immense social value on being able to say that you were part of the largest social gathering around. Local exhibitors and distributors played with and into these desires; most films were screened for only one day or maybe two. Thus, if you wanted to see a new film, you needed to see it the day of its premier—otherwise, you would likely miss it entirely. People paid close attention to the coming attractions; if a film by an applauded director or featuring a popular star was announced, news quickly traveled through the town. If rumors spread that tickets for the most prized seats were selling on the black market, everyone rushed to the ticket windows to book while they could, rather than risk being left out of the party.

Tanzanian exhibitors and distributors had to innovate on more standard industrial practices in order to meet the demands of these large and insistent audiences. In India, Europe, and the United States, first-run open-ings at numerous theaters were made possible by the simultaneous release of hundreds of prints of a new film. But in East Africa, importers and dis-tributors could rarely afford to buy more than one print. African ingenuity, agility, and ability to make the most of a limited situation saved the day. Depending on anticipated demand, Tanzanian distributors and exhibitors would agree to release a new film in two to four of the largest theaters in a given town simultaneously. By staggering start times by twenty minutes and employing "reelers"—agile men with well-tuned bicycles who sped reels of film from one venue to the next—multiple theaters could run a premier using a single print. At the time, films were wound on a series of small reels, each of which contained roughly twelve minutes of run time for a given production. Indian films, which were the only ones ever "reeled," typically consisted of nine to twelve reels. As each reel finished at the first theater, it was quickly rewound and handed over to a reeler, who hopped on his bicycle, raced through town, and delivered it to the second theater in line. The second theater would then send its first reel to the third cinema in the line, after starting the second reel that had just arrived by bicycle from the first cinema. All nine to twelve reels of a film would be sped around town in this way.[72] Moving-picture technology may have been somewhat standard-ized across the globe, but it required the ingenious application of indige-nous tools to overcome local constraints when operating in Tanzania.

In most respects, however, Tanzanian exhibition practices were com-mensurate with global standards of technological sophistication and mo-dernity. Local exhibitors brought talkies, CinemaScope projection, spring-loaded seats, air-conditioning, and stereophonic sound to their theaters as soon as they were able to do so, often within months of an innovation's debut in New York or London. The latest global architectural trends were also featured at movie theaters in East African towns. Cinematic entre-preneurs consciously built dynamic regional and transnational networks to keep abreast of the world's latest developments in the art, craft, and industry of film and exhibition, and they were committed to giving local audiences access to the best product they could possibly deliver.

The glamour and sophistication exuded by the film industry accentu-ated East African entrepreneurs' innate predilections for using their busi-nesses to project not just films but modernity, elegance, and style as well. Modernity was a prominent discursive and developmental category of the

Figure I.4 Plaza Cinema, Moshi, c. 1947. From the personal collection of Chunilal Kala Savani

twentieth century, as important in Tanzania as anywhere in the world. But how *the modern* was defined, measured, valued, and imagined was open to considerable debate. Drawing on a rich Africanist scholarship exploring the contested nature of modernity, successive chapters in this book illustrate how differently positioned historical actors conceived of the modern; how they imagined and gave form to their place within it; and how, to cite Lynn Thomas, they used the term to make political claims for inclusion or articulate visions of "new—often better—ways of being."[73]

SOURCES AND METHODS

My first waged job, when I was thirteen years old, was working as a ticket and concession stand girl at a small local theater. Years of working at this theater clued me in to the fact that a lot more goes on at the show than watching films. This was where uptown girls met downtown boys and relationships crossed the tracks, often behind parents' backs. Bold young couples sneaked upstairs to the baby cry room—a soundproofed enclosure with seats and a large glass window looking out on the screen—to make

31

out. Teens too young to purchase alcohol found willing buyers among the slightly older men who hung out at the adjacent hot dog stand. Those with cars, tricked-out bicycles, and hot stereos to sell positioned themselves on the streets outside the theater to take full advantage of the crowd. Adults probably socialized and made deals too, but none of us teens paid much attention to them. The owner taught me how to sell a single ticket over and over again, but it was only while doing this research that I came to appreciate how critical such acts of subterfuge were to the economic survival of American small exhibitors. The mysteries of projection were also first revealed to me there, although our projectionist was gruff and rather creepy and deemed us girls unworthy of learning the trade. But the older girl who filled in for the owner each Monday, his sole day off, more than made up for the creepy projectionist. She spiked the orange fountain drink with gin for employees and let us dance in the lobby after the patrons were gone. She also took me to my first rock concert, Bruce Springsteen's, and later helped me learn how to drive. My job at the theater later spurred me to ask Tanzanian cinema employees not only about the movies they screened but also about the characters they worked with and the people in the neighborhood they got to know from working at the show.

Data gathered from beyond the traditional archive form the bedrock on which this book is built. Interviews turned my attention from the films people went to see to what going to the movies meant and how people made use of films in their own lives. Kiswahili terms such as *mshabiki* (fan, fanatic), *mpenzi* (lover), or *mteja* (addict) were often used by people to describe their relationship both to particular genres of film and to the filmgoing experience in general. A surprising number of Tanzanians went to the movies at least once a week, and many self-described fans went two times a week or more. I also sponsored an essay contest by distributing flyers, in English on one side and Kiswahili on the other, outside schools, businesses, and bus stops. Respondents were able to write on one of eight different prompts. My fantasy was that this exercise would inspire young people to talk to their elders about the past, but in neoliberal Tanzania literate youth scoffed at the paltry prize money I offered. Older people, however, responded enthusiastically, providing detailed descriptions of nights at the drive-in, fashions borrowed from films, and the place of moviegoing in their lives.

Places are containers of memory; as Annette Kuhn has beautifully shown, memories have topography.[74] Walking down memory lane might be a cliché, Kuhn argues, but getting people to take such steps is incredibly useful to the oral historian, providing a pathway into the past. In her own study of moviegoing in 1930s Britain, Kuhn found that encouraging respondents in their seventies and eighties to speak of walking to the cinema had the effect of transporting them back to their early years. In the process, films became situated in a larger network of physical, social, and emotional experiences. Setting the scene in this way gave events and facts a context, without which there would have been no purpose for recall. In the United States, nursing homes have recently started making extensive use of music from years gone by to revive the memories of patients plagued with dementia. The sound stirs regions of the brain that trigger physical, mental, and emotional ties to more vibrant times in elders' lives. My own research revealed that memories of the cinema and moviegoing were surprisingly vivid for many Tanzanians, which I suspect is because such memories activate and draw on so many different parts of the brain. Thinking back to significant films triggered visual, aural, sensual, emotional, and physical recollections for many respondents. Thus, memories of the drive-in made more than one person salivate because the drive-in was intimately connected with a favorite food that was consumed only there. Others began to sing or dance while recalling a particular Egyptian or Indian film. And several cried and many laughed in remembering the antics of a partner, sibling, or age-mate with whom they went to see films. Memories of moviegoing were often powerful because they were not just about a film but also about the emotional relationships that were forged—between families, peers, and lovers—in the process of going to the show. Cinema memories went well beyond celluloid. They were infused with sensuality and affect; they were poignant, sentimental, and nostalgic.

Nostalgia loomed large in these recollections of nights at the show. This nostalgia was informed by specific longings and cultural desires, needs that "the future can no longer supply."[75] Nostalgia for nights at the movies combined deep yearnings for a lost time and a distant place, and in these recollections, the personal and the political were often intertwined. For many of those who were interviewed, childhood, adolescence, or the early years of parenthood corresponded with the hopeful years leading up to or immediately following national independence. These were years of triumph for many, as well as faith that the future's promise would be fulfilled. Nights at the movies were remembered nostalgically in part because they

33

were associated with the fleeting glories and excitement of youth, a time in both individual and national life cycles that could never be retrieved. Like parents who have grown estranged from their adult children, Tanzanians looked back to the 1950s, 1960s, and 1970s and longed for the confidence and closeness of those early years. Nostalgia for the golden years of moviegoing was also filled with longing for large public outings. For elders who rarely left the house anymore except to attend funerals, this hunger for public sociability and laughter was particularly strong. Critics might argue that interview data cloud my interpretation precisely because facts and feelings are intertwined. But my interest is not just in what happened in the past; I also want to know what it meant to *live* that past—how experiences produced feelings that gave meaning and pleasure to life.

Over the course of three summers and one academic year of fieldwork, I conducted over a hundred interviews with exhibitors, distributors, employees, black marketers, and men and women who went to the cinema. Interviews were typically an hour in length, but a few extended over several days. Many enthusiastic, knowledgeable, or accommodating interlocutors were pestered too many times to formally cite. With the help of research assistants, I also made an effort to do somewhat random surveys in Zanzibar, Dar es Salaam, Tanga, Bagamoyo, Moshi, Arusha, Morogoro, and Iringa to get a larger sample of attendance patterns and cinematic tastes, including the views of those who never went to the movies at all. The plan was to conduct surveys in Mwanza, Ujiji, and Lindi as well, but life, and death, intervened. Some three hundred surveys and interviews were conducted in these towns to ascertain how the cinematic habits of local moviegoers compared to those of the larger urban population. Sociologists have every right to laugh at my "random samples": I made no effort to survey every fifth household, but I did consciously query men and women from a range of ages, religious faiths, races, and neighborhoods. In addition, I hired research assistants to target populations different from those I was interviewing myself. My own random samples involved asking people of relevant ages—in the markets, on the streets, on buses, at restaurants, at soda stands, at football matches, at concerts, or in any public venue where I had the opportunity to engage someone in conversation—about their film and moviegoing experiences. This method gave me a way to start a conversation with a stranger while fixing a shoe or waiting for a bus. If a shop was open but had few customers, I took the opportunity to query employees.

Taxi drivers too were frequently canvassed. I also stopped in restaurants, bars, and roadside eateries that catered to people of different classes and offered to buy a drink for anyone willing to chat about his or her experiences. In several cases, employees took it upon themselves to spread the word with members of their cohort, arranging hours of conversations for me over the course of several days. If people were avid cinema fans, we made plans for more lengthy formal interviews. But even with folks who never went to the movies, it was important to understand why. Without these random surveys or the help of research assistants, I would have talked only to fans.

Personal photo collections also provided invaluable insights into how films were mediated and made use of in daily lives. Scholars have studied fan magazines to understand how and why certain stars appealed to audiences, and they have explored the tactile efforts men and women made to replicate the glamour, bravado, and drama of the screen in their own lives.[76] Tanzania had no fan publications, but the stories I was told by people as we looked through their photo albums resonated in significant ways with what fans elsewhere articulated in print.

Fans do not merely watch movies; they make tangible links between what they see on screen and their own emotional and material realities. Some fans collect pictures and memorabilia related to idolized stars, and Tanzanian youth were as prone to pasting their bedroom walls with images of their favorite heroes and heroines as kids anywhere. Fans also translate what they see into a cultural activity by sharing their feelings and thoughts with like-minded others. In literate cultures with commercial print media, this is often made evident by subscribing to fan magazines or joining fan clubs. In Tanzania, this type of fan engagement was more likely to take place on the streets, in kitchens, or in classrooms than in published form. People displayed their affinity for various stars by adopting hairstyles, hats, clothing, and modes of comportment modeled on a character in a film. Nearly all the self-identified movie fans who shared their photo albums with me had pictures of themselves in dresses, shirts, shoes, or hairstyles worn by film heroes or heroines and incorporated into their own fashion repertoires. Fan clubs as such did not exist, but this in no way precluded the existence of an expressive fan culture.

Much of the written data used in *Reel Pleasures* was found outside the official archive. The sources range from the uncollected holdings of departments, ministries, offices, and parastatals to private, personal collections of papers and business records. The potential significance of uncollected state records alone is astounding. For instance, in the national archives in Dar es Salaam the sum total of material related to the Tanzania Film Company—the parastatal that effectively took over the film distribution industry in 1968—was contained in just one file with a few pieces of paper. But in the buildings that formerly housed TFC staff, I found not only files but also films made by TFC that many, including the company's filmmakers, presumed were forever lost. The private archives of TFC employees, as well as theses written by students at the University of Dar es Salaam, were far more useful on the topic of postcolonial state film policy and practice than the material in the national archives. Similarly, nearly all the records of the postcolonial censor board cited in this volume, including wonderfully illuminating confidential files revealing internal struggles between the party, the TFC, and the censors, were found in a closet in an office building that has since been demolished. Members of the staff generously opened the door and allowed me to spend weeks occupying one of their desks. The Office of the Registrar of Companies, part of the Ministry of Industries and Trade, was a gold mine for information on corporate accounts. As Jean Allman has argued, to produce innovative new studies of the African past scholars need to begin aggressively pursuing alternatives to what has been conveniently collected, sorted, and cataloged in the national archives.[77] This is all the more true for the postcolonial period, when far less was written down and even less was collected and archived.

This is not to dismiss the importance of data gleaned from colonial archives. Without these records, I would have few dates indicating when cinemas were established, and without the obsessive compulsion of British censors in recording the name and origin of every film that entered the country, I would have no idea how many movies were imported or how diverse their origins were. Yet as Charles Ambler asserts in his work on moviegoing on the Zambian Copperbelt, censor records tell us a lot more about European anxieties than about the pleasures Africans derived from watching films.[78] Published newspapers are also invaluable, but like every type of source, these too skew our attention in particular ways. According to newspaper ads, Hollywood films dominated Tanzanian screens, accounting for more than 80 percent of what was shown during the colonial era. Based on this evidence, it would be easy to conclude that Hollywood shows were what most Tanzanians went to see. But my three months of fieldwork in

Zanzibar, Wete, and Tanga, in 2002, shattered this image. None of the interviewees who went to the movies during the 1950s and 1960s could name a single American film, and the names of American actors were nearly as difficult for people to recall.[79] The issue was not failing memories or a lack of interest in films: at times, the names of Indian films and directors and favorite Indian stars rolled off the tongues of respondents more readily than the names of their own children and grandchildren. The point is that even though Hollywood films dominated the press, they were not, by and large, what Tanzanians chose to see. Talking to people about their moviegoing experiences and film preferences during that initial exploratory phase of research completely transformed this project.

Reading newspapers alone and being largely unfamiliar with Indian films before I began this study, it would not have occurred to me that Indian movies were what everyone went to see. From the 1920 through the 1950s, these films were often not even advertised, since newspapers were not most urbanites' principle source of information about what was happening in town. And rarely did any town but Dar es Salaam or Zanzibar make the press. Yet as it turns out, in the 1950s and 1960s East Africa was the most lucrative overseas market for Indian films in the world. By 1960, export earnings on Indian shows screened in East Africa totaled some $700,000 (or $5.4 million in 2016 dollars, after adjusting for inflation).[80] In the 1960s, India films garnered a mere 5 percent of global screen time, and producers typically realized less than 2 percent of their box office earnings in foreign markets. This was largely because Hollywood screen contracts kept competitors out of many markets.[81] To get Hollywood films, exhibitors generally had to agree to forgo all others. Not one of the sixteen thousand theaters in the United States screened Indian films at the time, and the situation in Europe was little better. In fact, in the 1950s and 1960s Indian films earned ten times as much in East Africa as they did in the United Kingdom. Audiences in East Africa were obviously a critical—and lucrative—overseas market for Indian producers. This region is where Bollywood first really went global.

Private personal and business records are another set of sources I used to enhance the image of cinematic history projected by official archives. The largest cache of written documents was a vast trove of box office receipts kept by Abdulhussein Marashi, owner of the Majestic Cinema in Zanzibar. Abdul meticulously preserved the box office receipts presented to distributors and state officials between 1972, when he took over the business from his father, and 1993, when he screened the last 35 mm film. These records provide detailed accounts of attendance over time, as well as information on every film that was screened. They also give information on changing tax rates and the relative earnings of the Majestic, the state, and the distributors. Abdul's was one of the last theaters operating in Tanzania when I began this project, and many other proprietors said they had burned their remaining records just a few years (and in one case just weeks) before my arrival. If only someone had dared to follow in Bill Nasson's pioneering footsteps back in the 1980s, we could have amassed and preserved countless personal memories and business records that are now forever lost.[82] Asad Talati, owner of United Film Distributors—the largest and most important provider of films for Tanzanian theaters after independence—was another exceptionally generous source of knowledge and documentation. For years, he responded to my e-mail queries and provided details on international suppliers of films, costs of prints, and relative earnings. He also shared family and business archives and photos dating back to the 1930s. A list of films distributed during the waning years of commercial 35 mm exhibition, from 1992 to 2002, and returns and attendance details were also provided by his associate in Zanzibar. Members of the Savani family in Kenya and Tanzania also shared business records from their film distribution and exhibition companies. Without these individuals' willingness to share their personal archives and knowledge, I would know almost nothing about the economics of the industry, and I would not be able to corroborate the rich oral evidence on audiences' cinematic preferences with precise numbers of ticket sales.

This book joins a very small number of studies examining commercial exhibition, distribution, and cinemagoing in Africa. Now, the tide of neglect is beginning to turn, and scholars have started to publish books on what was obviously a significant form of leisure on the continent. In 2013, James Burns published *Cinema and Society in the British Empire, 1895–1940*, a pathbreaking, comparative study of the growth of cinemas and moviegoing cultures across Africa, the Caribbean, and Asia. Burns documents that the enthusiasm for commercial film and moviegoing was widespread throughout the tropics, and he makes us wonder how academics could have ignored such a vibrant facet of leisure life for so long. His book also emphasizes that we have only begun to scratch the surface in understanding film and audiences, as well as business across the British Empire.

The myriad ways in which local factors influenced the development of commercial cinema are further highlighted in Odile Goerg's *Fantômas sous les tropiques: Aller au cinéma en Afrique coloniale*. Published in 2015, this is the first book-length study of commercial cinema and urban audiences in sub-Saharan Africa. Goerg makes clear that Tanzanians' affection for film was far from exceptional. In western Africa too, urban Africans became avid moviegoing fans early in the twentieth century. The composition of the audience, the genres of films that were popular, and how people appropriated visual images and made use of them in their own lives are topics we have only begun to appreciate. And, as Gareth McFeely has argued, historians have neglected a significant component of African urban lives by ignoring the forty thousand people who went to the movies each week in Accra in the mid-1950s. Examining the Ghanaian businessmen who ran the theaters, he asserts, also fundamentally transforms our understanding of the economy.[83]

I am the first to concede that a regionwide study like Goerg's for East Africa could quite conceivably destabilize some of the claims I make about Tanzanians' unique position in the regional cultural economy. My initial aim was to do a comparative study of Zanzibar, Tanzania, Kenya, and Uganda, but once I began doing the research with two small children in tow, that plan was quickly revised. Until we have detailed studies of Uganda and Kenya, as well as Mauritius, Comoros, Sudan, Ethiopia, and Mozambique, it is impossible to say how the Tanzanian experience compares. The works of McFeely and David Gainer, on African moviegoing and the cinema industries in Ghana and South Africa, respectively, highlight the critical importance of detailed country-specific studies. These scholars illustrate the immense variations in business practices and cinematic experiences between the two countries, each of which in turn differed quite markedly from Tanzania, Senegal, and the Congo.[84] And as Lakshmi Srinivas demonstrates in her recent book, *Full House*, we urgently need more ethnographically rich and varied studies of moviegoing to destabilize both the textual approaches that have dominated examinations of film and traditional reception studies. *Reel Pleasures* offers just a glimpse at what will eventually become a more complex, colorful, and nuanced picture of moviegoing in Africa through the contributions of others.

There are few advantages to taking as long to write a book as I took in finishing this volume. But one of the good things that has come from

spending over a decade with this project is that a new media technology—
the internet—has developed, allowing readers to access nearly all of the
films mentioned. Whereas I spent extensive amounts of time and money in
the first decade of the 2000s hunting down copies of Indian classics, Italian
westerns, Hong Kong action films, and German soft porn, today you can go
to YouTube and watch everything from the remaining reels of the first Indian feature film, *Raja Harishchandra* (Phalke, 1913), to the Tanzania Film
Company's *Vita vya Kagera* (1980)—with live footage of the Tanzanian war
against Idi Amin in Uganda—from the comfort of your own couch.

Chapter 1

BUILDING BUSINESS AND BUILDING COMMUNITY

The Exhibition and Distribution Industries in Tanzania, 1900s–50s

THE ENTREPRENEURS who built the exhibition and distribution industries in East Africa were businessmen, and like their counterparts the world over, their aim was to turn a profit. But business cultures everywhere are also historically situated and socially constructed. In early twentieth-century East Africa, the capitalist profit imperative was tempered by local cultural norms and religiously sanctioned obligations that made sharing wealth and investing in community corollaries of individual accumulation. Wealth was revered—but all the more so when it was shared. "Big men," esteemed women, and respected families earned their social status by financing cultural troupes, religious festivals, or large public parties that brought the community together. Privately investing in public infrastructure (such as wells, waterworks, schools, mosques, and hospitals) was another common means of redistribution. Immigrants and the children of immigrants abided by these customary standards as much as the native born did, for this was an effective way to signal their commitment to belonging and to foster social bonds in their new home.[1]

For the men who built the exhibition industry in Zanzibar and Tanganyika in the early 1900s, one critical factor in evaluating business returns was the degree to which a capital investment helped build a good city and put one's town on the map. As of the 1930s, only nine towns were able to boast of regular film screenings (see map I.1). These towns were in their infancy at the time—a small fraction of their size and population today—and were built largely of impermanent materials such as mud and stick and thatch. Investing in a building like the Royal in Zanzibar, the Regal in Tanga, or the Tivoli in Mwanza signified a man's belief in the solidity and prosperity of the future, as well as his commitment to the beautification of a town's built environment. Cinemas were among the largest and most architecturally innovative buildings in any town, and bringing the latest global media to the community added a touch of cosmopolitan spark to local life. Building a public space where hundreds came together demonstrated one's willingness to invest in urban civic and artistic culture.

The men who built the industry incorporated elements of preexisting leisure and business customs into cinema's commercial culture. Like turning a profit, the desire to outdo a rival was a basic business motivation. But in East Africa, the rivalry between theaters was infused with elements from local song, dance, and football competitions. Leisure group competitions were at their most intense when a club had a known competitive rival, and the same was true for cinematic exhibition. Through innovative architectural styles, technological acumen, and the display of the best and most recent films, rival exhibitors continuously strove to win the contest for loyal fans, and moviegoers benefited as a result. This may sound like business competition anywhere, but in the small, face-to-face environment of East African towns, it took on a distinct quality. Business relationships between distributors and exhibitors also incorporated elements of the patron-client relations that infused nineteenth-century business and leisure networks. Building social capital and enhancing a reputation as a trustworthy, dependable individual were deemed far more critical to business success than amassing quick profits. And in the industry in Tanzania, unlike in some other capitalist cultures, the goal was never to eliminate one's rival but rather to outclass him.

The earliest displays of moving pictures were introduced to East Africa by merchants, traders, and sailors traveling the oceans aboard British and Indian vessels. By 1904, if not before, exhibitions of moving pictures had become an exciting and regular feature of urban nightlife in Zanzibar Town.[2] Local audiences could never be sure when a man carrying a hand-cranked projector and a few reels of film along with his other goods would arrive, but when he did, word quickly spread.[3] Little was required to muster a crowd other than finding a place to hang up a sheet as a makeshift screen: by nightfall, a sizable audience was virtually guaranteed. Given the public's enthusiasm, what began as an itinerant sideshow quickly grew into a permanent venue with regularly scheduled displays.

Hassanali Adamjee Jariwalla began as an itinerant showman when he was barely twenty and went on to pioneer the formal industry in East Africa. Jariwalla was actually employed by a firm in Bombay as a cloth merchant and traveled by dhow on the monsoon winds taking goods from India to Madagascar and Zanzibar each year. On one trip, according to his grandson, someone in Bombay offered him films and a portable projector to carry together with his other wares,[4] and just for fun, he took them along. Soon, he was providing itinerant shows when the dhow he was traveling on reached port, and the enthusiastic welcome that greeted his arrival each season encouraged him to start putting on regular shows. In 1914, he settled permanently in Zanzibar, choosing to make it his new home. That same year, he opened the region's first semipermanent exhibition hall inside a khaki tent adjacent to the central market, in the neighborhood of Mkunazini. He named the theater the Alexandra, and Zanzibar's *Official Gazette* proudly advertised that the latest releases from India, Europe, and the United States could be seen there each night. Within two years, Jariwalla was operating two such venues in Zanzibar, as well as a third in the Upanga neighborhood of Dar es Salaam.[5]

Business was brisk, inspiring him to draw up plans to transform his exhibition venues from makeshift tents into rock-solid picture palaces. He took what certainly must have seemed a crazy risk, investing his hard-earned savings from the cloth trade in erecting East Africa's first luxurious cinema — the Royal Theater, which opened in 1921 on the site now occupied by the Majestic Cinema. The Royal was one of the grandest public buildings in

43

Figures 1.1 a,b Alexandra Cinema, Dar es Salaam, c. 1916. Images courtesy of the
Melville J. Herskovits Library of African Studies Winterton Collection, Northwestern University

Zanzibar and certainly the only piece of architecture of its stature devoted
to entertainment.[6] Designed by the British resident, J. H. Sinclair, who was
trained as an architect, the theater was built in the Saracenic style popularized across the British Empire by those who sought to incorporate so-called
Muslim domes and Indian arches into imperial design.[7] Sinclair may have
dictated the facade, but Jariwalla insisted on the content. The Royal was a
large and modern theater on a par with the best operating anywhere in the
world at the time. With room for nine hundred seated patrons, as well as box
seats and a balcony, the latest projection equipment, and new releases from
three continents, the Royal was as impressive as its name implied.[8]

Why would a young South Asian merchant risk his savings by sinking everything into an unproven industry and an outlandishly expensive
building in Zanzibar? To be sure, the crowds drawn to the moving pictures

Figure 1.2 Royal Cinema, Zanzibar, opened 1921 (renamed the Majestic in 1938). Photo by Ranchhod T. Oza, courtesy of Capital Art Studio, Zanzibar

in the town seemed insatiable, and Jariwalla was clearly of an entrepreneurial spirit. But if it was possible to make people happy showing them silent films inside a tent, why invest something on the order of a million dollars to build a picture palace?[9] This was Africa, after all. Wouldn't a makeshift tent suffice? And when the average weekly attendance was five hundred patrons who paid less than ten cents for each ticket, how many shows over how many decades would it take to pay off the cost of construction, let alone turn a profit? Furthermore, how sure could anyone be in the 1910s that cinemagoing would be an enduring pastime—especially in East Africa, which was in the early, brutal years of imperial conquest? To comprehend the rationale behind building a cinema in colonial Tanzania, we need to see that investments of this type were about much more than monetary profit: they earned proprietors, townspeople, and even colonial officials valuable social and cultural capital.

Building Business and Building Community, 1900s–50s

All the men who built cinemas in Tanzania were either immigrants or the children of immigrants, but after settling in Zanzibar or Tanganyika, they invested heavily in developing not just business and commercial networks but also the physical, social, and cultural infrastructure of their towns. Sinking their capital literally into the ground spoke louder than any words could about their commitment to making East Africa home. The architectural history of the region is largely a lacuna, but Robert Gregory estimates that upwards of 90 percent of the cityscape in East African colonial towns—from private homes to markets, courthouses, and schools—bore the mark of immigrant Asian contractors, architects, craftspeople, financiers, and laborers.[10] From private homes and shops to public buildings of many types, South Asians played a major role in giving East African towns concrete form. Privately owned buildings offered opportunities to display artistic style, architectural competence, and financial power.[11] And cinemas, as monuments to the idea of a collective public sphere, enabled businessmen to demonstrate their commitment to building a beautiful town and a social community as well.

The religious traditions and personal experiences of many South Asian immigrants helped generalize expectations that financial success came with communal obligations. Many early immigrants were from regions prone to drought, famine, and debt. Most had fled because they had few other options. A common trope in the stories of late nineteenth- and early twentieth-century immigration is the young man, perhaps barely in his teens, who arrives in East Africa poor and alone. He is saved from abuse and the vagaries of life only by the generous intervention of some kind soul who takes him in; provides food and shelter; gives him a job; and helps him mature into a solid, successful, and respected man.[12] In fact, a number of poor immigrant boys became some of the wealthiest and most powerful men in East Africa. And according to individual and communal narratives, they never lost sight of where they came from. Personal experience both inspired and obligated them to help others.

In neither India nor East Africa did the colonial state invest substantially in health, education, or social welfare. Consequently, such obligations fell largely on local communities. South Asians built many formal and informal institutions for fund-raising and communal development; the annual tithe of 10 percent of one's income collected by Shia Ismailis and Bohora Ithnasheris for communal investment was but one expression of the strong commitment to social improvement. These acts of philanthropy were, of course, just as fraught with struggles over class, gender, and religious norms and decorum as benevolent donations by the Fords, Rockefellers, or Gateses, but they were still critically important for feeding the hungry, healing the sick, and housing the poor. They also reinforced the conviction that financial success came with communal obligations. Many of the first public hospitals, clinics, and maternity wards in East Africa were built and endowed by successful South Asians, as were some of the best public libraries, the first universities and preschools, sports stadiums, social halls, cultural centers, and public parks. In many instances, these institutions were the first of their kind serving all, regardless of race, religion, or class.[13] By making charitable gifts, endowing public institutions, and supporting critical social welfare institutions, individuals and families displayed their wealth, demonstrated their generosity, and enhanced their own social standing as patriarchs and communal elders. Through generous giving, they acquired blessings in the afterlife and social power in the here and now.

Cinemas were certainly not charities like orphanages or medical clinics, but they were nonetheless treasured gifts to the community: they healed souls, opened minds, and provided aesthetic and emotional nourishment for old and young alike. They were, to be sure, businesses first and foremost. But investing in a business enterprise that simultaneously provided a social good was a culturally and historically specific ideal of prudent spending. The men who built East Africa's cinemas were typically of much more modest means than those who endowed the universities and hospitals, yet in giving what they could, they too sought to endow their communities with cultural facilities. Cinemas were also frequently given over to charity organizations for fund-raising events, further demonstrating the owners' commitment to philanthropy. As early as 1920, for example, Jariwalla was dedicating the proceeds from various evening shows to charity, a tradition that was followed by proprietors up through the 1980s. Exhibitors were also known to dedicate proceeds to fledgling political parties or public institutions, including the police, schools, and sports teams. In addition, owners and managers frequently allowed local social groups to utilize their facilities rent-free for music, dance, and theatrical shows.[14] Charitable donations enhanced the personal and institutional bonds between theaters and the people of the town.

47

PROJECTING MODERNITY, TECHNOLOGICAL
SOPHISTICATION, AND COSMOPOLITAN CULTURAL STYLE

The social capital that came from having a cinema accrued to the community at large as well as to the proprietor. One recurring theme across the hundreds of interviews conducted for this project was that having a cinema of any kind, especially one as beautiful and impressive as the Royal, dramatically enhanced the cachet of a town and, by extension, the prestige of its people. Haji Gora Haji, a poet and film fan from Zanzibar who worked as a sailor on a *jahazi* (sail-powered cargo boat) in his younger days, described the status he and his crewmates enjoyed as Zanzibaris when they docked in "sleepy backwater towns" along the coast where few had ever witnessed the wonders of moving pictures. The two main islands comprising the Zanzibar archipelago, Unguja and Pemba, boasted six cinemas during much of Haji's life, making it the equivalent of a regional cultural Mecca.[15] Coming from a place with so many cinemas also gave young, economically poor but culturally rich Zanzibaris, Haji among them, artistic license to weave enraptured tales of evenings at the moving pictures for adoring crowds—tales that allegedly inspired others to stow away onboard boats headed to Zanzibar.[16]

Like picture palaces erected elsewhere in the world, the architecturally opulent theaters built in East Africa were intended to serve as spectacles and as sources of visual pleasure in and of themselves. At a time when the vast majority of Tanzanians lived in mud-and-wattle homes and almost no one had electricity, entering such a monument to modernity thrilled patrons nearly as much as the film entertained them. Going inside these glorious buildings evoked luxury and delight. As one woman said of the cinema in Tanga, "The Majestic was a classy theater, a truly chic, modern space. You felt elegant simply going in. Everyone dressed in their best clothes. You wanted to dress up, dress for your part, because the theater was such an elegant place."[17] Remarking on the Majestic Cinema in Zanzibar, one man recalled, "The building itself was astonishing, truly modern. When it opened our whole neighborhood felt proud. It was really something to be able to say you lived next door to the Majestic."[18] Another man made similar comments about the opening of the Sultana Cinema at the other end of town. "I was only a dockhand at the port, a day-laborer. You know, a man of little consequence or stature," he said. "But I remember when the cinema opened and my son was so proud. He kept telling all his friends that his father worked next door to the cinema [laughing]. It was like I built the place or something."[19] The general public claimed cinemas as their own and drew personal pride from their affiliation.

The architectural grandeur and names of the cinemas built in the first half of the twentieth century articulated the owners' perception of their towns' parity with cultural capitals across the world, as well as their commitment to enhancing residents' stature as fully engaged cosmopolitans and discerning cultural connoisseurs. Names such as the Globe, the Empire, the Alexandra, and the Metropole captured this sense of global cosmopolitan connection. The name Majestic was given to several picture palaces built along the coast, communicating each benefactor's sense of the grand, dignified, and aesthetically sumptuous contribution his theater made to the town. Paradise too was a popular name, evoking the heavenly, delightful nature of the experience afforded patrons once they stepped inside. There was also the Regal, the Empress, the Sultana, and the Elite. Proprietors and citizens alike had strong feelings that the names given to local theaters needed to convey the splendor and importance of the buildings and of the people who lived nearby or went inside.[20] In the early twentieth century, East Africans who patronized theaters such as the Royal, the Empire, or the Majestic suffered no illusions of inferiority or backwardness, and indeed, the owners and managers of these fine picture palaces did all they could to ensure that the patrons in their towns, no matter how big or small, felt thoroughly "first class" while they were at the show.

The white colonial elites were just as proud to have a theater in their town or territory. The British resident of Zanzibar was obviously inspired by the opportunity to draw plans for the Royal, and he proudly attended the grand opening and made a habit of treating visiting dignitaries to a film. Zanzibar may have been just a small crumb in the great scheme of the British Empire, but it was the only place between Egypt and South Africa with a picture palace in 1921.[21] When Jariwalla's second picture palace, the Empire, debuted in Dar es Salaam in 1929, it was opened by the governor of Tanganyika, who entered on a red carpet to the applause of white dignitaries and the fanfare of the army band. Colonial officials took delight in cutting the ribbons at cinema openings, and press coverage of these events was extensive. Film screenings were also big events for the European community. The *Tanganyika Standard* covered one such event at the Avalon

49

Figure 1.3 Christmas/New Year's greeting card from colonial Zanzibar. From the personal collection of Asad Talati

in Dar es Salaam in 1946. Attended by the governor of Tanganyika, the screening was described as "the most brilliant social function held in the center of town for many years."[22] A few years later when the Avalon was refurbished, the mayor spoke at the grand reopening, noting how venues like the Avalon provided him and others with an immense sense of civic pride. White journalists frequently emphasized how these modern cinemas served as proof of the tangible rewards of colonial development

Tanzania exhibitors continually strove to enhance the physical pleasure of patrons and improve the associated pleasures afforded to passersby. Jariwalla's first effort to update his khaki tents in Zanzibar came in the form of Cinema ya Bati, a permanent structure built of corrugated tin. The building, which had previously served as a potter's warehouse, was located on the poor side of town, across the bridge from the central market, in Ng'ambo (literally meaning "the other side"). The building was more permanent than a tent but far from regal. Inside, it was stifling hot during most of the year, and patrons sat on the floor. This was a step up from a tent—but only a small one. Jariwalla knew he and his town could do better than Cinema ya Bati. Thus, he began negotiating with the British resident of Zanzibar and designing plans for the Royal Theater—which would be built just down the street from the colonial court and the home of the resident. As World War I drew to an end and the Tanganyikan mainland fell from German to British hands, he also upgraded his exhibition venues in Dar es Salaam. There, he retired several of his khaki tent venues and moved the projection equipment to renovated buildings renamed the New Cinema and the Bharat (later the Globe). These venues were solid but small, seating only two hundred and three hundred patrons, respectively. Again, his vision was grander than the available architecture. So in 1929, he opened a second picture palace, the Empire, which was built in the Victorian style and was located, like the Royal, adjacent to the commercial and administrative centers of power. The Empire accommodated nearly six hundred patrons and quickly became a node of urban social life in the Tanganyikan capital.[23] Like the Royal in Zanzibar, the Empire in Dar es Salaam was a rare public space drawing all ranks of urban society—from the British governor to the average urban resident—into the same place at a time when colonial policy invested heavily in reifying difference and segregating space by race and class.

During the 1920s and 1930s as theaters spread across the land, Tanzanian proprietors worked hard to provide their communities with the most up-to-date and technologically sophisticated experience possible. Few theaters erected in these years were as impressive as the Royal or the Empire, but exhibitors did the best they could given their resources and the size of their towns. Most entrepreneurs began small. The first theaters in every town were tents, converted storerooms, or parts of warehouses. Regional differences in entrepreneurs' rates of capital accumulation and patrons' wages and access to cash impacted the timing and extent of upgrades. In Tanga, the tents used for exhibition were replaced in 1929 with two permanent theaters: the Regal Cinema and the Novelty Cinema.[24] In Pemba too, makeshift venues were replaced with permanent theaters at that time. By 1931, Pemba had three cinemas, one in Wete and two in Chake-Chake.[25] Nearly as soon as synchronized sound films hit the market, Jariwalla upgraded his equipment to accommodate "talkies." By 1932, both the Royal in Zanzibar and the Empire in Dar es Salaam featured the latest sound films. Three years later, striving to provide the most recent films to the widest public, Jariwalla also upgraded the projection equipment at the Globe to accommodate talkies.[26] Keeping up with trends in global technology and style was a hallmark of the cinema industry from its earliest days.

Shavekshaw Hormasji Talati was another Zanzibari cinematic entrepreneur who dedicated himself to bringing the latest cinematic technology and the best in global films to East Africa. Born in Zanzibar in 1889, he retired from the colonial civil service in 1932 and purchased the Cinema ya Bati from Jariwalla. The cinema would provide Talati with a little income after retirement, said his son, and it would help him stay active and engaged in the community.[27] After a few years of running the theater, it became clear to Talati that commercial cinema had financial potential, but he also realized that if his business was to grow and prosper, he needed to upgrade to sound and modernize the viewing experience for his patrons. So in 1939, Shavekshaw Hormasji Talati partnered with three other small businessmen from Zanzibar—Abdullah Mohammed Thaver, M. S. Sunjit, and Manilal Madhavji Suchak—and opened the Empire Cinema in Zanzibar, adjacent to the main city market. Being men of fairly modest means, they leased an old stable in a prime location and converted the interior to accommodate four hundred seated patrons. The structure afforded no room for a balcony, but what the partners' renovation lacked in physical attraction it made up for with cinematic style. The Empire featured first-rate projection and sound equipment and easily competed for customers with the more ostentatious Royal (which had been renamed the Majestic in 1938 when a new owner, Hassanali Hameer Hasham, purchased it from Jariwalla). Making the most of their personal and business connections, the partners quickly gained a reputation for bringing some of the best and most recent films from India, Egypt, Europe, and the United States to the isles. Thaver, for instance, had connections to the Egyptian film world that rivaled Jariwalla's in India; through the 1960s, Thaver was recognized across East Africa as the source of the best Arabic-language films in the land.[28] Actually, it is a wonder that the men were able to secure any films at all, given that they opened their theater and struggled through the first years of operating a new business just as World War II was heating up and global shipping lanes were closing down. But succeed they did, and from the modest beginnings of screening silent films inside a corrugated iron godown where patrons sat on old gunnysacks on the floor, these partners became, over the next two decades, the premier exhibitors and distributors in Tanzania.

Crowds thronged to the Empire in Zanzibar, and many consistently rated it as their favorite cinema, but the owners had grander visions for their town.[29] A converted barn simply did not live up to their idea of a modern cinema. The Empire lacked a balcony, which by the 1940s many patrons considered essential for theatrical savoir faire. The absence of a balcony also made it difficult to accommodate the sultan and his family, who wanted to see more movies but required semiprivate seating at public screenings. The high-class films the partners screened also frequently attracted crowds that exceeded the available seating capacity. Thus, by war's end the owners were organizing to build a larger, more striking venue than the Empire. Ideally, they wanted to build on the site of the former Cinema ya Bati, opposite the main city market, as the spot had sufficient frontage to allow the theater's architecture to "impress passersby."[30] They also wanted a site that was equally accessible and inviting to Africans, Arabs, Indians, and Europeans and that could accommodate patrons arriving by foot, bicycle, bus, and private automobile. The spot adjacent to the Darajani Bridge would have been perfect, but it was never approved. It took five years of struggle with the colonial authorities to finally agree on a site. This group of showmen refused to build the small, merely functional cinema the administration deemed adequate for Zanzibar; they insisted on erecting a classy, modern theater in a prominent part of town.

While negotiating with planning authorities and other officials, the partners temporarily rented a facility from the colonial government, at the newly constructed Raha Leo Civic Center on the outskirts of town. But from the beginning, this venture was plagued with difficulties and endless professional compromise. The partners were interested in running a proper business that would cater to the local demand for good films and thus turn a profit. The colonial officials, by contrast, tried to control and contain the venture and make it fit with their own visions of a cinema appropriate for Africa and Africans. The partners had to negotiate hard for the right to screen 35 mm commercial films, rather than merely 16 mm educational materials. They also fought administrative efforts to subject films previously screened at the Empire to additional censorship in order to make them "appropriate" for the largely African audience attending Raha Leo. Beyond that, colonial administrators tried to limit the number of nights per week the theater could operate as well as the hours of operation, two additional points on which the partners refused to budge.[31] The authorities ended up conceding on nearly every point in these negotiations, but it was exasperating for the partners to have to argue what seemed obvious: if you planned to open a theater or run a business of any type, you had an obligation to give your customers the best available — otherwise, they would look for better options, and you would fail.

The partners ran the cinema at Raha Leo for less than three years because in many ways it remained utterly below the standard they and their public demanded. Opening night foreshadowed the difficulties that would be faced by the partners: shortly after the first film, *King Kong* (Cooper, 1933), got rolling, the electricity failed, leaving the audience in the dark for more than an hour. The electricity started and then failed, started and then failed, frustrating everyone and potentially damaging new and costly projectors. By the time the power was restored, the crowd was in an uproar, and most people demanded their money be returned. Inadequate electrical service continued to plague Raha Leo throughout the cinema's remaining years, for the government flatly refused to upgrade the service to the degree required. In addition to losing money every time they had to cancel a show because the electricity failed, Talati and his partners lost face before their audiences. As owners of the Empire with plans to build a new picture palace for Zanzibar, Talati, Suchak, Sunjit, and Thaver had reputations to uphold, so they got out of their lease with the colonial government as soon as possible and forged partnerships with other East African Asians committed to running a proper enterprise.

During World War II, they took what was then a rare legal step for East African businessmen: they incorporated into a limited company, Indo-African Theaters Ltd. This allowed them to protect their families and personal property from liability for any calamities at their theaters, and moreover, it enabled them to seek other investors with capital to build proper, modern cinemas and secure business loans from banks.[32] The Zanzibari founders of Indo-African had the entrepreneurial spirit and technological knowledge to advance the cinema industry in East Africa, but as civil servants and small shopkeepers, they lacked the capital to turn their vision into reality. They saw great market potential in the Tanganyikan town of Dar es Salaam, whose population and wealth grew substantially during the war. They approached Kassum Sunderji Samji, a politically prominent and economically successful Ismaili businessman in Dar es Salaam, and offered him a share in Indo-African Theaters. Kassum Sunderji was a known film

fan who made something of a habit of attending the cinema after evening prayers. He recognized the need for an additional venue in the mainland capital in the 1940s, so when the partners of Indo-African approached him, he readily agreed to finance their expansion to Dar es Salaam. He funded the transformation of a godown near the port into the Avalon Cinema, which he leased back to Talati and his partners to run.

Kassum Sunderji was precisely the type of partner the men from Zanzibar needed to expand onto the mainland: he was wealthy and had liquid assets on hand; he was politically connected and well regarded by Europeans, which would help in getting building plans approved; and he was the head of the Ismaili community—a man with a well-deserved reputation for marshaling resources to support public infrastructure and charitable institutions. He personified the rags-to-riches success story that generations of South Asian immigrants passed on to their children and grandchildren. He had left his family of cowherds in India at the tender age of fifteen. Alone and uneducated, he immigrated to Dar es Salaam in the 1890s, where he found work as a shop assistant with a German company. After the war, he opened his own shop, catering to European tastes for cheese, chocolate, alcohol, and other imported goods. He did well financially and politically. He became the president of the Ismaili Council of Tanganyika and was made a count by a close friend, the Aga Khan. He was also appointed as an unofficial member of the Legislative Council by the British governor in the 1940s, another rare honor in those days.[33] Having a prominent business, religious, and political leader in their group allowed the owners of Indo-African Theaters to quickly and dramatically expand their operations. With

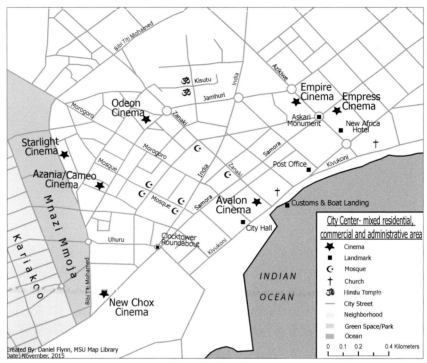

Map 1.1 Cinemas of Dar es Salaam city center

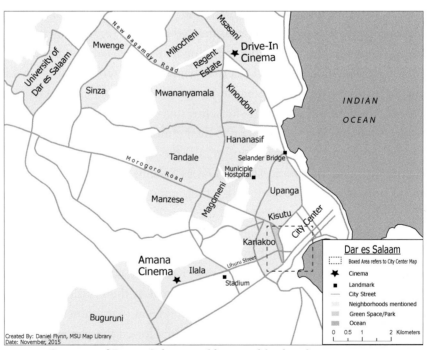

Map 1.2 Cinemas of Dar es Salaam and key neighborhoods

World War II still roiling, their business brought a bit of comfort to the citizens of Dar es Salaam. They opened the Avalon in 1944 with the premier East African screening of *Random Harvest* (LeRoy, 1942), a film about a British officer's dual lives and loves induced by shell-shocked amnesia, starring Ronald Colman and Greer Garson; the movie was nominated for seven Academy Awards and represented the high-caliber films the Avalon became known for offering.[34]

The accolades Kassum received from his connections to the Avalon spurred him to finance the building of two additional cinemas in Dar es Salaam in the 1950s: the Amana and the New Chox. According to his son and his projectionists, Kassum's affiliation with the Avalon significantly enhanced what was already a very solid reputation, making his name known to even wider segments of the population. The New Chox, like all theaters, was multiracial, but it came to be regarded as the premier cinema for the European community in Dar es Salaam, featuring films that catered to that crowd.[35] The Amana, located in the African suburb of Ilalla and adjacent to the football stadium, was the only theater ever built during the colonial era away from a city center. Kassum Sunderji's goal in financing the construction of the Amana, his son reported, was to provide a lower-priced venue where the urban poor could take in a film. At the opening of the Amana, Kassum argued that cinema was "a necessity of modern times" that should be available to all. Unlike the colonial authorities who built Raha Leo, he was fully committed to providing Africans on the outskirts of the city with a first-class venue, complete with a grand balcony seating 250 patrons. Enthusiasm for the Amana was overwhelming. Attendance at the Wednesday night opening was estimated at more than 1,000, well exceeding the theater's generous seating capacity of 750.[36] And when films were not being shown, the facility doubled as a community center and social hall.

In up-country towns, building a cinema enhanced a benefactor's self-esteem and buttressed his family's social value at least as much as it did along the coast. One benefactor, known as Mr. Khambaita, told me with pride about his escapades designing and constructing the Everest, which opened in Moshi in 1953 when he was a mere lad of twenty-nine. "I built the Everest all by myself! It is 60 by 40 feet without any I-beams. Myself I built that! It was quite an architectural feat for the time, and it is still standing in the center of town," he declared, positively glowing as we spoke.[37] From the age of thirteen, when he still lived in India, Khambaita

Figure 1.5 Everest Cinema, Moshi, opened 1953. Photo by the author, 2005

regularly went to the movies, and he became an avid reader of film magazines. During the war, he joined the British service as a construction contractor and was sent to Tanganyika. He had extended family in Moshi and
decided to stay after the war, in large part because he managed to convince
his elders, who had a transport business and auto repair shop, to invest a
small fortune in building the Everest. As a civil engineer, he oversaw the
construction of countless buildings in future years, but none made him feel
as accomplished as an architect or as proud as a citizen as his work on the
Everest. And as for Khambaita's family, though they had long been well
known in Moshi, they acquired regional fame after the Everest opened.
"People would come from fifty, even seventy miles, to see a movie on Sunday!" he recalled. "They waited all week for that day! On Saturdays too,
farmers would come. Instead of just doing business, they could now bring
their families. For women and children who spent nearly all their time on
the farm it was wonderful to come to town and enjoy entertainment."

Back in the 1920s, Moshi had had a venue for the occasional screening of silent films, and it acquired a dedicated theater, the Kilimanjaro,
by 1940. But like many of the earliest cinemas, that was a small, makeshift

Figure 1.6 (*above*) Playhouse Cinema (later renamed the Shazia), opened 1947, and (*right*) Highland Cinema, opened 1961, both in Iringa. Photos by the author, 2005

affair in a converted garage, and neither the venue nor the films attracted a particularly enthusiastic crowd. This changed dramatically after the war. In the early 1940s, Moshi's population and economic stature grew as the town became a regional trade and transport hub. This growth in turn spurred local entrepreneurs to invest in new venues for public leisure. The Plaza Cinema opened in 1947, followed by the Everest in 1953 as already described. Thus, in just a few years the seating capacity at Moshi's cinemas increased from under two hundred to nearly one thousand. The new structures were bold and beautiful, and the proprietors knew enough about film to select movies that would attract a crowd. Khambaita, for example, drove each week to Nairobi for other business and to pick out English films from the stock of Warner Brothers and MGM. He made a similar trip twice a month to Mombasa, where he loaded up his 1-ton truck with general goods in the morning and stopped by the warehouse of a film supplier to pick up Indian films in the afternoon.

Building Business and Building Community, 1900s–50s

After the war, the number of cinemas on the mainland mushroomed, as countless people endeavored to elevate the social and cultural status of their up-country towns and shake off their collective status as "country bumpkins" woefully behind their coastal cousins. The vast majority of the cinemas that eventually spanned Tanzania were built in the late 1940s and early 1950s. What is truly astounding is not how widespread the desire for cinematic entertainment was but the degree to which local entrepreneurs were willing to invest in meeting the demand. Of course, many of the cinemas built up-country were substantially smaller than those along the coast, averaging between 450 seats in bigger towns and 250 seats in smaller locales. But then, many of these up-country towns were tiny in comparison to Zanzibar and Dar es Salaam. Bukoba, Mbeya, Musoma, and Shinyanga, for instance, all had urban populations that barely reached three thousand in 1948.[38] And though many other towns saw their populations double or even triple between the 1930s and the end of the war, the populations of Lindi, Morogoro, Dodoma, and Moshi numbered only eight thousand each. Nonetheless, families like the Khambaitas—infused with postwar optimism and confident that a cinema would modernize the town and advance its stature as a regional economic, social, and cultural hub—invested their capital in putting on a show.[39] And indeed, the bright lights and spectacles of the cinema drew endless numbers to the center of town. Businessmen who invested in building a cinema saw slow returns from ticket sales, but the social capital they amassed certainly exceeded any they might have garnered by opening a dry goods store.

The increasing number of cinemas on the mainland was part of a much larger pattern of urban infrastructural growth across East Africa in the 1940s and 1950s. I was repeatedly told by interviewees that "a lot of people made a lot of money" during the war, and after it was over, many converted their liquid cash into solid investments in property. The downtown areas of urban centers across the region exploded with new commercial, housing, and office construction, and a few people invested in building spaces for public entertainment. In some towns previously considered sleepy backwaters, businessmen either established cinemas for the first time or built up-to-date facilities to replace makeshift theaters that already existed.[40] Like early investors along the coast, they hedged their bets and incorporated additional options in their designs. Thus, should a theater flop, which never really happened, the auditorium was constructed so that it could easily be

Figure 1.7 Metropole Cinema (later renamed the Shan), Morogoro, opened 1953. Photo by the author, 2005

converted into a storage facility or garage. Office suites and retail facilities were also integral components of building designs. Theaters along the coast incorporated office space as well, but the cinema was always the heart of the building and the main reason it was constructed. But in Moshi, Arusha, Mwanza, Iringa, Morogoro, and many other regional towns that blossomed in the 1950s, the pressures for office and retail space were nearly as intense as the demand for modern theaters. Building design thus catered to the multiple demands of the town, while simultaneously allowing investors to diversify their holdings. In these regional towns, the rent earned from office and retail space and small restaurants housed in the same building as the cinema often exceeded the theater proceeds.[41]

Asian businessmen and traders generally avoided putting their savings in an established bank at that time, preferring to hide their cash, loan it to others, or pool it in communal savings societies until they had enough to do something substantial.[42] Prior to the nationalizations of the 1970s, when Asians in Tanzania and Uganda lost most of their property, real estate investments were considered grounded and relatively secure.

They also tended to earn rates of return that surpassed the interest offered by banks.

A fair amount of the capital used to finance the construction boom of the 1950s was acquired from the "illicit" trade and transport of food, clothing, and other items deemed nonessential by colonial authorities in the preceding years. As the British turned their attention and resources toward the war effort, steamers and railways were requisitioned to transport military supplies, materials, and personnel. East Africans' notions of essential commodities often differed substantially from those of the British and included rice, cloth, matches, and kerosene, all of which were rationed by the state. Private traders stepped in to fill the void between consumer demand and official supply, and soon, alternative forms of transport, supply, and finance moved goods between East Africa and India, Arabia, China, and Japan. The dhow trade in and out of East Africa made a resurgence during the war, and men with lorries moved goods throughout the continent.[43] Some dhows docked at established ports, where their cargoes were subject to standard duty rates, but many used smaller landing stations to avoid paying taxes. There, they were met by men with private motor vehicles who transported goods for export and traded them for imports. The risks in transporting goods across the ocean were steep, and the consequences for being caught "smuggling" on land were great; combined with a general shortage of goods, this translated into high black market prices. Individuals willing and able to provide transport earned handsome profits, and by war's end, they had substantial cash reserves.[44] Many of the men who built up-country cinemas after the war earned their capital by operating lorries and buses or by providing spare parts and mechanical services for those who did. Such contributions to the urban built environment served multiple economic, social, and political purposes. They also served to cleanse somewhat dubiously earned cash.

The families who built the cinemas that opened in regional towns were at the center of dense social networks built around the show. Theaters were social institutions that brought life to the town and the region: they were where people went to see and be seen, to share news and gossip, to make connections and solidify potential deals. In the adjacent restaurants, offices, and snack bars or on the benches in front of the theaters, individuals with both problems and opportunities came together to share their thoughts, flaunt their successes, or seek counsel and support. As their hosts, the Khambaitas and other proprietors brought in not only money from

ticket sales but also contacts and customers for the families' other businesses. Through the cinema they not only secured contacts for themselves
but shared their knowledge, gossip, and connections with those who came
to the show, thus further enhancing their position as people with people.

COMPETITIVE RIVALRY: TECHNOLOGY, FILM, AND STYLE

The entrepreneurs who built and ran East Africa's cinemas aimed to demonstrate their knowledge of global cinematic and technological trends, as well
as their commitment to bringing the best films and facilities they could
to the citizens of their towns. Their efforts were spurred in part by innate
predilections but certainly enhanced by local business and entertainment
cultures, where friends and patrons insisted that proprietors live up to expectations and rivals always pushed them to do just a bit more. For centuries,
East Africans had prided themselves on acquiring the latest, the hippest, and
the most up-to-date commodities circulating the globe.[45] The growth and
expansion of the cinema industry created a new venue for expressing this
inclination, and changing cinematic technologies, architectural fads, and
communal standards kept owners from resting on their laurels. To keep their
customers coming back to the show, they had to invest in frequent updates
to stay on the cutting edge of their industry. The costs of maintaining a cinema—and thus a reputation—intensified dramatically in the 1950s due to
the combined effects of new cinematic technologies, larger amounts of capital in the regional economy, and the entry of new rivals into the industry.

The introduction of sound at the Royal Theater in Zanzibar in 1932,
just a few years after the new technology debuted, was symbolic of East
African entrepreneurs' commitment to running world-class theaters and
keeping their customers abreast of technological developments. Hassanali
Jariwalla did not really need to upgrade to talkies in 1932; in fact, it took
most of the 1930s for the majority of theaters in North America, Europe,
and India to be outfitted with sound, and the demand for silent films in
Zanzibar was showing no sign of decline. At Cinema ya Bati, the antics
of Charlie Chaplin remained incredibly popular through the 1930s, frequently drawing sellout crowds. (Charlie Chaplin became such an icon
that the term *chale* was adopted into Kiswahili to denote a joker or clown
and is still used today.) Issak Esmail Issak was one of many who recalled
the indelible mark Chaplin left on island audiences. On walks during the

1950s, a young Issak noted that his grandfather pointed to the former lo-cation of Cinema ya Bati every time they crossed the bridge, proudly pro-claiming, "This is where I saw . . . the great epic *Raja Harischandra* [the first Indian full-length feature film (Phalke, 1913)] and the mustachioed tramp Charlie!"[46] Mwalim Idd and Haji Garana were two others who fondly reminisced about flocking to the silent films with other children at Cinema ya Bati, where admission was a mere two cents.[47] Asad Talati, whose father purchased the cinema from Jariwalla in 1932, recalled that the silent films continued to attract large numbers of patrons, including many adults, for years. Action and adventure films and the slapstick comedies of Stan Laurel and Oliver Hardy were widely adored, and many people identified Fearless Nadia, a circus performer who became the first female action star of Indian film in *Hunterwali* (Wadia, 1935), as one of the most popular personalities of that generation.[48] But regardless of the ongoing al-lure of silent films, Jariwalla knew that talkies were the wave of the future, so the proud provider of the first picture palace in East Africa installed synchronized sound as soon as the equipment was available.

Indo-African Theaters Ltd. exemplified entrepreneurs' commitment to operating with the latest technology and the most impressive architec-tural style during these early years. In the 1930s, Talati and his partners tran-sitioned from silent films to talkies, and after their initial efforts with the Empire in Zanzibar proved successful, they began pursuing options to build a larger, more modern building in town. After five years of wrangling with the colonial administration to get their permits, Shavekshaw Talati and his partners took out a thirty-year mortgage to build the contemporary theater they felt the Zanzibari public deserved. (See fig. I.2.) The Sultana opened on New Year's Eve in 1951 with John Payne's *Tripoli* (Price, 1950); this was followed on Sunday by *Sargam* (Santoshi, 1950), starring Raj Kapoor, Re-hana, and Om Prakash.[49] The crowd at both shows exceeded the available six hundred seats, inaugurating the box office melee that would be a defin-ing feature of filmgoing at the Sultana for the remainder of its existence. Opening ceremonies were graced by the British resident and the sultan, who publicly expressed their gratitude to the investors for adding such a sophisticated institution to local life. Talati also spoke at the opening, say-ing that it had been his dream for years "to open a theater in Zanzibar as up-to-date as those in Dar es Salaam."[50] But within a year, the Sultana was rendered nearly obsolete by new developments in cinematic technology, requiring the partners to invest even more capital to maintain their status as premier providers of cinematic entertainment, not proprietors who were willing to shrug and tell their clients that last year's model was good enough.

In 1953, 20th Century Fox released the first CinemaScope picture, accompanied by stereophonic sound. Shot with a new type of lens, CinemaScope inaugurated panoramic filming, which all the major studios then adopted in various forms. The use of these innovative wide-angle lenses allowed for more encompassing views. They also produced an illusion of three-dimensionality, making patrons feel they were part of the action. But to display CinemaScope, one needed new, expensive projection equipment as well as a significantly wider, concave screen. The use of multiple microphones during filming, required to capture a more dispersed subject, led to the development of stereophonic sound. This too required changes to a theater's sound equipment and numerous additional speakers. Almost immediately after opening their cinema, the owners of the Sultana updated all their equipment, at a substantial cost. And while they were at it, they decided to transform the facade of the building too, eliminating some of the Saracenic elements that had been insisted upon by the colonial administration's chief secretary, Eric Dutton. In addition, all the original chairs, which had been locally produced, were replaced with spring-loaded, upholstered seats imported from the United Kingdom. Ultimately, more than TSh 400,000 (or over $57,000) was spent renovating the Sultana.[51] A commitment to excellence came at a cost.

"Keeping up with the latest" and good-natured competition were key elements of the capitalist ethos permeating East Africa's exhibition industry. When Hassanlai Hameer Hasham purchased Zanzibar's Royal Theater from Jariwalla and renamed it the Majestic, he vowed to do all he could to cater to the tastes of "the modern public."[52] With his rivals showing silents in a tin shed or even talkies in a venue half the size of the Majestic, he felt secure in his place at the apex of the local cinematic economy. But by the 1950s, the original picture palace of East Africa was some thirty years old and was now being challenged by the Sultana. He needed to modernize or risk losing customers to the new venue, so he and his manager installed new projection, sound, screen, and seating equipment. Unfortunately, just before the theater was to reopen in 1954, an electrical fire destroyed the entire building, resulting in a loss of at least $140,000 (or more than $1.2 million in 2016 dollars). Undeterred by the calamity, Hassanali Hameer

Figure 1.8 Majestic Cinema, Zanzibar, c.1956. Photo by Ranchhod T. Oza, courtesy of Capital Art Studio, Zanzibar

Hasham rebuilt the Majestic from scratch. He redesigned the exterior to reflect the modern era, replacing the earlier Saracenic architecture with art deco elements, and infused the interior with panoramic projection, screen, and stereophonic sound.[53] The new theater comfortably sat 750, and it boasted a large, steep balcony with seats for 200.

Letters to the editor in the Tanganyikan press show that by the 1950s, audiences expected theater management to keep them entertained and to offer the latest cinematic technology—and if the managers fell behind, patrons were not afraid to publicly call attention to their failings. Throughout the 1950s, few subjects garnered as much consistent attention in the newspapers as cinemas, films, and the moviegoing experience. Although many articles heralded the opening of new cinemas, the introduction of 3-D films and screens, or expensive renovations, letters to the editor tended to feature complaints about all manner of problems, including broken chairs and "substandard" seating, poor lighting, failed sound, scratched films, delayed start times, and extended intermissions. Audiences in regional cinemas lamented local owners' reluctance to accommodate CinemaScope and stereophonic sound. Feeling relegated to second-class status vis-à-vis their coastal cousins, they complained bitterly about watching endless repeats of releases made before production studios switched to the new technology or, worse still, viewing new releases but having large portions of the picture flow over the walls, audience, and ceiling. Some owners tried a local, less expensive fix by switching from a 35 mm lens to a 70 mm one, which at least contained the image to the screen, but the projection quality was not nearly as good as CinemaScope. Like the owners of the Sultana, many of the men who owned up-country cinemas had only recently built and outfitted their venues, and they found it frustrating to abandon nearly new projection, sound, and screen equipment—and expensive to replace it. But to protect themselves from charges of incompetence in the national press, they made improvements as soon as they could. Their earnings, their status as patrons of community leisure, and their personal reputations as top-notch businessmen all depended on their willingness to invest in the new technology.

The introduction of CinemaScope projection and stereophonic sound inaugurated something of an arms race in Dar es Salaam. In 1954, the Odeon and Avalon were vying for the title of "the first CinemaScope in East Africa"—a title won by the Avalon and proudly displayed in its corporate logo.[54] Less than a decade after opening the Avalon in 1944, the investors in Indo-African spent $56,000 to secure the title. They installed CinemaScope projectors, a new screen, and stereophonic sound incorporating fifteen speakers. They also added upholstered seating, enlarged the legroom between rows, increased the number of balcony seats to 239, and enhanced the ventilation and air-cooling equipment. It took nine agonizing months and another $140,000 to refurbish the Avalon, but the owners were determined to do the job right. They also renovated the facade of the theater to make it look more modern and less like the godown that it once was.[55]

Figure 1.9 Business letterhead of the Avalon Cinema, Dar es Salaam

67

Rising to meet the challenge, Hassanali Hameer Hasham, owner of the Majestic Cinema in Zanzibar and the main competitive rival of Indo-African, opened the Empress Cinema in 1954, just a short walk away from the Avalon. Built and equipped at a cost of $420,000 (or roughly $4.2 million today), the Empress was the largest theater in the nation, accommodating 793 patrons—47 more than the refurbished Avalon. The Empress also bragged of the largest balcony in Tanzania, with room for 330 people in widely spaced and deeply terraced rows.[56] Of course, the Empress also featured CinemaScope projection, a wide screen for both CinemaScope's panoramic films and the latest 3-D features, specially designed acoustic ceiling tiles, and multiple speakers for stereophonic sound. According to the European press, however, its crowning glory was a functioning air-conditioning system, indicative of the owners' determination to assure every aspect of their patrons' comfort. Even the European population of Dar es Salaam applauded the owners for their attention to detail, comfort, and design.[57] Such competition guaranteed access to films and venues that were every bit the equal of midcentury London and Bombay.

By the mid-1950s, adding an adjoining bar and restaurant to a cinema also became de rigueur for a modern leisure venue on the mainland. Despite the fact that many key investors and members of the moviegoing public were Muslim, nearly all the cinemas that were opened or renovated after the war featured a bar. The Odeon was the first theater in Dar es Salaam to serve alcohol, and according to some, this helped it retain its edge even when better pictures were shown at the Avalon and the Empire.[58] When the Avalon was renovated, $70,000 was invested in building an adjoining restaurant and two bars. The Empress again one-upped its competitors, including two restaurants in its building as well as a large bar with a parquet dance floor that could be viewed by the patrons in the upper restaurant, adjacent to the cinema's balcony seating. The bar provided an added enticement for Europeans as well as "modern" urban men, for they could fulfill their gendered obligation by taking the family out to see a movie but then excuse themselves to join others who found the bar more entertaining. It was not uncommon in the 1950s for Muslim men to mix business and pleasure in venues where alcohol was served: being open to others' social drinking was one of many signs of being modern.

After the war, discourses of modernization circulated widely in East Africa, spurred in part by the imam of the Shia Ismailis, Sultan Muhammed

Shah, the Aga Khan III. Regarded as a liberal innovator on many social issues, he actively encouraged Muslim women to pursue advanced degrees, enter the workforce, and abandon the hijab in favor of Western dress. In East Africa, he also inaugurated numerous large-scale investments in public welfare, including health care facilities, educational institutions, and modern affordable housing. He owned numerous prize-winning thoroughbreds, and he was the father of Aly Khan, the third husband of the American actress Rita Hayworth.[59] Presumably, he had no problem with the head of the Ismaili religious community in Tanzania, Kassum Sunderji, owning a cinema that featured a bar. Kassum, after all, made his initial fortune selling spirits and wine to Europeans, and that did not keep him from praying each day or donating generously to philanthropic endeavors. Practicality in business matters allowed him to fulfill his religious and social obligations. For those familiar with the competitive rivalry in Tanzanian football, dance, and music groups in the 1950s, the persistent one-upmanship that typified the business dealings of cinema owners surely strikes a chord.[60]

Of course, business rivalry centered on film and turning out the largest weekly crowd. When tickets for a theater's movie turned up on the black market or when patrons had to be seated on soda crates in the aisles due to overcrowding, the reputations of the theater's owners and workers blossomed; they and their public had scored. Authorities repeatedly chastised cinema managers for not working harder with the police to end the black market trade in movie tickets, but those authorities failed to realize how much black market sales augmented prestige.

In Dar es Salaam, the Empire might run *Pyaar* (Kapoor, 1950), featuring Raj Kapoor and Nargis, against the Avalon's premier of Guru Dutt's *Baazi* (1951), with heartthrobs Dev Anand and Geita Bali. The smaller Azania would counter with an Egyptian film such as *Gharan Rakissa* (Rafla, 1950) featuring Muhammed Fawzi and Noor el-Hooda, making it a tough choice all around for film fans on Saturdays and Sundays. In 1953, if the Empire in Zanzibar started the week with *Ivanhoe* (Thorpe, 1952), starring Robert Taylor and Elizabeth Taylor, the Majestic might counter with a tried but true offering of *Samson and Delilah* (DeMille, 1949), with Hedy Lamarr and Victor Mature. In general, theaters in Zanzibar and Dar es Salaam screened films within six to nine months of their opening in New York or Bombay, though credit, connections, or shipping difficulties sometimes resulted in a delay. The aim was also to open a new film at each

69

screening, but if the new movie on hand could not compete with a rival's offering, then managers pulled the best from available stock to remain competitive in the battle for the public's affection and leisure spending. A film such as *Samson and Delilah* might have been five years old in 1953, but as chapter 4 shows, it had all the elements that Tanzanians prized in movies. As late as 2004, it still held audiences spellbound when screened on ferries running between Dar es Salaam and Zanzibar.

Despite their no-holds-barred rivalry in putting on the best shows and attracting the most fans, competing owners and managers maintained friendly professional and personal relations. If one man's projectors went down, his rival would offer a spare to tide him over. If someone needed a film because his supplier sent him a dud, his competitor supported him with the best film he had available. Owners, managers, and workers from different theaters conversed frequently, sharing news about business and global industrial developments, national and community politics, local gossip, films, and their children's studies. They shared laments and commiseration in their common battles with censors, customs officers, and municipal authorities. They invited each other to their children's weddings and stood by each other at family funerals. And any worker from any theater could get a free seat or two at a rival's place simply by showing up. All this gave the industry a particular character and appeal. For East African cinematic capitalists, being known as a decent human being was more valuable than pushing a rival to fail.

EARNING SOCIAL CAPITAL IN THE DISTRIBUTION AND EXHIBITION INDUSTRIES

Exhibition and distribution were always and everywhere mutually dependent, but there was no consensus on how the profits from ticket sales would be shared or what the nature of the social, economic, and political relationships between exhibitors and distributors would be like. Tracing the growth and development of exhibition and distribution in Tanzania illuminates how entrepreneurs built industries that supported profitable local businesses while adhering to local social values. Generating profit from the supply of films was, of course, a goal of distributors across the globe. The greatest profits came from screening each film before the widest possible audience, and because distributors and exhibitors had to share box office proceeds, the greatest returns to distributors came when they also controlled exhibition. In the United States and South Africa, the law allowed distributors to consolidate theaters under their ownership and monopolize film supply, making it difficult for independent alternatives to survive. Distributors in these places also maintained control over exhibitors by requiring them to sign contracts for exclusive supply, thereby precluding the showing of others' films. These contracts typically lasted for years and often committed an exhibitor to accepting certain quantities of low-grade product for every hit provided. Vertical integration, hostile takeovers, "block booking," and harsh legal contracts may have comprised one way of organizing these businesses, but this model was flatly rejected by industry pioneers in Tanzania.

Though profit making was always the focus of the East African cinema business, it never eclipsed the importance of having a reputation for honesty and doing right by others as a basis for securing credit and making sales: business was a personal, not a contractual, affair.[61] There was no monopoly on distribution; rather, a plethora of players—some large, some small—brought in a diverse range of films, and exhibitors had the ability to search for the best product and the best terms. And because there were no excessively large conglomerates controlling exhibition, distributors had to cultivate clients to get their films screened and earn back the money they spent on obtaining prints and securing the legal right to distribute product in a given territory. No one ever starved another man out of business by refusing to give him good films, nor were there any hostile acquisitions. On the contrary, as both distributors and exhibitors the Tanzanians involved in the industry actively helped others get involved. Culturally specific standards of capitalism and manhood demanded that those with means help those without.

From 1900 through the 1950s, the economics of the exhibition and distribution industries had more in common with nineteenth-century East African patron-client relations than with American or South African cutthroat capitalism. In Tanzania, each party had duties and obligations, and business relations were often couched in ethical terms. Several prominent distributors supplied the majority of the films, but they did not monopolize first-run screenings within their own theaters, passing them along to rivals only after most people in town had seen a film. Instead, the aim was for each theater in the nation to be a first-run venue. Only when supply was exceptionally restricted or when a film was so popular that fans demanded to see it again and again did theaters screen shows for a second or third time. Typically it was owners and managers who requested to run a repeat, not a distributor who made the determination as a means of punishing someone with a film that would flop. Profit-sharing arrangements also reflected a recognition that exhibitors and distributors were mutually dependent. Through the 1950s, box office returns were split evenly between them, rather than having 70 percent or more go to distributors as happened where monopolies or oligopolies prevailed.

When Hassanali Adamji Jariwalla began importing films for display in Zanzibar, he was already a trader enmeshed in networks handling the finance, supply, and distribution of cloth from India across East Africa. The early film import, distribution, and exhibition business was built upon these established patterns. Many of the South Asian traders who immigrated to East Africa in the late nineteenth and early twentieth century started their businesses with no money. Personal connections or membership in a particular religious community secured them an advance of goods with which to begin trading.[62] Wealthier merchants advanced goods to trustworthy clients, who paid for the merchandise only after it was sold. Typically, payment was due after thirty, sixty, or ninety days, but "payable when able" agreements were not uncommon.[63] In this way, those with little or no capital could get a start in business, and more established merchants and manufacturers could expand their sales territory and thus their profits while simultaneously enhancing their reputations as benevolent patrons. Although Jariwalla was an established cloth trader, he was a novice when it came to importing and showing films. Initially, he took limited risks and invested only a small amount of capital. He purchased several hand-cranked projectors, which were reasonably priced by the 1910s and available from manufacturers in India. A small piece of white cloth or an old boat sail served as the screen at his early shows, and the dark tropical night was the auditorium. Jariwalla was fronted his films by suppliers in Bombay, and he paid for them only after they were screened. He provided projectors to others up-country, to whom he also advanced cloth and films as new supplies arrived. He was reimbursed for the films and cloth according to whatever terms he and his partners agreed on.[64]

In the 1910s, Jariwalla received his prints from Ardeshir Irani and Abdulally Esoofally, owners of Alexandra Company in Bombay.[65] By that time, Jariwalla was showing some fourteen different short films each week, changing his program every Wednesday and Saturday, so he really needed a top-notch supplier.[66] He chose well when he partnered with Irani and Esoofally, who were industry pioneers of incredible magnitude. Like Jariwalla, Esoofally had begun with traveling exhibits and then established regular tent venues in Bombay. In 1914, he partnered with Irani, and four years later, they opened a picture palace named the Majestic, at a time when there were only a handful of permanent venues in all of India. Irani and Esoofally purchased their prints—even of American films—from secondhand outlets in Britain that supplied most of the British Empire.[67] But Irani was not content with showing foreign films, and he quickly expanded into production. His studio grew into one of the best in India. Irani produced nearly 250 films over the course of his life, including the first Indian talkie, *Alam Ara* (Irani, 1931).[68] Jariwalla did business with the best, and the East African audiences benefited.

The cost of a print was finite, yet returns from that print could expand exponentially in proportion to the number of people who paid to view it. Irani and Esoofally increased their profits by advancing secondhand prints previously circulated in India to Jariwalla, who in turn tried to circulate these same prints as widely as possible within East Africa. To meet the demands of the local cinemagoing audience and satisfy his own need to boost returns, Jariwalla operated several theaters from the earliest days. In the 1910s, he quickly expanded from one khaki tent in Zanzibar to two, with a third in Dar es Salaam. He then sent his films to other tent venues in Pemba, Tanga, Moshi, Tabora, and Ujiji. (See map I.1.) When he upgraded to more solid structures, he replaced his Zanzibari tents with the Royal and Cinema ya Bati and his tent in Dar es Salaam with the Bharat and the New Cinema, eventually replacing these with the Empire. A short while later, he helped his son build the Azania (which would be renamed the Cameo), a modest venue with seats for some three hundred, built on top of what had been the city dump.[69] In the 1920s, there was also another small theater in Dar es Salaam, run by Hassanli Nurbhai and located on Kisutu Road.[70] None of these cinemas accommodated even half of the patrons served by the Empire, but they remained important venues, permitting Jariwalla to circulate the same films that opened at the Empire before a wider audience. To boost his earnings further, he expanded into potentially lucrative markets in Kenya. A year after he opened the Royal, he began construction on a modest cinema in Mombasa—the Kenya Kinema, which opened in 1923. Four years later, he opened the Alexandra in Nairobi, which he leased to associates to run.[71] By the time he opened the Empire in Dar es Salaam in 1929, he was operating six theaters in three territories. For reasons that remain unclear, Jariwalla later pulled out of Kenya as a direct investor, but he continued to be a prominent mentor and supplier for other Asians who entered the industry in subsequent years. As other proprietors came into the market, he rented his prints to them after screening them in his own theaters, beginning the circuit in Zanzibar.

In the early 1930s, Jariwalla updated his two picture palaces, the Royal in Zanzibar and the Empire in Dar es Salaam, to show talkies; although this was great for local audiences, keeping them engaged with the latest developments in the industry, it made his distribution business significantly more expensive. Now, Jariwalla needed to import two types of prints, one featuring synchronized sound and another for theaters that could only show silent films. In the early 1930s, distributors across the world were facing this same conundrum. The best theaters in the largest urban markets updated to talkies by the middle of the decade, but many small-town and rural theaters took years to make the transition. Most studios therefore produced dual versions of their films, one with sound and one without. Jariwalla imported both types of films, beginning his circuit in Zanzibar, where silent films were screened at Cinema ya Bati and sound films premiered at the Royal.

For Jariwalla and many of the entrepreneurs who entered the industry in the ensuing decades, cinema was a side business, a way to indulge and share one's passion for film and earn a little extra money in the process. But by the 1930s as the East African industry began to take off, Jariwalla partnered with another Zanzibari, Hassanali Hameer Hasham (commonly known as Hameer Gozi, from the Kiswahili *ngozi*, meaning "skin," because his main line of business was trading in hides). Hameer harnessed additional networks with producers in India to augment Jariwalla's supply. These films were screened first at the Royal (renamed the Majestic in 1938 when Hameer bought the theater from Jariwalla) and then sent to Jariwalla in Dar es Salaam, who screened them at the Empire or Azania before

Figure 1.10 Mohanlal Kala Savani (Samji Kala), founder of Majestic Film Distributors Ltd. and Majestic Theaters, Tanga. Photo courtesy of his son, Chunilal Kala Savani

releasing them to other exhibitors across East Africa. Ideally, a film would be paid for entirely through screenings at the Majestic in Zanzibar and the Empire and the Azania/Cameo in Dar es Salaam; then, revenue generated through screenings in other men's venues would accrue as profits. Jariwalla could have consolidated his hold on the industry in the 1930s by building a vertically integrated business along the South African model, but he did not do so. Instead, he supported others getting their start in the industry, including three men who would become major players—and competitors—in the 1940s and 1950s: Hassanali Hameer Hasham, Mohanlal Kala Savani, and Shavekshaw Hormasji Talati. Hameer Hasham later returned the favor, further strengthening the patron-client ties that bound the families together: he appointed Jariwalla's twenty-one-year-old grandson, Shabir, as manager of the Empress Cinema in Dar es Salaam. Good deeds (and bad) were recalled, repaid, and reinvested over generations.

Mohanlal Kala Savani was an early entrepreneur in the cinema industry in Kenya who began as an importer of five to ten films a year into East

75

Africa and within three decades became the key link in a family-firm chain that distributed Indian films to every corner of the world.[72] But like Jariwalla, he started out quite small. He followed his brother from Gujarat to Mombasa in 1918, with only a few shillings in his pocket. Like legions of other young South Asian men at that time, he was deemed trustworthy by someone with capital in Bombay and was employed as an East African agent, receiving imports of flour and dry goods from India and forwarding them across East Africa. By 1925, he had amassed enough capital to start trading on his own. He switched from foodstuffs to textiles and, with a prod from a friend in Bombay, movies too. He had no theater of his own but screened the occasional films that arrived by clearing space in a storeroom near the port. He then passed the films on to those with cinemas, such as Jariwalla, whom he knew because they both dealt in cloth. By 1935, Mohanlal Kala Savani—commonly known as Samji Kala—had saved enough money from his cloth trade to indulge his lifelong fantasy of opening a proper cinema. With advice and support from Jariwalla, he built the Majestic Cinema in Mombasa, which he rented to Jariwalla's protégé, Hameer Hasham, to run. Although Samji Kala obviously saw potential in the industry, according to his son all his friends thought he was insane for squandering ten years of hard-earned savings on an enterprise dedicated to projecting fantasy and providing entertainment.[73] But like others who took the plunge and invested their capital in building a theater when returns were far from guaranteed, he built modestly and in such a way that the seats could be removed and the structure converted into a godown if the cinema failed. In the 1930s and 1940s, Samji Kala focused his energies on the cloth trade; film remained a pleasant diversion but only a modest source of income.

In these early years, box office receipts were split—as they were in India—with most of the proceeds going to the exhibitor. East African exhibitors kept 50 percent of gate takings, and the remaining fifty percent was shared equally between the supplier in India and the middleman who linked Indian suppliers with East African exhibitors. Samji Kala recognized that he could earn significantly more from each print he imported if he controlled more theaters, but he could not expand for several reasons. For one, he was still quite young in the 1930s and did not have the capital to build more than a single theater. Then too, the political and economic situation in Kenya impinged on the development of a vibrant moviegoing culture among the Asians and Africans who were the primary audience for the films he imported. Members of both groups had difficulty freely walking the streets of the city center, especially in Nairobi. In the 1930s, white businessmen, all integrated with the Schlesinger organization out of South Africa, also owned the main cinemas in Nairobi—the Empire, the Capital, and the Playhouse—and restricted Asians' ability to open other venues. The best that Samji Kala could do was to lease the Empire, along with the Green Cinema next to the New Stanley Hotel, to show Indian films. And the only time when white owners were willing to concede their space to Asians was on Sundays, when Europeans were supposed to be devoting the day to church and family.[74] So in Kenya, Sundays were when Indian films were screened and nonwhites went to the show. Only on the eve of independence, in 1960, was Samji Kala finally allowed to open a cinema in Nairobi, the Kenyan city with the largest and most economically empowered population.

With his extensive import-export skill and knowledge, Samji Kala amassed significant capital during the war, which he invested in building regional cinemas in the 1950s. In 1953, he opened the 600-seat Queen's Cinema in Mombasa (renamed the Kenya after independence), followed by the nearly 700-seat Majestic in Tanga, Tanganyika, which he gave to his sons and nephew to run. Three years later, he helped a brother build the 800-seat Neeta Cinema in Kampala, which became the premier theater in Uganda.[75] Another friend, also in the cloth business, built the Plaza in Moshi, Tanganyika, after the war, but by the mid-1950s, he needed to sell it, so Samji Kala bought the Plaza too, in 1955. Over the span of twenty-five years, his situation had changed dramatically. In the early 1930s, he had films but no theaters. By the mid-1950s, he had theaters but needed to step up his game significantly to supply them with films.

Securing access to enough good-quality films necessitated building transnational business networks, networks that often either began with or developed into deeply personal relationships. Back in the 1930s, when Samji Kala opened his first theater in Mombasa and Hameer Hasham bought the Royal in Zanzibar from Jariwalla, the two men formed Majestic Theater Company Ltd., a film import and distribution firm that allowed them to pool their resources and more efficiently trade films across Zanzibar, Tanganyika, and Kenya. Jariwalla had been the main supplier up to that time, but he was aging (he was sixty-six in 1938) and content to see younger men build upon the foundation he laid. Independent of Jariwalla's suppliers,

77

Samji Kala and Hameer Hasham each had access to only some ten films annually out of India, which was less than half the number they needed to be able to change films each week of the year. Moreover, not all the films were top-class productions, which did not help them build public enthusiasm for regular evenings out at the show. So the partners built bridges to Jariwalla's contacts in India and reached out to friends and encouraged them to either import what films they could or help them make additional connections to some of the hundreds of independent distributors operating in India. By the 1950s, the Majestic Theater Company was able to supply some forty Indian films a year to the East African market.

Business models from the cloth trade also influenced sales and marketing in film. Jariwalla and Samji Kala made their initial fortunes importing and distributing cloth; they knew that the kanga cloths worn by East African women sold best when they were attractive and of good quality but available for only a limited time. The most successful cloth merchants carried high-quality, limited-edition prints—limited not necessarily in quantity but in the time they were sold in local shops before being shipped off to partners in smaller towns—in order to boost demand. This strategy was applied to film exhibition. Distributors aimed to give East African audiences access to a new Indian film each week, and in towns with more than one cinema, they wanted each to offer a different product. By pooling their collective supply of films and changing them out after only one or two days of screening, the distributors enticed the public to go to the theater to see "the latest," just as women rushed to the shops to purchase the newest limited-edition kanga cloths. If you wanted to see a film, you needed to go to the theater on opening day or risk missing the film entirely.

Indo-African Theaters, discussed earlier in this chapter, was another group that became a major film supplier in East Africa. Like Hameer Hasham and Samji Kala, the men who formed this group had been given a leg up by Jariwalla, and they too ventured into film import and distribution because they needed to supply their own theaters. Shavekshaw Hormasji Talati, the lead partner, purchased the Cinema ya Bati from Jariwalla and showed silent films there until 1939, when he and his partners—Abdullah Mohammed Thaver, M. S. Sunjit, and Manilal Madhavji Suchak—opened the Empire in Zanzibar. To make a success of the Empire, they needed to attract patrons by showing films that rivaled those screened at the neighboring Majestic. But by the time Talati and his group got into the business

Figure 1.11 Shavekshaw Hormasji Talati, born in Zanzibar in 1889. Talati partnered with Abdullah Mohammed Thaver, M. S. Sunjit, and Manilal Madhavji Suchak to open the Empire Cinema in Zanzibar in 1939.

of screening talkies, Jariwalla and Hameer Hasham already had an established network of theaters that they were obligated to supply with films. If the Empire wanted these same films, they would have to wait at the back of the line. Meanwhile, their chances of attracting patrons to see repeats months after their initial screening were about as good as the odds of getting Zanzibari women to pay full price for last season's kangas.[76]

To secure enough new movies to compete with the Majestic, the partners pooled their resources and worked with their connections in India, Egypt, Japan, and Europe to get films. Rather quickly, they developed a reputation as premier suppliers not just of Indian films but also of films from regions of the world no one else had yet tapped. Thaver's connections to the Egyptian film industry, in particular, were widely praised.

The partners in Indo-African were then left with the same conundrum that faced others: a single, 400-seat venue could not earn enough to cover the cost of importing good films. Clearly, they had to secure additional venues, and with the profit-sharing ratio as it was, owning or leasing the theaters was the most lucrative option. In the 1940s, they brought Kassum

Sunderji Samji into the group. He built the Avalon and leased it back to the partners to run, and in the 1950s, he also financed the New Chox and the Amana, where he appointed his son and another client as managers.[77] Harbanslal Sohanlal Ghai, from Nairobi, joined the group after the war, and with his connections and collateral, the company secured a loan for TSh 300,000 to construct a beautiful theater in Mombasa, the Naaz.[78] As Asian businessmen across Tanganyika built theaters during the 1950s, Indo-African brought them into the group, renting to up-country theaters films they themselves imported and first screened in their own cinemas in Zanzibar, Dar es Salaam, and Mombasa. Eventually, the Indo-African partners owned some of the premier theaters in the most lucrative markets in Tanzania, but unlike Schlesinger in South Africa, they made no effort to push others out of the exhibition business. They were quite content running 10 percent of the theaters in Tanzania (four out of forty) and earning a reasonable profit. Over a little more than two decades, Shavekshaw Hormasji Talati's business burgeoned from one modest, tin building showing silent films to a firm with international partners and investors operating world-class theaters in Zanzibar, Tanganyika, and Kenya.

In the 1950s, Dar es Salaam became the top market for cinematic entertainment, generating half or more of the industry's total earnings in the country.[79] Before the war, the city had only three theaters: the Empire, the Odeon, and the Azania, with a combined seating capacity of a "mere" 1,400. With the addition of the Avalon, the New Chox, the Amana, and the Empress in the 1950s, the available seating increased nearly threefold: with the exception of the New Chox, each of these venues sat between 750 and 800 patrons. The theaters competed wildly, not only in terms of size and architectural style but also for films to delight their fans. Diversity, variety, and novelty were highly prized by citizens in Dar es Salaam, so distributors did their best to make every theater a first-run venue, with each offering a unique film. Exhibitors could ask to keep a film or show it again after a few months, but they were offered a steady supply of new product. Only later did reeling and running the same film at multiple venues became increasingly common.

The number of films that moved through the Tanganyikan capital during any given week in the 1950s was truly astounding. There were seven different theaters, and each changed its pictures three to four times a week. From Monday through Friday, when crowds were smaller, American and British films filled the bills. On Sundays, each theater typically offered a different Indian or Egyptian musical feature, and the Avalon, the Azania, the Odeon, and the Empress frequently held their feature over for an afternoon ladies-only screening. Indo-African and Majestic were the main local suppliers of films for the Sunday market, importing more than a hundred films a year through Zanzibar by the 1950s.[80] Their selections were augmented by a similar, if not larger, number of films coming from other small, independent local distributors as well as large conglomerates out of India with subsidiaries in Nairobi. Exhibitors took movies from whichever distributor offered the best films on the best terms. Although the Majestic and Indo-African groups were rivals, the Azania—built by Jariwalla and thus part of the Majestic group—frequently screened Egyptian films provided by Indo-African. Rivalry did not preclude cooperation.

Dar es Salaam was a key market, but distributors could rarely turn a profit on films screened in just this single town, even when they owned the venues. Consequently, they needed to secure additional playing time for their products up-country, and to that end, they competed in culturally specific ways. Like a bachelor seeking a lady's hand, they had to woo and charm to get their films shown in other men's venues, and they also had to fulfill their promises. More than one up-country exhibitor I interviewed likened these relationships to marriage, suggesting that business partners were chosen based upon reputation and that relationships remained strong only when they were mutually beneficial. As one exhibitor put it, "You see, everyone had their connections, their personal connection to get movies, good movies. If your man couldn't fulfill your needs you looked for another who could."[81] An exhibitor was not bound by exclusive, long-term contracts to any one supplier. When a new exhibitor opened a theater, he talked to elder "uncles" with experience in the industry, who shared their knowledge of players' reputations and began making inquiries and offering proposals to distributors on the junior man's behalf. As with marriages, there were occasionally partners who lied, cheated, or disrespected their vows, but the community of exhibitors and film suppliers in East Africa was small and tightly knit. If a man was dishonest or disloyal, others were sure to find out. Gossip served to discipline and punish. A good reputation was as critical to success as good product. Many experimented with distribution, but only a few survived over time.[82]

The fifty-fifty split of box office receipts was a concrete expression of a mutually beneficial relationship, and once again, trust was key: a distributor had to trust his exhibitor to honestly report earnings. If he doubted the exhibitor's accounting, he had two options: either end the relationship or require that films be paid for on a flat-fee basis, known in the industry as a minimum guarantee (or MG). Here, a flat fee was paid to the distributor regardless of how a film did at the box office. MGs worked to the distributors' advantage financially and were common in countries with oligopolistic distribution systems, but they were rarely utilized in Tanzania before independence. If a Tanzanian exhibitor was placed on MG terms, the subtext was that he was not honest. Although he had other distributors he could turn to, word of his status as an MG client would soon circulate through the grapevine, and he would have difficulty negotiating a percentage-based deal with a new partner. In the 1950s, local distributors were reluctant to demand an MG, in part because they needed clients to screen their films and had to offer attractive terms to secure partners. A distributor with a habit of demanding an MG also signaled that he was not the kind of man most wanted to have a relationship with: he did not trust his partner, and he selfishly demanded the lion's share of the profits.

Following the lead of American producer-distributor cartels, which made heavy use of the diplomatic core in negotiating import agreements in foreign territories, Indians too worked to consolidate overseas distribution after independence, with the aim of securing a greater share of the profits. In the late 1950s, two of the largest distributors from India, Indian Film Combine and Overseas Film Distributors, opened branches in Nairobi.[83] They marketed aggressively in East Africa, attempting to force out locally based, independent distributors and consolidate their control over imports. But it took years for them to make substantial inroads into the Tanzanian market because local exhibitors saw value in maintaining their "locavore" economy. Unlike local suppliers, foreign distributors presumed their own superiority in negotiations: if a percentage deal was offered, it was 70 percent to the distributor and 30 percent to the exhibitor, but more typically, flat-rate MG rentals prevailed. Contracts, rather than negotiated personal relationships, were the rule. Whenever possible, Tanzanian exhibitors kept their supply relationships with local men.

Direct communication and the ability to negotiate over needs and desires were two other components of local business relationships that partners on both sides of the equation valued. Each exhibitor had a primary supplier, but rarely was this a strictly exclusive relationship. The manager of the Azania took most of his films from the Majestic group, but if Indo-African had a film he wanted, he usually could contact someone and get what he sought. If there was an opening in his program that local suppliers could not fill, he would turn to one of the Indian distributors to complete his bill. Theaters primarily supplied by Majestic also sometimes wanted to screen Egyptian or other films imported by Indo-African. And again, with a little face-to-face negotiation, a manager could clear a spot in his monthly schedule for the film he wanted, without being punished by his main supplier. Independent exhibitors in South Africa, by contrast, were bound by block-booking contracts and could not take a film from another supplier. Those who tried to do so found themselves in court for breach of contract and were often subsequently forced out of business entirely.[84] Shabir Jariwalla reiterated what I was told by many when he described business arrangements in Tanzania, "We did not write things down. We talked, we came to an agreement, and that was that. We did not need papers or a court. Business was done man to man."[85]

Good-natured rivalry between locally based suppliers—fueled by exhibitors—served the interests of the grassroots moviegoing public. By the 1950s, many towns in Tanzania had two cinemas, each of which was independently owned, largely supplied by a different distributor, and equally invested in being voted "the best" by local fans. Exhibitors paid close attention to what their local competitors were screening and pushed their distributors to provide them with films of a similar or superior quality. Again, if their man could not deliver, they looked to someone who could. To keep their clients, the distributors worked tirelessly to provide the best films. Managers at Indo-African Theaters Ltd., working with someone in Raj Kapoor's studios, secured a deal in the 1950s that gave them exclusive rights to distribute Kapoor's films—arguably some of the most popular of the era—in East Africa. This meant that fans of Raj Kapoor (and other stars linked to him) were drawn to theaters supplied by Indo-African. In response, the Majestic group worked out a deal with Bhagwan—who was also a director, producer, and actor and famous for his comic antics and allegiance to the proletariat—to become his exclusive East African distributor.[86] If a theater supplied by Indo-African screened *Awara* (Kapoor, 1951), starring Raj Kapoor and Nargis, the rival theater supplied by the Majestic group countered with Bhagwan's *Albela* (Bhagwan, 1951), featuring Bhagwan and Geeta Bali. On such days, nearly everyone in town was at the movies.

Building Business and Building Community, 1900s–50s

In his nostalgic recollections of this era, Natwar Joshi recalled how this competitive rivalry between theaters and distributors enhanced the options for local fans. Before the Naaz opened its doors in Mombasa in the early 1950s, he reported, "Samji Kala and their company Majestic Theaters ruled the roost." He claimed that without competition, "films lay canned in Samji Kala's warehouse [for ages] before being released."[87] But when Indo-African opened the Naaz, "Majestic declared an all-out war—fortunately to the advantage of the film going public." Like men's football clubs and women's dance troupes during this era, each theater and its core fan base wanted to be able to claim they put on the best show. Having patrons sitting on soda crates in the aisles or standing for three hours along the back wall meant that both exhibitors and distributors had met their mark. The fact that an average cinemagoer like Joshi took the time to write an extended Internet posting about these competitions some sixty years after the events indicates how long these reputations could last and how invested local citizens were in their relationships with neighborhood cinemas.

Tanzanian exhibitors' relationships with suppliers of English-language films were categorically different from their relationships with local distributors, but even in this regard, Tanzanians exhibited an unusual degree of strength in negotiations over films and rental terms. In the 1910s, Jariwalla purchased used prints of American and British films from the same suppliers of Indian films that he dealt with in Bombay. Others were ordered directly from London, where many prints for English-language films could be purchased secondhand after they had finished their UK run. Most theaters around the world at the time found it cheaper and quicker to order used prints from London than to deal with American suppliers directly.[88] Hollywood executives put an end to the secondhand market out of the United Kingdom in the 1920s, demanding that all American films be purchased through one of their licensed agents. Isador Schlesinger had by that time also secured the license to serve as the sole distributor for the majority of British and American studios in South Africa. By 1938, he had secured monopoly rights to distribute for these same studios in all of Africa south of the equator, as stipulated in a contract he repeatedly tried to interpret as giving him exclusive control to everything south of the Sahara.[89] But through this entire period, Tanzanians maintained their rights to play the field, categorically refusing to concede to Schlesinger's monopoly or dictatorial terms.

Jariwalla chafed at Schlesinger's demands and set the stage for future Tanzanians' rights to negotiate. Through the 1920s, he continued to import used prints from suppliers in India; only with the advent of talkies did he sign a limited agreement with Schlesinger. But when Jariwalla learned of the rivalry between United Artists, Metro-Goldwyn-Mayer, and 20th Century Fox, which spent the 1930s in protracted legal and theatrical battles fighting Schlesinger's monopoly on distribution in South Africa, he chose to deal with the three American studios instead. Jariwalla signed with United Artists and 20th Century Fox to supply the Empire in Dar es Salaam and with Metro-Goldwyn-Mayer to supply the Royal in Zanzibar, cutting Schlesinger out of the Tanzanian market almost entirely. When Talati and his partners switched to sound and opened the Empire in Zanzibar, they too signed with United Artists and Fox.[90] Following the advice of elder "uncles" in the business, many Tanzanians who opened theaters in the 1940s and 1950s did their best to avoid dealing with Schlesinger. But his films were indeed quite good, and with all the theaters striving to offer original product, some ultimately ended up working with him—but only on reasonable terms. Rather than having exclusive agreements to show the films of just one of the distributors operating out of South Africa, Tanzanians negotiated to choose English-language films from a buffet of options. "You would take five from this guy, three from that one, four from another," explained one exhibitor. "And each one would fight to get the end of the month dates, because that was when people got paid and when business was best."[91] Exhibitors could play distributors off against each other to get the best films on the best days and for the best terms. Typically, each theater received the bulk of its films from one agent, but East Africans refused to sign exclusive contracts during this period, which also gave them leverage in negotiating rental terms.

Block booking and blind selling were other standard features of contracts in oligopolistic markets that East Africans avoided, and as a result, Tanzanians enjoyed the best films produced by the major studios, rather than the B- and C-grade movies screened in much of the rest of the continent. Under block-booking and blind-selling arrangements, a distributor was given the power to book anywhere from twenty-six to fifty-two weeks of a theater's schedule, sending the exhibitor films of various qualities with no guarantee that particular titles or stars would be included. Once signed, these contracts lasted for years.[92] From the earliest days, Jariwalla refused to capitulate to such terms; he chose what films were screened in his theaters, and as a result, Tanzanians were treated to some of the best American product. During any given week in the 1930s, the Royal might screen an American or British drama on Monday and Tuesday followed by an Abbott and Costello or Laurel and Hardy comedy or an adventure film such as *The Wizard of Oz* (Fleming, 1939) or *King Kong* (Cooper, 1933) on Wednesday, Thursday, and Friday. Saturday's bill would cater to the European crowd, often featuring a musical starring Bing Crosby, Ginger Rogers, Ethel Merman, or Shirley Temple.[93] Sundays were always reserved for Indian and Egyptian films. Never did a Tanzanian theater run the same English-language film for days or weeks on end, which was standard practice where oligarchy and block booking prevailed. Tanzanian exhibitors also felt free to swap out a scheduled title for something else on hand if they thought the scheduled feature would flop; in South Africa, Schlesinger was reputed to put men out of business if they tried such a stunt. Reiterating what many exhibitors told me, one interviewee said, "The distributor might get mad and send you a letter, 'Why didn't you show this film on the dates we told you to?' But it is just a letter, so you stick it in the file and that is it. Business continues as usual. Really though, they rarely found out." In East Africa, distance—combined with competition between distributors—increased an exhibitor's ability to run his show as he liked.[94]

Tanzanians continued to demand high-quality English-language films throughout the colonial era, which also set them apart from exhibitors elsewhere on the continent. Often, exhibitors who catered to non-white audiences could only access films of the poorest quality. In Zambia, Zimbabwe, and Ghana, second- or third-rank films, dominated by B- and C-class westerns, comprised the majority of English-language films. In those countries, westerns and the cinema often became synonymous, so prevalent were the westerns of "poverty row" studios. In Ghana, according to Gareth McFeely, fewer than one film in ten came from a major production company.[95] In Tanzania, by contrast, westerns were also screened but not excessively, and they came from major studios and featured top stars such as Alan Ladd, Gary Cooper, and Robert Mitchum. Tanzanian exhibitors knew global films and their local fans, and they insisted on choosing movies that would please the crowd. Musical westerns, starring the singing duo Roy Rogers and Dale Evans or the singing cowboy Gene Autry, were chosen over the films of John Wayne because singing cowboys were more popular in Tanzania than tough-talking ones.[96] In the category of dramas too, Tanzanian exhibitors often chose stars with musical skills. The most acclaimed actors and actresses graced local screens. Over the course of just a few months in 1950, films starring Ginger Rogers, Lon Chaney, Dorothy Lamour, Carmen Miranda, Frank Sinatra, Judy Garland, Elizabeth Taylor, Susan Hayward, Cary Grant, Ingrid Bergman, Bud Abbott, Lou Costello, Bette Davis, and many others were shown.[97]

Across the globe, the highest earnings were amassed by those who controlled both exhibition and distribution as a single unit. But the fact that Tanzanian theaters were all independently owned and that local distributors did not consolidate into vertically integrated distribution-exhibition companies further enhanced the quality of the local cinematic scene. Indo-African and Majestic were the largest distribution groups in East Africa, but each controlled less than a handful of theaters as integrated distribution-exhibition units, or some 10 percent of the theaters in the nation. During interviews, I repeatedly pushed interviewees to explain why neither Indo-African nor Majestic made efforts to buy up independent theaters or assume oligarchic control of the industry. The answer in part was that Dar es Salaam and Zanzibar were by far the two most lucrative markets, so financially, it simply did not make sense to purchase up-country theaters given the investment costs and slow rates of return. But in the United States, Britain, Australia, and South Africa, this did not stop dominant chains from taking over small theaters in regional towns or forcing independents out of business. In those countries, the business culture venerated monopolies, and power was asserted through aggressive dominance. Taking it all made one a man. East Africans, in contrast, did not think a monopoly was beneficial, even if it did yield higher profits. None of the independent exhibitors I interviewed had ever been pressured to consolidate, sell, or capitulate, prior to nationalization. The business dictum was different in Tanzania, they maintained: live and let live was the motto. Putting others out of business was not only petty and vindictive, it was also socially and economically counterproductive. A good businessman created possibilities for others; he acted as a contact in a circuit, facilitating the circulation of information, opportunities, cash, connections, experience, and skill. Doing so, he established himself as a good man. In East Africa, entrepreneurs in the first half of the twentieth century balanced the desire for profits against other expectations, obligations, and rewards.

87

PROFITS, RISKS, AND COSTS

Through the 1950s, local distributors took half or more of the film earnings in the country, but they also shouldered the greatest financial risks. It was expensive to secure copyrights and buy prints. The distributors had to know what local audiences liked as well as what kind of global product was available at a price they could afford. They needed to maintain contacts with production studios so that they knew what was in the works and when it might be available for display on the local circuit. And sometimes, they had to commit to taking films from Indian studios while they were still in production and no one had any idea what the final products would actually look like.[98] They could never be certain, no matter who the stars were, that a given film would earn enough to cover costs. Certain films, even some that were quite expensive to buy, utterly flopped at the local box office. A blockbuster or superhit could earn back the cost of purchase in Dar es Salaam alone, but importers hit this mark only once or twice a year even if everything worked just as they planned.

If earnings in Dar es Salaam and Zanzibar paid for a film, a distributor could count up-country proceeds as profit. In a good year, perhaps 20 percent of the films imported by a distributor would turn a decent profit; an equal number would lose money.[99] The vast majority simply broke even. Asad Talati began running United Film Distributors (UFD) for his father after returning from his studies in London. (UFD was the distribution arm of Indo-African when the company split into exhibition and distribution firms in 1958.) He recalled that their highest-grossing film before independence was *Junglee* (Subodh Mukherjee, 1961). They opened it at the Sultana, their own theater in Zanzibar, where it earned the equivalent of $4,600, and they ran it for an unprecedented five Sundays and Mondays. But legal rights and print costs for a movie such as *Junglee* were on the order of $12,000. The film was a superhit by audience standards in Zanzibar, but UFD still had quite a way to go to break even, much less see a profit. Without extensive knowledge of both the local market and global supply, as well as trustworthy and dependable local and international partners, a distributor could easily go bankrupt.

For exhibitors, the profits accrued from operating a cinema were more social than economic. All the exhibitors in Tanzania had other businesses or professions before they opened a cinema. Many from the coast were traders or importers of manufactured goods and exporters of Tanzanian raw materials. Others earned their living as gold- and silversmiths or merchants selling everything from food and clothing to automotive spare parts. Some operated small factories producing soda or nails. Still others were professionals, including contractors, engineers, lawyers, and civil servants. What they had in common was that, to a man, they considered their cinemas a side business, a hobby, or something for personal and communal entertainment. Operating a cinema, I was told again and again, was "a labor of love." As one proprietor said, "The actual financial profits earned from the cinema were meager. These were the kinds of profits that could feed you, but little more. If you wanted to build a house, or educate your children, you needed to have another type of business."[100] Thus, for example, K. R. Juma, who built the Highland Cinema in Iringa in the 1950s, ran a transport business with lorries, as well as a store, a soda factory, a gas station, and an automotive spare parts store. "It was these other businesses that really earned him money," said his nephew Feroz. "It wasn't easy for anyone to live off of cinema alone. Everyone had to have another type of business to survive, and yet another to support the cinema." Someone else laughed when I asked about profits: "Profits? We earned pennies. But boy did we have a good time."[101]

The accuracy of these remarks was confirmed by my analysis of available returns and accounts. The archival, tax, and business records are limited, but they indicate that even large theaters in the most lucrative markets made only modest profits. In Zanzibar in the 1940s and 1950s, average earnings were roughly equivalent to $3,000 a year (or about $30,000 in 2016 dollars).[102] In 1960, the reported profits earned by Indo-African's cinemas in Zanzibar, Dar es Salaam, and Mombasa—three of the best markets in the region—were the equivalent of $7,644, and that sum had to be split between six investors.[103] Moreover, returns were slow and incremental. Repaying the initial capital outlays used to build and equip a theater typically took twenty-five to thirty years.[104] Gross receipts from ticket sales were indeed laudable, but after subtracting what was owed to distributors, plus mortgage or investor capital repayments and operating costs, exhibitors were left with relatively little. The operator of the Raha Leo Civic Center in Zanzibar claimed gross earnings of some TSh 81,614 (roughly $12,000) in 1951, which was certainly not bad for a second-run cinema on the poorer side of town. But more than three-fourths of this amount went to covering the basic costs of doing business.[105] After costs, the average net to exhibitors was less than ten cents on every dollar earned at the box office.[106] Nonetheless, relative to exhibitors in the United States, where average earnings were a mere 3.5 percent of the gross, East Africans did comparatively well.[107] Across the globe, exhibition was without doubt penny capitalism.

Taxes, fees, and the day-to-day operating costs associated with running a cinema were also quite substantial. A typical cinema might have ten or more employees. Their combined salaries were the largest monthly expenditure, often amounting to 50 percent more than the owner stood to earn as profit.[108] Cinema owners also incurred substantial costs for machinery and building maintenance, as well as electricity, water, and municipal taxes. And then there were expenses particular to this industry, such as fees charged by the government to cover the costs of censorship. Exhibitors complained about other costs associated with censorship as well, for members of the censorship board commonly expected free admission for themselves and their families—and of course they wanted prime seats. In Dar es Salaam and Zanzibar, where the main censorship boards were based, the cost in terms of lost sales could be substantial.[109] In addition, there were annual fees for a municipal business license and permit fees for each film, short, and trailer. During the colonial era, the government found it too cumbersome to impose taxes on profits, preferring the simpler method of charging flat-rate licensing fees for businesses and charging cinemas fees on each film they screened. In Zanzibar, these fees were the highest in the region, amounting to $1,000 per year per theater in 1952 (or roughly $10,000 in today's dollars).[110] Exhibitors were also obliged by distributors to pay the freight costs for shipping the films on to the next theater in the circuit; these costs varied considerably depending on how far one had to ship the films, as well as the relative ease of getting them from point A to point B. Other costs of doing business were more typical: accountancy fees, telephone charges, postage, bank fees, and advertising costs. When all was said and done at the end of the month, an exhibitor would be left with very little to show in terms of financial profit. In small up-country towns or in theaters in Pemba, exhibitors frequently had to borrow money—from another self-owned business or a friend—to keep the cinema afloat, particularly if they were faced with sudden, unanticipated costs related to expensive repairs.

The distribution industry was increasingly consolidated in the late 1950s, and for East African exhibitors, this meant that the share of the gross they retained declined. Hollywood distributors paved the way. First, they began opening regional offices across the continent, including in Nairobi, to improve their knowledge of and control over African markets. In 1956, Schlesinger also sold his distribution company, African Consolidated Films, to 20th Century Fox, leading to a monopoly that even by South African corporate standards seemed excessive.[111] The new organization, known as Anglo-American Film Corporation, moved agents to Nairobi to cover its East African territories. By the 1960s, rental terms for East African exhibitors rose to 70 percent of box office earnings for Hollywood films. Following suit, distributors of Indian films—beginning with international firms based in Nairobi—also raised their rates. By the mid-1960s, the previous fifty-fifty split of returns had changed to seventy-thirty in favor of the distributor in most cases. Nationalization of the distribution industries in Kenya and Tanzania in the late 1960s further transformed business relations. Patron and client give-and-take over films, terms, and scheduling was replaced by a new business model in which the state was the dominant partner. Terms were offered, and one could take them or leave them, but that was the end of the official discussion. These transformations are discussed at length in chapter 8.

The monetary rewards from running a cinema may have been limited, but the social capital earned was priceless. Cinemas were centers of urban social and cultural life, yielding returns for proprietors and townspeople that were beyond measure if calculated in good times and in people connecting with people.

Chapter 2

THE MEN WHO MADE THE MOVIES RUN

OWNERS WERE not the only ones who accrued social capital from their connections to film. Cinemas were vibrant urban institutions made all the more dynamic by the often larger-than-life characters who brought the shows to life. Managers, ticket sellers, projectionists, and concession stand operators made the buildings hum, and reelers, human billboards, and black market sellers of cinema tickets—occupational categories that were somewhat unique to this part of the cinematic world—added local flare. Entire neighborhoods were known by the cinemas in their midst, and the men from a range of class and ethnic backgrounds who worked at these theaters were regarded by many as local stars. These men drew immense pride from their ties to the cinema and their ability to bring fantasy, drama, and pleasure to others' lives. Sociability, commitment to community, professionalism, and pride in a job well done were hallmarks of being a good man in early twentieth-century East Africa. And working at a cinema or simply being affiliated in a tangential way allowed men to demonstrate these qualities before a large and appreciative audience.

It was the people who brought the buildings to life, not those who built and endowed them, who held the warmest spots in communal hearts.

Their names were known by everybody in town. As one man said of his father, who worked as an usher at the Empire Cinema in Zanzibar in the 1950s, "Everyone knew [him]. If you walked with him you were constantly being greeted, 'Eh Amir, how are you today? How is the family?' Cinema was highly valued, so if you worked at the cinema you were popular and people respected you."[1] Many residents could also tell you where cinema workers lived and who their relatives were. Being able to situate these men within the elaborate nexus of the crosscutting social networks of urban life meant that one was better able to connect to power should the need arise for an extra ticket to a sold-out show or should young kids with no money hope to gain entrance by pressuring an "uncle" who worked at the theater to let them in for free.[2] But it was not merely the power they exercised over goods in limited supply that brought them prestige: these men were loved because they gave the town a good time. Their charming smiles, twinkling eyes, and willingness to engage anyone and everyone in conversation about matters both grave and mundane added to their charisma. When I think back to my interviews and conversations with the men who ran the shows, *engaging, generous,* and *joyful* are the first adjectives that come to mind. At the time I met them, the industry was largely dead and the men were all well past middle age. I can only imagine how contagious their smiles and cheer were when they and the industry they ran were in their prime.

To make their cinemas a success, most theater owners had to employ from ten to twenty men. From a management standpoint, some positions were clearly more vital than others, but from the perspective of each employee—or even from that of a patron—they were all critical to a truly successful show. Beyond that, cinema workers added verve and vitality to the cast of characters that made up a town, coming as they did from various racial, religious, class, and communal backgrounds. When not at work, they were all interwoven into the wider tapestry of urban life, bringing news of cinematic happenings to their neighborhoods and likewise bringing their friends and families in touch with happenings at the central fixture of urban life.

House managers were certainly at the top of the management hierarchy in terms of responsibility, pay, and communal prestige. Owners often

93

conceded complete control over operations to a trusted house manager, who was paid a respectable but not exorbitant salary to run the theater from day to day.[3] Whether the house manager was given the authority to arrange bookings depended on his knowledge of films, his professional relationships with suppliers, and the degree of involvement and control maintained by the owner. But even if the manager was simply given a program of upcoming attractions to bill each week, he still had a lot to do.

Managers typically determined how many times to run a given film, and if a movie flopped, they were the ones who had to scramble to fill its spot with something more enticing. They supervised advertising and made sure that movie posters were prominently displayed. They oversaw the selling of tickets, the collection of money, the keeping of books, and the delivery of daily proceeds to the owner or the bank. When the theater was closed, they ensured that it was properly cleaned, painted, and maintained. If the projector was broken, the sound system blown, the roof leaking, or the electrical lines down, it was the manager who had to locate and organize repairmen, tools, and supplies. The day of the show, managers greeted guests and made them feel welcome—and when throngs tried to push through the doorway, or ticket window lines got totally out of control, they fought to restore order. Often, they were responsible for things that were simply beyond their control. If a film did not run, if patrons were turned away, or if (heaven forbid), the theater had to be closed for major structural repairs, the house managers found themselves in deep trouble. Their greatest fear was not the wrath of the owner but the disappointment of the fans whose needs they could not meet. Because cinemas were central hubs of neighborhoods and towns, a manager whose theater was closed could not go to the market or get a cup of coffee without encountering endless questions about the status of repairs and the expected date of reopening. It was this pressure from mere acquaintances that could produce ulcers or drive a man near to collapse.

Since the men who built the cinemas were patrons not just of the arts but of sundry clients and extended family members as well, house managers were sometimes chosen simply because they were a son, a nephew, a client, or a close friend's relative who needed a job.[4] The patron-client ties that were forged at the cinema were often inaugurated by the poor and needy. Ally Khamis Ally's relationship with his fictive-kin father is but one of numerous examples. In his sixties at the time of this writing, Ally was

Figure 2.1 Ad for *Mother India*, Zanzibar Central Market. Photo by Ranchhod T. Oza, courtesy of Capital Art Studio, Zanzibar

still commonly known as Ally Rocky, a nickname he was given as a child because he followed the proprietor of the Wete cinema, a Goan named Rocky, absolutely everywhere; people even teased him about being the Goan's illegitimate son.[5] But Ally ignored the taunts and bore the name of his fictive father with pride. He was fascinated by films, and eventually, his persistence at the theater paid off. While in his twenties, he was bequeathed the management of the Novelty Cinema in Pemba by his fictive father, making him one of the happiest lads in the land. Ahmed Hussein, a poor boy from Dar es Salaam, forged a similarly productive fictive kinship with Hassanali Kassum Sunderji, the eldest son of Kassum Sunderji Samji, who built the Avalon, Amana, and New Chox. Hassanali Kassum Sunderji was nicknamed "Chocolate," shortened in daily parlance to "Choxi," because of his love of the treat. His desire for the sweet things in life was indulged by his father, who reputedly allowed him to eat as much chocolate as he liked

95

from the family store. Then, in the 1950s, Kassum Sunderji Samji also built his son a cinema to indulge his passion for film. The cinema was named the New Chox. Ahmed Hussein also had a taste for film, and from the age of ten or twelve, he hung out around the New Chox daily picking up soda bottles, sweeping aisles, or doing whatever chores he could to make himself modestly useful and thus earn admission to the show. At fourteen or fifteen, pesky little Ahmed was finally taken into the projection room, where he would learn his trade. Around town, he then became known as Ahmed Choxi, with his father's name supplanted by that of his patron and the theater where he was now officially employed.[6] As a projectionist, he earned more than double the monthly minimum wage, which was considered quite grand for a young man with only a fourth-grade education. A few years later, he was promoted to house manager of the New Chox, which made his parents exceptionally proud. Both Ally and Ahmed were adopted by men of different class, religious, and ethnic backgrounds from their own. But a love of movies bound them with their fictive fathers for life, allowing both boys to turn a childhood passion into a respectable adult profession.

House managers were nearly always avid film fans; in fact, most were the equivalent of walking, talking film encyclopedias. Typically, they were gregarious crowd pleasers, and more than one was considered quite the ladies' man. Their skills were first and foremost people skills. Lacking business and accounting abilities did not necessarily make them bad managers. Being able to please a crowd and woo patrons was more critical to business success. A curmudgeonly accountant or even a manager's mother could keep the books, but it took a big smile and a big heart to manage one of the central institutions of urban life. In more than one instance, a cinema was handed over to a party boy to manage, with the hope that his natural inclinations could be channeled in a respectable, responsible business endeavor. There were few better jobs for a man who loved to be the life of the party. "Not only did you get to watch films, but you got to meet people all of the time, make people happy and really get to know and talk to members of the community," said one interviewee, Eddy. "Running a cinema was a business that was also a pleasure! Really it was pure pleasure, but you could earn a living off of it as well."[7]

Managers were not the only employees who reveled in the ability to show the town a good time and be at the center of urban social life; nearly everyone I interviewed, from doormen to sweepers, stressed the pleasure and benefits they got from their associations with the show. One man who worked as a gatekeeper from the age of eighteen until he was thirty-five told me, "Really I did it just for the fun. It was just a pastime really, the salary was very little, but it was fun seeing all of the people coming and going. It was a *great* way to make contacts. I enjoyed it a lot!"[8] Many stressed how they got to know *everybody* in town. "Everyone knew me," said one man who worked at the Empress in Dar es Salaam, "and . . . many people came and begged me, begged me to help them get tickets to the show." A man who worked at a theater in Moshi had similar recollections of his power and popularity: "I remember *Andhaa Kaanoon* [Rama Rao's 1983 production, starring Amitabh Bachchan and Hema Malini]. If you could get people tickets to that one, oh people will kiss your feet! Oh I had so many friends, so many friends in those days."[9] "Oh yes, and the women," said another, "they were the highlight of the job! Every beautiful woman in town knew my name."[10] Another doorman who considered himself quite the Romeo in his day echoed those remarks, "The ladies, the ladies were the highlight of the job. All dressed up in their finest and perfumed! And they all knew who I was."[11]

To spread the word about their offerings, exhibitors often displayed movie posters at the central market or near a clock tower in the central business district, as well as at the front of their cinemas, and some played music outside their venues in the evenings to draw potential customers' attention. From the earliest days, movie ads and showtimes were also featured in the English- and Gujarati-language press. But prior to independence, African literacy rates were limited, so if exhibitors wanted to ensure a large crowd, they took their advertising to where the people were and presented the information in a mode designed to communicate with the nonliterate. Thus, human billboards walked the streets of the central business district and the African neighborhoods, ringing bells, honking bicycle horns, or pushing carts festooned with posters and playing gramophone music from an upcoming Hindi film. As casual laborers, they were paid peanuts or simply offered free admission in exchange for their work. Managers did not really need to go to such lengths to garner a crowd, but they were often inundated with pesky young men eager to cement their association with the show: hiring some to walk around promoting movies was simply a way to get them out of the managers' hair. But to hear the human billboards tell

The Men Who Made the Movies Run

Figure 2.2 Human billboards, drawing by Dr. Juli McGruder, 2016. Based on a photo of advertising done by the Majestic theater, Tanga, in *Showman* 3, no. 3 (1954): 12, published by African Consolidate Films Ltd., Johannesburg, South Africa

the story, they were as central to the organization as the Jariwallas or Talatis themselves! Their shows in the streets were yet another manifestation of the excitement and revelry the cinema added to urban life; their antics earned them accolades and fond recollections for generations to come.[12]

Much less visible but arguably more central to the success of the shows were the projectionists. These men were typically far more reserved than managers, doormen, or walking billboards but no less revered. As Abdul, manager of the Majestic Cinema in Zanzibar, said, "*Everyone*, everyone wanted to be a projectionist. It was the dream of nearly every young man."[13] This job carried immense prestige because, in addition to being highly paid, it was—as trade publications described—"the heart and soul" of the show. Being a projectionist was highly technical and required a great deal of craftsmanship, mechanical ability, and engineering skill. The knowledge needed for the job increased exponentially over the years as films, projectors, and sound systems became more advanced. Only in the twenty-first century has this trajectory reversed, allowing one person to operate seven or eight multiplex screens with the touch of a few buttons. In the early years, projectors were hand-cranked, and films were rarely more than a minute or two long. Later, typical Indian movies ran for three hours and came on as many as thirteen reels of film, each of which had to run in order and be started as soon as the previous reel reached its end. It was incredibly easy to drop a reel of film or mishandle the take-up reel and end up with a tangled mess on the floor. Heaps of unspooled film were the nightmare of every projectionist but something nearly everyone encountered at least twice—once when he was learning to operate a projector and again when he was teaching the trade to someone else.

Fire was also an ever-present threat. Film was coated with nitrates and highly flammable, and until quite recently, the light that illuminated the pictures came not from a bulb but from a flame burning just behind the celluloid. It was extremely easy for the film to catch fire if it was not in continuous motion. If a film combusted and the operator was inattentive, a fire could quickly get out of control, potentially burning the entire building to the ground. Indeed, the earliest and most elaborate municipal fire regulations often emerged from quite legitimate fears of fire at moving-picture shows—which was as true in Chicago and Birmingham as it was in Zanzibar, Mwanza, and Dar es Salaam. Usually, projectionists were equipped with buckets of water, blankets, or fire extinguishers, and most learned a variety of tricks for putting out a fire before it spread. But the nitrates on the film produced nitric acid when burned, so even if a man managed to save a cinema, burning film harmed his lungs. Fortunately, most projectionists were quite skilled operators, and no one I interviewed had ever seen such a fire.[14] A much more common threat was the malfunctioning of the carbon rods used to produce the flame that illuminated the celluloid. Every projectionist I spoke with mentioned how fickle and problematic carbons could be, and they emphasized the skill required to maintain just the proper distance between the two rods to produce the precise amount of illumination required. Readers might recall watching videos of old black-and-white films, where the picture fades to gray or even black and then returns with vivid luminosity: this is what happened if a carbon burnt out and a new one was installed but not properly adjusted.

A young man learned how to run a projector, handle film, and adjust carbons by serving as an apprentice to a skilled projectionist. Every theater had a gaggle of youth eager to learn the trade, and managers often had to set limits on the number of people allowed in a projection booth. A boy given the honor of entry into the projection room would spend years simply watching the professional at work, picking up knowledge as time went along. If he was lucky and trusted, he then advanced to working as a rewinder, using a separate machine to put a finished reel back onto its original spool. If he was paid at all, he might earn sixty-two shillings a month, compared to the four hundred shillings earned by the projectionist, but many times, his only payment was simply the social cachet that came from sitting next to the projectionist or maybe free admission for his siblings and friends.[15] The position of assistant projectionist was the next step up the professional ladder, where one earned half as much as a full-fledged operator. The assistant could be trusted to keep the reel running or even start the next reel while the projectionist stepped outside to smoke a cigarette or nodded off for a nap. Being left in charge like that was a huge sign of professional maturation—and a huge responsibility. If a film jumped the sprocket, the gate tension slipped, or a splice broke, the projector could jam or the film could flutter into a pile of spaghetti in no time at all. There was no hiding such mistakes from the projectionist, for he would be roused from his sleep or his smoke by angry cries from the audience lamenting his incompetence or shouting evil things about his mother and the dubious circumstances of his conception.

In many cases, the only way an assistant projectionist could become an operator was through the death or retirement of his boss or through relocation to a town that was opening a new cinema and had no one to run its machines.[16] Suresh Solanki began his training in Tanga at the Majestic. Over the course of his five-year apprenticeship, his salary increased from half of what the cinema spent on rat poison, when he began, to one-third of what the full-time projectionists made, when he was promoted to assistant projectionist. His family then took over the management of the Plaza Cinema in Moshi, near Kilamanjaro; Solanki moved from the coast to join them and at last became a full-fledged operator there.[17] Had he remained in Tanga, he might never have advanced to the status of a projectionist—a job men coveted for life.

The talents required of a projectionist went well beyond running a machine and included splicing and editing film as well. Considerable skill and a steady hand were required to make a straight and clean splice, and since few projectionists in East Africa owned a splicer, most relied on a simple razor blade to make their cuts. Care had to be taken to join a film so that missing parts were unnoticeable, and sprocket holes had to be aligned to ensure a consistent feed. In addition, emulsion had to be gently scraped off the film and a special cement applied before the two pieces were carefully joined and then held together until the glue dried.[18] If not properly done, a splice would result in considerable disruption for the viewers, or it could cause a film to jump the sprocket and unravel, jam, and start a fire or damage the machine. And if a projectionist forgot to use a black marker to cover the sound track on the back side of the film, the audience would also be subjected to annoying audio thumps when the splice fed through the machine. Poorly joined films caused projectionists innumerable headaches. Splicing required adjustments to tension on reels: if the tension was too tight a splice might break, bringing an unwelcome intermission at a key moment of dramatic tension in a film. Cutting and splicing made projectionists the local technical and creative equivalent of film producers.

Censorship of films was routine during the colonial and postcolonial eras, and it was extremely common for certain types of scenes to be deleted, which of course required frequent splicing. In the colonial era, scenes depicting violence, juvenile crime, "unladylike" behavior, nudity, drunkenness, lovemaking, or the ridicule of Europeans—along with nearly a dozen other censored subjects—had to be cut. The particulars changed somewhat during the postcolonial era, but the list of forbidden visual fruit remained long. Given that there was often only a single print of a film circulating in all of East Africa and that Zanzibar, Tanganyika, Kenya, Uganda, and many regional towns all had their own guidelines and censorship boards permitting and excluding different material, every projectionist had to be adept at splicing, joining, and fixing botched jobs done by others.[19] The last projectionist to show a film in a region governed by a censorship board had to reinsert all the parts that had been cut before the film was passed to others in the regional circuit. By the time a print had completed the circuit, it was often a cut-and-glued mess. Projectionists did sometimes have fun with splicing, joining miscellaneous cut parts from various films on hand into an original montage of sex, nudity, and violence to entertain fellow workers or friends on rainy days.

A good projectionist was not only an artist and craftsman but an engineer as well. Maintaining and repairing a set of projectors was no simple job, especially in a region of the world where spare parts were nearly

The Men Who Made the Movies Run

impossible to find. Because the first line of defense against costly and time-consuming repairs was proper maintenance of the machines, a good projectionist "coddled his projectors like his babies," I was told.[20] Machines had to be cleaned, adjusted, and oiled daily. Mirrors and lenses needed to be spotless, and the distance between the mirrors and the aperture had to be precise; otherwise, the projection would be distorted. Tensions on rollers, valves, and springs had to be checked and adjusted. Amplifiers needed to be regularly cleaned of cockroaches, since, for some reason, the bugs found them to be extraordinarily suitable places for building nests. But no matter what a man did, his equipment eventually broke down. Consequently, in addition to understanding how his equipment worked, a projectionist had to be able to tell a metalsmith or electrician precisely how to fix it. Simply going to the store to get a new part was out of the question, and if a new one needed to be ordered, it could be weeks or months before it arrived on the next boat. There were no trained projector technicians because there were not enough cinemas in the region to support such specialization. So managers and projectionists had to be jacks of all trades.

Ally Khamis Ally, mentioned earlier, was a precocious child and an avid movie fan, and having weaseled his way into the projection room in Wete as a youth, he delighted in helping the projectionist find both the cause and the cure whenever equipment broke down. When he was a grown man, he managed two cinemas in Pemba and also ran a repair shop fixing radios, sound systems, appliances, televisions, water pumps, small engines, and of course projectors.[21] As an engineer, Ally traveled as far as Tabora and Bukoba to help other managers modify and fix their machines. Often managers were forced to take their equipment to a local *fundi* (repairman), who typically specialized in auto or bicycle repair. "Every time something went wrong you had to hunt around and get it fixed under a mango tree. You know how it is, local, local," said one manager, Nitesh. "If the guy is good, it will work. If not, your parts are in worse shape than when you started out." Nitesh's troubles were compounded by the fact that the theater he ran in the 1980s was the only one in the country that had Soviet projectors, making the odds of finding original spare parts next to impossible. Most theaters had some model of British Kelly projectors, and parts were frequently interchangeable with only slight modifications. One man with an auto repair shop regularly fixed the projectors for the Shan theater in Morogoro, and for him, modifications were no problem: a sprocket was a sprocket, a shaft a shaft. Length and thickness mattered; what it went into did not. In exchange for his services, his family members got complimentary tickets to the movies whenever they wanted.[22] It helped that he, his father, and his uncle had all worked in the projection room at the Majestic Theater in Tanga before moving to Morogoro to open the auto repair business in 1954.

One did not have to be wealthy, highly educated, or technically skilled to benefit from the social capital that came with being affiliated with the show. Small vendors, black marketers, and concessionaires—men who otherwise may have remained small fish in a very big urban pond—became, according to them, central movers and shakers in town. Dozens of men attached themselves to every local cinema. These relationships were mutually beneficial but typically informal and unpaid. Part of the social capital owners and managers acquired resulted from their ability to provide a space where others could create opportunities for themselves. They did not necessarily condone or get involved in all that took place outside their doors, but they tolerated and even welcomed it because it added vitality to cinematic life. The streets outside theaters were humming most of the day and at least half of the night, and the owners and managers generally appreciated the buzz. People gathered there to look at movie posters, share news, drink coffee, and peddle their wares, making the theater a vibrant node of urban life.

Men earned their livings and built their reputations through their affiliations with the show in myriad ways. Those who sold peanuts, fruit, coffee and *dafu* (coconut juice) outside the theaters made claims about how their connections to the cinema put them at the center of the town's social life. They had front-row seats to the evening promenade, and no rumor, scandal, or accomplishment passed them by. They also had ample opportunity to chat with men from all walks of life and thus expand their social networks of people with people. The man who sold coffee outside the Cine Afrique in Zanzibar in the early 1990s said that, the area in front of the cinema was an attractive venue for making sales and getting to know folks he otherwise would not encounter. Haji, whose uncle sold fruit and dafu outside the Majestic in Zanzibar, said that the connections his uncle

103

made through the cinema later helped Haji himself secure credit to open a small shop.[23] Haji's family was poor, and even if all his father's brothers had pooled their resources, they still could not have mustered the capital required to open a regular store and help the young men in their family get started in life. But in the course of a casual conversation outside the cinema one night, Haji's uncle mentioned the family's conundrum, and one of the wealthy men who regularly stopped for coffee after prayers offered to supply the money they needed. Over years of mingling with men on these *barazas* (seats or regular hangouts) in Zanzibar, I witnessed firsthand how the personal connections made there helped men negotiate the familial, legal, bureaucratic, and political trials and tribulations that life threw their way.

Black marketers were another group of men who attached themselves to the show in an informal way that allowed them to earn a living and simultaneously helped the theater earn prestige, for black market sales enhanced a venue's cachet. Though black marketers often came from poor families and had only a rudimentary formal education, they amassed incredible esteem, and often, they literally held other people's fates in their hands. A thriving black market for cinema tickets existed in Dar es Salaam from the early 1950s and well into the 1980s.[24] In Zanzibar too, avid fans would pay whatever it cost to be part of the opening-day crowd for hot new Indian releases. Markups varied depending on the stars and the films, but patrons were so insistent on seeing these shows that black marketers found they could easily charge two, three, or four times the face value of the tickets they held. I spoke to several men who lived their entire adult lives — building homes, raising and educating their children, and clothing their wives — on nothing other than what they earned from selling cinema tickets on the black market. Khamis told me he could readily make in one evening as much as the monthly minimum wage for an unskilled laborer; he also recalled earning more in a weekend than most people in Dar es Salaam earned in a month. Rashid said he earned between thirty and one hundred shillings a month as a casual laborer in Zanzibar, but he could make two or three thousand shillings in a single day if he held sought-after tickets to a popular film. And it was his earnings from dealing in black market tickets, not his regular wages, that allowed him to build a home. Msafiri claimed that one of his friends earned enough from one movie to put a new roof on his house.[25] As Kasanga said of black marketeering, "This was a great job! It was pure joy. It is rare to find work that is both profitable and highly enjoyable. How many lines of work are there where you make a very good living while hanging out with your buddies, watching a movie or two each night, and taking Monday and Tuesday off?"[26]

Working as a black market dealer in cinema tickets was also a highly prestigious way to earn a living. According to the men who sold these tickets, people respected their ingenuity and adored them for providing a way to see popular shows without having to fight the crowds at the ticket window. Those who wrote to the newspapers complaining about black marketers clearly disagreed, of course, yet the homes of ticket dealers were urban landmarks, almost as well known as the cinemas themselves, said the traders. People dropped by all the time to get tickets for upcoming shows or seek advice on which film to see. Black marketers had many friends, and if they had unsold tickets, they gifted them to those who would otherwise not be able to go. It was like the film *Robin Hood*, observed one black marketer: "We took only from the wealthy, redistributing cash and tickets to those of us who were poor."[27]

Being a black marketer was a skilled job, and like projectionists, these men often learned their trade by watching others or working as an assistant to a professional in their youth. Kasanga began learning the trade when he was in the fifth grade. His school was next to the Cameo in Dar es Salaam, and at the time, the government was in the midst of one of many short-lived, futile efforts to curb the black market. Under the new rules, each patron was limited to purchasing ten tickets, so one of the black marketers enlisted some schoolboys, including Kasanga, to purchase tickets on his behalf. Since the boys were tipped generously for their efforts, Kasanga made a habit of helping the man out and learned from him when, where, and how to buy and sell. When he finished seventh grade, the highest level of schooling completed by most Tanzanians in those days, he took up the trade in earnest, buying and selling tickets on his own. For the next thirty years, that was his principal form of employment.

Black marketers needed to know more than just what seats to buy and how many tickets to hold; they also needed to know about films and stars and how to read trailers and film posters if they were to accurately gauge what they should buy or how much they could charge. Like most everyone in the industry, these men adored film and had been avid connoisseurs since they were children. But black marketers realized there was often a difference between their personal preferences in film and the tastes of the urban crowd. "You had to be skilled and knowledgeable to appreciate which ones would make for good business," said Taday. "Just because it was a hit in America did not mean it would be a hit in this town. You had to know what people liked." Dar es Salaam was the best market in the nation by far, and a serious black marketer there might hold two hundred tickets for various films at different theaters each week. Each show was a gamble, but skill allowed a man to hedge his bets. "Sometimes you would lose your money," said Kasanga, "and on those days we would eat cassava [a cheap starch] without any fish. But other times you would win. Losing and winning was all part of the job. The most important thing was not to lose your capital. So long as you kept your capital safe it was all ok."[28] Typically, he added, he had most of his tickets sold before the day of the show. If not, on show day he went down to the theater, where people would fight to get their hands the few remaining tickets. Khamis preferred the presales to the frantic scrambles in the final minutes before the show; he recalled having to buy a new shirt after the debut of *The Rise and Fall of Idi Amin* (Patel, 1980) because the crowd outside the Avalon was so frantic for tickets that people tugged at him until his shirt was in tatters.[29] Few men in Dar es Salaam had the honor of being fought over, and it was a testament to his knowledge and skill that he had tickets to such a popular show.

Anything the censors attacked or tried to ban also became an instant hit with the urban crowd and was likely to be a sure winner for black marketers. In 1949, *No Orchids for Miss Blandish* (Clowes, 1948) was banned by some but not all local censor boards in Tanganyika, resulting in specially organized bus excursions from one town to the next for fans anxious to see the banned gangster film.[30] In the early 1970s, *The Shoes of the Fisherman* (Anderson, 1968), starring Anthony Quinn and Laurence Olivier, was banned, allegedly because the Chinese, who were then building the Tanzania-Zambia Railway Authority (TAZARA) railroad in Tanzania, objected to the film's portrayal of their regime. But somehow, Shabir, the manager of the Empress, was able to convince the censors to allow the movie to be screened for a charity show. He recollected, "Once the film had been banned, but not for the charity show, people went crazy to get tickets. The normal price of a ticket was ten or fifteen shillings, but the black-marketeers were selling them for one thousand shillings instead. Can you imagine? This was the early 1970s, one thousand shillings was a lot of money! Our eyes bugged out of our heads."[31] The charity did well with its sold-out show, but the black marketers did better yet.

James Bond films were also huge hits with the audience—and maligned by the censors, who found them to be crass Cold War propaganda. *From Russia with Love* (Young, 1963) was banned on the mainland and in the isles in 1964, but it was later released as *From 007 with Love* after extensive pressure from exhibitors and James Bond fans caused the censors to relent. Black marketers also scored, for nothing boosted a film's popularity with urban crowds like the censors' wrath. The following year when *Goldfinger* (Hamilton, 1964) was released, all the tickets were sold within hours, but before the film was screened, the censorship board banned it. Dar es Salaam was in an uproar. For more than two weeks, letters to the editor in the national press were filled with scathing attacks on the censors, making letters complaining about the black market for tickets seem pale in comparison.[32]

Black marketers operated independent of cinema owners and managers, but they shared many elements of the capitalist ethos that permeated the industry at large. For one, they strove to be the best at what they did and competed—in a good-natured way—against others in the business for the right to be recognized for their success. They also helped each other out in a bind. If someone lost all his capital, others would chip in to help him get started again. If another hit the jackpot, he shared with his fellow black marketers and other friends to celebrate the success. "If one of us won big we would all shout, 'Hey, today he is going to slaughter a goat and feed us all!'" said Khamis, and rather often the man actually did.[33] If a man was ill and could not get to the theater on the day tickets went on sale, others bought up tickets for him. If police came around and tried to interfere with sales, they all pitched in to offer a sufficient bribe or a few tickets to make the police go away. And on the rare occasion when a man landed in jail for dealing in black market sales, the others pooled their resources to bail him out and make sure his case never made it to court. Just how many men earned their livings selling black market cinema tickets during the colonial era is unclear, but published estimates put the figure at twenty to thirty. By the 1970s, according to men in the trade, there were six or seven known dealers in Zanzibar and nearly fifty in Dar es Salaam.[34]

I grew up south of Chicago in a town where the Mafia ran nearly everything—not just liquor licensing, horse tracks, drugs, and prostitution but also garbage pickup, park maintenance, office cleaning, and ice cream trucks. So the most surprising thing for me about the East African black market was that the men involved cooperated and helped each other, rather than staking out turf, breaking legs, or finding other ways to control territory. All the men worked all the theaters and all kinds of films: there *was* no turf or territory. Like the exhibitors and distributors I questioned about monopolies, these black marketers were as perplexed by my suggestion that staking turf was a common (and credible) way to do business as I was by their insistence that sharing and helping one another was profitable. In numerous ways, I tried to rephrase the question and press the point, and on each occasion, I was regaled with a lengthy list of specific examples to illuminate how helping, rather than harming, was the best course. There was enough wealth to go around, they argued, so why shouldn't everyone get a share? What was the point of gorging after you were full and others had not yet had a chance to eat? These guys clearly did not grow up near Chicago.

The institution of reeling is a further example of the ways in which the men who made the movies run in Tanzania actively worked to enable each other's successes and improve the community at large. Reelers, who ran each of the eight to twelve reels of a film from one theater to the next on their bicycles, comprised another group of men who operated somewhat behind the scenes but without whom the film-loving public could not have survived.[35] They made it possible for eighteen hundred fans, rather than a mere six hundred, to see the evening premier of a film in Zanzibar or for six theaters in Dar es Salaam to screen *Hum Paanch* (Bapu, 1980) for sixteen shows in a single weekend using just one print.[36] Each theater in the system employed one or more reelers whose sole job was to jump on a bike and race reels of film across town to the next theater in line. These were stressful and exhausting jobs: since each reel only ran for twelve or so minutes, reelers were riding hard for the entire duration of a three-hour film, often working multiple shows a day.

Distributors with cinemas could have easily hoarded top films—and the earnings from them—rather than spreading the wealth among patrons and owners of several theaters across a town. Instead, though, they found a novel solution to make a limited commodity as widely available as possible. In the process, they also created employment for other men and helped them lay claim to the glamour and cachet that came from working at the show. Reelers were proud of their speed and dexterity, and managers in turn were awed by their ability to maneuver through the crowded streets.

In Zanzibar, where there was less than a mile between the city's three the-aters, the reeling system worked quite well. But in Dar es Salaam, where the distances could be greater and the streets more crowded, exhibitors and projectionists often spent Sunday nights on pins and needles, worrying that their current reel would finish before the next one arrived. If this hap-pened, and indeed it occasionally did, an unscheduled intermission was declared, often to the great annoyance of those in the auditorium. And a breakdown at one theater of course meant delays at all other theaters down the line. Nonetheless, managers reported that the pleasure of satisfying the majority of their customers most of the time was worth the anguish brought on by the pressures of reeling. "As a businessman there is nothing more gratifying than being able to give your patrons what they want," said Abdul, the manager of the Majestic. Ameri, his reeler, was equally proud. "My job was hugely important," he said. "If they trusted this to someone who was lazy or distracted they would be late and the entire theater full of people would be disappointed and annoyed. Their whole experience would be sub-par."[37] An African man who earned his main living as a houseboy for a cinema owner said he was promoted to reeler because of his reputation for being trustworthy, reliable, and punctual. "Reeling wasn't a job you could give to just anyone," he declared with pride.[38] "The whole town depended on me doing an excellent job." Reelers' dedication made them much-admired and respected men about town.

Concession stand operators were another group of people who earned a living and social stature from their connection to the show. Said one con-cessionaire, "I am now famous, very famous, because of my concession stand at the cinema! Ask anyone and they will tell you who Gigri is, they will also tell you where to find me. That cinema has been closed for twenty years now, but ask anyone and they will tell you about Gigri's food."[39] The concession stand was by far one of the most lucrative aspects of the cin-ema. Concessionaires across the globe typically grossed 25 to 30 percent of what the box office earned, but they did not have to fork over most of their earnings to a distributor. At the small theater where I worked as a teen, the owner prided himself on the quality of his popcorn and constantly extolled its virtues to our patrons. We teased him relentlessly about his popcorn ser-mons, but he taught us that if patrons bought popcorn, they nearly always bought a drink as well. He also swore that he earned almost nothing on the movies; it was the concession stand that kept him in business. Only much

The Men Who Made the Movies Run

later did I learn that this was typical for the industry at large.[40] Cinema managers' ticket sales were carefully registered and checked by distributors and tax collectors, but concessionaires' earnings were largely off the books. Certainly, something had to be reported, but it might be only a fraction of what was actually sold.

As in other sectors of the industry, profits from the lucrative concession operations were widely shared, rather than hoarded. It was extremely rare for owners or managers to run the concessions themselves; instead, they gave the opportunity to others. Furthermore, there were no signs on theaters barring outside food and drink, so licensed and unlicensed hawkers gathered to sell their wares around these venues and even hawked them inside the auditorium. Savory pastries known as *sambusas* together with grilled chicken and kabobs, were offered at the official concession stands and at neighboring restaurants and countless outdoor stalls as well. So too were mangoes, bananas, oranges, and peanuts. The concessionaires did not try to prevent others from selling in order to make more money; rather, they prided themselves on having the best products available, knowing that if they did, they would also secure the majority of the patrons.

In East Africa, the restaurant, bar, or concession stand was typically leased to someone in town whose wife had a reputation for producing large quantities of delectable treats for weddings, religious festivals, or communal celebrations. The male concessionaire was always the public face of the operation, but in reality, it was the wife or other women in his household who, much like the projectionist, did the work behind the scenes that guaranteed success. Rent for the concession stand was extremely small, and restaurateurs and cinema managers claimed that concessionaires often cleared more each month than the cinemas themselves. Responding to my questions about the rent he was charged to run his restaurant at the theater, one man said, "Next to nothing, almost nothing at all. The owner said, 'I am not interested in your rent, I am interested that people enjoy your food. If the customers are happy that is payment enough!'" Other concessionaires echoed his remarks. Managers wanted to ensure that their customers were satisfied, and tasty concessions were an important part of the experience.[41]

Working at or being connected in some way to a theater boosted men's self-esteem and bolstered their status in the community. Here a party boy, houseboy, or precocious teen could find his place and become a popular and well-respected man. Cinemas were spaces that absorbed the character of the men who ran them as well as the neighborhoods that embraced them.[42] Each cinema was unique and had its own feel; it was known not only for particular types of films and crowds but also for its employees' individual styles and odd quirks. These intimate and deeply personal relationships were hugely significant in transforming local cinemas from mere spaces where movies were shown into places that gave a town life.

Every theater was also like a second home for the people who worked there, and fellow employees were like a second family. The bonding that took place among employees crossed social boundaries and helped to create a unified sense of urban citizenship and belonging among the

Figure 2.3 Abdulhussein Marashi and Rashid Abdalla, proprietor and employee of the Majestic Cinema, Zanzibar, coworkers and friends for sixty years, December 2014

The Men Who Made the Movies Run

heterogeneous groups in the city: schisms between their religious faiths meant nothing to Jariwalla, a Bohora Ithnasheri, and Hameer, an Ismaili, when both shared a passion for film. All the cinema owners and managers were either Asian or Arab, and nearly all the cleaners and human billboards were African, but this did not preclude the development of affective ties. Projectionists, doormen, reelers, and managers attended each other's weddings and funerals and provided moral and material support when someone was ill. A love of films and a commitment to the cinema as a social institution united these men like a family across boundaries of race, class, and creed. Talati's Indo-African Theaters Ltd. is but one small example. The founding members came from different religious traditions and communities—Parsi, Ithnasheri, and Ismaili. Employees were mostly Sunni Muslims, but there were some Shia and Hindu as well. When the group expanded to the mainland, Catholics and Lutherans found employment at the cinemas too.[43] Like members of a large and diverse Swahili family with a common father (the cinema) and a number of mothers, the men who worked at Indo-African Theaters became brothers through their love of movies. And they all staked their family reputations on delivering the best show in town.

Chapter 3

MAKING LOVE IN THE INDIAN OCEAN

Hindi Films and Zanzibari Audiences in the 1950s

CONDUCTING MY first round of research for this book, I asked Zanzibaris to identify what they considered to be the best films of all time. To my surprise, some two-thirds of those who attended the cinema in the 1950s and 1960s—regardless of class, ethnicity, education, or gender—named the same film, *Awara*, as their favorite. *Awara* hit the isles six months after its 1951 release, and played for repeated sold-out shows the following year. This was one of those rare films that could travel the circuit again and again, never failing to fill an auditorium. In fact, *Awara* could still pack the house more than a decade after its initial release. According to Zanzibaris, when people heard that it was returning after being screened up-country or elsewhere in East Africa, tickets would sell out before the film physically reached the isles.[1] Most people saw it more than once, with many claiming to have watched it three, five, or even more than ten times. It was a film that boatmen and traders would watch repeatedly as they traveled from Zanzibar to Pemba, Tanga, Mombasa, and Dar es Salaam; a film whose themes and music inspired poets and musicians across the littoral; and a film that tugged at the heartstrings and spoke directly to the romantic longings of a generation.

This chapter examines the social dimensions of *Awara's* reception, arguing that understanding the cultural, political, and historical contexts of film consumption is key to appreciating the relationship between movies and audiences. *Awara* was a brilliant film, but that really explains little about why so many Zanzibaris identified it as a personal favorite and one of the best films ever made. To understand the resonance of this film, we need to look at what exactly attracted Zanzibaris and, more important, how they used the film to interrogate and enrich their own lives. Exploring the social context in which *Awara* was viewed illustrates how films were used by the moviegoing public to materialize ideas, mores, and desires. Daily discursive practices centered on film shaped generational aspirations and divisions. A plethora of strong characters enmeshed in complicated relationships gave viewers much to think about, debate, and analyze. Questions concerning the meaning of love, the purpose of marriage, and the rights of young people to date and choose their own partners were central concerns in the 1950s, the world over. *Awara* and the debates it inspired remind us that the movements for independence in the 1950s and 1960s were not narrowly confined to questions of the state and politics but also involved calls to transform intimate family relations, romance, sexuality, and love.

Using art to talk about matters of the heart has a long history among coastal East Africans. Whether through sexually suggestive dances performed in puberty initiation rituals, through lengthy poems composed as reminders of gendered duties and obligations within marriage, or through popular *taarab* orchestral performances filled with a nuanced use of double entendre and forlorn lamentations on the pain of a broken heart, coastal East Africans have had a widespread appreciation for the power of art to express, rehearse, and instruct.[2] Film may have been a relatively new medium, but the didactic uses to which people put it were not. One reason folks said they went to the movies was to learn, and one of the things they sought to learn about was making love. In the 1950s, "making love involved far more than wiggling the body," as one informant put it. It involved emotional connection and mutual support. Kiswahili oral poetry and taarab music from the era also spoke eloquently about romance and longings for romantic love. But up until the 1980s or 1990s, nearly all first marriages in coastal societies were arranged. Though many couples in such marriages grew to appreciate each other deeply over time, the Swahili have historically had one of the highest divorce rates in the world. Second and subsequent marriages, however, were often rooted in romances initiated by the couples themselves; these marriages did not necessarily last any longer or go any more smoothly than arranged marriages, but they often began with a romantic spark. The midcentury rise of the amorous couple as a key cinematic trope in Hindi films spoke to the romantic desires of young men and women to inaugurate a "love marriage" on their first go-round.

Historians have linked fiction and print culture to the rise of romantic love in numerous times and places.[3] Yet when *Awara* was first playing, fewer than 6 percent of the people in the islands comprising Zanzibar had been to school, where they might have become literate in Kiswahili written in roman script. Educational opportunities for women were smaller still. Only around 1 percent of women in the isles had been to secular school, and as late as 1953, there were only ninety-three women enrolled in the Government Secondary School for Girls, where they were given instruction in English and literature, among other subjects.[4] Poetry, taarab music, and Hindi films, however, spoke eloquently about romance and longings for romantic love through media that were accessible to all. Movies could be enjoyed by anyone with a few pennies and three hours to spare on a Sunday. In her pioneering study of video culture on the nearby island of Lamu, Minou Fuglesang argues that watching Hindi movies gave viewers an opportunity to vicariously explore a range of emotions, together with "a language" for dealing with love.[5] Like the readers of romantic fiction in Ghana who were examined by Stephanie Newell, film fans in Zanzibar stressed the educative potential of Hindi films, which "opened their eyes" to new ways of thinking about life's possibilities as well as new strategies for coping with life's heartbreaks and constraints.[6] Watching Hindi melodramas in no way inaugurated dreams of romance in Swahili society, but these films certainly made the issue a more frequent topic of discussion.

In the West, romantic fiction is largely considered a feminized genre, but in Indian films and island life, men too were encouraged to express their emotions and to yearn for the deepest of loves.[7] As Haji Gora Haji, a well-known Zanzibari poet, taarab composer, author, and avid Hindi filmgoer, has explained, "The love between Raj and Rita [in *Awara*] was of

115

a totally fictional kind, but the kind that everyone, everywhere longs to have."[8] There was nothing like the proverbial chick flick in Tanzania. African and Asian men adored Indian tear-jerkers just as much as women did, and many a man told me that his favorite movies were those that made him cry or left him emotionally moved for days. An equal number of men and women named *Awara* as the best film of all time.

SETTING THE PROVERBIAL SCENE: *AWARA*

Unknown by most North Americans, *Awara* is perhaps "the most successful film in the history of cinema at large," having been seen in more countries and by more people, more times than any other film in history.[9] *Awara* was dubbed into Turkish, Persian, Arabic, English, and Russian; in Russia, the popularity of Kapoor's character apparently inspired a generation of Soviets to name their sons Raj, and explicit references to *Awara* were even included in Alexander Solzhenitsyn's *Cancer Ward*.[10] It was also said to have been a favorite film of Mao Tse-tung. One Zanzibari friend recalled a time when Chinese doctors who were stationed in the island in the 1970s made a house-call and the Zanzibaris and Chinese all ended up singing several rounds of "Awara Hoon," the film's signature song, the only thing they could directly communicate about without the assistance of a translator.[11] Although no film was ever dubbed into Kiswahili, many people with whom I spoke along the Swahili coast claimed to have watched so many Hindi films that they could understand the dialogue completely. But even without words, the passion, longing, and commitment between Rita and Raj almost ooze from the screen. What is certain is that these two characters spoke to deep human yearnings that transcended political, geographic, and linguistic divides.

Many elements in *Awara* attracted audiences and kept them coming back for more. The film starred two of the most widely acclaimed actors in Indian film history: Raj Kapoor and Nargis. Although this was not the first film in which they costarred, it was certainly the one that placed their romance center stage and lifted them to the status of the iconic romantic couple.[12] On screen and off, their romance was larger than life. Articles about their very public affair filled the newspapers and film magazines, and despite Kapoor being married with children and from a different religion—he was a Hindu and she a Muslim—their romance was rarely portrayed as a transgression. Drawing on their characters as Raj and Rita in the film, their love was commonly portrayed as "pure, blind, an all-consuming passion, and even divine."[13] Raj Kapoor and Nargis were household names and icons of true romance across the world.

Like all good Hindi films, *Awara* has many twists and turns and intricate plotlines that take nearly three hours to develop and unfold. Love across class boundaries and marriage in defiance of family and community are two of the central themes explored. Raghunath, the emblem of patriarchy and power in the film, defies convention and the wishes of his family to marry a widow named Leela. During the early years of their devoted marriage, the indulgent couple escapes from the watchful eye of the extended family by sailing away for a romantic weekend to a remote island. There, Leela is abducted by a villain and spends four days in his lair. When she turns out to be pregnant, rumors swirl that perhaps she was raped by the villain, casting Raghunath's paternity and masculinity—and the family's honor—in doubt. Raghunath's love is weakened by unceasing pressure from his family and his own questions about the legitimacy of Leela's child. When his associates from the upper echelons of society threaten his advancement from magistrate to judge, he caves to social pressure and throws Leela to the gutter, where she gives birth to their son, Raj.

Told from the perspective of Raj, *Awara* (Vagabond) considers the issues of social legitimacy, criminality, and class privilege from the vantage point of the poor. Modeled in part on characters played by Charlie Chaplin, Kapoor's Raj addresses the class system head on. Leela too refuses to play the role of victim. As a single mother, she struggles valiantly for years to feed her son, send him to school, and raise him to be an upright man who can rise above the slums in which he was born. Effort, education, moral strength, and a belief in oneself, she tells her son, are the keys to success. She expends every ounce of her energy in trying to raise her son to be a gentleman, but ultimately, ill health and poverty conspire against her. Raj loses his place at school because his mother cannot keep up with the school fees, despite the fact that they both work tirelessly at petty jobs. When Leela becomes ill, they quickly descend down that slippery slope from the dignified poor to the criminal. Trying to save his mother, who is on the verge of death from malnutrition, Raj steals some bread and ends up in a reformatory. There, he is schooled in the arts of petty crime. As a young adult, he becomes an important player in an underworld gang, run by none other than Jagga, the villain who abducted his mother.

117

One of the major themes developed throughout the film is the relative power of birth, social circumstance, and personal will to define one's fate. The dacoit who kidnapped Leela did so as revenge on Raghunath, who had sentenced him to prison as a young man for a crime he did not commit. Repeatedly, Raghunath proclaims that morals are inherited. He is convinced that the son of a thief will become a thief, whereas the son of an upright citizen will surely be upright as well. Jagga, the villain, sets out to prove him wrong. Jagga serves as a surrogate father to Raj, teaching him to steal cars, rob banks, or do whatever is necessary to keep his mother housed, clothed, and fed and living in a respectable part of town. Raj is tormented by his deceit, for he leaves home each day in a suit and pretends he is in business. But his criminal record haunts his life, and he is unable to secure honest work because no one will look beyond his conviction for stealing bread as a child. Committed to returning his mother's dedication and unfaltering love, he does whatever it takes to make her life easy and bring her joy.

Throughout the film, Raj incessantly speaks truth to power, and I for one am deeply appreciative of the subtitles that allowed me to fully appreciate his words. In one scene, he defines "the new world order" as a system in which the biggest crooks dress in first-class suits and are regarded by society as gentlemen when, in reality, these capitalists, bankers, and traders are nothing but thieves stealing from people whose labor and sweat produce the real profits. In a final scene where Raj is being tried for attempted murder, he addresses the court, accepting his guilt and sentence but reminding the powers that be that killing him is but a drop in the bucket. "Now that I am convicted of murder I have your attention," he tells the court. "But had anyone cared when I was a child I would not be here right now. . . . I did not inherit crime from my parents, it is from the gutter of life that I picked up this disease . . . and countless children who live in the slums fall prey to the same virus every day." Individuals certainly have choices to make, but why, asks the film, are the poor sent to prison for stealing so they can eat while thieving capitalists and politicians gorge themselves at the expense of others and are vigorously protected by the law? By combining stories of political struggle with those of love, this and other Hindi films have inspired viewers to imagine that they too might find happiness and fulfillment despite physical poverty and political powerlessness.[14]

Yet a third major plotline in *Awara* revolves around the developing romance between poor, illegitimate, but totally lovable Raj and his wealthy and spoiled childhood sweetheart, Rita, with whom he is reunited after twelve years when he tries to snatch her purse and steal her car. Despite the divergent paths their lives have taken since they were in school together, the flame of love is rekindled between them in a heartbeat. Because of his desire for Rita, Raj attempts to renounce his life of crime and go straight, but even the best efforts of this passionate couple cannot overcome the objections of Rita's guardian (who, as only an Indian film could have it, is also the father who abandoned Raj at birth). Raghunath reemerges as the patriarch protecting a woman's honor, and he refuses to hear of Rita's infatuation with a man well below her in class, status, and education. Despite his objections, Raj and Rita engage in a long and languid romance and publicly pronounce their eternal love. Their love is socially affirmed when Rita, who has been studying law, defends Raj in court against charges brought by her guardian and in the process reveals that her lover is really a son of prominence to whom fate has dealt a nasty hand. In the end, Raghunath accepts Raj as his son and admits that his theories of genetics as the basis of social deviance and class are wrong.

This bare-bones sketch of the major plotlines—devoid of the emotive potential of stars, cinematography, and songs—suggests that this film left audiences with a lot to discuss and debate. Raj and Rita were the characters that audience members most identified with, but people had a lot to say about the patriarch Raghunath as well. Some of those with whom I spoke in Zanzibar pointed to his failures—and the costs born by his wife and son—as evidence that marrying for love against the wishes of family and community would result only in tragedy for all concerned: love was, in the end, a very shaky foundation on which to build a family. Others, however, used Raghunath's story to illustrate that wealth and social power did not necessarily confer moral strength and to illustrate that any marriage could end in tragedy if the partners abandoned their commitments and obligations. After all, Raghunath was weak and failed to stand by Leela, the woman he claimed to love. Still others used the plot of *Awara* to suggest that fundamental social change, such as moving from arranged marriages to love marriages, takes time. Even though Raghunath failed to stand up to his family and community and stand by the woman he loved, his children refused to relent to patriarchal pressure, and in the end, their romance and abiding love stole the show.

Like academics, Zanzibaris examined the texts of movies for evidence but drew on that evidence to support their own diverse points of view. Films such as *Awara* were widely popular because they provided men and women in the audience with characters they could identify with and relate to, as well as others they could hate. Ultimately, these films offered ample opportunities for public sociability and endless fodder for moral debate. In public and private spaces, whenever people came together they discussed, critiqued, debated, imagined, and interacted with the issues that were presented on-screen. Even people who did not go to the show themselves were drawn into the public discussions the films sparked. As one Zanzibari woman said:

> Personally I wasn't a big fan, in fact I really didn't like films at all. But my sister and her friends were huge fans. They went to the cinema every Sunday, every single Sunday, and all week long they would talk about the film. Whether I wanted to, or not, I knew all about the latest movie. One of them might identify with this character, another with that, and they would argue back and forth about different scenes and the lessons they conveyed. I vividly recall how they argued and argued about characters and conclusions and how these debates would go on and on, at least until the next Sunday, when there would be a new film to discuss.[15]

These Zanzibari women were not alone. Nearly everyone I interviewed said that discussions about the latest movies were a central feature of urban conversations. At home, at work, and among classmates at school, everyone talked about films, characters, and stars. "Heck," said one man in Dar es Salaam, "even on busses and ferries people talked about films. You could always get a conversation going, even between complete strangers, if you turned the topic to the latest films."[16]

Indian films regularly packed the cinemas, drawing capacity crowds each Sunday. In Zanzibar, it was not uncommon for more than thirty-five hundred people to go to the movies at least two or three Sundays each month. Good Indian films, among them *Awara*, were typically held over on Mondays and perhaps again for a special ladies-only show on Tuesdays or

Wednesdays. By the end of its first-week run, *Awara* had been seen by some 10 percent of the local population, and it quickly became the talk of the town.

During the 1950s, more than half of all films shown in Zanzibar were US productions. These films also often centered on romance and love, yet Zanzibari audiences were not drawn to them to nearly the same degree as to their Hindi counterparts. In US films, as in US children's literature, parents were often entirely absent, leaving youthful characters to sort out their dilemmas on their own. During the mid-twentieth century, many Africans viewed such independent youth either as dangerous social characters or as completely beyond imagination. Hindi films from the 1950s and 1960s echoed African concerns.

Indian films revolved around individual protagonists, but they were always nestled within a family and the family within a community. And it was these larger groupings that defined the parameters for individual choice. Individuals were never alone. Their decisions and actions impacted the entire family, whose honor and respectability were sacrosanct. Characters, male as well as female, who forgot this or openly disregarded cultural norms landed in trouble. Yet Indian films also placed generational struggles, of all types, center screen. Beginning in the 1950s, generational differences regarding the purpose of marriage and changing ideals of love became increasingly prominent points of contention.[17] Patriarchal authority was seriously called into question, and the desires of youth to marry for love were foregrounded. But at the same time, the affective family also served as the symbolic locus of resolution in Hindi films. Youth were not obliged to rebel entirely. They might run off for a spell, but by the end of the film they were reunited and back in the warm embrace of their families. In Indian movies, youth disobeyed but within limits, and due to their pressure, patriarchs became kinder and gentler over time.

In *Awara*, Raghunath ignored social strictures regarding the untouchability of widows when he married Leela, convincing his family members that such ideas were wrong. Society too could change and become more accepting. But society was far less loving and embracing than family, and the social ostracism one had to endure to push the process of change took

121

a toll. Raghunath was not strong enough to fight social pressures condemning and blaming Leela when she was allegedly raped, and his weakness had devastating consequences for himself, his wife, and his child. The children of the following generation, Rita and Raj, were more determined and strong. They persevered, not only affirming their love for each other in the face of patriarchal opposition but also publicly challenging the orthodoxies of guilt, blame, and shame surrounding illegitimacy and crime. Clearly, meaningful social change sometimes takes generations.

In his study of Hausaland in northern Nigeria, Brian Larkin has found that there too Indian films were preferred because they raised issues and framed questions in ways that were more culturally resonant with the moral framework of the Muslim Hausa.[18] Indian films, argues Larkin, provided a "parallel modernity" to the West, a cinematic script that addressed a complicated range of issues facing modern youth but did not necessitate "selling out" to be resolved. Indian films addressed global generational tensions, yet they resolved them in ways that affirmed local moral codes. Hindi films were preferred to American ones in part because the Hausa and Swahili were attracted to fictional narratives that promised individual happiness could be achieved without sacrificing family honor or the family as a multigenerational whole. In the end, Raghunath accepted that he was the guilty party for having abandoned his wife and child; it was his fault that Raj turned to Jagga—the outlaw—as a surrogate father and was raised into a life of crime. Leela never lost faith in the potential of her son. On her deathbed, she counseled Rita to nurture him and give him the love he needed to turn his life around. Thus, though the children challenged the bedrocks of family honor, they were ultimately enveloped in the patriarchal fold.

Hindi films also developed themes and issues in ways that were far more relevant to East African life than those dreamed up by Hollywood. Social melodrama was the dominant mode of filmmaking in postindependence India, and many of the artists involved in the Bombay film industry were also leftists, including K. A. Abbas, who wrote the screenplay for *Awara*.[19] Class and the social divisions separating the wealthy from the poor were given center screen in these movies, whereas in Hollywood films, self-censorship and the production code made resolving class conflict in favor of the poor taboo.[20] Although poverty was never glamorized in films made by Kapoor or others of his generation, spectators were encouraged to empathize with the plight of the poor and to respect the honesty and integrity of the underclass. Heroes and heroines came from the downtrodden; the villains were wealthy and powerful.[21]

In the film *Awara* Kapoor makes this explicit. Raghunath, the patriarch, is the son of a feudal lord who has studied his lessons well in colonial schools and now serves as a pillar of the legal system protecting the interests of the propertied. Lawyers, judges, and industrialists attend each other's parties. Throughout the film the cinematography juxtaposes the living conditions of urban workers with those of their factory bosses and members of the legal community. The wealthy are portrayed as shrill, emotionless, and uncaring. The powerful never get to sing a song. Raghunath is always filmed from an angle that makes him large and imposing, like the systems of class and patriarchal privilege he represents. His physical features are never flattering; the way he is filmed reminds the viewer of Frankenstein. He is a monster built of male class privilege. He has no heart.

Raj, on the other hand, is always depicted as affable and lovable, a man who has committed some unsavory acts, to be sure, but is really good at heart. The mise-en-scène used during the title song from the film, "Awara Hoon," is a case in point. As the song begins, the camera is focused in on Raj's worn shoes and rolled-up pants legs, set in contrast with the well-polished shoes and nicely tailored pants of nearly all the others on the street. The camera then quickly moves out to show Raj singing, smiling, and picking pockets while moving down the street in a Chaplinesque sort of way. Quickly the scene changes and Raj is pictured in the midst of the poor neighborhood where he lives, which resembles neighborhoods in Zanzibar. Here he greets everyone he meets, including a group of women washing dishes at a communal water tap. The lengthiest shots are of him with two dark-skinned, naked toddlers, whom he affectionately carries and plays with. All the while he sings the film's title song, "I'm a tramp, I have no home, I'm not rich, I am just a tramp. My heart is full of wounds, but the songs I sing are merry songs, my eyes are always full of smiles." It is clear from the visual imagery that everyone who knows Raj adores him, and the viewer too finds it difficult to blame him for his faults. He is merry, gentle, and kind. If given the chance, we know he could be this way all the time.

Raj Kapoor was not only an actor but a producer and director as well. In many of his movies, including *Awara*, he directly references the work and characters of Charlie Chaplin, which added to his films' resonance in Zanzibar. Both men's films empathize with the struggles of the "tramps" of the

123

Figure 3.1 *Awara* film still from the third song, "Awara Hoon"

world, and they also work to reveal the corruption and deceit of those commonly regarded as respectable.[22] In *Shree 420* (Kapoor, 1955), again starring Raj Kapoor and Nargis, Raj's character is also a tramp newly arrived in the city. There, he encounters "a barren world of stone-hearted people who worship only money." He is warned by a beggar that there is no way for an honest, hardworking man to earn a living in modern Bombay but 420 ways to get rich by cunning, deceit, and fraud. The title of the film and this scene in particular refer to section 420 of the Indian Penal Code, which makes it a crime to intentionally defraud others. Kapoor and Abbas blatantly expose the hypocrisy of existing systems of law and justice in numerous films, and they repeatedly illustrate how the wealthiest are never prosecuted for their crimes. In one scene in *Awara*, where Raj is struggling to leave his life of crime and find a way to earn an honest living, we see him sweating and striving to learn a trade. The scene then cuts to a meeting between Raj and his boss, where Raj is fired after the boss learns that he has served time in jail. Recounting his woes to Rita, Raj asks, "What are the industrialists, millionaires, politicians? Thieves like me [but on a grander scale]."[23] Kapoor's films repeatedly emphasize the social construction of crime and the class inequalities endemic in the pursuit of justice. Those who live in the slums or on the social margins are poor because the economic system defrauds them of the wealth they produce, not because they are lazy.

Social theorist and film critic Ashis Nandy has aptly explained the popularity of movies such as *Awara* among the masses in urban India: these films provide a "slum's eye view of politics and society."[24] This point of view was shared by many in East Africa, who were themselves not only poor and disenfranchised but also keenly aware of the ways in which their poverty was exacerbated, criminalized, and institutionalized by the state. As one woman who saw *Awara* at least four times said of her appreciation for the plots in films from this era:

> Many stories were about the life of the poor, the trouble the poor had making ends meet. The films showed the real life conditions of the poor and how difficult it was. The stories were also about the wealthy and how they exploited the poor, how the poor were despised and looked down upon. That is what the stories were like in the old days. Many of the stories were like this, showing how the rich exploited the poor, or how the poor struggled and struggled, but never succeeded.[25]

Although solidly middle class by the time of our interview, this woman knew how easy it was to quickly descend into poverty. To achieve the comfortable life she and her husband now enjoyed, they had worked for decades, he in a shop and she for endless hours each day in a kitchen preparing food for a corner restaurant. When her first husband died, she was left financially destitute and forced to sell the gold she was given as her wedding dower (*mhari*) in order to clothe her son and pay his school fees. Her own father had died a few years earlier and her mother before that. She described herself as a vagabond, an *Awara Hoon*, living with one sister for a while and then another before meeting and marrying her second husband. She sang me the title song from *Awara* and first told me about a Kiswahili version recorded by Yaseen, a taarab musician from Mombasa. Yaseen recorded "Sina Nyumba" (I Have No Home) in the 1950s, a song in which the vocalist evokes the sorrow and suffering of all orphans in a mournful minor key: "I have no home, I have no mother, I have no father. I am an orphan, oh world, please take pity on me." Yaseen translates the visual imagery of Raj's wanderings through the slums, making them emotionally and linguistically Swahili. One of the reasons *Awara* was so widely popular, people said to me, was because it echoed local understandings that poverty

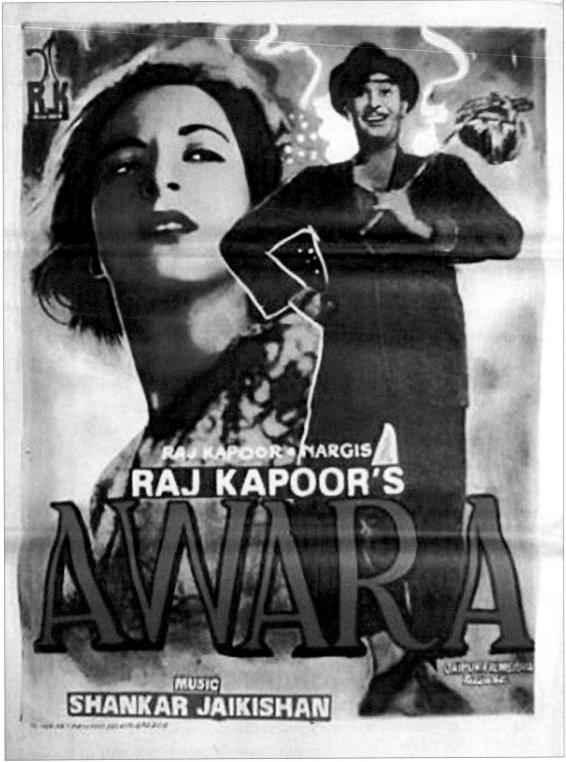

Figure 3.2 *Awara* poster. From the author's collection

and homelessness were bad breaks that could happen to anyone. Being poor or homeless, I was repeatedly told, should not be a crime.

Moral choices were as clear in Indian movies as the black-and-white film on which they were depicted, and this resonated with patterns known from African folktales. The evil and mean were always obvious, but the road traveled by most humans was depicted as a murky space—and that was where the hero or heroine confronted numerous dilemmas and endless temptations and obstacles. Indian films from the 1950s and 1960s directly addressed the Third World modernist dilemma: how to incorporate technological and scientific "advancement" into society without succumbing to a hollow mimicry of Western individualism, consumer capitalism, moral bankruptcy, and spiritual emptiness.[26] Moral and modernist dilemmas were often resolved through a reassertion of traditional values, whereby the hero or heroine was ultimately drawn back into the virtuous arms of the mother/family/nation.[27] Morally upright, traditional characters were often juxtaposed with others who dressed, talked, and drank like characters from Hollywood. These latter characters often manipulated state power or wealth to advance selfish ends, sending the message that individuals who carelessly mimicked the West were morally bankrupt even though they might be wealthy. In Hausaland and Zanzibar, people were deeply attracted to films that displayed modernity while simultaneously critiquing the West.[28] Indeed, many people in Zanzibar stressed that one of the reasons they went to the movies was "to learn something," "to expand [their] mind[s] to other possibilities," or "to compare [their lives] with those of people in other places."[29] The lessons people took were not necessarily that "the West is the best." As Mwalim Idd explained, "In those films you get to see [that the West] is more advanced in terms of technology, education or economy . . . but in terms of social life, social relations, and social values, we are ahead."

The lessons on love that people took from Hindi films were also far more resonant with local social life. In most Indian films, the love of the young couple is complicated by love and commitment to their extended families—complications that mirrored realities in the isles. In partial explanation of her attraction to *Awara*, one woman who saw it at least four times remarked, "The actors in this film were superb, truly superb! They could make you feel the pain that they felt right down to your core. You empathized with their struggles and hardships, and experienced their pain

127

from their perspective." Having watched several friends and sisters raise children without any financial or emotional support from the fathers, she had a deep appreciation for Leela's character. "This problem of women being abandoned by their husbands, for whatever reason, was a common problem here in Zanzibar as well. . . . She portrayed that pain and those problems in a way that really hit home."[30] Adam Shafi echoed her remarks when he exclaimed, "*Awara*, I loved that film. I saw it more than ten times. Raj Kapoor and Nargis were outstanding! And the film shows real life, the inside of life, and the ways in which family, traditions and culture can cause problems." Speaking to the power of social norms to undermine romantic relationships, he continued, "The plot shows how a man [Raghunath] can abandon his wife [Leela], even though he loves her very much. Family pressure has ruined many a loving relationship."[31] Couples did not always live happily ever after, and island audiences appreciated films that explored, rather than ignored, the marital truths that were part and parcel of real lives.

MARRIAGE, SEX, AND ROMANCE: BETWEEN THE REEL AND REAL LIFE

Casual visitors to Zanzibar are often struck by the many women covered in the black *buibui*, or hijab, and presume that this is an indication of sexual repression and gender oppression within the isles. Such facile conclusions belie a much more complicated reality. In Zanzibar and in Swahili culture more generally, modesty in dress and appearance is upheld as a virtue, for men and women alike, but this does not mean that sexuality is considered a sin. On the contrary, sensuality is regarded as an art form, and young women have historically been given ritualized instruction at puberty on how to enhance their own and their partners' erotic pleasures. In the course of female initiation rituals older women teach young women, using songs, dances, and play, about the mysteries and wonders of sex, marriage, and procreation.[32] Through ribald movements and lyrics performed in the context of *Chakacha, Unyago,* and many other types of women's dance, girls are given an opportunity to recognize and validate their sexual desires. They are encouraged to "dance out" anticipated events and in the process relieve some of the anxiety and fear associated with sex and marriage.

In ritual preparation for a wedding, the older women physically prepare and beautify the bride—massaging her entire body with sandalwood;
perfuming her with aloewood (*udi*); and adorning her with henna, silk, and
gold. They again perform the songs and dances the bride was taught during
the course of initiation, trying to relax her, allay her fears, and encourage her
to enjoy the consummation of her wedding night. These lessons and skills
are refined throughout a woman's life. After a young woman is married, she
is recognized as an adult and is able to participate regularly in the full range
of rituals that accompany other women's weddings. In the course of her own
marriage, she will also continue to beautify herself with sandalwood, perfume her clothes and bedroom with udi, and entice her husband by wearing
strings of jasmine flowers (jasmine is considered to be an aphrodisiac) in
provocative places or sprinkling these flowers on their bed.

The importance—or lack—of love within a relationship has also
been widely discussed and debated through poetry and song. Poets have
a long and revered history among the Swahili. Great poets have used
very complicated forms of rhyme and meter to praise the Lord, condemn
their political rivals, issue edicts on moral reform, instruct youth, give
thanks, and address a host of other topics both worldly and divine.[33] The
intense emotions associated with love, yearning, and heartbreak have
also been expressed through classical poetic Swahili forms, but it was
really only in the mid-twentieth century that romantic love and longing,
rather than love of God or family, became common topics in classic
metered verse. Nowhere near as bawdy or direct as the poems composed
for performance within the homosocial environment of women's wedding and initiation rituals, these love poems—often shared in the public
forum of taarab musical performance—focused on emotion and intense
spiritual devotion to the object of one's desire.[34] Romance, as expressed
through taarab songs, explored the "deep mental and spiritual inclination toward a pleasurable love experience."[35] In the 1950s, male taarab
poets and performers in Zanzibar began to move away from religious,
social, and political commentary and instead emphasize romantic love
and longing in their works.

The songbooks of Zanzibar's male taarab bands from the 1950s and
1960s were filled with poems that idealized a loved one and likened her to
the most beautiful of flowers, the brightest of stars, or the sweetest of fruits
in the isles.[36] Poets and performers for the two most prominent male clubs,

129

Michenzani and Ikhwan Safaa, also spoke openly of their frustrations in consummating their romantic desires. Swahili may have considered sex far from sinful, but to be condoned, it had to be confined to the bedroom of a properly married, heterosexual couple. As young men bursting with desire, these poets and performers expressed their frustrations with local cultural patterns that kept genders largely segregated in public spaces and that gave elders, rather than youth, the power to arrange first marriages. By the 1950s, women in Zanzibar were increasingly attending schools, and in the following decade, a few were even finding waged employment outside the home, where they met and sometimes mingled with members of the opposite sex. Brief public encounters at times sparked "love at first sight," but men's songs from the period tell us that women might as well have been the stars and the moon, so far were they out of reach.

Again, these desires and frustrations were given cinematic expression in films such as *Awara*, where the love the characters seek is nearly as impossible to achieve.[37] The sky, the moon, and the stars, common symbols in local taarab songs, are also prominent in the cinematographic visualizations accompanying *Awara*'s sound track. In every love song the moon figures prominently. In the first song where Rita and Raj pronounce their love to each other, "Dum Bhar Jo Udhar" (the sixth song in the film), they are looking up at a glowing full moon, wishing it could turn its face so that they could make passionate, romantic love, utter a thousand sweet nothings, gaze deep into each other's eyes, and not be seen. In the following song, a fantastic dream sequence in which Raj is tormented by a life of burning hell without Rita, he is allowed to ascend a spiral staircase to the heavens where Rita awaits, glittering like the stars that surround her, singing in a white star-studded sari, wearing a half-moon *bindi* on her forehead, nearly touching the full moon in whose light she basks. The divine, spiritual nature of their love is again reinforced by the fact that when they are united it is before temples and statues of gods and goddesses, amidst the clouds. In the next song, as Rita pines for Raj after her guardian Raghunath forbids her from seeing him again, she sings on a balcony to a moon and stars covered by clouds, begging them to come out, to help her through this darkest of hours. The idioms, euphemisms, and emotionality resonated with Zanzibaris' musical aesthetics as well as their insights on love.[38]

Figure 3.3 *Awara* film still from the sixth song, "Jab Se Balam Ghar Aaye"

Ethnomusicologists studying Swahili taarab, as well as Arab and Indian musics with which taarab shares certain affinities, have found that
one of the key criteria used to define good music is its emotionality and,
more specifically, its ability to evoke rapture, bliss, ecstasy, and the divine.
In Indian films, music and song are central media through which deep
emotions, particularly romantic longings, are expressed. The music and
song sequences in Hindi films convey the spiritual element of love, evoking
this "sojourn to an inner-world."[39] The love is romantic, not physical or
sexual. It is pure and transcendent. Comparing the love depicted in films
of the 1950s, including *Awara*, with that in today's movies, one woman said,
"These [earlier films] were serious stories, and the love, it was a deep, deep
love. The actors and actresses knew how to love each other, really love each
other. Love is still a theme in the movies today, but their love is superficial,
it is about wiggling the body, not that deep love of the heart like in the
old days."[40] Songs have long been "the heart and soul" of Indian films,[41]
and *Awara* certainly boasted a superb sound track. Indeed, gramophone
records of the songs from the film were among the best-selling Hindi releases of the 1950s.[42] Fifty years later, in 2002, I had youth in their twenties
playing me songs from the movie that they had in their cassette collections
as they—and their seventy-year-old mothers and fathers or grandparents—
sang along.

Making Love in the Indian Ocean: Hindi Films, 1950s

CINEMAS AND THE CONSUMMATION OF LOVE

In the 1950s and 1960s, cinemas were among the few public places where men and women could enjoy an evening of respectable leisure together. At a time when nearly all first marriages were still arranged by elders, newly married couples used the opportunities afforded by cinemas to date.[43] Going to the movies gave young couples, who often did not know each other at all before marriage, an opportunity to be together and alone. (Until fairly recently, it was rare for young marrieds to have a home that was separate from the joint or extended family.) In such cases, couples rarely had time or space, outside of their bedroom, to talk. As one African woman said of the movie dates she and her husband enjoyed, "Going to the cinema helped us to get to know each other better. It gave us things to talk about, things to share, and most importantly it gave us time alone."[44]

Numerous men and women in similar circumstances mentioned that their visits to the cinema helped them develop a relationship as a couple.[45] Issa, a Swahili cabdriver in Dar es Salaam, also recalled the importance of cinemas as physical and imaginary spaces in his early married life: "When we were first married my wife and I use to regularly go to the cinema. It was the only time we really got to be alone. . . . She preferred Indian films, those long, long love-story types. I liked action films better, but to make her happy I would take her to see these love-stories, and she too would accompany me to see action films."[46] He fondly reminisced about how they would make a day of it, casually starting off for the theater in late afternoon, watching the film until nine o'clock, and then talking about the show the whole way home. "One of the things about these Indian movies," he said, "was that when you see them they force you to talk about love, about what real love means and how to love each other. This wasn't something we usually talked about after an action film."

On Sundays, thousands of people would crowd theater lobbies and nearby streets before and after the shows, giving young people an opportunity to see members of the opposite sex in public and perhaps even "fall in love at first sight," I was told. They may not have been able to speak, but at a time when cultural mores kept youth strictly segregated by sex, even being in the same room together provided a thrill. On those occasions, small groups and individuals would mill about, greeting friends and neighbors and quietly checking out members of the opposite sex. In the company of their families, young people who met at the show rarely engaged each other in direct conversation. "We might smile and look," said Nitesh Virji, "but rarely had the nerve to talk."[47] If he or his male friends spied someone they wanted to meet, they would encourage a cousin or sibling to go and address a friend in the other group, allowing their eyes to follow and thus meet those of a new potential lover. Looks and glances were often far more communicative during those years than speech, and again, Hindi films provided visual models of evocative communication via the eyes. One man who did a lot of big-game hunting as an adult likened these adventures from his youth to a photo safari. "You get an image rather than an actual trophy, but you get the excitement and adventure none-the-less. Sometimes," he added, "a good picture is better than an actual [trophy] mount anyway."[48] Like the spouse you see every day, he explained, the animal mounted on the wall is taken for granted, whereas "the one who got away" remains fresh and alive, evoking the thrill of future pursuit.

Another woman who used to go to the cinema with her sisters and cousins confessed that she regularly met her boyfriend there. When asked how they arranged to sit together at these clandestine meetings, she exclaimed, "Sit next to each other? Heavens no! We were much too shy for this. Besides, if you ever did something like that you could be certain some auntie or cousin would see you and word would reach home before you did, and would you ever be in trouble then! It would be a long, long time before you were allowed to go to the cinema again."[49] You did not have to sit next to each other or touch to experience love, she explained. True love, like that in the Hindi melodramas, was an emotive, not a physical, love. Never in a Hindi film did you see a couple kissing, but the characters' love was of the most passionate kind. Another woman who similarly rendezvoused at the theater described it this way:

> You would sit here, and your lover would sit in front of you 6–8 rows, on the side. We would glance at each other, and make love with our eyes before the show started and during intermission. It was all so romantic! Simply seeing each other gave you such a thrill! And the entire time you and your lover were watching the movie you were experiencing together the love you saw on screen. I still get goose-bumps remembering my first love from those days.

133

Comparing the love depicted in today's films with that of the past, several men also said they found modern love superficial. In earlier times, they added, true love was emotional, elusive, and divine.[50]

One self-proclaimed romantic described her marriage to a man chosen by her parents as simply a marriage—he provided her with safety at a time when young women of her community were being forcibly wed to members of the Revolutionary Council in Zanzibar—and together they had children.[51] But the love of her life was a young man she had clandestine meetings with at the cinema. They too never sat next to each other and never even touched, yet she stated:

> My heart still races when I recall our affair. We were so in love. It was like this movie playing now, *Veer Zara* [Chopra, 2004] about a young couple who cannot marry because of the partition [of India and Pakistan]. He spends twenty years in solitary confinement, but he never forgets her, nor she him. Their love was true. It was divine. Politics separated us as well, but who knows, maybe someday we can be together again too.

Numerous men and women echoed her remarks, suggesting that in a society in which divorce held no stigma and subsequent marriages were common, Hindi films kept the flame of romance burning throughout their adult lives.

As texts, Hindi films may have inspired dreams of true love, but as places, cinemas allowed some couples to advance a romance to the physical plane. Cinema seating was assigned, and occasionally, a young couple would be so bold as to purchase their tickets ahead of time, thus assuring adjacent seats even if they arrived separately. One trick was for a young man to make an advanced booking for himself, his girlfriend, and her friends. When she approached the ticket window, the agent, who was well aware of the plan, could let her know which seat to take to sit closest to her man. Sitting in the dark during a film was as intimate as most youngsters would ever get with a member of the opposite sex prior to marriage. Part of the thrill of such a romantic adventure was the risk (despite one's fervent hope to the contrary) of being caught.

Older lovers took more advantage of the time offered by the cinema, rather than its space, to advance their romance to a new level. Hindi movies are usually at least three hours in length, leaving ample opportunity for a romantic tryst. So lovers might pretend they were going to the show and simply head someplace more intimate instead. Such romantic trysts were eulogized in a famous taarab song from the era, known as "Ladies' Show," by the Mombasa stars Yaseen and Mimi.[52] Going to the ladies' show was a widely popular pastime for so-called respectable women observing purdah who did not attend the regular shows where men and women mixed. The song—or at least the stories surrounding it—suggests that *purdah* and *propriety* were not necessarily synonymous. A man named Farouk told me that for members of his mother's generation, *ladies show* was a common euphemism for an adulterous affair.

Another ruse, I was told by cinema employees (who saw it all), was for a man and a woman to each take their separate seats and then at an agreed-on point in the film, such as the second song-and-dance number, leave the show. The cover of a veil was useful when attempting such feats. If a brother or father was expected to come and escort the woman back home, the couple would return to the theater in time for her to emerge with the rest of the crowd as though she had been in the theater all along. Such plans had the potential to go awry, however, as in the case of one infamous married man who regularly used the cover of three-hour Indian movies to meet his lover. One day after such a tryst, he returned to catch the end of the film and found his wife sitting in his seat, outing him before the entire crowd in the theater. In that particular case, it was *his* story rather than that of the film that circulated throughout town for the remainder of the week. Twenty years later, the tale continued to generate exuberant laughs.[53]

Even as the physical place of the cinema helped inaugurate new loves, the imaginary space opened up by films inspired men and women (and particularly youth) to fantasize about romance, love, and marriage in somewhat novel ways. The transnational flow of mass media has always allowed people to interact with narratives and imaginaries beyond their own lived reality.[54] Loves like that of Rita and Raj, depicted in *Awara*, provided intellectual fuel for the smoldering fires of romantic love sparking up along the coast during that period. Youth of the 1950s were not the first generation to chafe under the yoke of arranged marriages, but they were among the first to be nourished on a regular diet of Hindi romantic melodramas. As individuals and as a generation, they drew on the characters and plots from these films to rewrite the narratives for their own emotive lives. Few real-life

135

heroes or heroines had the chutzpah of Rita and Raj: forging a relationship across the chasms of class and communal divides, committing to each
other despite patriarchal opposition, and defending one another in the face
of immense social pressure—these were feats that few mere mortals could
manage. But as Janet Radway and others have argued, fantasizing about
what it would *feel like* to accomplish such feats is one of the main draws of
romantic fiction.[55] Films offer "alternatives, hopes, wishes . . . the sense that
things could be better, that something other than what is can be imagined
and maybe realized," in the words of Richard Dyer; they give us a vicarious
sense of fulfillment and the momentary bliss of living in utopia.[56]

Numerous self-defined romantics said that the power of Hindi melodrama to ignite deeply felt emotion and to keep dreams of romantic passion
alive was one of the factors that drew them to the show and to films such
as *Awara* again and again. As one woman said of the love between Raj and
Rita, "They died inside of each other's hearts, and if you got a male friend,
well you wanted it to be the same . . . without you he couldn't see, he
couldn't hear, until you died you were together, inseparable in fact. This
is what we saw in the films and this is how we wanted our loves to be."[57]
Despite her dreams, though, this woman had been married at fourteen to
a man at least three times her age.

Women often married in their teens, but many young men had to
suffer, both physically and emotionally, until well into their twenties or
thirties before they had sufficient resources to marry and provide for a wife
and children. The guardians who arranged most marriages typically chose
a husband based on his ability to provide financially, and in this regard,
an older man was perceived as a safer bet. If he came from a wealthy and
respected family, all the better, and missing teeth, warts, gray hair, and
fat bellies were to be overlooked in favor of the improved status he would
bring to the bride, her future children, and by extension her entire family.
One woman spoke quite dramatically of her marital life history in this way:
"I was married at the age of fifteen to a man who [was] not to my liking
at all. He was arrogant, unattractive and patronizing, and treated me like
I was nothing other than a slave."[58] Most women were less dramatic in
their descriptions, yet many shared similar disappointment in their first,
arranged marriages. But for some of the women I interviewed, the dreams
of romance and passion remained alive, fanned by their devotion to Hindi
films, and several made arrangements for divorce. One woman remarried

a cinema manager who shared her passion for life and romantic love. She showed me numerous pictures of their picnics and parties to illustrate the joy they brought to one another. These pictures were also offered as proof that love like that seen in the movies could be achieved in real life. The woman quoted a few lines earlier remarried as well "to the man of her dreams," although for her, the dreams quickly faded once they lived together. "Now that I'm older," she explained, "I know that the passion you feel when you first meet, that deep, deep desire fueled by emotion, you know, like what you see in the films, is something that leaves after a spell. But I cannot help it, I am a romantic, and I live for that feeling." Now in her sixties, she still speaks of her boyfriends or the men she is currently flirting with like an amorous and excited teen.

LOVE AND REVOLUTION IN THE 1950s

The back cover of Adam Shafi's Kiswahili novel *Vuta n'kuvute* describes the central themes driving the protagonists as "love and revolution." The novel, set in the 1950s, opens with a moving description of Yasmin, the desolate Asian heroine, who has been married off by her parents at the tender age of fifteen to Raza, a fifty-two-year-old small-time shopkeeper in Zanzibar. Yasmin detests Raza. He is old enough to be her grandfather, his teeth are stained, and his breath reeks from the pipe he constantly has in his mouth. He is often so busy in his shop that he regularly goes four or five days without shaving, and many a night, he falls down in bed next to her without even bothering to bathe. Yasmin, we are told on page two, "would rather die than give her body to this man."[59] Going to the cinema is one of the few things they do for mutual enjoyment, yet even there, Yasmin's pleasure is tempered by the fact that she has to sit next to Raza in public.

Confined by purdah to the inside of their small home, Yasmin finds her days are filled with longing and loneliness. The only joy she experiences during the early period of their marriage is when she winds up Raza's gramophone and dances in the kitchen, pretending to be a Hindi film star. One day, while joyfully lost in her fantasy, dancing around the kitchen and making eyes at her imaginary lover, she is brought back to earth at the end of her performance by clapping and cries of "*Shabash! Shabash!*" (Wonderful! Wonderful!) from the window across the narrow lane. Thus, while

137

dancing out her romantic fantasies to the tune from a Hindi film, Yasmin meets her future lover, the young and attractive Swahili man Denge, who has studied in the Soviet Union and is now organizing for the overthrow of the British in Zanzibar.

Romantic love and political revolution are the central themes explored in *Vuta n'kuvute*. When I first read the novel, it resonated quite intensely with the oral histories I had gathered in Zanzibar. While doing research for my first book, *Pastimes and Politics*, I was made aware, in no uncertain terms, that the nationalist organizing of the 1950s and the "revolution" of 1964 framed the lives of nearly everyone who lived in the isles. Arranged marriage, communal integrity, and cross-class and inter-racial sex were also issues that came up in this context, particularly as they had to do with the forced marriages that were part of state policy during the so-called revolutionary years. These themes emerged as well, with surprising frequency, during the interviews I conducted on the history of cinema. When I asked about the place of cinemas in urban social life or about what some of the best movies of all time were and why, I was told by many elders of their own revolutionary struggles to marry for love, rather than wedding the partner their parents had arranged for them. Shafi's novel seemed to capture these twin struggles that people had talked so much about. Yet when I asked Shafi, who was himself a young man involved in the era's revolutionary fight, if it was his intent to portray the struggle to choose one's own partner and the struggle for national independence as two sides of the same coin, he said:

> No. The novel is about nationalism and the struggles of young
> men, like Denge, to overthrow the British. I use Yasmin to
> locate the novel in Zanzibar, and describe her life because
> I wanted to describe how life was in Zanzibar at this time.
> Young people were taught to respect the elders, and girls their
> husbands, and never to question. In the 1950s there were many
> cases of old men like Raza marrying young girls like Yasmin.
> The beginning of the novel is intended to describe how her life
> was like, how circumscribed it was, and as the novel unfolds
> she too opens up and is exposed to many things she never
> knew existed before. I just wanted to describe how life was, not
> necessarily to link it with a dual colonialism.[60]

I include this exchange to illustrate that in the course of reading or watching, readers or viewers always invest a narrative with their own meanings. As a feminist, it could not be more obvious to me that this novel linked personal freedom and national independence. Obviously, though, this was not Shafi's intent. The point is that people take the narratives that are available to them and then rework them to give them meanings in the context of their own lives. As Sabrina, a young Zanzibari said, "Films are filled with lessons—it's like reading a novel. There is a story and different issues inside, but it is up to you to interpret them, to think about them and decide what the meaning of the story is for you. . . . Each person comes with their own interests and takes from it what is meaningful to them."[61]

In coastal East Africa, the growth of romance, the rise of nationalism, and the avid consumption of Hindi films were intertwined. The 1950s were a watershed decade for both lovers and nationalists on the African continent. It was during this decade that the struggles of peasants and wage laborers, women and men, ex-soldiers and students, and frustrated entrepreneurs and heady intellectuals coalesced and gave rise to the nationalist movements that swept the continent toward independence. Although no nationalists I know of ever proclaimed that ending the patriarchal control of youth and marriage was among their goals, the growth of nationalist movements fueled the development of romantic love in several important ways. Most significantly, both nationalism and romantic love were based on fantasies—often very elaborate fantasies—of what one wanted but did not have. Similarly, they both projected into the future and infused their subjects with hope that their dreams of fulfillment would come to pass. The 1950s were a decade in which nearly everyone on the continent was inspired to dream of liberation. *Freedom, independence,* and *self-determination* were words voiced in a thousand different languages. People across the continent struggled to define the meaning of these imprecise terms and imagine what they meant when applied to individual, communal, and national lives. The wide-ranging debates about politics and economics helped make this period—like that of the French Revolution described by William Reddy—an era of emotional liberty as well.[62] As nationalists from the Cape to Cairo and Cameroon took to the stage to rally support for national independence and freedom from colonialism, youth applied these vocabularies to more immediate personal concerns.

139

With the passing of time, newlyweds and nationalists everywhere have been forced to come to grips with the reality that the mundane management of daily affairs is far more complicated and conflictual than they ever dreamed. But in the 1950s, the elderly men and women with whom I spoke were still quite young, and their dreams were still alive. Many of them directly commented on their own nostalgia for the past, for a point in their personal and national lives when everything seemed possible — a time when the future was guaranteed to be more fulfilling and their lives less filled with compromise than those of their parents. Such is the folly of youth, I was told. But many also commented on the significance of the larger changes taking place all around them in terms of inspiring them to dream of different emotive and romantic lives. If nationalists could talk of overthrowing political economies based on colonialism, then why not talk of overturning the patriarchal control of marriage as well? If politicians found attentive audiences for proposals to end racial segregation and ethnic privilege, then why couldn't parents hear of Asian daughters like Yasmin falling in love with Swahili men like Denge? Scholars studying fiction and nationalism have found a similar pattern in other parts of the globe, where narratives of love conquering all have blossomed during periods of nationalist awakening.[63] From Argentina and Ecuador to India and Zanzibar, the romantic couple emerged as an emblem for imaginary nations struggling to overcome deep historic divisions of class, race, language, region, and religion.

The 1950s did not mark the first time in African history that youth and elders fought over marriage. Generational conflict about these issues had long been endemic. But in Zanzibar, the 1950s marked a turning point in public, as opposed to merely private, debate. Cinema certainly was not the only factor that contributed to the growing prevalence of these public deliberations, but it was a vital one. By providing a regular infusion of narrative material to fuel imaginations, films inspired debate. The fact that there was such widespread consumption of films also meant that the dilemmas presented on the screen became real as men and women, elders and youth argued among themselves over plots and the relative morality and immorality of characters and scenes. In bedrooms, on the streets, and in shops and tearooms and buses, thousands of people discussed and debated these texts each week.

For the most part, people were unable to make their real lives as dreamy or steamy as those depicted in film, but the movies opened up possibilities of fulfillment and gave them something to dream about. And many carried these dreams well into their old age. I know several sweet, quite elderly husbands who still get a thrill out of bringing a special treat home for their wives, the loves of their lives. The women, too, though now in their seventies, still perfume their rooms with aromatic incense and sprinkle jasmine flowers on their beds. Most of these couples dated regularly at the cinema during their early married lives, and for them, the romance lives on. Others lamented that although they dared to love across class or communal lines, they never managed to consummate their romance like Rita and Raj did. Instead, they married the partners of their parents' choosing and, in many cases, learned to accept conjugal love as a useful antidote for a broken romantic heart. Still others said that though they were not inspired to choose their own loves, the narratives from Hindi melodramas nonetheless did become the sound tracks for collective discussions in their day about the rights of young people to choose their own partners. Most of those married in the 1950s and 1960s were not able to follow their hearts in choosing their first mates, but when their children—and especially their grandchildren—came of age in subsequent decades, they were far more willing to empathize and compromise than their own elders had been at midcentury.

Awara was a special film. Indeed, according to many, it was the best film ever made. Its continued resonance in Zanzibar, more than fifty years after its first premier, alludes to the often enduring impact of texts on society. But *Awara* was far from alone in stirring communal passions, longing, and debate. There were many films, from many places and from many different genres, that had the power to light up local lives. What made a film important and its impact enduring was the degree to which viewers were able to relate to it, translate it, and incorporate it into their own lives.

Chapter 4

GLOBAL FILMS AND LOCAL RECEPTION

Audience Preferences, 1950s–80s

TANZANIAN TASTES in film were amazingly cosmopolitan. Already in the 1920s, movies produced in Britain, continental Europe, the United States, and India were being screened before enthusiastic audiences. As creative talents and new national industries flourished in the 1940s and 1950s, local importers secured films from Egypt, Japan, and Russia that they thought would resonate locally.[1] After independence, they again sought out new and novel sources of supply to meet the changing tastes and demographics of local audiences and to keep their fans abreast of the newest trends in global cinema. Action films from Hong Kong and Italy captured an important niche market and began to consume an ever-larger percentage of screen time. But even though commercial films from nearly every corner of the world were screened in Tanzania, it was Indian films of the Hindi-Bombay variety that won the most consistent applause. Other national cinemas and various genres appealed to small segments of the overall audience, but Hindi films were attractive to the largest portion of the movie-going public. Not surprisingly, Hindi-language films and Indian actors and actresses consistently ranked on the top of my respondents' lists of favorites, regardless of gender, age, race, religion, or region.[2]

Tanzanians relished exposure to new types of films but generally demanded that movies incorporate a broad but consistent set of elements if they were to succeed at the box office. First and foremost, they had to be visually engaging and able to express a plot cinematically, since there was no subtitling or dubbing and few in the audience spoke the languages in which films were made. Tanzanians also had a penchant for melodrama, and many of the films that were popular, regardless of national origin, fell loosely into this genre. Tanzanians went to the theater anticipating that their heartstrings would be pulled: they wanted a movie to make them feel yearning, anger, hope, fear, love, and the pain of loss, all in a single evening if possible. Stories in which the distinctions between good and evil were obvious, action was constant, or romantic longing and family crises were played out in the context of communal pressures to conform were also exceptionally popular. A stunning sound track, to complement and intensify the emotional roller coaster of story and action, was equally important; moving music made a film stand out. Films that brought crowds to their feet—dancing, boxing, and hollering—were also much preferred to those that left audiences sitting in their seats and pondering a character's inner struggle. Of course, talented actors and actresses who could pull the audience into the drama and action were also highly prized. The best films of all were those that lit an intellectual or artistic spark that spread from audience members to the community at large, kindling a fire that engulfed the town.

When questioned about the benefits of moviegoing, people said they went to the cinema not only to relax but also to get exposed to other cultures and different ways of living and being in the world. Among the many things they gleaned from films—and remade with the help of talented tailors and friends—were global fashion and music trends. Men's and women's hairstyles, shirts, dresses, and trousers were impacted by visions from the screen. Simple mimicry was never the goal, but refashioning was a revered local art. Musical rhythms and dance moves, strut, and swagger were also incorporated into individual performative styles. Films that people remembered years later were those that provided multiple mnemonic hooks: songs that they played, sang, or danced to; dramas that they debated and deliberated over; or concrete material that they reworked and relocated.

Records on film censorship are extensive and in fact constitute the most replete body of archival material on any aspect of the industry in Tanzania. From these accounts, we have quite comprehensive tallies of

143

how many films were imported each year, where they were produced, how they were rated by members of the boards of censors, and what if anything needed to be cut. These records tell us nothing, however, about what local audiences liked, ignored, or adored. To answer much more complicated questions about reception and audience tastes, interviews, surveys, and personal photo collections are most useful. Box office records from the Majestic Cinema in Zanzibar, covering the years 1972 to 1993, also provide exceptionally rare data on which films packed the house, which were utter flops, and which could draw a crowd for a repeat run. Combined with interview and survey data, these box office returns allow us to gauge how class, age, and gender impacted audience composition for different genres of film, as well as how these dynamics changed over time. This chapter provides a broad overview of the films that were screened in Tanzania, highlighting the audience preferences that explain why Indian films remained perennial favorites, despite competition from films produced all over the world.

HOLLYWOOD HEGEMONY? HARDLY: MARKET SHARE VERSUS CULTURAL MEMORY

From the 1930s through the 1960s, Hollywood distribution systems dominated global markets, and Tanzania was no exception in this regard. Hollywood movies comprised 75 to 90 percent of all films shown on Tanzanian screens between the 1930s and 1950s,[3] and it was not uncommon to find American productions consuming 80 to 90 percent of screen time in places as diverse as El Salvador, Iraq, Angola, Thailand, and Ireland.[4] Censorship and industry records from the 1950s through the mid-1960s indicate, however, that Hollywood movies lost some of their influence over time, dropping to an average of 55 percent of the films screened in Tanzania between 1954 and 1963.[5] Independence from colonialism in the 1960s initially did little to further alter what East Africans found playing at their local cinemas; reviews of newspaper ads from the first decade after independence reveal that 50 to 60 percent of all films screened were produced by one of the big Hollywood studios. Only in the 1970s did the preponderance of American products on Tanzanian screens begin to wane, for reasons that are explained more fully in chapter 8.

But even if Hollywood films monopolized screen time, they did not necessarily dominate people's minds or their memories of going to the show.

Only a small handful of filmgoers—of the hundreds who were asked—mentioned an American as their favorite actor; in fact, few people who frequented the movies in the 1950s and 1960s could even name an American actor aside from Elvis Presley. Egyptian films, which never constituted more than 4 percent of the movies screened in Tanzania, were named far more frequently as favorites than American films, highlighting the dissonance between market share and cultural memory. Egyptian films were screened less than once a month in the 1950s and 1960s, but Egyptian actors and actresses ranked high on lists of personal favorites, particularly among respondents who lived along the coast. Westerns, the quintessential American genre, were outgunned in Tanzania by their Italian counterparts. Alan Ladd, who starred in the western *Shane* (Stevens, 1953), was named as a memorable star by a few men who had the privilege of going to school and learning English during the colonial era, but the Italian Giuliano Gemma outranked Ladd in my surveys by a wide margin. Gemma (also known as Montgomery Wood) was identified as a favorite by many men who attended films in the 1960s and 1970s, and his classics—*One Silver Dollar* (Ferroni, 1965), *Adios Gringo* (Stegani, 1965), and *A Pistol for Ringo* (Tessari, 1965)—topped many a list of most memorable films. The American actors Lee Van Cleef and Clint Eastwood became household names among a generation of Tanzanians in the late 1960s and early 1970s but again only as a result of their roles in the Italian westerns *A Fistful of Dollars* (Leone, 1964) and *The Good, the Bad and the Ugly* (Leone, 1966). Richard Roundtree in *Shaft* (Parks, 1971), Fred Williamson in *Hell up in Harlem* (Cohen, 1973), and Pam Grier in *Foxy Brown* (Hill, 1974) were also named as favorites from the 1970s, but typically, their names were at the end of a list that began with Amitabh Bachchan, Dharmendra, Mithun Chakraborty, Waheeda Rehman, and Hema Malini, followed by Bruce Lee. American films may have dominated screen time, but this bore no relationship whatsoever to their long-term social, cultural, or intellectual impact in Tanzania.

Theater owners varied the price of admission to shows based on how much they believed audience members would pay, and Indian and Egyptian films consistently commanded the highest ticket prices. In the 1950s, even poorer patrons from the African side of town who frequented the cinema at the Raha Leo Civic Center in Zanzibar were willing to pay up to 50 percent more (TSh 1/50) for a ticket to see an Indian or Egyptian film than they were to see a Hollywood film (1/-).[6] Even at higher prices, well

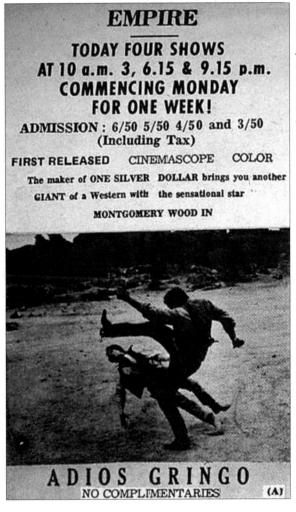

EMPIRE

TODAY FOUR SHOWS
AT 10 a.m. 3, 6.15 & 9.15 p.m.
COMMENCING MONDAY
FOR ONE WEEK!
ADMISSION : 6/50 5/50 4/50 and 3/50
(Including Tax)
FIRST RELEASED   CINEMASCOPE   COLOR
The maker of ONE SILVER DOLLAR brings you another
GIANT of a Western with the sensational star
MONTGOMERY WOOD IN

ADIOS GRINGO
NO COMPLIMENTARIES   (A)

Figure 4.1 Ad for *Adios Gringo*, starring Giuliano Gemma (aka Montgomery Wood). From *Sunday News*, June 26, 1966, p. 4

more than twice as many people attended Indian and Egyptian movies. And at the commercial cinemas in town, ticket prices for Egyptian and Indian films were often two times the price of admission to Hollywood films. Island audiences knew what they liked, and they were willing to pay to see it.

Available records suggest that these patterns of preference for Indian films persisted for decades. During the first six months of 1975, a total of 40,224 tickets were sold for Indian films at the Majestic Cinema in Zanzibar. Ticket sales for American films during this same period numbered just 1,340. Dividing these absolute numbers by the number of films screened and the number of shows, we find an average of 60 tickets were sold for each screening of an American film and more than four times as many patrons were paying to watch the average Indian show. In 1981, thirty-seven different Indian films played for sold-out houses at the Majestic, pushing annual ticket sales at the theater to 171,392. Films that were popular enough to reel between theaters were also always Indian films. In the 1970s and 1980s, usually two or three Indian films each month packed the Majestic and were reeled to at least one and sometimes two additional theaters in Zanzibar.[7] I have no box office records for any other theater in the nation, but interviews with managers and film fans indicate that these patterns of attendance, ticket pricing, reeling, and audience preference were consistent across the country.

In examining twenty years of ticket sales books from the Majestic, it was difficult to find American films that did anywhere near as well as their Indian counterparts. *Jaws* (Spielberg, 1975) was one exception. On its re-peat run through Zanzibar in 1978, it packed the house for two shows on a Wednesday night and then for another two shows on Saturday, as well as selling out a Sunday matinee. Between 1972 and 1993, no other American film came anywhere close to drawing such an audience. Yet in the twelve weeks after *Jaws* was screened, there were eight Hindi new releases and one classic Indian repeat that filled the Majestic nearly to capacity. Many of these films—including *Junglee* (Mukherji, 1961), *Dharam Veer* (Desai, 1977), *Dream Girl* (Chakravarty, 1977), *Aakhri Daku* (Mehra, 1978), *Fakira* (Dixit, 1976), *Raeeszada* (1976), *Lagaam* (Gautam, 1976), *Jaggu* (Ganguly, 1975), *Parvarish* (Desai, 1977), *Aafat* (Ram, 1977), *Chalta Purza* (Sonie, 1977), and *Don* (Barot, 1978)—not only sold out all the seats at the Majestic but also were reeled to one or more additional theaters in Zanzibar, where they presumably did equally well.

Dream Girl, starring Hema Malini as a modern-day female Robin Hood who steals from the wealthy to fund an orphanage and costarring Ashok Kumar and Dharmendra, was the most popular film of the balmy January to March 1978 season. Despite the fact that the film was reeled to all three theaters, there were not enough tickets to go around. Black marketers could simply name their price and be assured of getting what they asked. The melee in front of the ticket window at the Majestic was so intense, with people pushing, shoving, and catapulting friends forward, and dragging others back, that the steel bars on the ticket window were

147

permanently bent. In fact, *Dream Girl* was such a hit that it not only played for two sold-out shows at all three theaters on Sunday but also sold another 2,253 tickets at the Majestic on Monday and Tuesday. Thus, though *Jaws* did quite well, *Dream Girl* was a far more spectacular box office draw.

The beautiful and talented Hema Malini, who has appeared in more than 150 films, was repeatedly named by Tanzanians as one of their favorite actresses and a star whose new films they would never miss. Both male and female respondents were attracted to her glamour and accomplished classical dancing. The electricity between her and her costar (and future husband) Dharmendra added to her screen appeal in many of her early films. But Tanzanians across the country also said they were attracted to Malini because her characters made them think differently about women's social roles, as well as their physical and intellectual abilities. Respondents were drawn to the unconventional characters she played, such as the rambunctious and determined Geeta in *Seeta aur Geeta* (Sippy, 1972); the dancer and drug runner Seema in *Charas* (Sagar, 1976); and Basanti, a feisty young woman who earns her living driving a horse cart in *Sholay* (Sippy, 1975).

Good Indian films had incredible repeat value as well. On *Dream Girl*'s third run through the isles four years later, it could still draw 350 fans to the Majestic on a Wednesday night. There were many timeless Indian films, movies that could consistently attract large crowds decades after their initial release. *Mother India* (Khan, 1957), described by film scholars Ashish Rajadhyaksha and Paul Willemen as a massively successful national epic akin to *Gone with the Wind* in stature, was one such film.[8] *Mother India* stars Nargis, Sunil Dutt, and Rajendra Kumar in a beautifully told, heartbreaking tale of peasant struggle. Nargis plays a single mother who is left to raise her two sons after her husband, disabled in a farming accident, flees to diminish the number of mouths that had to be fed from a limited harvest. Nargis is then subjected to the sexual and monetary predations of the village moneylender, along with the physical and emotional burdens of raising her boys alone. One son remains dutifully bound to his long-suffering mother; the other grows up committed to direct, political action and the violent overthrow of the existing system. His political involvement thrusts the family into deeper dilemmas, raising questions that parallel those facing postindependence India. Tickets for *Mother India* were sold on the black market in Tanzania ten years after its initial release. Two decades later, the film was still drawing a respectable crowd to the Majestic for a ladies' show matinee.[9]

Many other Indian films could do equally well years and even decades after their initial release. According to Asad Talati and Shabir Jariwalla, one could always count on old films such as *Albela* (Bhagwan, 1951), *Awara* (Kapoor, 1951), *Anarkali* (Jaswantal, 1953), and *Mughal-e-Azam* (Asif, 1960) to please the crowds. "On a holiday," Jariwalla asserted, "people would go crazy for one of these films! Especially African people, they loved these old movies. The music was popular for generations. If you put [on] one of these classics for Christmas, African people would go crazy!" According to exhibitors and black marketers alike, tickets for any of these films would make their way onto the black market if the show was screened over on a holiday in Dar es Salaam as late as the 1970s.[10] *Junglee*, a 1961 film, was so popular that it could still sell out three theaters for six shows in Zanzibar in 1978, where it was shown on the second day of Eid al-Fitr, the Muslim holiday marking the end of Ramadan. The sound track to *Junglee*, including the all-time favorite "Yahoo!" combined with the youthful and rebellious performance of Shammi Kapoor, elevated the film to the status of a timeless classic. Complicated family dramas added further to the film's appeal. One of the main story lines involves a humorless mother who torments her children, refusing to permit laughter, play, or singing in the house. Both children end up falling in love with partners their mother condemns, and the daughter even has a child out of wedlock with her lover. *Sholay* (Sippy, 1975), starring Amitabh Bachchan, was another film that could fill the house decades after its initial release. Eddy, who ran the thousand-seat Starlight Cinema in Dar es Salaam, recalled, "*Sholay* was one of those timeless films. Anytime I showed it I knew I could just kick back in my office, put my feet up, and relax. It came out in 1975, and the last time I showed it was 1995 [on video] and it still packed the house!"[11] In contrast, American films with repeat value were a very rare exception; most were screened for a two-day run and never seen again.

Tanzanian audiences were not, however, undiscerning consumers of Indian kitsch. There were good movies that packed the house, and there were bad movies that simply filled the bill. Stars, directors, and singers all contributed to a film's potential draw, but shows that failed on one or all accounts could easily bomb. One example is the 1981 Indian film *Love Story*, starring Kumar Gaurav and directed by Rajendra Kumar (of *Mother*

149

India fame). The film had a five-star rating in India and thus was reeled to all three theaters in Zanzibar on opening night; it filled the Majestic to 70 percent of capacity for the evening show. But to local audiences, the movie was a dud, and at intermission, some patrons left and did not return. Word quickly spread around town about how bad the film was, and for the night show, the Majestic barely sold two hundred tickets. Usually, attendance figures at evening and night showings were fairly equal, but after more than fifty years of watching and debating films, island residents knew to trust the reviews offered by local critics. Talati, Tanzania's premier importer and distributor, explained that exhibitors had to know their audiences to succeed in the film business in Africa: "You could not rely on reviews or trade magazine promotions alone, because these were based on outside markets. It might get four stars with them, but that means nothing to us." The failure of *Love Story* is a compelling example of his point.[12] Yet even so, the Indian *Love Story* collected twice as much revenue at the Cine Afrique box office as the American film with the same title starring Ali MacGraw.[13]

American films were never popular enough to be reeled and opened at several theaters simultaneously. I asked cinema managers in Zanzibar and Dar es Salaam if they ever tried booking a first-run Hollywood film at several cinemas, but none could recall such an occasion. Abdul said that he did remember one English-language movie that played all three theaters in Zanzibar at once, "the film *The Rise and Fall of Idi Amin* [Patel, 1981]. That was a blockbuster! There was no Indian film that managed to pull together the material in that film. But it didn't happen frequently."[14] In mainland Tanzania as well, that was the only English-language film recalled by exhibitors as having the power to rival the typical Indian production in terms of audience demand. Even up-country exhibitors, who had much more difficulty filling their shows than colleagues along the coast, remembered the smashing success of the film. As one exhibitor in Morogoro said, "Yes, *The Rise and Fall of Idi Amin*, that was a spectacular film! . . . We had people coming from all over, even the villages, to see that film." Rural Maasai rarely went to the movies, but even they were going to town to see it, he added. "We'd never seen the Maasai coming to the cinema, but everyone was excited to see this film, even the Maasai. So we played that thing for almost a week up in here, five, six days. We used to run three shows, afternoon, evening and night and they were all packed! That was the only [English-language] film that I really remember doing so well."[15] He reported gross box office earnings from this film that were tenfold higher than up-country cinemas typically made with other films.[16]

The story of Idi Amin was of particular interest in Tanzania, where news circulated freely about the horrors suffered by civilians in neighboring Uganda during Amin's eight-year reign of terror and his brutal expulsion of Ugandan Asians. In November 1978, Amin's army invaded and annexed a section of Tanzania, resulting in the decision to utilize Tanzania's army to aid the Ugandan resistance and overthrow Amin. This singularly open use of Tanzanian military might beyond its borders was a resounding success, and by April 1979, the resistance had taken the Ugandan capital and forced Amin into exile. The timeliness of the Amin drama, together with the graphic depictions of the horrors of his reign, drew fans to this particular film. The state-owned Audio-Visual Institute and Tanzania Film Company (TFC) made a documentary about the events, titled *Vita vya Kagera* (the Kagera War) and released in 1980.[17] But even this color documentary heralding the bravery and determination of the Tanzanian armed forces — made by Tanzanians, starring Tanzanians, and shot as the troops marched into Kampala to rout Amin's forces — was no match at the box office for its gruesome dramatic rival. A British, Kenyan, and Nigerian coproduction, directed by the Uganda-born Sharad Patel and starring the Kenyan actor Joseph Olita as Amin, this singular example of an English-language film popular enough to rival Indian films was not a Hollywood production at all.

A handful of American films actually did quite well in Tanzania, and though they were not popular enough to reel or have their tickets appear on the black market, they could still pack the house. *Ben-Hur* (Wyler, 1959) was one such title.[18] *Ben-Hur* contained many of the aesthetic elements Tanzanians demanded in a movie. It was filled with stirring visual action — and it starred Charlton Heston as a merchant prince turned gladiator and charioteer. The plot and characters in the movie could also be comprehended visually: one did not need to know English or understand the nuances of the dialogue to get the picture. The story is set in the time of Christ and revolves around the struggles of the Jews against the Romans; thus, it appealed to East Africans' love of melodrama, as good and evil were easily deciphered and on full visual and emotional display. The main character, played by Heston, is a righteous Jewish prince condemned to slavery, as his mother and sister are imprisoned in a leper colony. He seeks justice for his people and his family and revenge for his own dethronement. Throughout

151

the film, Heston is depicted as but one individual in a larger community of slaves, all of whom are struggling to survive endless toil, cruel beatings, dire thirst, and gripping hunger. His righteousness and morality are foregrounded not only by his friendship with the Prophet Jesus and Balthasar — one of the wise old Arabs who followed the star of Bethlehem at the time of Christ's birth — but also by a stirring sound track that won an Oscar for best music, along with the film's eleven other Academy Awards. *Ben-Hur* was also the first film featuring MGM's version of the wide-screen, CinemaScope technology, which added to its local appeal when screened at the new and updated theaters in 1950s Tanzania.

Ben-Hur was somewhat atypical of American productions from that era, and it was also one of the few American films from the classic Hollywood days that I found playing again in the 1970s.[19] *The Ten Commandments* (DeMille, 1956) was another biblical epic from the 1950s that had enduring appeal. It was scheduled to run for a matinee at the Majestic on the morning of the Zanzibar Revolution in 1964, and it worked its way through the circuit again in 1972. Years later, as I was traveling by ship between the isles and the mainland in the early 2000s, I personally witnessed audiences mesmerized by each of these films. Though the videos were screened to entertain passengers and keep their minds off their seasickness, this level of enduring appeal was rare for Hollywood films.

There were certainly occasional action and adventure films in the late 1940s and 1950s that packed East African theaters, among them MGM's *The Three Musketeers* (Sidney, 1948) and the American and British coproduction *The Bridge on the River Kwai* (Lean, 1957). But for the most part, Tanzanians found it difficult to engage with American productions from that era. To begin with, few people spoke English, and classic Hollywood cinema relied extensively on dialogue to make its points. This emphasis on dialogue flowed from and reinforced Western film conventions where the individual — motivated by personal psychological concerns — was key. Individualism and the social isolation of characters were further emphasized by camera work in which medium and close-up shots dominated. The larger social and communal context was literally removed from the picture. This emphasis on the individual, with little attention to his or her placement within the family and community, neither reflected nor resonated with East Africans' sense of reality.[20] Consequently, though exhibitors and distributors could all recall the names of important American films that did well in Tanzania, not a single average respondent listed an American movie as a favorite. Comparing the relative merits of Hollywood and Indian films from that era, one man from Zanzibar stated it rather plainly: "American films were boring. You would sit in your seat trying to follow and eventually fall asleep. But this could never happen during an Indian film. You would never leave the theater tired, but exhilarated and anxious to see it again."[21]

MUSIC, MOVIES, AND THE ELVIS PHENOMENON

The one American actor whom Tanzanians readily identified as a star was Elvis Presley. Although his films contained many of the same elements that created cultural and emotional distance between Hollywood and the average Tanzanian, their pulsating musical scores and the visual and physical excitement generated by Elvis's thigh-thumping, hip-shaking, shoulder-shimmying dancing compensated for these deficiencies. Elvis was far from simply an American phenomenon. In the 1950s and 1960s, youth from Mexico to Argentina, Australia, and East Germany swooned to his records. His films were also among Hollywood's first to succeed in wooing a youthful demographic on a transnational scale.[22] His music and moves gave Tanzanian youth fun new things they could play with and numerous new styles they could incorporate into their repertoires. Local audiences had long appropriated music, fashion, and hairstyles from Indian films into their worlds, but Elvis was the first American star that Tanzanians adopted as their own, which accounts for his enduring memory among respondents. The centrality of music to his films also resonated with Tanzanian film aesthetics.

One of the many factors that made Indian films perennial favorites in Tanzania was the importance of music, song, and dance in those productions. The first sound film produced in India was *Alam Ara* (Irani, 1931). Containing seven songs with instrumental accompaniment, it was a major hit, and it basically set the formula for commercial Indian film for the next seventy years. From the 1930s through the present, nearly a quarter of the running time in an Indian film has been devoted to musical interludes that enhance emotionality, stir the audience, and help move the plot along. Hindi film music is also intentionally eclectic, adding to its transnational, cross-generational appeal. Sound tracks draw on music traditions from across the Indian subcontinent but freely mix these with instruments,

153

melodies, and rhythms from throughout the world.[23] Bengali, Punjabi, folk, devotional, cabaret, disco—any and every context and style has found its way into Hindi film music. By the 1930s, Indian film music composer-directors were already commonly incorporating Western orchestral instruments into their sound. The relative "modernity" or "traditionalism" of characters or their dilemmas was often expressed through the instrumentation and musical style of the songs with which the characters were associated. In the 1940s, as Latin-inspired music swept the globe, rumbas and calypsos were added to Hindi film tunes. Rock and roll, funk, and disco followed in the next decades. The hit *Sargam* (Santoshi, 1950)—the premier Indian film shown at the Sultana Cinema in Zanzibar when it opened—incorporated a rock-and-roll element even before that musical style became popular in movies from the United States. One thing that allowed Indian films to appeal across generations in Tanzania was their quite willful engagement with the global, together with their playful expressions of translocal orientations through musical cosmopolitanism. Particularly after World War II, it seemed that a new rhythm, style, and sound shook the world every ten years. These all found their way into Indian films and helped keep Tanzanians abreast of transformations in the transnational soundscape.[24]

Tanzanians consciously mined the movies for music, moves, and fashionable styles they could incorporate into their art, leisure, and daily lives. Egyptian and Indian film music of various kinds was quite intentionally incorporated into East African taarab and other musical genres. Mwalim Idd was one of several Zanzibari musicians who recounted going to Egyptian films to study orchestral composition and stage performance. Others cited specific taarab tunes, directing my attention to melodic or rhythmic references to Hindi film tunes. Dance steps too were creatively appropriated into local choreography. Reviews by Tanzanian film critic Bashir Punja, published weekly in the *Sunday News*, always noted the importance of the sound track to Indian films, and he typically identified the music director in his review; on one occasion, Punja described the director as the "hero" who saved an otherwise listless film by composing "tunes so hot they fire the blood."[25] Local singers, dancers, and musicians went to the movies for inspiration and then riffed off of what they had seen and heard in their own ways. In fact, it was often the musical elements of Indian movies that gave specific films repeat value. Although the preferred styles of music changed over time, one of the specific things Tanzanians sought when they went to the show was visual and aural information on global cultural trends. Elvis films fit wonderfully into these local expectations and uses of international films.

From the earliest days of synchronized sound, Indian studios released gramophone recordings of film songs before an opening to familiarize people with the music and garner publicity for the film's debut; in this too, Elvis films played to the score. The *Sunday News* published a weekly list of the ten top-selling records in Dar es Salaam, which was compiled in conjunction with one of the major outlets for vinyl in the city, Mahmood's Radio Service. In the months preceding the August showing of Elvis's film *Girl Happy* (Sagal, 1965), at least one and frequently two of the songs from the film made it to the Top Ten. The song "Do the Clam" was one of the most popular, holding steady on the local charts for months. Like Indian audio releases, Elvis records helped build familiarity and anticipation for the coming film. Friends and siblings danced to the vinyl that rocked the Top Ten, betting on whose style and moves might come closest to those in the film. Seeing how well records from the movie were selling, management at the Empire, in Dar es Salaam, screened *Girl Happy* for an unprecedented three shows on a Sunday and six more shows on Monday and Tuesday. In the 1960s, the Empire began to consciously cultivate young moviegoers as its niche crowd, and Elvis fit perfectly into that plan. Daring and youthful yet wholesome enough to attract young women, Elvis movies were recalled by several people I interviewed as marking the first time they split off from their parents on a Sunday and watched a film with their siblings and cousins instead.[26]

Elvis films were also singular examples of Hollywood movies that could garner a small segment of the ladies' show market. In January 1966, Elvis broke the mold when his *Viva Las Vegas* (Sidney, 1964), with costar Ann-Margret, rocked the zanana show crowd. Subsequent Elvis films were then featured in afternoon screenings at the Avalon for female fans. Nasra was one devout woman who gleefully recounted her youthful days enjoying Elvis. As a young girl, she began regularly attending ladies' shows with her aunt and cousins in Zanzibar, where Indian and Egyptian films were avidly consumed. But when Elvis films came to the Sultana, she recalled, "*everyone* rushed to get tickets before they sold out!"[27] Afternoon screenings gave an added option to women who missed tickets for the premier or who wanted to see a film again.

Tanzanians had long experienced a synergy between film, music, and local popular cultural styles; Nasra was but one of many who reworked Elvis for a local crowd. She and her cousins practiced for weeks after a film, perfecting their imitation of the star while giggling with delight in their bedrooms. Nasra's enthusiasm for music and dance stayed with her as she aged. Later in life, she became a renowned organizer of the Zanzibar women's taarab group, Sahib el-Arry. She was also a sought-after arranger of stage performances and choreography for nuptial celebrations. While doing her version of Elvis's moves for the small audience gathered in her sitting room on the day of our interview, she explained that one of the great draws of moviegoing was being exposed to different ideas about life and new cultural forms.[28] She was one of a great number who said they actively watched movies with an eye toward finding things that could enhance their local repertoires. She also relished remixing them to make them her own. Clothing and hairstyles seen on Indian actresses topped her list of imitated forms, but beats, instrumentation, and vocal styles were not far behind. Nasra could not recall where she got the idea for the shoulder shimmies she was teaching the young dancers practicing that day in her home. Was it from "Do the Clam" or from a bellydancing scene in an Egyptian film? It did not matter—it was an incredible move, one she frequently integrated into her own choreography and one that always earned applause from the crowd.

The music and wild, evocative dancing in Elvis films were major draws for Tanzanians. The films themselves were silly, said Ali, a man who grew up in the Kariakoo neighborhood of Dar es Salaam, and the stories did not resonate. "But the dancing was amazing, and unlike anything we had ever seen before," he declared. "Whenever there was an Elvis movie we went to every show to study his dance moves."[29] Like Nasra, Ali was a performer, and he culled the movies for material he could incorporate into his shows. Beginning as a young boy, he went regularly to the Azania Cinema in Dar es Salaam; by the time he was in his teens and twenties, he was going to the movies almost daily. Unlike most of the folks I interviewed, Ali liked Hollywood films as much as Indian ones, and his familiarity with American actors, actresses, and movies was by far the most detailed I encountered. His knowledge of English was critical to his appreciation for American films, he explained. Ali learned the rudiments of English at school, but he attributed his fluency to his avid consumption of Hollywood productions. Those English skills paid off immensely in his teens. For one thing, groups of kids pitched in and purchased his tickets for movies in exchange for his willingness to act as a translator during the show. For another, he was chosen as the lead singer for a group of Elvis impersonators because his command of English allowed him to give the most articulate, soulful renditions of Elvis's songs.

Like many youth in the capital city, Ali and his friends eagerly embraced music from across the nation, continent, and globe. Before the age of seven, he had publicly performed both Islamic *quasida* (poetry) and local taarab. Sneaking off to see nightly African *ngoma* (drum and dance) performances was a regular part of his childhood in Kariakoo. By his teens, he was frequently listening outside the dance halls, where Tanzanian jazz bands played, and buying recordings of Franco and OK Jazz from the Congo. His collection of Latin vinyl was also extensive, a collection he still cherished at the age of sixty-one. Over the years, he played in a number of bands that incorporated diverse musical genres into their mix. His first real success as a stage musician, however, came when he and a group of friends formed the band of Elvis impersonators known as the Big Five. For two years running, they won top honors in the rock-and-roll category of an annual youth talent contest held at the Avalon. Ali's stylish rendition of "Mean Woman Blues" and his band's artful choreography brought the audience to its feet at the theater. Their swinging hips, stylish steps, and Ali's vocals earned the Big Five the crown as "The Kings of Rock 'n Roll" in Dar es Salaam.

The success of the Big Five is a wonderfully illustrative example of Ahmed Gurnah's assertion that Tanzanians were not passively dominated by foreign cultural icons but instead "actively used them like so much change in their pockets to purchase extra excitement and power."[30] In his thoughtful and persuasive critique of theories of globalization and cultural imperialism, entitled "Elvis in Zanzibar," Gurnah explains how his own engagement with Elvis—which extended to sculpted Teddy Boy hair—was central to the development of his critical thinking. Elvis was not the only foreigner he studied; he also read Peter Abrahams, William Shakespeare, and Frantz Fanon. This was all part of a broad intellectual exercise among the youth of the 1950s generation, who were actively looking to expand their cultural, political, and intellectual horizons. Engagement with the foreign did not result in a rejection of the local but rather led to its enrichment. For Gurnah and Ali, playing with Elvis was akin to adding a bit more ginger or garlic to their mothers' pilaf: it was the youth who were the

157

Figure 4.2 The Big Five, Elvis tribute band, on the stage of the Avalon Cinema, Dar es Salaam. Photo courtesy of Ali Ghafoor (*center*), the lead singer

cooks. "Foreign" products were never swallowed whole; they were ground up, reconstituted, and transformed into signs with specific local meanings and lives.

Ahmed Gurnah, Ali Ghafoor, and the other members of the Big Five were among many East African men who sculpted their hair in imitation of Elvis during their teens and early twenties. Writing some thirty years later,

Gurnah admitted that the hair "was probably on the margins of good taste, but great fun at the time." As young people, they thought it was a "hoot [to imitate] the beautiful people," he said, "so we did."[31] Ali also had to laugh recalling all the trouble he went to trying to perfect his do, including borrowing his sister's straightening iron and soliciting tips on combs and oils from other girls. "It is crazy now to imagine all the time we had for such silliness," Ali added. "You couldn't believe how much time I spent on my hair! And those shirts and trousers, do you have any idea how much time and effort it took to procure the material for our matching outfits, not to mention the haggling with tailors?" But it was also endless fun and one of the memorable joys of being young.

According to Ali, the band's success at the talent contest held at the Avalon propelled each member of the Big Five to local stardom. He and his friends were simultaneously thrilled and terrified to be performing on stage before more than seven hundred very judgmental peers. "Man we were scared," he recalled. "You can't imagine the difference between being in the audience at the Avalon and being on that stage! The Avalon was the premier theater in the nation and here we were, a bunch of schoolboys, performing before such a crowd." But overcoming their fears paid off. "Everywhere we went people recognized us. Everyone knew who we were! None of us could walk down the street without being greeted with, 'Hey man, you were great at the Avalon!'" For young men in their teens, there was no greater glory. Elders and nationalists were far less enthusiastic about young people's embrace of Elvis; the hair, in particular, was viewed as a sure sign that the young men were "lost." But unlike many elders, Ali's parents voiced no objection to his participation in the Big Five. I asked Ali if his parents were concerned, in particular, about their Muslim son's mimicking of Elvis's wild dance moves and sensuality. His response was, "Absolutely not. As long as I read the Qur'an, went to mosque and continued to do well at school, all was fine."[32] His mother was also a performer in her youth, a singer in the women's taarab band Egyptian, which also performed on cinema stages in Dar es Salaam. She viewed his insistence on seeing every Elvis film as akin to her own attraction to the films of Umm Kulthum and Abd al-Wahab. She too used films for creative inspiration and appreciated that as the times changed, the forms of music popular with youth changed as well. She pointed Ali to the best tailors, confident that her son could be a great dancer and singer and a good Muslim and son as well.

To truly understand the global youth cultures that began to emerge in the 1950s and 1960s, we need to appreciate the ways non-Western youth were intimately involved in making them global. Elvis was most certainly American, but the Elvis phenomenon was not. Elvis films, music, and dance moves were as popular with Muslims in Tanzania and mariachi bands in Mexico as they were with white teens in Memphis. These signs and symbols of music and dance were eminently translatable. What made them attractive was not that they were American but that they were sensual, expressive, and novel. The young people who learned to shimmy, twist, and rock and roll used these cultural styles to speak to their local audiences and to help themselves stand out as individuals in a crowd. But the popularity of Elvis, the Beatles, and rock and roll more generally was also part of a transnational youth movement signaling a shift in global consciousness. In the succeeding decades, a new generation of youth who viewed themselves as explicitly "worldly" emerged. United by their resistance to colonialism, racism, the power politics of the Cold War, and to a lesser degree patriarchy, they searched out meaningful alternatives to the existing political and economic order. Experimenting with cultural repertoires was part and parcel of the process, and it often took them beyond the performative. "They sought cultural exchange to enhance their lives," argues Gurnah, and to broaden their mental and political horizons.[33]

NEW GENRES, NICHE MARKETS, AND ENDURING AUDIENCE STANDARDS IN THE 1970s AND 1980s

The youth of Tanzania who came of age after independence had many things in common with there parents, but like many young people across the globe, they were at pains to distinguish themselves from their elders in both stylistic and practical ways. For several generations, going to the movies had been a common form of urban entertainment. But during that era, going to the movies began to take on a new, youthful vibe. In the 1950s and 1960s, moviegoing was the quintessential form of family commercial leisure. In the 1970s and 1980s, many urban youth still went with the extended family to see the blockbuster Indian film on Sunday, but increasingly, if they wanted to be "cool," they also took in a flick with their friends, unchaperoned, from Tuesday through Friday. Khalid was one of many who frequented films with his parents, but once he turned eighteen,

Figure 4.3 *Checkbob* (cool cats), Dar es Salaam, sporting Pecos pants and hairstyles banned in Zanzibar

he began going almost exclusively with members of his cohort. Explaining the change, he said, "I often went once or twice a month with my parents to see Indian films. They had great, meaningful stories that you could understand without knowing the language. But by the 1980s the stories weren't as good and I myself had changed. Now I was spending more time with my friends." Noting the influence of his peers and the larger youth moviegoing culture of the time, he continued, "We young *checkbob* [hip cats], we fancied action films."[34] Bruce Lee, Fred Williamson, Jim Kelly—for young, hip dudes, that was where it was at.

Commensurate with changes in audience demographics were changes in film, both in Tanzania and across the world. In the 1960s and 1970s, the big American and Indian studios were struggling, in part because everlarger segments of their domestic and foreign markets were watching television. US attendance at the movies peaked just after World War II at 82 million, but it had sunk to 20 million by 1960 as a result of the growth of suburbanization and television viewership, as well as the large number of babies being born after the war. With several toddlers at home, young couples had less time, energy, and money to go to the movies. Similar phenomena played out to different degrees the world over, taking a toll on established studios' revenues.[35] But a decade later, these postwar increases in fertility and child survival meant that, globally, youth were far more numerous than ever before. They also had more disposable income and time for commercial leisure than their parents had ever had. Studios everywhere began producing films to specifically cater to this emergent youthful market. Action became more prominent, music more dominant, and those cast in lead roles younger and more politically oppositional. Independent studios also sprang onto the scene and garnered an expanding segment of the global B-movie market. Stylistically, their films were faster, more violent, and more erotic. Kung fu, blaxploitation, "spaghetti westerns," horror, and German erotica were new genres that became more and more prominent and financially successful. These genres all targeted the niche youth markets in the countries where they were produced, but new networks of independent distribution and young people's increasing embrace of the transnational allowed them to quickly become global phenomena.

In the 1970s, American blaxploitation films hit screens across the world, including those in Tanzania. When a Tanzanian respondent named an American actor in my surveys, the name was usually one of the African Americans associated with this genre: Fred Williamson, Richard Roundtree, Jim Kelly, or Pam Grier.[36] Movies in the blaxploitation genre were filled with visual spectacle and action. If most of the dialogue went over the heads of those in the audience, it was not a huge impediment; good and evil were easy enough to discern, and conflicts were resolved through action, not simply through words. The stories in blaxploitation also resonated with young Tanzanians in a way that earlier American films had failed to register with their parents. Struggles against racism, underdevelopment, and police brutality echoed Tanzanians' own 1970s experiences. The depictions of drug abuse, gang violence, and ghetto life that were featured in these films allowed Tanzanians to better appreciate the reasons for the growth of the Black Power movement in the United States and the increase in the number of African Americans, including numerous exiled Black Panthers, taking up residence in Tanzania.

The earliest circulation of these films coincided with the frequent appearance of African American activists in East Africa. Angela Davis, Malcolm X, Stokely Carmichael, Harry Belafonte, and many others gave speeches, held high-level meetings, and went on local tours, all of which were covered prominently in the press. Williamson, Roundtree, Kelly, and Grier became the Black Power activists' fictionalized counterparts. Tanzanians saw visual symmetry between Angela Davis's signature Afro, pantsuits, and commanding presence when she toured the country in 1973 and Pam Grier's no-nonsense character in *Coffy* (Hill, 1973). In that film, Grier is a nurse by day and an unstoppable communal hero by night, fighting to rid her community of heroin, corrupt police, the white mob, and black men who disrespect the women who raise and support them. Like Angela Davis, Coffy is gorgeous, smart, commanding, and determined to transform the world, regardless of personal cost. Talk on the streets and in the press indicated that the revolution was here and now; action on the screen provided vivid visual testament to the potential for both artistic and political black empowerment. Like the protagonists in Indian films, black superheroes were portrayed as powerful but also deeply enmeshed in complicated family and communal struggles. Riveting visual action was also typically accompanied by a stirring R & B, soul, or funk sound track. Thus, although there was a lot that was new and exciting about blaxploitation films, including black actors in lead roles, they also contained key aesthetic and narrative elements that Tanzanians valued in film.

Shaft (Parks, 1971), starring Richard Roundtree, was one of the first films of this genre screened in Tanzania. Backed by the Oscar-winning musical score composed by soul/funk legend Isaac Hayes, John Shaft quickly became an idol in Tanzania. In the film (and its sequels), Roundtree plays the stylish, competent, and sexy private detective. In the first movie, he rescues a Harlem kingpin's daughter from Italian mobsters, and in the third installment of the trilogy, *Shaft in Africa* (Guillermin, 1973), Roundtree's character goes undercover to break up a modern-day slavery ring, trafficking men from Ethiopia for gang labor in France. The sheer physicality and athleticism of Pam Grier, Fred Williamson, and Jim Kelly, who were all accomplished martial artists, also helped inspire a generation of Tanzanians to seriously begin training and building their bodies.

Tanzanian fashions, urban chic, and popular literature were heavily influenced by blaxploitation films. Tanzanian author Eddie Ganzel published numerous popular Kiswahili novels that showed the marked influence of the blaxploitation genre, distinguishing his novels from much of the socialist literature being published in East Africa in the 1970s and early 1980s. His characters ran diamond heists and confronted gangs. They were

163

Figure 4.4 Female compatriots of the *checkbob*, wearing a style of pants known as *bugaluu*, sewn by tailors across the mainland, 1977–78

cool like the black superheroes of the screen. Urban male youth also imitated the slang and strut of the African American stars and incorporated their demeanor into a personal style.[37] For a spell, youth across the country could signal their cool by chomping on a big wad of gum, just like Tony King (who played in *Shaft* and *Hell up in Harlem*). Numerous men who attended these films recounted how they practiced their stance and swagger in front of mirrors and younger siblings before taking them out on the street. Imitations of hip black style seen in *Hell up in Harlem* (Cohen, 1973) also induced mass consumer demand for platform shoes, known as *rizons* (rise on) in Tanzania, as well as shiny nylon shirts and boldly patterned synthetic pants. In *Three the Hard Way* (Parks, 1974), Jim Brown, Fred Williamson, and Jim Kelly, who were all household names in Tanzania, strutted the streets in their glorious 1970s fashions, while undermining a white supremacists' plot to poison the US water supply with a toxin that was lethal only to blacks. Afros also took the youth of the nation by storm, and many young people sported long hair even though that was banned by the ruling parties on the mainland and in the isles.[38] Tailors in Dar es Salaam, Morogoro, and Arusha noted that in the 1970s, they were increasingly being asked to sew pants and pantsuits for their female clientele, who brought them drawings and sketches after films such as Grier's *Black Mama White Mama* (Romero, 1972) and *Foxy Brown* (Hill, 1974) or Tamara Dobson's *Cleopatra Jones* (Starrett, 1973) came to town. Outside the Asian community, few Tanzanian women wore pants before that time, but on the mainland, female compatriots of the checkbob were increasingly donning trousers.

But popular though they were, films such as *Shaft* and *Hell up in Harlem* were hardly the kind of entertainment a couple would take the kids and granny to see. From cabdrivers in Dar es Salaam, barmaids in Arusha, professionals in Dar es Salaam, and casual laborers across the country, I heard vivid renditions of key scenes from such films, but these were movies that people saw with their age-mates, with dates, or alone, not with the extended family. When *Three the Hard Way* traveled the circuit for a second run, in 1982, screenings offered during the daylight hours at the Majestic drew fewer than seventy patrons. When screened on Thursday and Friday at night, however, attendance at each screening more than doubled. Blaxploitation films were always X rated, which might partially explain the low daytime attendance: some people were no doubt reluctant to be seen entering the theater for a matinee. X ratings were awarded not only for nudity but also and more typically for violence and fights with the law. An X rating meant that children under eighteen were denied admission, which only made adolescents and young adults even more eager to see the show. And of course, shots of naked breasts were de rigueur for the blaxploitation genre, and even films that featured strong female leads pandered to misogyny; the opening credits for *Foxy Brown*, for instance, roll for several minutes over close-ups of Pam Grier's breasts, in various states of undress. In addition, gratuitous rape scenes are exceptionally common.[39] According to censorship records and interviews, these scenes may have been shortened by managers and projectionists, but rarely did censors require them to be removed entirely.

A small number of women in Morogoro, Dar es Salaam, and Arusha spoke appreciatively of Pam Grier and Tamara Dobson, but on average, the gender composition of the audience for such films was almost entirely male.[40] The explicit sexuality in these films also meant that they lacked the multigenerational appeal that would allow them to be reeled to several theaters for simultaneous release. On its third run through Zanzibar, in 1979, *Foxy Brown* could still draw a respectable 1,000 fans to the Majestic over five shows. When *Hell up in Harlem* made a similar run that same year, it sold an impressive 688 tickets for three shows on a Wednesday night and another 1,100 tickets by the end of the week. According to the manager, there was not a single Zanzibari woman in the crowd. The same week that *Hell up in Harlem* ran, however, the second-run showing of *Adha Din Adhi Raat* (Doondi, 1977) sold more than three times as many tickets in a

165

single day. The Indian film's appeal across demographics meant that it was reeled to the 400-seat Empire Cinema at the same time that it was showing at the 750-seat Majestic. Even the most popular of American genres was no match for the popularity of Indian films, which appealed to men, women, and children of all ages.

Through the 1960s and 1970s, the main supplier of the major US studios, Anglo-American Film Distributors Ltd., had an on-again, off-again relationship with Tanzania. Shortly after independence, Tanzanian officials briefly halted all imports from the company because of its legal incorporation in South Africa. Tanzania had resolved not to do business with corporations benefiting from apartheid. Anglo-American then moved much of its Africa operation to Nairobi in the early 1960s. But when Tanzania nationalized film distribution in the 1970s, Anglo-American stopped supplying films to Tanzania to protest the principle of nationalization and the sudden increase in fees charged by the state for the right to do business in the country. These sudden, though short-lived, withdrawals left large voids in exhibitors' schedules, which independent Tanzanian importers quickly moved to fill. A growing number of films from Italy, including action films such as *Ursus* (Campogalliani, 1961) and *Ten Gladiators* (Parolini, 1963), were soon added to the bills. Risqué Italian titles such as *When Women Had Tails* (Campanile, 1970) and *Lady Medic on Maneuver* (Cicero, 1977) or any number of films containing the words "*World by Night*"—which featured strippers and exotic dancers from port cities across the globe—came to replace spots on marquees previously occupied by the films of MGM, Columbia, and 20th Century Fox.[41] By 1972, the proportion of American films screened in Tanzania dropped precipitously to a mere 17 percent, whereas Italian films rose to 40 percent of imports. With the exception of the drive-in cinema, which often received its movies directly from Nairobi, independent Tanzanian importers maintained most of the market share they developed during the years of struggle between Anglo-American and Tanzania Film Company. In the mid-1970s, the first Hong Kong films made their way into the Tanzanian market, which cut further into the US share of screen time. By 1977, the proportion of films screened in Tanzania that were made by US major producers had dropped to a mere 5.5 percent.[42]

Italian films were introduced to the country beginning in the 1950s by A. M. Thaver, of Indo-African Theaters (which was formally incorporated as United Film Distributors in 1958): *The Bicycle Thief* (De Sica, 1948) and *Anna* (Lattuada, 1951) were two of the first. Tanzanians gave them a cool reception. Only when the distributors began importing Italian westerns a few years later did they hit on a genre of Italian film that drew Tanzanians to the theaters. This new genre had all the elements local audiences demanded in good film: emotionality, ceaseless visual action, music, and an underclass hero. Created in the early 1960s as knock-offs of American westerns, spaghetti westerns really came into their own by the middle of the decade after the success of films by Sergio Leone.[43] Long-standing trade barriers and Hollywood monopolies of US theater chains kept the Italian films off American screens, but these movies took much of the rest of the world by storm, including Tanzania.

In 1966, United Film Distributors imported *One Silver Dollar* (Ferroni, 1965), which was screened across East Africa; a decade later, it was still being shown to appreciative crowds.[44] This was one of the rare non-Indian films that people said they never tired of seeing. An African cabdriver in Dar es Salaam, nicknamed Mr. India because of his knowledge of the Hindi language (which he said he learned from film), saw *One Silver Dollar* for the first time when he was a young man still living in Zanzibar, in 1966. After moving to Dar es Salaam six years later, he went to see the film repeatedly. He was far from alone. *One Silver Dollar*'s star, Giuliano Gemma, was the most frequently named Western actor in my surveys, and many said they saw his films numerous times. Four years after *One Silver Dollar*'s Tanzanian debut, the Empire Cinema in Dar es Salaam ran the film for three shows per day for four days per week, Wednesday through Saturday. Even with such generous amounts of screen time, the movie ad in the newspaper warned fans that "early booking [is] essential."[45]

In 1965, Gemma also starred in *A Pistol for Ringo* (Tessari, 1965) and *Adios Gringo* (Stegani, 1965), the latter of which also ran for four shows each day for an entire week at the Empire in June 1966.[46] Such extended runs were rare in Tanzanian theaters, where films typically changed three or four times a week. In *Adios Gringo*, Gemma plays an honest young man who is framed for murder by a man who stole his land. He narrowly escapes mob violence, and while on the run, he encounters, saves, and falls in love with a helpless, gorgeous woman who has been ruthlessly gang-raped and left in the desert to rot. One of the rapists is the son of a wealthy land baron, who bribes authorities to suit his needs. The homosocial world depicted

167

in these westerns, where women rarely appear except as victims of sexual violence or as fleeting objects of desire, resonated in and reinforced the male bonding that went on during screenings of these shows. In an audience where nary a woman was present, young men were free to hoot and holler or fight and swear to their hearts' content. According to those who attended, this was one of the great joys and particular pleasures of going to these movies. Men who frequented the cinemas in the late 1960s and early 1970s were far more likely than those from the previous generation to name a western star among their favorites. The most popular were Giuliano Gemma, Franco Nero, and Fernando Sancho. It is worth noting that not a single woman listed these stars among their favorites, nor did they mention a western of any type as one of the best films of all time. Westerns were a man's genre.

By the late 1960s, Tanzania was importing fifty or sixty of these films a year. A decade later, Italian films—which included far more than westerns but contained many similar aesthetic, narrative, and voyeuristic elements—accounted for some 40 percent of all screen time. Comparing Italian westerns to those made in Hollywood, a film reviewer and correspondent for the *Sunday News* in Dar es Salaam said the former made Hollywood "look pallid." Quoting the Italian director Sergio Corbucci, he added that the Italians "'have improved the American Western by removing all the boring parts [including] all that talk, talk, talk.' The result is pure action which pins the audience to its seat from beginning to end." The film Corbucci was working on at the time featured 150 killings in a 114-page script.[47] Action filled the screen. But like Indian films, Italian westerns also included stunning musical scores, as well as gorgeous and sensitive male stars. Protagonists were pushed to violence only as a last resort when the authorities failed to protect the ones they loved.[48]

The violent bravado expressed by the crowds viewing Italian westerns perhaps reflected some men's subconscious response to the pain and trauma they and their loved ones endured at the hands of a violent and marauding postcolonial state. The hero's ability to exact retribution was no doubt also appealing. In Zanzibar, *My Name Is Pecos* (Lucidi, 1967) achieved cult status among young, male audiences. It also was the most frequently named favorite film of the western genre in the isles. Its plot has many parallels to the violence experienced in 1964, when wanton rape and murder were carried out in the name of revolution. In the film,

Figure 4.5 *My Name Is Pecos* screen shot of Giuliano Gemma wearing the original Pecos pants

Pecos (played by Giuliano Gemma) returns to the village of his youth to track down a man who is now the leading politician, a man who had sadistically murdered his parents years earlier.[49] In his quest for vengeance, the hero leaves a trail of bodies belonging to those who directly or indirectly aided in his parents' murder. The ruling political, economic, and religious authorities are portrayed as gangsters and thugs, all of whom are eliminated by the protagonist. Pecos was many a young man's hero in Zanzibar. *Texas Adios* (Baldi, 1966), starring another frequently named favorite actor from this genre, Franco Nero, also centered around the hero's hunt for the man who stole his family's land and then murdered his father when the hero was young. In 1972, these Italian westerns sold an average of 120 tickets per show at the Majestic, although a double feature

169

of *The Legion of the Damned* (Lenzi, 1969) and *The Price of Power* (Velerii, 1969), which was about a plot to assassinate the president—ironically
screened just a week before Zanzibar's President Abeid Amani Karume
was assassinated—drew 800 fans over two shows when screened on a Saturday night. Given the plots, visual action, and male bonding that were
all part of the experience, it is perhaps not surprising that these westerns
were so popular.

The assaults on young men that were occurring in Zanzibar at the
time, conducted by police and Afro-Shirazi Party (ASP) members, only increased the oppositional politics and generational male bonding that took
place inside the theaters. According to Gary Thomas Burgess, between
1969 and 1976 hundreds, if not thousands, of young men were assaulted on
the streets, in schools, and at the cinemas by members of the party's Youth
League ostensibly because they wore bell-bottoms and Afros.[50] For their
"offenses," they were beaten, stripped, shorn, and arrested. Most of the
young men in Zanzibar who idolized Pecos never directly confronted the
state or the men who killed their loved ones, raped their mothers and sisters, or sent their friends and neighbors rushing into exile. Instead they adopted the fashion known as "Pecos pants," inspired by the movie hero's wide-
legged leather chaps. In 1991, while sifting through a High Court storeroom
of unarchived files, I came across a pile of cases, easily three feet high and
three feet wide, related to the unlawful wearing of Pecos pants and Afros.
Nearly every defendant was convicted, and repeat offenders were sent for
"reeducation" and hard labor at the state penitentiary. Fashion was at times
quite political.

In the 1970s, Hong Kong became a major new source of films for the
global market and one that was attractive to both Tanzanian importers and
urban (especially male) youth. In a few towns with multiple cinemas, one
theater was known explicitly for screening Hong Kong action films, which
were principally of the kung fu genre. In Zanzibar, the Majestic was where
young men gathered; in Dar es Salaam, it was the Empire; in Arusha the
Metropole; in Morogoro the Sapna; and in Moshi the ABC. In other towns
with more than one theater, exhibitors sometimes took turns screening
these films, depending on the desires of managers and the interests of the
town's overall clientele. In the 1970s, action films were most likely to draw
a solid crowd on nights that were otherwise fairly slow: Monday through
Thursday. At the Majestic, midweek ticket sales for kung fu films ranged

between 150 and 250 a show. If a film with actors known for their martial arts talents was shown on a Friday or Saturday night, it could sell as many as 500 tickets. The proportion of screen time devoted to films from Hong Kong at the Majestic grew from a mere 3 percent in 1975 to 25 percent by the early 1980s, eventually stabilizing at roughly 18 percent throughout the remainder of the decade.[51] Hong Kong films starring African American martial artists—such as Ron Van Clief in *Way of the Black Dragon* (Chen, 1979) or the ever-popular Jim Kelly, who costarred alongside Bruce Lee in *Enter the Dragon* (Clouse, 1973)—were known to easily sell out the 535-seat Empire in Dar es Salaam, forcing some patrons to sit in the aisles or stand at the back of the theater to watch the film.[52]

Young Tanzanian audiences loved martial arts films, but again, their love was not unconditional. As with every genre, certain actors, stories, and styles were definitely preferred over others. As Feroz, an exhibitor in Iringa, said, "I could earn twenty times as much showing a blockbuster hit, like *Super Ninja* [Wu, 1984], as a low-grade film like *Snake in Monkey's Shadow* [Cheung, 1979]."[53] Pankaj, an exhibitor from Morogoro, concurred: "We had people who were addicts, I tell you, this was their hobby and they would never miss a show. You know, some guys have to have their beer after work every day, these guys had to have their cinema. . . . But for most of the audience members there were definite preferences." According to Pankaj, Bruce Lee and his numerous imitators, known locally as Bruce "Lie," were far more popular than others. "You would pay more for a Bruce Lee film," he said, "but you would earn more too."[54] During interviews and surveys, respondents were nearly unanimous in saying that they preferred realistic visual spectacle—such as the stunts and fights of Bruce Lee—to "fakey special effects"—as offered by Jackie Chan.[55] Watching accomplished martial artists in action was also greatly preferred to camera tricks and guts and gore.

Figure 4.6 *Clones of Bruce Lee* ad

Nonetheless, it was still Indian films that stole the show. In 1978, Hong Kong films drew an average crowd of 280 patrons per show to the Majestic Cinema in Zanzibar and most certainly an even larger number to the Empire Cinema in Dar es Salaam. Yet nearly 50 percent more people attended the average Indian film. Among the best-attended films at the Majestic in 1982 were *Bruce Lee in New Guinea* (Yang, 1978), *Khoon Aur Pani* (Chand, 1981), and *Dada* (Kishore, 1979). The highest attendance for a single showing of Hong Kong's *Bruce Lee in New Guinea* was 261, whereas the two Indian films drew crowds of 668 and 680, respectively.[56] *Bruce Lee in New Guinea* definitely had repeat value: it ran for seven shows over the course of a week, drawing a total of 1,148 patrons to the theater. But *Khoon Aur Pani* played only one night, in two shows, and brought nearly 1,300 patrons to the Majestic. The film was also reeled to Zanzibar's two other theaters, where it opened on the same night.

During a typical three-month period between 1972 and 1982, seven or more Hindi films filled or nearly filled the Majestic. During that same decade, there was only one kung fu film that came anywhere close to selling out: *Bruce Lee I Love You* (Lo, 1976), a biography told from the perspective of Bruce's mistress, in whose apartment Lee died in 1973. The film sold a record 1,180 tickets for three shows when it opened on a Monday over the New Year's holidays, a clear rival to the Indian film *Fakira* (Dixit, 1976), which played on New Year's Day. Some 1,450 fans watched *Fakira* at the Majestic, but it was also reeled to the Empire and Cine Afrique theaters, which suggests that more than 3,400 people in Zanzibar were talking about the film the next day. With three more shows over the next two weeks, *Bruce Lee I Love You* sold another 380 tickets—a good total for midweek repeat showings but less than one-third of the revenue earned by the Indian film screened under similar circumstances.[57] Kung fu films were certainly popular, but their appeal was limited to a small slice of the general cinema audience, composed largely of young men, whereas Indian films appealed across boundaries of age, class, and gender. Bruce Lee was named by many as a favorite actor during the years when action reigned, but in surveys throughout the country, Amitabh Bachchan, who also did his own stunts, outranked Lee by a six-to-one margin. James Bond, Jim Kelly, and Giuliano Gemma, though popular, garnered only one vote for every ten cast for Bachchan.

In the 1970s and 1980s, Indian filmmakers also began to feature physical action, violent visual spectacle, and revenge in their productions. Melodramatic depictions of love triangles, siblings separated at birth, or families torn asunder by wealthy and politically powerful villains were key elements of plot progression, but action, explosions, fights, and violence increasingly supplemented the song-and-dance numbers that punctuated films.

Khoon Aur Pani, for instance, incorporates action and revenge into its story and visual imagery as a way of addressing changing audience interests and demographics. When a poor farmer diverts some water from the supplies hoarded by a wealthy land baron to save his drought-stricken fields and family, the wealthy neighbor has the farmer killed before his children's eyes. One son grows up to be a much-feared dacoit who protects the poor and victimized and takes revenge on the wealthy and powerful. In one scene, he bursts into a heavily guarded wedding to rescue a reluctant bride who is being forced to marry an old man to whom her father is in debt. In the course of rescuing the young woman, the hero and his band defeat the police guarding the wedding and steal their guns. One of the other main protagonists is a gun-totting, motorcycle-riding, female bounty hunter. By the 1980s, Indian action-oriented superheroes are no longer bound by gender. Everywhere, women's roles and character types in films are expanding at this time. But in Indian films, nonconforming, physically strong women can all still sing and dance. The sound track to *Khoon Aur Pani* boasts four top-grossing Bollywood hits. Thus, even those who attended musical melodramas with the family on Sundays got their fill of action in the 1980s.

By the mid-1970s, state agents emerge as central villains in Indian films. Police and politicians are identified as enablers and profiteers benefiting from economic and political corruption—or more directly as the assailants who molest the hero's mother, wife, or child. In India and Tanzania, anger and frustration fostered by widespread corruption and mismanagement by bureaucrats, politicians, and the police would find artistic release at the theater. In this context of fading hope for the social equality and justice promised by nationalists at independence, Amitabh Bachchan's "angry young man" becomes a national hero, giving brilliant fictionalized representation to a new generation's frustrations and desires for change. In all of Bachchan's films, his characters unveil corruption, misogyny, and naked profiteering. But rather than relying on the law and courts, these characters either take the law into their own hands or orchestrate mass civil action to set things right.[58]

173

Bachchan has starred in over two hundred films. His characters have ranged from the romantic, comic, and patriarchal to the angry young man roles in the 1970s and 1980s that catapulted him to the top of the charts. The first of his films in this genre was *Zanjeer* (Mehra, 1973), in which Bachchan grows from a young boy who witnesses the murder of his parents to an honest police inspector, Vijay, who fights gangs, gamblers, murderers, and corruption within the police force in an effort to atone for his parents' deaths. Over the next decade, Bachchan starred in more than fifty films, often playing a character named Vijay, an underclass hero living in the teeming slums who is forced to chose between moral duty, justice, and family loyalty or the easy money offered by gangs, drug lords, and politicians. Like Raj Kapoor's films, Bachchan's movies foreground class inequality perpetuated and intensified by law. They also highlight the ethical superiority of individuals most reviled by society and the moral bankruptcy of the wealthiest and most powerful. Every Bachchan film from that era that was imported into Tanzania (and there were many) scored big at the box office.

Bachchan's films were frequently named by those who went to the movies in the 1970s and 1980s as among the best of the era. One title that was mentioned often was *Coolie* (Desai, 1983), in which Bachchan plays a humble and hardworking baggage handler at a train station, whose family and community are destroyed during his childhood by a wealthy and evil man who blows up a dam and floods their region because Bachchan's mother has refused to be his mistress. As an adult, Bachchan's character leads a labor strike to improve conditions for the workers, but soon, corrupt politicians, bankers, and land barons unite in an effort to ruin his happiness once again. It turns out that Bachchan's mother, played by Waheeda Rehman (whom Tanzanians also adored), was abducted by the villain haunting Bachchan's life. After he destroys their village, the villain kidnaps Waheeda's character and forces her to live as his wife. She suffers amnesia after the fateful events that destroy her family, and to ensure that she never remembers, the villain has her treated with electroshock therapy in a mental hospital. He also gives her another stolen child to raise, in order to ease her maternal longing. As an adult, this son unites with Bachchan's coolie to uncover the plots of the evil villain and the politicians who profit from the destruction of other's lives. Despite the political core of the film, Bachchan's character wins the hearts of both the girl in the film and the

Tanzanian masses through his songs about the pain and pride of the working class and his enduring love for family and community.[59]

Thus, even as Indian movies changed in the 1970s and 1980s to meet the shifting demographics of moviegoers and to cater to the new cinematic emphasis on visual spectacle and explosive special effects, they remained true to the underlying elements that made them popular in East Africa over the years. Love, both romantic and filial, remains central and heroes and heroines continue to sing and dance, while villains never utter a musical note. The popularity of the sound track also helped maintain the film in people's memories. Twenty-five years after the movie's release, an interviewee named Amour began to hum a tune from the film and was immediately transported back to the day he first saw *Coolie*. I had never seen the movie when he first mentioned it, but he would not rest until he secured a VHS copy so I could see for myself why he considered this one of the best films ever made. We watched it together, and he offered extensive comments both on the film and on audience reactions during its initial run through Zanzibar. I then took it home to watch it again, and for the next ten days, every time I walked into the family sitting room—morning, noon, or night—some members of the household were watching the film. Regardless of gender or age, every family member viewed all or parts of it at least three times, often inviting friends, other relatives, and neighbors to join them and reexperience the joys of one of the greatest films ever made. Powerful acting, immensely talented stars, fabulous music, stirring anguish, relentless struggle, and the narrative perspective of the poor and humble combined to make this an unforgettable movie in households across the land.

Given the overwhelming evidence that Indian movies drew the largest crowds to the theaters and earned the greatest returns at the box office, why were these films not shown more often? Why didn't operators screen Indian films five or even seven days a week? The answer is rather complicated and requires attention to issues beyond film and audience preferences. A host of social, cultural, and economic factors came into play when deciding what to screen. For one, although Indian films had broad appeal, the leisure time available to most moviegoers was rather limited. Older men and women, in particular, had other, more pressing things to do than devote their days to watching three-hour-long films. From early in the colonial era, Sunday was the official day off in Tanzania. Offices and many businesses and shops were closed. Sundays were when people had time to relax and enjoy the leisure pursuits of their choice, including taking in a show. For many, discretionary income was also limited. Ticket prices, wages, and income opportunities often precluded indulging in commercial leisure of this kind more than one day a week. Young men of the postcolonial generation were one group to which this general rule least applied. A third factor was that, socially and culturally, "going out"—being part of a large crowd and a participant in the hottest event in town—was as important to many Tanzanians as what film was being shown. Exhibitors and distributors played into these desires, restricting the number of days when popular films were screened in order to help generate the largest possible turnout on Sunday.

Indian films were also expensive to import. Prices began rising in the 1950s and climbed substantially in the first decades after independence. This was one major economic factor contributing to the growth in reeling between 1960 and 1975. In the late 1970s and early 1980s, Tanzanian importers might pay $25,000 to $30,000 for a single print and the East African and Zambian distribution rights for a great film, such as *Disco Dancer* (Subhash, 1982) starring Mithun Chakraborty or Amitabh Bachchan's *Amar, Akbar, Anthony* (Desai, 1977). For the price of one Indian blockbuster, they could purchase five or six action films from Hong Kong, Italy, or independent distributors in the United States.[60] Importers and exhibitors had to be continually strategizing and balancing; there was no guarantee that they could break even, let alone turn a profit. The aim was to maximize ticket sales and encourage the most diverse slice of the public to attend the show, and this was best achieved by offering a range of movies on different days. I was repeatedly told by both exhibitors and distributors that they strove to satisfy as many kinds of customers as possible, not just those who paid the most for tickets. Providing exciting films for the masses was more important to them than showing expensive productions, at high prices, to a few.

The formula for sharing profits between importers/distributors and exhibitors also factored into the equation. Exhibitors sometimes earned more money per film by showing repeat kung fu movies, where they got to keep 50 to 60 percent of the box office earnings, than they did by showing

Figure 4.7 *Disco Dancer* (Subhash, 1982), starring Mithun Chakraborty, was a global sensation and a super-hit in Tanzania, riding a wave of enthusiasm for disco among urban youth. Propelled by an immensely popular soundtrack, it signaled for many Tanzanians a revolution in Hindi filmmaking, modernizing production and dance styles in a new idiom while presenting traditional Hindi film themes about family loyalty and the struggles of the poor.

first-release Indian films, where they only retained 30 percent of the money taken at the door. For example, when the Majestic closed out its accounts in 1978, it was found that after several weeks of running *Infernal Street* (Shen, 1973), a Hong Kong film about Chinese doctors who fight the morphine-dealing criminals running a Japanese nightclub, the theater earned TSh 2,890 ($390). The repeat run of *Jaws* that same month earned the Majestic TSh 4,268 ($575). Earnings from *Alaap* (Mukherjee, 1977), a family drama in which Amitabh Bachchan plays a rebellious son who prefers the slums and the company of a courtesan to the comforts of his father's home and the dignity of practicing law, were only TSh 1,420 ($192), even though it sold out the Majestic. Granted, *Alaap* showed only for one day and *Infernal Street* and *Jaws* for several, but the difference between keeping 30 percent and 50 to 60 percent of the gate was substantial. At the end of a typical month, however, the Majestic earned significantly more from Indian movies overall. Hollywood and Hong Kong films with the repeat potential of *Jaws* or *Infernal Street* were rare, but Indian films could always draw. It took a range of different types of films, with varied individual profit margins, to run a successful business. As Abdul explained, "You do make good money off of the repeats, so you don't complain about this. But you can't show repeats all the time, people will get tired. They want new films too, and to keep them interested you give them what they want."[61]

177

Repeats could also be screened for special matinee shows, which substantially bolstered the exhibitor's bottom line. Known in Zanzibar as "one-shilling-all-around" shows because all the seats in the theater were sold for the same low price, these matinees stand tall in urban memories. Beginning in the 1960s and continuing well into the 1970s, they typically featured action films and often filled 75 to 80 percent of a theater. For the boys and young men who frequented one-shilling-all-around shows, these matinees generated nearly as much excitement as the Sunday shows did for the community at large. In Zanzibar, repeat Indian films were also sometimes screened for ladies' show versions of the one-shilling-all-around. Tickets sold at this price were exempt from state taxes and levies, which encouraged exhibitors to dispense with issuing tickets. This added to the showtime craziness and the crush at the door, but the melee was a vital part of the adventure associated with the one-shilling-all-around. With no written records of admission, exhibitors were free to minimize the earnings they reported to distributors, if they reported earnings at all. Repeat films that were pulled from storage and screened at nearly giveaway prices went a long way toward improving the bottom line: if an exhibitor ran three of these shows each month, he could pocket, off the books, nearly as much as he earned from a Sunday first-run film. Varying the types of movies shown and catering to a diversity of crowds—willing and able to pay a variety of prices for entertainment—allowed exhibitors to earn the love and adoration of a wide swath of the public. And as chapter 8 details, when exhibitors' profit margins became increasingly marginal after nationalization, "extra money" and love from the community became all the more significant to exhibitors' lives.

Chapter 5

CINEMAS, CITIES, AND AUDIENCES

Cultural Geographies and Social Difference at the Show

THROUGHOUT MUCH of Tanzania's history, mass moviegoing was largely a coastal phenomenon. From the cultural and commercial epicenter of Zanzibar, cinemas spread across the region in the 1910s and 1920s, but the northern Swahili coast remained the most fertile ground for movie houses to take root and for audiences to grow. (See map I.1.) By the 1930s, twelve permanent cinemas were operating in Zanzibar, Pemba, Tanga, and Dar es Salaam, but in the remainder of the territory, there were only a few other towns where someone could see a moving picture—and often only periodically or in venues primarily used for other purposes. Up-country audiences no doubt found it easier to access cinematic pleasures after World War II, but the people along the coast continued to enjoy a privileged position in this regard. In the 1960s, half of the nation's cinemas were still located along the coast. And as the wealth and cultural power of the capital city grew, Dar es Salaam became home to one-quarter of the theaters in the country.[1]

What accounts for these differences in cinematic geography? And why do they persist over time? Chapter 1 offered a partial answer, exploring such questions from the perspective of entrepreneurs and capital. Here, we will examine the issue from the perspective of the audience. The argument is that understanding where cinemas were built and when tells us about Tanzanians' relationships not only with motion pictures but also with cities. Unpacking the cinematic map reveals a good deal about urban life overall. Africans' access to housing and cash income opportunities as well as their freedom to move across urban space directly impacted their ability to participate in the commercial leisure activity of moviegoing. In addition, the perspectives and power of local elders, religious authorities, and colonial officials regarding the morality of films affected people's willingness to take in a show. In certain places, cinemas had an immoral taint simply by virtue of being located in cities, which themselves were seen by some to be of dubious, if not outright dangerous, virtue. As Kathryn Fuller has found in her analysis of small-town audiences in the United States, "Geography, racial and ethnic prejudice, poverty, religion and local customs, and expectations about gender roles determined who went to the movies and how often."[2] Tanzanian cities varied enormously; they had different origins, forms, norms, and functions,[3] and these factors all affected the moviegoing culture and the relative passion for film that permeated populations in different towns.

Cinemagoing drew a larger and more diverse range of people together than any other activity (except perhaps going to the market), but at the same time, it allowed a patron to articulate difference and embody his or her sense of self. At the movies, one could often see great diversity—men and women; youth and elders; Muslims, Hindus, and Christians; Africans, Arabs, Asians, and a few Europeans; and the rich, the poor, and the middle class. Differences of race, class, gender, and generation were mitigated to some degree by collective entrance into the same social sphere, but inside the theater, social divisions were also written into the cinematic space and the bodies that occupied it. There were usually three or four different seat prices, so where one sat both expressed and reinforced class distinctions. Patrons with money sat farthest from the screen or in the balcony if there was one. Those with less money sat in front. Moviegoers were quite adamant about sitting in "their" section, which enhanced black marketers' ability to scalp tickets for the first-class seats. But even poor young men staked their territory in the cinema—in the rows closest to the screen—and few women or elders transgressed their bounds. In Zanzibar and Dar es Salaam, women also had the zanana, or ladies' show, which allowed females in purdah or those who preferred to socialize exclusively with other women to claim entire theaters for themselves. Accessing cinematic space was one means by which people became cognizant of their genders, and the movie theater was one of the key urban spaces where gendered identities were publicly performed.

COLONIALISM AND AFRICAN ATTENDANCE

The isles of Zanzibar and Pemba were not only the sites of the earliest cinemas in Tanzania, they were also home to the most enthusiastic moviegoers in the country. In the 1920s and early 1930s, the average weekly attendance in the isles was 4,200, four times the number then going to the show in the mainland capital, Dar es Salaam.[4] Compared to up-country attendance, however, Dar es Salaam's audiences were huge. In the early 1930s, for instance, weekly attendance in Mwanza amounted to only 150, that in Arusha a mere 50.[5] Although the isles were only a fraction of the size and population of the mainland, before the war more than twice as many people went to the movies each week in Zanzibar and Pemba as in the entire mainland territory combined.

The reasons for these remarkable differences in audience size are complex, and in many ways, they had little or nothing to do with people's appreciation for the thrills of moving pictures. The degree to which Africans felt themselves to be "legitimate" residents of the towns, with the right to walk the streets at night and fully enjoy urban leisure, was a critical factor influencing attendance at the show. Africans' claims to urban space were often strongest in cities and town that predated the arrival of Europeans. When motion pictures hit the town in Zanzibar and Pemba, local residents flocked to theaters in large numbers, just as they always had for the ngoma, taarab, and *beni* musical shows and competitions that regularly drew hundreds into the urban streets and squares each night. Tanga and Tabora, which were also vibrant market towns in the precolonial era, each had four hundred to five hundred people attending movies each week, whereas proprietors in Moshi were lucky to sell forty tickets a few nights each month.[6] To be sure, up-country residents also reveled in the delights of music and leisure, but by and large, such interests were pursued in rural, rather than urban, spaces. As late as the 1950s, the number of permits issued to Africans

181

for dance and music celebrations in the town of Moshi for an entire month was less than the number issued in Zanzibar for one night.[7] That does not mean the people in Moshi never danced or partied—they just did not do a lot of it in town after dark. This in turn impacted attendance at the shows. People from the coast typically went to the movies far more regularly, in much greater numbers, and at an earlier time both in history and in their individual lives than those who lived up-country. One of the pivotal questions driving this chapter is, Why?

Although urban population size was one factor that influenced the crowds attending the show, it was not the most important. The size of the urban population cannot, for example, explain why the towns of Wete and Chake-Chake on Pemba, each with under 2,000 residents, had more people going to the show each week in the 1930s than Dar es Salaam, whose population was 33,000.[8] Nor can it explain why Tabora, with an urban population of 12,500—the third largest on the mainland—could only keep a single cinema afloat during the earliest period for two years, from 1929 to 1931, whereas Tanga, with a slightly smaller urban population of 11,000, had enough patrons to keep two and eventually three cinemas in business during the 1930s. By the 1940s, Moshi, Arusha, Iringa, and Dodoma had populations equal to or greater than those of Pemba's towns, but combined ticket sales for an entire month in those towns were significantly less than the total attendance at the movies in Pemba in a single week.[9] Obviously, population alone cannot explain these differences in audience size. Local leisure cultures and the relative degree of colonial power in various towns were far more significant factors.

In Zanzibar and Pemba, the urban populations were large and racially mixed long before the British claimed the territories in 1890. In the Zanzibar Protectorate, which was administered separately from the Tanganyika Territory and the Kenya Colony, British policies of segregating and restricting African mobility, living, and leisure patterns were comparatively lax. Colonial authorities in Zanzibar certainly fretted as much as any about the allegedly immoral impact of movies on the "child-like minds" of African audiences, but in the isles, they were far less successful in keeping Africans from going to the show. In fact, they never even tried. The earliest records of attendance in Zanzibar, dating to 1926, note that Africans constituted half of those going to the theaters, with Asians (46 percent) and Arabs (4 percent) making up the remainder of the audience.[10] In the

1940s, Africans constituted a full 75 percent of attendees at the movies in Zanzibar.[11] By the time the British wrote their first report on cinemas and censorship and began contemplating restricting access to the show, Zanzibaris had been watching moving pictures for a generation: putting an end to a habit that was well ingrained was a losing battle. Moreover, in the late 1920s the colonial administration was already engaged in a number of extremely explosive battles with island residents over substantive changes in land policy, currency, export crop prices, and religious law. Zanzibaris did not take kindly to British efforts to transform their social and economic lives; they responded with mass jailbreaks, riots at the courts, and the murder of a colonial official at the central market. In this context, the call by censors to restrict African access to the movies was a very low administrative priority.[12]

On the mainland, the colonial authorities made a much more concerted effort to keep Africans out of commercial theaters. The British assumed control of the Tanganyika Territory from the Germans after World War I, just as a moral panic over the influence of movies on children was building toward a crescendo in Britain. Believing that the mind of an adult African never developed beyond the stage of a British adolescent, colonial censors sought to keep Africans from watching any films they would not allow their own children to see.[13] As the rules of censorship were written in the 1920s and 1930s, the classifications delineated what was appropriate for all, what was appropriate for none, and what was appropriate for "nonnative" audiences only. Members of the censorship board in Dar es Salaam took their new role as the moral guardians of African leisure quite seriously. They were known to be strict and less than generous in their assessment of films that supposedly would be harmful to natives.[14] As a result, films passed by censors in India, Burma, South Africa, Kenya, Uganda, and Zanzibar were sometimes banned in Dar es Salaam. The police and censors worked in tandem to restrict African access to the movies in the mainland capital: they were in constant dialogue about the potential for films to inspire a breach of public order, and if Africans were banned from a particular film, the late-night policing of streets surrounding the cinemas intensified.

But even with police support, colonial authorities had a difficult time enforcing their restrictions and faced opposition on numerous fronts. Africans continued to arrive at the theaters eager to purchase tickets, and Jariwalla and his managers complied with their requests, seeing little reason to

183

turn paying customers away. Jariwalla owned cinemas in Zanzibar, Nairobi, and Dar es Salaam and was thus acutely aware of the difference racialized restrictions on attendance made to his theaters' bottom lines. In Zanzibar, where there were no restrictions on African attendance, his theaters were frequently filled. In stark contrast, his theater in Kenya, which had the most draconian system of racial segregation in the region, rarely sold tickets for more than 30 percent of its seats.[15] As both a businessman and a citizen, Jariwalla worked to push the new colonial overlords in Dar es Salaam closer to the policies in the isles, and he actively encouraged African attendance at the show. Pricing was one strategy he used to attract African moviegoers. In two of his smaller theaters, the New Cinema and the Bharat/Globe, he offered seats for as little as ten cents, and even at his picture palace, the Empire, one-third of the seats were attractively priced for average laborers. He also built bridges to the African activist community, offering the African Association the use of his Globe Theater in 1935 for a fund-raiser to aid Ethiopia in its fight against Italian aggression, to which the British were turning a diplomatic blind eye.[16] Jariwalla also directly engaged the highest levels of the colonial administration in dialogue, attempting to persuade them to eliminate race as a criterion for film certification.

Censorship was an extremely heated political issue in Dar es Salaam.[17] Disputes over films led to mass dissatisfaction with authorities and embroiled officials in seemingly endless struggles with local businesspeople and fans. In one case in 1930, Jariwalla offered to let an Asian sports club use the Empire Cinema for a fund-raiser. Over a thousand tickets were sold, at the hefty price of five shillings apiece, suggesting that the event would be a smashing success. But then, the censors attempted to ban the scheduled film. The town was in an uproar. A spate of meetings took place over several days between interested parties, including the commissioner of police, members of the board of censors, Jariwalla, and a hundred members of various Asian organizations in Dar es Salaam. An incredible amount of professional time and energy was expended negotiating over the "appropriateness" of the chosen film, *The Light of Asia*, a biography of Buddha; organizers were sure it would pass muster with the censors, since it had already been approved by similar colonial censor boards in Zanzibar, Tanga, India, Burma, Kenya, South Africa, and Uganda. But rumors about the movie—circulated by people who had never seen it—led to trouble in Dar es Salaam. Ultimately, the censors relented and allowed a public screening of the film, but because they had taken up the scheduled evening screening time with their own viewing and debates, half of those who had purchased tickets and donated to the charity event were turned away at the nine o'clock show. Riding the wave of discontent, delegates from the African community went to the district officer that same week to press for the elimination of race as a criterion for exclusion.

The African Association, based in Dar es Salaam, was another thorn in the administration's side when it came to censorship. Between 1930 and 1935, the organization sent endless delegations to the offices of relevant officials and submitted numerous written petitions demanding the elimination of race as a criterion in censorship. They pointed out that in Dar es Salaam too, Africans had been going to the show for nearly a generation before the British tried to curtail their access to this pleasure by forming the censorship board in 1929. A year after the board was formed, a deputation from the African Association visited the district officer to try to convince him that racialized distinctions were utterly arbitrary, particularly along the mixed-race Swahili coast where many men who were considered Arabs had African mothers and were married to African wives. When that approach failed, they pointed to the absurdity of equating mental capacity with race, arguing that civilized, literate, well-heeled African men—like themselves—were intellectually and emotionally more mature than Asian and Arab common laborers, who were not barred from films. They argued that class and education, not race, could be legitimate criteria for admission. In later appeals, they continued to press the point, requesting that "educated natives [of] good character" be granted special permits to allow them into films rated for nonnatives only. The cinema licensing board refused all requests.[18]

In the early 1930s, Africans were legally barred from roughly one in three films screened in Dar es Salaam, and many found it not only annoying but also embarrassing to be turned away at the ticket window. Suleiman Bajuma wrote a letter (which apparently was never published) to the government-run Swahili-language newspaper, *Mambo Leo*, complaining of such a fate. He also objected to the offensive Kiswahili translation of the censorship regulations stating *"Mshenzi Asiruhusiwe"* (No barbarian shall be admitted), thus equating being African with a host of unsavory attributes.[19] By 1935, public pressure was mounting, spurring the chief secretary to query other East African territories about their use of race as a criterion

185

for censorship. He found only Kenya had a special rating that banned Africans. It is unclear whether it was political pressure or an inability to enforce these restrictions at theaters that ultimately pushed the administration to change its tune, but in 1936, the "nonnatives-only" rating was formally abolished in Dar es Salaam.[20]

Despite this development, a few Europeans in Tanganyika continued to press for the use of race as a criterion for admission to films, creating rifts within the colonial administration and fueling heated disputes with African filmgoers in regional towns. In 1940, several members of the censors board in Dar es Salaam tried to have the nonnative-only category reinstated. Their efforts put them in direct confrontation with men at the highest levels of the colonial administration. The chief secretary, for one, adamantly fought the board's efforts, arguing racial discrimination could not be allowed in a British-administered League of Nations Mandated Territory.[21] He further suggested that such petty discrimination was legally untenable as well as politically shortsighted. In Dar es Salaam, the board lost the battle, but in regional towns across the territory, where locally based censorship boards held sway, Africans were periodically barred from seeing certain films into the 1950s. In Iringa, the Playhouse Cinema opened in 1947, but even after it had been doing business for several years, Africans made up just a modest 20 percent of an average night's audience due to persistent discrimination.[22] In the 1950s, growing consternation among African would-be filmgoers grew to a feverish pitch. A number of men who had been denied entrance to the theater took their concerns to the local indigenous authority, who in turn warned British members of the local administration about mounting resentment and anger among his constituents. He counseled an end to the practice of using race as a basis for admission to certain films before it exploded into a volatile political issue. A short while later, in 1951, his warning materialized: there was "a near riot" at the box office when a number of Africans were once again turned away.

According to the local African authority, these box office skirmishes were undermining Iringa's reputation among Africans, who felt unwelcome, harassed, and discriminated against in town. More broadly, these encounters with racism at the show during the early years of the business undermined the growth of moviegoing as a mass form of leisure. "People from Iringa never developed the habit of going to the cinema," said Feroz Mukhadam, whose uncle built the Playhouse Cinema and later the Highland in

Iringa.[23] Persistent discrimination as late as the 1950s reinforced Africans' reticence about going to the show. Only in the 1970s did their children and grandchildren begin to feel welcome enough and daring enough to take in a movie, yet even then, Iringa's ticket sales and earnings remained a fraction of what similar-sized theaters made in Tanga.

The net effect of colonial law, policing patterns, and local custom was palpable, combining to differentiate the cinematic cultures of various towns in significant ways. Urban authorities in Arusha were perhaps the most restrictive in the territory when it came to recognizing and accommodating Africans' rights to inhabit urban space and walk the streets unmolested. After the British took power from the Germans, African rights in Arusha were increasingly curtailed. Africans and Asians who had lived in mixed residential quarters were segregated by the British, with Africans officially prohibited from residing in the town proper. Waarusha, or ethnic Africans drawn from the immediate surrounding area, were specifically targeted for eviction and removal. During World War II, Africans were required to carry passes validating their presence in town, and they were routinely arrested, especially at night, for walking the streets. In 1951 and 1952, the number of Africans "repatriated" (in other words, thrown out) from Arusha was three times the number sent out of Dar es Salaam, despite the fact that the population of the capital was nearly one hundred thousand and that of Arusha a mere five thousand.[24] Township authorities there authored numerous reports calling for the segregation of Africans into South African–styled locations. They also advocated allowing Africans into the city center only for employment or official business. Although these policies never became law, such discourses and sentiments infused urban life in important ways. For Africans in the 1950s, life in Arusha was more akin to black life in Nairobi or Johannesburg rather than in Chake-Chake or Dar es Salaam.

The explicit racism that permeated the air in Arusha impacted patrons' cinemagoing experiences as well. Exhibitors there pandered to the white expatriates who made up a sizable section of their clientele. One example of this involved the film that was chosen to open the Paradise theater in 1948. The movie was *The Drum* (Korda, 1938), the second feature in Zoltan Korda's trilogy glorifying the British Empire in South Asia. A box office smash in Britain, the film was so offensive to South Asians that it caused riots in Bombay before being withdrawn from theaters.[25] It was thus a questionable film for an Asian-owned theater in Tanzania to screen,

187

Figure 5.1 Paradise Theater (renamed the Elite), Arusha, showing tripartite entrances, where Africans entered farthest on the right, Asians through the middle door behind the car, and Europeans on the far left

Figure 5.2 Ticket windows for Europeans and Asians inside the Paradise/Elite

unless the goal was to explicitly attract the white colonial population to the show. Brij Behal's grandfather, Bhagwandas Behal, who migrated to Arusha from Kenya in 1922, built the Paradise Cinema (later renamed the Elite). The younger Behal said that the family felt pressured to segregate audiences and discourage African attendance during the colonial era. At the theater, he showed me a separate ticket window and entrance for Africans, who would proceed through this door to their seats at the front of the auditorium. At the main entrance, Asians and Europeans had separate entrances and ticket windows as well. The European ticket window was closest to the stairs, allowing white patrons to proceed directly up to the balcony and thereby minimize contact with other races. Gamdul Sing Hans, who ran the second theater in Arusha, the Metropole, told me similarly segregated seating patterns were followed there too. Africans always occupied the seats closest to the screen, Asians the seats toward the back of the main hall, and Europeans the balcony. "This wasn't law like it was in Kenya, mind you, but just custom," said Brij Behal. "That is just how people did it here in Arusha, up until independence."[26] With so-called customs like this, it is no wonder that Africans did not go to the cinema in large numbers.

Arusha was the only place in Tanganyika where racial segregation was explicitly marked with separate queues, entrances, and seating. Shabir Jariwalla, who managed the Empress Cinema in Dar es Salaam beginning in the 1950s, was aghast when I queried him about the existence of such patterns of segregation in the capital city. People sat wherever they wanted, he stated. They were free to buy tickets for any section they could afford, a claim that was confirmed by countless interviews with other exhibitors and cinemagoers. Shabir lived in Arusha at the time I interviewed Brij Behal and Gamdul Sing Hans, having moved there from Dar es Salaam in the 1970s, but he had never heard of such policies in Arusha. Given his experience in the capital, he expressed surprise that even in the 1950s theater owners could survive if they excluded Africans.[27]

Along the coast, selling tickets to Africans was widely regarded as crucial to the success of a theater: in fact, the industry boomed in Zanzibar, Dar es Salaam, and Tanga in the 1950s precisely *because* Africans went to the show in large numbers. In contrast, many up-country theaters struggled through their early years in large part because of the unwelcoming atmosphere for Africans. As late as 1952 in Iringa, for example, average attendance was a mere forty people per show, or 15 percent of capacity. The

189

audience there was composed almost entirely of European government officials and settlers or Asian clerks and traders.[28] During these same years in Zanzibar, Tanga, and Dar es Salaam, where Africans comprised 75 percent of the audience, there simply were not enough seats to meet demand.[29]

The importance of ticket sales to Africans was made poignantly clear to the colonial administration when one of the few commercial films it financed hit the market. The film was *Muhogo Mchungu* (Bitter Cassava), produced by the Colonial Film Unit in 1952 as part of a publicity campaign to stem the tide of rural-to-urban migration. It was the first feature-length film starring East Africans that was ever released in the region. The lead role was played by Rashid Kawawa, who went on to become prime minister and vice president after independence. Kawawa was employed by the Social Development Department, where his European supervisors were apparently quite taken by his charm and potential appeal to a mass audience. The film portrays the antics of a rural bumpkin trying to make it in the big city, where he is robbed, beaten, hoodwinked, and hit by a car before deciding to return to a quiet and productive life in the village.[30] The intended audience for the film was Africans, and in addition to being toured around the villages in the cinema vans, it was commercially screened in urban theaters. When it played in Dar es Salaam, it earned £214 sterling at the box office. In Nairobi, where Africans were actively discouraged from going to the movies and regularly hassled by the police for being downtown after dark, it earned a paltry £8.[31]

The Nairobi earnings were no doubt hurt by the fact that the film was released at the height of the crackdown on members of the Kenya Land and Freedom Army and the mass arrests of people allegedly sympathetic to Mau Mau. Understandably, Africans in Nairobi generally eschewed moviegoing altogether before independence. But in Dar es Salaam, things were dramatically different. In the twenty years since the lifting of racialized restrictions on attendance in the capital, moviegoing had come into vogue. When J. A. K. Leslie conducted his pathbreaking research on African social life in Dar es Salaam, in 1956, he found that African men, women, and children were all big cinema fans. Young men boasted about the glamour of taking a date to see a film, and women reportedly evaluated potential suitors by their willingness to treat them to the show;[32] a man who could score a ticket for a sold-out film showed persistence and determination to please his partner and thus immense potential as a spouse.

Urban planning and colonial geography, along with housing and transportation policies, helped keep Africans in many regional towns from feeling they belonged in and had a right to urban space. In Moshi, the political connection between African rights to the city and cinematic space was made explicit in the 1950s when organizers of the Tanzanian African National Union (TANU), including Julius Nyerere, used the Plaza Cinema to hold meetings and rallies. Denied permits for open-air public venues for their meetings, TANU leaders urged supporters to buy tickets to "special screenings" at the Plaza, where they were treated to nationalist speeches instead of a film.[33] But if, as this situation suggests, Africans in and around Moshi did not feel explicitly unwelcome in local theaters, other factors contributed to keeping their attendance levels comparatively low during the colonial era. In the 1930s, when nearly three thousand people went to the movies each week in Zanzibar, the number in Moshi was closer to fifty.[34] Mr. Khambaita, whose family built the Everest Cinema in Moshi, explained that as late as the 1950s and 1960s, "Africans did not come to the cinema very much . . . it wasn't like the coast, Tanga or Zanzibar where Africans enjoyed the cinema, here Africans went very little."[35]

According to my own survey data, more than 90 percent of the people who regularly went to the movies got there by foot, so distance could be a real impediment. As a result, many of those who lived far from the city centers where cinemas were built simply did not go. As late as 1957, less than 6 percent of the African population around Dodoma, Moshi, Iringa, or Mbeya lived in town, making access to cinemas difficult for the vast majority.[36] An interviewee named Edward, who grew up in a squatter area outside Arusha, put it plainly: "Cinemas were in town, and for us they were simply too far." There was no street lighting and no public transportation, he added, and he and his friends were not eager to walk long distances in the deep tropical dark. Deo, who lived in a village outside Moshi, gave a similar reason to explain why he never went to the cinema: he was also afraid of being attacked by animals while walking home in the dark. Explaining the relatively low numbers of Africans who attended the movies before independence, one cinema manager summed it up in one word, "Geography. Geography was a very big issue in Moshi. During the colonial

191

era most Africans lived outside of town, not in the town center. People lived so far away it often took them the better part of two hours to get back home. Even offices closed officially at 4:30 rather than 5 p.m. so that people could be home before dark."[37]

The combination of residential segregation and lack of transportation had profound implications for nightlife. Before independence, few people had private automobiles and public transportation was limited; buses were few and far between, and most stopped running well before dark.[38] As one man commented, "If people came in for work and had a long way to travel they were anxious to leave and head back home. Few Africans wanted to stay around and wait for a movie."[39] My surveys of attendance in and around regional towns confirmed this. Until independence, many folks told me, they rarely went to town at all except for official business, and when their business was done, they headed home. And because few Africans lived in the town proper, it was difficult for people visiting the city to simply spend the night with family or friends. Thus, the distance to town was not only physical but emotional and psychological as well: with no urban friends and no place that might serve as a home away from home, many found that the town was a foreign and unwelcoming environment.

In Dar es Salaam, less than a mile separated Kariakoo or Magomeni, the main African residential quarters, from the city center. People could stroll from their homes to any number of cinemas in less than thirty minutes. Dockworkers, who numbered in the thousands, only had to cross the street after work to take in a show at the Avalon. (See maps 1.1 and 1.2.) On their way to and from work or during breaks, stevedores and baggage handlers said, they made a habit of checking out film posters, and they argued during their shifts about which film looked most promising. From the Avalon, it was only three or four blocks to the Odeon, Empire, or Empress. Numerous men and women who lived in the Kariakoo neighborhood told me that even as children and teens, they regularly walked across Mnazi Mmoja Park to take in films at the Azania/Cameo, where Egyptian movies frequently packed the house. In Tanga, Zanzibar, Wete, and Chake-Chake, the walking distance to the cinema from key African neighborhoods or likely places of employment was even shorter. There, cinemas were mixed right in with residential neighborhoods; many could literally walk out the door of their homes and join the crowd gathering for the evening's entertainment.

Figure 5.3 Azania Cinema, opened in 1939 (renamed the Cameo in 1965).

In Zanzibar, Pemba, Tanga, and Dar es Salaam, long histories of urban-rural integration also facilitated emotional proximity to town. Years before there were cinemas, rural villagers walked from the countryside to take their goods to town for the big weekly markets. Men stayed to participate in prayers at the mosques, which furthered their sense of belonging to the *umma* (community). After selling their wares, men and women sometimes stayed for the weekend, taking part in urban festivals and dance competitions or attending weddings and funerals of urban friends and relatives. In this way, Africans' long historical precedent of going to town for both business and pleasure fostered familiarity with and comfort in the city, which eventually empowered them to travel to the urban center in order to take in a movie.

In the isles, affordable and accessible public transportation also facilitated rural-urban connections as well as visits to the cinema. Again, historical precedents eased the transition: long before motorized transportation, many people from the farthest corners of the isles traveled to town by sailboat. By the 1940s, limited bus service was available between select villages in Zanzibar and Pemba and the urban centers. Initially, buses were used predominantly to transport goods to market, but it did not take long before villagers were commandeering the vehicles to take large groups into town for an evening at the show. BiMaryam was one interviewee who recalled how she and her husband organized busloads of young couples from their village, in Uroa, to go to movies in town during World War II. Another woman, who lived in Nungwi (a village at the northern tip of Zanzibar Island), said that people in her village would spend days planning such outings. They had to rent a bus, collect money to purchase tickets, prepare food for the journey, and figure out what to wear. Because town was far by the standards of the day—some 25 miles—and the roads were uneven tracks through mud and tire-puncturing coral rock, they had to set out at midday to be in town for the evening show. Often, it was one or two o'clock in the morning by the time they returned home. On one occasion, she recalled, the bus ran out of tires after repeated punctures, and the party had to spend the night on the road before being rescued by the first bus at dawn. Such challenges made the adventure all the more memorable. Yet unlike rural dwellers on the mainland, at least stranded passengers in the isles did not have to fear attacks by lions, elephants, or hyenas.

Sultan Mohammed, who grew up in rural Pemba, also reminisced about taking such trips in his youth. His children were amazed by the verve and vitality that returned to his voice when he began telling me about his exploits organizing groups of young men and women from a village near Mkoani to go to the cinemas in the town of Chake-Chake. He had friends who were bus drivers, and they were a constant source of information about what was going on in town. Sultan always inquired about the movies that were showing. When he heard that *Mughal e-Azam* (Ashif, 1960), which he had seen while visiting relatives in Zanzibar, was finally arriving in Pemba, he immediately started organizing a village outing to see it. *Mughal e-Azam* is a grand historical epic, set at the time of the Mughal Empire in India. The film revolves around the socially forbidden love between Prince Salim (played by Dilip Kumar) and a court dancer named Anarkali (played by Madhubala), a love complicated by war, by tensions between Muslims and Hindus, and above all by the king's refusal to let his son marry a woman whose family cannot help cement the empire. The king condemns Anarkali to prison, but when his son orchestrates a jailbreak, the king seeks revenge by having her entombed alive. It is one of the most universally acclaimed Indian films of all time due to its larger-than-life drama, fabulously rich sets, poetic use of dialogue, and the explosive emotionality of the actors and the sound track.[40] As a result, it did not

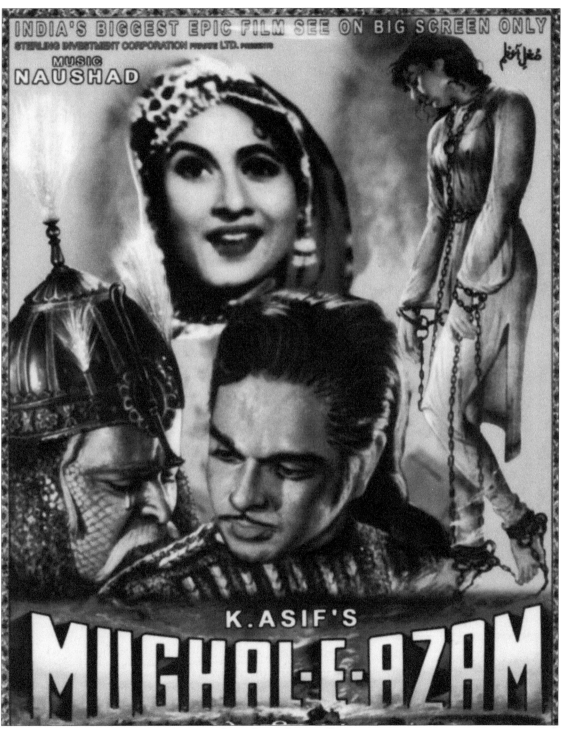

Figure 5.4 *Mughal-e-Azam* poster, from the author's collection

take long for Sultan Mohammed to convince a large group of youth from his village to join in an outing to the show. The trip was such a success, he worked out a deal with the cinema manager: for each busload of patrons he brought from the village he and two or three friends received free admission. Sultan spent the next seven years organizing such parties and group trips to the cinema in Chake-Chake, in the process making film fans out of those who dwelt far from town. These outings were a huge social event for his village, and his role in organizing them made him very popular with the youth who participated. When asked if women took part in these events too, I was told, "But of course! Everyone went! This was a big social event. Besides, we were all going as a group, so nothing bad could happen. Girls, boys, friends from school, even a few older couples; this was a huge public event. Everyone went!"[41] That many participants had relatives who lived in Chake-Chake also made nighttime visits to town seem less daunting.

Going to town for leisure enhanced people's sense of general comfort with urban life and their affective ties with the city overall. Many people I spoke with who grew up in rural areas in Zanzibar and Pemba said these trips to the movies in their teens marked their first occasion to go to town. Their pals walked them around before the movie, pointing out landmarks, specialty shops, and key points of urban geography. By going to the movies, they literally saw the town.[42]

For the owners and employees of the theaters in urban centers, having busloads of villagers arrive regularly added to the festive atmosphere of their venues. Ameri Slyoum, who worked as a gatekeeper at the Majestic in Zanzibar, recalled the many people who came from villages on the east coast, especially Chwaka and Uroa, which had the best road leading to town. Having grown up in the village of Kizimkazi, which was 25 miles from Uroa as the crow flies but had no good road or regular bus service, he was jealous when he first saw forty or fifty villagers alighting from a bus outside the Majestic. "You would think they had just ended a war or won the Champion's League Cup they were so exuberant!" he exclaimed. "And then, on the way home, the bus was ringing with song as they all improvised singing the film's hit tunes. Oh they had a lot of fun!"[43] Rashid, who sold black market tickets outside the theater, also told vivid stories about busloads of people coming from the villages for weekend shows and the boon this meant for his business. "If they came all the way from the countryside to see a film, they would pay whatever they had to, to get in.

Or, if they were smart, they would send someone to town to buy the tickets early, but this also meant that other customers would arrive at the box office and tickets would be all sold out. Either way, it made for good business for us!" Rashid said he did not gouge the villagers too badly with his prices, just enough to make it worth his while to do business. According to him, they did not mind having to buy black market tickets—they were just glad to get tickets at all: "'They were jubilant coming out of the show!" he recounted. "On a Sunday the film wouldn't let out until after midnight. By the time they got home it was nearly dawn. This was really a night on the town!"[44]

Until independence, colonial geography served to define up-country towns as fairly alien spaces for many Tanzanians. Few people had knowledge of and experience in the city, and beyond that, law, custom, and the police worked to make Africans feel less than welcome in many towns, particularly after dark. Prior to independence, the number of Africans actually living inside the urban boundaries of many regional towns was small. And for them, distance to the city centers where cinemas were built, lack of public transportation, and sometimes racialized receptions at the theaters undermined the desire to go to the show. It was not that up-country Africans were not interested in the movies, for they certainly were. When cinema vans rolled into their villages, they showed up to view the films in large numbers, but for up-country Africans, going to the city to see a movie was a rare occurrence.[45] This helps explain the somewhat common depiction in party publications, written after independence, of cinemas as racially exclusive spaces, owned and frequented primarily by Asians. Although this was far from true along the coast, it accurately reflected the experience of many who grew up outside provincial towns.

CHILDREN, YOUTH, AND ELDERS AT THE SHOW

In the racially mixed communities of coastal Tanzania, the location of the cinemas—in the heart of the town and amid residential space—helped define moviegoing within acceptable bounds. In these towns, the spaces where cinemas were located were perceived as extensions of the home; thus, they were deemed safe spaces where even children and youth could go alone. In other parts of the country, where most Africans lived outside the town proper or on the outskirts, African parents generally felt far less comfortable allowing their children to wander over to the show.

197

From at least the 1930s—the decade when the oldest people I spoke with grew up—children in Zanzibar and Pemba regularly attended the show unaccompanied or with small groups of friends, siblings, and cousins. By the 1950s, this had become an increasingly common practice in Dar es Salaam and Tanga as well. But up-country, it was not until the 1970s that African youth began going to the show unchaperoned, although Asians and Arabs who lived in the vicinity of movie theaters went without adults at a much earlier age.

The age at which people first went to a cinema also varied substantially. In Zanzibar, many began attending at eight, nine, or ten, whereas most of those I interviewed in up-country towns did not do so until they were in their late teens or early twenties. Because celluloid was intimately connected with the spaces in which it was consumed, this variation in ages largely reflected parental perceptions about the safety and morality of cities. Moviegoing was often grounded in elders' own familiarity and comfort (or discomfort) with the towns where cinemas were built. Children's access to cash was also a factor, as were ideas about the relative affordability of tickets to the show.

Children in Zanzibar were far more likely than any other youth in the country to go to the movies; the combination of a diverse economy and the proximity of the cinemas to residential spaces afforded these children easy access to the show. From the earliest days at Cinema ya Bati, youngsters made up a large portion of the audience. Mwalim Idd, who was born in Zanzibar in 1926, remembered the enthusiasm he and other children had for the silent films they saw. "It was only a few cents to get in," he said. "It would be packed with kids like myself." He recalled that films featuring Charlie Chaplin or cowboys attracted young boys to the theater in droves. "We sat on simple mats on the floor, there were no proper seats in that cinema, but we didn't mind." More children could fit into the theater, he explained, if they squished together on the floor. "We were just thrilled to be able to see the spectacle of moving pictures. Seeing things move across the screen was like magic. Moving pictures were a very big deal in those days!"[46] Haji, born in 1934, shared similar memories. "I started going when I was only six or seven, maybe eight years old at the most. We kids went by ourselves. Our parents didn't mind. And it was cheap, only a few cents to get in."[47] The fact that children in Zanzibar went to the movies alone spurred theaters to offer special children's shows, featuring films that appealed to juvenile tastes. This also helped keep the silent-movie theaters running after adults turned to the "talkies" that were featured at the Royal.

Children were free to wander through town in those days, both to go to the show and to earn a little cash if their parents would not give them the money for tickets. Idd recalled that his parents gave him a few cents each week, which he always saved for the movies. Along the coast, many parents or grandparents rewarded children with pennies for their regular attendance at Qur'anic school. Haji's parents were too poor for this indulgence, but his uncle sold fruit juice outside the Majestic and got him in for free once a week. At the age of ten, Haji started working to earn his own entrance fee so that he could frequent the show more often. He ran errands for neighbors or stall keepers at the market. After the movie was over, he also collected soda bottles left behind. From the 1950s through the 1970s, many young boys earned their entrance to the theaters in Zanzibar by collecting returnable bottles.[48]

Cinemas that were located in the neighborhoods of these young children were as familiar to their families as their own homes. When I asked interviewees if their parents ever worried about them disappearing for three or four hours inside a theater, most responded with a quizzical gaze. Haji, Idd, and a host of others said that, on the contrary, their parents felt secure when the children headed to the cinema, since they would be safe there and looked after by adults they knew. Men who worked at the cinema were commonly referred to as *mjomba* (uncle) by neighborhood youth, revealing the intimacy, affection, and kinship that bound them with children in the neighborhood. Fatma shared a delightful story about the time her older sister, who was then a teen, took Fatma, age seven or eight, and their younger brother to an Indian matinee. Resentful about having to babysit, the sister appealed to the gatekeeper at the Majestic Cinema to let the children in for free. Knowing they were from the neighborhood and that their family attended regularly on Sundays, he obliged. When the film ended more than three hours later, Fatma and her sister were so enraptured with the movie that they left with their heads in the clouds, utterly forgetting the little brother who was fast asleep in an adjacent seat. While sweeping up after the show, one of the employees found the sleeping boy and took him home. Fatma's mother, who had just returned from her own outing, answered the door, and needless to say, she was not amused. The oldest daughter was given the severest form of punishment: she was banned from the movies for several months.[49] As this anecdote shows, in Zanzibar the cinema really was "just like home," a place where "uncles" frequently babysat for young ones and then safely delivered them back into their mothers' arms.

Up-country, neither cinemas nor the cities in which they were located inspired such a sense of ease among most parents. Many Africans told me that even as teens and young adults, they had to sneak off if they wanted to go to a show. For Asians and Arabs, who lived in the town centers, going to the cinema was nearly as acceptable as it was along the coast, but for Africans, things were different: even after independence, parents who had grown up in the village retained an animosity toward the movies and refused to let their children attend. Christopher was one of many in Moshi whose parents explicitly forbade him from going to the show. They had never been to the cinema themselves, and they believed that dope smokers, gamblers, and fighters went to films in large numbers. Christopher went anyway in the 1970s by pretending to be going to church and then sneaking off to the cinema instead. Baltazar faced similar problems with his parents and employed a similar ruse in the 1980s. He went to church in the late morning on Sunday and sneaked out after a bit to the matinee; in fact, Sunday matinees were the only shows he ever saw. Young women found it even more difficult to attend the show. As Margareth said, "Going to the cinema wasn't a common thing for a girl to do, most parents vehemently objected. Boys could sneak out, for us it was much more difficult." She went to the movies for the first time when she was twenty-four, after moving to Dar es Salaam and being introduced to the pleasures of the cinema by her older brother and sister, who lived in the capital.

Many of the individuals I interviewed who later went on to have prominent careers in filmmaking, acting, or television had their first exposure to the cinema when they were in boarding school or at university.[50] Raymond's comments were illustrative: "As a child growing up in the village outside of Bukoba I was only allowed to go to town for school or to do errands for my parents at the post office." When we spoke, he was the manager of the first multiplex in the nation. "'But growing up," he said, "I was forbidden to go to the cinema. The only films I ever saw were religious education films or those of the Department of Health that would occasionally be screened in our village." He went to a cinema for the first time only as an adult. Belleghe, who was teaching film production and camera work at the University of Dar es Salaam when we spoke, also said that as a child, the only films he saw were cowboy movies brought by the cinema van to his village. The first time he went to a theater was in 1978, when he moved to Morogoro to attend boarding school. These examples reflect the patterns found in my surveys, as provincial African youth first began attending the cinemas in large numbers only in the 1970s and 1980s. Moviegoing was as central to the urban educational experience as learning to read and write.

There were, of course, exceptions, such as Freddy Macha, who shared stories of his parents taking him to the cinema when he was quite young. His parents were both musicians and recording artists, and they frequented the movies to get a look at international dance moves and to study stage style. They took him to see Elvis in *Viva Las Vegas* (Sidney, 1964) at the Plaza Cinema in Moshi when he was only eight years old.[51] But Freddy was an outlier in many ways. Few other up-country Africans attended movies at such a young age or were introduced to the cinema by their parents.[52] This early exposure to film affected Freddy's life profoundly. He went on to have a prolific career as a cultural critic, writing for several government newspapers after independence. Frequently weighing in with lengthy and thought-provoking film reviews and discussions of urban cultural practices, his voice was a rare breath of unabashed youthful opinion in an otherwise rather stodgy party publication.

How people spent their recreational time and money continued to be marked by regional and generational differences long after independence. A household budget survey conducted in 1969 found that Dar es Salaam residents spent 63 percent of their entertainment budget going to the cinema, whereas those who lived in nine smaller up-country towns spent only 5 percent in a similar way.[53] Across the country, drinking was the most popular form of entertainment, but in rural areas, people spent more than six times as much on alcohol as on other forms of leisure or entertainment.[54] Because public drinking was a form of leisure indulged in primarily by men, household recreational shillings were inequitably distributed, with the lion's share consumed by fathers. By the late 1970s, however, the popularity of moviegoing had grown significantly in up-country areas; people in regional towns now spent more than twice as much of their entertainment and recreation budgets going to the show. Moviegoing was also an increasingly common form of family recreation, which suggests that families across the nation were spending more of their leisure time together—and perhaps that fewer fathers were off drinking up the household's budget. Yet going to the cinema remained an urban form of recreation. Few rural households spent any money at all on films.[55]

Christianity also played a major role in fostering perceptions of cinemas and cities as sinful spaces. According to an interviewee named Soloman, everyone in his largely Christian town referred to the cinema as the "house of the devil." Youth were excoriated for even suggesting a visit there. Only sinners went in, Soloman was told. Similarly, many Christians I spoke with in Arusha and Moshi said that they never went to movie theaters because both their preachers and their elders portrayed them as houses of sin. Joyce, whose main forms of leisure and recreation included going to church and praying, told me that her grandmother, who raised her in Moshi, vehemently opposed moviegoing. "Cinema-going causes you to do bad things, contrary to God's plan," she said, and then added, "The people who went were hooligans interested in watching portrayals of sinful sexuality." Mama Erik also told me that in her church, the only films youth were allowed to see were those shown by the fathers themselves. She recalled a film she saw in her teens about Jesus's resurrection, which was screened in the church social hall before Easter—the only moving picture she ever saw before the introduction of television in the mid-1990s. Coastal Muslim populations commonly spent their Sundays at the cinema, but many up-country Christians preferred to pass their weekend leisure hours at their church, where they also spent a large portion of their discretionary income.[56]

CLASS AND ATTENDANCE AT THE SHOW

Class and relative degrees of wealth also impacted regional variations in cinemagoing. In interviews and surveys, people in Zanzibar and Pemba typically described cinema tickets as "cheap" or "affordable," but many on the mainland placed going to the movies in the category of a luxury expense, especially during the colonial era. Accordingly, young people in Zanzibar and Pemba generally found it easy to get a few cents from their parents or otherwise scrape together the money to go to the show, but youth on the mainland rarely had cash for such indulgences. Deo's remarks were representative of those who grew up near Moshi. He said that his parents had little access to cash themselves and certainly would not part with what little they had so that he could indulge in frivolity. After independence, however, fortunes began to change. More and more people on the

mainland began to go to the movies as their incomes increased and perceptions about the importance of commercial leisure began to change. By the
1970s and 1980s, movies were affordable and attractive enough that some
ten thousand to fifteen thousand people were going to the show across the
country each day.[57]

One reason why more people from a wider range of class backgrounds
went to the movies in the isles was simply because ticket prices were lower
there. Colonial officials were not particularly happy about the modest cost
of cinema tickets in Zanzibar and Pemba; in fact, they complained that
tickets were so cheap that juveniles and seasonal clove pickers regularly
attended the show. But exhibitors set the prices, and officials were largely
powerless to intervene.[58] From the 1920s through the end of the colonial
era, the minimum price of a ticket in Dar es Salaam was more than double
the price in the isles, and up-country, the cheapest seats were often four
times more expensive than in the isles. Of course, prices varied depending on the film, but at the Civic Center Cinema in Zanzibar, an English
movie could be seen for as little as twenty-five cents in the 1950s or one shilling at the regular theaters in town. In Pemba too, admission to an English
film was twenty-five cents, and an Indian film could be seen for as little
as forty cents. In Iringa and Dodoma the cheapest tickets available in the
1950s cost one shilling—roughly the equivalent of an unskilled laborer's
daily wage. Some up-country cinemas priced their cheapest seats as high as
three shillings, which was clearly beyond the reach of an average laborer.[59]
Obviously, ticket pricing was yet another important factor contributing to
regional variations in Africans' attendance at the movies.

In Iringa, the high price of tickets meant that most of those who went
to the movies were Europeans or civil servants. Half of the Asians and 70
percent of the Africans who attended the cinema there in the 1950s worked
as clerks, although they constituted a minuscule proportion of the overall population.[60] These relatively well paid, salaried men were among the
few nonwhites who could afford a night at the show. In Dodoma as well,
Africans were a small percentage of the audience, and most were salaried
clerks. Rather than working in offices, the majority of those surveyed and
interviewed in Zanzibar earned independent incomes as shopkeepers,
craftspeople, traders, fishermen, landlords, food sellers, or independent
businesspeople. In fact, clerk did not even make the list of occupations
available to Africans in the 1948 Zanzibar census, and fewer than 14 percent

of Asians there identified their main occupation as clerk.[61] According to Anthony Clayton, wages in Zanzibar in the 1930s and 1940s were some of the highest in eastern and north-central Africa, but still, few Zanzibaris found such jobs to be worth the effort, preferring self-employment whenever possible as it was more lucrative and gave them greater independence. The combination of relatively well-paid entrepreneurial opportunities and low ticket prices made it possible for people from all walks of life to afford a night at the movies in Zanzibar.

In the mainland capital of Dar es Salaam in 1957, the minimum wage was set at TSh 80–85 per month, and skilled masons could earn as much as 225.[62] At 1/-, a cinema ticket was affordable for most. As in Zanzibar, however, many in Dar es Salaam preferred casual labor over formal minimum-wage employment. A man could earn 7/- to 10/- in a day unloading goods at the port or moving packages from lorries to shops. At that rate, he would only have to work eight to ten days a month to earn the minimum wage. He would also have far more control over not just when but where he worked.[63] The large urban population meant that there were also numerous ways to earn an independent living, such as selling fruit, fish, or wood; renting rooms; brewing beer; driving a taxi; or making clothes, bread, or baked goods and selling them to others. These ways of earning a living were regarded as "informal" by authorities, but according to Leslie's survey of Dar es Salaam the profits were often substantial. African fishmongers, beer brewers, bread sellers, and other "casually employed" individuals built substantial homes from their earnings. And once their homes were built, many retired from backbreaking physical labor, choosing to live off the rent they earned from letting out rooms instead. Africans in Dar es Salaam did comparatively well economically, allowing them to indulge in a range of commercial and noncommercial leisure activities.

Women in Dar es Salaam also fared quite well economically. Although females were largely barred from formal waged employment during the colonial era, the opportunities available in the informal and service economies were extensive. Dar es Salaam was a large port town, teeming with traders and migrant male laborers longing for "the comforts of home," which women eagerly supplied, for a price. Leslie noted the high proportion of female homeowners in Dar es Salaam, with women in some of the oldest neighborhoods owning 20 to 50 percent of all the houses. Many lived quite well by renting rooms in their homes. Unlike many of his contemporaries in the colonial service who found female independence a cause for concern, Leslie applauded the industry of women who built substantial homes from "petty-trade," selling cakes, fritters, beans, and other goods.[64] He was also extremely open-minded about prostitution, describing it as a simple fact of life in any port town. He noted that a low-class prostitute could earn 1 to 2 shillings by turning a quick trick, and a "higher-class" woman earned 5 to 10 shillings if she agreed to let a man spend the entire night.[65] Beer brewing was another skill women in many towns throughout Africa used to earn a living, eventually establishing themselves among the propertied middle class.[66] As early as the 1930s, E. C. Baker reported that women beer brewers in Dar es Salaam earned between 150 and 180 shillings a month, which was eight to nine times what an average man employed by the government made.[67] With admission to the cinema as low as 1 shilling, a night at the movies was affordable for most, regardless of gender.

Almost immediately after independence, wages began to rise in Tanzania. By 1965, the average wage of those who were formally employed was more than TSh 265 per month. There were still large differences between urban and rural earnings, however. By 1969, the average per capita monthly income was roughly TSh 230, falling to 175 in rural areas and rising to nearly 1,000 in Arusha, Bukoba, Dodoma, Iringa, Mwanza, and Tanga. People in Dar es Salaam had substantially higher average incomes—almost TSh 4,000 per month.[68] Not surprisingly, the population of the capital exploded after independence. Between 1969 and 1974, average earnings on the mainland nearly doubled, allowing most people to feel they could afford to treat themselves to a show, even if inflation made them realize they did not quite have money to burn.[69] Through the 1980s, regional differences in wages and prices continued to make going to the show much cheaper in the isles than on the mainland and much more affordable in Dar es Salaam than in regional towns.

Enabling patrons to mix in public but still maintain physical distance by class and "respectability" was a key element of the social cartography of movie halls. Following British and Indian custom, seats in all theaters were sold at varying prices, effectively dividing patrons by wealth and status within the theater. Like purchasing a ticket for a seat on a train, people could choose

Figure 5.5 Classes of seating inside the Metropole, Arusha

between first, second, or third class. In some theaters, the difference between the physical seats in different sections was minimal, but in other venues, the seats in the cheapest section were rough and hard and sometimes without backs, whereas those in the first-class section were plush, upholstered, and soft. In every theater, the cheapest seats were closest to the screen, the first-class seats at the rear. Picture palaces in many towns had balconies as well, and those were the most expensive seats of all. Patrons who considered themselves middle class typically paid two times as much for a ticket as the poor, and members of the elite paid three to four times as much or even more.[70]

Patrons were quite particular about where they sat. Cinema seating both embodied and conveyed self-perceived status and class aspiration. Theoretically, anyone could sit anywhere he or she chose, but most people sat with others "of their kind." Educated Africans in Dar es Salaam during the 1950s wrote to the newspaper—another public venue for articulating perceptions of one's relative place in society—complaining about a lack of accommodation for members of the educated middle class. Why, asked one man, were there three classes of seats for Indian films but only two classes for English dramas? To him, this was an affront, depriving him and other "respectable middle-class patrons" of seats separate from the typical laborer. He and others felt it was important that educated, "civilized" Africans be

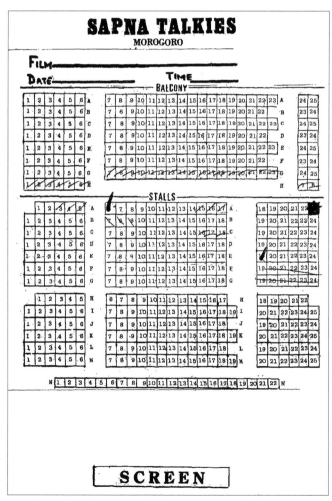

Figure 5.6 Seating chart showing permanently reserved seats for regular Sunday customers, at the Sapna Cinema, Morogoro. Courtesy of Pankaj Valambia

able to distance themselves from the "unwashed" African masses. His rancor increased in the context of English-language films because Europeans occupied the high-priced seats in the balcony, and when they looked down, he wanted them to be able to see that he was plainly apart from the African crowd.[71] But the number in his class was small indeed. According to Leslie, only some 2 percent of Dar es Salaam's African population was educated enough in the 1950s to write such a letter in English, and fewer than 2 percent could read the *Tanganyika Standard*, where the letter appeared.[72]

Ally, who managed several theaters in Pemba, speculated that perhaps one of the factors that contributed to the declining diversity of cinema audiences in the 1990s was that he and most other managers began selling tickets at a flat-rate price. There were no longer class distinctions determining where one sat. Commenting on the fact that his audience in 2002 was all male and mostly young, he said, "Perhaps elders and respectable people no longer want to come because theaters are no longer divided by class? Now an old man could come and next to him could be a young boy who doesn't show proper respect, who swears or acts like a hooligan. Perhaps this is why elders and women no longer come."[73] Class also determined who ended up paying black market rates, as the men who worked the business only bought tickets for seats in the balcony and the back of the theater. As Rashid explained, "Those people were the ones with money. I never bothered to try and buy or sell the cheap seats in the front, since there was no business for those."[74] Kasanga concurred: "I bought tickets for the back of the theater, since those seats were in highest demand. I bought tickets for the balcony as well, but never for the front!"[75] When I asked Haji why anyone would pay the black market rate for a ticket if he or she could simply buy a ticket at the window for a seat closer to the screen, he laughed and exclaimed, "They were rich! Those wealthy people were embarrassed to sit in front, they had to sit in the back. Perhaps they thought we smelled."[76] A spate of letters to the editor published in the newspaper, written by elite patrons complaining of drunken, disorderly, loud, and smelly people in the theaters, seem to confirm Haji's suspicions.[77] At any rate, the integrative potential of the theater was not entirely fulfilled. Many elite men and women might gladly engage poor and working-class people in a discussion of a film, but others were far less willing to literally rub elbows with them while seated in the theater.

Although theaters obviously made more from each ticket sold at a higher price, they grossed far more from seats sold to their poor and middle-class patrons. In Zanzibar from the 1950s through the 1980s, 60 to 80 percent of their income came from selling tickets to those who sat in the front and middle sections of the theater, as opposed to those who sat in the back or the balcony.[78] In Dar es Salaam, similar patterns held true. Though an exhibitor could earn four times as much on "first-class" tickets, often less than 3 percent of these tickets would actually sell for English movies in the 1950s. Overall sales were significantly better for Indian films, where an exhibitor could generally count on selling at least 80 percent of the tickets in each section. But even there, some 60 percent of the income was derived from sales in the lower two sections.[79] Despite a general reticence in African moviegoing in Iringa and Dodoma, even there exhibitors sold the majority of their tickets to lower- and middle-class patrons. This simple economic fact was one reason why exhibitors and distributors were opposed to European policies restricting access to the theaters by race or class.

LADIES' SHOWS AND YOUNG MEN'S ROWS: GENDER AT THE CINEMA

Although virtually everyone went to the show, claiming space both in cities and at the cinema was a gendered experience. This was part and parcel of how young women and men learned about and embodied their gendered identities. Going to the cinema was a central component of being recognized as a citizen in urban towns. Walking through the streets to the center of the city fostered familiarity with people, places, and practices beyond one's immediate home. The more women and young men walked the streets to attend the show, the less they felt strange and out of place in city spaces. In general, men had more money and more mobility than women, allowing them greater freedom to go to the cinema at night. Patriarchy and cultural expectations regarding gendered norms also impacted who went to the movies, when, and how often. These unwritten rules instructed young women and men about their place in the family and society. But such norms were not static, nor were they uniform across the nation. Women's access to the movies was greatest along the coast. And contrary to current popular perception, purdah provided them with added autonomy; ladies-only shows enhanced their access to the cinematic public. Unlike other public leisure spaces—including football grounds, coffee shops, and drinking halls, which were gendered almost exclusively male—cinemas encouraged women's movement across urban spaces and facilitated their participation in the discursive public sphere centered around films.

Men, however, constituted the majority of the cinema audience except on Sundays, when, according to exhibitors, audiences were largely balanced in terms of gender. Patriarchy was the principle force affording men more time, money, and freedom to move about: in Tanzania, this was a constant across regions, religions, and generations. As Subira told me, "Men went to the movies more often. Our culture and traditions tend to deprive women of many opportunities men take for granted, like the time and freedom to enjoy oneself or relax."[80] Semeni concurred, saying he went frequently "because I am a man. Our customs give men more freedom."[81] He explained that women's time-consuming domestic obligations, such as cooking, washing, and taking care of the young and the elderly, left less time for leisure. Echoing Phyllis Martin's findings about the gendered nature of leisure in colonial Brazzaville, John said plainly, "African customs don't give women a lot of time for relaxation. Women didn't have the time to indulge in leisure or movies." Across the nation, a reoccurring theme in my surveys was a recognition—on the part of both men and women— that leisure time was something men simply had more of. When asked what other types of leisure they participated in, the vast majority of women surveyed said, "*Sina*" (None). Women found moviegoing all the more empowering simply because it was one of the most commonly sanctioned forms of leisure they were allowed to enjoy.

The gendered privileges afforded men were acquired from an early age, and access to the cinema was one of many social spaces where lessons on such privileges were learned. Young girls, be they African, Asian, or Arab, were often kept at home helping their mothers and aunts with domestic responsibilities, but young boys frequently spent their days outside the home. For many small boys and youth, the cinema house became a refuge, a tranquil place to pass the time. "While my sisters stayed at home and helped with the wash and cooking, boys in our family were expected to be out of the house most of the day," said Haji. "When I was young my only obligation was Qur'anic school. Beyond that I was free. I played a lot of football, but when I wasn't doing that there wasn't much to do. Where can a young boy go and not be tempted to get in trouble?" he asked. "Going to the cinema gave me somewhere safe to spend my time." Others echoed Haji's remarks, saying freedom to roam was a double-edged sword, giving them time for leisure but also putting them in situations where they were not always comfortable. For these young boys, the cinema was a quiet refuge from the streets. From the tender age of eight or nine, many boys in Zanzibar began going to the cinema several times a week, if not daily. By the time they were in their teens, many had become self-described junkies, people who just had to get their fix of the latest film.

It was as teenagers and youth, prior to marriage, that young men enjoyed their most privileged access to the cinema.[82] By this point in their lives, most were struggling hard to figure out a means of earning an independent income, and one of the most common ways they rewarded themselves for their success was by going to the show. In the 1950s, J. A. K. Leslie found that young, casually employed men in Dar es Salaam frequently spent both their leisure time and their pocket money at the show. Similar patterns held true into the postcolonial era. When Abel Ishumi conducted his study of the urban jobless in 1984, going to the movies ranked third among their favorite leisure pursuits, after hanging out and talking with friends or listening to music. Nearly twice as many men in Ishumi's sample went to the movies as watched or played football or enjoyed cards or the board game *bao*.[83] Some 30 percent of the youth surveyed in the 1950s and again in the 1980s also said that what drew them to the city and what made them determined to stay no matter what was the "glamour of big town life." "Jobless" or not, they could not imagine living without the fun and freedom they found in town.[84] According to Ishumi, though they lived day to day and rarely had savings to tide them over, young men would rather have been "kings" for a night, blowing all their hard-earned money rather than saving for a rainy day. My own survey and interview data confirm these findings. Jecha, for instance, earned two shillings a day making *chokaa* (lime whitewash or cement made from burning coral rock) in the 1970s, yet he went to the cinema regularly even though admission was half of what he earned daily. Back when he was young and single, he said, his attitude was, "What is the point of earning the money if you don't use it to reward yourself when you can? You can always make more money the next day."[85] His tune changed after marriage and with age, but like many men I interviewed, he said that being able to blow his daily earnings on simple pleasures was one of the principal joys of being a young, single man.

Young men's and teens' access to the movies was also enhanced by the fact that theaters reduced the price of admission for the least desirable seats—those closest to the screen. The number of rows so designated varied from theater to theater, but in every cinema, the seats nearest the screen could commonly be purchased for less than half of the average ticket price. From the earliest days, these were marked as the "hooligan hangout" or "ruffian rows." Abdul, who managed the Majestic in Zanzibar and was particularly sympathetic to the desires of these young fans, said, "We cut the lower stall, closest to the screen, into two sections, and the price of tickets in the lowest section, closest to the screen, was one shilling, or less than half the price of the section behind that. It would fill up with those wild-ones, those who liked to scream and shout, the young men."[86] Cinema owners and managers along the coast consciously priced admission with the goal of maximizing the number of people who could enjoy a show. By reserving a substantial section of the theater for those without a lot of money, they ensured that everyone, not just the wealthy, had access to the cinema. Khalid, who grew up in the Dar es Salaam neighborhood of Magomeni and worked as a youth in the 1970s moving goods in a warehouse, said that these front-row seats were affordable to every young man he knew: "Even the guys who sold peanuts on the street could afford to get in. And man, did we go! Daily, daily we went to the movies!"[87]

Front rows also provided young men with a space where they were allowed and even encouraged to physically express their youthful gendered identities; these ruffian rows vibrated with male physicality. According to managers, one almost never found a female sitting in these seats, and not once did I interview a woman who confessed to having sat in the front. Unencumbered by social expectations of propriety and restraint, young men acted as if the world was theirs to do with as they pleased. They sang, danced, shouted, and frequently threw peanuts and orange rinds at the screen. Asked to describe the atmosphere in this section during the action films he frequented, Abdulrahim exclaimed, "It was crazy! Fists were flying, people were hooting and hollering at the villain, cheering for the hero. Oh man, we had a good time!"[88] Along the same lines, Bakari reported, "Oh when the action in the film reached a climax, everyone would be on their feet shouting. It was like a football match in the heat of the battle. And for Indian films too, we would strut about, we would sing, we'd dance like we were the young couple on screen!"[89] This was male bonding at its best.

Young men relished having what they regarded as their own unique space, a place where they were in control. As Ali put it, "This was our section, ours alone. We could dance along with the Indian belles or do Kung Fu with Bruce Lee. Everyone knew what to expect from the young men up in front. If you didn't like it you sat in the back. This space was ours."[90] During the colonial era, the educated, middle-class, African male elites were somewhat appalled by such "uncivilized" behavior. In the 1950s, the letters to the editor in the *Tanganyika Standard* frequently featured complaints, authored by the well-heeled and literate 2 percenters, about the "hooligans," the "ill-behaved," and the "mentally deficient" who shouted during movies and threw things at the screen.[91] Others, however, were more forgiving, adopting a "boys will be boys" attitude toward such behavior; these folks simply opted to buy tickets near the back of the theater, as far from such shenanigans as their pocketbooks would allow. Mwalim Idd said appeals in the newspapers were pointless; it was more effective to simply buy tickets for a higher class of seat. Having once been young himself, he viewed things philosophically: "If you sat in the young men's section you had to be prepared for people who acted like young men."[92]

Luckily for more "respectable" patrons, the youth preferred going to the late show, rather than the evening show where elders and women made up the majority of the crowd. In Zanzibar, it was (and remains) something of an unwritten rule that young men had to stay out late at night with a group of peers. Going home before their parents were asleep somehow undermined their status as real men. The night show gave them something to do while fulfilling this gendered expectation. As one anonymous man explained, "Every night, every night I went to the cinema. Back then [in the 1950s and 1960s] there was nowhere else to go. So I would go to the movies from 9 pm until midnight, which was then a reasonable time to go home and go to bed." When I asked Ameri which show he preferred to attend, he declared without hesitation, "Me, I went at night. The night show was better, it was more enjoyable. If you went to the six o'clock show you had to be out of the theater by 9 pm and then there was nowhere else to go and it was too early to go home." But if he went to the 9:00 show, he could easily stay occupied until midnight. "You weren't rushed out of the theater to make way for the next show, so you could relax and really enjoy it and stay out late."[93] When a film that appealed particularly to a young male audience played—such as *Mean Johnny Barrows* (Williamson, 1976), one of the first blaxploitation films starring Fred Williamson, or Italian thrillers such as *The Spy Who Loved Flowers* (Lenzi, 1966) or Hollywood

213

action films such as *Dixie Dynamite* (Frost, 1976)—attendance for the 9:00 p.m. show was often two to three times that of evening performances of the same film.[94] In Moshi and Dar es Salaam in the 1970s and 1980s, there were also all-night shows at the holidays. Two or three films would be run in succession, from midnight to 6:00 a.m. Ninety-five percent of those in attendance were young, unmarried men.[95] Youth also went alone, something no woman I spoke with ever did. Across the nation, feeling free, safe, and financially secure enough to go to the cinema by oneself was yet another privilege gendered male.

One of the questions I specifically asked in the course of interviews and surveys was whether going to the cinema was considered a respectable thing for a woman to do—or whether that in any way compromised a woman's reputation. Responses were markedly different up-country and along the coast, and they varied by religion as well. Hindu women often had the greatest difficulty getting permission to attend the cinema. In this, gender expectations, religious mores regarding caste, and class coalesced. All girls had to ask their parents for money as well as permission to see a film. For Hindu parents of the poorest children, the price of cinema tickets was prohibitively expensive. And wealthy Hindu families typically forbade their daughters to go to any screenings other than the ladies' shows. Nearly all the Muslims I consulted, whether male or female, indicated that going to the cinema was a perfectly respectable thing for a woman or girl to do. Interestingly, a number of Shia Ithnasheris I interviewed remarked that communal opinion became somewhat divided on this topic in the mid-1980s as a wave of more conservative teachers and clerics began to proselytize in Tanzania after the Iranian revolution. Several women who had grown up in Zanzibar, Dar es Salaam, and Mwanza regularly attending the movies with their families on Sundays said that they stopped going in the mid-1980s because of communal perceptions that such practices were now *haram* (forbidden). Not all Ithnasheris agreed, however, and many continued to go to the show.

Cinema managers, many of whom were themselves Muslim, also stressed that they worked to ensure that theaters were perceived as respectable spaces. Despite the young and boisterous crew in the front rows, respectability permeated the atmosphere. As one Ithnasheri cinema manager explained, "Going to the cinema was a normal, typical thing for a woman to do. Inside, no one would challenge a woman's honor. . . . And if a man did I would not admit him again."[96] Managers across the country made similar comments about their responsibility as proprietors to guarantee women's safety and dignity while at the show. Young men's hooliganism was allowed, but it was safely contained in the front rows; their freedom to mimic, mock, and make advances toward women was limited to interactions with the screen. In the mixed space of Sunday screenings or where large numbers of women were in the crowd, these men were also far more reserved than at midweek screenings of actions films, where they were often the only ones in the theater.

Christians often considered both cities and cinemas to be dangerous places for women, particularly during the colonial era. Far fewer Christian women went to the movies compared to Muslims or even Hindus. According to Josephine and many others, if a young woman went to the cinema in Moshi, she was pegged as a rebel (*mhuni kabisa*) or a woman of ill repute.[97] "Going to town to go to church was one thing," said Semeni from Bagamoyo, "but if a girl went to town simply to go to the cinema she would be seen as wandering about for no good reason, and she might miss getting a husband. No one would want to marry a girl who wandered about like that."[98] Numerous people told me that both preachers and parents instilled in them the idea that girls who attended the cinema were "practicing prostitution." A female interviewee named Gladness explained her parents' prohibitions on going to the show quite simply: "They didn't want me to get pregnant before marriage."[99] In the tightly controlled patriarchal parishes around Moshi, where both Catholic and Protestant leaders promoted female obedience and subordination to male and church-based authority, few women or girls were willing to be ostracized just to go to a movie.[100] Actually, I had a difficult time finding African women who grew up around Moshi during the colonial era who even expressed a desire to go the cinema. Moviegoing just was not something that appealed to Christian women of their generation.

The fact that theaters were located in cities, beyond the culturally and morally sanctified space in which village elders were comfortable and in control, added an extra dimension to their social marginality. Colonialism also played a pivotal part in conflating cities and sin, particularly for women. As new towns and cities grew near mines and railway termini, women quickly discovered a ready market among male migrants for their domestic skills. From Abeokuta to the Zambian Copperbelt, Nairobi to Johannesburg, and nearly everywhere in between, cities provided women with opportunities for economic and sexual autonomy that many of them found attractive but that rural elders simultaneously found quite threatening.[101] Women's agricultural and domestic labor was key to rural economic survival, and male patriarchs and colonial authorities across the continent collaborated to try to keep women "down on the farm." In the 1920s, the first moral panic over urban women reached a peak. Male authorities tried, with limited success, to mandate that women carry passes, signed by husbands and chiefs, to demonstrate that they had permission to travel to town. Indigenous and colonial authorities also attempted to prevent women from boarding trains or buying urban property, again with only limited success. In the 1940s, this crisis in male control over women again came to a head.[102] Unmarried women and others deemed beyond control were rounded up by local authorities, ethnic associations, and colonial police across the continent, including in Tanzania. What this meant for moviegoing was that just when coastal people began attending the movies in the largest numbers, there was heightened discourse in much of Tanzania about the idea that women who went to town were "lost." Only prostitutes went to the cities, or so the saying went, and unless a woman was willing to stand up to such accusations, she stayed far from town.

Both J. A. K. Leslie and Susan Geiger noted that religious affiliation impacted perceptions about the appropriateness of women moving independently in urban space. Geiger found that female TANU activists emerged from those who relished the class, ethnic, and social diversity of urban life. She also observed that women's organizing work for nationalism, which was done on foot and often alone, required knowledge of the city and a feeling of security within it. The most active female TANU organizers were Muslims from Dar es Salaam. In general, she found that the views of the Christian-educated elite were conservative regarding women's movements: a woman's "place" was domestic and dependent. Leslie also noted that Christian women participated far less often in mixed social activities, independent businesses, and trade. Comparing the economic autonomy and social freedom of Muslims and Christians in the capital city, he cited the example of one member of the educated Christian elite who said she had no permission to go out anywhere, except to the police, when her husband was not at home. This same woman told him she did not really like to mix with "random" people in town. Those not of her tribe and class—like most she would encounter at the cinema—were deemed a bad influence. Female TANU activists and Muslim moviegoers, by contrast, relished multiethnic, cross-class leisure pursuits and the opportunity they provided to move beyond the domestic sphere.[103]

In regions of the country where Christians predominated, women were a distinct minority in the audience well into the 1970s and 1980s. Pankaj Valambia, whose father built the Sapna Cinema in Morogoro, said that women rarely went to the theater unless it was with their husbands; there was no ladies-only show at the Sapna. Pankaj ran the theater beginning in 1978, when action films, including kung fu, reigned. He estimated weekly attendance at 95 percent African and 5 percent Asian and noted that roughly 70 to 80 percent of the audience was male.[104] Suresh Solanki, who managed the Plaza Cinema in Moshi during these same years, said that over the course of a week, 70 percent of his audience was also male. In these towns, I had difficulty finding any African women over fifty who had gone to the movies more than occasionally. In Iringa, Moshi, Arusha, and Morogoro, all the managers estimated that even for Sunday Indian films, women still comprised well less than half the audience, and they added that most of the women in attendance were Asian or Arab. Age differences among women were also stark: Asian and Arab women of every age went to the movies, but nearly all the African women were in their late teens and early twenties. Going to the movies was a new thing for African women in regional towns, something many only began to consider doing in the 1960s and 1970s (see chapter 7). Lulu was one of several women who told me about "sneaking" to the movies while in her teens. Her family moved to Arusha in the 1970s, and neither of her parents had ever been to a cinema. Based on what they had learned about the evils of moviegoing in their rural church, they forbade Lulu to go. But in the 1970s, *everyone* in her generation was talking about Bruce Lee, Pam Grier, Mithun Chakraborty, Hema Malini, and Amitabh Bachchan, and she just *had* to see what the fuss was all about. Lulu was among the first generation of up-country African women to go to the show.[105]

Cinemas, Cities, and Audiences: Cultural Geographies and Social Difference

Along the coast, women attended movies from the earliest days, and the consensus among interviewees was that the gender and generational demographics of the theater reflected that of the town. In Muslim families, everyone went to the show. Women's attendance at the movies was further encouraged by *ladies-only* shows held in the afternoon. From the 1950s through the 1970s, women had the privilege of attending at least one and often two or more weekly screenings reserved for them alone.[106] In Dar es Salaam, the Odeon, Empress, Avalon, Empire, Chox, and Cameo all offered zanana shows, and in Zanzibar too, one or more theaters held special screenings for women each week. The films were mostly Indian or Egyptian, and those featuring popular female stars such as Hema Malini, Nutan, Mumtaz, Rekha, or Asha Parekh could easily draw hundreds of women to the theater any afternoon.[107] Managers sometimes also offered repeat films for ladies-only versions of the one-shilling-all-around shows.

Often, going to the cinema was the only opportunity women had to leave their homes, walk the streets, and mix in public. Weddings and funerals were important social events, but moviegoing offered a more regular opportunity for outings. Between puberty and their first marriage, most girls had particularly restricted and supervised movement, so moviegoing was even more important to their social lives. Sofia and her sisters rarely got to leave the house unchaperoned. "But zanana shows, we went to all the time!" she exclaimed. Zanana shows were the only occasion her father allowed her to walk the streets with her friends. "So we really took advantage of the opportunity."[108] Numerous adult women also stressed how they were empowered by ladies' shows, which allowed them to take over an entire theater as well as the city streets before and after the show. Like the young men in the front rows on other occasions, women could claim the cinema as theirs and theirs alone during zanana shows.

With two hundred to four hundred women in attendance, such shows were easily the largest all-female gatherings in town. "There were few other places we got to see our friends in such numbers," said Khadija. "Nowhere else we got to see so many women, including all the members of the extended family."[109] Another women said, "Anyone and everyone you wanted to see was there." Others described the festive atmosphere as akin to a giant communal party but far more diverse, since the guests at most of the parties women attended were primarily from their own religious or ethnic communities. Ladies' shows drew women from all walks of urban life. "It was like a wedding," said another woman, "only better, because so many people came. It was packed!"[110] For young women, zanana shows were a rare and critically important venue for encountering various models of adult womanhood. Here, girls learned that not every woman behaved or thought like their mothers or aunts. Maryam, who was a regular at the shows but otherwise rarely left the house, explained the significance of these events: "I did not go to school, and I cannot read, so going to the movies really opened my eyes. At the movies I got to see women from all walks of Zanzibar life and I got to see women from other countries, like India, and see how their life compared to mine."[111] At the shows, coastal women saw Indian actresses, many of whom were also Muslim, as glamorous screen stars and as lawyers, teachers, mothers, and bandits in the roles they played. These portrayals opened up imaginative possibilities for Tanzanian women; few of them held professional jobs in the 1950s, but growing numbers were receiving more than just a rudimentary education. Interviewees said that seeing women portrayed as professionals encouraged them to recognize the value of school or seek additional professional training. Both the action on the screen and the action in the aisles allowed women to broaden their understandings of femininity.

Going out, being seen, and viewing others was a critical part of the ladies' show experience. Women and girls making their way to the cinema transformed the streets into runways or fashion promenades through the city center. One employee at the Empress in Dar es Salaam fondly recalled his heart palpitating wildly each Monday as the women gathered outside the theater for the show. "These ladies' shows, oh they were crazy! The show would start at 2 o'clock and by 12 o'clock people would be lining up, trying to get a good seat. . . . The theater would be packed, packed with all these beautiful women, all dressed up in their finest."[112] Ladies' shows added visual pleasure to urban life, not just from films, but from the hundreds of gorgeous women seen on the streets.

Zanana shows also offered women a rare opportunity to claim time for themselves. Regardless of how often they went, women described the chance to leave their domestic responsibilities behind as a real treat. In Nasra's household, all the women, young and old, would periodically go to these shows. "The men would be left to care for the little ones. For once, we got to relax and enjoy," she said.[113] Zanana shows provided women with

220

the opportunity to enter the public sphere as well as the socially sanctioned opportunity to require hubands and fathers to manage the domestic sphere, which in many households was equally rare.

The comparative size of cinemas built in Tanzania during the colonial era reflected the general population's sense of ease in the city and Africans' positions as citizens of the town. In the 1920s, when the 900-seat Royal opened in Zanzibar, the cinema in Moshi sat 120 and the theater in Mwanza 200, and rarely in either case were more than one-quarter of the seats filled.[114] Even in the 1950s, as the number of theaters on the mainland multiplied, the differences between coastal and provincial towns remained. New cinemas in Shinyanga, Morogoro, Bukoba, and Mpanda sat fewer than 300 people, whereas the Majestic in Tanga had nearly 700 seats and the Empress in Dar es Salaam almost 800.[115] More people went to any of the coastal theaters on a single Sunday than frequented the Playhouse in Iringa in a month. The two theaters owned by Sheriff Alwi El-Beity reflected the stark regional variations in urban audiences. He first operated the Enterprise Theater in Mbeya, which sat 344, and like most up-country cinemas, it rarely sold 100 tickets on its best days. After independence, he moved to Dar es Salaam and built the Starlight Theater, which accommodated more than 1,000 and was just one of several cinemas in the capital city's reeling circuit that brought thousands into the streets each Sunday.[116]

Only with independence did cinemas—and the cities where they were located—gradually begin to feel more welcoming to populations in many towns. Still, it often took a generation for moviegoing to become a common leisure pursuit. As coming chapters elaborate, participating in the social life surrounding movies also helped integrate immigrants into new urban social networks, thus making the city both more familiar and more embracing. Wiping tears, singing songs, and sharing laughter after a show created affective attachments between friends and between them and the urban environment. These ties helped transform cities that were alien to parents and grandparents into the postindependence generation's idea of home. Moviegoing also became a shared experience that helped integrate people from disparate regions into a nation.

Chapter 6

DRIVE-IN SOCIALISM

Debating Modernities and Development in Dar es Salaam

IN MAY 1966, the first—and perhaps only—socialist drive-in on the planet opened in the nation's capital, Dar es Salaam, on the site of what is today the American Embassy.[1] The brainchild of C. C. Patel, a cunning and well-connected insurance magnate with business, political, and family ties throughout East Africa, with the assistance of Prime Minister and Second Vice President Rashid Kawawa, a former actor, the drive-in was heralded by leading Tanzanian politicians as a stunning example of the modernist development opportunities achievable through African socialism.[2] At the ribbon-cutting ceremony, the minister of commerce and cooperatives, Abdulrahman Mohamed Babu, an avowed Marxist and an avid supporter of state socialism, hailed it as an "exemplary project of co-operation" between private enterprise and the socialist state.[3] The capital for building and operating the drive-in was provided entirely by Patel. The Tanzanian government acquired a 30 percent stake in the venture through a "donation" of land, and unnamed officials were granted shares in the company in exchange for their support.[4] In the spirit of the African socialism that was sweeping the nation at the time, the corporate name of the drive-in was Sisi Enterprises, with the "C. C." of Patel's initials superseded by *Sisi*, the Kiswahili word for "we" or "us."[5]

Yet why, one might reasonably ask, would a young nation like Tanzania—striving to dig its way out from under the problems caused by decades of colonial underdevelopment—choose to invest its limited resources in a drive-in? How could state ownership of a drive-in possibly help advance a socialist agenda? Didn't the drive-in—predicated as it was on the commercial consumption of foreign films and propelled by the urban amenities of electricity, cars, and leisure—directly contradict President Julius Nyerere's vision of village-based African socialism? Why would a righteous communist like Babu or a man like Kawawa, who launched several campaigns against youthful "debauchery" in the 1960s and 1970s, be motivated to participate in the opening festivities for a space that was commonly regarded as a passion pit?[6] How did the same government that banned television broadcasting until the mid-1990s and arrested private owners of televisions and VCRs in the early 1980s rationalize owning a drive-in? And why would a regime that frequently vilified Tanzanian Asians in the state-owned press and nationalized their property in the name of equality choose to partner with Patel, one of the wealthiest men in East Africa? The most obvious answer to these questions is that states, like the individuals who comprise them, are complicated and often contradictory entities that sometimes say one thing and do another.

Although the anomaly of a socialist drive-in cinema may complicate our understanding of state-centered development, we can use it to explore the complex and contradictory visions of socialism, modernity, and independence that were debated in Tanzania in the 1960s and 1970s. Sisi Enterprises was but one of many high modernist commercial leisure and industrial projects presaged by the National Development Corporation (NDC) in its published reports and magazines, championing the state's ability to fulfill not only needs but desires as well. Socialism and communism were conceived by many as alternatives to capitalism when it came to the fulfillment of consumptive desires. The aim was to achieve abundance; the goal was to do so without the cutthroat antagonisms and inequalities associated with capitalism. Somewhat akin to Joseph Stalin's 1930s campaign to provide champagne, caviar, and chocolate to Soviet stalwarts who had endured decades of economic deprivation, the drive-in allowed NDC to point to particular pleasures and make the claim, as Stalin had, that "life has become more joyous, Comrades."[7]

Interviews conducted with former patrons of the theater and en-tries that were submitted to an essay contest on the theme of moviegoing provide exuberant evidence of the joys experienced at the drive-in. The drive-in captured Tanzanians' historical enthusiasm for film and moviego-ing and compounded it, adding the glories of automobility and the latest exhibition technology to the show. More than twenty years after the last film was shown there, the bus stop at that location is still marked and referred to as "Drive-In," which speaks volumes about the affective power of this place in urban social cartography. Nostalgia looms large in many recollections.[8] Interview questions about evenings spent at the drive-in elicited cherished memories of a bygone era—a visceral longing for a time when both respondents and the nation were young. Those I spoke with expressed a sentimental yearning for the public space where families solidified, communities were built, and urban *ujamaa* (African socialism) was given tangible form.

Almost instantly, the drive-in became one of the premier destinations for leisure in Dar es Salaam. In 1966, its first year of operation, the busi-ness realized a little over 1.3 million Tanzanian shillings (TSh) in sales, roughly the equivalent of $1.3 million in 2016 US dollars.[9] At a time when the city's population was less than 273,000, nearly three times as many people visited the drive-in during that first year.[10] On a typical Sunday, families would head out early and get in line beginning at three in the afternoon, even though the show did not start until sundown, at roughly seven. By four o'clock, the line at the drive-in gates was often more than a mile long. Spending hours on a Sunday in that line at the drive-in was a defining generational experience for those who lived in Dar es Salaam between 1966 and 1986. During those formative years of nation building, the Sunday queue was somewhere one could actually see, rather than merely imagine, a diverse cross section of the populace patiently working toward a common goal.

Although the socialist credentials of a drive-in might seem suspect, Sisi Enterprises provided an architectural space where urban ujamaa and socialist citizenship were lived and where many newly arrived middle-class Africans first experienced the pleasures of collective moviegoing. In that space, one could see Asians and Africans side by side in their cars and youth and elders in dialogue about the same films and stars. There, not just men but women and youth too were allowed to enjoy public nightlife without jeopardizing their reputations. Those at the drive-in admittedly enjoyed a higher socioeconomic status than the average Tanzanian, but in addition to the spots for 650 cars, there were 100 seats for walk-in patrons. Those seats, as well as mats laid on the ground surrounding the cars, were regularly filled by less affluent fans who walked over from nearby neighborhoods, rode over on their bicycles, or alighted from the public bus that stopped right outside the entrance gates. In Tanzania in the 1960s and 1970s, it was not necessary to be a member of the elite to enjoy an evening at the show, and whether one arrived on foot, by bus, in the back of a pickup truck, or in a private sedan was irrelevant once the movie began.[11] The Sunday films that played at the drive-in were often being shown at the traditional theaters in town as well, so it was not uncommon for some ten thousand people to view the same movie on opening day. Come Monday morning, car owners, bus riders, and pedestrians were once again *wajamaa* (social equals or members of the same family) as they began to dissect and debate the latest scandal and drama to hit the screen. Being able to contribute an informed analysis of the latest film was a hallmark of urban citizenship. It did not matter how you got to the cinema, said many of the poorer people; the point was that you were there and could engage in these debates.

NDC relished the success of the drive-in. In its publications, it pointed to Sisi Enterprises as a potent symbol of the modernization and technological advancement that Africa could achieve by following a path of socialist development. Across the continent, modernist technocratic projects were all the rage. Nearly everyone welcomed large technological innovations—dams, tractors, and chemical fertilizers in the countryside and industrialization in the towns—as a way to bring Africa into the so-called modern age.[12] Millions on the continent, from miners in Zambia to technocrats in Ghana, believed that everyone's standard of living would soon rise to a level previously enjoyed only in the West.[13] Nationalists across the continent claimed—and citizens truly wanted to believe—that independence indeed marked a radical rupture with the past. The time-space continuum of colonialism that had somehow seemed to relegate Africans to the undeveloped past had been overturned by independence.[14] Sisi Enterprises allowed Tanzanians to drive right into the modern age.

It is important to note that socialism, like modernity, was never precisely defined in Tanzania. The road leading to socialist development was never definitively mapped out, and there was no general consensus on how to measure or evaluate socialist economic and communal progress. The term *ujamaa* was coined by Nyerere to distinguish Tanzanian socialism from its Russian, Cuban, and Chinese predecessors. Socialism, he asserted, was not about class conflict, overthrowing capitalism, or radically transforming production; it was "an attitude of mind," a political and moral commitment to ensuring that everyone's needs were met and that wealth and work were evenly distributed.[15] Nyerere's philosophy of socialism was rooted in a bucolic vision of the precolonial extended family: *ujamaa* literally translates as "familyhood." In precolonial Africa, he argued, families and communities lived together happily, cooperated willingly, worked hard to contribute to the economic pursuits of the collective, and shared unselfishly—all under the gentle guidance of a benevolent patriarch. That was the model independent Tanzania should emulate. According to Nyerere, the nation's future development rested on utilizing the resources it had—land, peasants, and fortitude. There was no point in wishing for money the nation did not have; it was better to harness the assets it could control.[16] Six years after independence, the president announced the Arusha Declaration (1967), which laid out the party's creed on socialism, inaugurated the nationalization of major components of the economy, and initiated the push for rural development in earnest.[17] He pointedly criticized the use of state resources for urban and industrial projects that exacerbated the gap between rural and urban living standards.[18] Only when farmers and their families also had access to electricity, piped water, primary schooling, basic health care, and adequate housing, he argued, should the nation consider spending resources on additional urban amenities. Nyerere's book *Uhuru na Ujamaa* (Freedom and Socialism) contained key policy statements, but citizens, bureaucrats, party members, and others offered myriad alternative readings of the text.

Although Nyerere was considered by many to be the father of the nation, he was not the only member of the ujamaa family with a vision or a voice. Within the extended family of his TANU party, among fictive kin in government bureaucracies, and amid the disobedient sons and daughters of the nation who fought their father at every turn, a wide variety of ideas and

225

ideals circulated regarding how, by whom, and for whom the household that was Tanzania should be run. The chairman of NDC and all members of the board of directors, many of whom were also cabinet ministers, were appointed by the president, but that did not necessarily mean that they shared his vision or his values. Most of those who were involved with NDC believed that only through industrialization could Tanzania's national economy progress. Some advocated for industrialization because they were staunch believers in modernization theory and regarded industrialization as key to raising the people's standard of living. Others were classic examples of the bureaucratic bourgeoisie, eager to cement their ties to foreign capital and reap the rewards of the ruling class.[19] Some argued that industrialization was key to curbing the flow of capital out of the country for the purchase of commonly used imported goods. A small number pushed for industrialization because their intellectual commitment to Marxism meant that they viewed the industrial working class as the most dynamic class in history, the one destined to lead Africa to a more prosperous future. Several, including Minister Babu—who cut the ribbon at the opening ceremony for the drive-in—pointedly argued that peasants were not only docile but also dumb.[20]

The push for industrialization began nearly a decade before efforts to promote socialist rural development.[21] Within six months of independence, in December 1961, the parliament created the Tanganyika Development Corporation.[22] It was renamed the National Development Corporation in 1965. NDC was a massive commercial organization involved in finance, mining, manufacturing, agriculture and agricultural processing, transportation, publishing, import-export trading, petroleum processing, and hotels and tourism. By the late 1960s, it was the whole or part owner—on behalf of the people of Tanzania—of forty-nine companies employing twenty-four thousand people, most of whom lived in towns.[23] Large, mechanized industrial facilities producing steel, concrete, textiles, tires, and lumber were the norm. Modernization via industrialization was central to NDC's vision of development.

Although a drive-in might seem to be a categorically different type of project than a railway, cement factory, or textile plant, at that time drive-ins were quite modernist, and Tanzania's claim to ownership placed it among a relatively small number of nations to realize such an achievement. The first "automobile movie theatre" was built in the United States in 1933, but it was only in the 1950s that drive-ins really took off. Tanzanians began attending the drive-in at roughly the same time as millions of their American

Figure 6.1 Drive-in audience watching a screening of the launch of *Apollo 11*.
From NDC, *Fifth Annual Report and Accounts*, 1969, p. 90

and Australian counterparts and years before many people in Europe.[24] By the end of the 1960s, in fact, there were reportedly only a handful of drive-ins on the European continent. As late as the 1980s, entrepreneurial efforts in this direction in Britain remained something of a joke, having more in common with the Colonial Office's mobile cinema van shows than with the slick modern venues operating in the United States or Dar es Salaam.[25] It was almost unheard of for Tanzanians to claim technological superiority to their former colonial masters on any front, but the drive-in

Drive-In Socialism: Debating Modernities and Development

gave them legitimate bragging rights on at least one score. With room for more than six hundred cars, a children's playground, a personalized loud-speaker, a call button for placing orders from the restaurant and bar, and the latest screen and projection equipment, it was on a par with anything operating in American suburbs at the time.[26] At the drive-in, Tanzanians did not have to imagine catching up to the West; there, they were in the lead. In interviews, they boasted that European expatriates even showed off the drive-in to visitors from home. Countless expats, development workers, faculty members at the university, and leftist activists from abroad shared their own fond memories of the modern splendors afforded by the drive-in and confirmed that this was a common place to take a visiting guest.

Sisi Enterprises also gave Tanzanians bragging rights over most of the African continent, as few other nations had a drive-in. South Africa was the exception, boasting more than seventy by the 1960s.[27] Yet nearly all of them were segregated, and most were reserved for the white population. Kenya, another colony with a large number of wealthy white settlers, was the only other nation on the continent to have a drive-in in the 1950s. Africans were not directly involved in the race into outer space, but they *were* involved in their own competitions for modernity, and in this, automobility was a key measure of success.[28] Uganda pulled in second behind Kenya, opening a drive-in just a few months before Tanzania did. Neither Ghana nor Nigeria had one, and only in the mid- to late 1970s did Namibia, Zambia, and Rhodesia join the race.[29] Tanzanians were aware and proud of the fact that their drive-in was one of only a few on the continent and that along with Uganda's it was the only one not linked with white owners from South Africa.[30] At a time when Tanzania served as the African base for freedom fighters from across southern Africa who were struggling to break the economic and political stranglehold of apartheid, the drive-in provided major symbolic capital. Odd though it may seem, Sisi Enterprises performed vital political work for the state, bolstering claims that African socialism could provide the masses not just with goods but with good times as well.

In addition to being one of the most modern ways to view a movie, the drive-in utilized the latest innovations in cinematic and telecommunications technology, enabling Tanzanians to experience and be part of the most modern advancements of the age. The NDC annual report of 1969 proudly displayed a photo of a drive-in audience witnessing the launch of *Apollo 11*, the first space mission to land a man on the moon, on July 20, 1969. Media

Figure 6.2 On the dance floor in Dar es Salaam during the age of *Apollo*. Photo courtesy of Ali Ghafoor

advancements of the era thus put Tanzanians in touch not only with Hollywood and Bollywood stars but also with the man on the moon. Across the globe, people felt triumphant as they witnessed Neil Armstrong utter those now-famous words as he stepped down onto the lunar surface: "One small step for man, one giant leap for mankind." Project Apollo epitomized the entangled geographies of modernization, with technological wonders that people across the globe claimed as their own. Space exploration was a frequent front-page news item in Tanzania. And in Dar es Salaam, Tanzanian youth signaled the simultaneity of their own modernity by embodying this giant leap for mankind in a new dance craze that swept the city that year. According to several men who recalled the moves, "the Apollo" involved both a leap into the air, replicating the launch, and slow-motion steps across the dance floor, emulating Armstrong as seen in newsreels at the cinemas.[31]

Leftists considered many of NDC's investments to be less than revolutionary. According to Issa Shivji, 30 percent of NDC's holdings by 1968 were in luxury commodities, including breweries, cigarette factories, and safari game parks, compared to only 10 percent of investments in companies producing necessities such as the cloth, hoes, and bicycles used by average Tanzanians.[32] In the 1970s and 1980s, numerous hard-hitting critiques of NDC were published by those on the left. Central points of critique were that Tanzania's development was overly reliant on foreign partners—including the World Bank—for both initiating and financing projects; that technical, management, and royalty agreements involved the heavy loss of foreign exchange; that the majority of NDC projects entailed large-scale capital- and import-intensive technologies ill suited to the realities of Tanzania; that a large percent of investments went toward producing primary products for export to traditional colonial trade partners rather than goods for local consumption; that many industrial projects were highly automated rather than labor-intensive, thus doing little to enhance local employment; that worker's concerns, interests, and ideas were undervalued or ignored in management decision making; and that, in sum, NDC had done little to alter the colonial and capitalist economic structures inherited at independence.[33]

Issa Shivji was perhaps one of the most vocal and persistent critics of NDC, but he had many allies. His article "Tanzania: The Silent Class Struggle" and his larger work *Class Struggles in Tanzania* provide detailed analyses and trenchant critiques of the neocolonial underdevelopment policies pursued by NDC, including an amazing analysis of the web of transnational capital flows siphoning profits from Tanzania to countries and corporations outside of its borders. Students of globalization and neoliberal economics should go back and read his rich and timeless analysis. From the dairy industry to sugar and transportation, the international bourgeoisie, rather than Tanzanians, remained in control of the national economy. As one example, Shivji details how the nationalized Dar es Salaam Motor Transport Company was one of some fifty-five subsidiaries and associated companies in Africa owned by the giant British transport concern United Transport Overseas Ltd. (UTOS). In 1966, UTOS made net profits after tax of more than £1.7 billion from its holdings in eastern and southern Africa.[34] C. E. Barker et al. detail similar patterns of "surplus" capital extraction with Tanzanian Breweries. First incorporated in Tanganyika in 1922, Tanzania Breweries was a subsidiary of East African Breweries Ltd , based in Kenya, which was itself linked to two larger British brewing interests in England. When the industry was nationalized, NDC came to hold a majority of shares in the company, yet management fees, interest paid on loans for equipment, and remittance of expatriate salaries for brewers and sales staff based in Kenya and the United Kingdom meant that most of the income generated by the sale of beer in Tanzania was drained from the country.[35] Tanzanian Breweries may have been among the more profitable NDC holdings, far outstripping the sales and profits of Sisi, but most of the proceeds left the country.

UTOS and Tanzanian Breweries were typical rather than exceptional examples of NDC relations with foreign firms. Aart van de Laar estimated, in 1972, that 70 to 80 percent of the total industrial production in Tanzania was controlled by foreign firms, that expat employees accounted for 47 percent of the total wages paid by NDC firms, and that 70 percent of the calculated net profit of NDC holdings had been transferred abroad through one means or another.[36] Other critics challenged NDC's decision making by illustrating how significant drains on the national economy resulted from the organization's willingness to grant its foreign partners control in choosing the technology for projects, which often led to the purchase of secondhand, obsolete machinery for new factories. Tanzania Bag Company, a sisal bag factory that had accumulated more than three million shillings in losses by 1973, and Kiltex, a textile factory in Arusha built with obsolete equipment purchased from Britain, are two examples of production facilities that operated well below efficiency, when operating at all, due to frequent breakdowns and the difficulty of obtaining spare parts.[37] Regardless of the factories' production, NDC was obligated to repay the loans (plus interest) taken out to finance the purchase of the equipment used in these plants.

Sisi Enterprises was different from these other companies in several pivotal ways. For one, it was among just a handful of companies in the portfolio that were not financed with loans or aid from abroad.[38] Financially, Sisi Enterprises epitomized Nyerere's call for self-reliance and economic nationalism (*kujitegemea*), employing local resources to foster development. The drive-in was also highly profitable, earning the state a 12 percent

Drive-In Socialism: Debating Modernities and Development

return in its first year of operation.[39] Gross earnings increased a further 37 percent from 1968 to 1969.[40] Dividend payouts jumped from roughly $5,000 in 1969 to nearly $27,000 in 1970.[41] At a time when the state needed millions of dollars to build schools, dispensaries, sewage and water facilities, railways, and roads, Sisi offered a glimmer of hope for self-financed development. In contrast to the vast majority of NDC projects, the managers, technical experts, projectionists, electricians, sound system engineers, builders, and employees were also all Tanzanian. The 75,000 shillings spent annually on wages stayed and recirculated entirely within the country, thus furthering local economic development.[42] Unlike the rubber, steel, and cement plants, which often suffered "technical difficulties" because of their reliance on external inputs or local water and electrical systems that could not meet their needs, the drive-in utilized networks of film distribution and exhibition practices that had been honed and perfected over several generations by Tanzanians. The location of the theater was also chosen in part because the area was among the least likely in the nation to suffer power outages, owing to its proximity to the homes of leading politicians, including the president. Having local partners with local knowledge and a lifetime of personal connections definitely had its advantages. The screen, projection equipment, and films were imported from abroad, but unlike the NDC's cashew and cloth plants, the drive-in was no secondhand affair. All the equipment was new and met the most up-to-date standards in the industry.

NYERERE AND THE 'NIZERS DEBATE AUTOMOBILITY

The successful operation of a drive-in theater is predicated on the widespread ownership of private cars, another issue that was a source of vociferous debate among those formulating and implementing state policy in Tanzania. For many, automobility epitomized the urban bias of national development, as private car ownership was largely confined to urban centers and especially to Dar es Salaam. In the early 1970s, some 60 percent of all vehicles in the country were registered in the region surrounding the capital.[43] Other people questioned the very existence of private transportation in a nation where equality was an alleged goal and where most of the people continued to rely on their own two feet to get them and their goods where they needed to go. Nyerere was not alone in advocating for investment in public transportation or more affordable means of enabling the masses to get around, but it was not until 1970 that bus service in the nation's capital was nationalized or that the state made its first investments in bicycle manufacturing.[44]

Many citizens, civil servants, and aspiring members of the middle class viewed car ownership as symbolic of their drive for modernity, and thinking of oneself as modern was an important first step in being recognized as such. In the years immediately following independence, private car ownership skyrocketed. In 1947, there were a mere eight thousand motor vehicles in the country, and most of those were either owned by the government or employed in public and goods transportation. By 1970, however, there were eighty-four thousand vehicles operating in Tanzania, with the vast majority in private hands.[45] Car ownership was the pride of many a Tanzanian man. The occasional woman owned a car too, but in the 1970s, men owned most of them, did most of the driving, and held most of the well-paying salaried jobs. By all accounts, cars were relatively affordable for members of the male professional and middle classes, many of whom also benefited from the government's *karadha* scheme, which granted state-financed loans to individuals for the purchase of automobiles. According to a 1963 survey, half of all midgrade African civil servants living in Dar es Salaam owned a car.[46] Housing was often a perk provided for those employed in the upper echelons of state-owned enterprises, and the Africanization of management, which led to the appellation "'Nizers" for members of this class, meant that increasing numbers of men had discretionary income they could spend on cars and other amenities. Businesspeople and even members of the working class also owned (or aspired to own) cars. Agnello Fernandez, whose father had been a cook and who had been employed as a mechanic in the 1960s and 1970s, recalled that cars were relatively affordable and that bank loans were easy to get for those who had a salaried job. He said that an inexpensive car could be had for TSh 7,000 (roughly $1,000 in 1970 US dollars). He bought a Peugeot 404 for TSh 11,000 when he was earning TSh 1,200 per month.[47] In the mid-1960s, the average family income for civil servants of all ranks in Dar es Salaam was TSh 1,160 per month, putting car ownership within the grasp of many.[48] Godwin Kaduma, who was then a teacher at a school of performing arts, bought his Peugeot in 1968.[49] These two men were not alone; within a decade of independence, 26,555 passenger cars had been imported into Tanzania.[50]

Although car ownership was widespread and largely unquestioned, Nyerere launched numerous campaigns to combat it. In an address in 1965 to the first graduating class of University College, he chastised the graduates for their aspirations for ostentatious, pampered lives, and he specifically criticized their desire to own cars. He chided government employees who took out loans for cars as soon as they began to receive their government salaries, and he said that he expected better from university graduates whose education had been financed by revenue raised from the sweat of peasants. The president considered the use of limited foreign exchange to purchase luxury items such as personal cars to be arrogant, pompous, and irresponsible.[51] According to Cranford Pratt, the ostentatious consumption of cars by members of the government, including the minister of regional administration who ordered seventeen Mercedes-Benzes for regional commissioners despite being told not to, was one of the final straws that led Nyerere to issue the Leadership Code. First articulated as part of the Arusha Declaration in 1967 and reiterated in 1971 as *Mwongozo*, the Leadership Code was intended to instill a socialist ethos among those employed by the government and the party.[52] For 'Nizers (bourgeois wannabes) who lacked "a socialist frame of mind," it was designed to clarify expectations.

Yet at the same time that Nyerere was reprimanding graduates and government employees for their pursuit of automobility, Vice President Kawawa and the board of NDC were finalizing plans for the drive-in with C. C. Patel. Nyerere walked whenever he could as a way to demonstrate his allegiance to and solidarity with the peasants who had to go by foot to get water, take their children to the doctor, or deliver their goods to market. To drive his point home, he even walked 134 miles to Mwanza for the 1967 TANU National Conference, where he announced the Leadership Code.[53] Clearly, performativity was by no means limited to the cinematic screen. Through personal example and pressure on the state-owned press, the president repeatedly questioned whether a nation committed to socialism should be "wasting" its foreign exchange in buying personal cars.[54] But while he was walking across the country in support of the Arusha Declaration's renewed commitment to socialist development and equality, other members of the state were holding a fund-raiser for the Arusha Declaration Fund at the drive-in. As Nyerere was feeling his blisters grow on his way to Mwanza, the general manager of NDC

Figure 6.3 Screening of *Ram aur Shyam* at the drive-in as a fund-raiser for the
Arusha Declaration fund; *left to right:* F. R. Karim (NDC), George Kahama
(NDC general manager), Mrs. Jamal, Mr. A. H. Jamal (minister of finance), Paul
Bomani (minister for economic affairs and development planning), Mrs. Vellani,
and Mr. Vellani (NDC). From *Jenga*, no. 2 (1968): 20

(George Kahama), the minister of finance (A. H. Jamal), and the minister
for economic affairs and development planning (Paul Bomani), accompanied by their wives, were watching the heartthrobs Dilip Kumar and
Waheeda Rehman in the film *Ram aur Shyam* (Chanakya, 1967) from the
comfort of their sedans.[55]

The drive-in satiated some of the specific desires of Tanzania's aspiring middle class. As car ownership increased in the decades following independence, the drive-in gave people a new place to go. It was where those
with cars went to see and be seen; it gave members of the political elite and
the aspiring middle class both an opportunity and a reason to show that
they were on the move. In his analysis of drive-ins in the United States,
Kerry Segrave argues that in order for a drive-in culture to thrive, citizens have to be relatively well off economically and "enjoy an emotional
relationship with their cars."[56] What Tanzanian men lacked in the first
category, they made up for in the second; they bathed and coddled their
cars nearly as often as they did their children; they "tropicalized" them to
make them more comfortable in the African heat; and they personalized
them through the application of painted names, prayers, witticisms, and
art.[57] Cars represented not just class aspirations but also social and political

235

dreams fulfilled. Nyerere may have seen personal cars as a sign of bourgeois affectation, but many others viewed car ownership as proof that national independence had delivered tangible goods.

The 'Nizers were not the only ones who thought that the whole point of independence was to break with the deprivations of the colonial past and celebrate by enjoying a little fun; so did many Marxists, who considered themselves far to the left of Nyerere on economic and political issues. Babu spent his youth learning from leading communists in China, Europe, and the Soviet Union. He was known in Tanzania for his strident denunciations of Western imperialism but also for his appreciation of African jazz bands and fine whiskey.[58] Ali Sultan Issa, a leading comrade from Zanzibar, was more unapologetic than most about his taste for pleasure, revealing in his life story as told to G. Thomas Burgess that he routinely indulged in drinking, smoking marijuana, and extramarital sex. Along with many Soviet stalwarts, he also adored ballet and had a penchant for ballerinas. As a further illustration of the complexity of ideology when embodied in human beings, he also began sharing his recollections of important revolutionary events, noting the erotic movie he was coming out of when each of them happened.[59] Clearly, revolutionary man did not live by politics alone.

INDEPENDENCE AND THE CITY

The drive-in appealed to aspirations for mobility and cosmopolitanism that were part of average citizens' imaginary *uhuru* (independence or freedom) as well, and from the late 1950s through the 1980s, many of those citizens were on the move. Dar es Salaam's African population nearly tripled between 1957 and 1967, and the total population then increased again by 40 percent from 1967 to 1972.[60] Whether across town or across the country, people were increasingly on the go.[61] A key element of British colonial policy was to try to keep Africans living in the countryside, "allowing" them into towns only when it was necessary to meet British labor needs. Africans who resided in colonial cities were also supposed to stay out of the so-called European sections of town except when they were going to work, and in Dar es Salaam, there were laws intended to keep them out of the city center after dark.[62]

The very existence of the drive-in was predicated on mobility—being able to cross town as well as colonial zones of racialized space to get where one wanted to go. Mary Morley Cohen argues that drive-in theaters "literalized the cinema's illusion of mobility by addressing spectators as voyagers." In the United States, the Oasis Theater in Bensenville, Illinois, took the travel theme to the extreme; it was designed around a desert motif, with patrons ushered through the neo–Taj Mahal entrance by a turbaned "'Arab."[63] For Tanzanians, simply being able to enter the previously exclusive white zone was novel enough. The drive-in invited and encouraged Africans to travel the streets of Msasani, a part of Dar es Salaam where they had been welcome only as houseboys, cooks, nannies, and gardeners a decade earlier. Those who usually walked or bicycled frequently described the journey itself as an adventure that brought them pleasure and entertainment. Traversing elite neighborhoods on their way to the drive-in from their homes in working-class and poor neighborhoods was a show in and of itself.[64]

Unlike the fancy hotels and safari game parks that were also owned by NDC, Sisi was by no means an exclusive space for the new elite. Women and children from nearby fishing villages and hawkers who came to sell fruit, drinks, and cigarettes were let in for free by employees. Men from African poor and working-class sections of town enthusiastically shared stories about entire football clubs jogging 3 to 6 miles to the drive-in or piling—along with friends and supporters—into a pickup truck to head to the show.[65] There were also fantastic tales told by men who said they had transported two, three, or even four people on a bicycle. Like Tanzanian transport vehicles, the drive-in rarely turned anyone away. When asked whether they felt out of place for not having a private car, people answered with a resounding "No!" The point was that they were at the show. Khalid Saloum said that it did not really matter to him and his young pals if they even went inside; there was always a group of young men they could join sitting on the hill or perched in the trees, watching the film from outside.[66] Jane Sarkodie recalled how the grassy slopes outside the cinema would regularly fill up with crowds of youth or families who could not afford the entrance fee. They could not hear the sound, she said, but they enjoyed an evening of free entertainment nonetheless: "There were worse ways to pass the evening than sitting in the warm night air watching a strange and wonderful world unfold."[67] Overcoming the "racialist habits of thought" that were the inheritance of colonialism was a necessary component of building a socialist society, said Nyerere, and the drive-in encouraged many to enter a space previously designated "white."[68] It also allowed them to travel

Drive-In Socialism: Debating Modernities and Development

to the far-flung corners of the globe and be exposed to other worlds, if only for the night.

For those who moved to Dar es Salaam from rural regions of the country, the drive-in held a special allure. The vibrant sociability of urban cinemas shared much with the exuberant crowds that gathered when Colonial Film Unit (CFU) vans visited villages, but now, citizens were in the driver's seat: in the city, one could go to the movies any day of the week, whereas villagers were lucky to see a film once or twice in a lifetime.[69] Even those who had attended exhibitions in up-country theaters said that the unique combination of automobility and film added to the drive-in's cachet. Freddy Macha, an arts and culture critic for the national press, attended many movies in his youth, but he said of his first drive-in experience, "It was like being given a glimpse of heaven."[70] John, who moved to Dar es Salaam from Iringa at the age of twenty in 1976, was a regular at the Empire Cinema downtown, but he felt that he had not fully arrived as a modern urban man until a friend with a car took him to the drive-in. He remembered that night as being like his *jando* (initiation), signifying a physical mark of maturity and transformation. He later had use of a car and became a cab driver, but because the vehicle was for work (and was owned by someone else), he typically continued to walk to the cinemas in town with his friends. Yet whenever guests from up-country came to visit, he took them to the drive-in as the highlight of showing them the capital. In Iringa, people also had cars, but their purpose remained largely functional: though folks wanted to cruise, there was nowhere to go to like the drive-in.[71] Using a car for leisure and pleasure, not just as a means to make a living, was automobility at its most refined, said John. If the goal of independence was social mobility or, in Donald Donham's words, to "get hip fast," the drive-in was where it was at.[72]

SOCIALISM AT THE SHOW

In addition to providing a visible, tangible example of the modernizing potential of African socialism, the drive-in and cinemas more generally were stunningly and perhaps singularly successful examples of Tanzania's interracial, multiethnic, cross-class public sphere. In a city where there was still residential segregation by race and class and where most sport, dance, and social clubs were neighborhood based, cinemas were one of the few attractions that brought people from across the city into the same leisure space. Equally important, films provided common texts for people to discuss. Ministers, their office boys, drivers, and maids frequently talked about films, and in this context, they had equal authority and a shared cultural experience. The crowd on an average night at the drive-in ranged from the poorest of the poor to the wife and children of the president.[73] Though the sense of social equality fostered by moviegoing may have been fleeting, there is no denying that it enabled people to momentarily transcend class and ethnic exclusivity and helped bridge gender and generational cleavages as well.

The drive-in was a popular destination for families, in part because admission was cheap and each car could bring two children in for free.[74] Just as Americans often prided themselves on sneaking into the drive-in, Tanzanian families devised intricate ruses to get their other youngsters in without having to pay for them. Many people laughed during their interviews as they recalled being hidden in a *kikapu* (a woven basket for carrying goods) and forced to lie still as their parents negotiated their way past the payment kiosk. A man named Eddy described hiding his younger brothers in the trunk when he took them and some visiting cousins from Mbeya to the drive-in on a Saturday night.[75] John, who took his wife and children to the drive-in every Saturday or Sunday, said that during a recent visit with his children in Texas, they all laughed heartily as they recalled fighting over whose turn it was to be hidden under blankets and baskets so that all five kids could get in for free. A man who worked the drive-in gate for fifteen years said that he and the other employees were well aware of the ruses, but they let people get away with sneaking the kids in as "our way of helping the poor." He justified their ticket-taking laxity as a token expression of employees' commitment to ujamaa—the equal distribution of wealth and pleasure for all.

Sisi's policy of limiting free admission to two children seemed to do little to reduce the number of youngsters in attendance, but it added substantially to the excitement of seeing a show, and sneaking a car full of kids into the venue became the stuff of many fond memories. As Annette Kuhn has argued, people working with oral histories need to pay attention not just to what people say about their memories but also to *how* they say it.[76] The individuals who were interviewed in Dar es Salaam enthusiastically volunteered story after story of "getting over" on the gatekeeper, sneaking into the show, and planning their next adventure.

239

Like their American counterparts in the 1950s and 1960s, many people I interviewed said that once they had children, they started frequenting the drive-in, rather than the cinemas in town, because it was cheaper and easier to go there with their kids.[77] Godwin Kaduma explained, "You could take the kids to the show and they got in free, so it was a good, cheap thing to do with the family on Saturday. You could put down your *mkeka* [mat] next to the car, and the kids could play, wrestle, sleep or whatever and you could sit and watch the movie with your wife."[78] An Asian woman in Zanzibar who had been an avid film fan since her youth lamented how she had had to stop going to the movies when she had young children. "I couldn't enjoy the cinema with my children in tow," she said. "There is too much noise and distraction with the kids. You can't follow the story properly if your children are bothering you, and there is no point in going if you are just going to get frustrated!"[79] Had she lived where there was a drive-in, she said, she and her husband would certainly have continued to enjoy evenings at the show, sending the kids off to the playground or to visit with cousins in an adjacent car.

At the core of Nyerere's vision of African socialism was a society modeled on a happy family under the leadership of a generous patriarch who prided himself not on exploitation but on redistribution.[80] During these pivotal years of building socialism, there were few better places to find a harmonious family or generous patriarch who lived up to these expectations than at the show. In the years immediately following independence, there was immense social pressure on men to provide their families with outings, leisure activities, and time together. National independence heralded a renegotiation of gender relations on many fronts, and the drive-in was one of numerous social arenas where these new norms and expectations were played out. Said John, "Saturday and Sunday, it was your *obligation* as a father to take the family out." Godwin stated that taking his children to the drive-in each week "made him *proud* as a father." "Every Saturday," he noted, "the kids knew: Today we get to go to the drive-in! Today we get to go to the drive-in! They would be ready hours before it was time to go. As a father, it made you happy to see your kids excited and happy. It was a *pleasure* to bring them to the drive-in because it gave them so much joy." Similarly, Kamal recalled that his father, as the head of the extended family, "felt it was his *responsibility* to take everyone out to the drive-in, to bring them together, at least once a week, for an evening of fun." He paid admission for several cars full of junior family members and untold numbers of children because that was what a generous patriarch was expected to do. Joseph recalled that the drive-in was one of the few places his family went together *as* a family, and Jane Sarkodie, his mother, said that the drive-in "was our only form of entertainment" and the only place all members of her family could enjoy themselves in public.[81]

Definitions of what it meant to be a good man or a responsible husband and father varied over the years. Yet, as was the case across the continent at different points in time, increased incomes and higher standards of living often came with new obligations toward dependents.[82] In Dar es Salaam during the first two decades after independence, a man's ability to take his family out for a night on the town and his willingness to spend his leisure time not only with his male friends but also with his wife and children were important measures of a family's modernity, as well as social markers of responsible adult urban male behavior. Ujamaa was not only about reimagining the nation; it was about reimagining genders, generations, and socialist families as well.

As a social space, the drive-in also created a public place where women and youth could express and experience their new status as urban citizens; it was a new venue for entering public space in a respectable way. "An evening at the drive-in wasn't just about the film," said Jane. "It was a night out, a sociable event where you *always* met up with someone you wanted to talk to."[83] Other entrants in the essay contest I sponsored agreed. Nabila Ally said that one of the best parts of an evening at the drive-in was "the chance to get out, to get exposed to new things and different people you didn't interact with every day." Yusuf too described the opportunity to get out of the house and his "normal surroundings" as the best part of the night. In hindsight, he was embarrassed at the way he had gawked at the wide range of people he encountered at the show. But he was young at the time and had not yet come to appreciate the diverse range of humanity in Dar es Salaam.[84] He was not alone. Many people described the opportunity to mix and mingle in a diverse cross section of the public as a central part of the show, and for many African and Asian women and youth, such public mixing was a defining transformation of the early independence era.[85] For a new nation that was desperately trying to foster a sense of unity, the drive-in was a place where its citizens could see themselves as one: a heterogeneous community whose members had something tangible in common.

241

Of course, the drive-in attracted groups of teens and young adults by the score. During holidays or on nights when Sisi offered special events, youth were often given the chance to go on their own, unchaperoned by parents, uncles, or aunts. Repeatedly, I pressed people to tell me if girls really got to go too. "Yes" was the overwhelming response. Things were different in those days, I was told. "Life was freer, kids could be trusted, and besides you were going together as a group," said one anonymous Hindu woman. "No one could compromise your honor," Adija, an African woman from Kariakoo, stressed. "You were in public, and you were there with your friends." "The children of three, four or five families would go together," said Mulji. "Boys and girls together, they were with their families, not with hooligans!"[86]

The ethos of sharing and cooperation at the core of ujamaa was taken to new heights by youth when it came to transportation to the drive-in. It was rare for a young person to own a car or drive, but those who did quickly became the most popular fellows in town. Several men told me how they first entered the transportation business during the 1970s, when they were in their twenties, by "borrowing" vehicles from work or family and using them to take groups of youth to the show. Some drivers had designated stops within their neighborhoods where young people needing a lift knew to gather. Others simply volunteered to fill their vehicles with as many people as possible as long as the passengers would pay for gas and the driver's admission to the show. Akhmed, who lived in Kariakoo, remembered his entire football team piling in the back of a pickup truck owned by a team-mate's distant cousin. "Any time we were able to pay for gas he would take us, so team-mates would get together and do a little cooperative business. We would buy fish or fruit wholesale and then sell it around town and then use the money to go to the show."[87] Agnello and Mulji, who worked at the drive-in, said it was not uncommon to see cars packed with as many as twenty teens coming to the show. "The best was when the *Herbie* movies were shown, because everyone with a Volkswagen Beetle got into the drive-in for free. We had so much fun watching these kids to see how many people they could cram in a car!" recalled Agnello.[88] Saloum and Fatuma were among the many Beetle-driving youth who entertained these drive-in employees with their exploits. They shared stories of going to see both *The Love Bug* (Stevenson, 1968) and *Herbie Rides Again* (Stevenson, 1974) at the drive-in. "Everyone in town with a Beetle was there," said Fatuma, proudly boasting that circus clowns pouring out of a minicar had nothing on Dar es Salaam teens trying to get as many friends as possible into a movie for free.[89]

In the 1970s, the drive-in also began sponsoring charity nights on Wednesdays, where the admission fee was charged by the car, no matter how many people were inside. Proceeds from the sale of tickets were donated to the Rotary, the Lions Club, the Red Cross, an orphanage, or some other cause. One woman remembered her father—a civil servant—letting her take the family station wagon, driven by his driver, to a charity show; she filled it with nearly twenty of her closest girlfriends and enjoyed an evening of revelry at the biggest late-night event for youth in town. Charles, an American, also watched shows from the cramped back end of his friend's pickup truck. His recollections centered on endless rows of other trucks "full of partying Indian kids, girls with an attitude . . . Indian boys serenading a car full of girls with the latest Bollywood hits, and Peace Corp volunteers slowly getting stoned."[90] These shows were hugely successful, drawing a younger crowd than usual and packing the drive-in during the middle of the week when attendance was usually down. In fact, charity shows frequently sold out.[91] Those who got involved with transporting others were guaranteed a booming business once these shows began. They could make money, have a good time, meet some new girls, and provide a much-valued service to other young citizens in Dar es Salaam.[92]

AN OASIS OF ABUNDANCE

Lines featured prominently in many people's memories of Tanzanian socialism, yet unlike the ubiquitous and annoying queues at state-run stores, the long, slow-moving line to get into the drive-in was one that people thoroughly enjoyed.[93] Being part of that "long, long line" on Sunday was pure pleasure. Fatma and Shanin shared their memories of outings to the drive-in as teenagers, when waiting in line was more like a picnic, they said, than something one dreaded and had to endure. "My mother brought food and drinks, and of course the bottle of chai—without which no picnic was complete," said Shanin. "If the show didn't start until sundown, by four in the evening we were in the queue, talking, making a picnic, and slowly, slowly working our way inside."[94] During the wait, people would get out of their cars and spread mats on the side of the road where they could relax.

243

Many folks visited with others in line, sharing news and gossip, showing off new clothes, and admiring each other's kids and cars. Men set up makeshift tables and played cards. Teens giggled and struggled to look cool. Boys pulled out the ubiquitous soccer ball and kicked it about. Nearly everyone described the atmosphere as festive and filled with food, family, friends, and fun. Kamal characterized the experience of standing in line as "incredible," positively beaming as he recalled, "You'd move an inch at a time, but you'd enjoy it all the same."

Queues in Russia and Romania have been described as places where one could hear the most vitriolic of statements against the regime and where feelings of anger, frustration, anxiety, and antagonism reigned.[95] There, queues represented shortages and failures of distribution. But the line to get into the drive-in was different in nearly every way: the longer it was, the better, for no one was competing for limited supplies.

Scarcity and austerity are terms commonly associated with socialism and communism, and in Tanzania, the late 1970s and 1980s were years of exceptional want. Food, clothing, spare parts, gasoline, paper, cassette tapes, sugar—everything was rationed at some point or was available only in limited supply. Scarcity turned respectable schoolteachers, nice old ladies, and unemployed youths into criminals—smugglers of illicit toothpaste and soap taken across the borders and back to Tanzania to be traded for cash or other goods.[96] A woman named Leonne laughed hysterically during her interview as she recalled an evening at the movies in 1983 when gasoline was in extremely short supply. When a bandit in the film hit a man over the head with a club and then proceeded to pour an entire can of gasoline on him and light him on fire, the crowd erupted with shouts of "Oh my god! He used an entire gallon of gasoline!" "He could have just finished him off with the club," others cried. "What a thoughtless use of precious petrol."[97]

The Tanzanian drive-in, by contrast, was an oasis of abundance where consumptive desires were fulfilled. The city's women prided themselves on the food they prepared for the Sunday picnic at the theater. They set out their mats and food and invited others to share in the feast, even the drive-in workers. These picnics epitomized Nyerere's vision of socialism, with everyone contributing what they could, collectively enjoying far more than any single family could produce on their own. Memories of the drive-in evoked recollections of opulent luxury because, as Ina Merkel has written of the former German Democratic Republic, luxury meant not only extravagance and pleasure but also the opposite of shortage.[98]

The concession stand and bar at the drive-in functioned in the way that citizens thought state-run stores and co-ops should. "Best of all," said one woman, "you could buy food! Even when shortages of just about everything held the country in the grip of hardship, we could always get something to eat at the cinema."[99] Gigri, who ran the concession stand, was extremely proud of his ability to satisfy his customers' hunger with chicken and chips, sambusas, chops, burgers, and kabobs.[100] On an average Sunday, he recalled, he went through four hundred pounds of potatoes, as many as two hundred chickens, five hundred sambusas, and four to five hundred kabobs. Although his numbers may have become inflated over the years, others confirm that the concession stand was a place of nearly unimaginable bounty. Gigri's chips (french fries) were legendary, looming large in people's memories of the drive-in. Chips were apparently nowhere near as ubiquitous then as they are today. One iconic memory from many childhoods was the chips they got to indulge in only at the drive-in. Godwin remembered his children's weekly chant of "Chipsi, chipsi, chipsi!" which started as soon as they got to the show, and Jane said that for her daughter, "the magic of the cinema was contained in a plate of chips."[101] The power of the drive-in as an affective landscape was enhanced by the multisensory associations it conjured.

Drinkers relished the well-stocked drive-in bar. "People knew that sodas and beers were hard to come by; there was shortage, shortage," said one employee. "But they could always count on the fact that if they came to my place at the drive-in, they would get a good cold soda or a beer."[102] Like many things during those difficult years, he explained, it was a matter of who you knew and of having a good working relationship with people who had access to supply. In the years of shortage in Tanzania, as in the *blat* (informal) economy in the Soviet Union, having friends in the right places or knowing someone who knew someone was often more important than having money if you needed supplies.[103] Two men who were interviewed in a somewhat seedy bar volunteered their own stories of going to the drive-in in the 1980s to find beer when every other place was dry. They and others said that it was one of the few spots where common citizens and party bureaucrats had equal access to alcohol. The socialist ethos of sharing also applied to drink: Charles Franzen, an American Peace Corps volunteer living in Tanzania who submitted an entry for the essay contest, recalled, "The great thing about Dar es Salaam during those socialist rationing, post-Ugandan war years was that nothing was available officially and yet everything was available in one way or another. At the drive-in if someone had a bottle of Konyagi [Tanzanian gin], well, someone else would have a large bottle of orange squash." As with the picnics provided by the women, through sharing their individual contributions with others, people had it all.[104] The drive-in was much more than a venue for watching a film: it was an affective space where longings both physical and emotional were satisfied.

There was much that went wrong with Tanzanian socialism, but the drive-in was one place where some things went right. There, the state and private entrepreneurs provided the basic infrastructural architecture, and enthusiastic urbanites used it to give the abstract ideals of socialism and participatory citizenship tangible form. Independence, too, was made concrete and brought to life. Political self-determination for the nation was included in most imaginative bundles defining independence, but for most people, the term also inspired dreams of personal transformation, social liberation, economic ease, and comfort. Sisi Enterprises was a place where these imaginings were given substance. For several decades, the drive-in was the pride of Dar es Salaam. It was locally owned, managed, and operated and among the most modern venues for viewing film on the continent. By combining modern viewing with automobility and family-centered leisure, the drive-in helped transform social life in the capital city. Much of the nostalgia associated with the drive-in comes from the conflation of the early years of national independence and times in the life cycle of respondents when they and their families were young. Both nationally and personally, these were years of vitality, aspiration, and imaginative possibility—an era when everything one wanted to achieve seemed possible. Who could not look back wistfully to such a time?

Many members of the professional middle class that swelled the capital city had not experienced the urban pleasure of moviegoing before, having grown up in the countryside. For them, the drive-in was particularly attractive because it allowed them to engage with the novelty of global films while simultaneously showing off their new cars and socializing with peers. Yet not all of the new immigrants to the city shared in the privileges of having education, professional jobs, or personal cars. As the next chapter details, most new immigrants were young and struggling. But they were no less enthusiastic about the potential for mobility and urbanity to usher in personal empowerment in the years immediately following independence. They too took to the cinemas as a new space for leisure and sociability, as well as a place where networks were forged and dreams of personal metamorphosis were inspired.

Chapter 7

THE INDEPENDENCE GENERATION GOES TO THE SHOW, 1960s–80s

THE POPULARITY of moviegoing soared after independence. In addition to the thousands who thronged to the new drive-in each week, there were another ten to fifteen thousand going to the movies across the country every day. As a mass form of urban leisure, moviegoing was no longer confined to the coast; by the 1970s, Tanzanians everywhere were taking in a show. Annually, more than four million tickets were sold.[1] Urbanization and the popularity of moviegoing increased hand in hand. In the first three decades after independence, the number of urban Tanzanians rose from less than 5 percent of the total population to more than 20 percent. In many regional towns, including Mbeya, Kigoma, and Shinyanga, the rate of population increase was as high as 2,000 percent during these years.[2] For many people, one of the particular delights of urban living was the novelty of spending afternoons or nights watching a film with friends. This chapter picks up on themes developed at length in earlier chapters and explores both continuity and change in the postcolonial era. As chapter 8 will detail, the socialist state transformed the political economy governing the film industry, yet despite pervasive structural changes, moviegoing remained a key means of familiarizing oneself with downtown neighborhoods, making new friends, and learning about city ways.

One thing that was distinctive about the 1960s, 1970s, and 1980s was that the majority of urban newcomers and moviegoers in those years were young and single; they gave both cities and cinemas a new and youthful vibe. In the 1960s, 75 percent of all migrants to town were under thirty years old, and most were between the ages of fourteen and twenty-four.[3] By 1978, a quarter of a million people in Dar es Salaam were from fifteen to thirty years of age, which was actually more than the total population of the city at independence.[4] That same year, youth outnumbered those over forty by a five-to-one ratio in Moshi, Morogoro, and a host of Tanzanian towns.[5] Demographically speaking, the city was a great place to be if you were young. Life was far from a perpetual party, but with such an overwhelming preponderance of young people, the vibrant pulse of youthful style was palpable. Most young migrants came in search of economic opportunities, but many towns, including Iringa, Morogoro, and Tabora, to name just a few, were also educational hubs. Regional towns hosted numerous boarding schools, and the postcolonial state's massive investment in education meant that by the 1970s and 1980s, a sizable number of young Tanzanians were entering secondary school for the first time. The student population at the University of Dar es Salaam also grew astronomically. At independence, the university enrolled a mere fourteen students, a figure that increased to two thousand a decade later and nearly doubled again by 1984.[6] Urban commercial nightlife blossomed like never before. With new genres of global film aimed directly at this youthful audience, young people swarmed to the theaters like bees to their hive.

As large public spaces, cinemas provided unique opportunities for hundreds of kids to gather, socialize, and consort. Legions of adolescent fans congregated at the theaters to watch the action—on the screen, in the aisles, and on the streets. This was where urbanizing young people between fifteen and twenty-five learned what it meant to be an urban kid. A full 60 percent of youthful moviegoers surveyed in Dar es Salaam attended the movies at least once a week, and half of those went twice a week or more.[7] From Mwanza to Iringa and Morogoro, two-thirds of the people who went to the movies were under thirty years of age. Nearly all of those who went daily were young.[8] Moviegoing was a generationally defining experience for most of the newly urbanized. Going to the show with friends, talking about the film after the show, and weaving the cosmopolitan cultural threads pulled from films into the tapestry of daily life helped solidify them into a definitive cohort and distance them from their elders' ways and time. Even youth whose parents were city dwellers took to the movies in distinctive ways after independence: moviegoing became more of a peer-led experience, rather than (or in addition to) a family phenomenon. Young people were also increasingly using the theaters as places to go with members of the opposite sex on dates prior to marriage, thereby pushing generational transformations in romantic relationships yet again.

The 1960s, 1970s, and 1980s were marked by a progressively globalized youth culture—and Tanzanians were as central to this process as people anywhere in the world. This was certainly not the first generation with a transnational sense of political and cultural engagement, but youth in these decades self-consciously borrowed, blended, and appropriated like no generation before. Transformations in travel, global communications technologies, and media circulation made it easier for styles and ideas from one corner of the world to travel to another. These flows were far from unidirectional. Their circular travels make it difficult to decipher exactly who borrowed from whom. Bell-bottoms, platforms, and maxi dresses were trending from Bukoba to Bombay to Brighton. Dashikis from Africa and salwar kameez from South Asia adorned the bodies of the hip and happening in Europe, the Caribbean, and North America. It took less than five years from the time Bob Marley and the Wailers released their first recording of "One Love" for the world to be aflame with the sounds of reggae and the "smokin'" Rasta vibe. The music youth listened to, the clothes they wore, and the movies they watched became important signs of this generation's awareness of and commitment to a globally integrated world. In the words of May Joseph, a Tanzanian Asian who grew up in Dar es Salaam during these years, the global circulation of films and music offered young people like herself "the possibility of cultural citizenship, of 'integrating' through an international Black cool."[9] Tanzania was a hotbed of transnational Black Power, and even those who were not directly involved were politicized by the discourse in the air. Tanzanian youth took new global genres of film— kung fu and blaxploitation—blending and bending them to speak to their own realities, as well as to signal their entanglement with the global, revolutionary cosmopolitan.

The spread of martial arts in the 1970s is a brilliantly redolent example of Tanzanians' ability to refashion global practices and make them local. Inspired by Hong Kong action films and the Chinese American martial artist and actor Bruce Lee, Tanzanians warmly embraced an African American karate expert, trained in Okinawa, into their families and communities in Dar es Salaam. Transnational and cross-cultural integration did not stop there. In cities across the nation, youth whose native languages numbered in the hundreds took up martial arts training in Kiswahili, the language of the city and the nation, offered by other Tanzanians. Young men and women strengthened and toned their bodies, at the same time expanding their minds. In the studios, on the streets, and in the auditoriums of cinemas across the country, the teachings of Bruce Lee were blended with Nyerere's philosophies of ujamaa. What made postcolonial youth culture a global phenomenon was that it was indeed truly global. And Tanzanians were central players in the process.

BRUCE LEE, URBAN YOUTH, AND THE KUNG FU CRAZE

In 1971, Bruce Lee released *The Big Boss* (Wei), also known as *Fists of Fury.* The next year, replicating the lighting speed of his fighting style, he released *Fist of Fury/The Chinese Connection* (Wei, 1972) and then wrote, directed, choreographed, coproduced, and starred in *The Way of the Dragon* (Lee, 1972) followed by *Enter the Dragon* (Clouse), released six days after Lee's death in 1973.[10] These four films, which hit the screens in quick succession over the course of three years, inaugurated a new era in global film production, distribution, and consumption. *The Big Boss* quickly stormed to the top of international box office charts, marking the first time a film made in Hong Kong seriously penetrated global markets. Produced by an independent studio and featuring a nonwhite actor in a powerful lead role, the film destabilized the industry on many levels. The new visual style and fast-paced action resonated loudly with youth. Lee's films highlighted themes of cultural nationalism and antiracism, as well as the urgent need for exploited peoples to take aggressive action against the politically and morally corrupt. These issues were at the core of popular political discourse in Tanzania, adding to the films' local appeal.

The kinetic energy of Lee in action seized viewers across the world, inspiring millions to take up martial arts. As Carl Douglas sang in his "B-side" recording that quickly rose to the top of the global charts, from Hong Kong to Oakland and Bombay to Kingston, "everybody was kung fu fighting."[11] I have African American friends, now more than sixty years of age, whose e-mail addresses still reference their obsession with martial arts as young adults. In Tanzania too, kung fu and Carl Douglas took the nation by storm. Martial arts studios mushroomed in towns across the country. Youth practiced their moves anywhere and everywhere. Tree trunks, veranda pillars, and passing city buses were all fair game. And woe to the unsuspecting pedestrian who had the misfortune of walking past the Empire Cinema—the central shrine of kung fu action cinema in Dar es Salaam—as a movie let out. On more than one occasion, city elders and portly politicians were caught in the fray as hundreds of punching, kicking, chopping, and "hay-yahing" youth spilled from the Empire after watching the latest film. Although Douglas neglected to mention it, in Tanzania too "those cats were fast as lightning!"

Elders and socialist politicians found these youthful actions more than just a little bit frightening. As G. Thomas Burgess, Andrew Ivaska, and Emily Callaci have all argued, marshaling the energy of youth and directing it toward "proper" nation-building ends was a central feature of early socialist praxis in Tanzania.[12] Moviegoing, it was argued by party ideologues, not only drained the country of foreign currency reserves but also encouraged youth to pursue hedonistic pleasures and imitate imperialist culture.[13] In the words of one critic, Hong Kong "Karate Choppers" were among the "slew of mindless trash" screened in Tanzania that needed to be banned. But Tanzanian youth did not read Lee's films in the same way. For many, Lee and his movies spoke directly to the social, economic, and political goals espoused by the nation's socialist leaders and the struggles being faced by the people of their country.

When Tanzanian youth went to the movies, they saw fictionalized versions of their own struggles depicted on the screen: the films were foreign, but the drama was theirs. In *Big Boss* and *Way of the Dragon*, Lee's characters confront situations remarkably similar to those facing tens of thousands of young people living in urban Tanzania at the time. In both films, the main character is a young, newly arrived immigrant from the countryside who is utterly reliant on a network of extended kin for food, housing, and employment. In *The Way of the Dragon*, Lee's character is embarrassingly out of place and hopelessly lost in the city before his city cousins show him the ropes. Told in the visual style of Indian films, where dialogue helps but is not essential for understanding the gist of the story, we see Lee struggle because he cannot speak the language used in town, does not know how to read, and cannot find any food he is familiar with. He is also constantly getting lost. When audiences laughed at Lee, they were also laughing at themselves.[14] In several scenes any guest in a foreign city could relate to, Lee's character is seen visibly suffering from an urgent need for a bathroom, which he has no clue how to locate or even ask for. In scenes depicting his efforts to make his bodily needs known, we see urbanites turning away from a young man they perceive as rude and utterly lacking in civility. As a young rural migrant newly arrived in the city, Lee is an outcast, someone respectable urban citizens do their best to avoid.

The importance of kinship, loyalty, and brotherhood are also central themes in Lee's films, much as they were in the lives of those in the Tanzanian audience. In both *The Big Boss* and *Way of the Dragon*, for instance, Lee's character is taken in by cousins who provide food, shelter, and connections for finding work. Similarly, nearly 70 percent of urban immigrants in Tanzania lived with extended kin when they first arrived in town, and most relied on social networks tied to home to find their first jobs.[15] Officially, many urban migrants remained nominally jobless for years, meaning that they never secured formal waged or salaried employment. Instead, they hustled, traded, and worked as day laborers. Yet very few considered returning to the countryside no matter how difficult or precarious life in the city was.[16] Having grown up in the village, they knew both its limits and its potentials. The city, by contrast, was unknown, and thus, urban life could be imagined as filled with prospects: an immigrant's big break could be coming tomorrow. Returning to the village was tantamount to going backward, admitting defeat, or accepting and acceding to the social and economic constraints they had been born into. These youth left for the city to strike it rich, and many harbored dreams of emerging as the family hero, the big brother or sister who financed their siblings' place at school and made parents' lives a little more secure. Movies such as *The Big Boss* and *Way of the Dragon* nourished these narrative dreams.

Plotlines centered around the poor and downtrodden taking on the economically powerful were dominant in Lee's films, and these too resonated with political discourse heard daily in Tanzanian. Newspapers, radio broadcasts, and public speeches continually reminded Tanzanians of their importance in supporting those fighting to end colonialism and white rule around the world. Exiles, organizers, and freedom fighters from South Africa, Namibia, Rhodesia, Angola, and Mozambique were a palpable presence in Dar es Salaam. Nyerere was also at the forefront of a south-south alliance voicing the need to build a new economic order free from the dictates of neocolonialism. Fidel Castro, Che Guevara, Malcolm X, Angela Davis, Samora Machel, Stokely Carmichael, Ruth First, and legions of other internationally revered revolutionaries regularly visited and toured Tanzania. Leading intellectuals at the University of Dar es Salaam such as Issa Shivji and the Guyanese-born historian Walter Rodney issued scathing critiques of global capitalism and the exploitation of peasants and the working classes by Western corporations. Students who attended these men's lectures during the day and consciousness-raising debates in the evening gathered, along with day laborers and the underemployed, at the Empire Cinema to watch Bruce Lee make things right. Freddy Macha was one young man who remembered the vibrant energy of the political and cultural scenes that coalesced in Dar es Salaam in 1973. He recalled that Rodney's classic book *How Europe Underdeveloped Africa* (with a prologue by Tanzania's minister of economy, Abdulrahman Babu) was published just as Lee's *Enter the Dragon* was released. Caught between Rodney and Lee, he and his fellow university graduates felt they were living at the fault lines of a world poised for revolution. In the words of May Joseph, "The air was thick with the promise of change."[17] Training their minds and bodies for the coming revolution was imperative. Macha and his friends were among thousands in Tanzania who took up the martial arts with gusto. The intellectual task of reimagining the world economic and social order was combined with physical and imaginative self-fashioning through martial arts.[18]

The beauty of Lee's body and the choreography of his fight scenes were also obvious draws. Lee was a champion dancer is his youth, and he carried his appreciation for choreography into his work in both the martial arts and film. Like anyone who has ever watched a Bruce Lee film, Tanzanian audience members were captivated by his fighting style, awed by his strength and agility, and inspired to immediately set about improving their own physiques. Bruce's body—nicely revealed in many fighting scenes as he removes his shirt before the action begins—provided a visual model Tanzanian men and women could relate to. Though buff and ripped, he was small in stature. Unlike Arnold Schwarzenegger or Sylvester Stallone, who were never terribly popular in Tanzania, Lee was similar in size to the average Tanzanian. He weighed a mere 126 pounds and stood only

5 feet 6 inches tall, but that did not stop him from taking on—and of course defeating—many who were bigger, including Chuck Norris, who outweighed him by nearly 40 pounds. When the pair face off in *Way of the Dragon*, the likelihood of Lee's defeat is foreshadowed by the staging of the fight inside the Coliseum. Lee has come to Rome to help his uncle and cousins save their restaurant from a Mafia boss intent on taking their property. Under the pretense of negotiating a truce with the mobster, Lee is tricked into fighting Norris, a hired killer. This trope of the small defeating the larger, more economically and physically powerful reoccurs in many of Lee's films. Through training, he defeats graft and nepotism, using his mind and body as his only weapons.

Lee's body and fighting style also provided visual inspiration for women to take up martial arts and imagine crushing male privilege with only their bare hands and feet. May Joseph, now a well-regarded professor of global studies and urban performance culture in New York City, was one of countless women in Tanzania who as a youth was inspired by Bruce Lee to begin training in martial arts.[19] Joseph notes that Lee's wing chun style was originally developed by a thirteenth-century Buddhist nun in mainland China as a form of self-defense for women and others with small frames. For Joseph, this creates an explicit link between kung fu and feminism. Although none of the women I spoke with in Tanzania were as knowledgeable about the history of different styles, they too made connections between kung fu films, the martial arts, and female empowerment. For many young women who moved to the cities in the 1970s, the changing social and material conditions of their lives required them to exude a new type of physicality. They reveled in the images of female power they saw displayed on screen. Kung fu films, like blaxploitation, often included voyeuristic and misogynistic scenes, but they were also among the first to portray women who were physically capable of protecting themselves or even taking on and defeating a man. Female martial artists who played lead roles in these films supported the fantasies of Tanzanian women who dreamed of taking the lead themselves and kicking butt in an imperfect, male-dominated world.

Angela Mao, who played Lee's sister in *Enter the Dragon* and then went on to star in more than twenty other films, including *Lady Whirlwind*

255

(Feng, 1972) and *Taekwando Heroes/Sting of the Dragon Masters* (Feng, 1973), was one female martial artist widely appreciated by Tanzanians. Among women, she was nearly as popular as Bruce Lee, and she was named repeatedly as one of the most impressive martial artists seen in film. Mao was highly skilled in the Korean art of hapkido as well as tae kwon do and several other forms of martial arts. Her style was as impressive as her stamina. Like Lee, she could believably defeat a room full of men single-handedly. The choreography of her fight scenes is breathtaking. Within the first fifteen minutes of *Lady Whirlwind*, she defeats a gang of more than twenty men armed with various weapons and reduces their lead fighter to tears. When he reports to his boss, he has to confess that he was whipped by a woman who "fights like a man, only better." Cynthia Rothrock was another female martial artist who inspired awe in Tanzania and was repeatedly named by women as a favorite star of this genre. Rothrock was an American martial artist with black belts in five different arts. She was also a five-time karate world champion. Rothrock burst onto the screen in 1985 with *Yes Madam/Police Assassins* (Yuen), and many Tanzanians followed both her martial arts career and her cinematic career with gusto. She defeated men on screen and in live competitions as well, something that several female practitioners of martial arts in Tanzania stressed in interviews.[20] Interestingly, even though many Tanzanian women identified Bruce Lee as one of their favorite film stars, no men gave Mao or Rothrock top billing.

During decades in which many women were struggling to break out of conventional roles and find their own places in the cities and nation, they were looking for narratives portraying female characters who were strong, smart, and capable of rising to meet new challenges. Kiswahili literature circulated widely during these years, but unfortunately for urban women, most published authors were male, and the female characters they invented were stereotypically weak. Despite the socialist ethos that allegedly permeated the publishing industry, men and women are far from equal in the land of Kiswahili fiction. Positions of domestic authority and economic power are gendered exclusively male. Women are portrayed either as in need of guidance and protection or as bloodsucking prostitutes and seductresses who lead good men astray. Female characters have the power to disrupt a stable and civilized male order but not to overturn it. In Kiswahili literature, women who challenge the dominant system or follow an alternative path toward empowerment invariably die or go to jail.[21]

Films featuring female martial artists flipped these narratives on their heads. There, women are independent masters of decisive action. They need no male protector; sisters and daughters can save a family as well as any son can. In *Lady Whirlwind*, Mao goes after the man who abandoned her pregnant sister, and along the way, she brings down a powerful gambling syndicate and overturns a complacent and corrupt local ruling class. Cynthia Rothrock is often cast as a capable and competent police officer, another role reserved in Kiswahili fiction for men. Rothrock not only battles drug lords and murderers, she also defeats corrupt officers of the law. Cast in leading roles, Mao and Rothrock always win in the end. These women might be sexy, but they are never reduced to their sexuality. They rely on their intellects to evaluate problems and their smarts and physical strength to solve them. Like the posters of Bruce Lee fighting Kareem Abdul-Jabbar (who was a foot and a half taller than Lee) that adorned the bedroom walls of countless Tanzanians, these films provided a visual reminder that you did not have to be big to be bad.

Female migrants to Tanzanian towns in the 1960s and 1970s confronted the same challenges as their male counterparts and others that were uniquely gendered. As Tanzania embarked on an intensive effort to industrialize, thousands of women found work in new factories. There were new coffee- and tea-processing plants in Bukoba, textile mills in Mwanza and Dar es Salaam, sisal bag plants in Tanga, and cashew-processing plants in Mtwara as well as factories producing shoes, hoes, cigarettes, beer, paper bags, and school notebooks scattered across the country. Like women around the globe who were among the first in their countries to enter factories, Tanzanian women struggled against many forms of gender-based discrimination in the workplace. They were clustered in industries and sectors that were lower paid, labor intensive, and unskilled. Managers, directors, and line bosses were nearly always male. Sexual harassment and gender-based discrimination on the job were common. Entering the urban workforce was no panacea; for most, social respect was much harder to earn than money.[22] Women who moved to the cities to go to school faced similar obstacles. In secondary schools, at colleges, and at the university, men outnumbered women by a ratio of four or five to one. Teachers, headmasters, and chancellors were typically male. Beyond that, sexual harassment in schools was often more extreme than that on the shop floor, since students tended to be younger than working women and less sure of their

257

ability or right to fend off unwanted advances.[23] Though the University of
Dar es Salaam was heralded for its progressive political stance on many
matters, when it came to women's issues in general and sexual harassment in particular the university was a difficult place to be. Many male
professors made a habit of demanding sexual favors in exchange for good
grades. Upperclassmen were also predatory. The ubiquity of sexual harassment on campus was highlighted in Austin Bukenya's 1972 satirical novel
The People's Bachelor, written after years of watching the predatory antics
of fellow students and faculty in Dar es Salaam. University women who
dared to speak out against misogyny were "'punched"—that is, publicly
ridiculed and condemned on posters that were mounted on billboards and
walls and circulated across campus. Anyone who dared to socialize with
a woman who had been punched was punched as well. Shamed and ostracized, many dropped out of school, and more than one committed sui-
cide.[24] The university administration largely dismissed women's complaints
and allowed the situation to go unchecked for years. Women in the 1970s
and 1980s could have used a sister like Angela Mao to take up their cause
and kick some butt in Tanzania.

At school, at work, and on city streets, women rightly feared for their
personal safety; female action heroes inspired them to take up martial arts
for protection and empowerment. As Gladness, a Maasai woman and a
big Cynthia Rothrock fan, said, "After seeing these movies and practicing
moves I knew I could protect myself. These films let us see that with training a woman really could beat a man." She began martial arts training at a
small, informal studio in Arusha, where she lived. It was a "mixed space,"
much like the cinema, where young men and women from diverse ethnic
and class backgrounds came together to learn kung fu. Gladness made
a habit of showing off some of her set moves on the street so that others
would know not to mess with her. She and other women she met at the
studio also wore loose-fitting, ankle-length pants known as "don't touch
my shoes" around town at a time when most women continued to wear
skirts and dresses. Wearing pants made it easier to execute kicks, and as
they walked about town, it subtly signaled that these young women were
empowered martial artists. Nights after movies were potentially dangerous
times. To discourage a potential assault or robbery, Gladness said, "on our
way home from the theater my friends and I would practice our kicks and
punches. No thug would dare to bother us. It was a great feeling to know

we could protect ourselves."[25] Nabila recalled that when she was in her twenties, she was struggling on numerous fronts against gender roles that she found restrictive; she too took up karate to enhance her self-image and sense of control. "Exercising is good," she added. "It is good for your body and enlivens your brain too. And in these movies you would see women who could do kung fu as well as men. This made me realize I could do it too. With training I could protect myself, and this made me feel far more confident in the city."[26] Mastering kung fu, she said, provided women of her generation with a means of protection, and equally important, it offered the sheer pleasure of perfecting their bodies and further testing the limits of self. Abby, who lived in Iringa and also began training in karate in the 1970s, said it was a revelation to see female martial artists on screen. "These women weren't like others, they believed in themselves, and could do anything. They were heroes, female heroes! We had never seen female action heroes before, it was amazing!" Abby said that after watching movies with women as stars she too was inspired to train. "Karate helped you to build self-confidence," she stated. "It made you physically stronger too, which helped at work, but it also gave you an inner strength."[27] A grandmother by the time we spoke, Abby said that she was still drawing on the mental exercises she learned while practicing the martial arts to cope with daily challenges.

May Joseph, who also had been inspired by films to begin training, argued that martial arts movies offered a powerful "visual representation of women breaking boundaries within public space." [28] In the first two decades after independence, the number of women entering Tanzanian cities surged. Previously, women had always migrated to cities in smaller numbers than their male counterparts, but by the early 1970s, they formed the majority of new migrants.[29] The number of unmarried women moving to town also increased significantly, from 13 percent in the early 1950s to 33 percent two decades later. By the late 1970s, 63 percent of women working in factories in Dar es Salaam were "husbandless."[30] These women broke numerous boundaries as they entered the public realms in cities, factories, schools, and even theaters. Urban women had always gone to the movies in Tanzania, but few of these new migrants or their mothers had ever been to the show. And though women were typically 50 percent or more of an audience for an Indian film, they were a distinct minority for action films. According to both exhibitors and fans, the number of women in attendance

259

at the average kung fu movie never totaled more than 30 percent of the audience; 10 to 20 percent was more the norm. Obviously, women had to be strong and willing to break boundaries just to see a martial arts film.

BRUCE LEE FILMS AND MARTIAL ARTS TRAINING IN TANZANIA

Tanzanians were further inspired to believe in their ability to become accomplished martial artists by the training regime followed by Bruce Lee; in both film and real life, he trained with a minimum of special equipment. He did sit-ups, push-ups, and leg-raises by the hundreds. Lee was famous not just for one-armed push-ups but also for push-ups done on one finger and a thumb. If he wanted an extra challenge, he added weight by having a man twice his size sit or stand on his back. In his films, he used isometric exercises to increase strength and shadowboxing to improve speed. No scene was ever shot inside a gym. Lee's training studio was literally everywhere—his bedroom, a field, a rooftop, or the alleyway behind the restaurant where he worked. For Tanzanians, this was one of the things that made him real. Fans soaked up information about his training from a range sources apart from the films. Newspapers, magazines, and books were shared by the continuous parade of sailors, traders, and boathands from across the globe who arrived in local ports each day.[31]

Tanzanians did not feel like second- or third-class citizens when they trained in storerooms, in alleys, or on the beach because even Lee—the greatest martial artist ever to live—trained in similar spaces. Both took advantage of all available opportunities to strengthen themselves mentally and physically. The fifty-pound sacks of flour, rice, and cement that men loaded and unloaded at work were reconceptualized as weights. Women who worked in factories said they also refashioned the sacks into punching and kicking bags. Kicks, punches, and set moves (*kata*) were incorporated into walks to the market or hanging up laundry to dry. Kung fu fans joined their friends who played football in running on the beach and across town to improve their stamina and cardio. It was these cross-training sessions that allegedly led to the inclusion of *vyura* (jumping squats across a field while grabbing opposing ears with hands) that became a mainstay of Tanzanian footballers' efforts to improve their quadriceps and balance.

But formalized training also took place. Tanzania's first internationally recognized karate studio was opened in Dar es Salaam in 1973, the

TANZANIA 75/- TANZANIA 75/- TANZANIA 75/-

BRUCE LEE 1940-1973 BRUCE LEE 1940-1973 BRUCE LEE 1940-1973

TANZANIA 75/- TANZANIA 75/- TANZANIA 75/-

BRUCE LEE 1940-1973 BRUCE LEE 1940-1973 BRUCE LEE 1940-1973

TANZANIA 75/- TANZANIA 75/- TANZANIA 75/-

BRUCE LEE 1940-1973 BRUCE LEE 1940-1973 BRUCE LEE 1940-1973

Figure 7.1 Bruce Lee stamps. From author's collection

same year *Enter the Dragon* was released. Known as Goju Ryu Karate, this studio was located in the Zanaki Primary School, a short walk from the Empire Cinema, and is still in operation today. The studio was founded by Sensei Nantambu Camara Bomani, an African American martial artist who trained in Okinawa and opened schools in the United States before moving

261

to Tanzania. A committed and politically engaged member of the Pan-African diaspora, Bomani later opened a studio in Ghana, where he lived until his death in 2009.[32] According to Sensei Malekia, who currently heads the school started by Bomani in Dar es Salaam, more than eight thousand Tanzanians have graduated from the institution since its founding. Bomani lived with his Tanzanian wife in Kariakoo, the mixed-race commercial and residential center of Dar es Salaam, and offered free lessons to kids in the neighborhood. Service to the community was something he emphasized to students through both word and deed. Tanzanians trained by Bomani passed these lessons on in ever-widening concentric circles.[33] Graduates include leaders of dojos in Mwanza, Arusha, Moshi, and Mbeya, as well as in Australia, the Netherlands, the United Kingdom, the United States, and Sweden. The transnational movement of ideas, expertise, and style through these dojos highlights how varied and multidirectional the cultural flows of the era were.

Cultural studies scholars speak of Lee as the "non-aligned superhero" — the global media icon who transcended the black-white and east-west binaries that dominated racial and political discourse prior to his time.[34] In Bomani's studio and those that grew from it, this theory was given concrete form. During its heyday, the studio on Zanaki Street was *the* place to be for the "hip and happening" of radical, transnational Dar es Salaam. Bomani was one of many black brothers from the United States who fled the racism of their native homeland for the warm embrace of socialist Tanzania. In addition to providing a haven for members of the Black Panthers, Dar es Salaam was also the epicenter of the southern African liberation struggle in exile. Inside Bomani's studio, one could find members of the African National Congress (ANC), the Mozambique Liberation Front (FRELIMO), and the South West Africa People's Organization (SWAPO) training among African, Asian, and Arab Tanzanian comrades. According to several who studied under Bomani, it was not uncommon for eighty to a hundred people to show up for training on any given night. Though their origins, talents, and future paths varied immensely, they bonded through martial arts. The prolific Tanzanian blogger and widely followed independent source of news and analysis Issa Michuzi, the University of California–Los Angeles (UCLA) Pan-African Studies professor C. R. D Halisi, the Tanzanian arts and culture critic Freddy Macha, and the music icon Juma Nature were among those trained at the Zanaki Street karate studio established by

Figure 7.2 Tanzanian martial artists, c.1974. From issamichuzi.blogspot.com, August 25, 2009. Courtesy of Issa Michuzi

Bomani.[35] As Japhet Kaseba, Tanzania's kickboxing champion, said of his own career as a kickboxer: "It all started with Bruce Lee. When I was kid I saw the movies, and that was who I wanted to be: Bruce Lee."[36]

JEET KUNE DO UJAMAA

Lee's films and fighting style resonated with common messages at the core of Nyerere's philosophies of ujamaa, in which notions of self-reliance were dominant. During the years when Lee's name was on nearly every young person's lips, Nyerere's ideas of socialism and self-reliance (*ujamaa na ku-jitegemea*) were daily features in the press, on the radio, and in public life. Neither Nyerere nor Lee believed in waiting for what one did not have; the key was to harness what one could control—self. Again and again in his speech delivered in 1967, "The Arusha Declaration," Nyerere stressed the notion that "it is stupid to rely on money as the major instrument of development when we know only too well that our country is poor."[37] Human effort, hard work, and intelligence, he argued, were central to Tanzania's future progress. In *Ujamaa ni Amani*, published in 1973, and in countless other speeches and publications before and after that date, Nyerere

263

emphasized the need for Tanzanians to believe in themselves, take pride in their roots, and recognize that the power to determine the future lay in their hands.

Nyerere's ideals found cinematic expression in Lee's films, where they took on a youthful verve and popular cultural vibe. Early on in *Way of the Dragon*, Lee is shown carving darts from bamboo with a pocketknife. Throughout the film, he then uses these handcrafted weapons to disarm and defeat men with manufactured guns. Greedy capitalists and gangsters are no match for Lee, with his command of simple technology and self. Kamal, an Asian from Dar es Salaam, spoke of the importance of such scenes in fostering his respect for Lee. Lee was the real deal, Kamal said. "He did not rely on fakey special effects. With Lee you got real action, great action. It was all him, and just him."[38] Many Tanzanians echoed his remarks. Unlike Sylvester Stallone's Rambo, who was not nearly as popular in Tanzania as he was in other parts of Africa, Lee did not rely on machines or technology to defeat the enemy. Like Nyerere's ideal of development in a socialist society, Lee depended solely on things he could control—his own labor and intellect—to transform his world. In May Joseph's terms, the ideals of Nyerere and Lee coalesced in a cultural "performance of frugality" among Tanzanian youth in the 1970s, a concept that continued to resonate for decades to come.[39] "Who needs a tractor that relies on spare parts and petrol to weed a field?" asked an acquaintance named Idi while sharpening my hoe one day. Paraphrasing Lee (and perhaps unconsciously channeling Nyerere as well), he instructed me, "Simplicity is the height of cultivation, not just on the farm, but in all of life. The simple way is also the right way. Rely on the power you can harness from within."[40]

Thus, it was under a mango tree on a bustling commercial street in Zanzibar, while getting a hoe sharpened before jumping on a crowded bus and heading out to the farm, that I received my introduction to the philosophical teachings of Bruce Lee. Idi and I went on to become good friends over the years, meeting more regularly on the beach where we both exercised each day in the early 1990s. As I swam with my girlfriend and her brothers at dawn, I noticed the guys who ran and did martial arts, but we had never spoken until Idi recognized me that day at his shop. Both sets of Idi's skills—as a metalsmith who could transform objects right before my eyes with only the simplest of tools and as a philosopher and sage—were equally impressive. Like most who came of age in Zanzibar in the first generation after independence, he was barely literate, but he was one of the most intelligent and self-reflexive people I have ever known. He did not know English, the language in which Lee wrote *The Tao of Jeet Kune Do*, but as Idi pointed out, he could not speak Arabic either but that did not prevent him from learning or committing to heart the Holy Qur'an. Idi was also well versed in the Hadith, the spiritual lessons of right moral living taken from the life and actions of the Prophet Mohammed and passed down orally over generations by his followers. Idi and others who trained at the beach learned of Bruce Lee and his philosophy of "intercepting the fist" in a similar way.

In the 1970s and 1980s, young aspiring martial artists like Idi sought out others with more knowledge than themselves, who passed on the wisdom and skills they had to share. Sometimes, these teachers were former students at established schools, such as the one in Dar es Salaam. At other times, they were sailors who learned of martial arts while traveling the seas with crews from across the globe or who picked up martial arts training and philosophies, rather than venereal diseases, in the ports they visited across the Indian and Atlantic Oceans.[41] In addition, books about Lee, martial arts, and a host of related topics in a variety of languages circulated throughout the country. Like other texts, they were read by those who were literate and then summarized, interpreted, and relayed to those who were not. By the early 1980s, there were also biographies, training manuals, and novels, all written in Kiswahili, that aimed to make these lessons available to a wider Tanzanian audience.[42]

If the politicians who abhorred the kung fu "fad" had bothered to sit down and talk with some of the hundreds of youth who swarmed to the cinemas each week, they would have found that many young people articulated numerous elements of Nyerere's philosophy of African socialism in their discussions of Bruce Lee and the martial arts. Like Nyerere, Lee stressed the importance of nonalignment. And both Lee and Nyerere took from China, Japan, and the United States, as well as a host of other nations, to craft something new.[43] *Jeet kune do* is an amalgamation of fighting styles developed by Lee after training with masters from a variety of schools. The point was not to become locked in a certain pattern or series of moves but to be conversant with a range of possibilities and to free oneself to adapt to the situation at hand. Lee instructed, "Absorb what is useful, discard what is not. Add what is uniquely your own." Like Nyerere's philosophies of

265

socialism, Lee said that the aim was not to mimic the master but, through experimentation and self-discovery, to find a unique style of expression that reflected the self.

Both Nyerere and Lee also read widely and encouraged their students and followers to do the same. Lee's personal library was extensive. He majored in philosophy in college and was as conversant with Descartes and Rumi as he was with Buddhism and Zen.[44] Nyerere's intellectual interests also spanned the globe and went so far as translating Shakespeare into Kiswahili. Both men advocated flexibility, pushing and stretching oneself until it was painful, and incorporating what was useful no matter where it was from. They both inspired materially poor Tanzanians to be content and proud of what they had. Going barefoot to kung fu films became something of a fad.

In the burgeoning cities of Tanzania in the 1970s and 1980s, Lee's philosophy also spoke to the intrinsic struggle of young people who were hundreds of miles from home, grappling with endless new cultural repertoires and striving to construct a mature urban self. Remaining true to one's core values and principles while being open to new styles and ideas was critical. The medium of movies was new to many of these individuals, but the lessons they took from this globalized form resonated deeply. In Tanzania's cosmopolitan cities, the nation's youth were struggling just as hard as the young nation to find a path toward a liberatory future. Jeet kune do and urban life required one to be limber and lithe. The ability to "go with the flow" was essential to survival for marginally employed urban residents, which included most of the youth who were kung fu fans. Frequent raids of streets where hawkers sold their wares or roundups of "superfluous" urban dwellers who were unglamorously returned to their rural homes made Lee's adage "Be water, my friend" extremely useful.[45] "When water is poured into a cup, it becomes like the cup. When water is poured into a teapot, it becomes the teapot. Become formless and shapeless like water," Lee counseled. As Dudly Mawalla, one of the senior instructors at a Dar es Salaam dojo, emphasized during a 2014 memorial organized by the Tanzania Karate-Do Federation in honor of Mwalimu Nyerere, "Karate is not about beating someone. It is about being patient in life and stay [sic] strong."[46]

Those who thronged to the Empire Cinema each week were not drawn by a mindless desire to mimic the foreign, as some of their elders feared. They were drawn to Hong Kong action movies because they provided grand and glorious fictionalized depictions of their own lives and struggles, depictions in which male and female heroes, though facing incredible odds, won out. Such narratives offered mental inspiration and hope to those who lived the Kiswahili saying "*Maisha ni mtihani*" (Life is a test). Kung fu action films and the martial arts allowed them to respond to the challenge by quoting Lee, "Do not pray for an easy life, pray for the strength to endure a difficult one."[47] Nyerere and his supporters should have been proud.

YOUTHFUL SPACES AND NEW CINEMATIC PLEASURES

Life in the cities for this new generation of urban youth was not solely about struggle; it was also about having the freedom to experiment, to learn, and to have a lot of fun. The trials of earning a living, avoiding assaults by the Youth League, or evading roundups by police were undeniably obstacles, but no life was free of difficulties. For youth in the cities, two obvious resources at their disposal in the pursuit of pleasure were their many peers and the space that the cinemas offered for them to gather and enjoy each other's company.

In the 1970s and 1980s, Tanzanian youth made cinemas their home away from home, and in every Tanzanian city, large numbers of young people went to the movies several times a week; a good 10 percent of any given audience went almost every night.[48] Regulars were on familiar terms with local cinema employees, who let them in for free on days when they could not pay. Every worker I queried could rattle off the names of a dozen people from surrounding neighborhoods who came to the theater nightly. Cinema managers not only tolerated youthful crowds, they actually welcomed and encouraged them. Obviously, this was partly motivated by the desire to sell tickets. But just as important was the sheer joy of filling the house at midweek and helping a new generation get turned on to pleasures of film. As the following chapter details, government policies, including the nationalization of theaters, made these exceptionally difficult years for exhibitors. The young people who thronged to the cinemas warmed the hearts of the men who made the movies run, affirming on a nightly basis why they got into this business in the first place.

The cinemas were a unique public space, allowing hundreds of urban youth to gather, free from a watchful and often condemning adult

267

gaze. From Tuesday through Friday and sometimes on Saturday as well, spaghetti westerns, gladiator dramas, Hong Kong action, and blaxploitation filled the screens at conventional theaters. Typically, the only adults in the venue were cinema employees—men who remained forever young at heart and who relished the thrills of a good action film as much as their adolescent audience.[49]

Young people went to the movies in pairs or, more frequently, in small groups of friends, neighbors, classmates, and coworkers and then mixed with dozens upon dozens of other small groups from across the town. Bakari, a construction worker who moved to Arusha from a village outside of Dodoma, spoke of the excitement moviegoing provided during his formative early years of urban life. He relished his weekly visits to the Metropole Cinema on Saturday, in part because this was the only time he ever really went downtown. Describing himself as a checkbob, or cool cat, back in the day, he reminisced about the thrill of strutting the city streets in his hippest clothes and the runway drama of youth on their way to and from the show. He also emphasized the bonds he built with the five or six buddies with whom he regularly went to the movies, as well as the pleasures of meeting and greeting hundreds of other youngsters from beyond his regular circles. He lived with other Muslims from the Dodoma region, but his checkbob, moviegoing pals included people who had moved to Arusha from all corners of the country. Neema, a Maasai woman who had to lie to her parents to go to the show, was equally enthusiastic about the thrill of "mixing it up" at the Metropole. When Neema started secondary school, she discovered that "all the students went to the movies. The Metropole was the great meeting place for urban young people in Arusha," so she too began going with her friends from school. "This was one of the few places we were free to mingle," she remarked, "and really the only place we got to meet youth from other schools."[50] She attended a Catholic girls' school, so the Metropole also provided a unique opportunity for her and her girlfriends to socialize in the presence of young men like Bakari and the other checkbob strutting like roosters at the show. Edward, another young Catholic who moved to Arusha from the Kagera region when Bruce Lee and then Mithun Chakraborty were at the top of the local charts, also went to the Metropole once or twice a week. "This was where I got together with friends," he said, "where we went to get some fresh air, get out of the house and see what was happening in town and around the world."[51] This self-conscious desire to mix it up in the city involved experiences and attitudes that set many apart from their parents.

Newcomers to the city also found community and made lifelong friendships through their attendance at the show. John, who moved to Dar es Salaam from the Iringa region in 1970, said a friend where he worked was a film fanatic (*mshabiki*) and got him "hooked." It was at the Empire Cinema that John made his first friends when he moved to the city. He introduced me to several of these men, with whom he had now been friends for more than forty years. Together they grew from being rowdy young men in the front rows into husbands who took their wives to see Indian films. Shabani, who also moved to Dar in 1970 from Rufiji, had a similar experience. "My first day at work I met this guy who was a huge fan and he insisted on taking me to the movies that night. He said, 'you just came from the village and you got a job! This is how we celebrate here in town. You *have* to go to the cinema!'"[52] Soon, Shabani too was a fan. Together they explored the city and their adolescence. They traveled the city analyzing movie posters to determine which film to see that night, and he bonded with his friend at work over their mutual appreciation for film. When I asked Shabani about the benefits of going to the movies, he said, "I made friends that I could depend on. As a young man who was new to the city, this was where I met guys I saw every night." He also recalled tense situations where there might have been trouble that were eased by recognizing someone he had seen at the movies. Tough talk could be eased with, "Hey man, anything good playing at the Empire?" *Washabiki* (film fans) shared a brotherhood among what might otherwise have remained an alien and potentially hostile urban crowd.

SOCIAL AND SEXUAL MATURATION AT THE SHOW

One of the more surprising themes in my surveys and interviews was how frequently both men and women equated moviegoing in the 1970s and 1980s with jando, unyago, or other puberty initiation ceremonies. Watching films and going to the show with friends was seen as a critical component of the social, sexual, and intellectual maturation of that generation. Neema, the young woman who sneaked out to the movies, was just one of many who equated this assertion of personal will as a defining step toward independent adulthood. She deceived her parents about little else, but *everyone* was going to the movies in the 1970s, and she was determined not

269

to be left behind. Neema made the explicit connection between this shared cultural experience with her classmates and the age-grade rituals forming cohorts in the countryside where she was born. The key difference, she and others noted, was that the groups formed at the cinemas were ethnically and racially diverse. Cinemas helped transform city youth of the 1970s into an age-grade cohort that spanned and integrated the nation.

Traditionally, initiation had involved pubescent youth being spirited away from their communities to undergo extensive instruction by elders; they learned about communal history, standards of propriety, social expectations, and sexual pleasure and reproductive responsibility. But with the rapid spread of schooling after independence and the mass influx of youth to the cities, many of these customs began to wane. Few urban immigrants in the 1970s and 1980s had undergone the extensive forms of instruction or ritual transformations that their parents and grandparents once experienced at initiation camps.[53] Peers schooled in the ways of the city were now the instructors.

By the 1980s, one new genre that appealed to many was erotica—films that most parents would have certainly found objectionable. As earlier generations of moviegoers had done, they looked to films for models of emotional and romantic love, but increasingly, they also turned to visual media to learn about the rudiments of physical sex. Edna recalled, "While we were in secondary school we were constantly being berated about moral laxity, and we were regularly checked for pregnancy. Each month we were inspected. . . . If a school-girl was found pregnant she was expelled."[54] But for Edna's generation, there was no such thing as sex education. "Those of us who went off to boarding school never went to initiation camps," she said. "We were warned not to get pregnant, but no one understood how that happened." For instruction, she and the girls in her Catholic boarding school turned to the movies. One evening, she and a group of girls sneaked off to the Empire Cinema in Dar es Salaam to watch *Young Lady Chatterley* (Roberts, 1977), an X-rated soft-porn film based on the D. H. Lawrence novel.[55] According to Edna, the film was "very dirty" but extremely popular—so popular in fact that she and her age-mates had to wait to see it on its second run because they could not afford the ticket price being charged on the black market when it first came out. When *Young Lady Chatterley* opened in 1983, it set a new record, being held over for more than six weeks, yet still leaving legions of aroused young people pleading for more.[56]

Generational tensions over premarital dating emerged as a major point of contention between parents and children during these years, and cinemas were often central to the dramas. Ebrahim Hussein's 1971 play, *Wakati Ukuta* (Generational Impasse/The Wall of Time), is one of many pieces of Swahili literature published in that period in which generational conflict over sexual standards and propriety drives the text. Hussein's play opens with a scene in which Tatu, a "modern," miniskirt-wearing Muslim girl of twenty-one living in Dar es Salaam, asks her mother for permission to go to the Empress Cinema on Friday night with her "friend" Swai. Her mother adamantly refuses, saying she can go to the ladies' show, but under no circumstances will her daughter be allowed to go to the theater on a Friday night with a man. Tatu protests, arguing that "all the girls go on dates, it is nothing foreign,"[57] and condemns her mother for being hopelessly old-fashioned and behind the times.

Whether *all* the girls were going on dates in 1971, as Tatu claimed, is debatable, but there was clearly a generation shift taking place, with youth pushing their elders to accept premarital dating as a legitimate practice; moreover, the movie theater was one of the most common places for dating couples to go. According to several different surveys done by students at the University of Dar es Salaam in the early 1980s, most girls continued to seek permission from their parents before embarking on such an adventure, and when permission was granted, it was often on the condition that a chaperone go along as well.[58] One man I interviewed recalled his own experience negotiating over the ability to date, saying that it involved concessions from both sides. Reflecting on taking a date to the drive-in, he said, "Dating then wasn't like it is now. That was 30 years ago! When you took a girl on a date back then you had to take her grandmother too!"[59]

Youth whose parents were still living in the countryside often found it easier than this man or Tatu did to arrange dates without a chaperone. One survey of moviegoing in Dar es Salaam that was conducted in 1982 found that 30 percent of the audience was composed of dating couples. Combined with newlyweds, young heterosexual couples accounted for half of the patrons. Another survey found that at a certain theater in Dar es Salaam on Friday night, as many as 70 percent of the patrons were young couples.[60] Friends who went to the university during these years said that

271

going to town on a Friday or Saturday night was common. Girls felt safe at the cinema, where you could be "alone" with your date but in a crowd of several hundred, which set limits on any sexual advances.[61]

Though it was as common in Tanzania as in the United States for some men to presume that if they bought a girl a ticket they should get something sexual in return, most young men had no intent of assaulting the women they took to the movies; their aim was usually to impress the girl and often to convince her that he was precisely the man she should want to marry. In the eyes of many, taking a girl to a movie displayed a man's modern urban sensibility, his command of English, and his ability and willingness to spend his money to entertain and please the woman he was fond of. Among those who responded to my surveys, many men said that they took their dates to the movies precisely because they wanted to demonstrate that they were gentlemen who were interested in long-term relationships, not casual encounters.

The cost of tickets to popular movies could sometimes be exorbitant; as a result of the rise in dating, black marketers found a new niche preying on young men eager to impress a girl. Usually, black market dealers in cinema tickets made their money from the Indian blockbusters shown on Sundays, but business was business, and black marketers who themselves had never made it beyond the seventh grade felt little affinity with university-educated 'nizers who were willing to part with their cash to impress a date. Some men relished the opportunity to flaunt their wealth in front of peers by paying two to three times the ticket window price to a black marketer, but most resented having to pay far more for a ticket than their limited budget made wise. Ultimately, though, peer pressure was often a far stronger motivator than economic self-interest: it would be an absolute embarrassment to take a girl to a movie and then turn away because you were unwilling to pay whatever price a scalper demanded.[62] Freddy Macha, the art critic and youth correspondent for the *Sunday News*, complained of black marketers' assaults on young men like himself, writing in one of his columns, "You have come with someone and you have to go inside the hall. You cannot go back home, it is too undignified. To hell with the budget, to hell with tomorrow. . . . You are going to see *Endless Love* today."[63] Meanwhile, newspaper ads depicted a tantalizing movie still of a topless couple moving toward a kiss. If that was not enough to entice young viewers, the accompanying text read, "She is 15, he is 17 . . . the love that every

Figure 7.3 Anti–black market cartoon. From *Nchi Yetu*, July–August 1977, p. 40

parent fears . . . the movie is the talk of the town." Legions of youth rushed to the Avalon to see the film, no matter the cost.

Endless Love (Zeffirelli, 1981) was one of the top hits of 1982 for young dating couples, playing for a nearly unprecedented five-week run in Dar es Salaam. Its title song, sung by Diana Ross and Lionel Richie, was heard everywhere.[64] One man confessed that when choosing a movie for a night out, he often tried to pick something slightly risqué with the hope of inspiring his date to be more physical. What title could be more innocuous or reminiscent of Indian melodramas than *Endless Love*? But in fact the film was quite risqué, showing teen sex on screen for the first time.[65] In his review of the film for the *Sunday News*, Freddy Macha stressed the educational over the erotic, likening the movie's central themes to those of Shakespeare's *Romeo and Juliet* or Ebrahim Hussein's *Wakati Ukuta*. The underlying lesson of these dramas, according to Macha, was the futility of parents' attempts to restrain their children's hearts. Generational change was inevitable.[66]

Like drive-in cinemas everywhere, Sisi in Dar es Salaam also developed a reputation as place for dating. Those who attended charity show events at the drive-in were adamant that no hanky-panky took place on

273

these nights: both the show and the cars were packed with people who could ruin your reputation or report you to your parents, said several people. I asked Akhmed if youth at these shows ever took advantage of the dark to kiss or do anything else. "Are you kidding?" he asked. "With four thousand prying eyes searching for something to gossip about? No way! If you ever attempted something like that you could be certain someone would see you, and then would you be in for it!" Few considered the risk worth the cost. Smiling, making eyes, or merely being in the same space with a romantic interest still constituted consummated love for many youth.

Yet nearly a dozen people, half of whom were cinema employees or their spouses, told me they met their partners at the show. Gigri first set his eyes on his future wife when she ordered from his concession stand. Impressed by her beauty, he took extra care with her order and then sent his brothers to inquire about her marital status and family position; he eventually proposed and then fell madly in love. A woman in Zanzibar reminisced about meeting her second husband, who was then a young man working evenings as an usher, in a similar fashion. Their eyes met, and it was mutual love at first sight. He sent his elders to propose. Shanin told me that one of the big anticipated thrills of Sundays at the drive-in was the opportunity to connect with her boyfriend once inside. Yet she said, "as close as we got was to see each other, not even to talk, because if you did some cousin would surely tell on you . . . and that would be the end of your freedom for some time."[67] Eddy also spoke of a rendezvous with a girlfriend at the drive-in: "We would agree to meet at a certain time, like the second song and dance number. I'd tell my mom or uncle that I had to go to the bathroom and hope that none of my younger siblings had to go too." If you were really bold, he continued, "you would slyly slip around the back of the concession stand, where it was pitch black and no one could see you. There you could talk—but never for longer than ten minutes—or the adults would start to wonder what you were up to taking so long to go to the bathroom."[68] The drive-in concession stand was apparently a real hot spot for young love. "Many people used to come to my place to make love stories!" said Gigri with glee. "Sometimes young men would come to me and say, 'I am coming to meet with my girlfriend, please give us ice, ice cold sodas, I want to impress her.'"[69] Youth did not need to go to the movies without their parents in order to date at the show, as dating rarely involved touching and only the bold ventured to talk.

Yet adults having affairs also used the drive-in for romantic meetings. When prompted by her friend to share her memories of the drive-in in the late 1980s, Irene exclaimed, "Legs! Legs in the air is all I recall!" Few had access to a home or a room of their own, but a car provided an enclosed private space, and the drive-in was a protected place to park. "If you went to the beach it was too secluded and you could be robbed," said one anonymous source, "and that would be the end to that date. She would never want to see you again. But the drive-in was safe." For women, the relative proximity of other cars also added to their sense of ease. A woman could leave the car, honk the horn, or make a public fuss if her partner wanted to take things too far.[70]

Late-night, midweek shows were somewhat notorious as make-out spots. "The night show, at 10 pm, was for lovers," said one drive-in employee. People would park far apart so that everyone was assured of privacy, or they would pull into "Lover's Lane," as the back row was commonly known.[71] "If you parked in Lover's Lane everyone knew you did not want to be disturbed," said one man who claimed to have regularly taken his girlfriends there. I expressed skepticism that there was much privacy involved, since everyone knew everyone else's car and could see who came with whom. "People came with their own business in mind," he replied. "They didn't really care what you were up to, and if a girl was really concerned about being found out she could cover her head with a *kanga* or a *buibui* until the lights went out and business got underway."[72] The number of young couples who made use of the drive-in in this way, however, was an exceedingly small percentage of cinematic patrons overall. Though premarital dating was increasingly common for modern young urbanites, the very real fear of pregnancy and the social expectations of parents, as well as peers, that women should remain virgins until marriage meant that most couples went to the movies to look, not to touch.

Every generation of young people, so it seems, is convinced of the novelty of their struggles and innovations, so different, so much more daring, they imagine, from anything their parents could have done. To be sure, there were certainly changes taking place in Tanzanian cinematic culture after independence, but there was also continuity with earlier years. For one,

275

Indian melodramas remained the most popular genre through the 1980s and the only films fit to be reeled. Youth who pushed their parents to allow them to date at the movies thought that they were revolutionary, but most were merely ignorant of the fact that their own parents or grandparents had drawn on films and cinematic culture to push for changes in intimate relations in the 1950s and had also utilized the space of the cinema to be alone and develop a relationship as a couple. While the feel of moviegoing changed as the cities and cinemas were overrun by people under thirty, there were innumerable continuities in the social experience of moviegoing from earlier years.

Chapter 8

THE POLITICAL ECONOMY
OF CINEMA, 1960s–80s

THE POLITICAL economy of cinema changed dramatically with independence. Alongside rapid urban growth and soaring numbers of moviegoers, big changes in state policies impacted the industry on numerous levels. Gone were the days of a laissez-faire colonial state, when entrepreneurs with a vision and the capital to see it through could operate a business with only minimal direct intervention from authorities. Aside from rating films and authorizing building permits, the colonial state had little impact on the film exhibition and distribution industries in Tanzania. During the colonial era, it was local citizens who ran the show. With independence, this all changed. State socialism demanded centralization of the economy and a bold new cultural policy. By the 1970s, Tanzania had one of the most centralized economies on the continent.[1] Between 1961 and 1971, the film industry too was harnessed to allegedly better serve the interests of socialism. New taxes were imposed; new censorship boards were appointed; and following the Arusha Declaration of 1967, distribution was nationalized. The Tanzania Film Company Limited (TFC) was created in 1968 to manage all aspects of the cinema industry.[2] As part of the larger assault on the

Asian community, cinema houses were nationalized—in 1964 in Zanzibar and 1971 on the mainland—although individual proprietors were both allowed and encouraged to continue operating their theaters *if* they were willing to give 50 percent of their annual profits to the state.

Despite this massive restructuring of the industry, average fans initially encountered few obvious changes when they went to the show. The Sultana Cinema in Zanzibar was forced to change its name to the more politically correct Cine Afrique, but in most cases, the same owners and managers remained in charge and greeted customers at the ticket windows and doors as they always did.[3] Fans continued to have their needs met by local operators who prided themselves on showing the town a good time, theaters remained packed to overflowing, and the talk of the town on Monday was still Sunday's Indian film. Thus, even though the economic and political structure of the industry was fundamentally altered, for several decades it appeared on the surface as though little had changed. But with each passing year, the cracks in this facade became more pronounced. The grassroots entrepreneurial spirit that had driven the industry in the first half of the century was eclipsed by centralized bureaucratic governance and the dictates of profit maximization at the top. The failure to reinvest in local cinematic infrastructure or to listen to local clients and managers meant that over decades the foundation of the industry became increasingly weak. As the epilogue details, the entire house collapsed by the turn of the millennium.

As with the socialist drive-in inaugurated by NDC, what was meant by *socializing* cinema was open to broad interpretation. At each and every level, there were at least two powerful interests, often with mutually antagonistic goals, trying to direct matters. Nationalizing the industry and transforming it to serve socialist ends were far from straightforward moves; cinematic policy was riddled with ambiguities, and TFC was full of contradictions. Under its articles of incorporation, TFC was saddled with no fewer than twenty-seven objectives; if it failed to meet these aims, one could legitimately argue that perhaps it was simply asked to do too much. One aim was to maximize profits, and on this score, TFC performed exceedingly well. Somewhat at odds with generating profits by circulating popular films, TFC was also called upon to support the intellectual and ideological revolution, preserve the national culture, and protect citizens from "the unabated hegemony of ideologically repugnant films."[4] Ideally, at least in some people's estimation, films promoting socialism and a socialist ethos should have completely replaced all the films previously discussed in this book.[5] But clearly, that never happened. Cold, hard cash held greater value for bureaucrats than socialist ideology. And as Kelly Askew, Marisa Moorman, Thomas Terrino, and Paul Schauert have all illustrated regarding postcolonial music policy, defining *national culture* was no simple task; determining the best way to use the national culture to promote socialism was more complicated yet.[6]

Ostensibly, the primary purpose of nationalizing distribution and heavily taxing exhibition was to secure funds for the development of an indigenous feature film–making industry. A few dared to imagine that Dar es Salaam could become the East African equivalent of Ouagadougou and that TFC could facilitate the rise of at least one Ousmane Sembene. But the artistic dreamers were marginalized within an organization that was top-heavy with bureaucrats who knew little about the arts and cared even less about film.[7] TFC employed many talented people in its filmmaking division, but they were allowed to produce very few films. It was only in the twenty-first century that a new generation of Tanzanian filmmakers, empowered by the relatively low cost, creative independence, and editorial freedom of digital technology, began to make films in large numbers. Consolidating profits at the top of the corporation was the primary achievement of TFC as a socialist parastatal. This chapter examines the multiple and competing forces struggling over cinematic policy and practice, from independence through the 1980s. Combined with the previous chapter, it illustrates how little state policies often appear to affect daily lives, as well the immense structural impact political and economic policies have in shaping options and future choices of every kind, including seemingly mundane ones such as, What shall we do tonight?

TAX POLICY AND THE STATE

Tax policy is a powerful tool. States can use taxes to raise revenues, reallocate wealth, and invest in social services and infrastructure. Or they can use them to penalize certain products and practices, with the aim of undermining their popularity or the businesses that profit from them. In the 1940s, authorities began debating the imposition of a sin tax on tickets for commercial cinemas, but it was only in the 1960s that such a tax was

279

finally imposed. The aims were twofold: first, to raise the price of tickets beyond the level average people could afford and thus "protect" Africans from the vices and ill effects of commercial film and, second, to raise a little bit of revenue from those who nonetheless continued to indulge. But as advocates of sin taxes on cigarettes and sugary drinks have discovered, it often takes a lot more than a tax to break sinners' beloved habits, and states can easily become addicted to a new source of revenue. As the growing popularity of moviegoing after independence attests, applying an entertainment tax to cinema tickets did not really work to undermine indulgence in film-based leisure. Yet bureaucrats capitalized on the elastic demand for cinematic entertainment, finding moviegoing a lucrative source of state revenue. On the eve of independence, there was no direct levy on cinema tickets, so 100 percent of ticket earnings went to those who ran the show and imported films. Twenty years later, however, 80 percent of the ticket price was taken directly off the top and delivered to the state. And most of the remaining box office earnings made their way into state coffers by the end of the tax year.[8]

In the three decades after independence, the profitability of operating a cinema declined tremendously even as the price for tickets and the volume of patrons increased. By the 1980s, between direct levies on tickets, payments to TFC for films, and business taxes on exhibition, the most profitable cinemas in Tanzania might be left with TSh 34,000 in net annual earnings ($2,525) on 3.3 million ($254,000) in gross ticket sales.[9] Quite literally, exhibitors kept a penny on every dollar they brought in the door. Taxes came in various forms, and new ones were continually being added. The state and TFC were the only real winners in the game. By 1984, TFC's annual revenues from film distribution alone exceeded TSh 40 million ($2,360,000).[10] Everyone who operated a cinema had other business concerns as well, and to a man, they said that the cinema industry was taxed far more heavily than any other business they ran. One proprietor, who ran a small cinema in a remote corner of Tanzania as well as several more successful small manufacturing companies making nails and processing hides for export, likened TFC to a hyena—a notoriously maligned scavenger in African folklore that eats after someone else has done all the work. "They ate and ate," he said. "We ran the business, but if we were lucky, they left us with a few bones." Another exhibitor described TFC similarly, saying, "We were like a milk-cow. But instead of thinking of our long-term health, providing us with good pasture and water, they just milked and milked until eventually they milked us dry." Across the country, the analogies and analysis were the same: the parastatal that was in charge of the cinema industry thought only about maximizing short-term profits, not long-term sustainability.

One might imagine that imposing and collecting taxes was the forte of colonial authorities, but in British Africa, the state was actually far more in-sistent about collecting direct taxes from African peasants than it was about collecting taxes on profits from businesses and corporations. Across the continent, colonial authorities invested heavily in constructing and mar-shaling an institutional structure for the collection of hut and poll taxes, often rationalized as a necessary "incentive" for getting the "lazy African" to work. In Tanganyika, these taxes were rigorously enforced by the Ger-man and British authorities. Failure to pay often resulted in imprisonment, forced labor, or both. Zanzibar was the only territory in British Africa with-out direct taxation.[11] Instead, authorities opted for a path of least resistance: indirect taxes collected at the port, whose costs were passed along to con-sumers by shopkeepers who simply added the tax into the prices charged for imported commodities. Export and customs duties along with excise taxes accounted for 60 to 70 percent of tax revenue in Tanganyika and 90 percent in Zanzibar.[12]

There were of course business income taxes in the colonies, but typically, only the largest foreign corporations were required to pay.[13] Tax authorities in Tanzania considered it too inefficient to try to collect taxes on the profits of small businesses. Shopkeepers encouraged this lack of oversight by claiming they did not keep written accounts or by keeping ac-counts in languages the British authorities could not comprehend. Annual licensing fees and import-export duties on specific commodities were con-sidered simpler and equally sufficient means of raising revenues.[14] Typical payments made by a cinema owner in Zanzibar during the 1950s included a TSh 400 ($57) fee for an annual exhibition license and permits for each film shown, which amounted to another TSh 6,300 ($900) per year.[15] Film importers also had to pay customs duties on each film retrieved at the port, which they paid for out of their share of box office receipts. Annual licensing

281

fees and flat-fee assessments on tangibles that can be easily counted—such as each film shown or each bed rented at a hotel—remain central to revenue collection in Zanzibar to this day.[16]

Cinemas were operating in Tanzania for nearly fifty years before authorities began to seriously consider them as potential sources of revenue. Annual licensing fees for exhibition were only imposed in Zanzibar in 1949, and not until 1962 was a direct levy on ticket sales, in the form of an entertainment tax, imposed either in the isles or on the mainland.[17] Legally, the power to collect an entertainment tax existed in Zanzibar from the 1930s. However, it was only in 1947 that authorities began a rather lengthy debate about the pros and cons of attempting to collect it. A few were certain that a tax on the cinemagoing public was a guaranteed revenue generator, but the majority in the administration—who apparently never walked the streets on a Sunday evening or read the letters to the editor in the newspapers complaining about the black market in cinema tickets—doubted that the income earned could possibly be worth the hassle of collecting it.[18] As late as 1960, the acting financial secretary was still arguing against an entertainment tax, saying, "The current system of taxes, which relies heavily on import duties, raises four times the money of a direct income tax. This of course is a regressive tax, since it falls heavily on the poor and less heavily on the rich, but it raises little objection since it is unseen."[19] He, like most other members of the local administration, feared that any clearly identifiable tax would meet resistance, and in the volatile political climate of 1960, the last thing the government needed, he argued, was "any measure that could be interpreted as an attack on the poor."

The entertainment tax was first imposed in Zanzibar in May 1962, and it provoked vociferous objections. Local exhibitors were outraged, in part because the administration imposed the tax without any consultation with business owners and in part because the new tax effectively raised the price of tickets 25 to 30 percent. Exhibitors claimed they had not increased ticket prices in more than eight years, allegedly out of concern for their patrons. Cinema owners in Pemba were even more displeased. Alleging that the depressed colonial economy left them barely hanging on to their establishments, they claimed to have recently slashed prices by more than 50 percent to woo patrons back to the show. Now the state wanted to raise prices 30 percent, and none of that would go to proprietors.[20] This was an outrage. Why, asked local theater owners, was the cinema industry being specifically targeted when other small businesses paid no direct tax at all? Would not a general business tax be more equitable and fair? In addition, they pointed out that this was yet another in a long line of utterly regressive taxes, falling hardest on the poor, who constituted the majority of the cinemagoing public in Zanzibar.

Proprietors who called for the elimination of the entertainment tax were joined by major international distributors, including MGM, 20th Century Fox, Anglo-American, and Indian Film Combine, who asserted that the new tax would make the isles of Zanzibar some of the most expensive places in East Africa to go to the movies. How, they asked, could the administration in Zanzibar expect a poor clove picker in Pemba to pay as much for a ticket as a business owner or settler in Nairobi? In Dar es Salaam and Kampala, these international distributors pointed out, there was no entertainment tax at all at that time. The general manager of Indian Film Combine, which was based in Bombay with a branch office in Nairobi, even went so far as to warn that the government might be confronted with a "rash of anti-social behavior as cinema moves beyond the reach of the poor man." Governments all over the world, he argued, had come to recognize that making cheap entertainment available to the masses was a useful check on so-called antisocial elements. Reminding authorities about the nationalist fervor rocking the streets of Zanzibar for the previous several years, he encouraged the government to reconsider their tax or at least the tax rates in hopes that riotous urban crowds plotting to end British rule might be persuaded to return to the relative passivity of a night at the movies.[21] These written appeals by local and international business leaders brought results: a month after the tax was first imposed, a new law was enacted cutting the effective tax rate in half. The cheapest seats in the house, roughly one-third of the seats in each theater or those with ticket prices of a shilling or less, were also exempt from the entertainment tax under the new provisions.[22]

Efforts to curtail the governments' tax avidity were much less successful after independence. Shortly after the entertainment tax was applied in Zanzibar, the newly independent government in Tanganyika imposed one as well. In 1966, the same year that NDC opened the drive-in, the mainland government doubled the tax rate per ticket, from one to two shillings. This was the headline story on the front page of the *Sunday News*, the national newspaper that cinema fans turned to for film news, reviews, and gossip.[23]

283

Governments on both sides of the channel quickly came to realize that large sums could be earned by taxing cinema fans for the pleasure of an evening at the show. Over the next fifteen years, the rates paid for the entertainment tax soared; by the 1980s, nearly 30 percent of a ticket's price went to pay for entertainment tax.[24] The aggregate earnings were considerable. The three theaters in Zanzibar Town alone were contributing nearly TSh 1.2 million ($144,000) annually to state revenues through the entertainment tax.[25] Between Zanzibar and the mainland, TFC collected an average of TSh 31 million a year ($2,341,389) in entertainment tax in the early 1980s.[26] Taxing people for their cinematic pleasures proved lucrative indeed.

As a sin tax, the entertainment tax did little to keep people away from the show, but as a revenue generator, it channeled large sums into state accounts; the entertainment tax was also just one of many tools used to redistribute income from the pockets of patrons and business owners to the parastatal. This tax was not directly taken from exhibitors, but it did significantly impact their potential profits. Because of steady increases in the tax, exhibitors were reluctant to raise the price of tickets, and each time they collectively contemplated such a move, the state beat them to it with yet another type of levy on tickets. The entertainment tax literally wasn't the half of it. Exhibiters were also required to pay a 10 percent "development" levy on the gross earnings from each show. There was also a flat CCM (Chama cha Mapinduzi—the ruling party after 1977) "development" levy of 1/- on each ticket and an additional duty charge of 2/- per ticket. In other words, a cinema on the mainland kept 4/20 on a 22/- ticket (19 percent), whereas cinemas in Zanzibar were allowed to retain 2/30 on every 14/- ticket sold (16 percent).[27] In Zanzibar, the Majestic Cinema paid TSh 1.2 million off the top of their 3.3 million gross ticket sales in entertainment tax, development levies, and CCM collections in 1985. Another 1.3 million was paid to TFC for film rental. There were also fees paid to the municipal governments for film permits and fees paid to censors for reviewing each film. Operating costs, including salaries, building repairs, equipment maintenance, film transportation, and advertising, were also substantial costs but typically amounted to less than half of what was paid in direct levies on tickets sold.[28] The vast majority of what cinemas took in at the door went directly to the state.

To add insult to injury, operators also had to pay rent for their facilities, which quite often their own fathers had built. The Majestic paid the Zanzibar government TSh 80,000 in annual rent in 1985, which amounted to roughly 20 percent of its total operating expenses for the year. After deducting payments to TFC and the Zanzibar government as well as business expenses, the Majestic netted TSh 69,000 in 1985 on 3.3 million in sales. Half of this 69,000 then had to be paid in corporate business tax, leaving the Majestic just under TSh 35,000 in profit on a year's labor. These earnings translated into $2,000 at the official exchange rate, or $195 at the black market rate—which is what a proprietor needed to figure at if he had to buy spare parts or equipment on the international market. Business accounts from the Majestic in Tanga show a similar breakdown in terms taxes, expenditures, and profits.[29] "Pennies, pennies on the dollar is all we earned," quipped one exhibitor. "Peanuts, peanuts is all we would make for our efforts," said another. A third lamented, "Between taxes and rent they killed us. By the 1990s there was no way the business could stay afloat." Sadly, archival, business, and tax records confirm the legitimacy of their claims. For readers who first encountered Tanzanian cinemas in the late 1980s or 1990s and doubted my depiction of once-grand picture palaces, these basic economic facts should help explain the dilapidated state of affairs in the late twentieth century. When the proprietor of one of the most profitable theaters in the nation retained only the equivalent of $195 for 365 days and nights of labor, how much could he afford to spend in upkeep?

Although all corporations on the mainland were officially subject to the 50 percent tax on profits, exemptions and reductions were not uncommon, provided one had friends in the right places. Oddly, foreign-owned businesses fared better in this regard than those that were locally owned. A detailed analysis of waivers and exemptions offered by the minister of finance and authorized by parliament between 1967 and 1983, conducted by Amon Chaligha, found that 75 percent of such waivers and remissions were given to foreign capital.[30] To my knowledge, the drive-in was the only cinema in the country that was offered leniency on taxes. I found petitions and letters requesting a reduction in the tax rates from cinema proprietors in the archives, yet (at least according to these records and interviews with exhibitors) none was ever granted.

NATIONALIZATION OF CINEMA HALLS

The lack of investment in theater maintenance was exacerbated by the fact that those who built and ran the theaters during the colonial period had their buildings nationalized during the socialist era. Overnight, these structures became the property of the state. Often, the former owners continued to operate the businesses, but the buildings were no longer theirs. The men who built Tanzania's cinemas were now merely tenants. They paid annual rent to the National Housing Corporation or the Registrar of Buildings but had no ability to demand that their landlords schedule maintenance. As Brij Behal, whose grandfather built the Elite Cinema in Arusha, lamented in a 2005 interview, "This building was built with love. But National Housing hasn't put any money into it to keep it up. Even paint, the outside hasn't been painted in more than thirty years."[31] Unfortunately, buildings such as the Elite, which were often the crowning architectural achievements of a town and the hallmark of an entrepreneur's social investment in the community, were left to languish and decay after independence. Watching their buildings crumble pained proprietors immensely.

Though the rents they paid were quite substantial, no cinema was maintained by the new landlord after nationalization. In 1985, to cite just one instance, the proprietor of the Majestic in Zanzibar paid the equivalent of $3,500 in annual rent, but the following year, he had to fix a leak in the roof with no assistance from the Registrar of Buildings, to whom the rent was paid. According to employees, the Avalon in Dar es Salaam was paying more than $1,000 per month in rent to the National Housing Authority in 2001.[32] At that time, the Avalon's projectionist earned $70 a month, which was twice the minimum wage, and the doorkeeper earned $45 a month for his nightly services.[33] Across the country, the story was the same. Yet despite these exorbitant rents, National Housing did no maintenance or repairs. Exhibitors continued to pay for the cleaning and maintenance of their halls, equipment, restaurants, and restroom facilities, considering such investments necessary for running an attractive business.[34] They also paid for the regular maintenance of screens, projectors, sound equipment, and seating. But by the mid-1980s, many buildings had not had roofs, walls, or major mechanical systems fixed or maintained for fifteen to twenty years. Fans and air-conditioning rarely functioned, making an evening at the cinema more like a trip to a sauna and less than attractive in the tropical climate. Numerous formerly avid film fans said their desire to go to the cinema diminished as the conditions inside the halls declined. Even state authorities admitted—behind closed doors—that the state's failure to repair and maintain the cinemas was negatively affecting attendance.[35] My own children cringed when I told them we were going to the show: having rats underfoot and getting flea-bitten bottoms was not their idea of a good time. By the late 1990s and early 2000s, formerly glorious picture palaces had deteriorated into dumps.

Exhibitors were understandably reluctant to invest their own meager earnings into building upkeep, but many did nonetheless. In the 1970s and 1980s, going to the movies was still the most important form of urban leisure, and exhibitors took pleasure in pleasing their customers and putting on a good show. If they prided themselves on providing this service, they had little choice but to keep their buildings up. Repairs to roofs were the most critical and expensive, and it was not uncommon for the men who ran the cinemas to spend thousands of dollars on important structural repairs of this type. But by the 1990s, as the crowds at the cinemas declined, repairs were more frequently put off. Several of the theaters I visited in the early 2000s had their roofs or walls collapse due to lack of structural maintenance. In many cases, all that remains today is literally the facade.[36]

The fact that rental contracts could be broken—and exhibitors evicted—at a moment's notice by National Housing also made proprietors reluctant to invest in equipment updates and technical innovation. "Nationalization had a big impact," said Asad Talati, who ran several of the premier theaters in the nation, including the Cine Afrique and Avalon. "If I want to put in digital sound and projection, how am I going to do that when it is not my building? Some day I might just get a letter, like [a colleague had just received in 2004] saying, 'Hey, we want this building,' and that is that."[37] During the first fifty years of the business, exhibitors prided themselves on keeping up with international standards and competed intensely to integrate the latest technologies into their theaters and shows. With nationalization, this too changed. Rather than updating projection equipment, until they closed, cinemas in Tanzania relied on carbon arc projection to illuminate films.[38] This technology dated from the turn of the twentieth century, but in the late 1960s and early 1970s, most theaters across the world switched to xenon arc lamps, which were easier to operate and less dangerous. It pained exhibitors who once had the most up-to-date equipment in the industry to fall behind, but many echoed Talati's remarks, saying they simply could not invest in such expensive improvements when they had no guarantee that their building leases would be renewed long enough to recoup the costs. With TFC now taking the bulk of box office

287

earnings, no one considered the purchase of new projectors and the sound systems they would require to be anything but a huge financial loss. Referring to Tanzanian's continued use of carbon rods to illuminate films into the twenty-first century, one of the nation's entrepreneurs said, "It was like others had sleek motor cars and we had donkeys. Really, by the end you couldn't find one cinema in the US, Canada or UK using carbons. Maybe some remote village in India, but nobody was using those things anymore, except us."[39]

Nationalization had profound impacts not only on the buildings but also on the owners and managers. Men who once bragged of the beauty of their buildings and the splendors of the shows they offered were crushed by nationalization. During the interviews I conducted, the mood invariably became gloomy when the conversation moved to this topic. People could talk casually but passionately about taxes or TFC, but discussing the nationalization of the halls themselves invariably elicited deep emotional pain. Some men changed the topic as soon possible; others were literally moved to tears in recalling the impact nationalization had on their fathers, who had invested their pride, joy, and honor in building their cinemas. Shabir Jariwalla, whose grandfather had pioneered the industry in Zanzibar in the early 1900s, relayed with tears in his eyes how his own father, Karimbhai H. Jariwalla, had a fatal heart attack after learning that his cinemas had been nationalized. "My father died because of this," he said. "When they nationalized his two cinemas, the Azania and the Empire, he collapsed and died. It killed him."[40] A man who was fifteen years old at the time of nationalization also recalled its devastating impact on his father's mental and physical health. The entire extended family eventually left town. Some moved to other towns in Tanzania and started again in another small business; others joined the tens of thousands who fled Tanzania. According to Richa Nagar, forty thousand Asians left the mainland within six months of the Building Acquisitions Act of 1971's promulgation. By the late 1980s, nearly 75 percent of the Asian population of Tanzania had left the country.[41] Previously, investing in building a home and living off the rent received from letting out rooms or flats in retirement was a common strategy for Asians and Africans alike. Suddenly, however, it became illegal for anyone other than National Housing to receive rent for a unit in which they did not personally reside. The suffering caused by the Building Acquisitions Act is powerfully portrayed by M. G. Vasanji in the novel *Book of Secrets*, where the nationalization of the home he has spent a lifetime building kills a key protagonist, as it did K. H. Jariwalla and countless others.[42]

Mr. Khambaita, who designed and built the Everest Cinema in Moshi, lamented the loss of his business, building, and investments but above all the loss of his extended family; most of his relatives left Tanzania after 1971. He stayed on in Moshi and continued to run his father's auto repair shop, with hopes that the government would relent and return their property. Like many Tanzanian Asians, however, he sent his wife and children to live in the United Kingdom, where they were more secure. As he explained, "After that time some eighty per cent of my family left the country straight away. We were about eighty members, now we are only five total. Myself, I am all alone here. All the rest have left because of nationalization. I am now eighty-one years old [in 2005], and to see my wife or children I must fly to the UK."[43] Imagine the disappointment and pain experienced by a man who designed, built, and ran a cinema for nearly twenty-five years but has never had the pleasure of taking his grandchildren to see a film.

Most of the men who built the cinemas remained in the country after the nationalizations of 1964, 1967, and 1971. Tanzania was home, and individuals who had invested their lives in building and operating successful businesses were not easily sent packing. And so, the vast majority of Tanzanian exhibitors continued on with the show. Although the buildings were no longer theirs and the profit margins of the businesses were increasingly slim, they continued to dedicate their evenings and weekends to providing entertainment for the ever-growing local crowds. Managers, projectionists, and gatekeepers too maintained their allegiance to the show. These men had always been employees who received a monthly salary for a job well done, and for the most part, nationalization did little to alter their employment or their commitment to showing the town a good time.

Most Tanzanians in the distribution business also stayed in the country and continued to run their enterprises as best they could. Like many Tanzanian Asians, they found that their skills, connections, and acumen were still vital assets—assets that the socialist state was eager to harness.[44] Despite taking these men's homes, the state—often in the form of President Nyerere himself—actively recruited many, asking them to take charge of the business, industry, and agricultural concerns their families had pioneered

289

over preceding generations.[45] This was true of the cinema industry as well. Asad Talati, whose father was one of the leading partners in Indo-African Theaters and founder of United Film Distributors, stayed in the exhibition and distribution business in Tanzania for nearly forty years after his theaters and the family home in Zanzibar were nationalized. His knowledge of the industry also made him a significant asset to TFC. Although many wealthier Asians, such as the Karimjees and the Chandes, were allowed direct control over industries their families had owned before nationalization, Talati was officially kept on the margins. He was encouraged to continue running his theaters and supplying TFC with films, but he was excluded from management decision making and from TFC's board of directors. Despite this, nearly everyone I interviewed in Tanzania stressed that without Talati, TFC could not have functioned. Naaz Rana, a distribution officer for TFC, said, "Talati taught me everything I know. When I was hired I knew nothing about films, buying or distributing. Without him I would not have had any idea what I was doing. No one in our office did."[46] This situation was typical of many parastatals.[47]

TANZANIA FILM COMPANY LTD., 1968–2000

The Tanzania Film Company was inaugurated in 1968 as a wholly owned subsidiary of the National Development Corporation, eventually emerging, in 1974, as an independent parastatal, affiliated with the Ministry of Information and Broadcasting.[48] The goals of TFC were laudatory, as well as daunting and contradictory. The company was charged with buying and distributing cinematic films; overseeing and expanding cinematic exhibition; making, directing, producing, and processing motion pictures; promoting and preserving "national culture"; and supporting and encouraging sociopolitical transformation. TFC was also commanded to: seek out talented singers, writers, musicians, and actors and assist them in realizing their artistic ambitions; expand the number of film, concert, and theater venues in the nation; dub imported films into Kiswahili; produce advertisements, newsreels, and educational films for other parastatals and government ministries; and, if all of that was not enough, promote national music culture by buying and renting musical equipment, recording local artists, and producing cassette tapes and vinyl records. It is perhaps not surprising that TFC failed to meet expectations.[49]

Officially, the aim of the organization was complete nationalization of the industry, but none of those appointed to manage TFC in 1968 knew how to run a projector, let alone a cinema; they knew even less about how to secure films on the international market or distribute them to forty theaters across the nation. Existing exhibitors and distributors were encouraged to continue their operations. Until 1971, the company did little more than collect a 10 percent fee on the earnings of private importers and film distributors operating in Tanzania. The nationalization of distribution was also delayed by diplomatic pressure from the US State Department on behalf of the Motion Picture Export Association of America's subsidiary companies working in East Africa, as well as Indian distributors with offices in Nairobi.[50] It took four years, but by 1972, TFC managed to consolidate its position at the apex of film distribution in Tanzania. It did this not by eliminating other suppliers and distributors but by bringing them under TFC's umbrella.[51] The existing distributors continued to import films that, in official terms, they supplied to TFC, which in turn distributed them to Tanzanian theaters.[52] TFC also acted as the middleman between the theaters and suppliers in the conveyance of box office receipts. As payment for its services, it kept 30 percent of the distributor's share of box office earnings. Nationalizing distribution meant little more than skimming 30 percent off the top, earning TFC more than $1 million a year for its services as a middleman in the early 1980s.[53]

Relations with the suppliers of American films were far more complicated for TFC than those with suppliers of films from other nations. At the height of the Cold War, the Americans were ideologically opposed to both socialism and nationalization, but practical business, political, and military matters meant they worked hard to maintain their ties to Tanzania.[54] As a prominent member of the frontline states fighting white rule in southern Africa, Tanzania was also ideologically opposed to businesses profiting from apartheid. On the eve of independence, all American films screened in Tanzania were supplied by companies based in South Africa; to eliminate that taint, a new entity called Anglo-American Film Distributors—a subsidiary of 20th Century Fox—was incorporated in Nairobi in 1960. After 1970, Anglo-American also briefly operated a sparsely furnished branch office in Dar es Salaam.[55] State Department diplomatic pressure on behalf of Anglo-American allowed the company to pay only 10 percent of its box office earnings to TFC, as opposed to the 30 percent paid by all other suppliers. Nonetheless, the relationship between TFC and Anglo-American remained tense. Between 1972 and 1982, Anglo-American halted distribution in Tanzania at least four times before finally pulling out entirely.[56]

TFC tried to secure its own films abroad, but because of a lack of experience, connections, capital, and credit, this remained more of an aspiration than an achievement. After more than a decade in the business, the company itself could rarely secure more than a handful of films in a given year, when the minimum number required was between 150 and 200. In 1980, TFC purchased and supplied only 5 of the 150 films circulated in the country that year. After ten years, its entire film library consisted of a mere 81 feature films,[57] and most of these came from the Soviet bloc and were notorious flops at the box office.[58] TFC purchasers were widely known to make bad choices when it came to selecting films for the local market: in 1985, they lost more than a million shillings on the films they purchased and distributed themselves, compared to the fourteen million they earned distributing films brought into the country by others.[59] Describing the competition that still drove exhibitors well into the 1980s, one exhibitor recalled a phone call when he and others in Dar es Salaam were required to reel a poor-quality TFC film. While calling the Avalon to check on the status of reels he asked, "How many [patrons] do you have?" "Only three people." "Three, oh you beat us! We have only two! At the Empress I hear they have only one, and at the Chox nobody. You win for the day with your three people!" To paraphrase what I was told by more than a dozen people in the industry, "Those guys at TFC did not know a thing about film."

To compensate for their own incompetence and the withdrawal of Anglo-American, TFC officials encouraged companies that began importing films during the colonial era to continue supplying films after nationalization. These included suppliers with offices in Nairobi, such as Indian Film Combine, Pan-African Film, and Overseas Film Distributors, as well as indigenous East African distributors. The Savanis, who imported and distributed as Majestic Film Distributors and had been doing business in Tanzania since the 1930s, provided TFC with a large proportion of their Indian films. Talati's United Film Distributors became one of TFC's most important suppliers of English-language films. In fact, each time Anglo-American halted its supply of American films to TFC, the parastatal turned to UFD to fill the void.

UFD had superb international connections to film suppliers across the globe. These connections, established over decades, allowed Talati to tap traditional suppliers as well as new, innovative, and independent producers from Hong Kong, Italy, Germany, and the United States. When Anglo-American and TFC severed their relationship in 1982, UFD went from providing some 30 percent of films screened in Tanzania in 1981 to 70 percent in 1985.[60] In an interview, Talati stressed that this near monopoly "was not a monopoly we sought, but one we saw no harm in pursuing once Anglo-American pulled out." TFC managers attempted to diversify their suppliers, securing product in the early 1980s from Gillespie Brothers, Deluxe Film Company, and Empire Film Company, but none of these suppliers could be relied on. They either sold TFC poor-quality films that lost the parastatal money or simply failed to deliver the quantity of films promised. According to internal TFC reports from the mid-1980s, UFD was the only company that promised to bring in sufficient product to keep Tanzanian theaters functioning, and equally important, it fulfilled its promises.[61] To keep the industry running, TFC needed both quality and quantity, so the socialist parastatal based on the mainland granted a near monopoly on supply to a private businessman from Zanzibar.[62]

Officially, UFD and all other importers were merely suppliers to TFC, but interviews with exhibiters across the country indicate that Talati's interventions in booking and distribution were critical to keeping the exhibition industry functioning. Echoing what I heard from numerous exhibitors, one up-country manager said, "Working with those guys from TFC was a joke. They would send you a totally junk film and tell you to run it on Sunday. They didn't even understand that Sunday was the day that kept us all alive." Exhibitors across the country shared tales of phone calls made to Talati for help. He would send them good films from UFD's library to substitute for the poor films scheduled by TFC managers. In interviews, Asad Talati made no mention whatsoever about such interventions. According to exhibitors, however, he was the real brains behind the business, and without him to turn to, TFC's monopoly on distribution decisions would have killed the industry long before it eventually expired.

Rampant corruption was another factor undermining TFC. The utter absence of any type of financial accounts or business records for the first decade of the company's existence suggests there was minimal oversight of earnings and expenditures. Most everyone in the industry, including

293

every TFC employee I interviewed, acknowledged that corruption was endemic.[63] (TFC general managers and chairmen all refused my repeated invitations to talk.) A consistent refrain in my interviews with exhibitors was that they often had to pay bribes in order to receive good films. Such pressures were intensified in small, up-country towns as well as towns with more than one theater. Off the record, numerous exhibitors said they made an arrangement with TFC officials to split the proceeds above the minimum guaranteed price (MG) they were charged for a film. Those who made such agreements received good films, and those who refused did not. Exhibitors who agreed to work with TFC officials were also charged lower MGs, thus increasing the amount flowing into pockets.

According to both exhibitors and TFC employees, by 1980 it was common for up-country cinemas to report only one-third of their box office earnings, keeping a third for themselves and giving the remaining third to the person they worked with at TFC. By the mid-1980s as corruption intensified, one man claimed, you could pay a bribe and your entire bill for the month or the year would simply disappear. Investigations by the Tanzania Audit Corporation seemed to confirm his allegations. In one year alone, auditors reported nearly TSh 13 million ($733,000) in outstanding balances from up-country exhibitors for films shipped and shown but payment not received. And these were only unpaid balances recorded in TFC's official accounts. The auditors noted that they wrote to the exhibitors asking for clarification of accounts but received not a single reply.[64] It seems investigations went no further. When I queried exhibitors about such practices, they claimed that they had no choice but to do as asked by TFC officials and that certainly it was better financially to cooperate than to raise a fuss about corruption.

TFC had a monopoly not only on film distribution but also on the legal importation of carbon rods. Carbons, I was repeatedly told, were also the rods used to bring exhibitors into submission: you might have films in your storeroom, but without carbons, you could not show them. According to several TFC employees, carbons were "big, big business" and "huge moneymakers." Several employees claimed that all the income earned from carbon sales went into management's pockets. Auditors again seem to confirm these allegations, noting that throughout the 1980s the money earned on carbons was conspicuously unaccounted for.[65] Financial data filed with the Registrar of Companies Office specifically mentioned carbon rod earnings, noting that TFC sold carbons for double what they paid for them, earning the company nearly TSh 300,000 ($35,000) in 1981.[66] In the six years of published annual reports, which included line-item accounts for a detailed range of income and expenses, projector carbon income was noted only once.

Auditors' analyses of TFC accounts in the 1980s found significant discrepancies and problems with accounting. Several years in a row, the auditors mentioned their inability to verify the existence of millions of shillings in alleged TFC assets. They also indicated that the records they received from TFC did not correspond to those of the company's account at the National Bank of Commerce, nor did individual receipts of expenditures for equipment and supplies given to auditors match with figures recorded in TFC office ledgers.[67] Moreover, receipts related to exhibition rentals were extremely difficult for auditors to sort out, and the earnings from the drive-in also disappeared entirely from state accounts after Sisi Enterprises was transferred to TFC in 1971.[68] TFC began running special live events known as premier shows, in 1979, where they hired a famous Indian actor for an evening of glamour, song, and dance. Premier shows became lucrative moneymakers, with gross earnings soaring from TSh 338,000 to 564,000 between 1979 and 1982, but after that point, all records of earnings and expenses disappeared from the books.[69] Again, a paucity of archival files pertaining to TFC's management makes it difficult to follow a paper trail — or even find the trailhead. But there is no evidence that problems noted by auditors were ever investigated or resolved, perhaps because, as oral sources allege, men at the highest levels of the government and the party were complicit in the raiding of TFC's accounts.

Published TFC annual reports supposedly approved by auditors showed wide discrepancies and large sums of money disappearing from page to page. To cite just one example, in the 1988 report, the chairman, F. J. Kibonde, proclaimed annual profits of TSh 7.99 million in 1985 on page one, a figure that was reproduced in the line-item statement of profits, costs, and loss on page ten. But on page three, profits for 1985 were reduced to just over 4 million, and it was this figure that was carried forward in the next published report.[70] But what's four million shillings between friends? Given the sketchy recordkeeping and minimalist records, all the budgetary information generated by TFC should be taken with a big grain of salt. Nonetheless, based on their own publications, TFC went from earning a sizable profit of somewhere between TSh 4 and 8 million in 1985 to end-ing 1990 with an accumulated debt of almost 35 million. By the end of the millennium, when TFC was officially handed over for liquidation, the company was TSh 49 million in the red.[71]

TFC was a parastatal dedicated to entertainment, but as one official who spent well over a decade working for the company confessed, the clients that most concerned management were not average moviegoers but high-ranking officials. The gala annual party for movers and shakers was just one example he mentioned. In 1985, the company spent nearly $6,000 on one evening's entertainment for guests.[72] For comparison's sake, the monthly minimum wage this same year was approximately $56. Entertaining members of the governing board was an additional line item in the budget, accounting for TSh 170,000 each year during the 1980s. Being on the governing board of TFC was a sought-after position, pushing the company to expand the board from six members plus the managing director in 1968 to twenty members by the 1980s.[73] Board membership was intentionally inclusive, bringing together men (and they were all men) from NDC, prominent civil servants, members of parliament, regional commissioners, ministers, principle secretaries, department directors, private businessmen, and one or two individuals affiliated with the treasury. Cultural expectations still demanded that wealth be widely shared. "These Ministers, Principle Secretaries and Commissioners weren't there to keep an eye on us, watch over us or impose policy on us," one long-serving member of the board explained. "They were there so that we could help pay for their entertainment and travels. We helped them get travel allowances to attend Board meetings. We would put them up at the Starlight hotel and pay for their room and meals while they were here." He said that TFC also paid for "pretty young ladies who made themselves available in the hotel lobby" and did what they could to make board members happy. "And this happiness would then translate into support for us . . . when we needed this or that."[74] TFC did its best to entertain.

Ostensibly, the principal aim of nationalizing distribution was to garner income to finance local film production and replace imports, but little of the money earned from commercial film distribution went in this direction. In 1986, only two-tenths of 1 percent of annual expenses went to film production.[75] Far more went to payroll, yet fewer than 40 of TFC's 250 employees were involved in making films.[76] Precisely what the other 200-plus employees did is unclear, especially if Talati and a small staff really did run imports and bookings from behind the scenes. Like most parastatals, TFC was mandated to provide employment opportunities, even if this meant few did productive work. But TFC employees were apparently always on the move, for expenses for motor vehicle operation consumed an even larger share of the annual budget. The year 1986 was not atypical: TFC spent more than TSh 2.3 million ($57,600) on vehicle expenses and less than TSh 38,000 ($936) making films.[77]

Tanzania never replaced foreign commercial films with local features. In fact, between 1973, when the filmmaking unit was begun, and 1999, when TFC was liquidated, only one feature-length film was produced for theatrical release, in 1976.[78] *Fimbo ya Mnyonge* (The Poor Man's Weapon) was a socialist drama/comedy depicting the trials and tribulations of urban life and promoting settlement in ujamaa villages as the key to individual, family, and national fulfillment. Technically and stylistically, *Fimbo ya Mnyonge* was not a bad first effort. The camera work and cinematography were varied and well composed, the acting good, and the editing clean. The response of the viewing public to the story line, which roughly paralleled the film Kawawa made back in the 1950s with the Colonial Film Unit, *Muhogo Mchungu*, was also moderately encouraging.[79] After I managed to secure a VHS copy from the corrupt archivist at TFC's former film library, in 2005, Tanzanian friends who remembered the film from their youth were eager to see it again.[80] Many fondly recalled the struggles of the lead character, Yombayomba, and more than once, I have heard befuddled rural immigrants to the city sarcastically called Yombayomba, suggesting the film's impact endured in local street culture.

Despite the relative success of *Fimbo ya Mnyonge*, members of the filmmaking unit were denied funding from TFC for the development of more movies. Independence as a parastatal required economic self-sufficiency: there were no handouts from ministries or central authorities, and the filmmaking unit was repeatedly told it would receive no funding from TFC central accounts. The company covered salaries but little more, so to make movies, TFC filmmakers needed to embark on coproductions.[81]

297

Aid from the Danish International Development Agency (DANIDA), in 1971, supported the initial training of local crews as well as the purchase of cameras and processing and editing equipment for both TFC and its sister organization, the Audio-Visual Institute (AVI). In 1973, both TFC and AVI began filmmaking, and each of the units released five short films during their initial year. Filmmakers at TFC then partnered with the prime minister's office, which was responsible for the socialist villagization project promoted by *Fimbo ya Mnyonge*. It was another decade before staff at TFC found coproduction partners willing to finance another artistically creative feature—*Harusi ya Mariamu* (1985), which explored individual and communal negotiations over indigenous and biomedical conceptions of health, illness, and healing.[82] Why TFC filmmakers had to seek out others to finance their films when TFC itself netted nearly TSh 23 million a year from its monopoly on the distribution of commercial films is perplexing, unless we accept the fact that promoting progressive art was far less important to the socialist state than making money.[83]

When *Fimbo ya Mnyonge* was released, the Ministry of Culture heralded the accomplishment and reiterated its desire to see all commercial films in Tanzania replaced by local productions. The managing director of TFC was summoned by officials in the Ministry of Culture, and the group brainstormed ideas for films. Members from the ministry also pointed to the burgeoning Kiswahili fiction market as an example of a successful effort to replace imported cultural products with locally created ones. Bureaucrats at the meeting were certain that if TFC committed itself, the nation could produce at least twelve films a year; thus, within five years it could have a sufficient quantity on hand to stop importing films entirely.[84] Apparently, no one at the meeting seemed aware or concerned that nations with "self-sufficient" film industries were typically producing more than three hundred films annually.

To keep busy, TFC filmmakers solicited jobs making documentaries and newsreels for various ministries, departments, parastatals, and governmental initiatives and programs. On average, they managed to make two films each year, but most were under ten minutes in length and all were either in a documentary or infomercial style.[85] They were also filmed in black and white and produced in a 16 mm format, which meant that they could not be screened in commercial theaters. Instead, the films of TFC and AVI were circulated primarily on those colonial era holdovers, the cinema vans. The style and content of the films was also far more reminiscent of Colonial Film Unit films than the commercial Indian, Italian, and Hong Kong films politicians wanted to replace. Titles included *Elimu ya Watu Wazima* (Adult Education), *Jembe ni Mali* (A Hoe Is Wealth), and *Miaka Kumi ya Azimio la Arusha* (Ten Years of the Arusha Declaration). A few of their films with a more progressive edge and of longer length included *Haki za Watoto* (Children's Rights) and *Somo Kasema* (As the Unyago Instructor Suggested), a film on family planning.[86] The audience for these films was not the urban youth who flocked to the Empire Cinema in Dar es Salaam but rather schoolchildren, prisoners, residents of ujamaa villages, and members of the armed forces stationed in military barracks.[87] The audience for TFC films was captive if not captivated.

The productivity of TFC's filmmaking unit was hampered by limitations that were imposed by superiors, not by a lack of talent and creative drive among those allegedly hired to make films. I interviewed numerous committed and talented producers, directors, actors, cameramen, screenwriters, and other staff who went on to have incredibly productive and exciting careers after years of languishing at TFC. Many echoed the assertion of Mark Leveri, TFC's general manager, that "managerial malaise" was the principal reason so few films were ever produced by the company, although their language was more pointed and less polite.[88] Many TFC employees lamented how their creative energy was drained by superiors with little commitment to cultural production. In the 1980s, Chairman F. J. Kibonde publicly declared that the organization's goal was to produce two feature films each year, but Godwin Kaduma, the senior production manager, shared with me a large private archive of screenplays and scripts written by staff from those same years that they were never allowed to produce.[89] Many complained about spending years working at TFC doing nothing. One cameraman who worked there for eight years in the 1980s said that in the entire time he was employed the company only produced one short documentary. Another described their time at TFC as "the most boring and frustrating job I have ever had." When pressed to explain what they did all day if they were not making films, I was told, "Come now. You've surely been to a government office. We slept at our desks when we had to come in. Mostly we reported to work, drank tea, and then left to take care of our own business or errands."

All these issues came to a head in the production of TFC's second feature film, *Yomba Yomba*. In this sequel to *Fimbo ya Mnyonge*, the lead

299

character travels to a number of ujamaa villages looking for members of his family, who had moved while he was away in the city. As Yombayomba continues his search, viewers are exposed to the various problems that plagued ujamaa villages over the years. The film was begun in 1980, but even at the scripting stage, it was hampered by interventions from above. The director, Martin Mhando, and the production manager, Godwin Kaduma, thought a film simply glorifying life in ujamaa villages would be dismissed by Tanzanian audiences as propaganda. Instead, they hoped to use the film to explore the reasons for socialism's failures at the village level: corruption, lack of democratic decision making, no grassroots participation in management, poor planning, and lack of respect for peasants' knowledge of farming.[90] But the film was funded by the prime minister's office, which wanted a more positive portrayal.[91] For more than two years, Kaduma and Mhando tussled over the script with the prime minister's office. Filming finally began in 1983, but it then took three years to complete. There was never enough raw film stock to complete shooting, and each time more was ordered it was commandeered for documentaries and parastatal infomercials, rather than being awarded for the feature film. Raw stock film supplies received no money at all in the annual budgets of 1984 and 1985 and a mere $700 in 1986. Actor salaries also figured nowhere in the budget, so office and production staff were cast as most characters in the film.

Once shooting for *Yomba Yomba* was finally completed, the film needed to be sent to Europe for processing because Tanzania had no color-processing studios. There, the film languished yet again. The production manager, Kaduma, recalled spending years trying to get someone in the government to release money so that he could pay for the rushes and move on to editing and production. He was told, "Look, we need medicine for the hospitals and clinics. You guys want money for a movie." Kaduma reported, "With attitudes like that it was difficult to get the financial support to make films. What they did not realize was that films and culture are medicines as well. Fine Arts and drama can make people feel better, and think better, too."[92] After nearly a decade, the film was finally completed in 1989. But that was not a terribly auspicious year for launching a film promoting socialism. It never had a theatrical release and a number of people who spent a decade of their lives working on that film never saw a finished version until I shared copies with them from the copy I received from the drawers of the corrupt archivist.

The contradictions that riddled TFC permeated national film policy at all levels—in part because there was no single national policy or single set of policymakers. In addition to the NDC, TFC, and various ministries, the party and the Board of Film Censors also sought to "improve" the quality and political content of films being shown. Their loud and consistent voices condemned the "mind-numbing" and "harmful" films screened in Tanzania, but they were effectively silenced by TFC bureaucrats who earned large sums of money from cinematic entertainment and shared that money in entertaining others. These antagonisms and contradictions illustrate what Ronald Aminzade identifies as perennial struggles between Tanzanian party officials and government bureaucrats—between desires for political legitimation as a nation-state and capital accumulation.[93] They also highlight the absurdities that sometimes resulted from a desperate attempt to reconcile profit maximization and ujamaa.[94]

Although the leadership at TFC refused to fund the filmmaking arm of the organization, there was persistent pressure from the highest levels of TANU and later CCM to promote a national filmmaking industry.[95] In 1969, the National Executive Committee of TANU (NEC) resolved, after a lengthy discussion of the deleterious effects of foreign films on national culture, that immediate steps should be taken for Tanzania to begin making its own films. The TANU-owned newspapers, the *Nationalist* and *Uhuru* (Freedom), ran lengthy articles covering the meeting.[96] Nineteen sixty-nine was a banner year for party efforts to cleanse the country of foreign influences. In addition to strong calls to transform film, the national newspapers gave prominent coverage to a number of other TANU efforts to expunge the foreign and promote "indigenous" culture. The TANU Youth League crackdown on so-called foreign fashions (including miniskirts) that were worn by Tanzanian women and the banning of soul music are but two of many examples.[97] TANU identified cinema as one of the worst offenders when it came to corrupting Tanzanian youth and indoctrinating them into a mindless mimicry of Western hedonism and hooliganism. As a corrective, NEC called for a demonstrated commitment to supporting a Tanzanian feature film industry. It also demanded that the Board of Film Censors be vigilant and relentless in banning "dirty" films.

301

But *Uhuru* and the *Nationalist* were just as guilty as any organ of the state for talking out of both sides of their mouths. As the official news outlets of TANU, these papers existed to inform citizens about government programs, slogans, and campaigns. But publishing was also costly, and like filmmakers, journalists needed to fund their own productions. So the papers sold advertising, and the most prominent advertisements were always for the cinemas. Typically, one and often two entire pages were devoted to ads and film reviews. Pragmatism had a way of impinging on ideology. Directly opposite the extensive coverage in *Uhuru* of NEC's resolutions on cinema were ads for what was playing at the theaters, ads that in many ways reinforced the party's arguments but nonetheless distracted the reader's attention from the need for reform. How many would head the party's call condemning cinemagoing when the opposite page featured a tantalizing picture of Raquel Welch in a bikini advertising a "breathtaking" show of *Fathom* at the Empress?

According to policy, 50 percent of these newspapers were to be devoted to news and editorials and 50 percent to advertising, which often resulted in utterly odd pairings. A few examples will illustrate this point. The front page of the New Year's Day edition of the *Nationalist* in 1969 featured praise for the TANU Youth League's Operation Vijana, a program intended to stamp out inappropriate dress among the young. As Andrew Ivaska has written at length, this program resulted in a mass mobilization of male party youth in Dar es Salaam who assaulted those wearing "indecent" dress, particularly women in miniskirts. On page eight of the same edition of the *Nationalist*, girls in Tanga were applauded for burning their miniskirts in support of this new campaign. The "half-nakedness" of females was derided, and women were encouraged to cover most, if not all, of their legs when in public. But between the first and eighth pages of the paper, there was extensive coverage of cinematic news, including an ad for the Wednesday night drive-in feature, *Blindfold* (Dunne, 1965), starring Rock Hudson and Claudia Cardinale—the Italian beauty queen turned actress who was known for her gorgeous legs and her willingness to reveal every inch of them. Opposite this ad was a summary of President Nyerere's new book, *Freedom and Socialism*. A few months later, copyeditors positioned a full-page review of a new collection of Ho Chi Minh's works under the banner *On Revolution*, opposite an ad for a barely clad Raquel Welch in *One Million Years B.C.* (Chaffey, 1966)—which was set in a savage world

Figure 8.1 Author's collage of film ads and headlines during Operation Vijana.
From *Nationalist*, January–March 1969

(according to the 20th Century Fox advertising) where humans and dinosaurs coexisted and the only law was lust![98] If cinema advertising allowed the party to distribute newspapers designed to "expose the poisonous absurdities of the imperialist propaganda as nothing but a calculated [*sic*] psychological warfare whose objective was to confuse and subvert the minds of our people," so be it.[99] The contradictions so visible in the paper permeated state socialism.

One might imagine that the drive-in cinema—being a state-sponsored project spearheaded by Vice President Rashid Kawawa, who also led Operation Vijana—worked harder to meet TANU calls for banning so-called dirty films, but as the screening of *Blindfold* attests, one would be wrong. Advertisements and films shown at the drive-in were actually some of the worst offenders. One example was the X-rated film *Woman Times Seven* (De Sica, 1967), described as seven ministories of female adultery or "Everything that a man should know and a motion picture could show about a woman! As naughty as a black lace nightgown!" Another film shown at the drive-in during these campaigns against Tanzanian women's alleged immorality was *The Secret Life of an American Wife* (Axelrod, 1968), in which a bored housewife poses as a call girl. The published ad for the film quite unabashedly depicted the lead actresses' sexy and unclothed legs—emanating from the smiling face of Walter Matthau—as well as a couple in bed. The March

303

6, 1972, edition of the *Nationalist* carried a full-page editorial on page four about socialism and foreign aid under the title "False Consciousness," and then on page five, there was an ad for a film at the drive-in entitled *Carry on Camping* (Thomas, 1969) about two men who lure their girlfriends to a nudist colony—rather than the wholesome campground the girls imagined—with the hope of getting them to "loosen up." Such films were the drive-in's forte. In fact, X-rated films, "strictly for adults only," dominated the drive-in's midweek bill until the middle of the 1970s.[100] Verbally, Kawawa and TANU condemned Western hedonism and immorality, but at the state-owned Sisi Enterprises, Hollywood films featuring scantily clad white women and illicit affairs figured prominently. Sisi Enterprises even appears to have intentionally solicited risqué advertising to pique audience interest. Films were often released internationally under multiple titles, with various types of marketing materials to accommodate different audience interests and censorship standards. In May 1969, Sisi featured the film *Spy in Lace Panties*, which was released in the United States as *The Glass Bottom Boat* with a much less erotic title and an utterly different film poster.

Although the drive-in was known as a great place to take the family on Sundays, when films appropriate for all ages were screened, it had another reputation altogether at midweek, a reputation that was encouraged by the frequent screening of X-rated films. When such films were on the bill, Lover's Lane overflowed.[101] Like the lead characters in *Carry on Camping*, some men in Dar es Salaam took women to the drive-in for X-rated films with high hopes of turning them on. Rumor has it that prostitutes also frequented the streets leading up to the gate at the drive-in during midweek. It was widely believed that TFC and party officials not only knew about such antics but also often parked at the show themselves. According to one man who regularly visited the drive-in during the 1960s and 1970s with his family, "By the late 1980s or early 1990s the drive-in was no longer a respectable place to go." Mostly, it was the big make-out spot, he said: "You would see cars rocking, blankets flopping—it was just way too embarrassing to take your mom or kids to the show."[102] Others stated that in the late 1980s, the space became so sullied by rumors of "big men" and prostitutes that Sunday attendance fell off entirely.

During their daylight meetings, TANU officials called on censors to ban the alleged dirty films completely, but bannings were exceptionally rare. Records held in the offices of the National Board of Film Censors

Figure 8.2 Drive-in advertising. From *Nationalist*, February 2, 1970

indicate that between 1963 and 1993, less than 1 percent of imported films were banned.[103] Derogatory depictions of Africans and incendiary representations of political allies provoked more orders to ban a screening than anything else. Films that promoted violence, vice, or banditry could also be banned, though few were, and those featuring excessive swearing, nakedness, or sexual violence were similarly subject to being outlawed. But if *The Ribald Tales of Robin Hood, His Lusty Men and Bawdy Wenches* (Kanter and Dietrich, 1969) was approved, what exactly counted as a dirty film? Voyeuristic and misogynist portrayals of women were common, yet censors rarely even mandated that particular scenes be cut. Titles that explored male homosexual relationships were singled out for consistent banning, but surprisingly, *The Christine Jorgensen Story* (Rapper, 1970), based on the biography of

305

the first American transgendered woman to have sex-reassignment surgery, passed without mention and was screened across the country in 1972. Films with nudity and sexual content, as well as those with violence and horror, were simply rated X to keep people younger than eighteen out of the show.

The Board of Film Censors became the whipping boy for TFC's failure to provide a sufficient supply of movies that were more politically correct. Letters to the editor in the press and speeches by party stalwarts frequently excoriated the board and its members for laxity in executing their duty. But Y. A. Marsha, chairman of the board for more than a decade, was always writing letters and memos to critics explaining the difficulty of his job. He repeatedly begged for understanding, noting that even his supervisors in the ministries he served often failed to grasp the basic fact that the board was only empowered to rate films, not to import or distribute them. Several times each month, he reminded critics in writing that TFC had far more influence over what was screened than the censors did.[104]

Initially, the censors had tried diligently to pursue their political mandate by banning films deemed contrary to socialism, but invariably, their efforts were overturned by appeals from importers, distributors, and TFC officials who had friends in higher places. Ultimately, they simply settled on expanding their use of the X rating, in hopes of at least shielding children from exposure to inappropriate material. Over the decades, the proportion of X-rated films grew from less than 6 percent in the 1960s to 25 percent in the 1970s and 1980s.[105] The explicit sexual and violent content of films increased significantly in the those decades. Debating cuts to such films was also a laborious process, one that busy censors with other full-time jobs preferred to avoid if not being paid overtime rates for their efforts. To get done quickly, censors in Zanzibar and Dar es Salaam told me they would simply give a film an X rating and dispense with haggling over the cuts that were needed to make it suitable for an A rating (adult accompaniment required).[106] Exhibitors actually liked X ratings, especially because they boosted ticket sales among young males, the demographic group most likely to be attracted to a film such as *The Vengeance of She* (Owen, 1968). According to men who read the movie posters with anxious anticipation in their youth, an A rating meant that most of the exposed flesh in the film was already shown on the poster displayed outside the cinema. An X rating, by contrast, allowed their imaginations to run wild with lusty anticipation of what they might see at night.

Figure 8.3 *The Vengeance of She* ad. From *Nationalist*, February 2, 1970

I had incorrectly presumed that TFC, as a socialist parastatal governing film, and the National Board of Film Censors would work in tandem toward the same goals. In fact, they worked at cross-purposes, and their relationship was utterly fraught. As one member of the TFC board of directors said of the relationship with the censors, "You could say that we were outright enemies. We hated them."[107] Censors said the feelings were mutual. Censorship generated headlines in the press, but censors were definitely the weaker party in the scuffle. The censors were so powerless that they spent the better part of the 1970s just trying to get someone from TFC to meet with them to discuss their concerns.[108] When I pushed exhibitors, distributors, and TFC employees to explain how they survived in the face of what I perceived, from press accounts, to be relentless political pressure, they scoffed. One TFC employee stated categorically, "Censors? Ha. They had no influence whatsoever on the types of films we distributed, none." When I queried him further about the barrage of letters and articles published in the national press criticizing TFC's choice of material, he stated matter-of-factly, "We didn't care. Even if it was a Minister and he signed his name, so what?" When I posed similar questions to a long-serving TFC board member, the response was similar. "They could write whatever they wanted," he said, "but not once, not even once were we reprimanded or told we needed to change what we were doing. Not once!" Looking at the titles and types of films screened, it seems these men had a point: there was no discernable "improvement" in the intellectual or leftist content of film over time, despite relentless criticism in the press. Hamza Kasongo, who also served for twenty-five years as a member of the board of directors of TFC, explained, "We did not even bother with these questions of politics, not at all. Our goal was entertainment. . . . Worrying about sex, violence, capitalism, this was not our concern. Our concern was to make money, and to do that we needed films that were popular with our audiences."[109] Sex and violence sold; socialist realism did not.

Boniface Sanjala, who served these same years on the National Board of Film Censors, lamented that TFC did indeed hold the reins. "TFC brought in money," he told me, "we on the other hand were an economic liability. Sure, we had ideological purpose, but we brought in no cash. So we had no power."[110] Walter Bagoya, a respected Tanzanian intellectual and book publisher who served a short stint on the censorship board, made similar comments: "Cultural policy was complicated by the fact that on the one hand there was the policy of *ujamaa*, or socialism, and on the other the need to generate a profit. TFC was a profit-making venture, not an educational one, and what drew were Kung Fu films and Hindi films with mindless songs and dances."[111] Bagoya resigned from the censorship board after quickly realizing the futility of its mission. Ultimately, he said, a great deal of cultural policy was *maneno tu*, which roughly translates as "a lot of hot air."

The lack of power felt by the censors was compounded by frequent ministerial moves that only exacerbated the board's marginalization. Over the years, the censorship board was moved between ministries no fewer than a dozen times. With each move, employees had to struggle to find their place, purpose, and legitimacy within a new ministerial and office environment. Typically, they had to fight just as hard for office space, frequently being denied even desks upon their arrival. Titus Lugendo, who served for five years as the chief film censor, said that by the time he joined the board, the censors had been literally reduced to occupying a closet. He had no staff, no telephone, and "no power."[112] Employees of the board also said that their efforts to push a political agenda only enhanced their marginalization. Attempts to ban films were frequently met with direct threats to their budget and staff or reshuffling to yet another ministry. Censors could annoy exhibitors and distributors with their ratings, but they were really the weakest players in the game.

In the 1970s, an industry that had grown and prospered over the preceding fifty years began a slow but perilous decline. Ironically, it was not demands for better socialist films that undermined the commercial industry but structural changes that featured the worst traits of monopoly capitalism. The vitality of the cinema industry in the first half of the twentieth century can be attributed in large part to the entrepreneurial proclivities of exhibitors, their daily and intimate interactions with clients, their satisfaction with marginal but steady profits, and their willingness to continually reinvest in their businesses. All of this was lost with the consolidation of the industry under a single corporation. Rather than entrepreneurs who prided themselves on their knowledge of the technical and cultural developments in the film and exhibition industries, bureaucrats whose overriding interest was directing profits into the hands of those at the top of the corporation took charge in TFC. As ticket prices rose in the 1970s and 1980s, the quality of the viewing experience gradually declined. The nationalization of cinema halls inaugurated a slow but steady deterioration in the nation's once-gleaming picture palaces and prevented reinvestment in new technologies of display. Local proprietors were also now powerless to seek out alternative sources of film supply. TFC bureaucrats in Dar es Salaam were oblivious to the pressures faced by exhibitors in Bukoba, Mpanda, or Mbeya for new films that would please their customers, and they never had to see the faces of disappointed fans who could not enjoy a night at the movies because the roof leaked, the cinema was out of carbons, or the advertised film simply never arrived. TFC's goal of profit maximization worked during the 1970s, when millions of new fans were discovering the urban pleasures of moviegoing for the first time, but persistent failure to reinvest in the industry caught up with them by the 1980s. The inconsistencies and contradictory agendas informing film policy also took a toll. Competing voices, aims, and directives are a normal part of any political process, but in the late 1980s and 1990s, such problems internal to the film industry were compounded by larger national and international political, economic, and technical transformations, changes to which we now turn.

Epilogue

A NEW WORLD

Transformations in Mediascapes, the 1990s and Beyond

WHEN I began my initial period of fieldwork for this book in 2002, the previously vibrant moviegoing culture in Tanzania was dead. Of the forty cinemas that once operated in the nation, only one, the Novelty in Pemba, continued to show 35 mm films. These films, however, were all repeats that patrons had seen numerous times. As the final stop on the circuit of film circulation in Tanzania, the Novelty became something of a default storage facility; the film prints remained in Pemba because no other theater wanted them. Within the previous year, the two remaining theaters in the circuit, the Cine Afrique in Zanzibar and the Avalon in Dar es Salaam, had permanently closed their doors. Cinema attendance remained strong through the late 1980s, but as the twentieth century drew to a close, a swirling mass of overlapping developments coalesced to undermine the cinemagoing culture of the nation. Over the course of four decades, average monthly attendance at the grand coastal theaters, such as the Majestic in Zanzibar or the Avalon, plummeted from 16,000 patrons each month in 1972, to a still respectable 14,000 in 1982, to fewer than 1,000 each month in 1992, and to a mere 100 in 2002.[1] As attendance declined, so did the number of theaters.

By 1995, there were only seven cinemas in the country still showing 35 mm films. But even there, ticket sales barely covered the cost of electricity, let alone the costs of film rental, building maintenance, or employee salaries.[2] Rents paid to the National Housing Corporation were also exorbitant, pushing lessees to either return their buildings to the state or convert them to other uses. Pentecostal churches, rent-to-own furniture stores, and warehouses for electronics were among the most common new uses for the old theaters, reflecting the immense social, political, and economic changes shaping Tanzania at the turn of the millennium.[3] In Arusha, Mwanza, and Tabora, a few theaters were still filled beyond capacity on Sundays, but the crowds now came to be part of an evangelical worship service, not to watch an Indian melodrama.

Numerous factors help explain the rather sudden drop in cinematic attendance; some are unique to Tanzania, and others are global. The massive transformations in media technologies that took place in the 1980s and 1990s hit movie theaters everywhere hard. In Tanzania, these problems were compounded by simultaneous and equally revolutionary changes in the national political economy. Structural adjustment policies decimated the disposable income of average Tanzanians and undermined importers' abilities to bring in the latest films. But as revolution rocked the technological and economic structures of Tanzania's media worlds, the laws governing the cinema industry remained moribund, locking existing players into a game whose rules were written back in 1968. Existing exhibitors found it impossible to respond to the technological and political-economic transformations in a way that would allow for survival. By the end of the century, it appeared that Tanzania's cinematic culture was nothing more than history.

But then, rather suddenly, a new industry took hold. At the turn of the millennium, TFC was liquidated, officially marking the end of state control of the cinematic economy. Liberalization of the markets in property and commodities made it possible for new players to enter the game. In 2003, a three-theater multiplex opened in Dar es Salaam. The theater was called the New World, and it was aptly named. The New World captured the vibe of twenty-first-century Tanzania and gave those who had benefited from the neoliberal economic reforms of the previous decade a new place to go. Plush and air-conditioned, the New World appeared identical to multiplex cinemas in Toronto, Dubai, or Cedar Rapids. The films, the screens, the Twitter feeds, the Facebook advertising, and even the concessions were similar to those found anywhere in the world. Over the next decade, shopping malls sprang up across Dar es Salaam, and each had a multiplex cinema to pull in customers. In the blink of an eye, the city went from having no screens to having fifteen, including several that offered 3-D viewing. Special accommodations for VIPs, for children's birthday parties, and for couples seeking private viewing rooms are now available for those who yearn for a personal yet public expression of their status as beneficiaries of the neoliberal turn. In the wake of the New World's success, the cinematic scene in the capital city transformed as quickly and as radically as Dar es Salaam's skyline and street-level architecture did. Apropos of the intense concentration of national wealth at the turn of the century, as of 2013 all but one of the nation's theaters were located in Dar es Salaam.[4] The new millennium ushered in a new world indeed.

A TECHNOLOGICAL REVOLUTION IN MEDIA LANDSCAPES

Across the globe, the once-hegemonic place of cinemas as a space for moving-picture entertainment was undermined by transformations in media technologies and viewing cultures in the second half of the twentieth century. In the United States and Europe, movie theaters faced their first big challenge after World War II when home television ownership first became widespread and growing numbers of people began moving out of city centers.[5] The previous public culture of viewing became increasingly atomized in the suburban home. Movie attendance in Europe and the States never returned to its prewar levels. Then, in the 1980s, the cinema industry was hit hard again by the development of VHS technologies and the proliferation of cable channels. Attendance plummeted yet again. Repeatedly, the mainstream cinema industry attempted to regain lost footing by deploying new gimmicks. Drive-in theaters, 3-D films, multiplex theaters built in malls, CinemaScope, surround sound, IMAX, digital projection, and 4-D seating were just a few of the strategies employed. But despite these efforts, cinema attendance continued to decline. By the 1980s, the number of patrons going to the movies each year in the United States was only a third of that in 1946. In the United Kingdom, the situation was even more dire, with 1984 marking the nadir for moviegoing there and ticket sales dropping to a mere 3 percent of their peak in 1946, despite a massive increase in population.[6]

313

In Tanzania, the impact of home viewing was compounded by the fact that television, VHS, DVD, satellite, cable, and computer technologies all hit the market in a very short period of time. In a little more than a decade, the entire landscape of media technology in Tanzania was utterly remade. Until 1994, television broadcasting was illegal on the Tanzanian mainland. Even owning a television was forbidden before 1985. This did not stop people from acquiring them, but in 1982 and 1983, police raids on "economic saboteurs" spurred hundreds of people in Dar es Salaam, Tanga, Moshi, and Arusha to literally dump their TVs—out of backroom windows as police mounted the front stairs or in public parks in the middle of the night. If caught with a television, the head of a household faced arrest and detention for criminal possession of illegal goods. The banning of television broadcasting was one of President Nyerere's ideas for promoting equality and minimizing urban bias in development. Until everyone in the nation had access to electricity, he argued, there was no reason to invest limited resources in developing television broadcasting that could be accessed only by the already privileged living in towns. During the campaigns of 1982 and 1983, owning a television was taken as symbolic of one's disdain for these principles of socialist equality, and because imports of televisions were illegal, having one also served as proof of involvement in smuggling and the equivalent of economic treason. For people on the mainland who were interested in film and visual media entertainment, the only legal option was to go to the cinema.[7]

Broadcasting was one of many "nonunion matters" under the legal framework governing the union of Tanganyika and Zanzibar when they formed Tanzania. Policy regarding television in the isles was the opposite of that on the mainland. In contrast to Nyerere, Zanzibar's first president prided himself on the development of television broadcasting in the isles. Tiny little Zanzibar even became the first place in Africa to broadcast in color, beginning in 1974. The government there actively encouraged people to buy televisions, even providing no-interest loans to state employees so they could purchase small televisions from the state store. But despite government efforts, fewer than 25 percent of island households had televisions by the early 1990s.[8] Nyerere was right: you needed to have electricity in order to run a television, and for most residents of the isles, this remained an unimaginable luxury. But public viewing of Television Zanzibar (TVZ) was encouraged by the governing party, which set up viewing portals at

Figure 9.1 Television Zanzibar TV (with TVZ logo on upper right), purchased by Bi Ramuna in 1974

party branches and neighborhood gathering spots. Transmitters were theoretically strong enough that people with televisions and electricity living anywhere in the islands of Zanzibar and Pemba could access TVZ, and as a result, so could those living in coastal towns on the mainland where televisions were illegal—such as Dar es Salaam, Bagamoyo, and Tanga. People along the border in Arusha, Moshi, and Musoma could also pick up limited transmission from Kenya.

But cinemas faced little competition from TVZ. There was only one channel, and it focused on educational and political broadcasting. Programming was limited to just a few hours each night and was more informational than entertaining. There were short news programs and a special half hour devoted to children's educational programming; another was devoted explicitly to adult education. Hours upon hours of broadcasting time simply featured lengthy speeches by the president or other high-level members of the state. But local programmers also sent crews across the isles to capture important events or film the launching of state-sponsored development projects. The police, the department of education, and the ministries of agriculture and health also worked with TVZ staff to develop half-hour programs on different issues. Some were nicely produced, but others were nothing more than a set camera offering a

315

single shot of a speech. Well-regarded storytellers, musicians, government-sponsored dance groups, and occasionally local drama troupes also had performances recorded for broadcast. These last productions were watched with delight: people were ecstatic to see local personalities and places on the screen and to hear broadcasts in Kiswahili. Until well into the 1980s, the vast majority of programming was locally produced. But by the late 1980s, structural adjustment policies began to take a toll on state budgets. Money to support film and production crews was increasingly in short supply. In the late 1980s and early 1990s, free programming donated by the Soviet Union, Yugoslavia, Japan, and the United States came to dominate airtime. Structural adjustment and globalization went hand in hand to radically remake TVZ. But few adults tuned in to anything other than evening news broadcasts anyway. Given the limited programming and the typically poor quality of reception, most adults turned on the television only to occupy the kids for a half hour to an hour each night. TVZ was no substitute for the cinemagoing experience of the islands' adult film fans, who continued to relish evenings out in public enjoying the melodrama, music, and action that TVZ lacked.[9]

With the advent of VHS technology, the cinema faced its first serious challenges. These innovations were officially illegal too, even in Zanzibar, where the government sought to limit access to anything other than TVZ. In the 1980s, all VCRs in the nation were smuggled in. Everyone I spoke to who owned a VCR in the 1980s told me that the devices were hidden inside the luggage of people returning from the Hajj to Mecca, as religious pilgrims were exempt from search at customs. In fact, a certain number of pilgrims each year financed their journey to Mecca by selling VCRs and VHS tapes acquired in the Holy Land upon their return. The cost of VCRs limited the development of any large-scale smuggling operations, however. Even in the United States and Europe, few households had a VCR before the late 1980s, when a single unit cost around $1,500 (the equivalent of $5,000 in 2016 dollars). But in the early 1990s, things quickly changed. Import restrictions on consumer goods were lifted in Zanzibar in late 1989, followed by a lifting of restrictions on access to foreign currency. Legal, open-market currency exchanges and "free-trade" took the isles by storm. TVs, VHS players, and other electronics flooded the islands and were then transported to the mainland. The price of electronics also dropped significantly on the international market in the 1990s, making TV and VHS technology affordable for Tanzanians.[10] By the dawn of the new millennium, it was rare to find a home with electricity that did not also have a television. I have personal photos dating to 2001, taken in some of the poorest neighborhoods in Zanzibar Town and villages on the outskirts, that show homes outfitted with palm-frond roofs or rusted, leaking tin ones all sporting large TV antennas. Most of those houses also had a home video system, which by then could be purchased in Tanzania for as little as $60.[11]

But things to watch on a VCR were also in limited supply before the 1990s. Major film studios released few films in video format, and in the United States, the studios filed a series of lawsuits in the 1980s charging emerging video rental stores with copyright infringement in an effort to protect theater revenues. By 1990, attitudes had changed considerably. In response to a rapidly growing home-viewing market and the burgeoning of media pirates, the studios determined that if they did not capitalize on the sale and rental of VHS copies of their films, others would. In both India and the States, studios began releasing a growing number of films in video format, typically six to twelve months after their theater release. Over the course of the 1990s, video rental shops became more and more common in Tanzania. Media pirates—some working right inside the studios—distributed from Los Angeles, Hong Kong, Pakistan, and Dubai to places with lax copyright enforcement, such as Tanzania. The quality of copies ranged from pristine prints clearly made by people with access to studio originals to copies made by someone sitting in a theater filming with a handheld camera. These latter films often included the bobbing heads of people in rows closer to the screen or images of people leaving the theater to go to the bathroom. But pirated videos were cheap, making lapses in quality forgivable. By 1995, an entire family and a gaggle of children from the neighborhood could watch a rented video at home for TSh 100, whereas the cost of admission for a single person at the theater ranged from 500 to 1,500. By the mid-1990s, few Tanzanians went to the theater. Instead, they watched movies the same way most people across the globe were now doing: they rented films from the local video shop and sat on their living room couches.

In 1993, most of the owners of traditional cinemas in Tanzania who wanted to keep their theaters running switched to VHS projection too, thereby eliminating the payments they had to make to TFC for films. Although such practices were officially illegal, this was the era of change (*mageuzi*). A small bribe could make an official look the other way, and 100

317

percent of the entrance fee could then be retained by the exhibitor. The switch to VHS projection inside theaters was prompted by the emergence of a major Tanzanian dealer in videos with excellent connections to bulk producers and distributors in Dubai. Chanu Vadgama, whose father had been a partner in several small theaters in Dodoma and Iringa back in the 1950s, took over the operation of the Empire Cinema in Dar es Salaam after it was confiscated from the Jariwallas, in 1971. He boasted that a little more than a decade later, he was the first in the nation to switch to VHS projection.[12] Chanu had dabbled in 35 mm film supply in the 1980s, providing a few movies here and there to TFC, but he never succeeded in becoming a serious supplier. But when the video market emerged, he found his niche. By the early 1990s, an exhibitor was paying anywhere from TSh 200,000 to 800,000—depending on the film, his location, and the nature of his relationship with TFC—to rent a 35 mm film. According to exhibitors, they could purchase a copy of a copy of a VHS from Chanu Vadgama for TSh 5,000. Chanu followed the block-booking and blind-selling practices of monopoly distributors of traditional films in the United States and South Africa: to get access to one high-budget new release, a theater had to agree to purchase a dozen films. But switching to VHS projection still saved theater owners money. It also gave them access to a wider range of films, and they could get new releases more quickly than if they rented 35 mm films from TFC. By 1993, TFC was circulating only seventy new films each year, and as had long been the case, it commonly took six months to one year for a legal print to arrive. In the 1990s, it was often possible to purchase a bootlegged copy of a new Hollywood or Bollywood film the same weekend the movie opened where it was made. Displaying and even producing VHS copies of internationally copyrighted material was technically not illegal under Tanzanian law because the country had no legislation protecting copyright and no office dedicated to enforcement.[13]

During this same period, new venues for public viewing also developed as enterprising Tanzanians began opening small viewing studios in the courtyards of their homes or renting space from bars, shops, or anyone with a walled space capable of seating a modest crowd. Patrons were typically the working poor—those who could not afford to own a TV and VCR or even have electricity in their homes. The entrance fee to these early video parlors was often a fraction of the cost at a larger theater. Admission to a cinema showing VHS films averaged TSh 200–500, but one could go to a small video parlor for a tenth of the price. Quickly, the market share of viewers previously monopolized by cinemas was undercut by video parlors. Small-time operators not only offered admission at a fraction of the cost, they also had more flexibility to cater to a narrower viewing public. With travel, trade, and import restrictions lifted in the 1990s, new suppliers dived into the VHS market, further expanding the number and types of films available. In the housing estates built for employees of the railroad in Morogoro, there were five different video parlors showing films by 1995. Low-budget action movies dominated, but one video parlor featured animated films for children and another specialized in porn. Neither of these latter two genres was screened in commercial theaters or distributed by TFC.

In the late 1990s, digital technology began to replace VHS, making bootlegging simpler, quicker, and less expensive. A single disc could now carry multiple films, and suddenly, the streets were swarming with young men selling DVDs or VCDs with five movies.. Prices varied, as they always had, with popular genres often costing twice as much as the average film. When they first emerged, DVDs offered mostly low-budget action films from the United States and Hong Kong, but gradually, the range of films available expanded to include anything produced anywhere in the world. Yet Tanzanian tastes still largely dictated supply and price. When Nigerian films began to appear on the local market, they often cost five times as much as the average Hollywood film. Once Tanzanians began producing their own movies, however, they quickly became the hottest commodities on the streets.[14] By 2005, a DVD carrying five Hollywood films or three Nigerian films could be purchased for TSh 5,000–8,000, whereas a single Tanzanian film sold for twice that price, reflecting the enthusiasm that greeted Tanzanian filmmakers once digital technology made indigenous production economically viable. As the supply of films available on the streets increased, the attraction of home viewing grew as well. Cinemas showing bootlegged films lost their niche, and high overhead costs forced most proprietors to close their doors in the late 1990s.

The mid-1990s witnessed major changes in the broadcast media landscape of Tanzania as well. In 1994, the first commercial television stations began broadcasting in the country. Cable providers also set up shop in half a dozen towns. Cable offered 40, then 100, and now nearly 200 channels to homes connected to the system, for a small monthly fee.[15] Satellite reception also took off, providing access to media produced anywhere across the globe. By 1998, one could sit at home and watch locally produced news and music videos; dramas from the United States; telenovelas from Mexico; melodramatic series from India; or the BBC, CNN, and Al-Jazeera. Several dozen channels specializing in Indian and American films were also carried by cable companies. Echoing the remarks of many, one formerly avid moviegoing fan said, "Why pay two thousand shillings go to the movies when you could sit at home and choose from fifteen or more movies each night for a cost of less than twenty cents a day?"[16]

In the remotest corners of Tanzania, when there was electricity someone with a satellite could pull down news and entertainment from Malaysia to Canada or Argentina, and this was all before computers, the Internet, or smartphones became common. Tanzanians who purchased cable access or a satellite also frequently shared with their neighbors, allowing them free access to programming through the installation of cheap routers and receivers or running cables to neighbors from the original home.[17] The media revolution even hit local football clubs, which began to lose fans. Starting with the 1998 World Cup, the first international competition widely received across Tanzania via satellite, many folks turned to watching their favorite international strikers on television—and many never went back to watching players live on their local grounds. Only in the mid-2010s were Tanzanian footballers able to finally strike back. Azam, a local company with a rising national team, ventured into media. Their mobile broadcasting vans now offer live streaming of competitions on televisions, computers, and cellphones.

Few of the youth I surveyed in 2005 had ever been to a cinema, and most were not particularly keen to go. Repeatedly, they told me that going to the cinema was old fashioned, something their elderly grandparents once did. In contrast, these youth positioned themselves as modern and developed. Facebook, WhatsApp, and Instagram are where they now go to see and be seen.

THE TRADITIONAL INDUSTRY AND POLITICAL-ECONOMIC REFORM

While all these technological innovations were transforming Tanzanians' media worlds, the traditional cinemas remained moribund, locked into a political-economic straitjacket that dated back to the late 1960s and early 1970s. Until TFC was "liquidated" at the turn of the twenty-first century, it remained the sole legal distributor of 35 mm films in the nation. Cinema buildings too remained the property of the state. These two basic economic and legal facts severely limited the ability of traditional theaters to respond to the revolutions in media technologies in any meaningful or creative way. When exhibitors were prevented from seeking out alternative sources of film supply, they were unable to innovate with IMAX, 3-D, or any of the other new theater technologies cinemas elsewhere in the world were using to lure back some segment of the audience. And if you did not own your own building and no serious maintenance had been done in twenty-five years, how much were you going to invest in retrofitting with new projection technology?

The rapid decline of the Tanzanian economy in the 1980s further undermined the industry at every level. Devaluation of the Tanzanian shilling, mandated by the signing of a Structural Adjustment Program with the International Monetary Fund (IMF) in 1986, had an immediate and deleterious impact on attendance and film supply. In 1983, the official exchange rate was 12.24 shillings to a US dollar. By 1986, it took 40.43 shillings to equal a dollar, and by the end of 1988, the rate was 123 shillings to the dollar.[18] What this meant for film importers was that the cost of a film on the international market skyrocketed. If it took TSh 100,000 to buy a good film from India in 1983, that same film cost over TSh 1 million in 1988 simply because of devaluation.[19] To keep buying the same number and quality of films in the next year, ten times as many people needed to go to the show just to break even, *if* there were no more devaluations. But the rate of devaluation intensified as the millennium drew to a close. Devaluation of the currency also meant that fewer and fewer people went to the movies. Wages remained stagnant, and over the course of the 1980s, their relative worth plummeted by nearly 60 percent as the basic costs of everything rose.[20] To compensate for rising costs and declining attendance, exhibitors raised ticket prices, but this merely aggravated the problem. In the 1970s and 1980s, the cost of a ticket to the show in Dar es Salaam averaged less than 2 percent of the monthly income of those earning the minimum wage; by 1990, a single ticket for the cheapest seat in the house equaled nearly one-quarter of the same wage.[21] It is no wonder attendance plummeted.

The rules and regulations governing foreign exchange transactions and imports further hampered the traditional industry. Although TFC was the only legal distributor, it relied almost entirely on independent importers, mainly United Film Distributors and Majestic Film Distributors, to supply its films. But no one legally doing business in Tanzania in the 1980s could possess hard currency or import goods that were not approved by various bureaucracies and paid for directly via the Bank of Tanzania. This made things extremely complicated—and increasingly untenable—for Asad Talati and Chunilal Savani, the individuals at the head of UFD and Majestic, respectively. Talati and Savani would choose their films and make agreements about price and distribution rights with their global suppliers. They would then submit their agreements to the central bank, which could approve or disapprove the purchases. Hard currency was in extremely limited supply at the Bank of Tanzania, so everyone seeking to use available funds had to compete to get their requests approved. As a result, the number of new films entering the country declined from nearly 400 per year in the 1970s to 134 in 1985 and then less than 50 in the early 1990s.[22] With fewer new films being imported, repeats began to fill the screens, and this too undermined attendance at traditional theaters. Who was going to spend a quarter of their monthly salary to see a film they had already seen when they could go to a video parlor and get a new release for less than the cost of a soda?[23]

TFC's Tanzanian suppliers were also increasingly caught in a financial bind between their own international creditors and the Bank of Tanzania. Each time UFD wanted to purchase a film from abroad, for example, the bill had to be approved by the bank and the equivalent cost in Tanzanian shillings had to be deposited there before the distributor was given legal approval to order the import. The bank would then be responsible for paying creditors, "subject to availability" of hard currency in national accounts. This process was known as the pipeline, and it was mandatory for all imports requiring payment in US dollars. In the early 1980s, it took only four to six weeks for payments to make their way through the pipeline, which meant there was little problem for Tanzanian importers whose international partners were willing to extend credit for a short time. But as the 1980s wore on, the length of time it took for a creditor to be paid kept growing. By the end of the decade, it was not uncommon for international suppliers of imported goods, including films, to wait three to four years for payment. This situation obviously undermined enthusiasm for doing business with Tanzanians, and it helps explain the scarcity of all imports in the late 1980s. By 1990, the pipeline closed down entirely. Unpaid accounts were only cleared when TFC was liquidated in 2000, and even then, creditors were rarely paid more than 15 percent of what they were owed—without adjustments for devaluation or inflation over more than a decade.[24] TFC was also less than prompt paying UFD and Majestic. In 1989, when Majestic stopped importing for TFC, it was owed tens of millions of shillings for films already supplied. Neither they nor their outstanding international creditors were paid after liquidation.

The cost difference between legally and illegally acquired films was enormous, and media piracy further undermined any hopes that UFD, the sole remaining supplier to TFC in the 1990s, might earn enough at the box office to pay for the films it imported. In addition to competing against small video parlors, bars, and home viewers, the remaining theaters still showing 35 mm films had to compete against television and cable stations, which also commonly aired pirated product. TFC did nothing to stop this. According to several of the last remaining cinema exhibitors, Asad Talati, owner of UFD, tried to bring a suit against broadcasters of pirated media, but his attempts were repeatedly undermined. Those in Tanzania's new media world had close friends among the younger generation of neoliberal politicians who were now governing.[25] Only in 1999, as a result of heavy diplomatic and trade pressure from the United States and India, was a copyright law finally passed in Tanzania, but application remains limited at best even today. Infringement also remains a civil, not criminal, offense. According to Stephen Mtetewaunga, CEO of the Copyright Society of Tanzania in 2005, one large distributor of pirated videos was tried and found guilty in 2004. He was fined the equivalent of $40, which he and others interpreted as a message condoning their business practices.[26] Tanzanian law also requires that the product at the center of any copyright infringement claim must be registered with the Tanzanian copyright office. As late as 2005, however, there were only four employees in the office. As Mtetewaunga asked, since Tanzania is half the size of Western Europe, how could four people possibly process a request for every product seeking registration and then supervise enforcement in every corner of the nation? Copyright also remains a nonunion matter, meaning that an artist, author, or film producer must register his or her material with the proper authorities in both the isles and the mainland and push for enforcement by both governments. Only in 2013 was any semi-earnest discussion of copyright taking place in the isles. Copyright law now protects Tanzanian musicians and filmmakers far more than in the recent past, but international artists and producers still find it rare for their creative rights to be respected or enforced.[27] As of 2014, it was still not uncommon to see pirated films broadcast on Tanzanian television and cable stations, a practice that cinema owners continue to battle.[28]

As late as 1999 and 2000, UFD continued to import some thirty new films a year to be shown in Tanzanian cinemas.[29] But even the hottest new movies rarely drew a crowd of more than fifty; more typically, attendance on any given night was less than ten. When new films opened in Bombay on Friday, pirated copies were shown on Tanzanian cable stations the following Sunday.[30] To acquire a legal print took far longer, and by the time it arrived in theaters, everyone had already seen the production on TV multiple times. In 1998, UFD spent well over $8,000 for a print and the legal rights to show *Titanic* (Cameron, 1997), but a television station in Dar es Salaam aired a bootleg copy of the film the same day it opened at the Avalon. A sizable crowd still filled the theater, eager to see the film on the big screen, but when it showed in Zanzibar the following week, it drew a meager sixteen patrons. Protests by the managers of the Avalon and Cine Afrique against violations of international copyright standards fell on deaf ears.

In such a situation, how could anyone rationalize spending $10,000 for the legal rights to release the latest film starring Shahrukh Khan in theaters in Tanzania? Many openly questioned Talati's sanity for his willingness to keep importing films. But he loved film and the cinema, and he remained committed to providing Tanzanians with a night on the town. He was also keenly aware of industry trends across the globe and believed that things would turn around in Tanzania—just as they had in other world markets—because people would eventually get tired of sitting at home and once again be eager to go out on the town for a night at the show. Between 2004 and 2014, things did indeed turn around, but by then, all the previous suppliers and exhibitors had gone out of business.

By 1998, there were only three remaining theaters in the nation still showing 35 mm films: the Cine Afrique in Zanzibar, the Avalon in Dar es Salaam, and the Novelty in Pemba. The first two, run by Asad Talati, were once the crown jewels in Tanzania's cinematic crown, having been built with love by Talati's father and other partners from Zanzibar and Dar es

Salaam. In 2001, the back wall behind the screen of the Cine Afrique collapsed, due to years of water damage from an unrepaired leak in the roof. Maintence had been minimal since the building was nationalized in 1964, and the lack of attention to needed structural repairs finally took its toll.[31] The following year, Talati returned the Avalon to the National Housing Authority, finally conceding that there was little point in continuing to pay nearly TSh 1 million in rent each month when on a good night, the Avalon attracted just twenty patrons and grossed a mere TSh 32,000. The National Housing Authority promptly awarded the building to a South African chain of rent-to-own furniture stores. The terms of the lease and the price paid by the South African company were never publicly disclosed, but none of the investors who built the Avalon earned a dime from the deal.

As of 2002, only the Novelty in Pemba remained, ironically sustained in large part by the island's notorious underdevelopment. The town of Wete, where the Novelty is located, had long been subject to a two days on–two days off (or one week on–one week off) power-rationing scheme in which the designated "on" time frequently failed to materialize. Ever since the 1960s, when Pembans voted overwhelmingly for political parties ousted in the revolution of 1964, the people had been punished by authorities in Zanzibar and ignored by politicians from the mainland. Suppressed tensions between the isles of Zanzibar and Pemba intensified in the 1990s, with the return of multiparty elections after thirty years of one-party rule.[32] Once again, Pembans paid dearly for their audacity in voting overwhelmingly for the opposition. Cuts to their development budget and more regular disruptions to the already erratic electric supply intensified. But the cinema was wired with the adjacent hospital, which often guaranteed it a much more regular supply of electricity; it also had its own generator, which the proprietor wisely kept in good working order. As a result, for decades the Novelty was one of the only buildings in town regularly emitting light after the sun set at 7:00 p.m. This allowed the theater to continue to attract a small but steady stream of customers who were tired of sitting at home in the dark night after night, year after year. Nightlife outside the Novelty also harkened back to earlier times, with all manner of street sellers and patrons attracted to the lights of the cinema like moths to a single bulb. Elsewhere in the nation but particularly in Dar es Salaam, a technological and economic revolution had ushered in a complete change in the media-viewing habits and preferences of would-be patrons. But in Pemba, most people remained too poor to purchase VCRs, DVDs, TVs, or satellite dishes, and even those who had these machines had no electricity with which to run them. Interestingly enough considering its name, the Novelty was the last of the old theaters to be showing 35 mm films in the nation.

A NEW WORLD

In late 2003, the first of a new generation of multiplex theaters opened in Tanzania. The New World was different from the Novelty on nearly every score. The economic class of patrons, the projection technology, the concession stand treats, and the social atmosphere at the show were just a few areas of difference. Another was that the New World (like all subsequent theaters opened in Tanzania during the next decade) was a multiplex, not a single-screen theater. Furthermore, it was not built in the city center but on the outskirts of town, catering to members of the ever-growing suburban and exurban population, who moved through space enclosed in private cars. Though millions of average city dwellers continued to walk, ride bicycles, or take public transportation across town, virtually no one went on foot to the cinema in the twenty-first century. Private cars were now the only way to go. A large, gated parking lot supervised by private security staff welcomed patrons to the New World. Any folks who arrived by foot were suspect, and unless they were white, they had difficulty getting past the gate. The overwhelming sentiment of those surveyed and interviewed at the New World and all theaters subsequently opened was that gated parking lots were now essential if a cinema owner hoped to attract patrons at night.

In the new millennium, everyone was afraid of strangers—and most people seemed increasingly strange. New World patrons lived in homes that were walled, gated, and secured by guards, and yet they still feared being robbed. Few knew their neighbors or the children from the neighborhood. Conversations with people outside of known circles were rare. But the proliferation of gates, security guards, and private transportation has only deepened perceptions that public space is hostile territory. Even at the theater, the conversations and debates with people from different class, race, and residential groups that used to take place after the film no longer occur. Patrons rarely talk to anyone they did not come with, and after the show, everyone quickly retreats to their private cars. In addition, cinemas now largely reinforce the social tendency toward economic segregation. In

Figure 9.2 New World Cinemas, 2005

2005, ticket prices at the New World averaged between $8 and $12, when the monthly minimum wage was less than $50. As late as the 1980s, the vast majority of a theater's earnings came from average or relatively poor urbanites. Now, only the rich go to the show.

Other aspects of the industry have also changed dramatically in the new millennium. For one, Hollywood is now the main attraction. Bollywood films play at select multiplexes, but they no longer attract the largest number of patrons or account for the highest box office gross.[33] In the twentieth century, Africans adored Indian films as much as Asians did. Today, it is extremely rare to find an African buying a ticket for a Bollywood film. The spread of English-medium, private school education, which also intensified during the neoliberal era, has contributed to the growing popularity of Hollywood. College students from the University of Dar es Salaam have long enjoyed English-language films. As the university liberalized admissions, student numbers at the university climbed from less than three thousand in 1990 to more than eighteen thousand in 2007.[34] Botswana-based developers saw an opportunity and opened the first indoor and air-conditioned mall in Tanzania in 2006, adjacent to the university

327

campus. The mall is anchored at one end by a three-screen cinema with five hundred seats, owned by Muslim Jaffer, the man who opened the New World. Although the university's relationship with the foreign mall developers was problematic for some, students found both the mall and the multiplex attractive. The cinema received nearly twelve thousand Facebook likes from young fans in its first years of operation. Despite ticket prices that rival those in North America, the movies remain a popular place for university students to go on dates.

Cinema ownership and distribution are far more concentrated now than in the previous century, with entrepreneurs consolidating ownership not just in Tanzania but also across the region and continent. In 2016, one man owned four of the five cinemas on the mainland, operated under the corporate banner of Century Cinemax, as well as several theaters in Kenya and Uganda. All but one of the five theaters operating in mainland Tanzania in 2016 were also located in Dar es Salaam. The regional and continental consolidation of distribution has also intensified. In 2005, the New World received its films from Nu-Metro, based in Nairobi, which supplied the theater with movies from all the major American studios as well as a number of Indian producers. As of 2016, all the theaters on the mainland were getting their films from the same supplier, Crimson Multimedia Ltd. Crimson, begun in 2011 by Trushna Buddhedev-Patel (who formerly worked at one of the Kenyan theaters taken over by Muslim Jaffer), controlled nearly 120 screens in Tanzania, Kenya, Uganda, Rwanda, Zambia, Nigeria, and Ghana as of 2016.[35] Crimson offers the digital release of the latest Hollywood films from a range of studios, as well as a limited selection from India. Only the fifty-seat Zancinema (built inside a hotel) in Zanzibar secures films from other suppliers.

Unlike the 1950s, when each cinema in the nation featured a unique movie, all five theaters on the mainland often show the same films. And unlike the twentieth-century pattern of each screen changing films several times a week, today's films now run for several weeks at a time. The internationally renowned Zanzibar International Film Festival or films screened at European cultural centers provide the rare alternative to large studio productions. Tanzanians now produce nearly one hundred films a year, but they are seldom screened in commercial theaters. Before his partnership with Crimson, Muslim Jaffer periodically featured the films of Tanzanians at his Oysterbay Theater in the Free Market Mall. But contracts managing screen time today make it difficult to negotiate room for independent productions and thus for local filmmakers to earn anything from theater screenings. At the same time, expansion to so-called emerging markets, including Tanzania, has been critical to the growth of American studios' earnings in the new millennium.[36]

In terms of genre preferences, Tanzanian tastes have also followed larger global trends, with action—and particularly 3-D action—being the biggest box office draw in the 2010s.[37] First marketed on a large scale in the 1950s in hopes of drawing audiences away from television, 3-D movies have seen a resurgence in recent years. Tickets for these films are generally more expensive, which has allowed Hollywood studios to show an increase in box office earnings despite drops in attendance. In East Africa, managers no longer aim to attract large numbers of poor or middle-income patrons as they did in the past; instead, they market to a small number of well-to-do fans, and 3-D has helped them to draw this demographic back to the theater. When the Nyali Cinemax in Mombasa, Kenya, opened the region's first 3-D screen in 2011, the manager claimed that the wealthy flew to the city just to see a film.[38] New theaters built in Dar es Salaam and Arusha since then were built to accommodate Digital 3D. At the newest cinema in Dar es Salaam, the Suncrest, 3-D film tickets are generally 25 percent more expensive than their 2-D counterparts, but they are typically preferred.

Catering to a juvenile crowd with animated films is another way East African exhibitors have mirrored recent global trends. Although children often attended movies in the twentieth century, neither studios nor exhibitors marketed specifically to youngsters. All this began to change in the 1970s, as youth between the ages of fourteen and twenty-four emerged as a lucrative new market, both in Tanzania and around the globe. Building on this success, studios started marketing to an ever-younger crowd. In North America, children between two and eleven years of age now account for 15 percent of ticket sales, and in Dar es Salaam, children account for 20 percent of earnings.[39] To draw children in, animated films are always at least one and frequently two of the films screened at Tanzanian theaters each week. When the New World first opened, operators marketed specifically to children and the wealthy parents who were eager to please them. According to Raymond Balemwa, the New World manager at the time, management even went so far as to encourage parents to drop off their kids and leave. The sons and daughters of the new elite expected to be entertained, but parents were often too busy—or too uninterested—to sit through a children's film. By encouraging parents to drop off the kids and then run errands or retire to a neighborhood bar, the New World catered to both children's and parents' desires.[40] In the New World on Saturday and Sunday mornings and school holidays, it is common to see children dropped off by the family's chauffeur so that parents can sleep in or attend to other affairs. The strategy paid off, in terms of ticket and concession stand sales. Unlike earlier days, when concessions were leased to others, theater owners in the twenty-first century retain control of all food and drink sales, and treats brought from outside are strongly discouraged. And like theaters showing animated films in North America, Tanzanian theaters can typically gross as much at the concession counter during such movies as they do at the door. For millennial children of the privileged classes in Dar es Salaam, going to the cinema is once again common.

Africa is often portrayed in development literature as a region that is decades, if not light-years, behind global trends. But in the areas of film exhibition and moviegoing, nothing could be further from the truth. From the earliest days of the twentieth century up until the present, the cinema industry in Tanzania has always been part and parcel of global developments. Culturally, technologically, and economically, Tanzania and the world have long been intertwined.

NOTES

1. Birgit Meyer, *Sensational Movies: Video, Vision and Christianity in Ghana* (Oakland: University of California Press, 2015), 4–5.

2. Brigitte Reinwald, "Tonight at the Empire: Cinema and Urbanity in Zanzibar, 1920s–1960s," *Afrique et Histoire* 5 (2006): 81–110.

3. Odile Goerg, *Fantômas sous les tropiques: Aller au cinéma en Afrique coloniale* (Paris: Vendémiaire, 2015), 14, 15, 18.

4. UNESCO, *Basic Facts and Figures: International Statistics Relating to Education, Culture and Mass Communications* (Paris: UNESCO, 1961), 135–36. According to United States Motion Picture Industry reports, the number of theaters elsewhere on the continent boomed in the 1950s. As of 1950, these sources list the number of cinemas in the Gold Coast as 10, Nigeria 24, Liberia and Sierra Leone 1 each, and British East Africa 44. The number of theaters in British East Africa grew to 59 by 1959, with those in the Gold Coast increasing to 35 and Nigerian cinemas then numbering 40. By 1963, the number of theaters in British East Africa had grown to 78, and those in Ghana and Nigeria to 59 and 67, respectively. Despite the growing importance of the industry in Africa, US industry reports paid no attention to markets or earnings outside South Africa. Jack Alicoate, *The Film Daily Year Book of Motion Pictures* (New York: Film Daily): 1950, 89; 1959, 120; 1963.

5. William Hance, *Population, Migration and Urbanization in Africa* (New York: Columbia University Press, 1970), 231–32, 38; Laura Fair, *Pastimes and Politics: Culture, Community, and Identity in Post-abolition Urban Zanzibar, 1890–1945* (Athens: Ohio University Press, 2001), 13.

6. "Films, Their Educational Uses and Censorship," 1927 memo contained in Zanzibar National Archives (hereafter cited as ZNA), AB 5/111: Memorandum on Films, Their Uses and Censorship, 1927–49; ZNA, AB 5/156: Pemba Cinemas.

7. James Burns, *Cinema and Society in the British Empire, 1895–1940* (New York: Palgrave Macmillan, 2013); Burns, "The African Bioscope—Movie House Culture in British Colonial Africa," *Afrique et Histoire* 5 (2006): 74–76; Burns, *Flickering Shadows: Cinema and Identity in Colonial Zimbabwe* (Athens: Ohio University Press, 2002); J. H. G. (a member of the Jaluo Tribe), "My First Visit to the Cinema," *Colonial Cinema* 8, no. 2 (1950): 60–61.

8. Hance, *Population, Migration and Urbanization*, 238.

9. Abdul Sheriff, *Dhow Culture of the Indian Ocean: Cosmopolitanism, Commerce and Islam* (New York: Columbia University Press, 2010); Alan Villiers, *Sons of Sinbad: An Account of Sailing with the Arabs in Their Dhows, in the Red Sea, around the Coasts of Arabia, and to Zanzibar and Tanganyika* (New York: Scribner, 1969); Stephen Rockel, *Carriers of Culture: Labor on the Road in Nineteenth-Century East Africa* (Portsmouth, NH: Heinemann, 2006); Jonathon Glassman, *Feasts and Riot: Revelry, Rebellion and Popular Culture on the Swahili Coast, 1856–1888* (Portsmouth, NH: Heinemann, 1995); Fair, *Pastimes and Politics*; Abdulrazak Gurnah, *Paradise* (New York: New Press, 1993).

10. Charles Ambler, "Popular Films and Colonial Audiences: The Movies in Northern Rhodesia," *American Historical Review* 106, no. 1 (2001): 81–105; Ambler, "Mass Media and Leisure in Africa," *International Journal of African Historical Studies* 35, no. 1 (2002): 119–36; Burns, *Flickering Shadows*; Charles-Didier Gondola, "Manhood and the Cult of the Cowboy," *Cahiers d'Etudes Africaines*, nos. 209–10 (2013): 173–99; Brian Larkin, *Signal and Noise: Media, Infrastructure, and Urban Culture in Nigeria* (Durham, NC: Duke University Press, 2008); Hortense Powdermaker, *Copper Town: Changing Africa—The Human Situation on the Rhodesian Copperbelt* (New York: Harper and Row, 1962); Glenn Reynolds, *Colonial Cinema in Africa: Origins, Images, Audiences* (Jefferson, NC: McFarland, 2015); Lawrence E. Y. Mbogoni, *Aspects of Colonial Tanzania History* (Dar es Salaam: Mkuki na Nyota, 2013), 81–101

11. Goerg, *Fantômas sous les tropiques*. In Northern Cameroon the first cinema was opened in 1955, with many of the remaining eight in the region opened in the 1970s. Honore Fouhba, *Les salles de cinéma au Nord-Cameroun: Des implantations aux transformations* (Yaounde: Editions Ifrikiya, 2016).

12. Caleb Owen, "Lands of Leisure: Recreation, Urban Space and the Struggle for Urban Kenya" (PhD diss., Michigan State University, 2016); R. Mugo Gatheru, *A Child of Two Worlds: A Kikuyu's Story* (New York: Praeger, 1964), 85; I thank Caleb Owen for sharing this reference. "District Officer to Provincial Commissioner Dar es Salaam, 8 December 1930," Tanzanian National Archives (hereafter TNA) 13038: Cinematograph Films Censorship and Control of Display.

13. Ambler, "Popular Films and Colonial Audiences," 88; Goerg, *Fantômas sous les tropiques*, 145; Charles Ambler, "Cowboy Modern: African Audiences, Hollywood Films and Visions of the West," in *Going to the Movies: Hollywood and the Social Experience of Cinema*, ed. Richard Maltby, Melvyn Stokes, and Robert

Allen (Exeter: University of Exeter Press, 2007), 348-63; Charles-Didier Gondola, *Tropical Cowboys: Westerns, Violence and Masculinity in Kinshasa* (Bloomington: Indiana University Press, 2016), 59–60.

14. Phil Bonner, "'Desirable or Undesirable Basotho Women?' Liquor, Prostitution and the Migration of Basotho Women to the Rand, 1920–1945," in *Women and Gender in Southern Africa to 1945*, ed. Cherryl Walker (London: James Currey, 1990), 221–50; Andrew Burton, *African Underclass: Urbanization, Crime and Colonial Order in Dar es Salaam* (Athens: Ohio University Press, 2005); George Chauncey, "The Locus of Reproduction: Women's Labor in the Zambian Copperbelt, 1927–1953," *Journal of Southern African Studies* 7, no. 2 (1981): 135–64; Frederick Cooper, ed., *Struggle for the City: Migrant Labor, Capital, and the State in Urban Africa* (Beverly Hills, CA: Sage, 1983); Garth Myers, "Sticks and Stones: Colonialism and Zanzibari Housing," *Africa* 67, no. 2 (1997): 252–72; Cherryl Walker, "Gender and the Development of the Migrant Labour System c. 1850–1930," in Walker, *Women and Gender*, 168–96; Luise White, *The Comforts of Home: Prostitution in Colonial Nairobi* (Chicago: University of Chicago Press, 1990); Justin Willis, *Potent Brews: A Social History of Alcohol in East Africa, 1850–1999* (Oxford: James Currey, 2002).

15. Andrew Burton, "Urchins, Loafers, and the Cult of the Cowboy: Urbanization and Delinquency in Dar es Salaam, 1919–61," *Journal of African History* 42, no. 2 (2001): 199–216; Burton, *African Underclass*.

16. Jan Lahmeyer, "Tanzania: Historical Demographic Data of the Urban Centers," 2001, accessed March 31, 2008, at http://www.populstat.info/Africa/tanzanit .htm.

17. James Brennan and Andrew Burton, "The Emerging Metropolis: A History of Dar es Salaam, circa 1862–2000," in *Dar es Salaam: Histories from an Emerging African Metropolis*, ed. James Brennan and Andrew Burton (Dar es Salaam: Mkuki na Nyota, 2007), 13–75; James Brennan, *Taifa: Making Nation and Race in Urban Tanzania* (Athens: Ohio University Press, 2012), 21–46; Burton, *African Underclass*.

18. Burton, *African Underclass*, 165.

19. "Films, Their Educational Uses and Censorship," 1927 memo contained in ZNA, AB 5/111: Memorandum on Films, Their Uses and Censorship, 1927–49; "Prices of Seats and Provisions Made for Africans in Cinemas in Dares Salaam [*sic*] and Nairobi, 1930," TNA 20496: Scheme for Establishment of Cinematograph Theaters in Native Areas; ZNA, AB 5/131: Censoring of State Plays and Cinematograph Exhibitions.

20. Goerg, *Fantômas sous les tropiques*, 46–48; Gareth McFeely, "'Gone Are the Days': A Social and Business History of Cinema-Going in Gold Coast/Ghana, 1910–1982" (PhD diss., Boston University, 2015), 152.

21. David Gainer, "Hollywood, African Consolidated Films, and 'Bioskoop-beskawing,' or Bioscope Culture: Aspects of American Culture in Cape Town, 1945–1960" (PhD diss., University of Cape Town, 2000); Gainer, "Man the People

333

Would Really Go Wild: The Bioscope, American Films, and South African Audiences, 1930–1960," paper presented at the African Studies Association Meeting 2002, now in possession of the author; Vashna Jagarnath, "Indian Cinema in Durban: Urban Segregation, Business and Visions of Identity from the 1950s to the 1970s," in *City Flicks: Cinema, Urban Worlds and Modernities in India and Beyond*, ed. Preben Kaarsholn (Roskilde, Denmark: International Development Studies, 2002), 165–76; Burns, *Cinema and Society*, 83, 175. Brian Larkin examines the impact of similar policies on architecture and attendance in Nigeria; see Larkin, "The Materiality of Cinema Theaters in Northern Nigeria," in *Media Worlds: Anthropology on New Terrain*, ed. Faye Ginsburg, Lila Abu-Lughod, and Brian Larkin (Berkeley: University of California Press, 2002), 319–38.

22. Yi-Fu Tuan, *Topophilia: A Study of Environmental Perception, Attitudes and Values* (Englewood Cliffs, NJ: Prentice-Hall, 1974); Annette Kuhn, "'That Day Did Last Me All My Life': Cinema Memory and Enduring Fandom," in *Identifying Hollywood's Audiences: Cultural Identity and the Movies*, ed. Melvyn Stokes and Richard Maltby (London: British Film Institute, 1999), 135–46.

23. For a thorough discussion of local naming practices, see Myers, "Sticks and Stones", and Garth Andrew Myers, *Verandahs of Power: Colonialism and Space in Urban Africa* (Syracuse, NY: Syracuse University Press, 2003).

24. D. W. McKiernan, *Cinema and Community* (Houndmills, UK: Palgrave Macmillan, 2008), 44. For a similar exploration in India see Lakshmi Srinivas, *House Full: Indian Cinema and the Active Audience* (Chicago: University of Chicago Press, 2016).

25. Larkin, *Signal and Noise*, 159–60; Elizabeth Thompson, *Colonial Citizens: Republican Rights, Paternal Privilege, and Gender in French Syria and Lebanon* (New York: Columbia University Press, 2000), 197–209; Kathryn Fuller, *At the Picture Show: Small-Town Audiences and the Creation of Movie Fan Culture* (Washington, DC: Smithsonian Institution Press, 1996), 28–35; Kathy Lee Peiss, *Cheap Amusements: Working Women and Leisure in Turn-of-the-Century New York* (Philadelphia: Temple University Press, 1986), 140–53; Lakshmi Srinivas, "Ladies Queues, 'Roadside Romeos,' and Balcony Seating: Ethnographic Observations on Women's Cinema-Going Experiences," *South Asian Popular Culture* 8, no. 3 (2010): 291–307.

26. Thomas Burgess, "Cinema, Bell Bottoms, and Miniskirts: Struggles over Youth and Citizenship in Revolutionary Zanzibar," *International Journal of African Historical Studies* 35, no. 2 (2002): 287; Andrew M. Ivaska, "'Anti-mini Militants Meet Modern Misses': Urban Style, Gender, and the Politics of 'National Culture' in 1960s Dar es Salaam, Tanzania," in *Fashioning Africa: Power and the Politics of Dress*, ed. Jean Allman (Bloomington: University of Indiana Press, 2004), 104–21; Ivaska, *Cultured States: Youth, Gender and Modern Style in Dar es Salaam* (Durham, NC: Duke University Press, 2011).

27. Kajole (aka Khamis), interview with the author, December 20 and 23, 2008, Zanzibar; Rashid, interview with the author, December 20, 2008.

28. *Jaws* was the number three all-time top-grossing film in Australia; Diana Collins, *Hollywood Down Under: Australians at the Movies, 1896 to the Present Day* (London: Angus and Robertson, 1987). Kajole (aka Khamis) interview. According to Clive Glaser, a Soweto gang also took its name from the film; Glaser, *Bo-Tsotsi: The Youth Gangs of Soweto, 1935–1976* (Portsmouth, NH: Heinemann, 2000), 69.

29. The film initially played at the Cine Afrique theater in Zanzibar, but I have no ticket sales data for those screenings. These numbers are based on ticket sale logs for the Majestic Cinema. Even on a repeat run in Zanzibar in July 1978, the film drew 1,619 fans to the Majestic on a Wednesday, followed by another 934 on Saturday.

30. Kajole (aka Khamis) interview.

31. Karen Tranberg Hansen, *Salaula: The World of Secondhand Clothing and Zambia* (Chicago: University of Chicago Press, 2000); Alusine Jalloh, *African Entrepreneurship: Muslim Fula Merchants in Sierra Leone* (Athens: Ohio University Press, 1999); Janet MacGaffey, *Entrepreneurs and Parasites: The Struggles for Indigenous Capitalism in Zaire* (Cambridge: Cambridge University Press, 1987); Myers, "Sticks and Stones"; Claire Robertson, *Trouble Showed the Way: Women, Men and Trade in the Nairobi Area, 1890–1990* (Bloomington: Indiana University Press, 1997); Aili Mari Tripp, *Changing the Rules: The Politics of Liberalization and the Urban Informal Economy in Tanzania* (Berkeley: University of California Press, 1997); Willis, *Potent Brews*; Jennifer Hart, *Ghana on the Go: African Mobility in the Age of Motor Transportation* (Bloomington: Indiana University Press, 2016); Kenda Mutongi, *Matatu: A History of Popular Transportation in Nairobi* (Chicago: University of Chicago Press, 2017).

32. Robert Gregory, *The Rise and Fall of Philanthropy in East Africa* (New Brunswick, NJ: Transaction Publishers, 1992).

33. Bill Nasson, "She Preferred Living in a Cave with Harry the Snake-Catcher: Towards an Oral History of Popular Leisure and Class Expression in District Six, Cape Town, c. 1920–1950," in *Holding Their Ground*, ed. Philip Bonner et al. (Johannesburg: Ravan, 1989), 285–310.

34. The development of theater chains began at a regional level before World War I; Douglas Gomery, *Shared Pleasures: A History of Movie Presentation in the United States* (Madison: University of Wisconsin Press, 1992), 61; Gomery, "Fashioning an Exhibition Empire: Promotion, Publicity and the Rise of Publix Theaters," in *Moviegoing in America*, ed. Gregory Waller (Malden, MA: Blackwell, 2002), 124–36; Mae Huettig, "Economic Control of the Motion Picture Industry," in *The American Film Industry*, ed. Tino Balio (Madison: University of Wisconsin Press, 1985), 285–310; Tino Balio, ed., *The American Film Industry*, 2nd ed. (Madison: University of Wisconsin Press, 1985), 103–31, 334–50. As of 2014, Regal was the largest theater circuit in the United States, controlling seven thousand screens. AMC, owned by the Dalian Wanda Group of China, was second, controlling five

335

thousand screens; "Regal, Big Theater Chain, May Be for Sale," *New York Times*, October 28, 2014, B4.

35. In the 1930s, Oscar Deutsch opened 136 new Odeon cinemas in Britain; Allen Eyles, *Odeon Cinemas: Oscar Deutsch Entertains Our Nation* (London: British Film Institute, 2002).

36. "Schlesinger Jubilee Supplement," *Tanganyika Standard*, April 11, 1953, 5–8; Thelma Gutsch, *The History and Social Significance of Motion Pictures in South Africa, 1895–1940* (Cape Town: Howard Timmins, 1972).

37. Gainer, "Hollywood, African Consolidated Films," esp. 87–113; David Gainer, "Exploitation: African Consolidated Films and Hollywood's Domination of South Africa's Bioscopes, 1930–1960," in *African Studies Meeting* (2001); Gutsch, *History and Social Significance*, 112–20; Kristin Thompson, *Exporting Entertainment: America in the World Film Market 1907–34* (London: British Film Institute, 1985), 33, 44–46. Schlesinger's counterpart in Australia was J. D. Williams, another American immigrant who finessed a similar stranglehold on the exhibition and distribution industries during that same period.

38. Gainer, "Hollywood, African Consolidated Films," 91n23.

39. South African National Archives (hereafter cited as SANA), Records of the Board of Trade and Industries. I am indebted to Jill Kelly, who secured copies of records held in the South African archives related to the film industry in South Africa and particularly a series of hearings related to Schlesinger's organizations in the 1950s and 1960s. SANA, RHN 181 2/101/9/2: Board of Trade, 1959–60; SANA, RHN 180 2/101/9/1: Investigation in Terms of Regulations of Monopolistic Conditions; SANA, RHN 178 2/101/9: Board of Trade Investigation in Terms of Monopoly Act in Specific Branches of Industry Trade: Motion Pictures, 1959–67; SANA, RHN 179 2/101/9/1: Investigation in Terms of Regulation of Monopolistic Conditions. Gutsch, *History and Social Significance*.

40. Gainer, "Hollywood, African Consolidated Films," 99–100.

41. Burns, *Cinema and Society*; Gainer, "Hollywood, African Consolidated Films"; Gutsch, *History and Social Significance*.

42. James Chapman, *Cinemas of the World* (London: Reaktion Books, 2003), 204.

43. Ashish Rajadhyaksha and Paul Willemen, *Encyclopedia of the Indian Cinema*, 2nd ed. (London: Fitzroy Dearborn, 1999), 30–32; Yves Thoraval, *The Cinemas of India, 1896–2000* (Delhi: Macmillan India, 2000), 51; Manjunath Pendakur, *Indian Popular Cinema: Industry, Ideology, and Consciousness* (Creskill, NJ: Hampton Press, 2003), 24.

44. Rikhab Dass Jain, *The Economic Aspects of the Film Industry in India* (Delhi: Atma Ram and Sons, 1960), 182–83; Pendakur, *Indian Popular Cinema*, 35; Thoraval, *Cinemas of India*, 47–49; B. Jha, *Indian Motion Picture Almanac* (Calcutta: Shot Publications, 1975); B. K. Adarsh, *Film Industry of India* (Bombay: Perfecta Printing Works for Trade Guide, 1963).

45. Jain, *Economic Aspects*, 192.

46. In the United States, typically 70 percent of the box office receipts went to distributors. In India, 50 percent was more the norm due to the greater ability of exhibitors to negotiate with a wider range of distributors. "Collections with Distributor's Share—Station-Wise," in Adarsh, *Film Industry of India*, 76/–/1.

47. Balio, *American Film Industry*, 117; Thomas Guback, "Hollywood's International Market," in *The American Film Industry*, ed. Tino Balio (Madison: University of Wisconsin Press, 1976), 463–86; Ian Jarvie, *Hollywood's Overseas Campaign: The North Atlantic Movie Trade, 1920–1950* (New York: Cambridge University Press, 1992); Michael Walsh, "The Internationalism of the American Cinema: The Establishment of United Artists' Foreign Distribution Operations" (PhD diss., University of Wisconsin, 1998), 45, 54; McFeely, "'Gone Are the Days,'" 191–92.

48. Tanzania Film Company Limited (hereafter TFC), *Annual Report and Account for the Year Ended 31 December 1984–31 December 1988* (Dar es Salaam: n.d., n.p.), 3; Tanzania Tourist Corporation, "Annual Report and Accounts, 1970–71" (n.p., n.d.), 52.

49. James Brennan, "Blood Enemies: Exploitation and Urban Citizenship in the Nationalist Political Thought of Tanzania, 1958–75," *Journal of African History* 47, no. 3 (2006): 389–413; Brennan, *Taifa*; Richa Nagar, "The South Asian Diaspora in Tanzania: A History Retold," *Comparative Studies of South Asia, Africa and the Middle East* 16, no. 2 (1996): 62–80; Gijsbert Oonk, *Settled Strangers: Asian Business Elites in East Africa, 1800–2000* (Mumbai: Sage, 2013).

50. Benjamin Amani Bruhwiler, "Moralities of Owing and Lending: Credit, Debt and Urban Living in Kariakoo, Dar es Salaam" (PhD diss., Michigan State University, 2015).

51. Brennan, "Blood Enemies," 387–411. Brennan gives this theme more sustained treatment in *Taifa*. For Zanzibar, see Jonathon Glassman, "Sorting Out the Tribes: The Creation of Racial Identities in Colonial Zanzibar's Newspaper Wars," *Journal of African History* 41, no. 3 (2000): 395–428.

52. Nagar, "South Asian Diaspora in Tanzania," 68–70.

53. Robert Gregory was among the first scholars to give sustained attention to the rich and varied histories of South Asians in East Africa, but few books have followed the publication of his in the early 1990s. Gregory, *Philanthropy in East Africa*; Gregory, *South Asians in East Africa: An Economic and Social History, 1890–1980* (Boulder, CO: Westview Press, 1993); Dana April Seidenberg, *Mercantile Adventurers: The World of East African Asians, 1750–1985* (New Delhi: New Age International, 1996); Gijsbert Oonk, *The Karimjee Jivanjee Family: Merchant Princes of East Africa, 1800–2000* (Amsterdam: Pallas Publications, 2009); Oonk, *Settled Strangers*; Sana Aiyar, *Indians in Kenya: The Politics of Diaspora* (Cambridge, MA: Harvard University Press, 2015).

54. G. Thomas Burgess, *Race, Revolution and the Struggle for Human Rights in Zanzibar: The Memoirs of Ali Sultan Issa and Seif Sharif Hamad* (Athens: Ohio University Press, 2009), 238. Abdulhussein Marashi, interview with the author,

May 15, 2002, Zanzibar; Asad Talati, interview with the author, August 31, 2004, Toronto, Canada.

55. James C. Scott, *Seeing Like a State: How Certain Schemes to Improve the Human Condition Have Failed* (New Haven, CT: Yale University Press, 1998).

56. James Ferguson, *Global Shadows: Africa in the Neoliberal World Order* (Durham, NC: Duke University Press, 2006); Ferguson, *Expectations of Modernity: Myths and Meanings of Urban Life on the Zambian Copperbelt* (Berkeley: University of California Press, 1999).

57. D. Iordanova, J. Goytisolo, A. K. G. Singh, A. Suner, V. Shafik, and P. A. Skantze, "Indian Cinema's Global Reach: Historiography through Testimonies," *South Asian Popular Culture* 4, no. 2 (2006): 113–40; Sudha Rajagopalan, *Indian Films in Soviet Cinemas: The Culture of Moviegoing after Stalin* (Bloomington: Indiana University Press, 2008).

58. Within a year of his first movie, Elvis shot to the number four spot among the top ten actors in Australia. Collins, *Hollywood Down Under*, 238; Eric Zolov, *Refried Elvis: The Rise of the Mexican Counterculture* (Berkeley: University of California Press, 1999).

59. Brian Larkin, "Indian Films and Nigerian Lovers: Media and the Creation of Parallel Modernities," *Africa: Journal of the International African Institute* 67, no. 3 (1997): 406–40; Larkin, *Signal and Noise*.

60. Burns, *Cinema and Society*; Richard Maltby, Melvyn Stokes, and Robert C. Allen, eds., *Going to the Movies: Hollywood and the Social Experience of Cinema* (Exeter: University of Exeter Press, 2007). The twenty chapters included in Maltby, Stokes, and Allen's edited volume also drive home how race, class, location, gender, and a host of other factors impacted audiences and the social practices of moviegoing.

61. For a further discussion of some of these tinkerers and innovators in India, see Thoraval, *Cinemas of India, 1896–2000*, 15. Brian Larkin, drawing on the work of Paul Virilio, adroitly connects the development of cinema not to photography but to war. Cinematic optics and revolutions inside the camera moving film were patterned on military sighting devices and repeating guns. Larkin, *Signal and Noise*, 82.

62. Thoraval, *Cinemas of India, 1896–2000*, 7. Trying to explain moving-picture technology to an uninitiated audience, Phalke advertised his first feature film, *Raja Harishchandra* (1913) as "a performance with 57,000 photographs, a picture two miles long," as cited by Patel in Rachel Dwyer and Divia Patel, *Cinema India: The Visual Culture of Hindi Film* (New Brunswick, NJ: Rutgers University Press, 2002), 101. The *East African Standard* was published in Mombasa, but the only advertisements for films in this publication were for those showing in the United Kingdom. *East African Standard*, May 6, 1911, 21, and October 26, 1912, 27.

63. Gomery, *Shared Pleasures*, 19; Peiss, *Cheap Amusements*, 139–62; Roy Rosenzweig, *Eight Hours for What We Will: Workers and Leisure in an Industrial City, 1870–1920* (Cambridge: Cambridge University Press, 1983), 191–221.

64. Chapman, *Cinemas of the World*, 67; Rachael Low, *The History of British Film, 1906–1914* (London: Routledge, 1973), 23; Burns, *Cinema and Society*, 13–54.

65. Lizabeth Cohen, "Encountering Mass Culture at the Grassroots: The Experience of Chicago Workers in the 1920s," *American Quarterly* 41, no. 1 (1989): 6–33

66. Bernhard Rieger, *Technology and the Culture of Modernity in Britain and Germany, 1890–1945* (Cambridge: Cambridge University Press, 2005), 98–99; Eyles, *Odeon Cinemas: Oscar Deutsch*; Jeffrey Richards, *The Age of the Dream Palace: Cinema and Society in Britain, 1930–1939* (London: Routledge and Kegan Paul, 1984); Gomery, *Shared Pleasures*; David Naylor, *American Picture Palaces: The Architecture of Fantasy* (New York: Van Nostrand Reinhold, 1981); Richard Butsch, *The Making of American Audiences: From Stage to Television, 1750–1990* (Cambridge: Cambridge University Press, 2000), 158–72; Paul Monaco, *Cinema and Society: France and Germany during the Twenties* (New York: Elsevier, 1976).

67. Annette Kuhn, *Dreaming of Fred and Ginger: Cinema and Cultural Memory* (New York: NYU Press, 2002), 133; Jackie Stacey, *Star Gazing: Hollywood Cinema and Female Spectatorship* (London: Routledge, 1994), 94–104.

68. Mwalim Idd Abdulla Farhan, interview with the author, May 25, 2002, Zanzibar. Such sentiments were echoed by many across the mainland and the isles. Balaban and Katz, leading industry strategists in the United States, also utilized trained, deferential, polite ushers, whose duty was to make patrons feel that their experience was on a par with that in a fine hotel or country club. Gomery, *Shared Pleasures*, 49–50.

69. Gomery, *Shared Pleasures*, 4–56.

70. Jim Crow legislation in the South effectively barred African Americans from nearly all indoor and outdoor amusements catering to whites. Latinos too were typically excluded from white shows. The net effect was that white audiences also lost out because in areas with large black populations movie theaters simply could not draw enough patrons to stay afloat. In the 1920s and 1930s, "black theaters" developed in many southern cities, from Washington, DC, to Atlanta. By 1930, there were some 460 black theaters across the United States, with almost 300 of them concentrated in the South. In regions of the country where people of color were allowed to enter the same theater as whites, they were often restricted to sitting in the balcony. In some towns, African Americans were allowed into the theater only at midnight, after the last of the white crowds had left the show. Gomery, *Shared Pleasures*, 155–70; Fuller, *At the Picture Show*, 33.

71. Charles Anderson, *A City and Its Cinemas* (Bristol: Redcliffe, 1983); Steve Derné, *Movies, Masculinity, and Modernity: An Ethnography of Men's Filmgoing in India* (Westport, CT: Greenwood Press, 2000); Sara Dickey, *Cinema and the Urban Poor in South India* (Cambridge: Cambridge University Press, 1993); Jain, *Economic Aspects*; Judith Mayne, "Immigrants and Spectators," *Wide Angle* 5, no. 2 (1982): 32–40; Ashis Nandy, "Popular Indian Cinema as a Slums' Eye View of Politics," in *The Secret Politics of Our Desires: Innocence, Culpability and Indian*

339

Popular Cinema, ed. Ashis Nandy (London: Zed, 1998), 1–18; David Nasaw, *Going Out: The Rise and Fall of Public Amusements* (Cambridge, MA: Harvard University Press, 1993); Peiss, *Cheap Amusements*; Srinivas, "Ladies Queues, 'Roadside Romeos,' and Balcony Seating;" Srinivas, *House Full*, 96–104, 122–29, 159–61, 217–24.

72. Abdulhussein Marashi, interview with the author, May 7, 2002, Zanzibar; Agnello Fernandez, interview with the author, March 10, 2005, Dar es Salaam; Ameri Slyoum, interview with the author, May 16, 2002, Zanzibar; Ahmed "Eddy" Alwi al-Beity, interview with the author, November 27, 2004, Dar es Salaam; Mwalim Idd Abdulla Farhan, interview of May 25, 2002.

73. Lynn M. Thomas, "Modernity's Failings, Political Claims and Intermediate Concepts," *American Historical Review* 116, no. 3 (2011): 727–40; Thomas, "Love, Sex and the Modern Girl in 1930s Southern Africa," in *Love in Africa*, ed. Jennifer Cole and Lynn Thomas (Chicago: University of Chicago Press, 2009), 31–57; Peter Bloom, Stephan Miescher, and Takyiwaa Manuh, eds., *Modernization as Spectacle in Africa* (Bloomington: Indiana University Press, 2014); Stephan F. Miescher, "Building the City of the Future: Visions and Experiences of Modernity in Ghana's Akasombo Township," *Journal of African History* 53, no. 3 (2012): 367–90; Bianca Murillo, "'The Modern Shopping Experience': Kingsway Department Store and Consumer Politics in Ghana," *Africa* 82, no. 3 (2012): 368–92; Ivaska, *Cultured States*. For a rich discussion of the plurality of imaginaries represented and given form in Pentecostal videos in Ghana, see Meyer, *Sensational Movies*.

74. Kuhn, *Dreaming of Fred and Ginger*, 16–17.

75. William Cunningham Bissell, "Engaging Colonial Nostalgia," *Cultural Anthropology* 20, no. 2 (2005): 240.

76. Rachel Dwyer, *All You Want Is Money, All You Need Is Love: Sexuality and Romance in Modern India* (London: Cassell, 2000); Rajagopalan, *Indian Films in Soviet Cinemas*; Stacey, *Star Gazing*.

77. Jean Allman, "Phantoms of the Archives: Kwame Nkrumah, a Nazi Pilot Named Hanna, and the Contingencies of Postcolonial History Writing," *American Historical Review* 118, no. 1 (2013): 104–29.

78. Ambler, "Popular Film." This is not to deny the import or richness of the studies that have been written from such sources. For the case of Tanzania, see Rosaleen Smyth, "The Development of British Colonial Film Policy, 1927–1939, with Special Reference to East and Central Africa," *Journal of African History* 20, no. 3 (1979): 437–50; Smyth, "The Post-war Career of the Colonial Film Unit in Africa: 1946–1955," *Historical Journal of Film, Radio and Television* 12, no. 2 (1992): 163–77; Burton, "Urchins, Loafers"; James R. Brennan, "Democratizing Cinema and Censorship in Tanzania, 1920–1980," *International Journal of African Historical Studies* 38, no. 3 (2005): 481–511.

79. In the 1950s, a number of American hits sold out shows, including *Rock around the Clock* (1956), *Samson and Delilah* (1949), *Ivanhoe* (1952), *Shane* (1953), and *The Guns of Navarone* (1961). Tony Curtis also turned more than a few heads

when he starred in *The Prince Who Was a Thief* (1951). But these titles were recalled by exhibitors and distributors, not by average audience members.

80. Adarsh, *Film Industry of India*, 46–47, 77; Jain, *Economic Aspects*, 180. A very special thank you to Ravi Vasudevan, who first pointed me to Adarsh.

81. Adarsh, *Film Industry of India*, 46–47, 77, 131–32, 77–78, 300; Manjunath Pendakur, "India," in *The Asian Film Industry*, ed. John Lent (London: C. Helm, 1990), 229–52; Manjunath Pendakur and Radha Subramanyam, "Indian Cinema beyond National Borders," in *Patterns in Global Television: Peripheral Vision*, ed. John Sinclair, Elizabeth Jacka, and Stuart Cunningham (Oxford: Oxford University Press, 1996), 67–82; Raminder Kaur and Ajay Sinha, *Bollyworld: Popular Indian Cinema through a Transnational Lens* (New Delhi: Sage, 2005); *Film Daily Year Book*: 1959, 97; 1963, 101; Madras Film Diary, "World Market for Indian Films,"; Adarsh, *Film Industry of India*, 178; "Export Earnings on Indian Films," ibid., 46.

82. Nasson, "She Preferred Living in a Cave."

83. McFeely, "'Gone Are the Days,'" 169–70.

84. Gutsch, *History and Social Significance*; Gainer, "Hollywood, African Consolidated Films"; McFeely, "'Gone Are the Days.'"

Chapter 1: Building Business and Building Community

1. Steve Battle, "The Old Dispensary: An Apogee of Zanzibari Architecture," in *The History and Conservation of Zanzibar Stone Town*, ed. Abdul Sheriff (Athens: Ohio University Press, 1995), 91–99; Abdul Sheriff and Javed Jafferji, *Zanzibar Stone Town: An Architectural Exploration* (Zanzibar: Gallery Publications, 2008); Khamis S. Khamis, "Lights of Zanzibar," accessed at http://zanzibarhistory.org /lights_of_zanzibar.htm; Gregory, *Rise and Fall of Philanthropy*.

2. *Zanzibar Offical Gazette*, December 7, 1904; 1904 is the first reference I have found advertising cinematic displays in East Africa. Throughout the early 1900s, regular references to displays of moving pictures can be found in the *Official Gazette*. The earliest references found in other regional print publication from Dar es Salaam, Mombasa, and Nairobi date to the 1910s. This does not, of course, mean that such shows did not take place, merely that they were not of note for those who read the paper.

3. *Zanzibar Gazette*, May 2 and April 4, 1911. I spoke with several individuals whose ancestors displayed films in this way in the ports of Mombasa and Zanzibar in the 1910s: Chunilala Kala Savani, interview with the author, June 17, 2005, Mombasa; Jitu Savani, interview with the author, January 29, 2004, Tanga, and May 26, 2005, Dar es Salaam; and Shabir K. Jariwalla, interview with the author, April 25, 2005, Arusha. As a result of the excitement generated by a show of moving pictures in Zanzibar in the 1910s, the audience exceeded the limited space of Victoria Gardens, forcing operators to move their exhibitions to the much larger Mnazi Moja grounds.

4. Shabir K. Jariwalla interview; "The Late Mr. Hassanali Jariwalla," *Samachar*, May 11, 1947, 4B; "Obituary of HA Jariwalla," *Zanzibar Voice*, May 9, 1947, 4.

341

Enterprising traders who traveled on from Zanzibar into the interior also brought projectors and films along when they could as a means of attracting attention to their other wares, entertaining themselves, astounding others, and earning a little extra cash at night.

5. Shabir K. Jariwalla interview; *Zanzibar Official Gazette*, May 2, 1911; Supplement to the *Zanzibar Official Gazette*, May 15, 1916; *Zanzibar Official Gazette*, September 11, 1916; *Zanzibar Official Gazette*, January 15, 1917. TNA, AB 356: Electric Current, Alleged Theft Of. See also Brennan, "Democratizing Cinema"; Reinwald, "Tonight at the Empire." I am eternally indebted to Joshua Grace for finding this picture in the Winerton Collection, held at Northwestern University, when it first appeared online and then sharing it with me.

6. Large and impressive stone homes and palaces had been part of Zanzibar's cityscape since the early 1800s, and ornate mosques and several churches were built later in the century. After the 1890s, the British too began making a sizable contribution to the island's architectural footprint, with Sinclair also designing the Peace Museum, the British Residency, the Aga Khan Secondary School (now TASCISI), and the High Court in a similar architectural style. Rustomvji Navroji Talati was the government building contractor who supervised construction of the High Court. Sheriff, *Zanzibar Stone Town*, 82–89.

7. Remarkably little has been written on the history of built forms in East Africa, particularly after the height of Swahili maritime trade. Sheriff and Myers provide the fullest accounts of architecture in Zanzibar. See Sheriff, *History and Conservation of Zanzibar Stone Town*; Sheriff and Jafferji, *Zanzibar Stone Town*; Myers, *Verandahs of Power*; Prita Meier, *Swahili Port Cities: An Architecture of Elsewhere* (Bloomington: Indiana University Press, 2016).

8. ZNA, AB 5/111: Films, Their Educational Uses and Censorship.

9. I do not have any precise figures on what it cost to build the Royal just after World War I, but it clearly required a substantial sum. When the building burned down due to an electrical fire in 1954, the cinema's owner, Hameer Hasham, estimated the loss at no less than $140,000. It seems doubtful that Hameer was exaggerating by much, if at all, as other cinemas built in Tanzania of a similar size and sophistication cost between $100,000 and $150,000 to build and equip at that time. In 1950, $100,000 would be the equivalent of nearly $1 million today. "Majestic Cinema Fire," *Tangayika Standard*, February 11, 1954, 3; *Tanganyika Standard*, August 15, 1954, 3; "A New Cinema for Dar es Salaam," *Tanganyika Standard*, June 9, 1954, 2; "New Avalon Cinema Rennovations Cost 75,000," *Tanganyika Standard*, March 10, 1955, 3; Files from the Office of the Registrar of Companies (hereafter RC), File 1546: Majestic Theaters Ltd., Tanga; RC, File 1488: Indo-African Theaters Ltd.; Asad Talati, interviews with the author, August 14, 15, and 16, 2004, Toronto, Canada; Asad Talati, e-mail correspondence with the author, March 27, 2005.

10. Gregory, *South Asians in East Africa*, 167–69. The artist Sarah Markes has provided the closest thing to an architectural history for colonial urban Tanzania

in her drawings from Dar es Salaam. She has also done us all a huge favor, capturing many old, unique, and delightful buildings just before they were leveled between 2005 and 2015 to make way for monolithic, multistory megastructures. Those interested in a visual slice of the vitality of urban street life should also check out her other wonderful drawings on "darsketches blog" at worldpress.com. Sarah Markes, *Street Level: A Collection of Drawings and Creative Writing Inspired by Dar-es-Salaam* (Dar es Salaam: Mkuki Na Nyota, 2011). On the absence of architectural history, see Akin Mabogunje, "Urban Planning and the Post-colonial State in Africa: A Research Overview," *African Studies Review* 33, no. 2 (1990): 121–203; Myers, "Sticks and Stones." 11. As Garth Myers has documented in his explorations of the architectural work of the Zanzibari Agit Singh Hoogan, even the most gracious of European supervisors were reluctant to give credit to their colonial "underlings" for their designs, drawings, and supervision of construction. Richard Harris and Garth Myers, "Hybrid Housing: Improvement and Control in Late Colonial Zanzibar," *Journal of the Society of Architectural Historians* 66, no. (2007): 476–93; Myers, *Verandahs of Power*. Rustomji Navroji Talati, Asad Talati's grandfather, supervised the construction of the High Court Building as mentioned earlier, but to my knowledge, his work, like that of most Asian contractors and builders, remains undocumented in writing. Asad Talati, e-mail correspondence with the author, August 30, 2004.

12. Among those whose life histories follow such patterns are Tharia Topan, Jivanjee Budhabhoy (father of the Karimjee Jivanjees), Allidina Visram, Nanji Kalidas Mehta, and Kassum Sunderji Samji, to name but a few. Gregory, *Rise and Fall of Philanthropy*; Al Noor Kassum, *Africa's Winds of Change: Memoirs of an International Tanzanian* (London: I. B. Tauris, 2007); Oonk, *Karimjee Jivanjee Family*; Battle, "Old Dispensary"; Seidenberg, *Mercantile Adventureres*, 66–92; Gaurav Desai, "Commerce as Romance: Nanji Kalidas Mehta's *Dream Half Expressed*," *Research in African Literatures* 42, no. 3 (2011): 147–65; Martha Spencer Honey, "A History of Indian Merchant Capital and Class Formation in Tanganyika, c. 1840–1940" (PhD diss., University of Dar es Salaam, 1982): 62, 264–312; J. C. Penrad, "The Ismaili Presence in East Africa: A Note on Its Commercial History and Community Organization," in *Asian Merchants and Businessmen in the Indian Ocean and the China Sea*, ed. D. L. A. J. Aubin (New Delhi: Oxford University Press, 2000). Poignant fictional depictions of youth facing similar circumstance are provided by M. G. Vassanji in his novel *The Book of Secrets* (New York: Picador, 1994) and in Gurnah, *Paradise*.

13. Gregory, *Rise and Fall of Philanthropy*; Desai, "Commerce as Romance"; Honey, "History of Indian Merchant Capital," 264–312; Shirin Walji, "A History of the Ismaili Community in Tanzania" (PhD diss., University of Wisconsin, 1974); Richa Nagar, "Making and Breaking Boundaries: Identity Politics among South Asians in Postcolonial Dar es Salaam" (PhD diss., University of Minnesota, 1995).

14. *Dar es Salaam Times*, February 25, 1920, 4. Ads for charity shows also appeared regularly in the *Zanzibar Official Gazette* during the colonial era, and in

343

the postcolonial period, these shows were commonly advertised or covered as news stories in the *Daily News, Mwaafrika,* and the *Sunday News.* Stars such as Dilip Kumar, John Wayne, Harry Belefonte, Sidney Poitier, and many others were also known to make guest appearances and mingle with the crowds at such events. Taarab, dance, and theater groups were also regularly allowed to perform in these venues. Bunny Reuben, *Dilip Kumar, Star Legend of Indian Cinema: The Definitive Biography* (New Delhi: HarperCollins, 2004), 365. *Tanganyika Trade Bulletin,* May 1961, 8; Agnello Fernandez interview; Ahmed "Eddy" Alwi al-Beity, interviews with the author, November 3 and 27, 2004, Dar es Salaam; Asad Talati, interview with the author, August 24, 2008, Toronto, Canada; Mr. Drive-In, interview with the author, March 11, 2005, Dar es Salaam; Mulji, interview with the author, March 13, 2005, Dar es Salaam.

15. Adam Shafi, interview with the author, May 18, 2005, Dar es Salaam; Ahmed Hussein Choxi, interview with the author, April 12, 2005, Dar es Salaam; Ally "Rocky" Khamis Ally, interview with the author, June 21, 2002, Wete, Pemba; Ameri Slyoum interview; Anonymous, interview with the author, May 18, 2005, Dar es Salaam; Aunti Sofia, interview with the author, February 12, 2004, Zanzibar; Bi Maryam, interview with the author, February 16, 2004, Zanzibar; Fatma Alloo, interview with the author, May 14, 2002, Zanzibar; Mwalim Idd Abdulla Farhan, interview with the author, May 25, 2002, Zanzibar; Mr. India, interview with the author, March 8, 2004, Dar es Salaam; Mzee Mohammed, interview with the author, February 5, 2004, Zanzibar; Robert Kibwana, interview with the author, July 2, 2002, Dar es Salaam; Shabir K. Jariwalla interview; Shanin, interview with the author, May 14, 2002, Zanzibar.

16. Haji Gora Haji, interview with the author, December 24, 2004, Zanzibar.

17. Asha, interview with the author, January 28, 2004, Tanga.

18. Mzee Mohammed interview.

19. Juma, interview with the author, May 23, 2002, Zanzibar.

20. "Standard Notes: Pemba Theater," *Tanganyika Standard,* April 1, 1953, 2; "New Talkies Opened," *Tanganyika Standard,* April 13, 1953, 2; "Lindi Cinema Opened," *Tanganyika Standard,* June 12, 1950, 2; *Tanganyika Standard,* June 17, 1954, 2, and June 24, 1954, 2. On the enhanced stature of residents and their neighborhoods with the building of a cinema, see *Tanganyika Standard,* July 15, 1954, 2, and July 16, 1954, 3; *Tanganyika Standard,* July 18, 1955, 2, and July 23, 1955, 2. Leading trade publications in the United States also encouraged theater owners to consider the naming of their theater with care, as the name of the theater provided the first impression of what patrons were to encounter. *Moving Picture World* went so far as to argue that the name of the theater was an important part of "helping pictures cast their spell," as cited in Fuller, *At the Picture Show,* 54–55.

21. "Obituary of HA Jariwalla."

22. "Brilliant Premier of 'Men of Two Worlds' in Dar es Salaam. Film—100 percent Tanganyika—Puts the Territory Prominently on the World Map," *Tanganyika*

Standard, July 17, 1946, as cut and included in TNA 16276: Feature Film in African Life (Two-Cities Films Ltd.); "Civic Pride," op-ed, *Tanganyika Standard*, March 21, 1952, 2.

23. Shabir K. Jariwalla interview; TNA 13038; TNA 61/172/1; TNA 20496; TNA AB 356. Brennan, "Democratizing Cinema."

24. "A. C. Donne, Chairman of the Cinematograph Licensing Board to Chief Secretary, 16 October 1931," TNA 20496: Scheme for Establishment of Cinematograph Theaters in Native Areas; TNA: District Officer's Report, Tanga District, 1929; TNA 13038, including "HA Jariwalla to Chief Secretary, 8 December 1930."

25. ZNA, AB 5/156: Pemba Cinema, 1935–54.

26. TNA 13038; TNA 13864; "Sound Comes to the Royal," *Supplement to the Official Gazette of Zanzibar*, February 27, 1932; "Twenty-One Years Ago: The First Talkies," *Tanganyika Standard*, February 2, 1953, 2.

27. Asad Talati interviews of August 14, 15, and 16, 2004.

28. Ibid.; Asad Talati e-mail of March 27, 2005; Reinwald, "Tonight at the Empire."

29. Issak Esmail Issak was not alone in saying that when he saw a supermarket where the Empire used to be, he wept. Many in Zanzibar described the Empire as their favorite cinema in the isles. Issak, "Cinema in Zanzibar," Internet posting forwarded to me by Asad Talati, 2008.

30. "Talati to Dutton, 23 July 1946," ZNA, AB 40/55: Application by SH Talati for Lease of Government Land for the Purpose of Building a Cinema in Zanzibar Town.

31. ZNA, AB 9/47: Civic Center Cinema. For more on the role of Ajit Singh Hoogan, who also struggled with his European bosses over "appropriate" built forms for Africa as he worked on the design and construction of Raha Leo, see Myers, *Verandahs of Power*, 76–105.

32. Thomas, "Advantages of Being Ltd.," 51–54. I thank Kenda Mutongi for this reference, which documents how rare it was for anyone other than Europeans to incorporate in East Africa during the colonial era. According to Thomas, among the many hindrances for Africans and Asians in East Africa hoping to move in this direction were the intricate legal and accounting requirements of registration. Indo-African was well placed in this regard, as the senior partner, Shavakshaw Talati, sent three of his sons to study law in England; they returned to Zanzibar in the 1940s and 1950s and presumably aided and encouraged their father in pursuing incorporation. Asad Talati interviews of August 14, 15, and 16, 2004.

33. Kassum, *Africa's Winds of Change*, 3–4. In 1941, Kassum's wife was appointed to a socially prominent position on the cinema censor board. TNA 26633: Cinema Censor Board.

34. Asad Talati e-mail correspondence with the author, April 17, 2004. Talati's love of films is so intense that sixty years after the opening, he could still recall not

345

only the movie the theater screened on opening night but also the actors, actresses, and story line and the particular features that made the film a hit. Kassum, *Africa's Winds of Change*, 14. ZNA, AB 5/131; TNA 13038.

35. Kassum, *Africa's Winds of Change*, 14; Ahmed Hussein Choxi interview; Msafiri Punda, interview with the author, October 21, 2004, Dar es Salaam. The New Chox was opened by the British governor of Tanganyika, the Avalon by the city's mayor.

36. "New Cinema Will Serve Tastes of All Communities," *Tanganyika Standard*, July 16, 1954, 3.

37. Mr. Khambaita, interview with the author, April 19, 2005, Moshi. Sixty years later, the building is still standing strong, though it is now called the ABC. Unlike many who designed their own homes and other buildings in Tanzania, Khambaita at least had some training in the field. He arrived in Tanzania from India in 1942, at the age of eighteen, as an employee of the British service and worked constructing buildings during the war. After the war, he stayed in Tanganyika, joining his extended family, whose main business was working as contractors for civil engineering projects in northern Tanzania. Moshi had had a silent cinema from the early 1930s and a "modern" proper theater, the Plaza, from 1947, but Khambaita's Everest boasted a balcony fully 50 percent larger than the Plaza's, with an enhanced slope to ensure that a short person's view was not blocked by a tall man in the row in front.

38. Lahmeyer, "Tanzania."

39. Akhmed "Eddy" Alwi al-Beity interview of November 3, 2004; Brij Behal, interview with the author, April 24, 2005, Arusha; Chunilal Kala Savani, interviews with the author, June 17, 21, and 23, 2005, Mombasa; Feroz Mukhadam, interview with the author, March 26, 2005, Iringa; Gamdul Sing Hans, interviews with the author, January 22 and April 19, 2004, Arusha; Jitu Savani interview of May 26, 2005; Mr. Khambaita interview; Pankaj Valambia, interview with the author, May 29, 2005, Morogoro; Suresh Solanki, interview with the author, April 23, 2005, Moshi.

40. United States Information Agency (USIA), *Communications Data Book for Africa* (Washington, DC: USIA, 1966), 69–71. TNA 13864; TNA 35999: Film Production by the Colonial Film Unit; TNA 435/B2/1: Dodoma Broadcasting and Films; TNA 435/ B/2/2: Iringa Broadcasting and Films, Cinematograph and Censorship Board; TNA 181/TA/: Mbeya Factory Cites, Cinema and Petrol Godowns.

41. Brij Behal interview; Feroz Mukhadam interview; Gamdul Sing Hans interview of April 19, 2004; Pankaj Valambia interview; Sapna Talkies Ltd. Morogoro, "Trading, Profit and Loss Accounts for the Year Ended 31 December 1994"; Suresh Solanki interview.

42. Many Asian entrepreneurs in the early twentieth century relied on such deposits or loans as a source of capital for starting or expanding businesses. Gregory, *South Asians in East Africa*, 98–105; Vassanji, *Book of Secrets*.

43. Erik Gilbert, *Dhows and the Colonial Economy of Zanzibar, 1860–1970* (Athens: Ohio University Press, 2004); Gregory, *South Asians in East Africa*, 117–58; Honey, "History of Indian Merchant Capital," 487–510.

44. Fair, *Pastimes and Politics*, 46–51; Brennan, *Taifa*, 98–103.

45. The extensive literature on Swahili archaeology and trade with Persia, China, and Great Zimbabwe illustrates the extent of this. For the nineteenth and twentieth centuries, see Rockel, *Carriers of Culture*; Jan-Georg Deutsch, Peter Probst, and Heike Schmidt, eds., *African Modernities: Entangled Meanings in Current Debate* (Oxford: James Currey, 2002); Laura Fair, "Identity, Difference and Dance: Female Initiation in Zanzibar, 1890–1930," *Frontiers: A Journal of Women Studies* 17, no. 3 (1996): 146–72; Fair, "Dressing Up: Clothing, Class and Gender in Post-abolition Urban Zanzibar," *Journal of African History* 39, no. 1 (1998): 63–94; Jeremy Prestholdt, *Domesticating the World: African Consumerism and the Geneologies of Globalization* (Berkeley: University of California Press, 2008).

46. Issak, "Cinema in Zanzibar." Amazingly, the film can be seen on YouTube. The movie also discusses the social and technical challenges of making a film in 1913.

47. Mwalim Idd Abdulla Farhan, interview with the author, May 25, 2002, Zanzibar; Haji Faki Mohammed (aka Haji Garana), interviews with the author, June 3 and July 1, 2002, Zanzibar.

48. Asad Talati, e-mail correspondence with the author, October 1, 2004. Sound first came to cinemas in Pemba only in 1938, when it was introduced at the Regal, in Wete; ZNA, AB 5/156. In the late 1950s, Chaplin was still filling the Majestic in Zanzibar. I myself attended the screening of several Chaplin films in 1989 inside a packed hall, filled with a boisterous crowd, at TASCISI. Fearless Nadia starred in some thirty-four films, many of which were produced by Wadia Movietone, an innovative movie studio in India owned by the Parsi brothers J. B. H. and Homi Wadia, the later of whom was married to Nadia; *Samachar*, January 19, 1958, 2A. See also Reinwald, "Tonight at the Empire."

49. *Samachar*, January 6, 1952, 7; Asad Talati e-mail of April 17, 2004; Asad Talati interviews of August 14, 15, and 16, 2004; ZNA AB 40/55.

50. "Sultana Opens," *Samachar*, January 6, 1952, 7.

51. Asad Talati, interview with the author, August 30, 2004, Toronto, Canada; Fuller, *At the Picture Show*, 195; Allen Eyles, *Odeon Cinemas: From J. Arthur Rank to the Multiplex*, vol. 2 (London: Cinema Theater Association, 2005), 43–44; Gutsch, *History and Social Significance*, 232, 237, 255.

52. "At the Majestic," *Samachar*, January 16, 1938, 2A.

53. "Majestic Cinema Fire," *Tanganyika Standard*, February 11, 1954, 3; *Tanganyika Standard*, August 15, 1954, 3; Nisar Sheraly, *Moto! Moto! Majestic Cinema Is on Fire!* (Dar es Salaam: Desk Top Productions, 2006); Abdulhussein Marashi interview of May 7, 2002.

347

54. In a newspaper article in the *Tanganyika Standard* dated February 16, 1954, the Odeon claimed to be the first theater in Tanzania (and one of a small handful in all of East Africa) to install the new wide screen. The article noted, however, that neither the requisite lens nor films had arrived to allow for a proper debut of CinemaScope technology. "New Wide Screen Comes to Dar es Salaam," *Tanganyika Standard*, February 16, 1954, 5.

55. "New Avalon Cinema Renovations Cost £75,000," *Tanganyika Standard*, March 10, 1955, 3; "Avalon Opening," *Tanganyika Standard*, March 12, 1955, 3. In the 1950s, the exchange rate was $2.80 to £1.

56. "A New Cinema for Dar es Salaam," *Tanganyika Standard*, June 9, 1954, 2; Shabir K. Jariwalla interview of April 25, 2005.

57. "New Cinema at Ilala," *Tanganyika Standard*, July 15, 1954, 4; "New Cinema Will Serve Tastes of All Communities," *Tanganyika Standard*, July 16, 1954, 3; "A New Cinema for Dar es Salaam," *Tanganyika Standard*, June 9, 1954, 2.

58. Agnello Fernandez interview; Gigri, interview with the author, January 17, 2005, Dar es Salaam; Mr. Drive-In interview of March 11, 2005; Mulji interview.

59. This marriage greatly enhanced the stature of Rita Hayworth in Tanzania. "If Rita Turns Moslem," *Samachar*, July 16, 1950, 5; "Rita Plans Her Fourth Marriage," *Samachar*, November 16, 1952, 7; Vassanji, *Book of Secrets*, 243.

60. Tadasu Tsuruta, "Simba or Yanga? Football and Urbanization in Dar es Salaam," in *Dar es Salaam: Histories from an Emerging African Metropolis*, ed. James Brennan, Andrew Burton, and Yusuf Lawi (Dar es Salaam: Mkuki na Nyota, 2007), 198–212; Frank Gunderson and Gregory Barz, eds., *Mashindano: Competitive Music Performance in East Africa* (Dar es Salaam: Mkuki na Nyota, 2000).

61. Trust and reputation remained central to finance and credit in many realms of business through the twentieth century. See, for instance, Bruhwiler, "Moralities of Owing and Lending."

62. Honey, "History of Indian Merchant Capital," 63–66; Gijsbert Oonk, "After Shaking His Hand, Start Counting Your Fingers: Trust and Images of Indian Business Networks, East Africa 1900–2000," *Itinerario* 18, no. 3 (2004): 70–88; Oonk, *Settled Strangers*, 63–110. As Oonk notes, many of those who tried their hands at trade and business ended up failing and returning to India or staying on in East Africa working for others.

63. Gregory, *South Asians in East Africa*, 102–15. Gregory's discussion of this practice includes a charming little vignette of his own experiences, as a graduate student in Kenya, in buying a car from an Asian used car dealer in this manner. For fictionalized accounts of these practices as well as trenchant critiques of the seedier side of such patron-client relations, see Vassanji, *Book of Secrets*, and Gurnah, *Paradise*. For the importance of these relations in the rice trade in Tanzania, see Bruhwiler, "Moralities of Owing and Lending."

64. Shabir K. Jariwalla interview; Chunilal Kala Savani interviews.

65. ZNA 5/127: "CO to Private Secretary 10 September, 1919"; Reinwald, "Tonight at the Empire," 95. This is most likely why Jariwalla named his first two cinemas Alexandra.

66. ZNA 5/127. By the late 1920s, films were longer, necessitating fewer changes for each night's program. In 1927, for instance, there were 123 films imported into Zanzibar. ZNA, AB 5/111: Memorandum on Films, Their Educational Uses and Censorship.

67. There were few permanent facilities for exhibition anywhere in the world at that time. In 1910, Bombay had four permanent venues, Calcutta one. Mexico City also had only one cinema, whereas Singapore and Shanghai each had three, Constantinople ten, and Johannesburg forty. Thompson, *Exporting Entertainment*, 33, 40, 44–45; Thoraval, *Cinemas of India*, 1–19. According to Thoraval, as late as 1927 some 85 percent of the films circulating in India were foreign, and 90 percent of those were American.

68. Rajadhyaksha and Willemen, *Encyclopedia of the Indian Cinema*, 109; Erik Barnouw and S. Krishnaswamy, *Indian Film*, 2nd ed. (New York: Oxford University Press, 1980), 3–10, 68.

69. TNA 13038; TNA 61/172/1; Shabir K. Jariwalla interview.

70. TNA 61/172: Morogoro Cinemas and Theaters.

71. Shabir K. Jariwalla interview.

72. As owners of a family firm, the Savanis grew to international renown by the 1960s and 1970s, operating theaters and/or supplying Indian films to family and associates in Uganda, Malawi, Zambia, Mauritius, Nigeria, Bahrain, Dubai, Muscat, London, Birmingham, Manchester, Bradford, New York, Trinidad, Fiji, Thailand, Afghanistan, and eventually Rotterdam, Amsterdam, Frankfort, and Lisbon as new waves of South Asian immigrants, including Mohanlal's youther brothers and cousins, moved across the globe. Mohanlal, based in Mombasa, was the head of the firm and the one who really knew films. His brother, in Bombay, purchased the copyright and ordered prints as instructed by Chunilal. When a brother went to the United Kingdom for studies in 1955, he leased theaters on Sunday and screened Indian films. Later in 1955, another brother left for Bahrain, and he did the same, and in the mid-1960s, the youngest brother moved to New York and began importing Indian films and distributing in the United States. Mohanlal handled everyone's ordering and booking from Mombasa.

73. Chunilal Kala Savani interviews.

74. Ibid.; Jitu Savani interview of May 26, 2005; "Schlesinger Jubilee Supplement," *Tanganyika Standard*, August 11, 1953, 4–8. When Samji Kala did finally enter the market in Nairobi, however, he entered in style. The Embassy, with eight hundredseats, allegedly was the first cinema in East Africa designed by an architect from London.

75. Chunilal Kala Savani interviews; Jitu Savani interview of May 26, 2005; Asad Talati, e-mail correspondence with the author, August 26 and March 27, 2004;

349

"Gala Opening of Majestic Cinema, Tanga," *Tanganyika Standard*, February 25, 1954, 1; Ministry of Industries and Trade, RC, File 4622: Majestic Film Distributors Tanzania Ltd.

76. Zanzibaris were indeed a fickle and discerning lot when it came to the consumption of global commodities. In the nineteenth century, they prided themselves on setting the fashion trends of East Africa. Goods first arrived in Zanzibar's ports, and what did not sell there was traded to Pemba and then to lesser markets on the mainland. Once something had passed out of fashion, it simply could not be sold in the isles. See Fair, "Dressing Up"; Prestholdt, *Domesticating the World*.

77. Kassum, *Africa's Winds of Change*, 14; Ahmed Hussein Choxi interview.

78. Ministry of Industries and Trade, RC, File 1488: Indo-African Theaters Ltd.; ZNA, AD 5/80: Correspondence of Censorship Panel, 1966–67; TNA 13038; Natwar Joshi, "A Nostalgic Look at Naaz Cinema," accessed at www.sikh-heritage.co.uk/sikhhert EAfrica/nostalgic-Mombasa.html.accessed March 18, 2015.

79. Asad Talati, interviews with the author, May 22 2004, and August 14, 15, and 16, 2004, Toronto, Canada.

80. Over the course of fifteen months, from February 1, 1954, to May 13, 1955, 360 Indian films and 35 Egyptian films were approved or renewed by the censorship board in Dar es Salaam. From January 1956 through August 1958, the board reviewed 616 Indian and 154 Arabic films. TNA 13038; Cinematograph Ordinance, permit records 1954–55 and 1956–58. Censorship records for Zanzibar indicate that 102 films were reviewed from India and Egypt in 1954 and 119 in 1955, jumping to 167 one year later. Films from Russia, Japan, Italy, and France were also imported by East African independent distributors, although these usually numbered fewer than 10 each year. ZNA, AD 5/75: Film Censorship, 1954–63.

81. Shabir K. Jariwalla interview.

82. Men dabbled in distribution over the years, but their success was limited by their bad reputations and less than honest practices. Only when I broke the ice and mentioned my own troublesome encounters with some of these individuals did others share their personal stories or their regret and remorse related to dealings with these people. Verbal contracts were typical of nearly all African and Asian businesses in the first half of the twentieth century, as was the importance of reputation and honesty for maintaining access to credit or supply. Christine Dobbin, *Asian Entrepreneurial Minorities: Conjoint Communities in the Making of the World-Economy, 1570–1940* (Richmond, UK: Curzon Press, 1996), 96; Oonk, "After Shaking His Hand"; Gregory, *South Asians in East Africa*, 98–101; Jalloh, *African Entrepreneurship*; Abner Cohen, "Cultural Strategies in the Organization of Trading Diasporas," in *The Development of Indigenous Trade and Markets in West Africa*, ed. C. Meillassoux (London: Oxford University Press, 1971), 266–84; Cohen, "The Social Organization of Credit in a West African Cattle Market," *Africa* 35 (1965): 8–20; Polly Hill, *Studies in Rural Capitalism in West Africa* (Cambridge: Cambridge University Press, 1970); Paul Lovejoy, *Caravans of*

Kola: The Hausa Kola Trade, 1700–1900 (Zaria, Nigeria: Ahmadu Bello University Press, 1980).

83. Pendakur and Subramanyam, "Indian Cinema beyond National Borders," 72–73; Adarsh, *Film Industry of India*, 127, 31–32, 300.

84. Gainer, "Exploitation"; Jagarnath, "Indian Cinema in Durban."

85. Shabir K. Jariwalla interview.

86. Asad Talati, e-mail correspondence with the author, August 31, 2004; Chunilal Kala Savani interviews; Mr. Khambaita interview; Joshi, "Nostalgic Look at Naaz Cinema."

87. Joshi, "'Nostalgic Look at Naaz Cinema."

88. Thompson, *Exporting Entertainment*, 33–40; ZNA, AB 5/111; ZNA, AB 5/127.

89. Gainer, "Hollywood, African Consolidated Films," esp. 87–113; Gainer, "Exploitation"; Gutsch, *History and Social Significance*, 112–20; Thompson, *Exporting Entertainment*, 4–46; Burns, *Cinema and Society*, 61–65, 74–75. Schlesinger's counterpart in Australia was J. D. Williams, another American immigrant who finessed a similar stranglehold on the exhibition and distribution industries during this same period.

90. Wisconsin Historical Society (hereafter cited as WHS), O'Brien Legal Files, US MSS 99 AN/2A, Box 39, Folder 11; WHS, "United Artists Foreign Sales Manager to O'Brien, 11 September 1934," United Artist Collection, Series 2A, O'Brien Legal Files, MS 99 AN/2A, Box 81, File 6; Bureau of Foreign and Domestic Commerce, US Department of Commerce, *Small Island Markets for American Motion Pictures* (Washington, DC: US Government Printing Office, 1931), 3; Gutsch, *History and Social Significance*, 230–58. Walsh, "Internationalism of the American Cinema"; "Ilalla Cinema," *Tanganyika Standard*, July 16, 1954, 3.

91. Abdulhussein Marashi interview of May 7, 2002. Jariwalla paid MGM and UA 35 to 50 percent of the box office in the late 1930s and early 1940s. Records for other periods and theaters are difficult to find. Available records in South Africa on the Schlesinger Corporation say almost nothing about finances during this early period. WHS, Center for Film and Theater Research, United Artists Corporation Records, Series 2A, O'Brien Legal File, 1919–51, MS 99 AN/2A, Box 81, File 6: United Artists Corporation and Culver Export Corporation, Foreign Sales Manager to O'Brien, September 11, 1934; WHS, MS 39/11, File 156: International Variety and Theatrical Agency, African Consolidated Films, License Agreement for Africa; WHS, United Artists Corporation, Series 2F: Foreign Correspondence and Legal File, 1930–1953.

92. Typical terms were block-booked contracts from two to five years in length, but in South Africa, Schlesinger was known to force small independents to sign for as long as ten years. SANA, Records of the Board of Trade and Industries, RHN 178 2/101/9/1: Board of Trade Investigation in Terms of Monopoly Act, Monopoly Conditions in Specific Branches of Industry Trade: Motion Pictures, 1959–1967; SAB, Records of the Board of Trade and Industries, RHN 181 2/107/9/2: Representation

352

Submitted by the Association of Motion Picture Exhibitors. I am deeply indebted to Dr. Jill Kelly for expending time and effort in tracking down these records in South Africa for me. Thompson, *Exporting Entertainment*, 126; Tino Balio, ed., *The American Film Industry*, 2nd ed. (Madison: University of Wisconsin Press, 1985), 117; Guback, "Hollywood's International Market," 463–86; Gainer, "Exploitation"; McFeely, "'Gone Are the Days,'" 191–92.

93. A review of ads in the *Samachar*, published in Zanzibar during the 1930s.

94. Abdulhussein Marashi interviews of May 7 and 15, 2002; Asad Talati interviews of August 14, 15, and 15, 2004; Asad Talati e-mail of April 17, 2004; Chunilal Kala Savani interviews ; Mr. Khambaita interview; Shabir K. Jariwalla interview.

95. McFeely, "'Gone Are the Days,'" 190–91 and also 21, 29–30, 48, 203. Powerdmaker's analysis of the films screened in Zambia reveals a similar pattern. Powdermaker, *Copper Town*; Ambler, "Cowboy Modern," 348–63; James Burns, "John Wayne on the Zambezi: Cinema, Empire and the American Western in British Central Africa," *International Journal of African Historical Studies* 35, no. 1 (2002): 103–17; Gondola, "Manhood and the Cult of the Cowboy," 173–99.

96. Film ads in the *Samachar* and *Tanganyika Standard*, 1950. Chunilal Kala Savani interviews; Asad Talati e-mail of August 31, 2004. 97. Film ads in the *Samachar*.

98. This became a common strategy used by producers from the 1950s on, both as a way to secure the necessary financing to finish a film and to guarantee commitments to purchase the product. The risks for distributors in such cases were exceptionally high, since there was also no guarantee when or even if a given film would be done.

99. Asad Talati interviews of August 14, 15, and 16, 2004; Chanu Vadgama, interview with the author, October 5, 2004, Dar es Salaam; Chunilal Kala Savani interviews; Feruz Hussein, interview with the author, June 25, 2002, Zanzibar; Jitu Savani interview of May 26, 2005.

100. Feroz Mukhadam interview. ZNA, AB 5/156; ZNA, AB 5/127; TNA 435/B2/1: Dodoma Broadcasting and Films: 1947–63; TNA 435/B/2/2: Iringa Broadcasting and Films, Cinematograph and Censorship Board, 1937–57.

101. Shabir K. Jariwalla interview.

102. ZNA, AH 17/30: Entertainment Tax, 1947–82; ZNA, AB 9/47: Civic Center Cinema; ZNA, DO/17: Reporti ya Sinema Majestic.

103. RC File 1488: Indo-African Theaters Ltd.

104. RC File 1546: Majestic Theaters Ltd., Tanga; RC File 5142: Dodoma Paradise Cinema Ltd.; RC File 7717: Novelty Cinema Ltd., Lindi; RC File 8747: New Chox Theater Ltd., Dar es Salaam. The Talatis borrowed the money for the construction of he Sutlana from the Public Trust (Mambo Msiige), taking out a thirty-year mortgage, which they had to refinance through Standard Bank after the revolution in 1964. In a rare exception, the members of the Indo-African group managed to pay off their debt of 300,000 shillings incurred for building their theater in Mombasa in a mere ten years. RC File 1488: Indo-African Theaters Ltd.

105. ZNA, AB 9/47: "Schedule A: Rasul's Estimate of Losses."

106. ZNA, AH 17/30; ZNA, DO 40/17. RC File 1546: Majestic Theaters Ltd., Tanga; RC File 2040: Empire Cinema, Dar es Salaam; RC File 8747: New Chox Cinema, Dar es Salaam; RC File 7717: Novelty, Tanga; RC File 6810: Metropole, Arusha; RC File 5142: Paradise, Dodoma.

107. *International Motion Picture Almanac* (New York: Quigley Publishing, 1978), 32A.

108. ZNA, AB 9/47; ZNA, DO 40/17; ZNA AH 17/30: "Majestic Theaters Zanzibar Ltd. Income and Expenditure Accounts for the Year Ended 31st December, 1973"; "Majestic Cinema Zanzibar, Trading, Profit and Loss Account for the Year Ended 31st December, 1985," private archive, in possession of author; RC File 1546: "Majestic Theater Ltd., Tanga, Film Exhibition, Profit and Loss Account for the Year Ending 31 December, 1986."

109. Owners also stressed, however, that the price of not providing free tickets could cost them more in the end, since censors did have the power to deny permits; require cuts of the most crowd-pleasing scenes; or file complaints with municipal authorities about lax attention to fire, cleaning, or other codes. Running a business that depended on public satisfaction and enthusiasm required that owners and managers be on good terms with everyone. Brennan, "Democratizing Cinema"; "Zamu za Kuchungua [*sic*] Sinema, October 1967," ZNA, AD 5/81: Correspondence Stage Plays and Cinematograph Censorship Panels, 1967 September–1968 August; "Bodi ya Ukaguzi wa Filamu za Sinema ya Taifa, Kazi ya bodi pamoja na misingi ya uamuzi inayotumiwa katika kukagua picha, 27 August 1976," Board of Film Censor Records. Even during the colonial era, distributors and exhibitors complained bitterly about having to provide free admission to censors for regularly scheduled screenings. MGM, 20th Century Fox, and United Artists sent numerous letters to colonial official in Tanganyika registering such complaints. This correspondence, dating from 1947 to 1949, can be found in TNA 13038, vol. 6.

110. ZNA, AH 17/30.

111. Indeed, all the documentation found on the Schlesinger organization in the South African archives was amassed and preserved as part of the hearings into potentially unfair trade and business practices developing in South Africa as a result of 20th Century Fox's acquisition of ACF. RC File 4298: Anglo-American Film Distributors Ltd.

Chapter 2: The Men Who Made the Movies Run, 1940s–90s

1. Akhtar Amir, interview with the author, June 26, 2002, Zanzibar.

2. *Mjomba* translates as "uncle," but it is often used by Swahili speakers to create fictive kinship ties or claims of reciprocity between themselves and an elderly or powerful man. Men who worked at the cinema were frequently called mjomba by many, especially by kids from the neighborhood.

3. Estimate of Expenses, "Savakshaw Talati to Secretary Central Development Authority 8 November, 1947," ZNA, AB 9/47: Civic Center Cinema. The wages of two operators were 225 shillings per month; three boys, 100 per month; two ticket sellers, 60; manager, 150; "Estimate of Costs, 17 November 1964," ZNA, DO 40/17: Ripoti ya Sinema ya Majestic, lists the number of employees at thirteen.

4. *Samachar*, January 16, 1938, 2A; "Lindi Cinema Opened," *Tanganyika Standard*, June 12, 1950, 2; "A New Cinema for Dar es Salaam," *Tanganyika Standard*, June 9, 1954, 2; "Majestic Cinema Fire," *Tanganyika Standard*, February 11, 1954, 3; "Hassanali Jeffer Hameer to Mkamao wa Rais, Bwana Abedi Amani Karume, 6 January, 1965," ZNA, DO 40/17: Ripoti ya Sinema ya Majestic, 1964–65.

5. Ally "Rocky" Khamis Ally interview.

6. Ahmed Hussein Choxi interview; Kassum, *Africa's Winds of Change*, 14. Such "adoptions" of young men by older, more experienced, and wealthy traders and merchants was also common in many other areas of African trade and business. Cohen, "Social Organization of Credit," 13; Abner Cohen, *Custom and Politics in Urban Africa* (London: Routledge and Kegan Paul, 1969), 86–92; Jalloh, *African Entrepreneurship*, 63, 125; Vassanji, *Book of Secrets*, 133–50.

7. Ahmed "Eddy" Alwi al-Beity interview of November 3, 2004.

8. Mulji interview.

9. Nitesh Virji, interview with the author, April 25, 2005, Moshi.

10. Shabir K. Jariwalla interview.

11. Romeo, interview with the author, March 15, 2005, Dar es Salaam.

12. The sound tracks for Hindi films were typically released on gramophone discs and later cassette tapes well before the film. The idea was to familiarize people with the music and entice them to view the film. Pictorial depictions of these men can be found in "Street Publicity," *Showman* 3, no. 3 (1954): 12; Sheraly, *Moto! Moto!*, 5; Abdulhussein Marashi interviews of May 7 and May 15, 2002; Ally "Rocky" Khamis Ally interview; Bi Maryam interview; Haji Faki Mohammed (aka Haji Garana) interviews; Jitu Savani interview of May 26, 2005; Kasanga, interviews with the author, December 16, 2004, and March 5, 2005, Dar es Salaam; Maryam Yahya, interview with the author, June 3, 2002, Zanzibar; Mr. Khambaita interview; Mwalim Idd Abdulla Farhan interview of May 25, 2002; Rashid Said, interview with the author, December 23, 2004, Zanzibar; Semeni Juma, interview with the author, March 20, 2002, Bagamoyo; Shabir K. Jariwalla interview.

13. Abdulhussein Marashi interview of May 7, 2002.

14. TNA 13038; TNA AB 264: Films, Control and Rules under the Township Ordinance; TNA 435/B2/1: Dodoma Broadcasting and Films: 1947–63; TNA 435/B/2/2: Iringa Broadcasting and Films, Cinematograph and Censorship Board, 1937–57; TNA 188/GEN/1/25: Mtwara Cinemas; TNA 18931: Cinematograph Ordinance, 1930; TNA 61/172: Morogoro Cinemas and Theaters; ZNA, AB 5/126: Pemba Cinema, 1935–54; ZNA, AB 5/127: Rules under the Stage Plays and Cinematograph Exhibitions Decree 1917–1943; ZNA, AB 5/111: Films, Their Educational Uses, and

Censorship. A fire occurred at the Ritz Cinema in Morogoro in 1953, damaging the projectors and projection room. *Tanganyika Standard*, March 24, 1953, 3. Fires at film warehouses were far more common and difficult to extinguish, often destroying the contents of the building before the fire could be contained. ZNA, AB 5/127; *Tanganyika Standard*, March 6, 1953, 1; Burns, "African Bioscope," 65; Larkin, *Signal and Noise*, 141–42.

15. Abdulhussein Marashi interview of May 7, 2002; Ally "Rocky" Khamis Ally interview; Saidi, interview with the author, April 26, 2005, Moshi; Msafiri Punda interview. ZNA, DO 40/17: Ripoti ya Sinema ya Majestic, 1964–65; ZNA, AB 9/47.

16. Abdulhussein Marashi interview of May 7, 2002; Ally "Rocky" Khamis Ally interview; Saidi interview; Msafiri Punda interview; Suresh Solanki interview; Pankaj Valambia interview.

17. Suresh Solanki interview; Tanga Messrs., Majestic Theaters Ltd., "Balance Sheet: Film Exhibition, Profit and Loss" (1980), "Film Exhibition, Profit and Loss" (1981), "Film, Exhibition, Profit and Loss Account for the Year Ended 31 December, 1982" (1982), "Film Exhibition, Profit and Loss" (1984), "Film Exhibition, Profit and Loss" (1985), "Film Exhibition Profit and Loss" (1986), "Film Exhibition, Profit and Loss" (1987).

18. *The Showman*, an industry newsletter promoting professionalization of the trade, produced by African Consolidated Films in South Africa, featured more articles on the importance, skill, and training of projectionists and the possible errors that could be made with splicing than any other topic related to the industry. Each monthly issue from 1948 through 1956 featured elaborate and often highly technical articles aimed at improving the professional knowledge and skill of projectionists. As the main distributor of American films in Africa, African Consolidated had a vested interest in preserving the quality of its prints.

19. The files on censorship are extensive, and only a few are cited here. Office of the Board of Film Censors, Dar es Salaam: Karatasi ya Uchunguzi wa Filamu za Cinema, 1977–1985 and 1993–2000; Board of Film Censors: confidential letters and memos, 1964–78; TNA 622/s1/B1: Bodi ya Filamu includes the postcolonial censorship rules and guidelines, which in many ways are mere translations of the colonial rules with but a few modifications; TNA 13038: Cineamtograph Films Censorship and Display; US Department of Commerce, *World Trade in Commodities*, February 1950, vol. 8, pt. 4, no 6, 1.

20. Nitesh Virji, describing the relationship of the projectionist at the Plaza with his machines.

21. Ally "Rocky" Khamis Ally interview.

22. Pankaj Valambia interview.

23. Haji Faki Mohammed (aka Haji Garana) interview of June 3, 2002.

24. Haji Garana, interview with the author, June 3, 2002; Mwalim Idd Farhan interview of May 25, 2002; Ameri Slyoum interview; Abdulhussein Marashi interview of May 7, 2002; Feruz Hussein interview of June 25, 2002; Haji Faki

Mohammed interview of June 3, 2002; Ahmed Hussein Choxi interview; Kasanga interview of December 16, 2004; Khamis Msellem, December 16, 2004, Dar es Salaam; Rashid Said interview; Taday, interview with the author, December 20, 2004, Dar es Salaam; Msafiri Punda interview. Complaints about the cost of black market tickets frequently generated two or more letters each month. See, for example, these letters to the editor : "Cinema Tickets," *Tanganyika Standard*, March 5, 1954, 2; "Cinema Racket," *Tanganyika Standard*, March 24, 1954, 2; "Cinema Tickets," *Tanganyika Standard*, April 9, 1954, 2; "Black Market in Tickets," *Tanganyika Standard*, October 22, 1955, 2.

25. Kasanga interview of December 16, 2004; Khamis Msellem, interview; Rashid Said interview; Taday interview; Msafiri Punda interview. On the difficulties of getting tickets and the role of the black market in India see Srinivas, *House Full*, 105–15.

26. Kasanga, interview of December 16, 2004.

27. Taday interview.

28. Kasanga, interview of December 16, 2004.

29. Khamis Msellem, interview.

30. The bus excursions to see banned films were mentioned by the acting colonial secretary in a memo dated November 24, 1948, TNA 13038, vol. 6.

31. Shabir K. Jariwalla interview. Set during the height of the Cold War, the film tells the story of a man suddenly released from a Siberian labor camp who becomes the pope and averts a nuclear war through diplomacy

32. In March 1965, the *Standard* printed numerous tirades against the banning of *Goldfinger*. Finally, the editors refused to print any more letters on the topic. Debates about the anti-Soviet and anti-Chinese nature of many popular films were rampant among those on the censor board. Office of the Board of Film Censors, Confidential Letters and Memos, 1964–78, "Richard Kisch to Yusuf Marsha, 23 February 1965" and "YA Marsha to All Ministers, 7 March 1964"; Joe Adelhelm John Mponguliana, "The Development of Film in Tanzania" (master's thesis, University of Dar es Salaam, 1982), 84; Abdulhussein Marashi interview of May 15, 2002; Brennan, "Democratizing Cinema," 481–511.

33. Khamis Msellem, interview.

34. Sultan Jessa, "Black Market of Cinema Tickets Still on in Dar," *Nationalist*, May 22, 1963, 7.

35. Abdulhussein Marashi interview of May 15, 2002; Agnello Fernandez interview; Ameri Slyoum interview; Ahmed "Eddy" Alwi al-Beity interview of November 27, 2004; Mwalim Idd Abdulla Farhan interview of May 25, 2002; Darwesh, interview with the author, February 7, 2004, Zanzibar.

36. *Daily News*, September 24, 1983, 9–10.

37. Ameri Slyoum interview.

38. Darwesh interview.

39. Gigri interview.

40. Movie-house popcorn is allegedly the most profitable commodity ever sold. American trade magazines kept rigorous statistics on concession stand sales. Typical theaters earned roughly seventeen cents at the concession stand for every dollar spent at the ticket window. At the drive-in, these rates increased to over forty cents on the dollar. Often, more than one-third of a drive-in owner's total net came from the concession stand. Blockbuster films such as *Spiderman* or children's movies also allowed profits to soar for concessionaires at brick-and-mortar theaters. Arthouse cinemas, by contrast, suffered not only because their audiences were small but also and more importantly because the patrons bought almost nothing at the concession stand. Statistics from South Africa too show that concession stand earnings were 25 percent of box office earnings. "Statement of Accounts for Shah Hanah Theaters, 1958, Including Milk Bar Takings," SANA RHN 179/2/101/9/1, vol. 1; 1959 *Year Book of Motion Pictures*, 105, placed US earnings on popcorn alone above $126,000; *Film Daily Year Book of Motion Pictures* 1969, 109; Deborah Allison, "Multiplex Programing in the UK: The Economics of Homogeneity," *Screen* 47, no. 1 (2006): 81–90; George M. Petersen, *Drive-In Theater: Manual of Design and Operation* (Kansas City, MO: Associated, 1953), 25–27; Kerry Segrave, *Drive-In Theaters: A History from Their Inception in 1933* (Jefferson, NC: McFarland, 1992), 89–98, 227–32.

41. Abdulhussein Marashi, interview with the author, February 4, 2004, Zanzibar; Ally "Rocky" Khamis Ally interview; Feruz Hussein, interview with the author, July 6, 2002, Zanzibar; Asad Talati interviews of August 14, 15, and 16, 2004.

42. Nasson, "She Preferred Living in a Cave," 285–310.

43. Asad Talati interviews of August 14, 15, and 16, 2004; Feruz Hussein interviews of July 6, 2002 and June 25, 2002; Msafiri Punda interview; Naaz Rana, interview with the author, October 21, 2004, Dar es Salaam; Robert Kibwana interview.

Chapter 3: Making Love in the Indian Ocean

1. TNA 435 B/2/2: Iringa Broadcasting and Films, Cinematograph and Censorship Board; TNA 246/c.5/10: Mwanza Cinema Censorship Board; Adam Shafi interview; Haji Faki Mohammed (aka Haji Garana) interviews; Haji Gora Haji interview; Mwalim Idd Abdulla Farhan interview of May 25, 2002; Adam Shafi interview; Shabir K. Jariwalla interview.

2. Kelly Askew, *Performing the Nation: Swahili Music and Cultural Politics in Tanzania* (Chicago: University of Chicago Press, 2002); Ann Biersteker, "Language, Poetry and Power: A Reconsideration of '*Utendi Wa Mwana Kupona*,'" in *Faces of Islam in African Literature*, ed. Ken Harrow (Portsmouth, NH: Heinemann, 1991), 59–77; Minou Fuglesang, *Veils and Videos: Female Youth Culture on the Kenyan Coast* (Stockholm: Department of Social Anthropology, Stockholm University, 1994); Jan Knappert, *Four Centuries of Swahili Verse: A Literary History and Anthology* (London: Heinemann Educational, 1979); Knappert. "Swahili Songs with Double-Entendre," *Afrika and Ubersee* 66, no. 1 (1983): 67–76; Fair,

357

"Identity, Difference and Dance," 146–72; Margaret Strobel, *Muslim Women of Mombasa, 1890–1975* (New Haven, CT: Yale University Press, 1979); Strobel, *Three Swahili Women: Life Histories from Mombasa, Kenya* (Bloomington: Indiana University Press, 1989). The didactic role of literary and performance cultures in West Africa also has a rich historiography. Karin Barber, *The Generation of Plays: Yoruba Popular Life in Theater* (Bloomington: Indiana University Press, 2000); Stephanie Newell, *Ghanaian Popular Fiction: "Thrilling Discoveries in Conjugal Life" & Other Tales* (Athens: Ohio University Press, 2000).

3. Beth L. Bailey, *From Front Porch to Back Seat: Courtship in Twentieth-Century America* (Baltimore: Johns Hopkins University Press, 1988); Keith Breckenridge, "Love Letters and Amanuenses: Beginning the Cultural History of the Working Class Private Sphere in Southern Africa, 1900–1933," *Journal of Southern African Studies* 26, no. 2 (2000): 337–48; Anthony Giddens, *The Transformation of Intimacy: Sexuality, Love, and Eroticism in Modern Societies* (Stanford, CA: Stanford University Press, 1992); Bryna Goodman, "All the Feelings That Are Fit to Print: The Community of Sentiment and the Literary Public in China, 1900–1918," *20th Century China* 27, no. 3 (2006): 291–327; Jeffrey Watt, *The Making of Modern Marriage: Matrimonial Control and the Rise of Sentiment in Neuchatel, 1550–1800* (Ithaca, NY: Cornell University Press, 1992).

4. In 1948, the total population of Zanzibar was 265,000, and only 15,000 had attended government schools. Fewer than 3,000 of this total were women. E. Batson, "Social Survey of Zanzibar Protectorate" (Cape Town: School of Social Sciences and Social Administration at the University of Cape Town, 1960), 10:1–10; Corrie Decker, "Reading, Writing and Respectability: How Schoolgirls Developed Modern Literacies in Colonial Zanzibar," *International Journal of African Historical Studies* 43, no. 1 (2010): 89–114.

5. Fuglesang, *Veils and Videos*, 157.

6. Newell, *Ghanaian Popular Fiction*.

7. Giddens, *Transformation of Intimacy*; Janice A. Radway, *Reading the Romance: Women, Patriarchy, and Popular Literature* (Chapel Hill: University of North Carolina Press, 1984).

8. Haji Gora Haji interview.

9. D. Iordanova, et al., "Indian Cinema's Global Reach," 114.

10. Barnouw and Krishnaswamy, *Indian Film*, 153; Gayatri Chatterjee, *Awara* (New Delhi: Wiley Eastern, 1992), 160–62; Wimal Dissanayake and Malti Sahai, *Sholay, a Cultural Reading* (New Delhi: Wiley Eastern, 1992), 42; Rajagopalan, *Indian Films in Soviet Cinemas*; Rosie Thomas, "Sanctity and Scandal: The Mythologization of Mother India," *Quarterly Review of Film and Video* 11, no. 3 (1989): 23; Rajadhyaksha and Willemen, *Encyclopedia of the Indian Cinema*, 321–22; Andrew Eisenberg, "The Resonance of Place: Vocal Expression and the Communal Imagination in Old Town, Mombassa, Kenya" (PhD diss., Columbia University, 2008).

11. Asad Talati, e-mail correspondence with the author, June 14, 2008.

12. Ravi Vasudevan, "Shifting Codes, Dissolving Identities: The Hindi Social Film of the 1950s as Popular Culture," in *Making Meaning in Indian Cinema*, ed. Ravi Vasudevan (New Delhi: Oxford University Press, 2000), 99–121.

13. Thomas, "Sanctity and Scandal," 23.

14. D. Chute, review of *The Kapoors: The First Family of Indian Cinema*, by Madhu Jain, *Film Comment* 42, no. 6 (2006): 79–97; Dickey, *Cinema and the Urban Poor*; Barnouw and Krishnaswamy, *Indian Film*; Lalit Mohan Joshi, *Bollywood: Popular Indian Cinema*, 2nd ed. (London: Dakini Books, 2002); Larkin, "Indian Films and Nigerian Lovers," 406–40; Vijay Mishra, *Bollywood Cinema: Temples of Desire* (New York: Routledge, 2002); Ashis Nandy, ed., *The Secret Politics of Our Desires: Innocence, Culpability and Indian Popular Cinema* (London: Zed, 1998); Rajagopalan, *Indian Films in Soviet Cinemas*; Rosie Thomas, "Indian Cinema: Pleasures and Popularity," *Screen* 26, no. 3 (1985): 116–31; Thomas, "Sanctity and Scandal"; Ravi Vasudevan, "Addressing the Spectator of a 'Third World' National Cinema: The Bombay Social Film of the the 1940s and 1950s," *Screen* 36, no. 4 (1995): 305–24; Vasudevan, "You Cannot Live in Society—and Ignore It: Nationhood and Female Modernity in Andaz," *Contributions to Indian Sociology* 29, no. 1 (1995): 83–108; Vasudevan, "Shifting Codes, Dissolving Identities."

15. Alwiyya, interview with the author, November 28, 2008, Bloomington, IN.

16. Juma Sultan, interview with the author, May 17, 2005, Dar es Salaam.

17. Thomas, "Sanctity and Scandal"; Vasudevan, "You Cannot Live in Society."

18. Larkin, "Indian Films and Nigerian Lovers."

19. Chatterjee, *Awara*; Vasudevan, "Shifting Codes, Dissolving Identities"; Jyotika Virdi, *The Cinematic Imagination: Indian Popular Films as Social History* (New Brunswick, NJ: Rutgers University Press, 2003); Tejaswini Ganti, *Bollywood: A Guidebook to Popular Hindi Cinema* (New York: Routledge, 2004), 28–29; Rachel Dwyer, *All You Want Is Money*; Rachel Dwyer and Christopher Pinney, *Pleasure and the Nation: The History, Politics, and Consumption of Public Culture in India* (New Delhi: Oxford University Press, 2001); Sanjeeve Prakash, "Music, Dance, and the Popular Films: Indian Fantasies, Indian Repressions," in *Indian Cinema Superbazaar*, ed. Aruna Vasudev and Philippe Lenglet (Delhi: Vikas Publishing, 1983), 114–18.

20. The Motion Picture Production Code was a set of guidelines adopted by all the major US studios in the 1930s. The code was commonly known as the Hays Code, after the chief censor at the time, Will Hays, who was also responsible for the establishment of the Motion Picture Association of America (MPAA). The code made an explicit list of thirty-six things that should not be portrayed in film (this included sex, interracial couples, crime, and sedition that did not result in conviction and imprisonment) or whose inclusion could result in the film being banned. The net result was that for more than thirty years, Hollywood largely self-censored its productions and agreed not to portray certain socially and politically questionable topics. Class tensions, the exploitation of the working class,

359

360 or armed struggle against capital were all studiously avoided. Thomas Doherty, *Hollywood's Censor: Joseph I. Breen and the Production Code Administration* (New York: Columbia University Press, 2007); Guback, "Hollywood's International Market," 463–86; Robert Sklar, *Movie-Made America: A Cultural History of American Movies* (New York: Vintage Books, 1994).

21. Mishra, *Bollywood Cinema*; Nandy, "Popular Indian Cinema as a Slums' Eye View," 1–18; Vasudevan, "You Cannot Live in Society"; Virdi, *Cinematic Imagination.*

22. Malti Sahai, "Raj Kapoor and the Indianization of Charlie Chaplin," *East-West Film Journal* 2, no. 1 (1987): 62–75.

23. Chatterjee, *Awara*, 32.

24. Nandy, "Indian Popular Cinema as a Slums' Eye View," 1–18.

25. Mama Ak, interview with the author, June 26, 2002, Zanzibar.

26. Vasudevan, "Addressing the Spectator"; Vasudevasn, "Shifting Codes, Dissolving Identities."

27. Thomas, "Sanctity and Scandal", Vasudevan, "Addressing the Spectator"; Vasudevan, "Shifting Codes, Dissolving Identities."

28. Larkin, "Indian Films and Nigerian Lovers."

29. Ameri Slyoum interview; Nasra Mohammed, interview with the author, May 21, 2002, Zanzibar; Mwalim Idd Abdulla Farhan interview of May 25, 2002.

30. Bi Maryam interview.

31. Adam Shafi interview.

32. Fuglesang, *Veils and Videos*, 238; Françoise Le Guennec-Coppens, *Wedding Customs in Lamu* (Nairobi: Lamu Society, 1980); Sarah Mirza and Margaret Strobel, *Three Swahili Women: Life Histories from Mombasa, Kenya* (Bloomington: Indiana University Press, 1989); Leila Sheik-Hashim, *Unyago: Traditional Family Life Education among the Muslim Digo, Seguju, Bondei, Sambaa and Sigua of Tanga Region* (Dar es Salaam: Tanzania Media Women's Association, 1989); Carl Velten, *Desturi Za Wasuaheli* (Gottingen, Germany: Dandehoed and Rupercht, 1901), 67–80, 86; Fair, "Identity, Difference and Dance"; Muhammed Saleh Farsy, *Ada Za Harusi Katika Unguja* (Dar es Salaam: East African Literature Bureau, 1965); Strobel, *Muslim Women of Mombasa*, 10–12, 196–203.

33. Mohamed H. Abdulaziz and Hajji ibn Muyaka , *Muyaka: 19th Century Swahili Popular Poetry* (Nairobi: Kenya Literature Bureau, 1979); Biersteker, "Language, Poetry and Power"; Ann Joyce Biersteker, *Kujibizana: Questions of Language and Power in Nineteenth- and Twentieth-Century Poetry in Kiswahili* (East Lansing: Michigan State University Press, 1996); Ali Jahadhmy, *Anthology of Swahili Poetry* (London: Heinemann, 1977); Knappert, *Four Centuries of Swahili Verse.*

34. Askew, *Performing the Nation*; Mwenda Ntarangwi, *Gender, Performance & Identity: Understanding Swahili Cultural Identity through Songs* (Trenton, NJ: Africa World Press, 2001).

35. Geoffrey Kitula King'ei, "Language, Culture and Communication: The Role of Swahili Taarab Songs in Kenya, 1963–1990" (PhD diss., Howard University, 1992), 131.

36. Song books of Ikhwan Safaa/Malindi, 1959–63, courtesy of Mwalim Idd Farhan.

37. Kishore Valicha, *The Moving Image: A Study of Indian Cinema* (Bombay: Orient Longman, 1988), 44.

38. Natalie Sarrazin, "Celluloid Love Songs: Musical *Modus Operandi* and the Dramatic Aesthetics of Romantic Hindi Film," *Popular Music* 27, no. 3 (2008): 393–411; Teri Skillman, "The Bombay Hindi Film Song Genre: A Historical Survey," *Yearbook for Traditional Music* 18 (1986): 133–44.

39. Valicha, *Moving Image*, 44.

40. Mama Ak interview.

41. Pendakur, *Indian Popular Cinema*, 119.

42. Rajadhyaksha and Willemen *Encyclopedia of Indian Cinema*, 300; Chatterjee, *Awara*, 127–40; Iordanova, "Indian Cinema's Global Reach," 124.

43. Mama Ak interview; Nasra Mohammed interview; Adam Shafi interview; Agnello Fernandez interview; Bibi Amour Aziz, interview with the author, June 20, 2002, Zanzibar; BiMkubwa Said, interview with the author, June 21, 2002, Zanzibar; BiSaumu, June 16, 2002, Wete, Pemba; Mwalim Idd Abdulla Farhan interview of May 25, 2002; Khamis Kombo, interview with the author, June 15, 2002, Zanzibar; Maryam Yahya interview; Mr. Drive-In, interview with the author, March 10, 2005, Dar es Salaam.

44. Bi Maryam interview.

45. Derné, *Movies, Masculinity, and Modernity*.

46. Issa, interview with the author, February 16, 2004, Dar es Salaam.

47. Nitesh Virji interview.

48. Patel, interview with the author, April 24, 2005, Moshi.

49. Fatma Alloo, interview with the author, May 14, 2002, Zanzibar.

50. Adam Shafi interview; Haji Faki Mohammed (aka Haji Garana) interview of July 1, 2002; Haji Gora Haji interview; Mwalim Idd Abdulla Farhan interview of May 25, 2002.

51. Laura Fair, "'It's Just No Fun Anymore': Women's Experiences of Taarab before and after the 1964 Zanzibar Revolution," *International Journal of African Historical Studies* 35, no. 1 (2002): 61–81; Glassman, "Sorting Out the Tribes."

52. I thank Andrew Eisenberg for his generous willingness to share copies of this recording, as well as Yasseen's *Sina Nyumba*, with me. See Eisenberg, "Resonance of Place," for a fuller discussion of the larger place of Hindi film music in Swahili taarab.

53. A friend, Ali Skandor, told me this story in June 2005, during a discussion of the various ways in which Indian films figured into Swahili love lives.

54. Jennifer Cole and Lynn Thomas, eds., *Love in Africa* (Chicago: University of Chicago Press, 2009); Lila Abu-Lughod, "Egyptian Melodrama—Technology

361

of the Modern Subject," in *Media Worlds: Anthropology on New Terrain*, ed. Faye Ginsburg, Lila Abu-Lughod, and Brian Larkin (Berkeley: University of California Press, 2002), 115–33; Larkin, "Indian Films and Nigerian Lovers."

55. Radway, *Reading the Romance.*

56. Richard Dyer, "Entertainment and Utopia," in *Movies and Methods: An Anthology*, vol. 2, ed. Bill Nichols (Berkeley: University of California Press, 1985), 222.

57. Mama Ak interview.

58. Anonymous, interview with the author, March 24, 2005, Zanzibar.

59. Adam Shafi Adam, *Vuta n'kuvute* (Dar es Salaam: Mkuki na Nyota, 1999), 2.

60. Adam Shafi interview.

61. Sabrina, interview with the author, May 5, 2004, Zanzibar.

62. William M. Reddy, *The Navigation of Feeling: A Framework for the History of Emotions* (New York: Cambridge University Press, 2001).

63. Doris Sommer, *Foundational Fictions: The National Romances of Latin America* (Berkeley: University of California Press, 1991); Vasudevan, "You Cannot Live in Society."

Chapter 4: Global Films and Local Reception

1. ZNA, AB 5/111, "Films, Their Educational Uses, and Censorship"; ZNA, AD 5/75: Film Censorship 1954–1963; TNA 622/s1/B1: Bodi ya Filamu; TNA 435 B/2/2: Iringa Broadcasting and Films, Cinematograph and Censorship Board, 1937–1957; TNA 435/B2/1: Dodoma Broadcasting and Films: 1947–63; Ticket Books for the Majestic Cinema, Zanzibar, 1973–93, private archives now in the author's possession, hereafter cited as Majestic Books.

2. As a broad gloss, I use *Hindi* and *Indian* interchangeably. The majority of films imported into Tanzania were produced in Bombay. During the period under discussion, films were produced all across the subcontinent and in some twenty different languages. The term *Bollywood* is commonly used today in both academic and common parlance, but it emerged as a tag only in the 1990s, and many of these films contain themes and production styles that distinguish them in important ways from earlier films produced on the subcontinent. The explicit aim of Bollywood films is often to appeal broadly to diasporic South Asian populations, particularly middle- and upper-class nonresident Indian populations in the West. Thus, I avoid the term *Bollywood*. Tejaswini Ganti, *Producing Bollywood: Inside the Contemporary Hindi Film Industry* (Durham, NC: Duke University Press, 2012); Thomas Blom Hansen, "In Search of the Diasporic Self: Bollywood in South Africa," in *Bollyworld: Popular Indian Cinema through a Transnational Lens*, ed. Raminder Kaur and Ajay J. Sinha (New Delhi: Sage, 2005), 239–60; Joshi, *Bollywood*; Mishra, *Bollywood Cinema*; Divia Patel, Laurie Benson, and Carol Cains, *Cinema India: The Art of Bollywood*, 1st ed. (Melbourne, Australia: National Gallery of Victoria, 2007); Dwyer and Patel, *Cinema India*; Dwyer and Pinney, *Pleasure and*

the Nation; Kaur and Sinha, "Bollyworld"; Sangita Gopal and Sujata Moorty, eds., *Global Bollywood: Travels of Hindi Song and Dance* (Minneapolis: University of Minnesota Press, 2008); Ganti, *Bollywood*, 1–23.

3. TNA 435 B/2/2; *Tanganyika Standard*, January to June 1950; *Samachar,*1952 and 1953.

4. *Film Daily Year Book of Motion Pictures* (Hollywood, CA: J. E. Brulatur, 1938), 1204; *Motion Picture and Television Almanac* (New York: Quigley, 1953), 9.

5. ZNA, AD 5/75: Film Censorship, 1954–1963; US Department of Commerce, *World Trade in Commodities* 8, no. 6 (1950): 1–2.

6. "Rasul's Estimate of Losses, Schedule A, 1951," ZNA, AB 9/47.

7. Majestic Books.

8. Rajadhyaksha and Willemen, *Encyclopedia of the Indian Cinema*, 350.

9. TNA 435/B2/1; Wizara ya Utamaduni wa Taifa na Vijana: Karatiasi za uk-aguzi wa filamu za senema kwa April 1977–March 1978, Board of Film Censors Office, Dar es Salaam; Majestic Books, 1978; Sultan Issa, "Black Marketing of Cinema Tickets Still on in Dar" *Nationalist*, May 22, 1966, 6.

10. Shabir Jariwalla interview; Taday interview; Kasanga interviews; Asad Talati, e-mail correspondence with the author, March 16, 2004, and July 7, 2004.

11. Ahmed "Eddy" Alwi al-Beity interview of November 3, 2004.

12. Asad Talati interviews of August 14, 15, and 16; Asad Talati e-mail of August 31, 2004.

13. Asad Talati interviews of August 14, 15, and 16; Asad Talati, e-mail correspondence with the author, October 13, 2004.

14. Abdulhussein Marashi interview of May 7, 2002.

15. Pankaj Valambia interview.

16. Feroz Mukhadam interview.

17. Hadji Konde, *Press Freedom in Tanzania* (Arusha, Tanzania: East African Publications, 1984), 95–96. *Vita vya Kagera* can be found on YouTube.

18. This was one of a dozen US or British films named by Asad Talati, who recalled them packing the house at various theaters in Zanzibar in the 1950s. I am deeply indebted to him for his willingness to read an earlier draft of this and correct my overzealous statements regarding the lack of appeal of American films. He rightly corrected my utterly incongruous comparison between Fred Astaire's *Belle of New York* and Raj Kapoor's *Awara*. Fred Astaire "was never Zanzibar's cup of tea," said Talati, only appealing to the "so called 'elite' audience of the colonial times." This did not mean, however, that there were not other styles of Hollywood films and other American and British actors from that era who could attract a crowd. Asad Talati e-mail of August 31, 2004.

19. The film played two shows Friday and Saturday in the 1970s at the Empress in Dar es Salaam.

20. Try watching the American film *Love Story* with the sound turned off and see how long it takes before you are utterly bored. I vaguely remembered the film

363

from my own youth, but when I watched it again as part of this research, I fully appreciated what Tanzanians said about the overreliance on dialogue in American films, as well as the obsessive focus on individual psychological drama and the exclusion of family, friends, and community from a story. The extensive literature on African film and filmmakers, only a few key works of which are cited here, emphasizes the importance of communal struggle and family in films made by those from the continent. Nwachukwu Frank Ukadike, *Black African Cinema* (Berkeley: University of California Press, 1994); Manthia Diawara, *African Cinema: Politics and Culture* (Bloomington: Indiana University Press, 1992); June Givanni and Imruh Bakari, eds., *Symbolic Narratives/African Cinema: Audiences, Theory and the Moving Image* (London: British Film Institute, 2000); Joseph Gugler, *African Film* (London: James Currey, 2003); Melissa Thackway, *Africa Shoots Back* (Bloomington: Indiana University Press, 2003); Françoise Pfaff, *Focus on African Films* (Bloomington: Indiana University Press, 2004).

21. Ameri Slyoum interview.

22. Zolov, *Refried Elvis*; Collins, *Hollywood Down Under*, 236–38; Juliane Furst, "Swinging across the Iron Curtain in Moscow's Summer of Love: How Western Youth Culture Went East," in *Transnational Histories of Youth in the Twentieth Century*, ed. Richard Ivan Jobs and David M. Pomfret (London: Palgrave Macmillan, 2015), 236–59.

23. Alison Arnold, "Popular Film Song in India: A Case of Mass-Market Musical Eclecticism," *Popular Music* 7, no. 2 (1988): 177–88; Sarrazin, "Celluloid Love Songs," 393–411; Sarrazin, "Songs from the Heart: Musical Coding, Emotional Sentiment, and Transnational Sonic Identity in India's Popular Film Music," in *Global Bollywood*, ed. Anandam P. Kavoori and Aswin Punathambekar (New York: NYU Press, 2008), 203–22; Skillman, "Bombay Hindi Film Song Genre," 133–44; Sarrazin, "Songs in Hindi Films: Nature and Function," in *Cinema and Cultural Identity: Reflections on Films from Japan, India, and China*, ed. Wimal Dissanyake (New York: University Press of America, 1988), 149–64; Biswarup Sen, "The Sounds of Modernity: The Evolution of Bollywood Film Song," in *Global Bollywood: Travels of Hindi Song and Dance*, ed. Sangita Gopal and Sujata Moorti (Minneapolis: University of Minnesota Press, 2008), 85–104.

24. This is a theme developed by numerous authors in the edited volume *Global Bollywood: Travels of Hindi Song and Dance*, where contributors discuss the influence of Hindi film music from Indonesia to Egypt, Israel, and the United States. Brian Larkin's work on Bandiri music in Nigeria is another stunning example of local appropriation and transformation. See Gopal and Moorti, *Global Bollywood*; Brian Larkin, "Bandiri Music, Globalization and Urban Space in Nigeria," in *Bollyworld: Popular Indian Cinema through a Transnational Lens*, ed. Raminder Kaur and Ajay J Sinha (New Delhi: Sage, 2005), 284–308.

25. Bashir Poonja, "Thrills Are Missing," *Sunday News*, June 26, 1966, 4, in his review of *Yeh Raat Phir Na Aayegi*.

26. Ali Ghafoor, interview with the author, May 19, 2005, Dar es Salaam; Khulsum, interview with the author, June 26, 2002, Zanzibar; Nasra and Maryam, interview with the author, May 22, 2002, Zanzibar; Shanin interview; Juma Sultan, interview with the author, May 25, 2005, Dar es Salaam.

27. Nasra Mohammed interview.

28. Ibid.

29. Ali Ghafoor, interview of May 19, 2005.

30. Ahmed Gurnah, "Elvis in Zanzibar," in *The Spaces of Postmodernity: Readings in Human Geography*, ed. Michael Dear and Steven Flushing (Oxford: Blackwell, 2002), 351.

31. Ibid., 349, 60, 53.

32. Ali Ghafoor interview of May 19, 2005.

33. Gurnah, "Elvis in Zanzibar," 353.

34. Khalid Saloum, interview with the author, October 12, 2004, Dar es Salaam.

35. Richard Maltby, Melvyn Stokes, and Robert C. Allen, "Introduction," in *Going to the Movies: Hollywood and the Social Experience of Cinema*, ed. Richard Maltby, Melvyn Stokes, and Robert C. Allen (Exeter: University of Exeter Press, 2007), 9; UK Cinema Admissions 1933–2001, accessed April 14, 2004, at http://www.bfi.org.uk/facts/stats/alltime/uk_admissions.html.

36. Sidney Poitier and Harry Belefonte toured Tanzania as part of a larger US diplomatic effort to build goodwill in Africa during the Cold War. Their visits were covered prominently in the press but left little impression on those interviewed. On the cultural tours of African Americans as part of State Department's "goodwill" missions, see Penny Von Eschen, *Satchmo Blows Up the World: Jazz Ambassadors Play the Cold War* (Cambridge, MA: Harvard University Press, 2004).

37. Subiria Sawasawa and Aidan Hyera, "The Effectiveness of Feature Films as a Communication Medium in Tanzania" (School of Journalism thesis, University of Dar es Salaam, 1982), 38; Luptatu Mussa Rashid, "Tanzania Film Company: A Measure of the Role of Movies in Tanzania—A Study of the Effects of the Movie on the Tanzanian Youth (School of Journalism thesis, University of Dar es Salaam, 1981), 25–26; Nkwabi Ng'wanakilala, *Mass Communication and the Development of Socialism in Tanzania* (Dar es Salaam: Tanzania Publishing House, 1981), 69; Edna Rajab, interview with the author, February 11, 2005, Dar es Salaam.

38. Freddy Macha, "My Name Is Check-Bob," *Sunday News*, July 4, 1982, 7. On banned fashions, see two articles in the Zanzibar newspaper *Kweli Ikidhihri Uwongo Hujitenga* [sic]: "Clothes Decree for All," April 19, 1973, 2, and "'Sheria Nam': 1 ya 1973: Sheria ya Kulinda Heshima na Adabu ya Taifa," April 26, 1973, 3. The latter was particularly instructive for laying out all the banned fashions and exceptions, as well as the punishments to be meted out for repeat infractions. Burgess, "Cinema, Bell Bottoms, and Miniskirts," 287–313; Ivaska, *Cultured States*, 79–82.

39. Gratuitous sexual violence permeated many films of this genre. Like Stephane Dunn, author of *"Baad Bitches" and Sassy Supermamas*, and many other

365

scholars who have studied this genre, I was shocked when I watched these films again, many years after they first came out. My recollection of Grier or Dobson focused on their uniquely powerful, strong, and smart characters. Somehow, I repressed and completely forgot the gratuitous rape scenes and antifeminist portrayals of black female sexuality that dominate the blaxploitation genre. In interviews I conducted, Tanzanians too emphasized the powerful representations of black women they recalled, not the sexual violence. Censorship records from Dar es Salaam say nothing about specific cuts to any of the films from this genre, although individual exhibitors and projectionists did note that they themselves sometimes removed scenes of sexual violence. See Stephane Dunn, *"Baad Bitches" and Sassy Supermamas: Black Power Action Films* (Urbana: University of Illinois Press, 2008).

40. Asad Talati e-mail of March 16, 2004; Asad Talati interviews of August 14, 15, and 16, 2004; Gamdul Singh Hans interview of April 19, 2004; Ahmed "Eddy" Alwi al-Beity interview of November 3, 2004; Kasanga interview of December 16, 2004; Feroz Mukhadam interview; Shabir Jariwalla interview; Nitesh Virji interview; Pankaj Valambia interview.

41. The plot for *When Women Had Tails* (Campanile, 1970) revolves around isolate cavemen on an island who find a woman and discover the joys of sex. The film also stars Giuliano Gemma, an icon in Tanzania popularized through roles in Italian westerns.

42. Majestic Books; Records from the Board of Film Censors, Dar es Salaam, 1977.

43. MaryEllen Higgins, Rita Keresztesi, and Dayna Oscherwitz, eds., *The Western in the Global South* (New York: Routledge, 2015).

44. *Standard*, March 23, 1966, 5; *Nationalist*, May 25, 1970, 5; Records from the Board of Film Censors, Dar es Salaam, 1977.

45. *Nationalist*, May 25, 1970, 5.

46. *Sunday News*, June 26, 1966, 5.

47. "Hollywood Cowboys Tame by Comparison," *Sunday News*, July 3, 1966, 4.

48. Thomas Weisser, *Spaghetti Westerns: The Good, the Bad, the Violent* (Jefferson, NC: McFarland, 1992).

49. Like films in the blaxploitation genre, *My Name Is Pecos* also reverses the typical racial hierarchy of good and bad displayed in film. Robert Woods, although six feet tall and white, plays a Mexican, Pecos Martinez, who clearly commands the moral high ground.

50. Burgess, "Cinema, Bell Bottoms, and Miniskirts"; Ivaska, *Cultured States*.

51. Majestic Books.

52. Chanu Vadgama interview.

53. Feroz Mukhadam interview.

54. Pankaj Valambia interview.

55. Kamal, interview with the author, February 4, 2005, Dar es Salaam.t

56. Majestic Books.

57. Ibid.

58. Ganti, *Bollywood*, 29–34; Mishra, *Bollywood Cinema*; Ashwani Sharma, "Blood, Sweat, and Tears: Amitabh Bachchan, Urban Demigod," in *You Tarzan: Masculinity, Movies, and Men*, ed. Pat Kirkham and Janet Thumin (New York: St. Martin's Press, 1993), 167–80; Koushik Banerjea, "'Fight Club': Aesthetics, Hybridization and the Construction of Rogue Masculinities in *Sholay* and *Deewaar*," in *Bollyworld: Popular Indian Cinema through a Transnational Lens*, ed. Raminder Kaur and Ajay J. Sinha (New Delhi: Sage, 2005), 163–85; Dissanayake and Sahai, *Sholay*; Anupama Chopra, *Sholay, the Making of a Classic* (Mumbai: Penguin, 2000); Dickey, *Cinema and the Urban Poor*; Dwyer and Pinney, *Pleasure and the Nation*; Nandy, "Popular Indian Cinema as a Slums' Eye View," 1–18; Ravi Vasudevan, ed., *Making Meaning in Indian Cinema* (New Delhi: Oxford University Press, 2000); Vasudevan, "Shifting Codes, Dissolving Identities," 99–121.

59. Every respondent who mentioned *Coolie*, and there were many, also told me that Bachchan almost died while making the film. Bachchan always did his own stunts. In one of the fight scenes, he was injured, and for nearly a year, he struggled against death. After his miraculous recovery, the director changed the ending of the film, as initially Bachchan's character was to die.

60. Asad Talati, e-mail correspondence with the author, April 17, 2004, April 11, 2005, and March 16, 2005.

61. Abdulhussein Marashi, interview with the author, May 18, 2002, Zanzibar.

Chapter 5: Cinemas, Cities, and Audiences

1. TNA 13864: Cinematograph Ordinance. Films were occasionally screened in many towns prior to the construction of a cinema. Dodoma, for instance, held screenings on and off for years before the first cinema was erected in 1944. During the waning years of cinemagoing in the 1990s, coastal audiences also remained the most steadfast. A. C. Donne, Chairman of the Cinematograph Licensing Board to Chief Secretary, 16 October 1931, TNA 20496: Scheme for Establishment of Cinematograph Theaters in Native Areas; District Officer's Report, Tanga District, 1929, held in TNA; HA Jariwalla to Chief Secretary 8 December 1930, TNA 13038: Cinematograph Films Censorship and Control of Display; ZNA, AB 5/156: Pemba Cinema, 1935–54; TNA 35999: Film Production by the Colonial Film Unit; TNA 435/B2/1: Dodoma Broadcasting and Films: 1947–63; TNA 41/B2/2: Mwanza; TNA 435 B/2/21: Iringa Broadcast and Films; Boniface Sanjala, interview with the author, January 14, 2005, Dar es Salaam. For more on the cultural connections that flowed from commercial caravan culture, see Rockel, *Carriers of Culture*.

2. Fuller, *At the Picture Show*, 28; Christopher J. McKenna, "Tri-racial Theaters in Robeson County, North Carolina, 1896–1940," in *Going to the Movies: Hollywood and the Social Experience of Cinema*, ed. Richard Maltby, Melvyn Stokes, and Robert C. Allen (Exeter: University of Exeter Press, 2007), 45–59; Srinivas, *House Full*, 73–75, 122–27.

367

3. Garth Myers, *African Cities: Alternative Visions of Urban Theory and Practice* (London: Zed, 2011).

4. "Films, Their Educational Uses and Censorship," 1927 memo, ZNA, AB 5/111: Memorandum on Films, Their Uses and Censorship, 1927–49; ZNA, AB 5/156.

5. ZNA AB 5/156; ZNA AB 5/111; TNA 13038; "Price of Seats and Provisions Made for Africans in Cinemas in Dares Salaam [*sic*] and Nairobi, 1930," TNA 20496: Scheme for Establishment of Cinematograph Theaters in Native Areas.

6. TNA 13038.

7. These permits were required by urban authorities for Africans interested in holding large or "loud" parties in town. They required, in essence, that an individual notify the authorities of the intent to have a gathering and that an individual accept responsibility for any breaches of the law engaged in by attendees. The number of permits issued in Moshi was less than ten each month. TNA 39/53: Moshi Ngoma Permits, 1953–60; Fair, *Pastimes and Politics*, 23.

8. Lahmeyer, "Tanzania."

9. "Price of Seats and Provisions," TNA 20496; ZNA, AB 5/156; TNA 435 B/2/2.

10. Memo citing the response of the Office of the Secretariate of Zanzibar, 29 November 1935, TNA 13038; ZNA, AB 5/111.

11. Talati to Dutton, the British Resident, 23 July 1946, Talati to Head of Town Planning, 5 September 1946, and Talati to Mr. Warren, Town Planning Board, 2 October 1946, all in ZNA, AB 40/55: Application by SH Talati for a Lease of Government Land for the Purpose of Building a Cinema in Zanzibar Town.

12. It seems that the first colonial inquiry into exhibition occurred only as a result of a fire in Jariwalla's film storage room, then located at his house in Zanzibar. It took two months after the fire for the administration to begin an investigation into the safety of film storage and exhibition. Two years later, a report was filed discussing the question of film censorship; it was concluded that censoring was too time-consuming for the administration, and the officials trusted Jariwalla to ensure the films were not immoral. Only in 1926, after growing pressure from the Colonial Office resulting from fears in England that pictures were the cause of growing juvenile delinquency there, did Zanzibar begin to censor films. November 26, 1917, clip from the *Samachar* about the house fire; "Commissioner of Police Report, 12 January, 1918," "Commissioner of Police to Private Secretary, 10 September 1919," all in ZNA, AB 5/127: Rules under the Stage Plays and Cinematograph Exhibitions Decree 1917–1943; Fair, *Pastimes and Politics*, 110–48, 185–209.

13. TNA 13038; TNA 61/172/1. On colonial censorship, see Ambler, "Popular Films and Colonial Audiences," 81–105; Brennan, "Democratizing Cinema," 481–511; Burns, *Flickering Shadows*; Burton, "Urchins, Loafers," 199–216; Burns, *Cinema and Society*; Larkin, *Signal and Noise*.

14. The precise number of films classified for "nonnatives only" during the late 1920s and 1930s is unclear; different notes in the archives claim anywhere from 25

to 75 percent of films were certified as unfit for native viewing. My sense is that the 75 percent estimate was most likely wishful/paranoid thinking. Most records indicate that 25 to 30 percent was more accurate. MD Kampf, East African Representative of African Films Ltd., to Chief Secretary, 18 September, 1929, Chair, Cinematograph Licensing Board, Mr. A. A Isherwood, to Chief Secretary, 5 June, 1931, Chair Cinematography Licensing Board to Chief Secretary, 22 June 1931, Acting Director of Education to Chief Secretary, 7 August 1931, all in TNA 13038. See also E. C. Baker, "Memorandum on the Social Conditions of Dar es Salaam," ed. District Officer (1931), 98; a special thanks to Benjamin Bruhwiler, who retrieved a copy of this "lost" report in the School of Oriental and African Studies, University of London archives and provided it to me.

15. TNA 13038.

16. TNA 20496. Also Jariwalla to Chief Secretary, 8 December 1930 and Jariwalla to Chief Secretary, 2 December 1935, both in TNA 13038. A cutting from the *Tanganyika Standard* contained in this archival file also called for increased penalties for proprietors who ignored censorship ratings and allowed Africans into films from which authorities thought they should be excluded. Apparently, several cinemas had been caught ignoring the "nonnatives only" designation. "Film Censorship," *Tanganyika Standard*, January 18, 1930.

17. Brennan, "Democratizing Cinema."

18. Acting Provincial Commissioner to Chief Secretary, 11 December 1930, District Officer Dar es Salaam to Provincial Commissioner, 8 December 1930, and Memo, 5 June 1931, all in TNA 13038.

19. Suleiman Bajuma, Dar es Salaam, to *Mambo Leo*, typed manuscript and administrative comments included in TNA 13038; Brennan, "Democratizing Cinema."

20. Acting Chief Secretary, 21 November, 1935, TNA 13038.

21. Sixteen of the eighteen members of the board of censors supported the motion to reimpose racialized classifications. The chief secretary refused. TNA 61/172/1; TNA 13038.

22. District Commissioner Iringa to Provincial Commissioner, Southern Highlands, 8 February 1952, TNA 435/B/2/2.

23. Feroz Mukhadam interview.

24. Rona Elayne Peligal, "Spatial Planning and Social Fluidity: The Shifting Boundaries of Ethnicity, Gender and Class in Arusha, Tanzania, 1920–67" (PhD diss., Columbia University, 1999), 138–80, 240–57; Burton, *African Underclass*, 1, 250–56.

25. Prem Chowdhry, *Colonial India and the Making of Empire Cinema: Image, Ideology and Identity* (Manchester: Manchester University Press, 2000), 57–123.

26. Brij Behal interview; Gamdul Singh Hans interview of January 22, 2004; McKenna, "Tri-racial Theaters"; Fuller, *At the Picture Show*, 29–34.

27. Shabir Jariwalla interview.

369

28. District Commissioner Iringa to Provincial Commissioner Mbeya, 19 December 1953, TNA 435/B/2/2.

29. "Indo-African Theaters Ltd., 17 December, 1947," ZNA, AB 5/131; Talati to Dutton, the British Resident, 23 July 1946, Talati to Head of Town Planning, 5 September 1946, and Talati to Mr. Warren, Town Planning Board, 2 October 1946, all in ZNA, AB 40/55.

30. TNA 50114: Production of African Films, Confidential. Andreas Eckert, "Regulating the Social: Social Security, Social Welfare and the State in Late Colonial Tanzania," *Journal of African History* 45 (2004): 467–89; Smyth, "Development of British Colonial Film Policy," 437–50; Smyth, "The Feature Film in Tanzania," *African Affairs* 88, no. 352 (1989): 389–96; Smyth, "Post-war Career of the Colonial Film Unit," 163–77; Mike Hillary Ssali, "The Development and Role of an African Film Industry in East Africa with Special Reference to Tanzania, 1922–1984" (PhD diss., University of California, Los Angeles, 1988), 71–97.

31. "Confidential Memo Dated 7 April 1953," TNA 50114: Production of African Films, Confidential, 1949–1950; David Anderson, "Master and Servant in Colonial Kenya," *Journal of African History* 41 (2000): 459–85.

32. J. A. K. Leslie, *A Survey of Dar es Salaam* (London: Oxford University Press, 1963), 105, 46–49, 228. On the prevalence of the black market in cinema tickets, see the many letters to the editor on this topic, such as *Tanganyika Standard*, June 22, 1951, 2; March 19, 1952, 2; April 9, 1952, 2; March 20, 1953, 2; October 20, 1953, 2; March 5, 1954, 2; March 24, 1954, 2; April 9, 1954, 2; October 22, 1955, 2. Brennan, "Democratizing Cinema," 500.

33. Suresh Solanki interview; Jitu Savani interview of January 29, 2004; Chunilal Kala Savani interviews.

34. ZNA, AB 5/111; TNA 20496.

35. Mr. Khambaita interview.

36. In Dodoma, 87 percent of the non-African population lived in town, compared to only 6 percent of the Africa population. In Arusha, comparable percentages were 77 and 7; in Morogoro, 61 and 5; in Iringa 67 and 4; and in Mbeya, 54 and 3. *Tanganyika Population Census, Report on the Census of the Non-African Population, 1957*, table 8, 19; "Tanganyika Population Census, 1957, Population of Main Towns" and "Tanganyikan Population Census, 1957, Analysis of Civil Population by District and Race," both in *Tanzanian Statistical Abstract* (Dar es Salaam: Government Printer, 1962), 16, 28.

37. Nitesh Virji interview.

38. Herbert Werlin's African friends offered similar explanations when he queried them on the lack of nightlife in Nairobi in the early 1960s, saying that decades of police harassment for *kipande* (pass), housing that was often 5 to 10 miles from town, and a lack of sufficient transportation all contributed to their lack of interest in looking to the city at night for their pleasure. Werlin, "Nairobi in the Time of Uhuru," *Africa Today* 10, no. 10 (1963): 10. I thank Kenda Mutongi for this

reference and also for her work on transportation in Nairobi, which provides a vivid portrayal of the rise of the *matatu* (informal transport) industry as a grassroots effort to meet urban Africans' transportation needs. See Mutongi, *Matatu*.

39. Mr. Ninga, interview with the author, April 11, 2005, Dar es Salaam.

40. The film was the first ever to be colorized and rereleased, in 2004. Once again, it broke records of all kinds across the globe.

41. Sultan Mohammed, interview with the author, July 25, 2005, Arusha.

42. Bi Maryam, interview with the author, May 14, 2002, Zanzibar.

43. Ameri Slyoum interview.

44. Rashid Said interview.

45. The 1948 tour report indicates that the van traveled some 4,500 miles across Tanganyika, doing 58 shows before a combined audience of 37,000. Audiences ranged from 300 to 3,000, but typically averaged between 400 and 600. TNA 36444: Mobile Cinema Units: Tours and Tour Reports; TNA 435/B2/1: Dodoma Broadcasting and Films, 1947–63.

46. Mwalim Idd Abdulla Farhan, interviews with the author, May 24 and 25, 2002, Zanzibar.

47. Haji Faki Mohammed (aka Haji Garana) interview of June 3 2002.

48. Abdulhussein Marashi, interview of February 4, 2004; Ameri Slyoum interview; Haji Faki Mohammed (aka Haji Garana) interview of July 1, 2002; Haji Gora Haji interview; Mwalim Idd Abdulla Farhan interview of May 25, 2002; Rashid Said interview with the author.

49. Fatma Alloo, interview with the author, December 23, 2008, Zanzibar.

50. Belleghe, interview with the author, February 14, 2005, Dar es Salaam; Godwin Kaduma, interview with the author, March 2, 2005, Bagamoyo; Raymond Balemwa, interview with the author, October 13, 2004, Dar es Salaam; Edna Rajab interview. The moral ambiguity of youth's relationship to consumerism and global culture continued to be debated well through the twentieth century. See Amy Stambach, "Evangelism and Consumer Culture in Northern Tanzania," *Anthropological Quarterly* 73, no. 4 (2000): 171–79.

51. Frederick Macha, e-mail correspondence with the author, April 12, 2005.

52. Abel G. M. Ishumi, *The Urban Jobless in Eastern Africa: A Study of the Unemployed Population in the Growing Urban Centers, with Special Reference to Tanzania* (Uppsala: Scandanavian Institute of African Studies, 1984), 64.

53. United Republic of Tanzania, *Household Budget Survey, 1969* (Dar es Salaam: Bureau of Statistics, 1972), 172, 81.

54. Ibid., 61–63. In urban areas, only slightly more was spent on alcohol than on other things classified as entertainment.

55. Statistics show that 93 percent of the money spent in the nation on movie-going was spent by people living in urban areas. United Republic of Tanzania, *Household Budget Survey, 1976/77* (Dar es Salaam: Bureau of Statistics, 1988), appendix 3.2.1., 169. The leisure category included books, magazines, newspapers,

music, sports, photography, and—by far the largest expenditure for people living anywhere—buying records and cassettes and the machines to play them on. David Giltrow's study of teen viewing habits found that 96 percent of urban teens had been to the movies in the previous year, with some 30 percent of boys and 20 percent of girls going at least once a month. Giltrow, "Young Tanzanians and the Cinema: A Study of the Effects of Selected Basic Motion Picture Elements and Population Characteristics on Filmic Comprehension of Tanzanian Adolescent Primary School Children" (PhD diss., Syracuse University, 1973).

56. The tendency for donations to religious charities to eclipse spending on leisure and entertainments was also strongest among the poor, who often spent seven to eight times more on religious contributions than entertainment. United Republic of Tanzania, *Household Buedget Survey*, 1969, 1:38, 48–50; Stambach, "Evangelism and Consumer Culture."

57. Nkwabi Ng'wanakilala, *The Liberating Effect of Mass Communication in Tanzania* (Dar es Salaam: Institute of Adult Education, 1979), 67.

58. ZNA, AB 5/127; ZNA, AB 5/126.

59. ZNA, AB 5/127; ZNA, AB 5/126; ZNA, AB 9/47; ZNA, AH 17/30: Entertainment Tax, 1947–82; TNA 188/GEN/1/25: Mtwara Cinemas; TNA 435/B2/1. Wages varied considerably depending on the type of job and for whom one worked, but average wages for unskilled African laborers who worked for the Public Works Department were TSh -/40 to 1/30 per day, whereas masons earned 1/- to 4/50. Cooks averaged TSh 90–120 per month, houseboys 25–90 per month. *Tanganyika Blue Book* (Dar es Salaam: Government Printer, 1948), 396–98.

60. District Commissioner Iringa to Provincial Commissioner Southern Highlands, 8 February 1952, TNA 435 B/2/2.

61. ZNA, BA 34/4: *Notes on the Census of the Zanzibar Protectorate* (Zanzibar: Zanzibar Government Printer, 1953), 8–10. Anthony Clayton, *The 1948 Zanzibar General Strike* (Uppsala: Scandinavian Institute for African Studies, 1976), 19, 52n14.

62. Leslie, *Survey of Dar es Salaam*, 74–83, 125.

63. Ibid., 121.

64. Ibid., 168.

65. Luise White found similar patterns in colonial Nairobi, where men would pay substantially more for "the comforts of home," including a bath, a nice bed, and breakfast. There too, women were a substantial proportion of homeowners. White, *Comforts of Home*.

66. Bonner, "'Desirable or Undesirable Basotho Women?,'" 221–50; Chauncey, "Locus of Reproduction," 135–64; Jane Parpart, "'Where Is Your Mother?' Gender, Urban Marriage and Colonial Discourse on the Zambian Copperbelt, 1924–1945," *International Journal of African Historical Studies* 27, no. 2 (1994): 241–71; Dorothy Hodgson and Sheryl McCurdy, eds., *"Wicked" Women and the Reconfiguration of Gender in Africa* (Portsmouth, NH: Heinemann, 2001).

67. Baker, "Memorandum on the Social Conditions of Dar es Salaam," 34, 87.

68. United Republic of Tanzania, "Household Budget Survey, 1969," 12, 26; United Republic of Tanzania, *Selected Statistical Series, 1951–1993* (Dar es Salaam: Presidents Office Planning Commission, 1995), 26 28.

69. United Republic of Tanzania, *Survey of Employment and Earnings, 1973–74* (Dar es Salaam: Bureau of Statistics, 1977), tables 22 (a) and 23. Wage rates actually rose 97 percent, but the consumer price index increased substantially as well. Real earnings, adjusted for inflation, increased 32 percent between 1969 and 1974, which was still quite substantial.

70. In Pemba in 1945, tickets for Indian films were -/40, -/80, and 1/-. In Zanzibar in 1949, they were -/50, -/75, and 1/25, rising in 1953 to 1/-, 1/25, and 1/50 for English films and 2/-, 2/50, and 3/- shillings for Indian and Egyptian films. In Dar es Salaam, where differences in wealth were greater, tickets at the Empire sold for 1/80, 2/80, and 3/80 in 1952. For India see Srinivas, *House Full*, 122–29.

71. Letter to the editor, *Tanganyika Standard*, September 12, 1950, 2; "Local Cinemas," *Tanganyika Standard*, April 15, 1952, 2.

72. Leslie, *Survey of Dar es Salaam*, 197–98.

73. Ally "Rocky" Khamis Ally interview.

74. Rashid Said interview.

75. Kasanga interview of December 16, 2004.

76. Haji Faki Mohammed (aka Haji Garana) interview of July 1, 2002.

77. See *Tanganyika Standard*, May to August 1951, where numerous letters in this vein appear.

78. In 1951, Rasul earned roughly twice as much from second-class ticket sales for Indian films as he did for first-class tickets. Nearly 80 percent of the income earned from English-language films at this theater came from second- and third-class ticket sales. In the 1970s and 1980s, 70 to 80 percent of tickets sold at the Majestic were for the front sections of the theaters. Majestic Books; ZNA, AB 9/47.

79. "Local Cinemas," *Tanganyika Standard*, April 15, 1952, 2.

80. Subira, interview with the author, February 3, 2004, Zanzibar.

81. Semeni Juma interview.

82. This was true for the United States as well, where twelve- to fourteen-year-olds accounted for 60 percent of admissions in 1975. Teens were also more than twice as likely as their adult counterparts to go to the movies more than once per month. *International Motion Picture Almanac, 1985*, 32A.

83. Ishumi, *Urban Jobless*, 64–65.

84. Ishumi never defines what it means to be "jobless." Nontheless, 75 percent of the unemployed surveyed in the towns of Dar es Salaam, Arusha, Tabora, and Mwanza said they planned to stay in town. Ibid., 68–69.

85. Jecha Saloum, interview with the author, June 15, 2002, Zanzibar.

86. Abdulhussein Marashi interview of May 7, 2002.

373

87. Khalid Saloum, interview with the author, October 12, 2004, Dar es Salaam. Many of the young men I spoke with who sat in these seats went to the movies not just once but often two to five times each week.

88. Abdulrahim Said, interview with the author, December 12, 2004, Dar es Salaam.

89. Bakari Juma, interview with the author, February 12, 2005, Dar es Salaam.

90. Ali Makame, interview with the author, December 15, 2004, Dar es Salaam.

91. A few of many letters to the editor in the *Tanganyika Standard* include "Hooligans in the Cinemas, March 20, 1953, 2; "Cinema Manners," January 5, 1954, 2; "Nuisance at Cinema," February 10, 1955, 2; "Nuisance at the Cinema," February 17, 1955, 2; "Nuisance at the Cinema," February 18, 1955, 2; two more "Nuisance at the Cinema" letters, February 22, 1955, 2; "Mbeya Cinema," March 9, 1955, 2; "Call the Police," March 10, 1955, 2. A special thanks to Joshua Grace and Lindsay Anderson, who worked as research assistants and found these references for me.

92. Mwalim Idd Abdulla Farhan interview of May 25, 2002.

93. Ameri Slyoum interview.

94. These films all played at the Majestic Theater in Zanzibar from April to July 1977. Majestic Books.

95. Nitesh Virji interview.

96. Abdulhussein Marashi interview of May 7, 2002.

97. Josephine, interview with the author, April 21, 2005, Moshi.

98. Semeni Juma interview.

99. Gladness, interview with the author, April 23, 2005, Arusha.

100. Marja-Liisa Swantz, "Church and the Changing Role of Women in Tanzania," in *Christianity in Independent Africa*, ed. Edward Fashole-Luke, Richard Gray, and Adrian Hastings (Bloomington: Indiana University Press, 1978), 136–50. Well into the 1990s, students in the Moshi region articulated ideas that girls who danced in clubs, particularly clubs in town, were "prostitutes" or women who were "asking for trouble" or "likely to get pregnant before marriage." Amy Stambach, *Lessons from Mount Kilimanjaro* (New York: Routledge, 2000), 151–53. Sally Falk Moore also noted in her study of the Kilimanjaro region that, well into the late 1970s, it was extremely difficult for women in the region to gain access to cash and that it was exceptionally rare for a woman to go to town. Moore, *Social Facts and Fabrications: "Customary" Law on Kilimanjaro, 1880–1980* (Cambridge: Cambridge University Press, 1986), 36–37, 118, 201.

101. White, *Comforts of Home*; Bonner, "'Desirable or Undesirable Basotho Women?'"; Judith Byfield, "Women, Marriage, Divorce and the Emerging Colonial State in Abeokuta (Nigeria), 1892–1904," *Canadian Journal of African Studies* 30 (1996): 32–51; Chauncey, "Locus of Reproduction"; Parpart, "'Where Is Your Mother?'"; Walker, "Gender and the Development of the Migrant Labour System," 168–96; Hodgson and McCurdy, *"Wicked" Women*; Jean Allman and

Victoria Tashjian, *I Will Not Eat Stone: A Women's History of Colonial Asante* (Portsmouth, NH: Heinemann, 2000).

102. Brennan, *Taifa*, 148–50; Kenda Mutongi, *Worries of the Heart: Widows, Family and Community in Kenya* (Chicago: University of Chicago, 2007), 139–48; Lynn Thomas, *Politics of the Womb: Women, Reproduction and the State in Kenya* (Berkeley: University of California Press, 2003), 68, 183.

103. Susan Geiger, *TANU Women: Gender and Culture in the Making of Tanganyikan Nationalism, 1955–1965* (Portsmouth, NH: Heinemann, 1997), 12–14, 23; Leslie, *Survey of Dar es Salaam*, 91–92.

104. Pankaj Valambia interview.

105. On the persistence of patriarchial pressures keeping women from the town; gendered consumption of popular culture in this region; and generational and gendered tensions over youth and leisure, see Stambach, *Lessons from Mount Kilimanjaro*, 111–60.

106. The earliest reference I have found for ladies-only shows in the newspapers dates to 1945. It is possible that they occurred even earlier but were not advertised in print or were advertised in publications I did not read.

107. Majestic Books. Large theaters such as the Avalon, Empress, and Empire frequently ran a special weekday afternoon screening of the Sunday new release. Smaller theaters, among them the Odeon and Cameo, tended to run repeats of earlier hits.

108. Aunti Sofia interview.

109. Khadija, interview with the author, June 28, 2002, Zanzibar.

110. Anonymous, interview with the author, June 26, 2002, Zanzibar.

111. Maryam Yahya interview. On gender differentials in education in Tanzania and the impact this had on jobs and professions, see Marjorie Mbilinyi, "The State of Women in Tanzania," *Canadian Journal of African Studies* 6, no. 2 (1972): 371–77; Stambach, *Lessons from Mount Kilimanjaro*; Decker, "Reading, Writing and Respectability," 89–114; Corrie Decker, *Mobilizing Zanzibari Women: The Struggle for Respectability and Self-Reliance in Colonial East Africa* (New York: Palgrave Macmillan, 2014).

112. Shabir K. Jariwalla interview.

113. Nasra Mohammed interview.

114. Moshi's theater sat 120, that of Mwanza 200. Theaters in Tabora and Ujiji were the largest, seating 250 people each. TNA 13038; TNA 61/172/1; TNA 20364; TNA 13864.

115. In 1953, the Playhouse Cinema in Iringa averaged only 40 patrons per show. In an entire month, attendance amounted to 1,012, with the highest number of tickets sold for any one show being 98. District Commissioner Iringa to Provincial Commissioner Mbeya, 19 December, 1953, TNA 435/B/2/2: Iringa Broadcasting and Films, Cinematograph and Censorship Board, 1937–57. The Shan in Morogoro was built in 1954 and seated 277; the Delight in Shinyanga 248; the Nulite in Bukoba 243; and the Dodoma350.

375

116. Ahmed "Eddy" Alwi al-Beity interview of November 3, 2004; Shariff Alwi al-Beity, interview with the author, April 6, 2005, Dar es Salaam. Makau and colleagues found regional disparities in Kenya too, with coastal audiences far more likely to take in a film (two-thirds of those under thirty) than audiences located up-country (12 percent). The number of women in the audience was also more than double along the coast. Nereah Makau, Mwenda Ngesu, Fred Kawuna, and Paul Mbutu, *Cinema Leo Survey: A Study of Viewer Characteristics, Viewing Habits, Preference and Attitudes* (Nairobi: Daystar University, 1988).

Chapter 6: Drive-In Socialism

1. Neither the Soviet Union nor Cuba, both of which had highly developed filmmaking industries and affective car cultures, had drive-in cinemas at that time. Havana, with the highest per capita concentration of Cadillacs outside Detroit, did have a drive-in before the revolution, but it was subsequently closed. I thank Louis A. Pérez, Jr., for this information. Moscow opened its first drive-in theater only in 1999. To my knowledge, no other socialist state had a drive-in, let alone one that was state owned. Pérez, *On Becoming Cuban: Identity, Nationality and Culture* (Chapel Hill: University of North Carolina Press, 1999); Michael Wines, "Moscow Journal: Drive-In Offers Cabbage and Promises of Popcorn," *New York Times*, June 21, 1999, at http://www.nytimes.com/1999/06/21/world/moscow-journal-drive-in-offers -cabbage-and-promises-of-popcorn.html. I thank Lewis Siegelbaum for this reference and his work on automobility; Siegelbaum, *Cars for Comrades: The Life of the Soviet Automobile* (Ithaca, NY: Cornell University Press, 2008).

2. Among the films made by Kawawa in the 1950s were *Chalo Amerudi*, *Meli Inakwenda*, and *Muhogo Mchungu*. TNA 435/B2/1: Dodoma Broadcasting and Films, 1947–63; TNA 50114: Production of African Films, Confidential,1949–50; Progress Report 15 March 1952, Department of Social Development, TNA 35999: Film Production by Colonial Film Unit; Tanga Report, June 24, 1953, Information and Publications, TNA 562/I2/22: Mobile Cinema Van; Eckert, "Regulating the Social" 467–89; Burton, *African Underclass*, 225; John M. J. Magotti, *Rashidi Mfaume Kawawa: Simba wa vita katika historia ya Tanzania* (Dar es Salaam: Matai, 2007), 12–14.

3. "Babu Opens Tanzania's First Drive-In Cinema," *Nationalist*, May 14, 1966, 1.r

4. In 1966, the Tanzanian government granted Sisi Enterprises 21 acres of land in the neighborhood of Msasani for the drive-in, under the terms of a ninety-nine-year lease. Thirty-three years later, almost to the day, Sisi signed a letter of intent with the US Department of State to sell the land for $3 million so that the United States could build a new embassy on the site. The following month, before the sale could take place, the government of Tanzania repossessed the property, invoking the Land Acquisition Act of 1967. The government then "gave" it to the United States for an undisclosed amount and offered to compensate Sisi with the sum of TSh 602,363,000. Sisi declined the offer and took the government to civil court in

2001, where it won the case. The government then appealed the decision (Civil Appeal 30, 2004). The appeals court judges, Justices Ramadhani, Msoffe, and Kaji, found that the state had no basis for acquiring the land under the 1967 statute. Yet in their decision, rendered in June 2005, they found that compensation in the amount of TSh 998,467 ($883.60), the value as estimated by the government, was adequate compensation. Civil Appeal 30 of 2004, *Attorney General vs. Sisi Enterprises*, Court of Appeals of Tanzania at Dar es Salaam. Various publications of the National Development Corporation (NDC) describe the relationship between Sisi Enterprises and the state in different terms. Some of those publications make no mention of the land but assert instead that the government provided a one-fourth share of the capital invested in the initial opening; others note that anonymous "leaders" were awarded private shares in Sisi Enterprises. NDC, *First Annual Report and Accounts for the Year Ended 31st December 1965* (Dar es Salaam, 1966), 61; NDC, *Third Annual Report and Accounts* (Dar es Salaam, 1967), 73.

5. Though Asian Tanzanians were often vilified in the press and though their homes and businesses were the primary quarry of nationalizations, many had prominent roles both in the ruling political party—the Tanzanian African National Union—and in government. Key Asian entrepreneurs also worked with or for various parastatals. Well-known examples include members of the Karimjee family, Al Noor Kassum, Sophia Mustafa, and Amir H. Jamal. Kassum, *Africa's Winds of Change*; Sophia Mustafa, *The Tanganyika Way* (1961; repr., Toronto: TSAR Publications, 2009); Oonk, *Karimjee Jivanjee Family*.

6. As Kelly Askew has argued, nationalism and national culture are highly contested. Within any single nation, there are multiple ideologies competing for dominance and acceptance. Askew, *Performing the Nation*, 10, 157–223. For Kawawa's campaigns, see Ivaska, "'Anti-mini Militants Meet Modern Misses,'" 104–121; Ivaska, *Cultured States*.

7. Sheila Fitzpatrick, *Everyday Stalinism: Ordinary Life in Extraordinary Times—Soviet Russia in the 1930s* (Oxford: Oxford University Press, 1999); Jukka Gronow, *Caviar with Champagne: Common Luxury and the Ideals of the Good Life in Stalin's Russia* (New York: Berg, 2003); Julie Hessler, *A Social History of Soviet Trade: Trade Policy, Retail Practices, and Consumption, 1917–1953* (Princeton, NJ: Princeton University Press, 2004); Siegelbaum, *Cars for Comrades*; Karen Petrone, *Life Has Become More Joyous, Comrades: Celebrations in the Time of Stalin* (Bloomington: Indiana University Press, 2000). Such expectations were widespread in the Eastern Bloc, as attested by the contributors to David Crowley and Susan E. Reid's rich edited volume *Pleasures in Socialism: Leisure and Luxury in the Eastern Bloc* (Evanston, IL: Northwestern University Press, 2010).

8. Nostalgia is an important concept that is beginning to receive scholarly attention in Tanzania. As M. Anne Pitcher and Kelly M. Askew note, postsocialisms on the continent have yet to receive even a fraction of the attention they have garnered in Europe. Pitcher and Askew, "African Socialisms and Postsocialisms,"

Africa 76, no. 1 (2006): 1–14; Askew, "Sung and Unsung: Musical Reflections on Tanzanian Postsocialisms," *Africa* 76, no. 1 (2006): 15–43; Jamie Monson, "Defending the People's Railway in the Era of Liberalization: TAZARA in Southern Tanzania," *Africa* 76, no. 1 (2006): 113–30; Bissell, "Engaging Colonial Nostalgia," 215–48.

9. NDC, *Third Annual Report and Accounts*, 20. By 1970, Sisi Enterprises had earned after-tax profits equal to $169,690 in 2013 US dollars. NDC, *Sixth Annual Report and Accounts* (Dar es Salaam, 1970), 90.

10. Richard H. Hosier, *Urban Development in Tanzania: A Tale of Three Cities* (Stockholm: Stockholm Environment Institute, 1994), 6; John Hutton, *Urban Challenge in East Africa* (Nairobi: East African Publishing House, 1970), 180; Lahmeyer, "Tanzania." In 1967, the population of Dar es Salaam was 272,800. There are no extant records of ticket sales or attendance for the drive-in. Estimates of attendance are based on published data of earnings divided by average ticket price. Depending on the film, ticket prices ranged from Tsh 1/50 to 5. Assuming an average price of Tsh 3, more than 435,000 tickets were sold to paying adults in 1966. Children were admitted for free.

11. James Brennan notes that various cars were associated with particular classes, with the Volkswagen Beetle owner being considered the working-class subordinate of the bureaucratic Peugeot owner or driver of a Mercedes Benz. Brennan, "Blood Enemies," 389–413. In figure 6.1, note the mix of automobile brands at the drive-in.

12. Jean Comaroff and John Comaroff, *Modernity and Its Malcontents: Ritual and Power in Postcolonial Africa* (Chicago: University of Chicago Press, 1993); Frederick Cooper, *Colonialism in Question: Theory, Knowledge, History* (Berkeley: University of California Press, 2005); Bloom, Miescher, and Manuh, *Modernization as Spectacle in Africa*; Bruce M. Knauft, *Critically Modern: Alternatives, Alterities, Anthropologies* (Bloomington: Indiana University Press, 2002); Stephan F. Miescher, "Building the City of the Future: Visions and Experiences of Modernity in Ghana's Akasombo Township," *Journal of African History* 53, no. 3 (2012): 367–90; Allen F. Isaacman and Barbara S. Isaacman, *Dams, Displacement, and the Delusion of Development: Cahora Bassa and Its Legacies in Mozambique, 1965–2007* (Athens: Ohio University Press, 2013).

13. Donald L. Donham, *Marxist Modern: An Ethnographic History of the Ethiopian Revolution* (Berkeley: University of California Press, 1999); Ferguson, *Expectations of Modernity*; Allman, "Phantoms of the Archives," 104–29; Cooper, *Colonialism in Question*; Miescher, "Building the City of the Future," 367–90.

14. David Harvey, *The Condition of Postmodernity: An Enquiry into the Origins of Cultural Change* (Oxford: Oxford University Press, 1989).

15. "'Ujamaa': The Basis of African Socialism" was published as a TANU pamphlet in 1962 and republished numerous times, including in Julius Nyerere, *Ujamaa: Essays on Socialism* (Dar es Salaam: Oxford University Press, 1968); quotation is from p. 20.

16. Nyerere wrote and published a number of pamphlets in which he advanced such arguments, including *Socialism and Rural Development* (1967), *The Arusha Declaration* (1967), and *The Purpose Is Man* (1967), all of which can be found in Julius Nyerere, *Freedom and Socialism/Uhuru na Ujamaa. A Selection from Writings and Speeches, 1965–1967* (Dar es Salaam: Oxford University Press, 1968).

17. Almost immediately after the pronouncement of the Arusha Declaration, the government nationalized private banks and many of the largest foreign export companies. Over the next several years, imports, manufacturing, mining, and other sectors of the economy were nationalized. The distribution of films was also nationalized, beginning in 1968.

18. Nyerere, *Ujamaa*, 28.

19. Many radical leftists considered most of the men associated with NDC, as well as many leading members of the national party, TANU, to be quintessential examples of the bureaucratic bourgeoisie. The classic denunciation of this class was produced by Frantz Fanon, whose *Wretched of the Earth* was then widely circulating in Dar es Salaam. Fanon, *The Wretched of the Earth* (1961; repr., New York: Grove Press, 1966); Lionel Cliffe and John Saul, eds., *Socialism in Tanzania: An Interdisciplinary Reader*, vol. 2, *Policies* (Dar es Salaam: East African Publishing House, 1973); Issa G. Shivji, "Tanzania—The Silent Class Struggle," in *Socialism in Tanzania: An Interdisciplinary Reader*, vol. 2, *Policies*, ed. Lionel Cliffe and John Saul (Dar es Salaam: East African Publishing House, 1973), 304–30. For a further discussion of the challenges posed by leftist intellectuals for state socialism in Tanzania, see Ivaska, *Cultured States*, 124–65.

20. Abdulrahman Mohamed Babu, *African Socialism or Socialist Africa?* (London: Zed, 1981), 3. Despite their disagreements, Babu was appointed by Nyerere to the NDC board, and he served for eight years in various ministerial roles, including minister of state for planning, minister of economic development, and minster of commerce and cooperatives/industry. He was later imprisoned by Nyerere and served six years in detention. While in prison, he authored *African Socialism or Socialist Africa?* in which he offered a trenchant critique of the economic policies pursued by Tanzania and Africa more generally, where African leaders and technocrats continued to serve as the handmaidens of international capital rather than initiating a fundamental transformation of national or continental economies. Babu's criticisms of Nyerere and his relationship with the United States and the World Bank are also found in his introduction to Amrit Wilson, *US Foreign Policy and Revolution: The Creation of Tanzania* (London: Pluto Press, 1989), 1–7. The union between Tanganyika and Zanzibar was another significant point of disagreement between the two.

21. Jamie Monson, *Africa's Freedom Railway: How a Chinese Development Project Changed Lives and Livelihoods in Tanzania* (Bloomington: Indiana University Press, 2009). With the exception of Monson's book, there have been few explorations of industrial policy in Tanzania since the 1970s. In part, this stems

379

from the paucity of archival sources available for such investigations. Most academic studies published in the 1960s and 1970s were authored by individuals working in key ministries, industries, and parastatals and were based on "insider" knowledge. The critical insights they offered are rare today. Andrew Coulson, *Tanzania: A Political Economy* (New York: Oxford University Press, 1982); Coulson, ed., *African Socialism in Practice: The Tanzanian Experience* (Nottingham: Review of African Political Economy, 1979); Bismarck U. Mwansasu and Cranford Pratt, eds., *Towards Socialism in Tanzania* (Toronto: University of Toronto Press, 1979); Ian Parker, "Contradictions in the Transition to Socialism: The Case of the National Development Corporation," in *Towards Socialism in Tanzania*, ed. Bismarck U. Mwansasu and Cranford Park (Toronto: University of Toronto Press, 1979), 46–71; Issa G. Shivji, *Class Struggles in Tanzania* (Dar es Salaam: Tanzania Publishing House, 1976); Shivji, "Tanzania." Although peasants were strongly encouraged to produce collectively from at least 1967, it was only in the early 1970s and particularly from 1973 to 1976 that state muscle was used to push them toward declared goals. Some 10 million peasants were forcibly relocated as part of the effort to socialize rural production and development. Michaela von Freyhold, *Ujamaa Villages in Tanzania: Analysis of a Social Experiment* (London: Heinemann, 1979); Goran Hyden, *Beyond Ujamaa in Tanzania: Underdevelopment and an Uncaptured Peasantry* (London: Heinemann, 1980); Mwansasu and Pratt, *Towards Socialism in Tanzania*; Cranford Pratt, *The Critical Phase in Tanzania, 1945–1968: Nyerere and the Emergence of a Socialist Strategy* (Cambridge: Cambridge University Press, 1976).

22. NDC, *First Annual Report and Accounts for the Year Ended 31st December 1965*.

23. "Report by the Chairman, the Hon. A. M. Babu, M.P., Minister for Commerce and Industries," in NDC, *Fifth Annual Report and Accounts* (Dar es Salaam, 1969), 16–18. The corporate public relations publication *Jenga: Magazine of the National Development Corporation*, published from 1968, highlighted the industrial nature of NDC's development strategies.

24. The United States, Australia, and South Africa were the nations with the most developed drive-in industries. Surprisingly, there is almost nothing written on drive-ins for any region of the world. Mary Morley Cohen, "Forgotten Audiences in the Passion Pits: Drive-In Theatres and Changing Spectator Practices in Post-war America," *Film History* 6, no. 4 (1994): 470–86; Collins, *Hollywood Down Under*, 223; Gainer, "Hollywood, African Consolidated Films"; Gomery, *Shared Pleasures*, 91–93; Segrave, *Drive-In Theaters*.

25. Operators in Britain took their projection equipment to parking lots in the backs of Land Rovers and showed films on the sides of buildings or on sheets hung from scaffolds. For the most extensive discussions of the British Colonial Film Unit and mobile cinema vans in Africa, see Burns, *Flickering Shadows*; Larkin, *Signal and Noise*; Smyth, "Development of British Colonial Film Policy," 437–50; Smyth, "Post-war Career of the Colonial Film Unit," 163–77; Segrave, *Drive-In Theaters*,

104–14. Cold and rainy weather, high land values, and common people's reliance on public transportation all conspired against the development of drive-ins in Britain.

26. "Government Joins in Drive-In Cinema Project in Dar," *Nationalist*, May 5, 1965, 2. Though some drive ins in the United States could hold several thousand cars, the average capacity was between five hundred and six hundred. *International Motion Picture Almanac* 1949–50, xv, and 1962, 60A.

27. Gainer, "Hollywood, African Consolidated Films, " 188–93. By the end of 1961, Johannesburg had nearly seventy drive-ins, whereas Cape Town had only four; thus, even within wealthy South Africa, access to the latest cinematic adventure was uneven. Gainer also notes that only a handful were open to "mixed" patronage or reserved for nonwhites. In the United States, drive-ins were among the first racially integrated public spaces in the South. Cohen, "Forgotten Audiences in the Passion Pits," 471.

28. The annual East Africa Car Rally, which pitted drivers, mechanics, and financiers from the region against each other in a race across East Africa, was one spectacular expression of this and was regularly covered in the East African press. In Ghana, President Kwame Nkrumah's push to reach the skies resulted in his employment of a female Nazi pilot as the head of the national aviation school. Allman, "Phantoms of the Archives."

29. I thank Caleb Owen for his research in East African and southern African newspapers confirming the mid- to late 1970s as opening dates in these countries. I am also grateful to Jan-Bart Gewald for sharing with me his memories of family excursions to southern African drive-ins. Gewald was the first to direct my attention to the widely popular song "Ag Pleez Daddy," in which children beg their father to cram eight, nine, or ten of them into the car and take them to the show. That song was subsequently shared with me by many people who had grown up in South Africa and Namibia. A video clip of a version of the song can be found at http://www.youtube.com/watch?v=6RAQP-2sODk.

30. The Nairobi drive-in was owned and managed by whites, and several of the members of the board were drive-in owners from South Africa. The Kenyan press clearly portrayed the drive-in as a space largely for whites, emphasizing the uniforms and showers provided for the "boys" employed there. "First Drive-In Cinema to Take 750 Cars," *East African Standard*, March 14, 1958, 19.

31. Field notes from informal interviews conducted during an evening with Shaaban, Ali, and Juma, May 22, 2005, Kigamboni, Dar es Salaam. Mentions of the "Apollo" dance appear in several published letters to the editor condemning the ban on "soul music" in November 1969. See especially the *Standard*, November 19 and 20, 1969.

32. Shivji, "Tanzania," 314.

33. Ibid.; Shivji, *Class Struggles*; C. E. Barker, M. R. Bhagavan, P. V. Mitschke-Collande, and D. V. Wield, *African Industrialization: Technology and Change in Tanzania* (Brookfield, VT: Gower, 1986); Parker, "Contradictions in the Transition

381

to Socialism," 46–71; Coulson, *Tanzania*; Coulson, *African Socialism in Practice*; Mwansasu and Pratt, *Towards Socialism*; Dean McHenry, *Limited Choices: The Political Struggle for Socialism in Tanzania* (Boulder, CO: Lynne Rienner, 1994).

34. Shivji, "Tanzania," 316.

35. Barker et al., *African Industrialization*, 75–77; NDC, *Annual Reports*.

36. Aart J. M. Van de Laar, "Foreign Business and Capital Exports from Developing Countries: The Tanzanian Experience," in *Socialism in Tanzania*, ed. Lionel Cliffe and John Saul (Dar es Salaam: East African Pulishing House, 1973), 83–87, esp. 85–86.

37. Barker et al., *African Industrialization*, 82–83. Numerous other examples can be found in Andrew Coulson, "Tanzania's Fertilizer Factory," in *African Socialism in Practice*, ed. Andrew Coulson (Nottingham: Spokesman, 1979), 184–90; Parker, "Contradictions in the Transition to Socialism"; and Cliffe and Saul, *Socialism in Tanzania*. See also Mukandala, as cited in McHenry, *Limited Choices*, 147–49.

38. In 1969, there were only five partners who were not foreign. NDC, *Fifth Annual Report and Accounts*, 11. Investments in posh hotels, safari game parks, and gold and diamond mines were particularly controversial. Hard-hitting critiques of the neocolonial economic ties fostered and encouraged by NDC partnerships with foreign capital also circulated widely. Cliffe and Saul, *Socialism in Tanzania*, esp. Van de Laar, "Foreign Business and Capital Exports," 1:83–87; Shivji, "Tanzania"; Shivji, *Class Struggles*.

39. NDC, *Third Annual Report and Accounts*, 73.

40. NDC, *Fifth Annual Report and Accounts*, 90. In 1971, Sisi Enterprises was transferred to the Tanzania Film Company, an NDC parastatal. All financial and corporate records related to Sisi disappear after this point.

41. NDC, *Sixth Annual Report and Accounts*, 90. Actual dividends were TSh 35,000 and 188,000, respectively.

42. NDC, *Third Annual Report and Accounts*, 73.

43. Rolf Hofmeier, *Transport and Economic Development in Tanzania: With Particular Reference to Roads and Road Transport* (Munich: Weltforum Verlag, 1973), 104.

44. Joshua Grace, "The People's Car of Dar es Salaam: Buses, Passengers, and the State in Urban Tanzania, 1960s to 1980s," paper presented at the 2010 Society of the History of Technology Annual Meeting, Tacoma, WA; James N. Karioki, *Tanzania's Human Revolution* (University Park: Pennsylvania State University, 1979); McHenry, *Limited Choices*, chap. 7; United Republic of Tanzania, *Bus Transport for Site and Service Areas, Dar es Salaam* (Dar es Salaam: Ministry of Lands, Housing and Urban Development, 1973). NDC held 50 percent of Raleigh Cycles East Africa Ltd., which was incorporated in September 1970. NDC, *Ninth Annual Report and Accounts*, 24.

45. Hofmeier, *Transport*, 101–3; United Republic of Tanzania, "New Registration of Motor Vehicles," *Monthly Statistical Bulletin* 19, no. 4 (August 1969): 22, table 18.

46. Republic of Tanganyika, Central Statistical Bureau, *Family Budget Survey of Middle-Grade African Civil Servants, 1963* (Dar es Salaam, 1963), 22. The number of Tanzanians in the upper echelons of the civil service increased from 1,170 (26 percent of the total) to 6,145 (80 percent) during the 1960s. Pratt, *Critical Phase*, 130. The centrality of cars to the identities of these men is powerfully portrayed in the novel *Ngumi Ukutani* by John Rutayisingwa (Dar es Salaam: Longman, 1979). I am indebted to Josh Grace for generously sharing the novel with me, as well as many of the newspaper references cited in this section.

47. Agnello Fernandez interview.

48. Central Statistical Bureau, *Family Budget Survey*, 24.

49. Godwin Kaduma interview.

50. United Republic of Tanzania, *Selected Statistical Series*, 67, table 13.2.2: Passenger Cars: Direct/Net Imports by Origin.

51. "Kununua mamotokaa, masuti au taiti-Ni kutia maji katika pakacha," *Ngurumo*, March 10, 1965, 1.

52. Among the rules articulated by the code were that employees of the government or party could not hold shares in a private company, receive more than one salary, own property that was rented to others, or employ others to work for them. Perhaps the fact that Sisi Enterprises was state owned made it acceptable for national leaders to be issued private shares. More likely, this accounts for the secrecy surrounding these shares. For debates at the university during these years among socialists and other members of the student body over cars, see Ivaska, *Cultured States*, 136–61; McHenry, *Limited Choices*; Pratt, *Critical Phase*, 232–33.

53. A photo of Nyerere comparing blisters with other members of the party who joined him on his journey is included in Nyerere, *Uhuru na Ujamaa*, photo 17.

54. "Editorial: Car Loans and Public Transport," *Nationalist*, June 17, 1970, 4; "Kununua mamotokaa, masuti au taiti-Ni kutia maji katika pakacha"; "Kutononoka kwa magari ya binafsi ni marufuku sasa!" *Ngurumo*, November 9, 1971, 1; "Sheria ya magari sawa na sheria ya bunduki," *Ngurumo*, November 15, 1971, 1. Such debates over automobility and socialism were not unique to Tanzania. See György Péteri, "Alternative Modernity? Everyday Practices of Elite Mobility in Communist Hungary, 1956–1980," in *The Socialist Car: Automobility in the Eastern Bloc*, ed. Lewis H. Siegelbaum (Ithaca, NY: Cornell University Press, 2011), 47–70, as well as other contributions to that volume.

55. *Jenga*, no. 2 (1968): 20.

56. Segrave, *Drive-In Theaters*, vii.

57. Jajada Verrips and Birgit Meyer, "Kwaku's Car: The Struggles and Stories of a Ghanaian Long-Distance Taxi Driver," in *Car Cultures*, ed. Daniel Miller (Oxford: Berg, 2001), 153–84; Olatunde Bayo Lawuyi, "The World of the Yoruba Taxi Driver: An Interpretive Approach to Vehicle Slogans," in *Readings in African Popular Culture*, ed. Karin Barber (Bloomington: Indiana University Press, 1997), 146–50.

58. Haroub Othman, "Introduction: A. M. Babu—A Life Well Earned," in *Babu: I Saw the Future and It Works—Essays Celebrating the Life of Comrade Abdulrahman Mohamed Babu, 1924–1996*, ed. Haroub Othman (London: E and D, 2001), 1–6.

59. Burgess, *Race, Revolution, and the Struggle for Human Rights*, 132–33, 58–61.

60. "Tanganyika Population Census, 1957: Population of Main Towns," in *Tanzania Statistical Abstract* (Dar es Salaam, 1962), table C.6; United Republic of Tanzania, *Bus Transport*, 14; United Republic of Tanzania, *1967 Population Census*, vol. 2, *Statistics for Urban Areas* (Dar es Salaam, 1970), table 2; Hutton, *Urban Challenge in East Africa*, 6, 12, 180; Hosier, *Urban Development in Tanzania*, 6; Lahmeyer, "Tanzania."

61. Monson, *Africa's Freedom Railway*; Grace, "People's Car of Dar es Salaam." In Dar es Salaam alone, the national bus service was selling some 7 million intracity tickets a month, or 90 million a year, by 1970. United Republic of Tanzania, *Bus Transport*, 19, 28.

62. Burton, *African Underclass*, 165; Brennan and Burton, "Emerging Metropolis," 13–75.

63. Cohen, "Forgotten Audiences in the Passion Pits," 474.

64. Comments made in the interviews by those who walked and rode bicycles to the cinemas often resonated deeply with arguments advanced by Michel de Certeau in *The Practice of Everyday Life*, trans. Steven Rendall (Berkeley: University of California Press, 1984). In this regard, I conducted interviews with Iddi Maganga, December 12, 2004, Dar es Salaam; Shabani Mkoga, October 20, 2004, Dar es Salaam; Juma Sultan and Ali Ghafoor, May 17, 2005, Dar es Salaam; Khalid Saloum, December 12, 2004, Dar es Salaam; Shaaban Kavitenda, September 22, 2004, Dar es Salaam. This was also noted by many who entered the essay contest, including Juma Mussa and Abby Joseph, who were both from Iringa; Yusuf Kajenje, Charles Franzen, and Felista Mwakale, who were from Dar es Salaam; and Nabila Ally, who was from Arusha.

65. Khalid Saloum interview; Shabani Mkoga interview; Iddi Maganga interview; Ali Ghafoor interview of May 19, 2005.

66. Khalid Saloum interview. Employees, patrons, and scholars also noted that the crowds on the grassy slopes outside the cinema were frequently dominated by young men. Giltrow, "Young Tanzanians and the Cinema.".

67. Jane Sarkodie, "An Evening at the Drive-In Cinema," essay contest submission.

68. Julius Nyerere, "Socialism Is Not Racialism," in his *Ujamaa: Essays on Socialism* (Dar es Salaam: Oxford University Press, 1968), 38–43.

69. Rural showings attracted hundreds of people within walking distance, from both near and far, with attendance averaging between 300 and 500. In exceptional cases, crowds could be as large as 2,000 to 3,000. "District Commissioner Pangani Report, October 27, 1953," TNA 562/I2/22: Information and Publications, Mobile

Cinema Van. Yet records from the ministries that ran these vans indicate that such shows were few and far between. In the late 1940s, there was only one van for the entire country, and it was on tour for only three months annually. One year, the van would tour villages in the northern portion of the country, the next year, villages in the south, and so on. Because of breakdowns, the tours rarely went beyond one region. By 1950, there were two vans in Tanganyika, yet rough roads, heavy rains, and troubles with the projection equipment meant that scheduled shows were frequently canceled. The "mobile" van also relied heavily on the train to transport it, so that villages far from the rails were even less likely to see a show. TNA 3644: Mobile Cinema Unit Tours and Tour Reports; TNA 562/I2/22: Information and Publications, Mobile Cinema Van.

70. Frederick Macha e-mail of April 12, 2005, with the subject line "History of Cinema in Tanzania."

71. Ibid.; John, interview with the author, February 8, 2005, Dar es Salaam.

72. Donham, *Marxist Modern*, 4.

73. Nyerere was certainly no fan, but according to others who frequented the drive-in, members of his family regularly enjoyed evenings at the show. On more than one occasion, Nyerere publicly criticized the drive-in as a capitalist luxury good and a waste of state resources that could be better spent on housing, health clinics, and schools. Apparently, even members of his own household begged to disagree.

74. Admission ranged between TSh 1/50 and 5/-, depending on the film, at a time when a beer or a pack of cigarettes cost 2/25. United Republic of Tanzania, Central Statistical Bureau, *Statistical Abstract 1966* (Dar es Salaam, 1968), 152. Beers and cigarettes were often consumed by men in spaces where wives and children were not particularly welcome. The price of admission to cinemas in town was on a par with rates charged by the drive-in, but since children took up seats in a conventional theater, they had to have tickets as well.

75. Eddy was shocked when I told him that I remembered hiding in the trunk of a car to get into a drive-in as a teenager. "Really?" he said. "I thought only us Africans did things like that."

76. Kuhn, *Dreaming of Fred and Ginger*. Nate Plageman's recent book is another fine example of an author's ability to hear and convey not only people's words but also the emotions behind them. Plageman, *Highlife Saturday Night: Popular Music and Social Change in Urban Ghana* (Bloomington: Indiana University Press, 2013).

77. Although mention of a drive-in frequently conjures up images of necking couples, drive-in patrons were overwhelmingly families in both the United States and Tanzania. Segrave, *Drive-In Theaters*. Segrave found that in the United States, 72 percent of all patrons in the 1950s were family groups. No such statistics are available for Tanzania, but I would estimate from interviews and survey data that Tanzania's figures are not far off that mark. On the growth of drive-ins as spaces for

385

386   postwar family leisure, see also Cohen, "Forgotten Audiences in the Passion Pits";
Collins, *Hollywood Down Under*; Gomery, *Shared Pleasures*, 92–93.

78. Godwin Kaduma interview.

79. Anonymous interview of June 26, 2002.

80. Nyerere, *Ujamaa*, 1–12.

81. Kamal interview; Sarkodie, "Evening at the Drive-In Cinema"; Abby Joseph,
essay contest entry.

82. Lisa A. Lindsay, "'No Need . . . to Think of Home'? Masculinity and Domes-
tic Life on the Nigerian Railway, c. 1940–61," *Journal of African History* 39, no. 3
(1998): 439–66; Allman and Tashjian, *I Will Not Eat Stone*; Stephan F. Miescher,
Making Men in Ghana (Bloomington: Indiana University Press, 2005); Lisa A.
Lindsay and Stephan F. Miescher, eds., *Men and Masculinities in Modern Africa*
(Portsmouth, NH: Heinemann, 2003).

83. Sarkodie, "Evening at the Drive-In Cinema."

84. Both Nabila and Yusuf submitted entries to the essay contest I sponsored in
April and May 2005. In the United States, as well, the diverse drive-in audience
was, according to Cohen, "a sort of side show," where one could view those one did
not typically come in contact with. Drive-in audiences, she argues, were far more
diverse than the audiences at indoor theaters, mixing urban and rural, black and
white, affluent and working class, and including the disabled. In the US South,
drive-ins were also the first theaters to racially desegregate. Cohen, "Forgotten Audiences in the Passion Pits," 471, 478–79, quotation is from p. 478.

85. Generational struggles over access to public space and a renegotiation of respectability and autonomy from patriarchal control are common themes in Kiswahili literature published in the postindependence era.

86. Mulji interview.

87. Akhmed, interview with the author, December 10, 2004, Dar es Salaam.

88. Agnello Fernandez interview.

89. Saloum and Fatuma, interview with the author, October 12, 2004, Dar es
Salaam.

90. Charles Franzen, essay contest response, May 2005.

91. Agnello Fernandez interview; Mulji interview.

92. Mbaruku, interview with the author, April 10, 2005, Dar es Salaam.

93. Tripp, *Changing the Rules*; Deborah Fahy Bryceson, *Food Insecurity and
the Social Division of Labor in Tanzania, 1919–85* (New York: St. Martin's Press,
1990); Grace, "People's Car of Dar es Salaam."

94. Fatma Alloo, interview of May 14, 2002; Shanin interview.

95. Hessler, *Social History of Soviet Trade*; Katherine Verdery, *What Was
Socialism, and What Comes Next?* (Princeton, NJ: Princeton University Press,
1996).

96. Such tales were shared by many who traveled between the mainland and
Zanzibar, Kenya, and Zambia. For obvious reasons, the names of those who spoke

of such matters are not given here. Smugglers were identified as high-level enemies of the state. In the early 1980s, large-scale traders in scarce commodities, particularly Asians, were arrested, imprisoned, and divested of their property in a mass campaign against "economic saboteurs." This campaign was launched in March 1983, resulting in more than four thousand arrests—according to the state-run *Daily News*—in a little over a month. Goods that were confiscated in large quantities included salt, cooking oil, sugar, flour, kerosene, soap, and hoes. The *Daily News* and *Sunday News* carried many articles in support of the campaign from March through June 1983. See also T. L. Maliyamkono and M. S. D. Bagachwa, *The Second Economy in Tanzania* (London: James Currey, 1990); Richa Nagar, "South Asian Diaspora," 62–80; Issa G. Shivji, "Liberalization and the Crisis of Ideological Hegemony," in *Re-thinking the Arusha Declaration*, ed. Jeannette Hartmann (Copenhagen: Axen Nielsen and Son A/S, 1991), 132–43.

97. Leonne, interview with the author, March 7, 2005, Dar es Salaam.

98. Ina Merkel, "Luxury in Socialism: An Absurd Proposition," in *Pleasures in Socialism: Leisure and Luxury in the Eastern Bloc*, ed. David Crowley and Susan Reid (Evanston, IL: Northwestern University Press, 2010), 53–70.

99. Sarkodie, "Evening at the Drive-In Cinema." In the United States, drive-in patrons spent forty-five cents on concessions for every dollar they spent on admissions. Segrave, *Drive-In Theaters*, 71, 89.

100. Gigri interview.

101. Sarkodie, "Evening at the Drive-In Cinema."

102. Anonymous [employee], interview with the author, January 16, 2005, Dar es Salaam.

103. Fitzpatrick, *Everyday Stalinism*; Gronow, *Caviar with Champagne*; Hessler, *Social History of Soviet Trade*.

104. Charles Franzen, "A Night at the Drive-In Cinema, Dar es Salaam," essay contest submission, May 2005.

Chapter 7: The Independence Generation Goes to the Show

1. Ng'wanakilala, *Liberating Effect of Mass Communication*, 67. "Mahudhurio na pato la Kampuni TFC kutokana na biashara ya sinema za kigeni hapa nchini," ZNA, EA 10/13: Report "Hali ya matarajio na mwelekeo wa sinema"; Mark Leveri, "Fiscal Planning and Control in Motion Picture Production: A Paradigm for a Costing Technique System at the Audio-Visual Institute" (MBA thesis, University of Dar es Salaam, 1984), 50. Ticket sales were 4 million in 1979, 4.2 million in 1980, and 3.9 million in 1981.

2. In the thirty years between 1957 and 1988, the overall urban population on the mainland increased from 245,105 to 2,811,954. By 1978, it had reached 1,775,218. Some towns, such as Dar es Salaam and Arusha saw their populations swell by 1,200 to 1,400 percent. Smaller towns often saw even higher rates of growth. Zanzibar town's increase during this same period was just under 200 percent. Hosier,

387

Urban Development in Tanzania, 6; Lahmeyer, "Tanzania"; United Republic of Tanzania, Bureau of Statistics, *Morogoro Regional Socio-economic Profile* (Dar es Salaam: National Bureau of Statistics and Morogoro Regional Commissioner's Office, 2002).

3. M. Bienefeld and R. Sabot, "The National Urban Mobility, Employment and Income Survey of Tanzania (NUMEIST)" (Dar es Salaam: Ministry of Economic Affairs and Development Planning and Economic Research Bureau, 1971); R. H. Sabot, *Economic Development and Urban Migration: Tanzania, 1900–1971* (Oxford: Clarendon Press, 1979), 85; P. P. Namfua, "'Age, Sex, Marital Status,' Analysis of the 1978 Population Census," ed. Bureau of Statistics (Dar es Salaam: Ministry of Planning and Economic affairs, 1982), 57–91.

4. United Republic of Tanzania, Bureau of Statistics, *1978 Population Census* (Dar es Salaam: Ministry of Planning and Economic Affairs, 1982), vol. 5, table 6, and vol. 7, 57–66.

5. United Republic of Tanzania, Bureau of Statistics, *Kilimanjaro Region Socio-economic Profile* (Dar es Salaam: National Bureau of Statistics and Kilimanjaro Regional Commissioner's Office, 2002), 12–13; ibid., *Morogoro Regional Socio-economic Profile,* 16–17.

6. In 1984, some thirty-five hundred students were enrolled at the University of Dar es Salaam. Brian Cooksey, David Court, and Ben Makau, "Education for Self-Reliance and Harambe," in *Beyond Capitalism vs. Socialism in Kenya and Tanzania,* ed. Joel Barkan (Boulder, CO: Lynne Rienner, 1994), 201–34.

7. Sawasawa and Hyera, "Effectiveness of Feature Films," 30–31. Sawasawa and Hyera gave questionnaires to 160 people. Thirty percent of respondents said they went to the movies once a week, 24 percent went twice a week, and almost 8 percent said they went every day. In his study of movie theaters in Mwanza and Dar es Salaam, Luptatu found that two-thirds of the weekly audience was composed of patrons under thirty years of age; Luptatu, "Tanzania Film Company," 23.8. Luptatu, "Tanzania Film Company," 23; Feroz Mukhadam interview. Such patterns were typical for the United States as well, where youth comprised some three-fourths of the moviegoing public in the 1970s.

9. May Joseph, *Nomadic Identities: The Peformance of Citizenship* (Minneapolis: University of Minnesota Press, 1999), 45.

10. All of these films were known by different titles when released in Hong Kong, on the global market, and in North America. Lee's first film with Golden Harvest Studios, based in Hong Kong, was released internationally in 1971 under the English title *The Big Boss.* This same film was titled *Fists of Fury* in North America. His second film with Golden Harvest was known as *Fist of Fury,* or *The Chinese Connection* in North America. *The Way of the Dragon* (1973) was known as *Return of the Dragon* in North America. In 1973, he also began shooting *The Game of Death,* which was released after his passing. See Stephen Teo, *Hong Kong Cinema: The Extra Dimension* (London: British Film

Institute, 1997), for a complete filmmography, including Lee's lesser known films from the 1950s.

11. The lyrics to this song were originally recorded by Carl Douglas in 1974 and released by Pye (in the United Kingdom and Canada) and 20th Century Fox (in the United States) records. It was subsequently covered by performers from across Europe, Latin America, and the Caribbean.

12. Burgess, *Race, Revolution and the Struggle for Human Rights*; Burgess, "Cinema, Bell Bottoms, and Miniskirts," 287–313; Ivaska, "'Anti-mini Militants Meet Modern Misses,'" 104–21; Ivaska, *Cultured States*; Emily Callaci, "Dancehall Politics: Mobility, Sexuality, and Spectacles of Racial Respectability in Late Colonial Tanganyika, 1930s–1961," *Journal of African History* 52 (2011): 365–84. Harnessing and disciplining youth was also important elsewhere on the continent. Jay Straker, *Youth, Nationalism and the Guinean Revolution* (Bloomington: Indiana University Press, 2009); Donham, *Marxist Modern*.

13. Ng'wanakilala, *Liberating Effect of Mass Communication*, 67–68; Ssali, "Development and Role of an African Film Industry," 141–42; E. E. Kaungammo, "'Mass Media and Youth,'" in *The Young Child Study in Tanzania, Age 7–15*, ed. I. M. Omari and Paul J Mhaiki (Dar es Salaam: Tanzania National Scientific Research Council, 1977), 77–97.

14. Akhmed interview; Ali Ghafoor interview of May 17, 2005; Juma Sultan interview of May 17, 2005; Belleghe interview; Brij Behal interview; Feroz Mukhadam interview; Gamdul Sing Hans interview of January 22, 2004; Kamal interview

15. Ishumi, *Urban Jobless*, 47–56; Joe Lugalla, *Crisis, Urbanization, and Urban Poverty in Tanzania: A Study of Urban Poverty and Survival Politics* (New York: University Press of America, 1995).

16. According to Ishumi's survey of jobless youth in Dar es Salaam, Arusha, Mwanza, and Tabora, 75 percent planned on staying in the city. Ishumi, *Urban Jobless*, 68–69.

17. Joseph, *Nomadic Identities*, 52.

18. Freddy Macha, "Sensei Bomani: Pioneer of Martial Arts in Tanzania," April 22, 2012, accessed October 18, 2015, at freddymacha.blogspot.com.

19. Joseph, *Nomadic Identities*, 49–69; Kajubi Mukajanga, *Bruce Lee—Mfalme Wa Kung Fu* (Dar es Salaam: Grand Arts Promotions, 1982).

20. Gladness interview; Neema, interview with the author, July 25, 2005, Arusha; Hawa, interview with the author, October 14, 2004, Dar es Salaam.

21. Patricia Mbughuni, "The Image of Woman in Kiswahili Prose Fiction," *Kiswahili* 49, no. 1 (1982): 15–24; Elena Zúbková Bertoncini, "An Annotated Bibliography of Swahili Fiction and Drama Published between 1975 and 1984," in special issue on Swahili verbal arts, ed. Carol M. Eastman, *Research in African Literatures* 17, no. 4 (Winter 1986): 525–62; Emily Callaci, "Ujamaa Urbanism: History, Culture and the Politics of Authenticity in Socialist Dar es Salaam, 1967–80" (PhD diss., Northwestern University, 2012); Ernesta Simon Mosha, "Discourse Analysis

389

of Gender-Based Violence in Contemporary Kiswahili Fiction: A Case Study of Selected Novels of the Past Three Decades (1975–2004) and Young Tanzanians' Interpretations" (PhD diss., University of Waikato, 2013).

22. "On Sexual Harassment," *Sauti ya Siti*, March 1989, 4–5; "How Common Is Sexual Harassment in the Workplace?," *Sauti ya Siti*, March 1992, 4–5; Deborah Fahy Bryceson, "The Proletarianization of Women in Tanzania," *Review of African Political Economy* 17, no. (January–April 1980): 4–27; Marjorie Mbilinyi, Patricia Mbughuni, Ruth Meena, and Priscilla Olekambaine, *Education in Tanzania with a Gender Perspective* (Stockholm: SIDA, 1991); Mbilinyi, "The State of Women in Tanzania," *Canadian Journal of African Studies* 6, no. 2 (1972): 371–77; Z. Meghji, "The Development of Women Wage Labour: The Case of Industries" (master's thesis, University of Dar es Salaam, 1977).

23. Bryceson, "Proletarianization of Women," 21–22; Austin Bukenya, *The People's Bachelor* (Dar es Salaam: East African Publishing House, 1972); Mbilinyi et al., *Education in Tanzania*.

24. Leila Sheik, "Tamwa: Levina's Song—Supporting Women in Tanzania," in *Composing a New Song: Stories of Empowerment from Africa*, ed. Hope Bagyendera Chigundu (London: Commonwealth Foundation, 2004), 95–128, on Mzee Punch see 99–101; Chemi Che-Mponda, "Why Did Levina Kill Herself?" *Sauti ya Siti*, January–March 1990, 4–5; "Seminar on Sexual Harassment and Violence against Women," *Sauti ya Siti*, July–September 1990, 6; Bukenya, *People's Bachelor*.

25. Gladness interview

26. Nabila Ally Salim, interview with the author, April 24, 2005, Arusha.

27. Abby Joseph Mwingeleza, essay contest response (Iringa, 2005).

28. Joseph, *Nomadic Identities*, 65.

29. Bienefeld and Sabot, "National Urban Mobility"; Sabot, *Economic Development*, 90.

30. Bienefeld and Sabot, "National Urban Mobility"; Bryceson, "Proletarianization of Women," 23; Sabot, *Economic Development*, 89–98.

31. Mukajanga, *Bruce Lee*; Bruce Lee, *Tao of Jeet Kune Do* (Valencia, CA: Black Belt Communications, 1975); Saumu Mwalimu, "Fighting for Change—the Kung Fu Way," *Citizen*, August , 2011, at www.thecitizen.co.tz/sunday-citizen/38-soundiving /14184-fighting-for-change-the-kung-fu-way.html. In this piece, Titi Robinson Michael describes how he and friends began training by mimicking moves they had seen on screen and then seeking out others who knew more. Titi is now a professional karate trainer in Dar es Salaam, using training as a means of instilling values of discipline and self-control in youth.

32. Obituary of Nantambu Bomani (Victor Phillips III), who was born in Ithaca, New York, and passed away in Ghana on August 22, 2009, *Ithaca (NY) Journal*, September 1, 2009.

33. Rumadha Fundi, one of many in the Tanzanian diaspora to comment on the Internet after Bomani's passing, spoke of being inspired by the man, who was

a neighbor from Kariakoo (Aggrey/Congo Streets). See also Freddy Macha's blog, accessed October 18, 2015, at goju-ryukaratemwanza.blogspot.com/2010/10/sensei-bomani-pioneer-of-martial-arts.html, and Issa Michuzi's blog, at issamichuzi .blog spot.com/2014/10/Tanzania-karate-awards-five-5-senior.html.

34. Teo, *Hong Kong Cinema*, 110–21; Joseph, *Nomadic Identities*, 59–61.

35. Googling "Sensai Bomani" returns thousands of hits. After his death in 2009, former students from across the globe turned to the internet to share their memories and articulate their grief. Among those who posted were Freddy Macha, in the Tanzanian newspaper *Citizen* on April 22, 2010, and Issa Michuzi, the Tanzanian blogger. In his introduction to *Black Political Thought in the Making of South African Democracy* (Bloomington: Indiana University Press, 1999), C. R. D. Halisi thanks Bomani and the other comrades and southern African freedom fighters he studied martial arts with in Dar es Salaam.

36. When he was eight, he started training under Bomani; he continued to train in karate for fifteen years before moving on to more mixed martial arts. See www.guhle.typepadcom/jespintanzania/training_with_the_champ, originally published as Jesper Gulhe Mogensen, "'Training with the Champ: Japhet Kaseba—Tanzania's World Kickboxing Champion," *ZanAir*, in-flight magazine, issue 9 (2009): 10–11.

37. Nyerere, *Ujamaa*, 22.

38. Kamal interview.

39. Joseph, *Nomadic Identities*, 49.

40. This is at the heart of Lee's jeet kun do philosophy and hybrid system of martial arts.

41. Historically, serving on board ships was a common occupation for young Swahili men. The prospect of traveling the globe and learning of different cultures and peoples was often as enticing as the prospect of earning money from such employment. When ships and dhows docked at ports, they typically spent anywhere from several days to several weeks and sometimes as long as a month. if the ship needed repairs, in port. In each port, networks established through other sailors helped men find ways to pass the time.Some opted to pursue drink and women, but others followed a range of divergent paths, from martial arts to training in skilled trades, politics, religion, music, and art.

42. Mukajanga, *Bruce Lee*; Kassim Musa Kassam, *Joto La Fedha* (Dar es Salaam: Kobe Publications, 1982). I recall many well-worn books containing both text and drawings circulating in Zanzibar in the early 1990s among martial artists.

43. Lee, *Tao of Jeet Kune Do*; John R. Little, *Bruce Lee: A Warrior's Journey* (New York: Contemporary Books, 2001); Mukajanga, *Bruce Lee*.

44. Kareem Abdul Jabbar said that both he and Lee were avid fans of Herman Hesse, whose works they frequently discussed while developing and testing new styles of fighting and self-defense; Jabbar as cited in Little, *Bruce Lee*, 38, 91, and 195. See also the introduction written by Linda Lee in Lee, *Tao of Jeet Kune Do*.

45. Tripp, *Changing the Rules*.

46. As quoted by Issa Mchuzi after the Mwalimu Nyerere Memorial show in October 2014. See issamchuzi.blog-spot.com/2014/10/Tanzania.karate-awards-five-%-senior.html.

47. This adage was first taught to me by Idi. When I Googled it on November 14, 2012, I came up with 1,620,000 hits.

48. Sawasawa and Hyera, "Effectiveness of Feature Films," 30–31; Luptatu, "Tanzania Film Company," 23.

49. Chanu Vadgama interview; Feroz Mukhadam interview; Gamdul Sing Hans interview of January 22, 2004;Abdulhussein Marashi, interview of May 7, 2002; Pankaj Valambia interview; Suresh Solanki interview.

50. Neema interview.

51. Edward, interview with the author, April 15, 2004, Arusha. On the importance of going with different groups of friends in India see Srinivas, *House Full*, 130–36.

52. Shabani Mkoga interview.

53. Stambach, *Lessons from Mount Kilimanjaro*, 72–79; Leila Sheik-Hashim, *Unyago*; Fair, "Identity, Difference and Dance," 146–72.

54. Edna Rajab interview.

55. Luke Ford, *A History of X: 100 Years of Sex in Film* (Amherst, NY: Prometheus Books, 1999), 21. The novel itself was banned in the United States until 1959.

56. *Daily News*, September–October 1983. It is possible that the film began its run even earlier in the year.

57. Ebrahim Hussein, *Wakati Ukuta* (Dar es Salaam: East African Publishing House, 1971), 11.

58. Luptatu, "Tanzania Film Company," 25; Sawasawa and Hyera, "Effectiveness of Feature Films," 30–34.

59. Paul Fernandez, interview with the author, February 8, 2005.

60. Luptatu, "Tanzania Film Company," 25; Sawasaw and Hyera, "Effectiveness of Feature Films," 30–34k

61. In the 1980s, *Ms. Magazine* conducted one of the first nationwide surveys of date and acquaintance rape in the United States, surveying students at thirty-two universities. The findings were that one in four women surveyed were victims of rape or attempted rape and that 84 percent knew their attackers. Robin Warshaw, *I Never Called It Rape: The Ms. Report on Recognizing, Fighting and Surviving Date and Acquaintance Rape* (New York: HarperCollins, 1988). Sadly, statistics on the incidence of rape on US college campuses remain largely unchanged to this day. Most date rapes continue to go unreported, but as late as 2014, 20 percent of women on college campuses surveyed in the United States had been victims of sexual assault by someone they knew. Tina deVaron, "At Colleges Plagued with Date Rape, Why 'No' Still Means 'Yes,'" *Christian Science Monitor*, June 28, 2011,

19; Jackie Calmes, "Obama Seeks to Raise Awareness of Rape on Campus," *New York Times*, January 23, 2014, 18; Jennifer Steinhauer, "U.S. Colleges Are Pressed to Combat Sex Assault," *International New York Times*, April 10, 2014, 4.

62. Luptatu, "Tanzania Film Company," 27; Khamis Msellem, interview with the author, December 16, 2004, Dar es Salaam; Taday interview; Kasanga interview of December 16, 2004.

63. Freddy Macha, "Cultural Images," *Sunday News*, February 21, 1982, 7.

64. In the United States, the song became a number one hit on Billboard Hot 100. The film, in contrast, earned numerous Golden Raspberry Awards, including worst actress, worst director, worst picture, and worst screenplay. Despite this, the film was remade in 2014.

65. Macha, "Cultural Images."

66. Three years later, in 1985, the film could still fill the Empire for five shows on Sunday. *Sunday News*, August 18, 1985, 5.

67. Shanin interview

68. Ahmed "Eddy" Alwi al-Beity interview of November 27, 2004.

69. Gigri interview.

70. Cohen's informants made similar comments about the relative sexual security of American drive-ins, where women felt they had more control to limit the extent of advances. Cohen, "Forgotten Audiences in the Passion Pits," 486n42.

71. Mulji interview; Mr. Drive-In interview.

72. Anonymous, interview with the author, March 12, 2005, Dar es Salaam.

Chapter 8: The Political Economy of Cinema, 1960s–80s

1. Tanzania Film Company was only one of more than four hundred state-owned-enterprises—easily twice the number found in Guinea, Ethiopia, Senegal, or Ghana. Andrew E. Temu and Jean M. Due, "The Business Environment in Tanzania after Socialism: Challenges of Reforming Banks, Parastatatals, Taxation and the Civil Service," *Journal of Modern African Studies* 38, no. 4 (2000): 683–712; John R. Nellis, "Public Enterprises in Sub-Saharan Africa," in *State-Owned Enterprises in Africa*, ed. Barbara Grosh and Rwekaza S. Mukandala (Boulder, CO: Lynne Rienner, 1994), 3–24, esp. 5.

2. TFC was established as a wholly owned subsidiary of NDC in 1968. A year later, it was designated a parastatal and transferred to the Tanzania Tourist Corporation. Its first managing director was appointed in late 1970. From July 1, 1974, TFC was transferred to the Ministry of Information and Broadcasting. NDC Public Relations Division, "A Beginning for a Tanzanian Film Industry," *Jenga: Magazine of the National Development Corporation* 11 (1972): 34; Tanzania Tourist Corporation, "Annual Report and Accounts" (n.p., 1973), 29.

3. The cinemas in Pemba were taken over and managed directly by a new government organization, known after 1970 as Shirika la Sinema Pemba. The Everest in Moshi was controlled directly by TFC, apparently because the former owner

393

refused the terms offered to continue with the business and no one else was willing to purchase the enterprise. In these cases, local managers were hired to operate the cinemas. "Halmshauri ya sinema za Serikali Pemba, 17 June 1974," Meneja Mkuu wa Shirika la UHNS to Msaidizi Meneja Mkuu shirika la UHNS, Chake, 10 September 1981, ZNA, AH 17/30: Entertainment Tax, 1947–82; Nitesh Virji interview.

4. The quote is from the master's thesis of the future general manager and secretary to the board of directors of Tanzania Film Company Limited, Mark Leveri; Mark Mbazi Eilinaza Leveri, "Prospects in Developing a Viable National Film Industry: A 'Close-Up' of a Decade's Performance of the Audio-Visual Institute of Dar es Salaam and the Tanzania Film Company Ltd. (1973–1983)" (master's thesis, University of Dar es Salaam, 1983), 7. In 1984, Leveri also completed an MBA and authored a thesis analyzing the budget of the Audio-Visual Institute.

5. Leveri, "Prospects," 7; Ng'wanakilala, *Mass Communication*, 70; Ssali, "Development and Role of an African Film Industry"; Mona Ngusekela Mwakalinga, "The Political Economy of the Film Industry in Tanzania: From Socialism to an Open Market Economy, 1961–2010" (PhD diss., University of Kansas, 2010); NDC, "Beginning for a Tanzanian Film Industry," 34; TFC, *Annual Report and Account, 1984–1988*; Konde, *Press Freedom in Tanzania*, 92–95.

6. Askew, *Performing the Nation*; Marissa Moorman, *Intonations: A Social History of Music and Nation in Luanda, Angola, 1945–Recent Times* (Athens: Ohio University Press, 2008); Thomas Turino, *Nationalists, Cosmopolitans, and Popular Music in Zimbabwe*, Chicago Studies in Ethnomusicology (Chicago: University of Chicago Press, 2000); Paul Schauert, *Staging Ghana: Artistry and Nationalism in State Dance Ensembles* (Bloomington: Indiana University Press, 2015).

7. The capital of Burkina Faso has been home to the famed African film festival FESPACO (Panafrican Film and Television Festival of Ouagadougou) since 1969. Sembene is widely regraded as the grandfather of independent African film. His films and those receiving awards at FESPACO have focused on themes relating to individual and institutional economic and social exploitation and liberation in the broadest sense. Diawara, *African Cinema*; Ukadike, *Black African Cinema*; Gugler, *African Film*; Pfaff, *Focus on African Films*; Thackway, *Africa Shoots Back*; Mahir Saul and Ralph A. Austen, eds., *Viewing African Cinema in the Twenty-First Century: Art Films and the Nollywood Video Revolution* (Athens: Ohio University Press, 2009).

8. N. Rana for the General Manager of TFC to Managers of Cine Afrique, Majestic and Empire Cinemas, 21 January 1982, ZNA, AH 17/30; Meneja Mkuu wa Majestic to Mkurugenzi wa Idara wa Mapato, Zanzibar, Malipo ya Taxes Kutoka Cinema Mwezi wa Mai, 1986, Majestic Cinema Zanzibar, Statement of Accounts.

9. Zanzibar Theaters Ltd. (Majestic Cinema), "Trading, Profit and Loss Account for the Year Ended 31st December 1984," "Trading, Profit and Loss Account for the Year Ended 31st December 1985," and "Trading, Profit and Loss Account for the Year Ended 31st December 1986," all in RC, File 1546: Majestic Theaters Ltd., Tanga. "Film, Exhibition, Profit and Loss Account for the Year Ended 31

December, 1981," "Film, Exhibition, Profit and Loss Account for the Year Ended 31 December, 1982." Asad Talati interviews of August 14, 15, and 16, 2004; Jitu Savani interview of May 26, 2005; Shabir K Jariwalla interview. Official exchange rates jumped from 9.2/$1 in 1982 to 17.73/$1 in 1985; my dollar conversion rate is an average of the two.

10. "Pato la Kampuni TFC kutokanan na biashara ya sinema za kigeni hapa nchini," ZNA, EA 10/13: "Hali ya matarajio na mwelekeo wa sinema." TFC's earnings were TSh 40.5 million, which at the official exchange rate of TSh 17.17/$1 equals $2,358,765.

11. Legislation authorizing income tax on "nonnatives" was introduced in East Africa in 1921 but was largely unenforced until 1940 due to settler objections. John F. Due, "Collecting Taxes South of the Sahara," *Challenge* 12, no. 1 (1963): 8–11; Fair, *Pastimes and Politics*, 110–68; John Iliffe, *A Modern History of Tanganyika* (Cambridge: Cambridge University Press, 1979), 118–20, 132–43, 306–9.

12. Amon Chaligha, "Taxation and the Transition to Socialism in Tanzania" (PhD diss., Claremont Graduate School, 1990); John F. Due, *Taxation and Economic Development in Tropical Africa* (Cambridge, MA: MIT Press, 1963), 26; Due, "Collecting Taxes."

13. According to Due, there were only 22 companies paying business taxes in Zanzibar and 633 in Tanganyika in 1960–61. In comparison, there were 4,553 in Rhodesia and 2,243 in Kenya. Only 10 percent of tax revenue in Zanzibar came from direct taxation of any type, but business taxes amounted to just 10 percent of this revenue. Due, *Taxation and Economic Development*, 50, 27. See also the Annual Tanganyika Territory Blue Books for extensive lists of duties, fees, and taxes imposed and collected between the 1920s and 1960.

14. A "profits tax" was introduced by the British in 1923 but abandoned in 1925 due to difficulty of collection. Honey, "History of Indian Merchant Capita," 349; Oonk, *Settled Strangers*, 151–53.

15. Owners and Managers of the Majestic, Empire and Sultana Cinemas to the Financial Secretary, 1 June 1962, ZNA, AH 17/30.

16. A flat fee on each tourist, paid by hotels, is one such example. In 2013, that fee was $8 per head, regardless of the room rental rate charged by the hotel. This is obviously a quite regressive but easy to administer system. Standard fees on film shows were equally regressive. The cost was the same regardless of whether one's theater accommodated two hundred patrons or six hundred and did not vary between films that drew a modest crowd and those that packed the auditorium. Import duties applied to basic commodities such as food and cloth are even more regressive, as the poor spend a much larger percentage of their income on basic necessities than the wealthy. Today's taxes on imported rice, sugar, cloth, and other basics are holdovers from the colonial era.

17. "Municipal Officer to Senior Commissioner, 16 July 1954," "Financial Secretary to HJ Hameers, AS Talati, AM Thaver, N Zaverchand, T Esmailji and LB

395

Desai, 22 June 1962," ZNA, AH 17/30; TNA 20374: Entertainment Tax. As of 1947, there was no entertainment tax on the books in Tanganyika Territory, and the file labeled "Entertainment Tax" was one of the thinnest in the archives I consulted. Shabir K Jariwalla interviewDar es Salaam. Bashir Punja, "This Film System Is Not Fair," *Sunday News*, June 12, 1966, 7; "Government Gets Tough with Cinemas," *Sunday News*, June16, 1966, 1; "Cinema Charges Too High," letter to the editor, signed "Disturbed," *Daily News*, March 1, 1983, 5; ZNA, EA 10/13.

18. In 1954, when the Legislative Council began to seriously debate the possibility of applying a tax on cinema tickets, the municipal officer estimated that it would generate about £1,500 per annum. When the bill was finally passed in 1962, the government estimated it would raise about £3,000 per year. Officials were pleasantly surprised when they collected nearly double their estimate. "Municipal Officer to Senior Commissioner, 16 July 1954," "Acting Permanent Secretary to Financial Secretary, 18 August 1962," "Accountant General to Permanent Secretary, 16 October 1962," "Acting Permanent Secretary, 22 October 1962," ZNA, AH 17/30.

19. "Acting Financial Secretary to Chief Secretary, 9 January 1960," ZNA, AH 17/30.

20. "Owners of Pemba Cine, Chake, Liberty, Chake, Novelty, Wete and Prabhat, Wete to Chief Minister, 1 June 1962," "Owners and Managers of the Majestic, Empire and Sultana Cinemas, Zanzibar to Financial Secretary, 1 June 1952," ZNA, AH 17/30.

21. "P. Makenshaw, General Manager Indian Film Combine, 13 June 1962," ZNA, AH 17/30.

22. Copies of the Bill, First Gazetted on 19 May 1962 and Amended andPassed as Bill 16 of 1962, ZNA, AH 17/30.

23. "Government Gets Tough with Cinemas," *Sunday News*, June 16, 1966, 1. On press ownership and circulation, see John C. Condon, "Nation Building and Image Building in the Tanzania Press," *Journal of Modern African Studies* 5, no. 3 (1967): 335–54; Ng'wanakilala, *Mass Communication*, 51–52; Konde, *Press Freedom*, 49–51. "Tanzania's Largest Daily Paper Joins the NDC Group," *Jenga* (May 1970): 3.

24. In Zanzibar, the tax amounted to shs 4/30 on an average ticket of price of 15/-. On the mainland, ticket prices were generally higher, at 22/-, with the entertainment tax comprising 6/- of that in 1982. "AS Talati, Owner of the Cine Afrique to Minister of Finance, 23 June 1982," "Naaz Rana, General Manager of the Tanzania Film Company to Managers of Zanzibar Theaters, 21 January, 1982," ZNA, AH 17/30.

25. This was as of 1981. "Othman Othman, Mkaguzi wa Mapato: Mapato wa Sinema Yaliyokusanywa," ZNA, AH 17/30. The tax collected from Cine Afrique amounted to TSh 516,718, that from the Majestic 427,571, and the Empire 231,631. Pemba cinemas were nationalized in the 1970s and combined into one group: Shirika la Sinema, Pemba. Although the group was obligated to pay taxes, the

general manager of cooperatives complained that none had been forwarded to the general fund since the cinemas were put under state control. "Meneja Mkuu wa Shirika la UHNS to Msaidizi Meneja Mkuu UHNS Chake, 10 September 1981," also in ZNA, AH 17/30.

26. "Pato la Serikali Kutokana na biashara ya sinema za kigeni hapa nchini," ZNA, EA 10/13. The official and unofficial exchange rates began to change dramatically in the 1980s. Here and elsewhere. I figure at the official exchange rate, since TFC was a government institution. In 1982, the official exchange rate was 8.32 shillings to the dollar; by 1984, it has jumped to 17.8. See Andrew Kiondo, "The Nature of Economic Reforms in Tanzania," in *The IMF and Tanzania*, ed. Horace Campbell and Howard Stein (Harare: Southern Africa Political Economy Series Trust, 1991), 23–47 and 33 for a table of exchange rates.

27. N Rana for the General Manager of Tanzania Film Company to Managers of Cine Afrique, Majestic and Empire Cinemas, 21 January 1982, ZNA, AH 17/30.

28. Zanzibar Theaters Ltd. (Majestic Cinema), "Trading, Profit and Loss, 1985."

29. In Zanzibar, this arrangement of sharing profits on a fifty-fifty basis was initially agreed upon informally between members of the Baraza la Mapinduzi (Revolutionary Council) and cinema proprietors. This arrangement was later formalized under Presidential Decree No. 15 of 1971. ZNA, AH 17/30. Corporate tax rates on the mainland increased from 37.5 percent in 1965 to 40 percent by 1967, eventually reaching 50 percent after 1976.

30. Chaligha, "Taxation and the Transition," 171–72.

31. Brij Bihal interview.

32. Zanzibar Theaters Ltd. (Majestic Cinema), "Trading, Profit and Loss" 1985; Feruz Hussein interview of July 6, 2002; Msafiri Punda interview; Robert Kibwana interview.

33. Msafiri Punda interview; Robert Kibwana interview.

34. RC, File 1546: Majestic Theaters Ltd., Tanga, "Film Exhibition, Profit and Loss," 1980, 1981, 1982, 1984, 1985, 1986, 1987; Zanzibar Theaters Ltd. (Majestic Cinema), "Statement of Trading, Profit and Loss," 1982, 1984, 1985, 1986. Abdulhussein Marashi interviews of February 4, 2004, and May 7 and 15, 2002; Ally "Rocky" Khamis Ally interview; Asad Talati, interviews of August 14, 15, and 16, 2004; Chunilal Kala Savani interviews; Feroz Mukhadam interview; Feruz Hussein interview of June 25, 2002; Gamdul Sing Hans interviews of January 22 and April 19, 2004; Jitu Savani interview of May 26, 2005; Pankaj Valambia interview; Rashid Said interview; Robert Kibwana interview; Sapna Talkies Ltd. Morogoro, "Trading, Profit and Loss Accounts, 1994"; Shariff Al-Beity interview; Suresh Solanki interview.

35. "Halmshauri ya sinema za Serikali Pemba," ZNA AH 17/30.

36. The Cine Afrique in Zanzibar is but one example. In 2002, the wall behind the screen of the theater collapsed due to water damage—damage that could easily have been prevented with a simple repair—which brought an inglorious end

397

to a building that had brought joy to untold millions for half a century. Because Stone Town received a UNESCO World Heritage Site designation in 2000, it was still somehow deemed important to maintain the facade of the former theater, although the interior of the building has completely changed. Many other theaters had had their interiors gutted by 2000. Among these were the Highland in Iringa and the Sapna in Morogoro, as well as the Chox, Avalon, Empress, and Odeon in Dar es Salaam. Popular new uses were godowns or rent-to-own furniture stores, owned by companies out of South Africa.

37. Asad Talati interview of August 14, 2004.

38. One can go on YouTube and search for "carbon arc projection" to see demonstrations of this technology.

39. Asad Talati interview of August 14, 2004.

40. Shabir K. Jariwalla interview.

41. Nagar, "South Asian Diaspora in Tanzania," 62–80; Oonk, *Settled Strangers*, 212–22. Both Nagar and Oonk found that people were fairly understanding of the nationalization of their businesses. It was assaults on their persons and the sanctity of the home that caused them to flee. In Zanzibar and Pemba, there were mass murders and sexual assaults of Asian and Arab women during and after the revolution. Thousands fled by any means possible. The majority initially moved to the mainland. Others left for Kenya, the United Kingdom, and Canada, and a few moved to India or Pakistan. Mass exodus from the mainland was not spurred by the Arusha Declaration of 1967, which nationalized businesses, but by the Building Acquisition Act of 1971, where people lost their homes. In both Zanzibar and the mainland, widespread anti-Asian rhetoric followed these political events, increasing people's sense of fear.

42. Vassanji, *Book of Secrets*, 311–13.

43. Mr. Khambaita interview. He was far from alone in choosing this path. According to Oonk, many Tanzanian Asians employed similar strategies, with the man acquiring Tanzanian citizenship and staying in the country to work and the women and children moving to the United Kingdom or Canada on a British passport. Oonk, *Karimjee Jivanjee Family*; Oonk, *Settled Strangers*, 175–228.

44. Many individuals went on to occupy prominent positions in the government after their families' assets were confiscated in the name of socialist economic transformation. Two examples are illustrative. J. K. Chande, whose family's private milling corporation was nationalized in 1967, was appointed the following year as general manager of the National Milling Corporation, the giant parastatal amalgamated from all of the previously independent companies. AbdulKarim Karimjee, whose family had at least fifty buildings nationalized in 1971 but managed to maintain control of several of their most profitable business ventures including their sisal estates and Toyota dealership, also served as the director of the National Development Corporation and the National Bank of Commerce after most of the family's buildings and some of their businesses were nationalized. J. K. Chande, A

Knight in Africa: Journey from Bukene (Manotick, Canada: Penumbra Press, 2005); Oonk, *Karimjee Jivanjee Family*, 112–13.

45. Gregory, *South Asians in East Africa*; Nagar, "South Asian Diaspora"; C. Voigt-Graf, *Asian Communities in Tanzania: A Journey through Past and Present* (Hamburg: Hamburg University Press, 1998); Honey, "History of Indian Merchant Capital"; Kassum, *Africa's Winds of Change*; Chande, *Knight in Africa*; Rwekaza S. Mukandala, "State Enterprise Control: The Case of Tanzania," in *State-Owned Enterprises in Africa*, ed. Barbara Grosh and Rwekaza S. Mukandala (Boulder, CO: Lynne Rienner, 1994), 125–47. Al Noor Kassum, whose father was a prominent investor in Indo-African Theaters and owner of the Avalon, Chox, and Amana Cinemas in Dar es Salaam, for instance, was appointed by Nyerere to serve in many key posts, including as minister of finance and administration of the East Africa Community; minister of water, energy, and minerals; and chairman of the National Development Corporation. Despite Al Noor's political appointments, his family's theaters were all nationalized. Al Noor was also appointed by Nyerere as the general manager of Williamson Diamonds—the main diamond mine in the country—and as Tanzania's representative to UNESCO in Paris and New York.

46. Naaz Rana interview.

47. Hanan Sabea, "Reviving the Dead: Entangled Histories in the Privatisation of the Tanzanian Sisal Industry," *Africa* 71, no. 2 (2001): 286–313; Deborah Fahy Bryceson, *Liberalizing Tanzania's Food Trade* (Dar es Salaam: Mkuki na Nyota, 1993), 16–24, 53–61, 68–70; Marjorie Mbilinyi, *Gender and Employment on Sugar Cane Plantations in Tanzania* (Geneva: ILO, 1995), 30.

48. From 1969 to 1973, TFC was under the Tanzania Tourist Corporation, before being granted independence. NDC, "Beginning for a Tanzanian Film Industry," 34; Tanzania Tourist Corporation, *Annual Report and Accounts 1973* (n.p.: n.p., n.d.), 29.

49. TFC, *Annual Report and Account, 1984–1988*, 1; Alex Perullo, *Live from Dar Es Salaam: Popular Music and Tanzania's Music Economy* (Bloomington: Indiana University Press, 2011), 287–97; Mponguliana, "Development of Film in Tanzania."

50. RC, File 4298: Anglo-American Film Distributors; TFC, *Annual Report and Accounts, 1984–1988*, 1; NDC, *Annual Report 1971* (Dar es Salaam: National Development Corporation, 1972), 73, 80; Guback, "Hollywood's International Market," 463–86; Guback, "Film as International Business: The Role of American Multinationals," in *The American Movie Industry: The Business of Motion Pictures*, ed. Gorham Kindem (Carbondale: Southern Illinois University Press, 1982), 336–50; Guback, "American Films and the African Market," *Critical Arts* 3, no. 3 (1985): 1–14.

51. *Jenga* 1972, Vol. 11, 34; "Memo from TFC 21 February 1972," ZNA, AH 17/30.

52. In actuality, distributors fought to retain control of both their films and their booking schedules as much as possible. Their ability to do so varied between distributors and over the years.

399

53. Kampuni ya Filamu Tanzania, *Taarifa ya mwaka na hesabu kwa mwaka ulioishia 31 December 1990*, table 1: Income, Profit and Loss, 1980–1990 (Dar es Salaam: TFC, 1991), 7. Actual earnings increased from TSh 8,826,171 in 1980 to 18,433,662 in 1985, but due to changes in the exchange rate, the value in dollars remained slightly more than US$1 million. The highest earnings were achieved in 1982 and 1983, at roughly US$1.25 million.

54. Wilson, *US Foreign Policy and Revolution*; Burgess, *Race, Revolution and the Struggle for Human Rights*; Don Petterson, *Revolution in Zanzibar: An American's Cold War Tale* (Boulder, CO: Westview Press, 2002); Anthony Clayton, *The Zanzibar Revolution and Its Aftermath* (Hamden, CT: Archon Books,1981); Ian Speller, "An African Cuba? Britain and the Zanzibar Revolution, 1964," *Journal of Imperial and Commonwealth History* 35, no. 2 (2007): 283–301.

55. RC, File 4298: Anglo-American Film Distributors Ltd.

56. Ibid., "Directors Reports and Balance Sheets of Anglo-American Film Distributors Ltd, 1968–1982"; Leveri, "Prospects." For a number of years, NDC and then TFC were also in dialogue with 20th Century Fox about the possibility of opening a multimillion shilling cinema complex in Dar es Salaam. This project was never completed. NDC, *Annual Report 1971*, 80.

57. Mponguliana, "Development of Film in Tanzania," 42–43; Luptatu, "Tanzania Film Company," 42–43; Sawasawa and Hyera, "Effectiveness of Feature Films," 12–15; TNA 622/sl/B1: Bodi ya Filamu; Records of the Board of Film Censors, 1974, 1979, 1984, 1986, 1993–2000.

58. Kaungammo, "Mass Media and Youth," 91.

59. ZNA, EA10/13; TFC, *Annual Report and Account, 1984–1988*, 10.

60. "Tanzania Film Company Limited Accounts for the Six Months Ended 30 June 1985," ZNA, EA 10/13.

61. "DM Mazanda, Mhasibu Mkuu, Kuongeza bei za tikiti za sinema na mwago wa filmu mpya kwa mwaka 1985, 14 December 1984," ZNA, EA 10/11: Kampuni ya Filamu Tanzania Bodi ya Wakurugenzi 1984.

62. "Tanzania Film Company Ltd., Accounts for the Year Ended 30 June 1985," ZNA, EA 10/13.

63. Comments made about corruption and illegal activities in interviews remain anonymous. Only a few of the many people interviewed asked explicitly to remain anonymous or to speak off the record, but for legal and ethical purposes, names are not cited related to this material.

64. "Report of the Auditors for the Year 1985, Signed and Delivered February 1987," TFC, *Annual Report and Account, 1984–1988*, 5.

65. RC, File 3570: Tanzanian Film Company Limited, "Auditor's Reports, 1980–1983"; TFC, *Annual Report, 1984–1988*. Among the items noted in line-item budget purchases, projector carbons were mentioned only once in six years.

66. RC, File 3570: Tanzania Film Company Ltd., "Auditor's Report, 1981," "Auditor's Report, 1982," "Auditor's Report, 1983."

67. "Report of the Auditors, 1984," "Report of the Auditors, 1985," "Report of the Auditors, 1986," "Report of the Auditors, 1987," TFC, *Annual Report 1984–1988*, 4–6. Auditors were paid TSh 1.5 million for their work.

68. NDC, *Fifth Annual Report and Accounts*, 90. In 1971, Sisi Enterprises was transferred to TFC. All financial and corporate records related to Sisi disappear after that point.

69. RC, File 3570, "Tanzania Audit Corporation, TFC Balance 1980" and "Tanzania Audit Corporation, TFC Report 1981–83"; "Report of the Auditors, 1987," TFC, *Annual Report, 1984–1988*, 4, 10. Oddly, a line item is given for these shows in the statements of profit and loss between 1984 and 1988. The only year anything is noted is 1984, when a loss of 58,494 shillings is indicated. In 1987, auditors noted that two premier shows were offered by TFC, but there were no records of any kind in the accounts.

70. TFC, *Annual Reports, 1984–1988*; TFC, *Taarifa ya mwaka na hesabu*, 7.

71. Mr. Ninga, interview of April 11, 2005; TFC, *Annual Reports, 1984–1988*, 10; TFC, *Taarifa ya mwaka na hesabu*, 11.

72. TFC, *Annual Reports, 1984–1988*, 22; TFC, *Taarifa ya mwaka na hesabu*, 20.

73. RC, File 3570 provides the names and official positions of board members.

74. Anonymous, interview with the author, May 21, 2005, Dar es Salaam.t

75. Leveri, "Prospects," 51; Luptatu, "Tanzania Film Company," 13.

76. "Schedule No. 9, Overhead Costs," TFC, *Annual Reports and Accounts, 1984–1988*, 22.

77. Mark Leveri, who became the general manager of TFC and secretary to the board, was critical of a similar ratio of expenditure when he analyzed the budget of TFC's sister organization, the Audio-Visual Institute, in 1984. Leveri, "Fiscal Planning and Control," 39–40.

78. A sequel to this film, *Yomba Yomba*, was released in 1989, but according to Mwakalinga, the film was never screened for the Tanzanian public. Mwakalinga, "Political Economy of the Film Industry," 59–61.

79. Leveri, "Prospects," 6–8; Mponguliana, "Development of Film," 38–40; Mwakalinga, "Political Economy of the Film Industry," 53–55; Ssali, "Development and Role of an African Film Industry," 109–33; Smyth, "Feature Film in Tanzania," 389–96.

80. I was initially asked to pay $300 for the VHS copy I eventually received. I refused but said I was perfectly willing to provide VHS tapes and pay someone a reasonable wage to make the copies. We eventually settled on $25 for copies of the film and its sequel. Although I thought we were making an above-the-board transaction, when I went to pick up the copies the archivist had me drive to a nearby gas station before he produced the films, which he retrieved from inside the front of his pants! It seems that the culture of corruption at TFC quite effectively trickled down throughout the organization. My field notes indicate that the archivist and

401

I began our conversation in his office, under a large poster hanging on the wall condemning corruption, proclaiming it illegal, and calling on those who witness corruption to report it.

81. Leveri, "Prospects," 58–61. According to Leveri, the Ministry of Economic Affairs and Development Planning issued a report in May 1972 directing the government to focus on distribution, where the money was, rather than filmmaking, which required substantial investment. In 1974, TFC became a full-fledged parastatal organization under the Ministry of Information and Broadcasting. As a parastatal, the organization was expected to be financially independent of government subsidies, to meet its goals and expenses from self-generated income, and to turn a profit that went to enhance central accounts. *Jenga* 1972, vol. 11, 34; NDC, *Annual Report 1971*, 73; Ssali, "Development and Role of an African Film Industry," 113–20.

82. Mwakalinga, "Political Economy of the Film Industry," 78–82.83. TFC, "Annual Reports, 1984–1988," 3. Heavy losses were attributed to an investment in a record-manufacturing plant, which was supposed to begin production in 1981 but failed for numerous reasons, including the exploding preference for cassette tapes over LPs for home and portable music listening.

84. "Mazungumzo kati ya viongozi wa TFC na Wizara kuhusu upigaji wa filamu za kibiashara za Kitanzania, 5 January 1976" and "Kumbukumbu za Mkutano wa Kurugenzi za Sanaa na Lugha ya taifa, Nyaraka Kukuu, Mambo ya Kale, Michezo na Vijana, na Utafiti na Mipango Kuongelea Ombi la Ushauri Kutoka TFC Kuhusu Suala la Utengenazaji wa Filamu za Kibiashara za Kitanzania, 14 January 1976," TNA 622/sl/t1/15. For a discussion of this fiction, see Callaci, "Ujamaa Urbanism."

85. TFC employees often found themselves in competition with AVI filmmakers, who made similar types of films. To make matters worse, AVI was within the state ministerial structure and thus had a regular, reoccurring budget that paid for the making of films. In a typical year, AVI produced four times the number of film shorts as TFC. Leveri, "Prospects," 6, 58–59; Mwakalinga; Edna Rajab interview; Godwin Kaduma interview; Belleghe interview

86. Mponguliana, "Development of Film," 38–40; Andrew John Josiah Mtekateka, "The Importance of Adult Education Film Shows to Adult Learners" (master's thesis, University of Dar es Salaam, 1987), 7; Smyth, "Feature Film in Tanzania"; Mwakalinga, "Political Economy of the Film Industry," 76–82.

87. Mponguliana provides a detailed list of distribution and lending from the national film library where TFC and AVI films were held. Mponguliana, "Development of Film in Tanzania," 49–54.

88. Leveri, "Prospects," 10.

89. "Chairman's Statement, F. J. Kibonde," TFC, *Annual Report and Account 1984–1988*, 1; Godwin Kaduma interview.

90. Godwin Kaduma interview; Belleghe interview; Martin Mhando, personal correspondance, 2008; Edna Rajab interview; Mwakalinga, "Political Economy of the Film Industry," 57–61.

91. Von Freyhold, *Ujamaa Villages in Tanzania*; Hyden, *Beyond Ujamaa in Tanzania*.

92. Godwin Kaduma interview.

93. Ronald Aminzade, *Race, Nation, and Citizenship in Post-colonial Africa: The Case of Tanzania* (Cambridge: Cambridge University Press, 2013), 10.

94. The National Development Corporation was riddled with such contradictions. In 1972, the organization's public relations magazine highlighted the importance of generating profits through parastatals, such as TFC, if the nation hoped to improve standards of living for the masses. Its news magazine, *Jenga*, featured an article by F. Csagoly, the Hungarian director of NDC's Department of Research and Development, entitled, "Profits Are Socialist." There, Csagoly derides the idea that "the bigger the losses, the better the socialist who makes them," proclaiming repeatedly that profits are socialist. *Jenga* 12 (1972): 2–5.

95. "Party Resolves on Films," *Nationalist*, March 22, 1969, 1.

96. Ibid.; "*Sinema*," *Uhuru*, March 24, 1969, 2.

97. "Sijaona Warns Saboteurs of 'Operation Vijana,'" *Nationalist*, January 1, 1969, 1; Ivaska, "'Anti-mini Militants Meet Modern Misses,'" 104–21; Andrew Ivaska, "Consuming and Contesting 'Soul' in Tanzania," in *New World Coming: The Sixties and the Shaping of Global Consciousness*, ed. Karen Dubinsky et al. (Toronto: Between the Lines, 2009), 169–78; Ivaska, *Cultured States*.

98. "On Revolution," *Nationalist*, March 17, 1969, 4; "Freedom and Socialism," *Nationalist*, January 1, 1969, 4. Cinema ads and film reviews appeared on p. 5. The *Sunday News* in October 1970 is particularly revealing. Each week, there was extensive coverage of women being arrested for "indecent" dress or willful sexuality, as well as numerous letters and editorials calling on the censor board to improve the quality of films that undermine Tanzanian culture and lead youth astray. Nearly naked women remained a common feature in the cinema advertising, nonetheless.

99. Obituary for the *Nationalist* written on the day of its merger with the *Standard* to form the *Daily News*, April 26, 1972, cited in full in Konde, *Press Freedom in Tanzania*, 67–73, 81.

100. In the mid-1970s, X-rated films were banned from the drive-in, allegedly because the child of someone with very powerful connections was traumatized by watching a late-night horror film from the family's balcony, adjacent to the drive-in. Horror films were almost always rated X, in an effort to protect children from precisely these kinds of frights. Supposedly, no more X-rated films were ever screened at the drive-in after this incident.

101. Mulji interview; Mr. Drive-In interview.

102. Ahmed "Eddy" Alwi al-Beity interview of November 27, 2004.

103. "*Sinema*," *Uhuru*, March 24, 1969, 2; Board of Film Censors Reports, 1963–1993, Office of the Board of Censors; ZNA, AD 5/81: Ministry of Education and Information, Correspondance Regarding Stage Plays and Cinematograph Censorship Panels; TNA 622/sl/B1. In many years, no films at all were banned. But 1974–75 was

403

an exception to the rule, with twenty-nine films banned in 1974 and twenty-two in 1975. The 1974–75 year was also remarkable in terms of the written records kept—and preserved—regarding censor decisions. Nineteen seventy-four was the first year that the Board of Film Censors served under the Ministry of National Culture and Youth, and it is likely board members and civil servants were working hard to justify their importance to their new bosses. Boniface Sanjala interview; Titus Lugendo, interview with the author, February 7, 2005, Dar es Salaam.

104. "Confidential Letters and Memos, 1964–1978," Office of the Board of Censors; TNA 622/Sl/B1; TNA 622/F2: Films, General Culture, 1969–78; TNA 622/ F2/5: Films and Theater, 1964–65; TNA 622/SL/T1/15: TFC 1977; TNA 622/ Sl/U/1/9: Utamaduni wa Mtanzania 1978; TNA 597/FA/S.40/2: Film Matters.

105. "Board of Censor Reports, 1963–1993," Office of the Board of Censors.

106. Boniface Sanjala, interview with the author, January 25, 2005, Dar es Salaam; Mwalim Idd Abdulla Farhan interview of April 2, 2002; Seif Bakari, interview with the author, April 4, 2002, Zanzibar; Titus Lugendo interview; Walter Bagoya, interview with the author, May 26, 2005, Dar es Salaam.

107. Hamza Kasongo, interview with the author, May 19, 2005, Dar es Salaam.

108. TNA 622/s1/B1.

109. Hamza Kasongo interview.

110. Boniface Sanjala interview of January 25, 2005.

111. Walter Bagoya interview.

112. Titus Lugendo interview The ministers under whom the board served were frequently overwhelmed with more pressing concerns, and it was not uncommon for employees of the board of censors to be denied a meeting with the minister before they were moved, yet again. Without ministerial backing and support, the Board of Censors was also hampered in its ability to call meetings or push its agenda. ZNA, AD 5/81; TNA 622/sl/B1; "Confidential Letters and Memos from 1964–1978," Board of Censors Office.

Epilogue: A New World

1. Majestic Books, 1972–93; Cine Afrique Books, 2002; Avalon ticket sales records, 2002.

2. United Film Distributors Distribution Records, 1992–2002.

3. The conversion of cinemas to Pentecostal churches became common in many parts of the continent in the 1990s. Birgit Meyer, "'Praise the Lord': Popular Cinema and Pentacostalite Style in Ghana's New Public Sphere," *American Ethnologist* 31, no. 1 (2004): 92–110; Meyer, *Sensational Movies*.

4. The only other cinema in the country was a multiplex in Arusha. In 2014, a small new theater opened in Zanzibar.

5. Butsch, *Making of American Audiences*; Collins, *Hollywood Down Under*; Gomery, *Shared Pleasures*; Kuhn, *Dreaming of Fred and Ginger*; Low, *History of British Film*; Robert D. Putnam, *Bowling Alone: The Collapse and Revival of*

American Community (New York: Simon and Schuster, 2000); Sklar, *Movie-Made America*; Robert Sklar, "The Lost Audience: 1950's Spectatorships and Historical Reception Studies," in *Identifying Hollywood's Audiences*, ed. Melvyn Stokes and Richard Maltby (London: British Film Institute, 1999), 81–92; Stokes and Maltby, *Identifying Hollywood's Audiences*; Melvyn Stokes and Richard Maltby, eds., *American Movie Audiences: From the Turn of the Century to the Early Sound Era* (London: British Film Institute, 1999); Gregory Waller, ed., *Moviegoing in America: A Sourcebook in the History of Film Exhibition* (Malden, MA: Blackwell, 2002). Anderson, *A City and Its Cinemas*.

6. UK Cinema Admission 1933–2001; "Motion Picture Statistics: Exhibition Grosses and Admissions," *International Motion Picture Almanac* (Groton, MA: Quigley, 2004).

7. It only became legal to own a TV and VCR in June 1985. The *Daily News* and *Sunday News* carried many articles in support of the campaign against economic saboteurs from March through June 1983. See also Maliyamkono and Bagachwa, *Second Economy in Tanzania*; Nagar, "South Asian Diaspora in Tanzania," 62–80; Issa G. Shivji, "Liberalization and the Crisis of Ideological Hegemony," in *Re-thinking the Arusha Declaration*, ed. Jeannette Hartmann (Copenhagen: Axen Nielsen and Son A/S, 1991), 132–43.

8. Between 1976 and 1979, the state sold roughly three hundred television sets per year. ZNA, ED 10/1; ZNA, ED 7/3: Vipindi vya Watoto, 1973–1976; ZNA, ED 7/1: Vipindi vya TV vya Watu Wazima, 1973–1976; ZNA, ED 10/2: Takrimu Mbalimbali Idara ya Televisheni; Martin Sturmer, *A Media History of Tanzania* (Mtwara, Tanzania: Ndanda Mission Press, 1998), 295–99.

9. In the late 1980s, as a "reward" for participation in the liberalization reforms promoted by the World Bank and IMF, the United States donated a satellite dish to TVZ, giving it access to a certain range of American products free of charge. Broadcasting times were doubled, and entertainment programs, including children's cartoons, were added to the educational and informational mix for the first time. Adbul Hamiri [program manager, TVZ], interview with the author, December 23, 2004, Zanzibar; Sturmer, *Media History*, 295–99; ZNA, ED 10/1; ZNA, ED 7/3; ZNA, ED 7/10; ZNA, ED 7/1; ZNA, ED 10/2.

10. Import restrictions were loosened gradually after 1985, but between 1990, when import restrictions were radically reduced, until 1997, when a value-added (VAT) tax was imposed and the mainland authorities imposed measures to move imports and trade to mainland ports, imports through Zanzibar soared.

11. Hussein and Shebi Muzamill, major retailers of electronics in Zanzibar, said that with the drop in the price of TVs and VCRs, sales took off. Their father had purchased the family's first VCR in Saudi Arabia in 1981 and paid $1,500 for it. Between 1995 and 2000, the sales of television sets from their store averaged between 150 and 180 per month. Hussein and Shebi Muzamill, interview with the author, December 23, 2004, Zanzibar.

405

12. Chanu Vadgama interview. RC, File 11882: Empire Video Center, Incorporated, 1986.

13. Board of Film Censors Records, 1993–2000; Feroz Mukhadam interview #308; Feruz Hussein interview of June 25, 2002, #26; Gamdul Sing Hans interviews of January 22 and April 19, 2004, #467; Jitu Savani interview of May 26, 2005, #472; Pankaj Valambia interview #502; Shariff Al-Beity interview #667; Suresh Solanki interview #457; Stephen Mtetewaunga, interview with the author, May 9, 2005, #897.

14. Claudia Bohme, "Bloody Bricolages: Traces of Nollywood in Tanzanian Video Films," in *Global Nollywood: The Transnational Dimensions of an African Video Film Industry*, ed. Matthias Krings (Bloomington: Indiana University Press, 2013), 327–46; Matthias Krings, "Nollywood Goes East: The Localization of Nigerian Video Films in Tanzania," in *Viewing African Cinema in the Twenty-First Century: Art Films and the Nollywood Video Revolution*, ed. Ralph Austen and Mahir Saul (Athens: Ohio University Press, 2010), 74–91; Krings, *African Appropriations: Cultural Difference, Mimesis and Media* (Bloomington: Indiana University Press, 2015). The history of Tanzanian video filmmaking is still waiting to be written.

15. With the installation of new digital cable systems. the costs to homes soared. In 2013, homes in Zanzibar with premium packages were paying nearly $100 each month. A decade earlier, no one I knew paid more than $6 for cable, and many received it free, courtesy of their neighbors.

16. Sultan Mohammed interview.

17. The process was known as "kurusha" meaning "to send into the air." The precise technological details are another topic worthy of further investigation. Although I never quite understood how it worked, many of the homes in which I lived or visited from the late 1990s on were linked to global broadcasting due to the generosity of neighbors. As of 2013, digital transmission of cable became dominant. As far as I can tell, this has also, at least temporarily, eliminated the ability of Tanzanians to "share" their signals without payment to the cable company.

18. Kiondo, "Nature of Economic Reforms," 33; Maliyamkono and Bagachwa, *Second Economy in Tanzania*, 141.

19. TFC, *Annual Report and Account, 1984–1988*, 2.

20. Tanzania Bureau of Statistics, Selected Statistical Series, 1951–1993, table 5.3: Minimum Wage and Average Wage for a Regular Adult Citizen Employee, 12; Maliyamkono and Bagachwa, *Second Economy in Tanzania*.

21. The minimum wage was 170 shillings per month in 1972, rising to 600 by 1982. Ticket prices in Zanzibar ranged from 1/- to 4/- for various classes of seats in 1972 to 5/50 to 11/- by 1982. Wages from Bureau of Statistics, table 5.3: Minimum Wage and Average Wage for a Regular Adult Citizen Employee, 12.

22. TNA 622/s1/B1: Bodi ya Filamu; Office of the Board of Film Censors: Board of Film Censor Reports 1984/85, 1990, 1993, 1995.

23. In 1993, the final year the Sapna theater in Morogoro showed films, the operators made twice as much money selling food and drinks as they did selling tickets. Unable to compete with nearby video parlors, they transformed the theater into a disco, which allowed them to meet a different entertainment need and sell even more at the bar. Sapna Talkies Ltd., Trading and Profit and Loss Accounts for the Year Ended 31 December 1994; Pankaj Valambia interview.

24. Asad Talati interviews of August 14, 15, and 16, 2004; Chunilal Kala Savani interviews; Jitu Savani interview of May 26, 2005; Mr. Ninga interviews with the author, April 11 and May 2, 2005, Dar es Salaam; Hamza Kasongo interview.

25. Abdulhussein Marashi interviews of May 7 and 15, 2002; Ahmed "Eddy" Alwi al-Beity interview of November 3, 2004; Feruz Hussein interview of July 6, 2002; Jitu Savani interview of May 26, 2005; Shariff Al-Beity interview.

26. Stephen Mtetewaunga interview.

27. Ibid., Alex Perullo, *Artistic Rights: Copyright Law for East African Musicians, Artists, Writers and Other Authors* (US State Department, 2012).

28. Muslim Jaffer, the owner of the New World Cinema and several other theaters in the Century Cinemax group, faced numerous challenges trying to get such broadcasts stopped when he opened New World. Ten years later, he continued to wage the same battles, although improvements had been made. Muslim Jaffer, interview with the author, May 30, 2005, Dar es Salaam; Muslim Jaffer, e-mail correspondence with the author, May 28, 2014.

29. Board of Film Censors, Dar es Salaam, Records 1993–2000; Cine Afrique Books, 1999–2000; Feruz Hussein interview of June 25, 2002; Msafiri Punda interview; Robert Kibwana interview.

30. Cine Afrique Books, 1999–2000; Feruz Hussein interview of June 25, 2002, Zanzibar; Asad Talati e-mail, of October 1, 2004.

31. A similar fate met the Beit-al-Ajaib Palace Museum in December 2012, when a large chunk of wall collapsed off of a top floor due to years of water damage from an unrepaired leak in a toilet. As of 2016, this wonderful museum remained closed and deterioration continued.

32. The move toward multipartyism began in 1990, and the first elections were held in 1995. Pembans largely supported the main opposition party, the Civic United Front. Both individually and collectively, they were punished again because of their intent to remove the ruling party. Violence and intimidation intensified with subsequent elections. In 2001, there were massive state reprisals, resulting in numerous civilian deaths at the hands of state forces and wanton destruction of property. Christine Otieno, "Eyewitness: Suspicion on Pemba," BBC, March 2, 2001, at http://news.bbc.co.uk/2/hi/africa/1199236.stm; "'The Bullets Were Raining': The January 2001 Attack on Peaceful Demonstrators in Zanzibar," Human Rights Watch, at http://www.hrw.org/reports/2002/tanzania/.

33. Muslim Jaffer interview; Muslim Jaffer e-mail of May 28, 2014.

407

34. Brian Cooksey, Lisbeth Levey, and Daniel Mkude, "Higher Eduction in Tanzania: A Case Study—Economic, Political and Education Sector Transformation," *World Education News and Reviews* 16, no. 1 (2003), online publication; University of Dar es Salaam page on the website of the Southern African Regional Universities Association, http://www.sarua.org/?q=uni_University+of+Dar+es+Salaam.

35. See www.crimsonmultimedia.com; "Tanzanian Tycoon Takes Over Silverbird Cinemas," *Daily Nation*, June 20, 2011, at allafrica.com.

36. Motion Picture Association of America Theatrical Market Statistics, 2014, 4–7.

37. "Tanzanian Tycoon Takes Over,", www.nation.co.ke/Features/smartcompany/Tanzanian+tycoon+takes+over+Silverbird+Cinemas; "Kenya—Local Cinema Is Not Dead," *Daily Nation*, July 9, 2011, at allAfrica.com/stories/201107111198.html. *BFI Statistical Yearbook 2013*, 24, 32, 37; Motion Picture Association of America Theatrical Market Statistics 2013, 2, 17, at www.mpaa.org/MPAA-Theatrical-Market-Statistics-2013.pdf.

38. "Tanzanian Tycoon Takes Over."

39. Motion Picture Association of America Theatrical Market Statistics 2014, 16, www.mpaa.org/MPAA-Theatrical-Market-Statistics-2014.pdf; Muslim Jaffer, e-mail correspondence with the author, May 29, 2014.

40. Raymond Balemwa interview.

SELECT BIBLIOGRAPHY

Public and Private Archives Consulted

Board of Censors Office, Dar es Salaam
Bodleian Library, Rhodes House, Oxford
Cine Afrique, Zanzibar, Tanzania
East Africana Collection, University of Dar es Salaam Library
Majestic Cinema, Zanzibar, Tanzania
Majestic Cinemas Ltd., Tanga, Tanzania
Michigan State University Library, Africana Collection, East Lansing, MI
Ministry of Industries and Trade, Registrar of Companies Office, Dar es Salaam
Public Records Office, London
Rhodes House Library, Oxford
Sapna TalkiesMorogoro, Tanzania
South African National Archives, Records of the Board of Trade and Industries, Pretoria
School of Journalism thesis, University of Dar es Salaam
Tanzanian National Archives, Dar es Salaam
United Film Distributors, Zanzibar, Tanzania
Wisconsin Historical Society Archives, United Artist Corporation Collection, Madison, WI
Zanzibar National Archives, Zanzibar, Tanzania

Almanacs, Newspapers, Magazines, and Trade Publications

Daily News, Dar es Salaam
East African Standard, Nairobi
Film Daily Year Book of Motion Pictures, New York
Indian Motion Picture Almanac, Calcutta, India
International Motion Picture Almanac, New York
Jenga: Magazine of the National Development Corporation, Dar es Salaam

410

Motion Picture and Television Almanac, New York
Mwaafrika, Dar es Salaam
National Development Corporation. *Annual Report and Accounts*, Dar es Salaam
Nationalist, Dar es Salaam
Nchi Yetu, Dar es Salaam
Ngurumo, Dar es Salaam
Sauti ya Siti, Dar es Salaam
Samachar, Zanzibar
Showman, Johannesburg, South Africa
Standard, Dar es Salaam
Sunday News, Dar es Salaam
Tanganyika Standard, Dar es Salaam
Truth Prevails Where Lies Must Vanish, Zanzibar
Uhuru, Dar es Salaam
US Department of Commerce, *World Trade in Commodities*, Washington, DC
Zanzibar Official Gazette, Zanzibar
Zanzibar Voice, Zanzibar

Interviews

All interviews were conducted by the author either in Kiswahili or in English. When only first names are listed, they are often pseudonyms, used for individuals who chose not to be identified. For especially sensitive material, where either the interviewee or the author thought it best for the source to remain utterly unidentified, individuals are listed as "Anonymous."

* indicates an owner, employee, or associate of a cinema

Abdul Hamiri, December 23, 2004, Zanzibar
Abdulhussein Marashi,* May 7, 15, and 18, 2002; February 4, 2004; along with casual conversations too numerous to cite, Zanzibar
Abdulrahim Said, December 12, 2004, Dar es Salaam
Adam Shafi, May 18, 2005, Dar es Salaam
Agnello Fernandez,* March 10, 2005, Dar es Salaam
Ahmed "Eddy" Alwi al-Beity,* November 3 and 27, 2004, Dar es Salaam
Ahmed Hussein Choxi,* April 12, 2005, Dar es Salaam
Akhmed, December 10, 2004, Dar es Salaam
Akhtar Amir, June 26, 2002, Zanzibar
Ali Ghafoor, May 19 and 22, 2005, Dar es Salaam
Ali Makame, December 15, 2004, Dar es Salaam
Ally "Rocky" Khamis Ally,* June 21, 2002, Wete, Pemba
Ameri Slyoum,* May 16, 2002, Zanzibar
Amina, February 12, 2005, Dar es Salaam
Anonymous, May 18, 2005, Dar es Salaam
——, January 16, 2005, Dar es Salaam

———, January 13, 2005, Dar es Salaam

———, October 11, 2004, Zanzibar

———, March 24, 2005, Zanzibar

———, March 12, 2005, Dar es Salaam

———, May 18, 2005, Dar es Salaam

———, May 21, 2005, Dar es Salaam

Asad Talati,* August 14, 15, and 16, 2004, Toronto, Canada, along with numerous personal e-mails and casual conversations over the years

Asha, May 19, 2005, Dar es Salaam

Asha, January 28, 2004, Tanga

Asha, November 28, 2008, Zanzibar

Aunti Sofia, February 12, 2004, Zanzibar

Bakari Juma, February 12, 2005, Dar es Salaam

Belleghe, February 14, 2005, Dar es Salaam

Bi Maryam, February 16, 2004, Zanzibar

BiMaryam, May 14, 2002, Zanzibar

BiMkubwa Said, June 21, 2002, Zanzibar

BiSaumu, June 16, 2002, Wete, Pemba

Blandina, February 6, 2005, Dar es Salaam

Boniface Sanjala, January 14 and 25, 2005, Dar es Salaam

Brij Behal,* April 24, 2005, Arusha

Chanu Vadgama,* October 5, 2004, Dar es Salaam

Chunilal Kala Savani *, June 17, 21, and 23, 2005, Mombasa

D, February 25, 2005, Dar es Salaam

Darwesh,* February 7, 2004, Zanzibar

Edna Rajab, February 11, 2005, Dar es Salaam

Edward, April 15, 2004, Arusha

Fatma, May 19, 2005, Dar es Salaam

Fatma Alloo, May 14, 2002, and December 23, 2008, Zanzibar

Feroz Mukhadam,* March 26, 2005, Iringa

Feruz Hussein,* June 25 and July 6, 2002, Zanzibar

Frida, January 14, 2005, Morogoro

Gamdul Sing Hans,* January 22 and April 19, 2004, Arusha

Gigri,* January 17, 2005, Dar es Salaam

Gladness, April 23, 2005, Arusha

Godwin Kaduma, March 2, 2005, Bagamoyo

Haji Faki Mohammed (aka Haji Garana), June 3 and July 1, 2002, Zanzibar

Haji Gora Haji, December 24, 2004, Zanzibar

Hamza Kasongo, May 19, 2005, Dar es Salaam

Hawa, October 14, 2004, Dar es Salaam

Hussein and Shebi Muzamill, December 23, 2004, Zanzibar

Iddi Maganga, December 12, 2004, Dar es Salaam

Issa, February 16, 2004, Dar es Salaam

Jecha Saloum, June 15, 2002, Zanzibar

Jitu Savani,* January 29, 2004, Tanga, and May 26, 2005, Dar es Salaam

John, February 8, 2005, Dar es Salaam

John, February 18 and 20, 2004, Dar es Salaam

Josephine, April 21, 2005, Moshi

Juma, May 23, 2002, Zanzibar

Juma Sultan, May 17, 22, and 25, 2005, Dar es Salaam

Kajole (aka Khamis), December 20 and 23, 2008, Zanzibar

Kamal, February 4, 2005, Dar es Salaam

Kasanga,* December 16, 2004, and March 5, 2005, Dar es Salaam

Khadija, June 28, 2002, Zanzibar

Khalid Saloum, October 12, 2004, Dar es Salaam

Khamis Kombo, June 15, 2002, Zanzibar

Khamis Msellem,* December 16, 2004, Dar es Salaam

Khulsum, June 26, 2002, Zanzibar

Leonne, March 7, 2005, Dar es Salaam

Machinga, April 4 and 5, 2005, Dar es Salaam

Mama Ak, June 26, 2002, Zanzibar

Maryam Yahya, June 3, 2002, Zanzibar

Mbaruku, April 10, 2005, Dar es Salaam

Method A. Kashonda, May 9, 2005, Dar es Salaam

Mr. Drive-In,* March 10 and 11, 2005, Dar es Salaam

Mr. India, March 8, 2004, Dar es Salaam

Mr. Khambaita,* April 19, 2005, Moshi

Mr. Ninga, April 11 and May 2, 2005, Dar es Salaam

Mrushwa, February 11, 2005, Dar es Salaam

Msafiri Punda,* October 21, 2004, Dar es Salaam

Mulji,* March 13, 2005, Dar es Salaam

Muslim Jaffer,* May 30, 2005, Dar es Salaam

Mwalim Idd Abdulla Farhan, April 2, May 24 and 25, 2002, Zanzibar

Mzee Juma, April 13, 2005, Dar es Salaam

Mzee Mohammed, February 5, 2004, Zanzibar

Naaz Rana, October 21, 2004, Dar es Salaam

Nabila Ally Salim, April 24, 2005, Arusha

Nasra and Maryam, May 22, 2002, Zanzibar

Nasra Mohammed, May 21, 2002, Zanzibar

Neema, July 25, 2005, Arusha

Nitesh Virji,* April 25, 2005, Moshi

Patel, April 24, 2005, Moshi

Pankaj Valambia,* May 29, 2005, Morogoro

Paul Fernandez, February 8, 2005, Dar es Salaam
Rashid, December 20, 2008, Zanzibar
Rashid Noorani, December 23, 2005, Zanzibar
Rashid Said,* December 23, 2004, Zanzibar
Raymond Balemwa,* October 13, 2004, Dar es Salaam
Richard, March 28, 2005, Iringa
Robert Kibwana,* July 2, 2002, Dar es Salaam
Romeo, March 15, 2005, Dar es Salaam
Sabrina, May 5, 2004, Zanzibar
Saidi,* April 26, 2005, Moshi
Saloum and Fatuma, October 12, 2004, Dar es Salaam
Semeni Juma, March 20, 2002, Bagamoyo
Shaaban, May 22, 2005, Dar es Salaam
Shaban Kavitenda, September 22, 2004, Dar es Salaam
Shabani Mkoga, October 20, 2004, Dar es Salaam
Shabir K. Jariwalla,* April 25, 2005, Arusha
Shanin, May 14, 2002, Zanzibar
Sheriff Al-Beity,* April 6, 2005, Dar es Salaam
Stephen Mtetewaunga, May 9, 2005, Dar es Salaam
Subira, February 3, 2004, Zanzibar
Sultan Mohammed, July 25, 2005, Arusha
Suresh Solanki,* April 23, 2005, Moshi
Taday,* December 20, 2004, Dar es Salaam
Titus Lugendo, February 7, 2005, Dar es Salaam
Walter Bagoya, May 26, 2005, Dar es Salaam
Warda, June 26, 2002, Zanzibar

References Cited

Abani, Chris. *Graceland:* Farrar, Straus and Giroux, 2004.
Abdalla Uba Adamu. "Islam, Hausa Culture, and Censorship in Northern Nigerian Video Film." In *Viewing African Cinema in the Twenty-First Century: Art Films and the Nollywood Video Revolution,* edited by Ralph Austen and Mahir Saul, 63–73. Athens: Ohio University Press, 2010.
———. "The Muse's Journey: Transcultural Translators and the Domestication of Hindi Music in Hausa Popular Culture." *Journal of African Cultural Studies* 22, no. 1 (2010): 41–56.
Abdulaziz, Mohamed H., and Hajji ibn Muyaka. *Muyaka: 19th Century Swahili Popular Poetry.* Nairobi: Kenya Literature Bureau, 1979.
Abu-Lughod, Lila. "Egyptian Melodrama—Technology of the Modern Subject." In *Media Worlds: Anthropology on New Terrain,* edited by Faye Ginsburg, Lila Abu-Lughod, and Brian Larkin, 115–33. Berkeley: University of California Press, 2002.

413

414

Adam Shafi Adam. *Vuta n'kuvute*. Dar es Salaam: Mkuki na Nyota, 1999.

Adarsh, B. K. *Film Industry of India*. Bombay: Perfecta Printing Works for Trade Guide, 1963.

Aidoo, Ama Ata, ed. *African Love Stories: An Anthology*. Banbury, UK: Ayebia Clarke, 2006.

Akyeampong, Emmanuel, and Charles Ambler. "Special Issue: Leisure in African History—Leisure in African History: An Introduction." *International Journal of African Historical Studies* 35, no. 1 (2002): 1–16.

Allen, Robert. "From Exhibition to Reception: Reflections on the Audience in Film History." *Screen* 31, no. 4 (1990): 1–16.

Allison, Deborah. "Multiplex Programming in the UK: The Economics of Homogeneity." *Screen* 47, no. 1 (2006): 81–90.

Allman, Jean. "Phantoms of the Archives: Kwame Nkrumah, a Nazi Pilot Named Hanna, and the Contingencies of Postcolonial History Writing." *American Historical Review* 118, no. 1 (2013): 104–29.

Allman, Jean, and Victoria Tashjian. *I Will Not Eat Stone: A Women's History of Colonial Asante*. Portsmouth, NH: Heinemann, 2000.

Ambler, Charles. "Cowboy Modern: African Audiences, Hollywood Films and Visions of the West." In *Going to the Movies: Hollywood and the Social Experience of Cinema*, edited by Richard Maltby, Melvyn Stokes, and Robert Allen, 348–63. Exeter: University of Exeter Press, 2007.

———. "Mass Media and Leisure in Africa." *International Journal of African Historical Studies* 35, no. 1 (2002): 119–36.

———. "Popular Films and Colonial Audiences: The Movies in Northern Rhodesia." *American Historical Review* 106, no. 1 (2001): 81–105.

Anderson, Charles. *A City and Its Cinemas*. Bristol: Redcliffe, 1983.

Anderson, David. "Master and Servant in Colonial Kenya." *Journal of African History* 41 (2000): 459–85.

Appadurai, Arjun. *Disjuncture and Difference in the Global Cultural Economy*. Middlesbrough, UK: Theory, Culture and Society, 1990.

Arnold, Alison. "Popular Film Song in India: A Case of Mass-Market Musical Eclecticism." *Popular Music* 7, no. 2 (1988): 177–88.

Askew, Kelly. *Performing the Nation: Swahili Music and Cultural Politics in Tanzania*. Chicago: University of Chicago Press, 2002.

———. "Sung and Unsung: Musical Reflections on Tanzanian Postsocialisms." *Africa* 76, no. 1 (2006): 15–43.

Babu, Abdulrahman Mohamed. *African Socialism or Socialist Africa?* London: Zed, 1981.

———. "Memoirs: An Outline." In *Babu: I Saw the Future and It Works*, edited by Haroub Othman, 7–96. London: E and D, 2001.

Bailey, Beth L. *From Front Porch to Back Seat: Courtship in Twentieth-Century America*. Baltimore: Johns Hopkins University Press, 1988.

Bakari, Imruh, and Mbye Cham, eds. *African Experiences of Cinema.* London: British Film Institute, 1996.

Baker, E. C. "Memorandum on the Social Conditions of Dar es Salaam." Edited by District Officer, 1931.

———. "A Report on the Social and Economic Conditions in the Tanga Province." Dar es Salaam: Government Printer, Tanganyika Territory, 1934.

Balio, Tino, ed. *The American Film Industry.* 2nd ed. Madison: University of Wisconsin Press, 1985.

Banerjea, Koushik. "'Fight Club': Aesthetics, Hybridization and the Construction of Rogue Masculinities in *Sholay* and *Deewaar*." In *Bollyworld: Popular Indian Cinema through a Transnational Lens,* edited by Raminder Kaur and Ajay J Sinha, 163–85. New Delhi: Sage, 2005.

Banfield, Jane. "Film in East Africa." *Transition* 13 (1964): 18–21.

Barber, Karin. *The Generation of Plays: Yoruba Popular Life in Theater.* Bloomington: Indiana University Press, 2000.

———. "Popular Arts in Africa." *African Studies Review* 30, no. 3 (1987): 1–78.

———. "Preliminary Notes on Audiences in Africa." *Africa* 67 (1997): 347–62.

Barker, C. E., M. R. Bhagavan, P. V. Mitschke-Collande, and D. V. Wield. *African Industrialization: Technology and Change in Tanzania.* Brookfield, VT: Gower, 1986.

Barnouw, Eric, and S. Krishnaswamy. *Indian Film.* New York: Columbia University Press, 1963.

———. *Indian Film.* 2nd ed. New York: Oxford University Press, 1980.

Batson, E. "Social Survey of Zanzibar Protectorate." Cape Town: School of Social Sciences and Social Administration at the University of Cape Town, 1960.

Battle, Steve. "The Old Dispensary: An Apogee of Zanzibari Architecture." In *The History and Conservation of Zanzibar Stone Town,* edited by Abdul Sheriff, 91–99. Athens: Ohio University Press, 1995.

Bertoncini, Elena Zúbková. "An Annotated Bibliography of Swahili Fiction and Drama Published between 1975 and 1984." Special issue on Swahili Verbal Arts, edited by Carol M. Eastman. *Research in African Literatures* 17, no. 4 (Winter 1986): 525–62.

Bickford-Smith, Vivian, and Richard Mendelsohn, eds. *Black and White in Colour: African History on Screen.* Athens: Ohio University Press, 2007.

Bienefeld, M., and R. Sabot. "The National Urban Mobility, Employment and Income Survey of Tanzania (NUMEIST)." Dar es Salaam: Ministry of Economic Affairs and Development Planning and Economic Research Bureau, 1971.

Biersteker, Ann Joyce. *Kujibizana: Questions of Language and Power in Nineteenth- and Twentieth-Century Poetry in Kiswahili.* East Lansing: Michigan State University Press, 1996.

———. "Language, Poetry and Power: A Reconsideration of 'Utendi Wa Mwana Kupona.'" In *Faces of Islam in African Literature,* edited by Ken Harrow, 59–77. Portsmouth, NH: Heinemann, 1991.

416

Biersteker, Ann Joyce, and Ibrahim Noor Shariff. *Mashairi Ya Vita Vya Kuduhu: War Poetry in Kiswahili Exchanged at the Time of the Battle of Kuduhu*. East Lansing: Michigan State University Press, 1995.

Binnie, Jon, Julian Holloway, Steven Millington, and Craig Young, eds. *Cosmopolitan Urbanism*. London: Routledge, 2007.

Bissell, William Cunningham. "Engaging Colonial Nostalgia." *Cultural Anthropology* 20, no. 2 (2005): 215–48.

Bloom, Peter, Stephan Miescher, and Takyiwaa Manuh, eds. *Modernization as Spectacle in Africa*. Bloomington: Indiana University Press, 2014.

Blumer, Herbert, and Philip Morris Hauser. *Movies, Delinquency, and Crime*. New York: Macmillan, 1933.

Bohme, Claudia. "Bloody Bricolages: Traces of Nollywood in Tanzanian Video Films." In *Global Nollywood: The Transnational Dimensions of an African Video Film Industry*, edited by Matthias Krings, 327–46. Bloomington: Indiana University Press, 2013.

Bonner, Phil. "'Desirable or Undesirable Basotho Women?' Liquor, Prostitution and the Migration of Basotho Women to the Rand, 1920–1945." In *Women and Gender in Southern Africa to 1945*, edited by Cherryl Walker, 221–50. London: James Currey, 1990.

Boym, Svetlana. *The Future of Nostalgia*. New York: Basic Books, 2001.

Bradley, A. "The Nationalization of Companies in Tanzania." In *Private Enterprise and the East African Company*, edited by Philip Aneurin Thoas. Dar es Salaam: Tanzania Publishing House, 1969.

Breckenridge, Carol Appadurai. *Consuming Modernity: Public Culture in a South Asian World*. Minneapolis: University of Minnesota Press, 1995.

Breckenridge, Keith. "Love Letters and Amanuenses: Beginning the Cultural History of the Working Class Private Sphere in Southern Africa, 1900–1933." *Journal of Southern African Studies* 26, no. 2 (2000): 337–48.

Brennan, James. "Between Segregation and Gentrification: Africans, Indians, and the Struggle for Housing in Dar es Salaam, 1920–1950." In *Dar es Salaam: Histories from an Emerging African Metropolis*, edited by James Brennan, Andrew Burton, and Yusuf Lawi, 118–35. Dar es Salaam: Mkuki na Nyota, 2007.

——. "Blood Enemies: Exploitation and Urban Citizenship in the Nationalist Political Thought of Tanzania, 1958–75." *Journal of African History* 47, no. 3 (2006): 389–413.

——. "Democratizing Cinema and Censorship in Tanzania, 1920–1980." *International Journal of African Historical Studies* 38, no. 3 (2005): 481–511.

——. "Radio Cairo and the Decolonization of East Africa, 1953–64." In *Making a World after Empire: The Bandung Moment and Its Political Afterlives*, edited by Christopher J. Lee, 173–95. Athens: Ohio University Press, 2010.

——. *Taifa: Making Nation and Race in Urban Tanzania*. Athens: Ohio University Press, 2012.

Brennan, James, and Andrew Burton. "The Emerging Metropolis: A History of Dar es Salaam, circa 1862–2000." In *Dar es Salaam: Histories from an Emerging African Metropolis,* edited by James Brennan and Andrew Burton, 13–75. Dar es Salaam: Mkuki na Nyota, 2007.

Brosius, Christiane. "The Scattered Homelands of the Migrant: Bollyworld through the Diasporic Lens." In *Bollyworld: Popular Indian Cinema through a Transnational Lens,* edited by Raminder Kaur and Ajay J. Sinha, 207–38. New Delhi: Sage, 2005.

Bruhwiler, Benjamin Amani. "Moralities of Owing and Lending: Credit, Debt and Urban Living in Kariakoo, Dar es Salaam." PhD diss., Michigan State University, 2015.

Bryce, Jane. "Donor Values and the Case of Film in Tanzania." In *Viewing African Cinema in the Twenty-First Century: Art Films and the Nollywood Video Revolution,* edited by Ralph Austen and Mahir Saul, 160–77. Athens: Ohio University Press, 2010.

Bryceson, Deborah Fahy. *Food Insecurity and the Social Division of Labor in Tanzania, 1919–1985.* New York: St. Martin's Press, 1990.

——. *Liberalizing Tanzania's Food Trade.* Dar es Salaam: Mkuki na Nyota, 1993.

——. "The Proletarianization of Women in Tanzania." *Review of African Political Economy* 17 (January–April 1980): 4–27.

Bukenya, Austin. *The People's Bachelor.* Dar es Salaam: East African Publishing House, 1972.

Burgess, Thomas. "Cinema, Bell Bottoms, and Miniskirts: Struggles over Youth and Citizenship in Revolutionary Zanzibar." *International Journal of African Historical Studies* 35, no. 2 (2002): 287–313.

——. "Mao in Zanzibar: Nationalism, Discipline and the (De)Construction of Afro-Asian Solidarities." In *Making a World after Empire: The Bandung Moment and Its Political Afterlives,* edited by Christopher J. Lee, 196–234. Athens: Ohio University Press, 2010.

——. *Race, Revolution and the Struggle for Human Rights in Zanzibar: The Memoirs of Ali Sultan Issa and Seif Sharif Hamad.* Athens: Ohio University Press, 2009.

Burns, James. "The African Bioscope—Movie House Culture in British Colonial Africa." *Afrique et Histoire* 5 (2006): 65–80.

——. *Cinema and Society in the British Empire, 1895–1940.* New York: Palgrave Macmillan, 2013.

——. *Flickering Shadows: Cinema and Identity in Colonial Zimbabwe.* Athens: Ohio University Press, 2002.

——. "John Wayne on the Zambezi: Cinema, Empire and the American Western in British Central Africa." *International Journal of African Historical Studies* 35, no. 1 (2002): 103–17.

Burton, Andrew. *African Underclass: Urbanization, Crime and Colonial Order in Dar es Salaam.* Athens: Ohio University Press, 2005.

418

——, ed. *The Urban Experience in Eastern Africa c. 1750–2000*. Nairobi: British Institute of East Africa, 2002.

——. "Urchins, Loafers, and the Cult of the Cowboy: Urbanization and Delinquency in Dar es Salaam, 1919–61." *Journal of African History* 42, no. 2 (2001): 199–216.

Butsch, Richard. *The Citizen Audience: Crowds, Publics, and Individuals*: Hoboken, NJ: Taylor and Francis, 2008.

——. *The Making of American Audiences: From Stage to Television, 1750–1990*. Cambridge: Cambridge University Press, 2000.

Byfield, Judith. "Women, Marriage, Divorce and the Emerging Colonial State in Abeokuta (Nigeria), 1892–1904." *Canadian Journal of African Studies* 30 (1996): 32–51.

Calas, Bernard, ed. *From Dar es Salaam to Bongoland: Urban Mutations in Tanzania*. Dar es Salaam: Mkuki na Nyota, 2010.

Callaci, Emily. "Dancehall Politics: Mobility, Sexuality, and Spectacles of Racial Respectability in Late Colonial Tanganyika, 1930s–1961." *Journal of African History* 52 (2011): 365–84.

——. "Ujamaa Urbanism: History, Culture and the Politics of Authenticity in Socialist Dar es Salaam, 1967–80." PhD diss., Northwestern University, 2012.

Campbell, Horace. "The Politics of Demobilization in Tanzania: Beyond Nationalism." In *The IMF and Tanzania*, edited by Horace Campbell and Howard Stein, 126–52. Harare: Southern Africa Political Economy Series Trust, 1991.

Campbell, Horace, and Howard Stein, eds. *The IMF and Tanzania*. Harare: Southern Africa Political Economy Series Trust, 1991.

Certeau, Michel de. *The Practice of Everyday Life*. Translated by Steven Rendall. Berkeley: University of California Press, 1984.

Chakravarty, Sumita. "National Identity and the Realist Aesthetic: Indian Cinema of the Fifties." *Quarterly Review of Film and Video* 11 (1989): 31–48.

Chaligha, Amon. "Taxation and the Transition to Socialism in Tanzania." PhD diss., Claremont Graduate School, 1990.

Chanan, Michael. *Cuban Cinema*. Minneapolis: University of Minnesota Press, 2004.

Chande, J. K. *A Knight in Africa: Journey from Bukene*. Manotick, Canada: Penumbra Press, 2005.

Chapman, James. *Cinemas of the World*. London: Reaktion Books, 2003.

Chatterjee, Gayatri. *Awara*. New Delhi: Wiley Eastern, 1992.

Chatterjee, Partha. "A Bit of Song and Dance." In *Frames of Mind: Reflections on Indian Cinema*, edited by Aruna Vasudev, 197–218. Delhi: UBS, 1995.

Chauncey, George. "The Locus of Reproduction: Women's Labor in the Zambian Copperbelt, 1927–1953." *Journal of Southern African Studies* 7, no. 2 (1981): 135–64.

Chindoya, Shimmer. *Harvest of Thorns*. Oxford: Heinemann, 1989.

Chopra, Anupama. *Sholay, the Making of a Classic*. Mumbai: Penguin, 2000.

Chowdhry, Prem. *Colonial India and the Making of Empire Cinema: Image, Ideology and Identity*. Manchester: Manchester University Press, 2000.

Chute, D. Review of *The Kapoors: The First Family of Indian Cinema*, by Madhu Jain. *Film Comment* 42, no. 6 (2006): 79–79.

Clayton, Anthony. *The Zanzibar Revolution and Its Aftermath*. Hamden, CT: Archon Books, 1981.

Cliffe, Lionel, and John Saul, eds. *Socialism in Tanzania: An Interdisciplinary Reader*. 2 vols. Dar es Salaam: East African Publishing House, 1973.

Cohen, Abner. "Cultural Strategies in the Organization of Trading Diasporas." In *The Development of Indigenous Trade and Markets in West Africa*, edited by C. Meillassoux, 266–84. London: Oxford University Press, 1971.

——. *Custom and Politics in Urban Africa*. London: Routledge and Kegan Paul, 1969.

——. "The Social Organization of Credit in a West African Cattle Market." *Africa* 35 (1965): 8–20.

Cohen, Lizabeth. "Encountering Mass Culture at the Grassroots: The Experience of Chicago Workers in the 1920s." *American Quarterly* 41, no. 1 (1989): 6–33.

Cohen, Mary Morley. "Forgotten Audiences in the Passion Pits: Drive-In Theatres and Changing Spectator Practices in Post-war America." *Film History* 6, no. 4 (1994): 470–86.

Cole, Catherine M. *Ghana's Concert Party Theatre*. Bloomington: Indiana University Press, 2001.

Cole, Jennifer, and Lynn Thomas, eds. *Love in Africa*. Chicago: University of Chicago Press, 2009.

Collins, Diana. *Hollywood Down Under: Australians at the Movies, 1896 to the Present Day*. London: Angus and Robertson, 1987.

Comaroff, Jean, and John Comaroff. *Modernity and Its Malcontents: Ritual and Power in Postcolonial Africa*. Chicago: University of Chicago Press, 1993.

Conant, Michael. "The Paramount Decrees Reconsidered." In *The American Film Industry*, edited by Tino Balio, 537–73. Madison: University of Wisconsin Press, 1985.

Condon, John C. "Nation Building and Image Building in the Tanzania Press." *Journal of Modern African Studies* 5, no. 3 (1967): 335–54.

Cooksey, Brian, Lisbeth Levey, and Daniel Mkude. "Higher Eduction in Tanzania: A Case Study—Economic, Political and Education Sector Transformation." *World Education News and Reviews* 16, no. 1 (2003): online publication.

Cooper, Frederick. *Colonialism in Question: Theory, Knowledge, History*. Berkeley: University of California Press, 2005.

——, ed. *Struggle for the City: Migrant Labor, Capital, and the State in Urban Africa*. Beverly Hills, CA: Sage, 1983.

419

Coulson, Andrew, ed. *African Socialism in Practice: The Tanzanian Experience.* Nottingham, UK: Review of African Political Economy, 1979.

——. *Tanzania: A Political Economy.* New York: Oxford University Press, 1982.

——. "Tanzania's Fertilizer Factory." In *African Socialism in Practice,* edited by Andrew Coulson, 184–90. Nottingham, UK: Spokesman, 1979.

Crowley, David, and Susan Reid. "Introduction: Pleasures in Socialism?" In *Pleasures in Socialism: Leisure and Luxury in the Eastern Bloc,* edited by David Crowley and Susan Reid, 3–52. Evanston, IL: Northwestern University Press, 2010.

——, eds. *Pleasures in Socialism: Leisure and Luxury in the Eastern Bloc.* Evanston, IL: Northwestern University Press, 2010.

De Boeck, Filip, and Marie-Françoise Plissart. *Kinshasa: Tales of the Invisible City.* Ghent: Ludion, 2006.

Decker, Corrie. *Mobilizing Zanzibari Women: The Struggle for Respectability and Self-Reliance in Colonial East Africa.* New York: Palgrave Macmillan, 2014.

——. "Reading, Writing and Respectability: How Schoolgirls Developed Modern Literacies in Colonial Zanzibar." *International Journal of African Historical Studies* 43, no. 1 (2010): 89–114.

de Luna, Katherine M. "Society and Affect in Precolonial South Central Africa." *International Journal of African Historical Studies* 46, no. 1 (2013): 123–50.

Derné, Steve. *Movies, Masculinity, and Modernity: An Ethnography of Men's Filmgoing in India.* Westport, CT: Greenwood Press, 2000.

Desai, Gaurav. "Commerce as Romance: Nanji Kalidas Mehta's *Dream Half Expressed.*" *Research in African Literatures* 42, no. 3 (2011): 147–65.

Desser, David. "Making Movies Male: Zhang Che and the Shaw Brothers Martial Arts Movies, 1965–1975." In *Masculinities and Hong Kong Cinema,* edited by Laikwan Pang and Day Wong, 17–34. Hong Kong: Hong Kong University Press, 2005.

Deutsch, Jan-Georg, Peter Probst, and Heike Schmidt, eds. *African Modernities: Entangled Meanings in Current Debate.* Oxford: James Currey, 2002.

Diawara, Manthia. *African Cinema: Politics and Culture.* Bloomington: Indiana University Press, 1992.

——. "Black Spectatorship: Problems of Identification and Resistance." *Screen* 29, no. 4 (1988): 66–76.

Dickey, Sara. *Cinema and the Urban Poor in South India.* Cambridge: Cambridge University Press, 1993.

Dissanayake, Wimal, and Malti Sahai. *Sholay, a Cultural Reading.* New Delhi: Wiley Eastern, 1992.

Dobbin, Christine. *Asian Entrepreneurial Minorities: Conjoint Communities in the Making of the World-Economy, 1570–1940.* Richmond, UK: Curzon, 1996.

Doherty, Thomas. *Hollywood's Censor: Joseph I. Breen and the Production Code Administration.* New York: Columbia University Press, 2007.

Donham, Donald. *Marxist Modern: An Ethnographic History of the Ethiopian Revolution.* Berkeley: University of California Press, 1999.

Dovey, Lindiwe, and Angela Impey. "*African Jim:* Sound, Politics and Pleasure in Early 'Black' South African Cinema." *Journal of African Cultural Studies* 22, no. 1 (2010): 57–73.

Dubinsky, Karen, Catherine Krull, Susan Lord, Sean Mills, and Scott Rutherford, eds. *New World Coming: The Sixties and the Shaping of Global Consciousness.* Toronto: Between the Lines, 2009.

Due, John F. "Collecting Taxes South of the Sahara." *Challenge* 12, no. 1 (1963): 8–11.

———. *Taxation and Economic Development in Tropical Africa.* Cambridge, MA: MIT Press, 1963.

Dunn, Stephane. *"Baad Bitches" and Sassy Supermamas: Black Power Action Films.* Urbana: University of Illinois Press, 2008.

Dwyer, Rachel. *All You Want Is Money, All You Need Is Love: Sexuality and Romance in Modern India.* London: Cassell, 2000.

Dwyer, Rachel, and Divia Patel. *Cinema India: The Visual Culture of Hindi Film.* New Brunswick, NJ: Rutgers University Press, 2002.

Dwyer, Rachel, and Christopher Pinney. *Pleasure and the Nation: The History, Politics, and Consumption of Public Culture in India.* New Delhi: Oxford University Press, 2001.

Dyer, Richard. "Entertainment and Utopia." In *Movies and Methods: An Anthology,* vol. 2, edited by Bill Nichols, 221–32. Berkeley: University of California Press, 1985.

Eckert, Andreas. "'Regulating the Social: Social Security, Social Welfare and the State in Late Colonial Tanzania.'" *Journal of African History* 45 (2004): 467–89.

Eisenberg, Andrew. "The Mouths of Professors and Clowns: 'Indian Taarab' and the Resonance of South Asia in Swahili-Space." Manuscript, in possession of the author, 2008.

———. "The Resonance of Place: Vocal Expression and the Communal Imagination in Old Town, Mombassa, Kenya." PhD diss., Columbia University, 2008.

Ewen, Elizabeth. "City Lights: Immigrant Women and the Rise of the Movies." In *Women and the American City,* edited by Catharine R. Stimpson, Elsa Dixler, Martha J. Nelson, and Kathryn B. Yatrakis, 42–63. Chicago: University of Chicago Press, 1980.

Eyles, Allen. *Odeon Cinemas: From J. Arthur Rank to the Multiplex,* vol. 2. London: Cinema Theater Association, 2005.

———. *Odeon Cinemas: Oscar Deutsch Entertains Our Nation.* London: British Film Institute, 2002.

Fair, Laura. "Dressing Up: Clothing, Class and Gender in Post-abolition Urban Zanzibar." *Journal of African History* 39, no. 1 (1998): 63–94.

———. "Hollywood Hegemony?—Hardly: Audience Preferences in Zanzibar, 1950s–1970s." *ZIFF* 1, no. 1 (2004): 52–58.

———. "Identity, Difference and Dance: Female Initiation in Zanzibar, 1890–1930." *Frontiers: A Journal of Women Studies* 17, no. 3 (1996): 146–72.

——. "'It's Just No Fun Anymore': Women's Experiences of Taarab before and after the 1964 Zanzibar Revolution." *International Journal of African Historical Studies* 35, no. 1 (2002): 61–81.

——. *Pastimes and Politics: Culture, Community, and Identity in Post-abolition Urban Zanzibar, 1890–1945*. Athens: Ohio University Press, 2001.

——. "Songs, Stories, Action! Audience Preferences in Tanzania, 1950s–1980s." In *Viewing African Cinema in the Twenty-First Century: Art Films and the Nollywood Video Revolution*, edited by Mahir Saul and Ralph Austen, 108–30. Athens: Ohio University Press, 2010.

Fanon, Frantz. *The Wretched of the Earth*. New York: Grove Press, 1966. First published in 1961.

Farhan, Idd Abdulla. "Historia Ya Cinema, Unguja." Manuscript, in possession of the author, 2002.

Farsy, Muhammed Saleh. *Ada Za Harusi Katika Unguja*. Dar es Salaam: East African Literature Bureau, 1965.

Fenster, Tovi. "Gender and the City: The Different Formations of Belonging." In *A Companion to Feminist Geography*, edited by Lise Nelson and Joni Seager, 242–56. Malden, MA: Blackwell, 2005.

Fenwick, Mac. "'Tough Guy, Eh?': The Gangster-Figure in *Drum*." *Journal of Southern African Studies* 22, no. 4 (1996): 617–32.

Ferguson, James. *Expectations of Modernity: Myths and Meanings of Urban Life on the Zambian Copperbelt*. Berkeley: University of California Press, 1999.

——. *Global Shadows: Africa in the Neoliberal World Order*. Durham, NC: Duke University Press, 2006.

Fitzpatrick, Sheila. *Everyday Stalinism: Ordinary Life in Extraordinary Times—Soviet Russia in the 1930s*. Oxford: Oxford University Press, 1999.

Forsher, James. *The Community of Cinema: How Cinema and Spectacle Transformed the American Downtown*. Westport, CT: Praeger, 2003.

Fourchard, Laurent. "Between World History and State Formation: New Perspectives on African Cities." *Journal of African History* 52, no. 2 (2011): 223–48.

Frater, Patrick. "Cinema Revolution Stirs as Revs Grow." *Variety* 409, no. 3 (2007): C4.

Freyhold, Michaela von. *Ujamaa Villages in Tanzania: Analysis of a Social Experiment*. London: Heinemann, 1979.

Fouhba, Honore. *Les salles de cinéma au Nord-Cameroun: Des implantations aux transformations*. Yaounde: Editions Ifrikiya, 2016.

Fuglesang, Minou. *Veils and Videos: Female Youth Culture on the Kenyan Coast*. Stockholm: Department of Social Anthropology, Stockholm University, 1994.

Fuller, Kathryn. *At the Picture Show: Small-Town Audiences and the Creation of Movie Fan Culture*. Washington, DC: Smithsonian Institution Press, 1996.

Furniss, Graham, and Malami Bub. "Youth Culture, Bandiri, and the Continuing Legitimacy Debate in Sokoto Town." *Journal of African Cultural Studies* 12, no. 1 (1999): 27–46.

Furst, Juliane. *Stalin's Last Generation: Soviet Postwar Youth and the Emergence of Mature Socialism*. Oxford: Oxford University Press, 2010.

———. "Swinging across the Iron Curtain in Moscow's Summer of Love: How Western Youth Culture Went East." In *Transnational Histories of Youth in the Twentieth Century*, edited by Richard Ivan Jobs and David M. Pomfret, 236–59. London: Palgrave Macmillan, 2015.

Gainer, David. "Exploitation: African Consolidated Films and Hollywood's Domination of South Africa's Bioscopes, 1930–1960." Paper presented at the annual African Studies Meeting, Boston, 2001.

———. "Hollywood, African Consolidated Films, and 'Bioskoopbeskawing,' or Bioscope Culture: Aspects of American Culture in Cape Town, 1945–1960." PhD diss., University of Cape Town, 2000.

Ganti, Tejaswini. *Bollywood: A Guidebook to Popular Hindi Cinema*. New York: Routledge, 2004.

———. *Producing Bollywood: Inside the Contemporary Hindi Film Industry*. Durham, NC: Duke University Press, 2012.

Gatheru, R. Mugo. *A Child of Two Worlds: A Kikuyu's Story*. New York: Praeger, 1964.

Geiger, Susan. *TANU Women: Gender and Culture in the Making of Tanganyikan Nationalism, 1955–1965*. Portsmouth, NH: Heinemann, 1997.

Giddens, Anthony. *The Transformation of Intimacy: Sexuality, Love, and Eroticism in Modern Societies*. Stanford, CA: Stanford University Press, 1992.

Gilbert, Erik. *Dhows and the Colonial Economy of Zanzibar, 1860–1970*. Athens: Ohio University Press, 2004.

Giltrow, David. "Young Tanzanians and the Cinema: A Study of the Effects of Selected Basic Motion Picture Elements and Population Characteristics on Filmic Comprehension of Tanzanian Adolescent Primary School Children." PhD diss., Syracuse University, 1973.

Givanni, June, and Imruh Bakari, eds. *Symbolic Narratives/African Cinema: Audiences, Theory and the Moving Image*. London: British Film Industry, 2000.

Glaser, Clive. *Bo-Tsotsi: The Youth Gangs of Soweto, 1935–1976*. Portsmouth, NH: Heinemann, 2000.

Glassman, Jonathon. *Feasts and Riot: Revelry, Rebellion and Popular Culture on the Swahili Coast, 1856–1888*. Portsmouth, NH: Heinemann, 1995.

———. "Sorting Out the Tribes: The Creation of Racial Identities in Colonial Zanzibar's Newspaper Wars." *Journal of African History* 41, no. 3 (2000): 395–428.

Goerg, Odile. *Fantômas sous les tropiques: Aller au cinéma en Afrique coloniale*. Paris: Vendémiaire, 2015.

Gokulsing, K. Moti, and Wimal Dissanayake. *Indian Popular Cinema: A Narrative of Cultural Change*. London: Trentham Books.

Gomery, Douglas. "Fashioning an Exhibition Empire: Promotion, Publicity and the Rise of Publix Theaters." In *Moviegoing in America*, edited by Gregory Waller, 124–36. Malden, MA: Blackwell, 2002.

424 ———. *Shared Pleasures: A History of Movie Presentation in the United States*. Madison: University of Wisconsin Press, 1992.

Gondola, Charles-Didier. "Dream and Drama: The Search for Elegance among Congolese Youth." *African Studies Review* 42, no. 1 (1999): 23–48.

———. "Le culte du cowboy et les figures du masculine à Kinshasa dans les années 1950." *Cahiers d'Etudes Africaines*, 52, nos. 1–2 (2013): 173–99.

———. *Tropical Cowboys: Westerns, Violence and Masculinity in Kinshasa*. Bloomington: Indiana University Press, 2016.

Goodman, Bryna. "All the Feelings That Are Fit to Print: The Community of Sentiment and the Literary Public in China, 1900–1918." *20th Century China* 27, no. 3 (2006): 291–327.

Gopal, Sangita, and Sujata Moorty, eds. *Global Bollywood: Travels of Hindi Song and Dance*. Minneapolis: University of Minnesota Press, 2008.

Grace, Joshua. "Heroes of the Road: Race, Gender and the Politics of Mobility in Twentieth Century Tanzania." *Africa* 83, no. 3 (2013): 403–25.

———. "The People's Car of Dar es Salaam: Buses, Passengers, and the State in Urban Tanzania, 1960s–1980s." Paper presented at the annual meeting of the Society of the History of Technology. Tacoma, Washington, 2010.

Graebner, Werner. "The Interaction of Swahili *Taarab* Music and the Record Industry: A Historical Perspective (Tanzania)." In *African Media Cultures: Transdisciplinary Perspectives*, edited by Rose Marie and Frank Wittmann Beck, 171–92. Cologne: Rudiger Koppe Verlag, 2004.

———. "The Ngoma Impulse: From Club to Nightclub in Dar es Salaam." In *Dar es Salaam: Histories from an Emerging African Metropolis*, edited by James Brennan, Andrew Burton, and Yusuf Lawi, 177–97. Dar es Salaam: Mkuki na Nyota, 2007.

Gregory, Robert. *The Rise and Fall of Philanthropy in East Africa*. New Brunswick, NJ: Transaction Publishers, 1992.

———. *South Asians in East Africa: An Economic and Social History, 1890–1980*. Boulder, CO: Westview Press, 1993.

Gronow, Jukka. *Caviar with Champagne: Common Luxury and the Ideals of the Good Life in Stalin's Russia*. New York: Berg, 2003.

Guback, Thomas. "American Films and the African Market." *Critical Arts* 3, no. 3 (1985): 1–14.

———. "Film as International Business: The Role of American Multinationals." In *The American Movie Industry: The Business of Motion Pictures*, edited by Gorham Kindem, 336–50. Carbondale: Southern Illinois University Press, 1982.

———. "Hollywood's International Market." In *The American Film Industry*, edited by Tino Balio, 463–86. Madison: University of Wisconsin Press, 1976.

Gugler, Joseph. *African Film*. London: James Currey, 2003.

Gunderson, Frank, and Gregory Barz, eds. *Mashindano: Competitive Music Performance in East Africa*. Dar es Salaam: Mkuki na Nyota, 2000.

Gurnah, Abdulrazak. *Paradise*. New York: New Press, 1993.

Gurnah, Ahmed. "Elvis in Zanzibar." In *The Spaces of Postmodernity: Readings in Human Geography*, edited by Michael Dear and Steven Flushing, 347–62. Oxford: Blackwell, 2002.

Gutsch, Thelma. *The History and Social Significance of Motion Pictures in South Africa, 1895–1940*. Cape Town: Howard Timmins, 1972.

Guyer, Jane. "Wealth in People, Wealth in Things." *Journal of African History* 36, no. 1 (1995): 83–90.

Hair, P. E. "The Cowboys: A Nigerian Acculturative Institution c. 1950." *History in Africa* 28 (2001): 83–93.

Hance, William. *Population, Migration and Urbanization in Africa*. New York: Columbia University Press, 1970.

Hansen, Karen Tranberg. *Salaula: The World of Secondhand Clothing and Zambia*. Chicago: University of Chicago Press, 2000.

Hansen, Thomas Blom. "In Search of the Diasporic Self: Bollywood in South Africa." In *Bollyworld: Popular Indian Cinema through a Transnational Lens*, edited by Raminder Kaur and Ajay J. Sinha, 239–60. New Delhi: Sage, 2005.

Harris, Richard, and Garth Myers. "Hybrid Housing: Improvement and Control in Late Colonial Zanzibar." *Journal of the Society of Architectural Historians* 66, no. 4 (2007): 476–93.

Hart, Jennifer Anne. *Ghana on the Go: African Mobility in the Age of Motor Transportation*. Bloomington: Indiana University Press, 2016.

Hartmann, Jeannette. *Re-thinking the Arusha Declaration*. Copenhagen: Axen Nielsen and Son A/S, 1991.

Harvey, David. *The Condition of Postmodernity: An Enquiry into the Origins of Cultural Change*. Oxford: Blackwell, 1989.

——. "The Right to the City." *New Left Review* 53 (September–October 2008), https://newleftreview.org/II/53/david-harvey-the-right-to-the-city.

Hearne, Joanna. "John Wayne's Teeth: Speech, Sound and Representation in Smoke Signals and Imagining Indians." *Western Folklore* 64, no. 3-4 (2005): 189–208.

Hecht, Gabrielle. *Being Nuclear*. Cambridge, MA: MIT Press, 2012.

Hessler, Julie. *A Social History of Soviet Trade: Trade Policy, Retail Practices, and Consumption, 1917–1953*. Princeton, NJ: Princeton University Press, 2004.

Higgins, MaryEllen, Rita Keresztesi, and Dayna Oscherwitz, eds. *The Western in the Global South*. New York: Routledge, 2015.

Hill, Polly. *Studies in Rural Capitalism in West Africa*. Cambridge: Cambridge University Press, 1970.

Hobson, Dorothy. *Crossroads: The Drama of a Soap Opera*. London: Methuen, 1982.

Hodgson, Dorothy, and Sheryl McCurdy, eds. *"Wicked" Women and the Reconfiguration of Gender in Africa*. Portsmouth, NH: Heinemann, 2001.

426

Hofmeier, Rolf. *Transport and Economic Development in Tanzania: With Particular Reference to Roads and Road Transport*. Munich: Weltforum Verlag, 1973.

Home, Robert. *Of Planting and Planning: The Making of British Colonial Cities*. London: Spon, 1997.

Honey, Martha Spencer. "A History of Indian Merchant Capital and Class Formation in Tanganyika, c. 1840–1940." PhD diss., University of Dar es Salaam, 1982.

hooks, bell. *Reel to Real: Race, Sex, and Class at the Movies*. New York: Routledge, 1996.

Hopkins, A. G. "The New Economic History of Africa." *Journal of African History* 50, no. 2 (2009): 155–77.

Hosier, Richard H. *Urban Development in Tanzania: A Tale of Three Cities*. Stockholm: Stockholm Environment Institute, in collaboration with SIDA, 1994.

Huettig, Mae. "Economic Control of the Motion Picture Industry." In *The American Film Industry*, edited by Tino Balio, 285–310. Madison: University of Wisconsin Press, 1985.

Hussein, Ebrahim. *Wakati Ukuta*. Dar es Salaam: East African Publishing House, 1971.

Hutton, John. *The Urban Challenge in East Africa*. Nairobi: East African Publishing House, 1970.

Hyden, Goran. *Beyond Ujamaa in Tanzania: Underdevelopment and an Uncaptured Peasantry*. London: Heinemann, 1980.

Iliffe, John. *A Modern History of Tanganyika*. Cambridge: Cambridge University Press, 1979.

Iordanova, D., J. Goytisolo, A. K. G. Singh, A. Suner, V. Shafik, and P. A. Skantze. "Indian Cinema's Global Reach: Historiography through Testimonies." *South Asian Popular Culture* 4, no. 2 (2006): 113–40.

Isaacman, Allen F., and Barbara S. Isaacman. *Dams, Displacement, and the Delusion of Development: Cahora Bassa and Its Legacies in Mozambique, 1965–2007*. Athens: Ohio University Press, 2013.

Ishumi, Abel G. M. *The Urban Jobless in Eastern Africa: A Study of the Unemployed Population in the Growing Urban Centers, with Special Reference to Tanzania*. Uppsala: Scandinavian Institute of African Studies, 1984.

Issak, Issak Esmail. "Cinema in Zanzibar." Internet posting forwarded to me by Asad Talati, 2008.

Ivaska, Andrew M. "'Anti-mini Militants Meet Modern Misses': Urban Style, Gender, and the Politics of 'National Culture' in 1960s Dar es Salaam, Tanzania." In *Fashioning Africa: Power and the Politics of Dress*, edited by Jean Allman, 104–21. Bloomington: Indiana University Press, 2004.

——. "Consuming and Contesting 'Soul' in Tanzania." In *New World Coming: The Sixties and the Shaping of Global Consciousness*, edited by Karen Dubinsky, Catherine Krull, Susan Lord, Sean Mills, and Scott Rutherford, 169–78. Toronto: Between the Lines, 2009.

———. *Cultured States: Youth, Gender and Modern Style in Dar es Salaam*. Durham, NC: Duke University Press, 2011.

———. "Movement Youth in a Global Sixties Hub: The Everyday Lives of Transnational Activists in Postcolonial Dar es Salaam." In *Transnational Histories of Youth in the Twentieth Century*, edited by Richard Ivan Jobs and David M. Pomfret, 188–212. New York: Palgrave Macmillan, 2015.

Jagarnath, Vashna. "Indian Cinema in Durban: Urban Segregation, Business and Visions of Identity from the 1950s to the 1970s." In *City Flicks: Cinema, Urban Worlds and Modernities in India and Beyond*, edited by Preben Kaarsholn, 165–76. Roskilde, Denmark: International Development Studies, 2002.

Jahadhmy, Ali. *Anthology of Swahili Poetry*. London: Heinemann, 1977.

Jain, Rikhab Dass. *The Economic Aspects of the Film Industry in India*. Delhi: Atma Ram and Sons, 1960.

Jalloh, Alusine. *African Entrepreneurship: Muslim Fula Merchants in Sierra Leone*. Athens: Ohio University Press, 1999.

James, Jeffrey. "Public Choice, Technology and Industrialization in Tanzania: Some Paradoxes Resolved." In *The Industrial Experience of Tanzania*, edited by Adam Szirmai and Paul Lapperre, 135–52. New York: Palgrave, 2001.

James, Nick, Ali Jaafar, and Kieron Corless. "Rushes." *Sight & Sound*, n.s., 17, no. 4 (2007): 6–8, 10, 12, 14.

Jancovich, Mark, Lucy Faire, and Sarah Stubbings. *The Place of the Audience: Cultural Geographies of Film Consumption*. London: British Film Institute, 2003.

Jarvie, Ian. *Hollywood's Overseas Campaign: The North Atlantic Movie Trade, 1920–1950*. New York: Cambridge University Press, 1992.

Jha, B. *Indian Motion Picture Almanac*. Calcutta: Shot Publications, 1975.

Jonsson, Urban. "Ideological Framework and Health Development in Tanzania, 1961–2000." *Social Science and Medicine* 22, no. 7 (1986): 745–53.

Joseph, May. *Nomadic Identities: The Performance of Citizenship*. Minneapolis: University of Minnesota Press, 1999.

Joshi, Lalit Mohan. *Bollywood: Popular Indian Cinema*. 2nd ed. London: Dakini Books, 2002.

Kaarsholm, Preben, ed. *City Flicks: Cinema, Urban Worlds and Modernities in India and Beyond*. Roskilde, Denmark: Graduate School, International Development Studies, Roskilde University, 2002.

Kamphausen, Hannes. "Cinema in Africa, a Survey." *Cineaste* 5, no. 2 (1972): 28–41.

Karioki, James. *Tanzania's Human Revolution*. University Park: Penn State University Press, 1979.

Kassam, Kassim Musa. *Joto La Fedha*. Dar es Salaam: Kobe Publications, 1982.

Kassum, Al Noor. *Africa's Winds of Change: Memoirs of an International Tanzanian*. London: I. B. Tauris, 2007.

427

428

Kaungammo, E. E. "Mass Media and Youth." In *The Young Child Study in Tanzania, Age 7–15*, edited by I. M. Omari and Paul J. Mhaiki, 77–97. Dar es Salaam: Tanzania National Scientific Research Council, 1977.

Kaur, Raminder, and Ajay J. Sinha. "Bollyworld: An Introduction to Popular Indian Cinema through a Transnational Lens." In *Bollyworld: Popular Indian Cinema through a Transnational Lens*, 11–35. New Delhi: Sage, 2005.

Kavoori, Anandam P., and Aswin Punathambekar, eds. *Global Bollywood*. New York: New York University Press, 2008.

Kiel, Hildegard. "Travel on a Song: The Roots of Zanzibar Taarab." *African Music: Journal of the African Music Society* 9, no. 2 (2012): 75–93.

King'ei, Geoffrey Kitula. "Language, Culture and Communication: The Role of Swahili Taarab Songs in Kenya, 1963–1990." PhD diss., Howard University, 1992.

Kiondo, Andrew. "The Nature of Economic Reforms in Tanzania." In *The IMF and Tanzania*, edited by Horace Campbell and Howard Stein, 23–47. Harare: Southern Africa Political Economy Series Trust, 1991.

Knappert, Jan. *An Anthology of Swahili Love Poetry*. Berkeley: University of California Press, 1972.

———. *Four Centuries of Swahili Verse: A Literary History and Anthology*. London: Heinemann Educational, 1979.

———. "Swahili Songs with Double-Entendre." *Afrika and Ubersee* 66, no. 1 (1983): 67–76.

Knauft, Bruce. *Critically Modern: Alternatives, Alterities, Anthropologies*. Bloomington: Indiana University Press, 2002.

Konde, Hadji. *Press Freedom in Tanzania*. Arusha, Tanzania: East Africa Publications, 1984.

Krings, Matthias. *African Appropriations: Cultural Difference, Mimesis and Media*. Bloomington: Indiana University Press, 2015.

———. "Nollywood Goes East: The Localization of Nigerian Video Films in Tanzania." In *Viewing African Cinema in the Twenty-First Century: Art Films and the Nollywood Video Revolution*, edited by Ralph Austen and Mahir Saul, 74–91. Athens: Ohio University Press, 2010.

Krings, Matthias, and Onookome Okome, eds. *Global Nollywood: The Transnational Dimensions of an African Video Film Industry*. Bloomington: Indiana University Press, 2013.

Kuhn, Annette. "Cinema Culture and Feminity in the 1930s." In *Nationalizing Feminity: Culture, Sexuality and British Cinema in the Second World War*, edited by Christine Gladhill and Gillian Swanson, 177–92. Manchester: Manchester University Press, 1996.

———. *Dreaming of Fred and Ginger: Cinema and Cultural Memory*. New York: New York University Press, 2002.

———. "'That Day Did Last Me All My Life': Cinema Memory and Enduring Fandom." In *Identifying Hollywood's Audiences: Cultural Identity and the*

Movies, edited by Melvyn Stokes and Richard Maltby, 135–46. London: British Film Institute, 1999.

Laar, Aart J. M. Van de. "Foreign Business and Capital Exports from Developing Countries: The Tanzanian Experience." In *Socialism in Tanzania,* edited by Lionel Cliffe and John Saul, 83–87. Dar es Salaam: East African Publishing House, 1973.

Lahmeyer, Jan. "Tanzania: Historical Demographic Data of the Urban Centers." 2001. http://www.populstat.info/Africa/tanzanit.htm.

Larkin, Brian. "Bandiri Music, Globalization and Urban Space in Nigeria." In *Bollyworld: Popular Indian Cinema through a Transnational Lens,* edited by Raminder Kaur and Ajay J. Sinha, 284–308. New Delhi: Sage, 2005.

———. "Indian Films and Nigerian Lovers: Media and the Creation of Parallel Modernities." *Africa: Journal of the International African Institute* 67, no. 3 (1997): 406–40.

———. "The Materiality of Cinema Theaters in Northern Nigeria." In *Media Worlds: Anthropology on New Terrain,* edited by Faye Ginsburg, Lila Abu-Lughod, and Brian Larkin, 319–36. Berkeley: University of California Press, 2002.

———. *Signal and Noise: Media, Infrastructure, and Urban Culture in Nigeria.* Durham, NC: Duke University Press, 2008.

Lawuyi, Olatunde Bayo. "The World of the Yoruba Taxi Driver: An Interpretive Approach to Vehicle Slogans." In *Readings in African Popular Culture,* edited by Karin Barber, 146–50. Bloomington: Indiana University Press, 1997.

Lee, Bruce. *Tao of Jeet Kune Do.* Valencia, CA: Black Belt Communications, 1975.

Lefebvre, Henri. *The Production of Space.* Oxford: Blackwell, 1974 (translation 1991).

Le Guennec-Coppens, Françoise. *Wedding Customs in Lamu.* Nairobi: Lamu Society, 1980.

Leslie, J. A. K. *A Survey of Dar es Salaam.* London: Oxford University Press, 1963.

Leveri, Mark. "Fiscal Planning and Control in Motion Picture Production: A Paradigm for a Costing Tequnique System at the Audio-Visual Institute." MBA thesis, University of Dar es Salaam, 1984.

———. "Prospects in Developing a Viable National Film Industry: A Close-Up of a Decade's Performance of the Audio-Visual Institute of Dar es Salaam and the Tanzanian Film Company Ltd. (1973–1983)." Master's thesis, University of Dar es Salaam, 1983.

Liebes, Tamar, and Elihu Katz. *The Export of Meaning: Cross-Cultural Readings of Dallas.* New York: Oxford University Press, 1990.

Lihamba, Amandina. "The Role of Culture." In *Re-thinking the Arusha Declaration,* edited by Jeannette Hartmann, 270–76. Copenhagen: Center for Development Research, 1991.

Lindsay, Lisa. "'No Need . . . to Think of Home'? Masculinity and Domestic Life on the Nigerian Railway, c. 1940–61." *Journal of African History* 39, no. 3 (1998): 439–66.

430

Lindsay, Lisa, and Stephan Miescher, eds. *Men and Masculinities in Modern Africa*. Portsmouth, NH: Heinemann, 2003.

Little, John R. *Bruce Lee: A Warrior's Journey*. New York: Contemporary Books, 2001.

Lovejoy, Paul. *Caravans of Kola: The Hausa Kola Trade, 1700–1900*. Zaria, Nigeria: Ahmadu Bello University Press, 1980.

Low, Rachael. *The History of British Film, 1906–1914*. London: Routledge, 1973.

———. *History of British Film*, vol. 2. London: Taylor and Francis, 2005.

Lugalla, Joe. *Crisis, Urbanization, and Urban Poverty in Tanzania: A Study of Urban Poverty and Survival Politics*. New York: University Press of America, 1995.

Luptatu Mussa Rashid. "Tanzania Film Company: A Measure of the Role of Movies in Tanzania—Study on the Effects of the Movie on the Tanzanian Youth." School of Journalism thesis, University of Dar es Salaam, 1981.

Lynd, Robert Staughton, and Helen Merrell Lynd. *Middletown, a Study in Contemporary American Culture*. New York: Harcourt, Brace, 1929.

Mabogunje, Akin. "Urban Planning and the Post-colonial State in Africa: A Research Overview." *African Studies Review* 33, no. 2 (1990): 121–203.

MacGaffey, Janet. *Entrepreneurs and Parasites: The Struggles for Indigenous Capitalism in Zaire*. Cambridge: Cambridge University Press, 1987.

Macha, Freddy. "Sensei Bomani: Pioneer of Martial Arts in Tanzania." *Citizen*, April 22, 2010, online.

Madi, Sacky, and Sarah Rashid. "The Distribution of Documentary Films in Tanzania." School of Journalism thesis, University of Dar es Salaam, 1982.

Magotti, John M. J. *Rashidi Mfaume Kawawa: Simba wa vita katika historia ya Tanzania*. Dar es Salaam: Matai, 2007.

Maingard, Jacqueline. *South African National Cinema*. New York: Routledge, 2007.

Makau, Nereah, Mwenda Ngesu, Fred Kawuna, and Paul Mbutu. *Cinema Leo Survey: A Study of Viewer Characteristics, Viewing Habits, Preference and Attitudes*. Nairobi: Daystar University, 1988.

Maliyamkono, T. L., and M. S. D. Bagachwa. *The Second Economy in Tanzania*. London: James Currey, 1990.

Maltby, Richard, Melvyn Stokes, and Robert C. Allen. "Introduction." In *Going to the Movies: Hollywood and the Social Experience of Cinema*, edited by Richard Maltby, Melvyn Stokes, and Robert C. Allen, 1–22. Exeter: University of Exeter Press, 2007.

Manuel, Peter. *Cassette Culture: Popular Music and Technology in North India*. Chicago: University of Chicago Press, 1993.

———. "The Cassette Industry and Popular Music in North India." *Popular Music* 10, no. 2 (1991): 189–204.

Markes, Sarah. *Street Level: A Collection of Drawings and Creative Writing Inspired by Dar-es-Salaam*. Dar es Salaam: Mkuki na Nyota, 2011.

Markovits, C. *The Global World of Indian Merchants, 1750–1947: Traders of Sind from Bukhara to Panama*. Cambridge: Cambridge University Press, 2000.

Martin, Phyllis. *Leisure and Society in Colonial Brazzaville*. Cambridge: Cambridge University Press, 1995.

Mascarenhas, Ophelia, and Marjorie Mbilinyi. *Women in Tanzania: An Analytical Bibliography*. Uppsala: Scandinavian Institute of African Studies, 1983.

Masey, Doreen. "A Global Sense of Place." In *Reading Human Geography*, edited by Trevor Barnes and Derek Gregory, 315–23. London: Arnold, 1997.

———. *Space, Place and Gender*. Minneapolis: University of Minnesota Press, 1994.

Masquelier, Adeline. "Lessons from Rubi: Love, Poverty and the Educational Value of Televised Dramas in Niger." In *Love in Africa*, edited by Jennifer Cole and Lynn Thomas. Chicago: University of Chicago Press, 2009.

Mayne, Judith. "Immigrants and Spectators." *Wide Angle* 5, no. 2 (1982): 32–40.

Mbilinyi, Marjorie. *Gender and Employment on Sugar Cane Plantations in Tanzania*. Geneva: ILO, 1995.

———. "The State of Women in Tanzania." *Canadian Journal of African Studies* 6, no. 2 (1972): 371–77.

Mbilinyi, Marjorie, Patricia Mbughuni, Ruth Meena, and Priscilla Olekambaine. *Education in Tanzania with a Gender Perspective*. Stockholm: SIDA, 1991.

Mbogoni, Lawrence E. Y. *Aspects of Colonial Tanzania History*. Dar es Salaam: Mkuki na Nyota, 2013.

Mbughuni, Patricia. "The Image of Woman in Kiswahili Prose Fiction." *Kiswahili* 49, no. 1 (1982): 15–24.

McFeely, Gareth. "'Gone Are the Days': A Social and Business History of Cinema-Going in Gold Coast/Ghana, 1910–1982." PhD diss., Boston University, 2015.

McHenry, Dean. *Limited Choices: The Political Struggle for Socialism in Tanzania*. Boulder, CO: Lynne Rienner, 1994.

McKiernan, D. W. *Cinema and Community*. Houndmills, UK: Palgrave Macmillan, 2008.

Meghji, Z. "The Development of Women Wage Labour: The Case of Industries." Master's thesis, University of Dar es Salaam, 1977.

Merkel, Ina. "Luxury in Socialism: An Absurd Proposition." In *Pleasures in Socialism: Leisure and Luxury in the Eastern Bloc*, edited by David Crowley and Susan Reid, 53–70. Evanston, IL: Northwestern University Press, 2010.

Meyer, Birgit. "Praise the Lord': Popular Cinema and Pentacostalite Style in Ghana's New Public Sphere." *American Ethnologist* 31, no. 1 (2004): 92–110.

———. *Sensational Movies: Video, Vision and Christianity in Ghana*. Oakland: University of California Press, 2015.

Meier, Prita. *Swahili Port Cities: An Architecture of Elsewhere*. Bloomington: Indiana University Press, 2016.

432

Miescher, Stephan F. "Building the City of the Future: Visions and Experiences of Modernity in Ghana's Akasombo Township." *Journal of African History* 53, no. 3 (2012): 367–90.

——. *Making Men in Ghana.* Bloomington: Indiana University Press, 2005.

Miller, Toby, Nitin Govil, John McMurria, and Richard Maxwell. *Global Hollywood.* London: British Film Institute, 2001.

Mirza, Sarah, and Margaret Strobel. *Three Swahili Women: Life Histories from Mombasa, Kenya.* Bloomington: Indiana University Press, 1989.

Mishra, Vijay. *Bollywood Cinema: Temples of Desire.* New York: Routledge, 2002.

Mitchell, Alice Miller. *Children and the Movies.* Chicago: University of Chicago Press, 1929.

Mitchell, Timothy, ed. *Questions of Modernity.* Minneapolis: University of Minnesota Press, 2000.

Monaco, Paul. *Cinema and Society: France and Germany during the Twenties.* New York: Elsevier, 1976.

Monson, Jamie. *Africa's Freedom Railway: How a Chinese Development Project Changed Lives and Livelihoods in Tanzania.* Bloomington: Indiana University Press, 2009.

——. "Defending the People's Railway in the Era of Liberalization: TAZARA in Southern Tanzania." *Africa* 76, no. 1 (2006): 113–30.

Moore, Sally Falk. *Social Facts and Fabrications: "Customary" Law on Kilimanjaro, 1880–1980.* Cambridge: Cambridge University Press, 1986.

Moorman, Marissa. *Intonations: A Social History of Music and Nation in Luanda, Angola, 1945–Recent Times.* Athens: Ohio University Press, 2008.

Morcom, Anna. *Hindi Film Songs and the Cinema.* Hampshire, UK: Ashgate, 2007.

Morton-Williams, P. *Cinema in Rural Nigeria: A Field Study of the Impact of Fundamental-Education Films on Rural Audiences in Nigeria.* Lagos: Federal Information Service, 1950.

Mosha, Ernesta Simon. "Discourse Analysis of Gender-Based Violence in Contemporary Kiswahili Fiction: A Case Study of Selected Novels of the Past Three Decades (1975–2004) and Young Tanzanians' Interpretations." PhD diss., University of Waikato, 2013.

Mponguliana, Joe Adelhelm John. "The Development of Film in Tanzania." School of Journalism thesis, University of Dar es Salaam, 1982.

Msina, Victoria. "Towards Understanding the Impact of Mass Media on Culture in Tanzania: A Case Study of Television in Dar es Salaam." School of Journalism thesis, University of Dar es Salaam, 2000.

Mtekateka, Andrew John Josiah. "The Importance of Adult Education Film Shows to Adult Learners." School of Journalism thesis, University of Dar es Salaam, 1987.

Mueller, Susanne. "The Historical Origins of Tanzania's Ruling Class." *Canadian Journal of African Studies* 15, no. 3 (1981): 459–98.

Mukajanga, Kajubi. *Bruce Lee—Mfalme Wa Kung Fu*. Dar es Salaam: Grand Arts Promotions, 1982.

Mukandala, Rwekaza S. "State Enterprise Control: The Case of Tanzania." In *State-Owned Enterprises in Africa*, edited by Barbara Grosh and Rwekaza S. Mukandala, 125–47. Boulder, CO: Lynne Rienner, 1994.

Murillo, Bianca. "'The Modern Shopping Experience': Kingsway Department Store and Consumer Politics in Ghana." *Africa* 82, no. 3 (2012): 368–92.

Mustafa, Sophia. *The Tanganyika Way*. Toronto: TSAR Publications, 1961 (reprint 2009).

Mutongi, Kenda. "'Dear Dolly's Advice: Representations of Youth, Courtship, and Sexualities in Africa, 1960–1980." *International Journal of African Historical Studies* 33, no. 1 (2000): 1–23.

———. *Matatu: A History of Popular Transportation in Nairobi*. Chicago: University of Chicago Press, 2017.

———. *Worries of the Heart: Widows, Family and Community in Kenya*. Chicago: University of Chicago Press, 2007.

Mwakalinga, Mona Ngusekela. "The Political Economy of the Film Industry in Tanzania: From Socialism to an Open Market Economy, 1961–2010." PhD diss., University of Kansas, 2010.

Mwangi, Meja. *Going Down River Road*. Portsmouth, NH: Heinemann, 1976.

Mwansasu, Bismarck U., and Cranford Pratt, eds. *Towards Socialism in Tanzania*. Toronto: University of Toronto Press, 1979.

Myers, Garth. *African Cities: Alternative Visions of Urban Theory and Practice*. London: Zed, 2011.

———. "Sticks and Stones: Colonialism and Zanzibari Housing." *Africa* 67, no. 2 (1997): 252–72.

———. *Verandahs of Power: Colonialism and Space in Urban Africa*. Syracuse, NY: Syracuse University Press, 2003.

Mytton, G. L. "The Role of Mass Media in Nation-Building in Tanzania." PhD diss., University of Manchester, 1976.

Nagar, Richa. "Communal Places and the Politics of Multiple Identities: The Case of Tanzanian Asians." *Ecumene* 4, no. 1 (1997): 3–26.

———. "Making and Breaking Boundaries: Identity Politics among South Asians in Postcolonial Dar es Salaam." PhD diss., University of Minnesota, 1995.

———. "The South Asian Diaspora in Tanzania: A History Retold." *Comparative Studies of South Asia, Africa and the Middle East* 16, no. 2 (1996): 62–80.

Nagar, Richa, and Helga Leitner. "Contesting Social Relations in Communal Places: Identity Politics among Asian Communities in Dar es Salaam." In *Cities of Difference*, edited by Ruth Fincher and Jane Jacobs, 226–51. New York: Guilford, 1998.

Namfua, P. P. "'Age, Sex, Marital Status,' Analysis of the 1978 Population Census." Edited by Bureau of Statistics, 57–91. Dar es Salaam: Ministry of Planning and Economic Affairs, 1982.

434

Nandy, Ashis. "Popular Indian Cinema as a Slum's Eye View of Politics." In *The Secret Politics of Our Desires: Innocence, Culpability and Indian Popular Cinema*, edited by Ashis Nandy, 1–18. London: Zed, 1998.

Nasaw, David. *Going Out: The Rise and Fall of Public Amusements*. Cambridge, MA: Harvard University Press, 1993.

Nasson, Bill. "She Preferred Living in a Cave with Harry the Snake-Catcher: Towards an Oral History of Popular Leisure and Class Expression in District Six, Cape Town, c. 1920–1950." In *Holding Their Ground*, edited by Philip Bonner et al., 285–310. Johannesburg: Ravan, 1989.

Naylor, David. *American Picture Palaces: The Architecture of Fantasy*. New York: Van Nostrand Reinhold, 1981.

Nellis, John R. "Public Enterprises in Sub-Saharan Africa." In *State-Owned Enterprises in Africa*, edited by Barbara Grosh and Rwekaza S. Mukandala, 3–24. Boulder, CO: Lynne Rienner, 1994.

Newell, Stephanie. *Ghanaian Popular Fiction: "Thrilling Discoveries in Conjugal Life" & Other Tales*. Athens: Ohio University Press, 2000.

———. *Literary Culture in Colonial Ghana: How to Play the Game of Life*. Bloomington: Indiana University Press, 2002.

Ng'wanakilala, Nkwabi. *The Liberating Effect of Mass Communication in Tanzania*. Dar es Salaam: Institute of Adult Education, 1979.

———. *Mass Communication and the Development of Socialism in Tanzania*. Dar es Salaam: Tanzania Publishing House, 1981.

Notcutt, L. A., and Geoffery Latham. *The African and the Cinema*. London: Edinburgh House, 1937.

Ntarangwi, Mwenda. *Gender, Performance & Identity: Understanding Swahili Cultural Identity through Songs*. Trenton, NJ: Africa World Press, 2001.

Nyatori, Abraham. "Video and Film: Pros and Cons of the Two in Business and Culture." Master's thesis, University of Dar es Salaam, 1992.

Nyerere, Julius. *Freedom and Socialism/Uhuru na Ujamaa: A Selection from Writings and Speeches, 1965–1967*. Dar es Salaam: Oxford University Press, 1968.

———. *Ujamaa: Essays on Socialism*. Dar es Salaam: Oxford University Press, 1968.

Olson, Scott Robert. *Hollywood Planet: Global Media and the Competitive Advantage of Narrative Transparency*. Mahwah, NJ: Lawrence Erlbaum, 1999.

Oonk, Gijsbert. "After Shaking His Hand, Start Counting Your Fingers: Trust and Images of Indian Business Networks, East Africa, 1900–2000." *Itinerario* 18, no. 3 (2004): 70–88.

———. *The Karimjee Jivanjee Family: Merchant Princes of East Africa, 1800–2000*. Amsterdam: Pallas Publications, 2009.

———. *Settled Strangers: Asian Business Elites in East Africa, 1800–2000*. Mumbai: Sage, 2013.

Othman, Haroub, ed. *Babu: I Saw the Future and It Works*. London: E and D, 2001.

Owen, Caleb. "Lands of Leisure: Recreation, Urban Space and the Struggle for Urban Kenya." PhD diss., Michigan State University, 2016.

Owens-Ibie, Nosa. "Programmed for Domination: US Television Broadcasting and Its Effects on Nigerian Culture." In *Here, There and Everywhere: The Foreign Politics of American Popular Culture*, edited by Reinhold Wagnleitner and Elaine Tyler May, 132–46. Hanover, NH: University Press of New England, 2000.

Packard, Philip. "Corporate Structure in Agriculture and Socialist Development in Tanzania: A Study of the National Agricultural and Food Corporation." In *African Socialism in Practice: The Tanzanian Experience*, edited by Andrew Coulson, 200–213. Nottingham: Review of African Political Economy, 1979.

Parker, Ian. "Contradictions in the Transition to Socialism: The Case of the National Development Corporation." In *Towards Socialism in Tanzania*, edited by Bismarck Mwansasu and Cranford Pratt, 46–71. Toronto: University of Toronto Press, 1979.

Parker-Pope, Tara. "'Chick Flicks' Can Double as Therapy for Couples." *International New York Times*, February 12, 2014.

Parpart, Jane. "'Where Is Your Mother?' Gender, Urban Marriage and Colonial Discourse on the Zambian Copperbelt, 1924–1945." *International Journal of African Historical Studies* 27, no. 2 (1994): 241–71.

Patel, Divia, Laurie Benson, and Carol Cains. *Cinema India: The Art of Bollywood*. 1st ed. Melbourne, Vic.: National Gallery of Victoria, 2007.

Peiss, Kathy Lee. *Cheap Amusements: Working Women and Leisure in Turn-of-the-Century New York*. Philadelphia: Temple University Press, 1986.

Peligal, Rona Elayne. "Spatial Planning and Social Fluidity: The Shifting Boundaries of Ethnicity, Gender and Class in Arusha, Tanzania, 1920–67." PhD diss., Columbia University, 1999.

Pendakur, Manjunath. "India." In *The Asian Film Industry*, edited by John Lent, 229–52. London: C. Helm, 1990.

———. *Indian Popular Cinema: Industry, Ideology, and Consciousness*. Creskill, NJ: Hampton Press, 2003.

Pendakur, Manjunath, and Radha Subramanyam. "Indian Cinema beyond National Borders." In *Patterns in Global Television: Peripheral Vision*, edited by John Sinclair, Elizabeth Jacka, and Stuart Cunningham, 67–82. Oxford: Oxford University Press, 1996.

Penrad, J. C. "The Ismaili Presence in East Africa: A Note on Its Commercial History and Community Organization." In *Asian Merchants and Businessmen in the Indian Ocean and the China Sea*, edited by D. L. A. J. Aubin, 222–38. New Delhi: Oxford University Press, 2000.

Pérez, Louis A., Jr. *On Becoming Cuban: Identity, Nationality and Culture*. Chapel Hill: University of North Carolina Press, 1999.

Perullo, Alex. *Artistic Rights: Copyright Law for East African Musicians, Artists, Writers and Other Authors*. US State Department, 2012.

436

————. *Live from Dar Es Salaam: Popular Music and Tanzania's Music Economy.* Bloomington: Indiana University Press, 2011.

Peteri, Gyorgy. "Alternative Modernity: Everyday Practices of Elite Mobility in Communist Hungary, 1956–1980." In *The Socialist Car: Automobility in the Eastern Bloc*, edited by Lewis Siegelbaum, 47–70. Ithaca, NY: Cornell University Press, 2011.

Petersen, George M. *Drive-In Theater: Manual of Design and Operation.* Kansas City, MO: Associated, 1953.

Petterson, Don. *Revolution in Zanzibar: An American's Cold War Tale.* Boulder, CO: Westview Press, 2002.

Pfaff, Françoise. *Focus on African Films.* Bloomington: Indiana University Press, 2004.

Phil Hubbard, Rob Kitchin, and Gill Valentine, eds. *Key Thinkers on Space and Place.* London: Sage, 2004.

Phillips, Joseph. "Film Conglomerate Blockbusters: International Appeal and Product Homogenization." In *The American Movie Industry: The Business of Motion Pictures*, edited by Gorham Kindem, 325–35. Carbondale: Southern Illinois University Press, 1982.

Piot, Charles. *Remotely Global: Village Modernity in West Africa.* Chicago: University of Chicago Press, 1999.

Pitcher, M. Anne, and Kelly M. Askew. "African Socialisms and Postsocialisms." *Africa* 76, no. 1 (2006): 1–14.

Powdermaker, Hortense. *Copper Town: Changing Africa—The Human Situation on the Rhodesian Copperbelt.* New York: Harper and Row, 1962.

Prakash, Sanjeev. "Music, Dance, and the Popular Films: Indian Fantasies, Indian Repressions." In *Indian Cinema Superbazaar*, edited by Aruna Vasudev and Philippe Lenglet, 114–18. Delhi: Vikas Publishing, 1983.

Pratt, Cranford. *The Critical Phase in Tanzania, 1945–68: Nyerere and the Emergence of a Socialist Strategy.* Cambridge: Cambridge University Press, 1976.

Prestholdt, Jeremy. *Domesticating the World: African Consumerism and the Geneologies of Globalization.* Berkeley: University of California Press, 2008.

Putnam, Robert D. *Bowling Alone: The Collapse and Revival of American Community.* New York: Simon and Schuster, 2000.

Pype, Katrien. "Fighting Boys, Strong Men and Gorillas: Notes on the Imagination of Masculinities in Kinshasa." *Africa: Journal of the International African Institute* 77, no. 2 (2007): 250–71.

Radway, Janice A. *Reading the Romance: Women, Patriarchy, and Popular Literature.* Chapel Hill: University of North Carolina Press, 1984.

Rajadhyaksha, Ashish, and Paul Willemen. *Awara.* London: British Film Institute, 1994.

————. *Encyclopedia of the Indian Cinema.* 2nd ed. London: Fitzroy Dearborn, 1999.

Rajagopalan, Sudha. *Indian Films in Soviet Cinemas: The Culture of Movie-Going after Stalin.* Bloomington: Indiana University Press, 2008.

Reddy, William M. *The Navigation of Feeling: A Framework for the History of Emotions*. New York: Cambridge University Press, 2001.

Reinwald, Brigitte. "Tonight at the Empire: Cinema and Urbanity in Zanzibar, 1920s–1960s." *Afrique et Histoire* 5 (2006): 81–110.

Republic of Tanganyika. "Family Budget Survey of Middle-Grade African Civil Servants, 1963." Edited by Central Statistics Bureau. Dar es Salaam: Bureau of Statistics, 1963.

Reuben, Bunny. *Dilip Kumar: Star Legend of Indian Cinema—The Definitive Biography*. New Delhi: HarperCollins Publishers India, 2004.

Reynolds, Glenn. *Colonial Cinema in Africa: Origins, Images, Audiences*. Jefferson, NC: McFarland, 2015.

Richards, Jeffrey. *The Age of the Dream Palace: Cinema and Society in Britain, 1930–1939*. London: Routledge and Kegan Paul, 1984.

Richards, Paul. *Fighting for the Rainforest: War, Youth and Resources in Sierra Leone*. London: James Currey, 1996.

Rieger, Bernhard. *Technology and the Culture of Modernity in Britain and Germany, 1890–1945*. Cambridge: Cambridge University Press, 2005.

Robertson, Claire. *Trouble Showed the Way: Women, Men and Trade in the Nairobi Area, 1890–1990*. Bloomington: Indiana University Press, 1997.

Rockel, Stephen. *Carriers of Culture: Labor on the Road in Nineteenth-Century East Africa*. Portsmouth, NH: Heinemann, 2006.

Rockwell, John. "The New Colossus: American Culture as Power Export." *New York Times*, January 30, 1994, 1, 30.

Roe, A. "The Company in Tanzanian Development," *Journal of Modern African Studies* 7, no. 1 (1969): 47-67. Rosenzweig, Roy. *Eight Hours for What We Will: Workers and Leisure in an Industrial City, 1870–1920*. Cambridge: Cambridge University Press, 1983.

Rutayisingwa, John. *Ngumi Ukutani*. Dar es Salaam: Ben, 1979.

Sabea, Hanan. "Reviving the Dead: Entangled Histories in the Privatisation of the Tanzanian Sisal Industry." *Africa* 71, no. 2 (2001): 286–313.

Sabot, R. H. *Economic Development and Urban Migration: Tanzania, 1900–1971*. Oxford: Clarendon Press, 1979.

Sahai, Malti. "Raj Kapoor and the Indianization of Charlie Chaplin." *East-West Film Journal* 2, no. 1 (1987): 62–75.

Salgia, Deepesh. "'Mughal-E-Azam': Restoration-cum-Colorization for 35mm Release." *Moving Image* 5, no. 1 (2005): 128–35.

Sardar, Ziauddin. "Dilip Kumar Made Me Do It." In *The Secret Politics of Our Desires: Innocence, Culpability and Indian Popular Cinema*, edited by Ashis Nandy, 19–91. London: Zed, 1998.

Sarrazin, Natalie. "Celluloid Love Songs: Musical *Modus Operandi* and the Dramatic Aesthetics of Romantic Hindi Film." *Popular Music* 27, no. 3 (2008): 393–411.

438

———. "Songs from the Heart: Musical Coding, Emotional Sentiment, and Transnational Sonic Identity in India's Popular Film Music." In *Global Bollywood*, edited by Anandam P. Kavoori and Aswin Punathambekar, 203–22. New York: New York University Press, 2008.

Saul, Mahir, and Ralph A. Austen, eds. *Viewing African Cinema in the Twenty-First Century: Art Films and the Nollywood Video Revolution.* Athens: Ohio University Press, 2009.

Saunders, Thomas. *Hollywood in Berlin: American Cinema and Weimar Germany.* Berkeley: University of California Press, 1994.

Sawasawa, Subiria, and Aidan Hyera. "The Effectiveness of Feature Films as a Communication Medium in Tanzania." School of Journalism thesis, University of Dar es Salaam, 1982.

Schauert, Paul. *Staging Ghana: Artistry and Nationalism in State Dance Ensembles.* Bloomington: Indiana University Press, 2015.

Scott, James C. *Seeing Like a State: How Certain Schemes to Improve the Human Condition Have Failed.* New Haven, CT: Yale University Press, 1998.

Segrave, Kerry. *Drive-In Theaters: A History from Their Inception in 1933.* Jefferson, NC: McFarland, 1992.

Seidenberg, Dana April. *Mercantile Adventurers: The World of East African Asians, 1750–1985.* New Delhi: New Age International, 1996.

Sen, Biswarup. "The Sounds of Modernity: The Evolution of Bollywood Film Song." In *Global Bollywood: Travels of Hindi Song and Dance*, edited by Sangita Gopal and Sujata Moorti, 85–104. Minneapolis: University of Minnesota Press, 2008.

Shannon, Jonathan H. "Emotion, Performance, and Temporality in Arab Music: Reflections on Tarab." *Cultural Anthropology: Journal of the Society for Cultural Anthropology* 18, no. 1 (2003): 72.

Sharma, Ashwani. "Blood, Sweat, and Tears: Amitabh Bachchan, Urban Demigod." In *You Tarzan: Masculinity, Movies, and Men*, edited by Pat Kirkham and Janet Thumin, 167–80. New York: St. Martin's Press, 1993.

Sheik, Leila. "Tamwa: Levina's Song—Supporting Women in Tanzania." In *Composing a New Song: Stories of Empowerment from Africa*, edited by Hope Bagyendera Chigundu, 95–128. London: Commonwealth Foundation, 2004.

Sheik-Hashim, Leila. *Unyago: Traditional Family Life Education among the Muslim Digo, Seguju, Bondei, Sambaa and Sigua of Tanga Region.* Dar es Salaam: Tanzania Media Women's Association, 1989.

Sheraly, Nisar. *Moto! Moto! Majestic Cinema Is on Fire!* Dar es Salaam, Tanzania: Desk Top Productions, 2006.

Sheriff, Abdul. *Dhow Culture of the Indian Ocean: Cosmopolitanism, Commerce and Islam.* New York: Columbia University Press, 2010.

———, ed. *The History and Conservation of Zanzibar Stone Town.* London: James Currey, 1995.

———. "An Outline History of Zanzibar Stone Town." In *The History and Conservation of Zanzibar Stone Town*, edited by Abdul Sheriff, 8–29. London: James Currey, 1995.

Sheriff, Abdul, and Javed Jafferji. *Zanzibar Stone Town: An Architectural Exploration*. Zanzibar: Gallery Publications, 2008.

Sherman, Daniel J., Ruud van Dijk, Jasmine Alinder, and A. Aneesh, eds. *The Long 1968: Revisions and New Perspectives*. Bloomington: Indiana University Press, 2013.

Sherman, Sharon R. "Introduction: An Expanded View of Film and Folklore." *Western Folklore* 64, no. 3-4 (2005): 157–61.

Shively, JoEllen. "Cowboys and Indians: Perceptions of Western Films among American Indians and Anglos." *American Sociological Review* 57, no. 6 (1992): 725–34.

Shivji, Issa. *Class Struggles in Tanzania*. Dar es Salaam: Tanzania Publishing House, 1976.

———. "Liberalization and the Crisis of Ideological Hegemony." In *Re-thinking the Arusha Declaration*, edited by Jeannette Hartmann, 132–43. Copenhagen: Axen Nielsen and Son A/S, 1991.

———. "Tanzania—The Silent Class Struggle." In *Socialism in Tanzania*, edited by Lionel Cliffe and John Saul, 304–30. Dar es Salaam: East African Publishing House, 1973.

Siegelbaum, Lewis. *Cars for Comrades: The Life of the Soviet Automobile*. Ithaca, NY: Cornell University Press, 2008.

———, ed. *The Socialist Car: Automobility in the Eastern Bloc*. Ithaca, NY: Cornell University Press, 2011.

Skillman, Teri. "The Bombay Hindi Film Song Genre: A Historical Survey." *Yearbook for Traditional Music* (1986): 133–44.

———. "Songs in Hindi Films: Nature and Function." In *Cinema and Cultural Identity: Reflections on Films from Japan, India, and China*, edited by Wimal Dissanyake, 149–64. New York: University Press of America, 1988.

Sklar, Robert. "The Lost Audience: 1950s Spectatorships and Historical Reception Studies." In *Identifying Hollywood's Audiences*, edited by Melvyn Stokes and Richard Maltby, 81–92. London: British Film Institute, 1999.

———. *Movie-Made America: A Cultural History of American Movies*. New York: Vintage Books, 1994.

Smyth, Rosaleen. "The Development of British Colonial Film Policy, 1927–1939, with Special Referrence to East and Central Africa." *Journal of African History* 20, no. 3 (1979): 437–50.

———. "The Feature Film in Tanzania." *African Affairs* 88, no. 352 (1989): 389–96.

———. "The Post-war Career of the Colonial Film Unit in Africa: 1946–1955." *Historical Journal of Film, Radio and Television* 12, no. 2 (1992): 163–77.

439

440

Sommer, Doris. *Foundational Fictions: The National Romances of Latin America*. Berkeley: University of California Press, 1991.

Speller, Ian. "An African Cuba? Britain and the Zanzibar Revolution, 1964." *Journal of Imperial and Commonwealth History* 35, no. 2 (2007): 283–301.

Spitulnik, Debra. "Mobile Machines and Fluid Audiences: Rethinking Reception through Zambian Radio Culture." In *Media Worlds*, edited by Abu-Lughod Ginsburg and Brian Larkin, 337–54. Berkeley: University of California Press, 2002.

Spurr, Norman. "A Report on Audience Reactions to Zonk." Edited by Public Records Office, CO 875 51/7.

Srinivas, Lakshmi. *House Full: Indian Cinema and the Active Audience*. Chicago: University of Chicago Press, 2016.

———. "Ladies Queues, 'Roadside Romeos,' and Balcony Seating: Ethnographic Observations on Women's Cinema-Going Experiences." *South Asian Popular Culture* 8, no. 3 (2010): 291–307.

Ssali, Mike Hillary. "The Development and Role of an African Film Industry in East Africa with Special Reference to Tanzania, 1922–1984." PhD diss., University of California, Los Angeles, 1988.

Stacey, Jackie. *Star Gazing: Hollywood Cinema and Female Spectatorship*. London: Routledge, 1994.

Stambach, Amy. "Evangelism and Consumer Culture in Northern Tanzania." *Anthropological Quarterly* 73, no. 4 (2000): 171–79.

———. *Lessons from Mount Kilimanjaro*. New York: Routledge, 2000.

Stokes, Melvyn. "Female Audiences of the 1920's and Early 1930's." In *Identifying Hollywood's Audiences*, edited by Melvyn Stokes and Richard Maltby, 42–60. London: British Film Institute, 1999.

Stokes, Melvyn, and Richard Maltby. *Identifying Hollywood's Audiences: Cultural Identity and the Movies*. London: British Film Institute, 1999.

———, eds. *American Movie Audiences: From the Turn of the Century to the Early Sound Era*. London: British Film Institute, 1999.

Straker, Jay. *Youth, Nationalism and the Guinean Revolution*. Bloomington: Indiana University Press, 2009.

Strobel, Margaret. *Muslim Women of Mombasa, 1890–1975*. New Haven, CT: Yale University Press, 1979.

———. *Three Swahili Women: Life Histories from Mombasa, Kenya*. Bloomington: Indiana University Press, 1989.

Suriano, Maria. "Clothing and Changing Identities of Tanganyikan Urban Youth, 1920s–1950s." *Journal of African Cultural Studies* 20, no. 1 (2008): 95–115.

Swantz, Marja-Liisa. "Church and the Changing Role of Women in Tanzania." In *Christianity in Independent Africa*, edited by Edward W. Fashole-Luke, Richard Gray, and Adrian Hastings, 136–50. Bloomington: Indiana University Press, 1978.

Tamale, Sylvia, ed. *African Sexualities*. Oxford: Pambazuka, 2011.

Tanganyika Territory. "African Census Report." Dar es Salaam, 1957.

Tanzania Film Company Ltd. *Annual Report and Account for the Year Ended 31 December 1984–31 December 1988*. Dar es Salaam: AS General, n.d.

———. *Taarifa ya mwaka na hesabu kwa mwaka ulioishia 31 December, 1990*. Dar es Salaam: TFC, 1991.

Tanzania, People's Republic. *Statistical Abstract 1962*. Dar es Salaam: Government Printer, 1962.

Tanzania Tourist Corporation. "Annual Report and Accounts, 1970–71." N.p., n.d.

———. "Annual Report and Accounts 1973." N.p., 1973.

Taylor, Helen. *Scarlett's Women: Gone with the Wind and Its Female Fans*. New Brunswick, NJ: Rutgers University Press, 1989.

Temu, Andrew E., and Jean M. Due. "The Business Environment in Tanzania after Socialism: Challenges of Reforming Banks, Parastatals, Taxation and the Civil Service." *Journal of Modern African Studies* 38, no. 4 (2000): 683–712.

Teo, Stephen. *Hong Kong Cinema: The Extra Dimension*. London: British Film Institute, 1997.

Thackway, Melissa. *Africa Shoots Back: Alternative Perspectives in Sub-Saharan Francophone African Film*. Bloomington: Indiana University Press, 2003.

Thomas, Lynn. "Love, Sex and the Modern Girl in 1930s Southern Africa." In *Love in Africa*, edited by Jennifer Cole and Lynn Thomas, 31–57. Chicago: University of Chicago Press, 2009.

———. "Modernity's Failings, Political Claims and Intermediate Concepts." *American Historical Review* 116, no. 3 (2011): 727–40.

———. *Politics of the Womb: Women, Reproduction and the State in Kenya*. Berkeley: University of California Press, 2003.

Thomas, P. A. "The Advantages of Being Ltd." *Transition* 36 (1968): 51–54.

Thomas, Rosie. "Indian Cinema: Pleasures and Popularity." *Screen* 26, no. 3 (1985): 116–31.

———. "Melodrama and the Negotiation of Morality in Mainstream Hindi Film." In *Consuming Modernity: Public Culture in a South Asian World*, edited by Carol Breckenridge, 157–82. Minneapolis: University of Minnesota Press, 1995.

———. "Sanctity and Scandal: The Mythologization of Mother India." *Quarterly Review of Film and Video* 11, no. 3 (1989): 11–30.

Thompson, Elizabeth. *Colonial Citizens Republican Rights, Paternal Privilege, and Gender in French Syria and Lebanon*. New York: Columbia University Press, 2000.

Thompson, Kristin. *Exporting Entertainment: America in the World Film Market, 1907–34*. London: British Film Institute, 1985.

Thoraval, Yves. *The Cinemas of India, 1896–2000*. Delhi: Macmillan India, 2000.

Tignor, Robert L. "The Business Firm in Africa: Literature Review." *Business History Review* 81 (Spring 2007): 87–110.

442

Tomaselli, Keyan G. *The Cinema of Apartheid: Race and Class in South African Film*. New York: Smyrna/Lake View Press, 1988.

Tomlinson, John. *Cultural Imperialism: A Critical Introduction*. Baltimore, MD: Johns Hopkins University Press, 1991.

Tripp, Aili Mari. *Changing the Rules: The Politics of Liberalization and the Urban Informal Economy in Tanzania*. Berkeley: University of California Press, 1997.

Tsuruta, Tadasu. "Simba or Yanga? Football and Urbanization in Dar es Salaam." In *Dar es Salaam: Histories from an Emerging African Metropolis*, edited by James Brennan, Andrew Burton, and Yusuf Lawi, 198–212. Dar es Salaam: Mkuki na Nyota, 2007.

Tuan, Yi-Fu. *Topophilia: A Study of Environmental Perception, Attitudes and Values*. Englewood Cliffs, NJ: Prentice Hall, 1974.

Turino, Thomas. *Nationalists, Cosmopolitans, and Popular Music in Zimbabwe*. Chicago: University of Chicago Press, 2000.

Ukadike, Nwachukwu Frank. *Black African Cinema*. Berkeley: University of California Press, 1994.

UNESCO. *Basic Facts and Figures: International Statistics Relating to Education, Culture and Mass Communications*. Paris: UNESCO, 1961.

United Republic of Tanzania. *1967 Population Census*, vol. 2: *Statistics for Urban Areas*. Dar es Salaam, 1967.

——. *1978 Population Census*. Dar es Salaam: Bureau of Statistics, 1983.

——. *Bus Transport for Cite and Service Areas, Dar es Salaam*. Dar es Salaam: Ministry of Lands, Housing and Urban Development, 1973.

——. *Family Budget Survey of Middle-Grade African Civil Servants, 1963*. Dar es Salaam: Central Statistical Bureau, 1964.

——. *Household Budget Survey of Wage-Earners in Dar es Salaam, 1965*. Dar es Salaam: Bureau of Statistics, 1967.

——. *Household Budget Survey, 1969*. Dar es Salaam: Bureau of Statistics, 1972.

——. *Household Budget Survey, 1976/77*. Dar es Salaam: Bureau of Statistics, 1988.

——. *Monthly Statistical Bulletin, August*, vol. 19. Dar es Salaam: Government Printer, 1969.

——. *Monthly Statistical Bulletin, August*, vol. 20. Dar es Salaam: Government Printer, 1970.

——. *Monthly Statistical Bulletin, August*. Dar es Salaam: Government Printer, 1969.

——. *Selected Statistical Series, 1951–1993*. Dar es Salaam: Presidents Office-Planning Commission, 1995.

——. *Survey of Employment and Earnings, 1973–74*. Dar es Salaam: Bureau of Statistics, 1977.

United Republic of Tanzania, Bureau of Statistics. *Morogoro Regional Socio-economic Profile*. Dar es Salaam: National Bureau of Statistics and Morogoro Regional Commissioner's Office, 2002.

United States Information Agency (USIA). *Communications Data Book for Africa.* Washington, DC: USIA, 1966.

Unsiker, Jeff. "'Tanzania's Literacy Campaign in Historical Perspective.'" In *National Literacy Campaigns: Historical and Comparative Perspectives*, edited by Robert and Harvey Graff Arnove, 219–44. New York: Plenum Press, 1987.

US Department of Commerce. "World Trade in Commodities: Motion Pictures and Equipment." 1–2. Washington, DC: US Government Printing Office, 1950.

US Department of Commerce, Bureau of Foreign and Domestic Commerce. *Small Island Markets for American Motion Pictures.* Washington, DC: US Government Printing Office, 1931.

Valicha, Kishore. *The Moving Image: A Study of Indian Cinema.* Bombay: Orient Longman, 1988.

Vassanji, M. G. *The Book of Secrets.* New York: Picador, 1994.

———. *Uhuru Street.* London: Heinemann, 1992.

Vasudevan, Ravi. "Addressing the Spectator of a 'Third World' National Cinema: The Bombay Social Film of the the 1940s and 1950s." *Screen* 36, no. 4 (1995): 305–24.

———, ed. *Making Meaning in Indian Cinema.* New Delhi: Oxford University Press, 2000.

———. "Shifting Codes, Dissolving Identities: The Hindi Social Film of the 1950s as Popular Culture." In *Making Meaning in Indian Cinema*, edited by Ravi Vasudevan, 99–121. New Delhi: Oxford University Press, 2000.

———. "You Cannot Live in Society—and Ignore It: Nationhood and Female Modernity in Andaz." *Contributions to Indian Sociology* 29, no. 1 (1995): 83–108.

Verdery, Katherine. *What Was Socialism and What Comes Next?* Princeton, NJ: Princeton University Press, 1996.

Verrips, Jajada, and Birgit Meyer. "'Kwaku's Car: The Struggles and Stories of a Ghanaian Long-Distance Taxi Driver'" *Car Cultures* (2001): 153–84.

Villiers, Alan. *Sons of Sinbad: An Account of Sailing with the Arabs in Their Dhows, in the Red Sea, around the Coasts of Arabia, and to Zanzibar and Tanganyika.* New York: Scribner, 1969.

Virdi, Jyotika. *The Cinematic Imagination: Indian Popular Films as Social History.* New Brunswick, NJ: Rutgers University Press, 2003.

Voigt-Graf, C. *Asian Communities in Tanzania: A Journey through Past and Present.* Hamburg: Hamburg University Press, 1998.

Walji, Shirin. "A History of the Ismaili Community in Tanzania." PhD diss., University of Wisconsin, 1974.

Walker, Cherryl. "Gender and the Development of the Migrant Labour System c. 1850–1930." In *Women and Gender in Southern Africa to 1945*, edited by Cherryl Walker, 168–96. London: James Currey, 1990.

Waller, Gregory, ed. *Moviegoing in America: A Sourcebook in the History of Film Exhibition.* Malden, MA: Blackwell, 2002.

444

Walsh, Michael. "The Internationalism of the American Cinema: The Establishment of United Artists' Foreign Distribution Operations." PhD diss., University of Wisconsin 1998.

Warshaw, Robin. *I Never Called It Rape: The Ms. Report on Recognizing, Fighting and Surviving Date and Acquaintance Rape.* New York: HarperCollins, 1988.

Watt, Jeffrey. *The Making of Modern Marriage: Matrimonial Control and the Rise of Sentiment in Neuchatel, 1550–1800.* Ithaca, NY: Cornell University Press, 1992.

Weinbaum, Alys Eve, Lynn M. Thomas, Priti Ramamurthy, Uta G. Poiger, Madeleine Yue Dong, and Tani E. Barlow, eds. *The Modern Girl around the World: Consumption, Modernity and Globalization.* Durham, NC: Duke University Press, 2008.

Werlin, Herbert. "Nairobi in the Time of Uhuru." *Africa Today* 10, no. 10 (1963): 7–10.

White, Luise. *The Comforts of Home: Prostitution in Colonial Nairobi.* Chicago: University of Chicago Press, 1990.

Willis, Justin. *Potent Brews: A Social History of Alcohol in East Africa, 1850–1999.* Oxford: James Currey, 2002.

Wilson, Amrit. *US Foreign Policy and Revolution: The Creation of Tanzania.* London: Pluto Press, 1989.

Wines, Michael. "Moscow Journal: Drive-In Offers Cabbage and Promises of Popcorn." *New York Times,* June 21, 1999, 4.

Wolfe, Ernie, and Clive Barker. *Extreme Canvas: Hand-Painted Movie Posters from Ghana.* New York: Kesho Press, 2000.

Zakharova, Larissa. "Dior in Moscow: A Taste for Luxury in Soviet Fashion under Krushchev." In *Pleasures in Socialism: Leisure and Luxury in the Eastern Bloc,* edited by David Crowley and Susan Reid, 95–120. Evanston, IL: Northwestern University Press, 2010.

Zhang, Yingjin. *Cinema, Space and Polylocality in a Globalizing China.* Honolulu: University of Hawaii Press, 2010.

Zolov, Eric. "Mexico's Rock Counterculture (La Onda) in Historical Perspective and Memory." In *New World Coming: The Sixties and the Shaping of Global Consciousness,* edited by Karen Dubinsky, Catherine Krull, Susan Lord, Sean Mills, and Scott Rutherford, 379–87. Toronto: Between the Lines, 2009.

——. *Refried Elvis: The Rise of the Mexican Counterculture.* Berkeley: University of California Press, 1999.

Filmography

*Following are the films mentioned in the text and viewed in Tanzania,
by country of origin:*

Egypt

Gharan Rakissa (Rafla, 1950)

Germany

The Ribald Tales of Robin Hood, His Lusty Men and Bawdy Wenches (Kanter and
Dietrich, 1969)

Hong Kong

The Big Boss (Wei, 1971)
Bruce Lee I Love You (Lo, 1976)
Bruce Lee in New Guinea (Yang, 1978)
Enter the Dragon (Clouse, 1973)
Fist of Fury/The Chinese Connection (Wei, 1972)
Infernal Street (Shen, 1973)
Lady Whirlwind (Feng, 1972)
Snake in Monkey's Shadow (Cheung, 1979)
Super Ninja (Wu, 1984)
Taekwando Heroes/Sting of the Dragon Masters (Feng, 1973)
Way of the Black Dragon (Chen, 1979)
The Way of the Dragon (Lee, 1972)
Yes Madam/Police Assassins (Yuen, 1985)

India

Aafat (Ram, 1977)
Aakhri Daku (Mehra, 1978)
Adha Din Adhi Raat (Doondi, 1977)
Alaap (Mukherjee, 1977)
Alam Ara (Irani, 1931)
Albela (Bhagwan, 1951)
Amar, Akbar, Anthony (Desai, 1977)
Anarkali (Jaswantal, 1953)
Andhaa Kaanoon (Rao, 1983)
Awara (Kapoor, 1951)
Baazi (Dutt, 1951)
Chalta Purza (Sonie, 1977)
Charas (Sagar, 1976)
Coolie (Desai and Raj, 1983)
Dada (Kishore, 1979)
Danka (Advani, 1954)
Dharam Veer (Desai, 1977)
Disco Dancer (Subhash, 1982)
Don (Barot, 1978)
Dosti (Bose, 1964)
Dream Girl (Chakravarty, 1977)
Fakira (Dixit, 1976)

445

446

Guide (Anand, 1965)

Hare Rama Hare Krishna (Anand, 1971)

Hum Paanch (Bapu, 1980)

Hunterwali (Wadia, 1935)

Jaggu (Ganguly, 1975)

Jagte Raho (Maitra, 1956)

Junglee (Subodh Mukherjee, 1961)

Kal Aaj Aur Kaal (Randhir Kapoor, 1971)

Khoon Aur Pani (Chand, 1981)

Koi Jeeta Koi Haara (Ganguly, 1976)

Lagaam (Gautam, 1976)

Love Story (Kumar, 1981)

Mother India (Khan, 1957)

Mughal e-Azam (Ashif, 1960)

Parvarish (Desai, 1977)

Pyaar (Kapoor, 1950)

Raeeszada (1976)

Raja Harishchandra (Phalke, 1913)

Ram aur Shyam (Chanakya, 1967)

Sargam (Santoshi, 1950)

Seeta aur Geeta (Sippy, 1972)

Sholay (Sippy, 1975)

Shree 420 (Kapoor, 1955)

Soorat Aueerat (Bahl, 1962)

Veer Zara (Chopra, 2004)

Italy

Adios Gringo (Stegani, 1965)

Anna (Lattuada, 1951)

The Bicycle Thief (De Sica, 1948)

A Fistful of Dollars (Leone, 1964)

The Good, the Bad and the Ugly (Leone, 1966)

Lady Medic on Maneuver (Cicero, 1977)

The Legion of the Damned (Lenzi, 1969)

My Name Is Pecos (Lucidi, 1967)

One Silver Dollar (Ferroni, 1965)

A Pistol for Ringo (Tessari, 1965)

The Price of Power (Velerii, 1969)

The Spy Who Loved Flowers (Lenzi, 1966)

Ten Gladiators (Parolini, 1963)

Texas Adios (Baldi, 1966)

Ursus (Campogalliani, 1961)

When Women Had Tails (Campanile, 1970)
World by Night (Vanzi, 1961)

Tanzania

Fimbo ya Mnyonge (TFC, 1976)
Harusi ya Mariamu (TFC, 1985)
Muhogo Mchungu (Colonial Film Unit, 1952)
Vita vya Kagera (TFC, 1980)
Yomba Yomba (TFC, 1989)

United Kingdom

Dr. No (Young, 1962)
The Drum (Korda, 1938)
From Russia with Love (Young, 1963)
Goldfinger (Hamilton, 1964)
The Rise and Fall of Idi Amin (Patel, 1980)

United States

Ben-Hur (Wyler, 1959)
Blindfold (Dunne, 1965)
The Bridge on the River Kwai (Lean, 1957)
Carry on Camping (Thomas, 1969)
The Christine Jorgensen Story (Rapper, 1970)
Cleopatra Jones (Starrett, 1973)
Dixie Dynamite (Frost, 1976)
Double Trouble (Taurog, 1967)
Endless Love (Zeffirelli, 1981)
Foxy Brown (Hill, 1974)
The Glass Bottom Boat (Tashlin, 1969)
Hell up in Harlem (Cohen, 1973)
Herbie Rides Again (Stevenson, 1974)
Ivanhoe (Thorpe, 1952)
Jaws (Spielberg, 1975)
King Kong (Cooper, 1933)
The Love Bug (Stevenson, 1968)
The Manchurian Candidate (Frankenheimer, 1962)
Mean Johnny Barrows (Williamson, 1976)
No Orchids for Miss Blandish (Clowes, 1948)
One Million Years B.C. (Chaffey, 1966)
Random Harvest (LeRoy, 1942)
The Robe (Koster, 1953)
Samson and Delilah (DeMille, 1949)

448

The Secret Life of an American Wife (Axelrod, 1968)

Shaft (Parks, 1971)

Shane (Stevens, 1953)

The Shoes of the Fisherman (Anderson, 1968)

The Spy Who Came in from the Cold (Ritt, 1965)

The Three Musketeers (Sidney, 1948)

Three the Hard Way (Parks, 1974)

Titanic (Cameron, 1997)

Tripoli (Price, 1950)

Twist around the Clock (Rudolph, 1961)

The Vengence of She (Owen, 1968)

Viva Las Vegas (Sidney, 1964)

The Wizard of Oz (Fleming, 1939)

Woman Times Seven (De Sica, 1967)

Young Lady Chatterley (Roberts, 1977)

INDEX

Abdulhussein Marashi, 37, 111
action, 140–43, 161–74, 217, 248–67
aesthetics, 16, 42–43, 46, 49, 98, 142–43,
    162–63, 260–67
affect, 10, 33–34, 92–112, 114–16, 168–70, 192,
    199, 220, 223, 235–36, 239–41, 244–46,
    267, 269, 285–90
Amitab Bachchan, 145, 149, 172–75
Apollo 11, 227–29
Asians, 15, 21–23, 41–53, 61–62, 68, 72–90,
    95, 111–12, 138, 140, 151, 159, 184, 187,
    214, 251, 278, 288–90
attendance, 5, 14, 32, 43, 57, 142–51, 161, 165,
    171–72, 176, 182, 223, 242–43, 249, 311;
    regional variations, 4–9, 59–63, 66–70,
    80, 142, 144–45, 147, 165, 179–220,
    248–50, 313
audiences: class composition, 1, 4, 8, 12,
    27–28, 49, 116–19, 122–25, 144, 180, 190,
    202–9, 224, 238–39, 272, 321, 326–29;
    gender composition, 1, 115–16, 144–45,
    148, 167–71, 181, 197–202, 209–19,
    239–47, 255–60, 269–75; interactive, 2,
    4, 12, 143, 152, 154, 224. *See also* film-
    inspired engagements/interpretation
automobility, 62, 89, 191–93, 224, 230,
    232–38, 242–43
Awara, 12, 83, 113–41

balcony seating, 28, 44, 57, 66, 67
Bhagwan, 83, 98, 149
black market, 1, 29, 62, 69, 104–8, 113,
    147–48, 196, 208, 244–45, 270, 272–73,
    285, 314, 316
blaxploitation, 145, 161–65, 250
Bond, James, 12, 107, 172
box-office receipts, 144–47, 165–75, 292,
    295–96, 311, 329

business cultures, 15–23, 41–47, 55,
    63–91, 92–111. *See also* entrepreneurial
    strategies

capitalism, 6, 8, 9, 15, 41–43, 70–72, 82, 222,
    230, 254, 316–23, 326–30
carbon rods, 99, 287–88, 294–95
censorship, 53, 101, 106–7, 143–44, 165,
    183–90, 301–9
Chaplin, Charlie, 24, 63–64, 117, 123–24
cinema: architecture, 16–17, 43–45, 49, 53,
    57, 59–62, 67–69, 223, 246, 285–90,
    326–27; and colonialism, 4–9, 43,
    53–54, 57, 60, 64, 179–220; and
    neighborhood, 10–11, 15, 29, 43, 48,
    55, 84, 92–112, 177–78, 197–202, 230,
    248–50, 264–68, 278
cinemas mentioned more than once
    Alexandra, 43–44
    Amana, 10, 57, 80
    Avalon, 10, 50–51, 54–56, 67, 69, 80, 158,
      192, 218, 273, 286–87, 311, 324–25
    Azania/Cameo, 69, 73, 80, 156, 193, 218,
      288
    Bharat/Globe, 51, 73, 184
    Cinema ya Bati, 51–52, 63–64, 74, 198
    Drive-in/Sisi, 56, 221–47, 295, 304
    Elite, 188–89, 286
    Empire, Dar es Salaam, 10, 49–51, 69,
      73, 80, 85, 155, 170–71, 184, 218, 252,
      254, 269–70, 288
    Empire, Zanzibar, 52–53, 69, 79, 85,
    Empress, 68–69, 75, 80, 106, 218, 271,
      307
    Everest, 57–58
    Highland, 59, 89
    Majestic, Tanga, 48–49, 75, 77, 98, 103,
      285